Explaining Corruption

The Politics of Corruption

Series Editor: Robert Williams
Professor of Politics
University of Durham, UK

Wherever possible, the articles in these volumes have been reproduced as originally published using facsimile reproduction, inclusive of footnotes and pagination to facilitate ease of reference.

For a list of all Edward Elgar published titles visit our site on the World Wide Web at
http://www.e-elgar.co.uk

Explaining Corruption

Edited by

Robert Williams

Professor of Politics
University of Durham, UK

THE POLITICS OF CORRUPTION 1

An Elgar Reference Collection
Cheltenham, UK • Northampton, MA, USA

Published by
Edward Elgar Publishing Limited
Glensanda House
Montpellier Parade
Cheltenham
Glos GL50 1UA
UK

Edward Elgar Publishing, Inc.
136 West Street
Suite 202
Northampton
Massachusetts 01060
USA

A catalogue record for this book is available from the British Library.

Library of Congress Cataloguing in Publication Data

Explaining corruption / edited by Robert Williams.
    — (The politics of corruption ; 1)
    Includes bibliographical references and index.
    1. Political corruption. I. Williams, Robert, 1946 Sept. 10– II. Series.

  JF1081 .E96 2000
  364.1'323—dc21
                                                   00–044234

ISBN   1 84064 489 3
        1 84064 115 0 (4 volume set)

Printed and bound in Great Britain by Biddles Ltd, *www.biddles.co.uk*

Contents

Acknowledgements

The editor and publishers wish to thank the authors and the following publishers who have kindly given permission for the use of copyright material.

American Journal of Economics and Sociology for article: M. Shahid Alam (1989), 'Anatomy of Corruption: An Approach to the Political Economy of Underdevelopment', *American Journal of Economics and Sociology*, **48** (4), October, 441–56.

American Political Science Association for articles: J.S. Nye (1967), 'Corruption and Political Development: A Cost-Benefit Analysis', *American Political Science Review*, **LXI** (2), 417–27; J. Patrick Dobel (1978), 'The Corruption of a State', *American Political Science Review*, **72** (3), September, 958–73.

American Society for Public Administration for article: Simcha B. Werner (1983), 'New Directions in the Study of Administrative Corruption', *Public Administration Review*, **43** (2), March/April, 146–54.

Blackwell Publishers Ltd for articles: M. McMullan (1961), 'A Theory of Corruption: Based on a Consideration of Corruption in the Public Services and Governments of British Colonies and Ex-Colonies in West Africa', *Sociological Review*, **9** (2), July, 181–201; Yves Mény (1996), '"Fin de siècle" Corruption: Change, Crisis and Shifting Values', *International Social Science Journal*, **149**, September, 309–20; Michael Johnston (1996), 'The Search for Definitions: The Vitality of Politics and the Issue of Corruption', *International Social Science Journal*, **149**, September, 321–35; Susan Rose-Ackerman (1996), 'Democracy and "Grand" Corruption', *International Social Science Journal*, **149**, September, 365–80; Paul Heywood (1997), 'Political Corruption: Problems and Perspectives', *Political Studies*, **XLV** (3), Special Issue, 417–35; Mark Philp (1997), 'Defining Political Corruption', *Political Studies*, **XLV** (3), Special Issue, 436–62; Paul D. Hutchcroft (1997), 'The Politics of Privilege: Assessing the Impact of Rents, Corruption, and Clientelism on Third World Development', *Political Studies*, **XLV** (3), Special Issue, 639–58.

Brown Journal of World Affairs for article: Moisés Naím (1995), 'The Corruption Eruption', *Brown Journal of World Affairs*, **II** (2), Summer, 245–61.

Cambridge University Press for articles: Colin Leys (1965), 'What is the Problem About Corruption?', *Journal of Modern African Studies*, **3** (2), August, 215–30; James C. Scott (1969), 'The Analysis of Corruption in Developing Nations', *Comparative Studies in Society and History*, **11** (2), 315–41; J.P. Olivier de Sardan (1999), 'A Moral Economy of Corruption in Africa?', *Journal of Modern African Studies*, **37** (1), March, 25–52.

Government and Opposition for article: Graeme C. Moodie (1980), 'On Political Scandals and Corruption', *Government and Opposition*, **15** (2), 208–22.

Johns Hopkins University Press for article: John Waterbury (1973), 'Endemic and Planned Corruption in a Monarchical Regime', *World Politics*, **XXV** (4), July, 533–55.

Journal of Law and Economics, University of Chicago for article: Edward C. Banfield (1975), 'Corruption as a Feature of Governmental Organization', *Journal of Law and Economics*, **XVIII** (3), December, 587–605.

Kluwer Academic Publishers BV for article: A.W. Goudie and David Stasavage (1998), 'A Framework for the Analysis of Corruption', *Crime, Law and Social Change*, **29** (2–3), 113–59.

MIT Press Journals and the President and Fellows of Harvard College and the Massachusetts Institute of Technology for articles: Andrei Shleifer and Robert W. Vishny (1993), 'Corruption', *Quarterly Journal of Economics*, **108** (3), August, 599–617; Paolo Mauro (1995), 'Corruption and Growth', *Quarterly Journal of Economics*, **CX** (3), August, 681–712.

Public Policy and Administration for article: Robert J. Williams (1976), 'The Problem of Corruption: A Conceptual and Comparative Analysis', *PAC Bulletin*, **22**, 41–53.

Review of African Political Economy for article: Morris Szeftel (1998), 'Misunderstanding African Politics: Corruption and the Governance Agenda', *Review of African Political Economy*, **76**, 221–40.

Sage Publications, Inc. for article: Nathaniel H. Leff (1964), 'Economic Development Through Bureaucratic Corruption', *American Behavioral Scientist*, **VIII** (3), November, 8–14.

Taylor & Francis Ltd for articles: Robin Theobald (1999), 'So What Really is the Problem About Corruption?', *Third World Quarterly*, **20** (3), June, 491–502; Robert Williams (1999), 'New Concepts for Old?', *Third World Quarterly*, **20** (3), June, 503–13.

John Wiley & Sons Ltd for article: Mushtaq H. Khan (1996), 'The Efficiency Implications of Corruption', *Journal of International Development*, **8** (5), 683–96.

World Bank for excerpt: Michael Johnston (1998), 'What Can Be Done about Entrenched Corruption?', in Boris Pleskovic (ed.), *Annual World Bank Conference on Development Economics 1997*, 69–90.

Every effort has been made to trace all the copyright holders but if any have been inadvertently overlooked the publishers will be pleased to make the necessary arrangement at the first opportunity.

In addition the publishers wish to thank the Library of the London School of Economics and Political Science, the Marshall Library of Economics, Cambridge University, B & N Microfilm, London and the Library of Indiana University at Bloomington, USA, for their assistance in obtaining these articles.

Introduction

Robert Williams

Corruption is ancient and modern. History is replete with cases of bribery and nepotism but the academic study of corruption is primarily a late twentieth century phenomenon. While historians have recorded the details of individual scandals and *cause célèbres*, the dominant perspective has been one which sees corruption as a deviant and probably transitory activity. Individual scoundrels and scandals attracted attention and lent colour to otherwise mundane accounts of economic and political history. At the same time, the rise and fall of political machines in the USA and the elimination of rotten boroughs and other forms of electoral malpractice in the UK also attracted critical attention. The supposition was that corruption, like adolescence, is a phase which countries go through before they reach maturity. Thus corruption was either linked to the demonization of particular individuals or seen as a particular stage or point on the path to modernity.

The study of corruption was transformed by the success of the independence movements of the 1950s and 1960s. The winds of change which blew through Africa and Asia created a large number of newly independent states. The study of the politics of underdeveloped, less developed, developing countries and now the South (the nomenclature shifted over time) became a social science industry and, it was widely noted, corruption was a major problem. The key question was whether corruption in such countries was different from or similar to corruption in developed countries. The developed countries had apparently experienced corrupt phases before getting corruption under control through a combination of political, judicial and administrative reforms. From this perspective, corruption was associated with forms of political and economic immaturity which educational and social progress would overcome. But subsequent events combined to render this sanguine interpretation and prognosis both inadequate and inaccurate.

It became clear that the corruption experienced in some newly independent states was pervasive and deep seated. It was simultaneously appreciated that the 'take off' phase of economic growth seen as necessary for political and social development had not materialized. Development was seen as the cure for all manner of social and economic ills and, without it, what was once seen as a transitional phase looked more like a permanent condition. Economic 'take off' in a global economy dominated by powerful industrialized states proved more difficult than was once envisaged. It was no longer legitimate to assume that development would resolve the multiple problems besetting the South and, if development was stalled, it was necessary to tackle the specific problems directly.

But just as the perception that corruption was a major problem in developing countries emerged, confidence in its decline in developed countries began to evaporate. The incidence of political scandals was hard to reconcile with the belief that corruption was a problem which had been solved. The implosion of the Italian political system after the 'tangentopoli' revelations revealed how deep seated a problem corruption still is in some developed states.

The last bastion of self righteousness was Britain where, as late as the 1970s and 1980s, public figures ritually extolled the high ethical standards that prevailed in British public life. When scandals did occur, they were attributed to the odd 'rotten apple' in an otherwise wholesome barrel. But the 'cash for questions' affair in the early 1990s set off a chain of events which proposed substantial structural reform in British government and politics. The corruption eruption is therefore a global rather than a regional phenomenon.

The perception of corruption has radically changed. Where it was once seen as deviant, peripheral and transitory, it is now seen as common, deep rooted and permanent. But is this only a problem of perception or does it signify a decline in standards of behaviour? Are corruption scandals the exceptions that prove the rule or only the tip of an iceberg? Is the multilateral action against corruption in the 1990s evidence of a timely response to a freshly perceived phenomenon or a sign of institutional panic borne of years of policy neglect?

Like poverty, corruption has always been with us. Like prosperity for all, absolute integrity in public life is rhetorical or idealistic rather than practical and real. Eliminating corruption completely from public life is an impossible dream. But electorates and citizenry in both North and South seem increasingly intolerant of corruption and its associated costs and consequences. Allegations of corruption have demonstrated a unique capacity to generate demonstrations and riots against regimes in many parts of the world. And just as the dispossessed of the world are angered by corruption, the priority and attention it attracts in the international agencies and financial institutions have reached unprecedented heights. The World Bank, the United Nations, US Aid and the UK Department for International Development are all parts of the consensus which argues that corruption is a major cause of poverty and a serious obstacle to development. The consensus further holds that something must be done, new policies devised and programmes of action implemented. This represents a significant shift in both policy and priorities. Before the late 1980s, corruption was seen by donor bodies as something regrettable but probably inescapable. In some cases, the geopolitical role of dictators such as Mobutu in Zaire was seen as important enough to condone the massive corruption associated with their regimes. The end of the Cold War removed the need to support every anti-communist regime, however brutal or corrupt, and produced a sea change in the attitudes and policies of the World Bank and other bodies. What was once perceived as undesirable but tolerable is now seen as completely unacceptable. Governments which have not responded to international calls for firm action against corruption, for example, Kenya, have found their flows of international assistance being reduced or even cut off.

Thus we see that interest in corruption has increased dramatically in a number of ways; corruption in the South has been identified as a major problem and many governments are taking active steps to combat it. Contrary to some expectations, corruption in the North has not declined or disappeared and there are heightened levels of political and public interest in confronting it. The international donor community has now recognized corruption as a serious obstacle to development. If corruption has always been with us, it has rarely attracted the intensity of global attention it now receives.

Fatalists would say that, because corruption has always been with us, it always will be. Its causes are rooted in basic human weaknesses such as greed, and therefore attempts to control corruption are largely futile. But this ignores the fact that levels of corruption vary dramatically from country to country. Greed may be a constant factor in human life but political and economic structures and processes clearly play important roles in determining to what extent this vice can be exercised. In terms of corruption, Denmark is very different from Nigeria but, more interestingly, so is Botswana. There can be striking differences in the incidence of corruption within continents, within regions, between adjacent states and even within states. In some states in the USA corruption is a way of life, while in others it is virtually unknown. The same observation could be made about corruption in local authorities in the UK.

Corruption not only varies from place to place but also from time to time. In every state's history, there are periods when corruption appears to be peculiarly high and others when its incidence seems to decline. The ebb and flow of corruption is difficult to predict but what is certain is that claims to have won the 'war against corruption' or to have found the cure for the 'cancer of corruption' are at least premature and probably misconceived. Corruption offers no grounds for complacency and experience of tackling corruption suggests that success is usually temporary and partial.

The 'corruption eruption' has given the subject a much higher profile in both the academic and policy-making worlds. Whereas corruption experts were once few in number and had difficulty in persuading publishers and journals to publish their research, the flow of publications on corruption has now turned into a raging torrent. It has become very difficult, even for specialists, to monitor, let alone read, everything written about corruption in newspapers, magazines, journals, books, think tank papers and the official reports, inquiries and publications of national and international governmental bodies.

This new collection of articles is therefore extremely timely. Corruption is a jungle and there is an urgent need for an authoritative guide to the flora and fauna. It would be a bold individual who laid claim to expert status in all aspects of corruption and, when invited to edit this collection, the need for specialist help was apparent. By a fortuitous piece of timing, the research group investigating corruption and anti-corruption strategies on behalf of the UK Department for International Development had just begun its work and assistance from my research colleagues, Alan Doig, Rachel Flanary, Jon Moran and Robin Theobald, was quickly forthcoming. The task was more challenging than originally anticipated because the literature is now substantial. Much of the literature is unsatisfactory in that there are significant problems of gaps, overlaps and duplication. In terms of geographical coverage, corruption has been extensively researched in some countries, patchily studied in others and hardly considered at all in still others. In dividing the material, it was difficult to arrive at criteria that allowed a clear demarcation between the volumes. Corruption seems to be a subject which invites varying mixtures of theory and empiricism, micro and macro analysis, explanation and prescription, and case studies and comparative analysis.

The first volume in this collection, *Explaining Corruption*, is more conceptual than empirical. But despite the giant lava flow of publications from the 'corruption eruption', the literature on this aspect of corruption still generates more heat than light. Many contributions appear ideological in character and corruption remains a highly contested concept. We still lack firmly grounded theories of corruption and the shortage of analytically informed empirical inquiries continues. Too many participants in the contemporary corruption debate content themselves with resurrecting tired clichés about the topic or with slaying long-dead dragons. In selecting material for this collection, two criteria have been employed; first, the contributions say something important, different or interesting about corruption. This is not to say that the editor necessarily agrees with what is said but rather indicates that the articles are intellectually provocative and stimulating and should be read by all serious students of corruption. The second and related criterion is that the article marks a particular point or phase in the study of corruption or has influenced the ways in which academics and policy analysts have subsequently thought about corruption.

The volume is concerned with the different ways in which scholars have sought to understand corruption and the range of theories and perspectives they have used to explain it. Thus it includes articles on definitions, on conceptual classification and distinctions, and on the salience of particular disciplines to the key explanatory problems posed by corruption. Such articles address a variety of deceptively simple questions: What is corruption? What form does it take? How can it be distinguished from similar or related concepts? What are its principal causes? What are its major political and economic consequences? In seeking the answers to these questions, scholars display a spectrum of rival and apparently incompatible theoretical frameworks and analytical approaches. In their attempts to understand and explain the concept, corruption has become something of a disciplinary football to be kicked backward and forward. It began life as a political or philosophical concept but was subsequently given a legal character before being appropriated successively by sociologists, anthropologists and, most recently, by economists. The issue remains of how to judge the outcome of this interdisciplinary competition for conceptual ownership.

This intellectual competition mirrored changes in broader political and ideological struggles. The collapse of the Soviet Empire had profound implications for the international order and patterns of political support. But while the perception of corruption has been dramatically reshaped by these international changes, the ground was already laid in changes in the internal politics of the USA and the UK. Ideological shifts in the USA and UK in the 1980s had implications not merely for the domestic policies of those nations but also for their perceptions of the external world and its problems. Thus, when President Reagan observed that 'government is not the answer to our problems, it is the problem', he pithily encapsulated a cluster of attitudes, ideas and policy strategies. This perception was brought to bear not only on the US budget deficit but on the debt crises of the South. The perceived need to limit the role of the state, to 'downsize' the federal government and to elevate the market and promote the virtues of individual responsibility and self reliance all made their impact on the ways in which international institutions conducted their affairs. Such institutions became more receptive to certain kinds of neo-liberal message which were incorporated into institutional thinking and policy making.

The intellectual ascendancy of neo-liberal thinking and the political dominance of Reagan and Thatcher helped ensure that the new forms of conditionality introduced into foreign assistance programmes would reflect the view that government was often the enemy of development and the prime source of corruption. To some, corruption was the unpleasant but inevitable by-product of the unwarranted distortion of markets by governments. The logic suggested that when the size and role of government were reduced, the opportunities and incentives for corruption would similarly decline. But this framework of analysis ran into a number of problems. In many contexts, there is an absence of other competent players ready to take up the roles previously performed by government. It seems that, if some activities or services are to continue, there is often no alternative to the government performing the role. The key policy prescriptions of neo-liberalism were privatization and de-regulation, and they brought their own crop of corruption-related problems. In many cases, privatization amounted to little more than the licensed theft of state property. To those unable to secure basic services without making an illicit payment, the issue of public or private ownership is largely irrelevant.

There are obvious indications that neo-liberalism has passed its political zenith and, while economists are still prominent in the contemporary corruption literature, their prescriptions have been modified in the light of privatization and de-regulation experience. Some current research suggests that, while corruption is obviously linked to the role and performance of the state, a more appropriate and effective response is not rolling back the state but reforming it. The debate goes on but it is clear that, in different periods, contrasting paradigms have dominated both academic and political discourse.

The first volume is therefore intended to set the scene for the volumes that follow. It identifies the evolution of the theoretical debates, their points of agreement and disagreement, and considers how corruption can best be understood. The range of contributions suggests that corruption is not a simple phenomenon susceptible to monocausal explanation. The intention here is not to resolve the debate but to expose more clearly its origins, development and current parameters.

The second and third volumes offer a global perspective on corruption. *Corruption in the Developing World* includes some selections that are intended to convey how thinking about corruption in such contexts has evolved. Some early contributions sought to explain corruption in terms familiar to students of American politics. Comparisons were made with political machines and with spoils and patronage politics. Max Weber's hitherto neglected concept of patrimonialism was re-discovered and subsequent analysis has conclusively shown that the social and political costs of patrimonial forms of politics have been extremely high for less developed countries. Most of the articles in this volume have been chosen to illustrate the dismal consequences for citizens, governments and the economy of the pervasive illegal appropriation of public resources. In extreme cases, the ravages of corruption have been so damaging as to culminate in acute civil strife and state collapse. The volume begins, however, with an article which demonstrates the scope and potential for corruption by presenting a peasant's eye view of the world and its dangers.

The other readings offer a representative range of case studies as possible given that Latin America is under-represented in the literature in English on corruption. But, even here, the selection illustrates the characteristic problems of institutionalized corruption, drug-related corruption and the transition from dictatorship to democracy, as well as an overview of the continental issues. In comparison, African states are relatively new entities and their political origins render their institutional structures particularly susceptible to abuse and, in extreme cases such as Zaire, this can lead to the effective privatization of the state. In such contexts a growing proportion of the population withdraw or 'exit' into subsistence farming or into the informal economy by means of smuggling, black marketeering and banditry. Corruption in its 'grand' and 'petty' forms plays a major role in the political and economic life of the continent but there are still exceptions and an article is included on Botswana which examines how one state has managed to combine political stability, administrative effectiveness and economic growth with low levels of corruption.

Selecting examples from Asia was a particular challenge given its somewhat imprecise geographical identity and the vast range of societies and states. The choices were made on the rough and ready assumption that it is possible to identify three broad types of Asian state: those which have endured long periods of authoritarian rule in which the military has been the dominant force, such as Indonesia, Thailand and the Philippines; formal democracies, albeit with an authoritarian tinge, such as Malaysia and India; and the command economies in the process of transition, such as the People's Republic of China and Vietnam. The final selections deal with the issue of to what extent certain developmental processes, notably marketization and democratization, exacerbate or ameliorate the problem of corruption in the developing world.

The third volume, *Corruption in the Developed World*, includes articles on Europe, North America, Australia and Japan. The contributions include reflections on corruption and social change, corruption and organized crime, and, in the Italian and Russian cases, reflections on the notion of structural corruption. They offer discussions of the inter-relationship of corruption with political culture and party finance, and with concepts of democracy, accountability and public ethics. While many analysts have principally focused their attention on the less developed states, the corruption scandals which have afflicted most developed states in the past twenty years have stimulated new analyses and revisions of once strongly held convictions about standards of public integrity in the developed world.

In some cases, the source of corruption can be traced to a particular characteristic of the political system; for example, campaign finance practices in the United States or the inter-weaving of party and state structures in Italy. In other cases, political transformation of the Russian sort has created new incentives and opportunities and has exchanged one kind of corrupt system for another.

Complacency has given way to concern and, across the developed world, anti-corruption reform is high on political agendas. It is no longer possible to tolerate corruption, to shrug one's shoulders and accept that a certain degree of nepotism and fraud is an unavoidable consequence of a particular national political style. Political cultures may vary but, as the European Commissioners discovered in 1999, it is increasingly the norm for common and rigorous standards to be applied. Countries which place a premium on combating corruption in the less developed world find it morally and politically necessary to tackle corruption at home.

The fourth volume in this series, *Controlling Corruption*, reflects the global consensus that corruption is a major problem which has a variety of negative impacts on political, economic and social systems around the world. But the consensus which shares the conviction that something must be done does not extend to agreement on what exactly needs to be done. If corruption is a common problem, are there common solutions? While the Independent Commission Against Corruption in Hong Kong is frequently hailed as a success, attempts to replicate it in very different political and economic contexts are fraught with difficulty.

This volume includes articles from the ever expanding literature on anti-corruption strategies. Anti-corruption strategies can be initiated at a variety of levels; international, regional, national, sub-national and local. The impetus for reform can come from international bodies such as the World Bank and from donor countries in the form of specific assistance and aid conditionality. But reform can also be domestically driven and evidence suggests that, without strong political will and commitment, reform programmes are likely to be cosmetic rather than substantive. But even where political commitment is not wholehearted, the demands and protests emanating from civil society can induce reluctant political leaders to conduct anti-corruption purges.

The articles selected represent different strands of thinking about how best to tackle corruption. Some approaches are holistic, arguing that corruption issues are a sub-set of governance problems and the governance problems are a manifestation of structural and systemic problems of the political economy of particular societies. The aim here is comprehensive reform but, however laudable the aims, it is not yet clear how such grand designs can be implemented. Even if wholesale reform of economies, societies and governance is thought feasible, it is still necessary to determine priorities, to provide co-ordination and to work out the sequencing of reform measures. The costs of anti-corruption strategies need to be identified, as does their impact on the effectiveness of organizations. Research suggests that striving to eliminate corruption completely can be counterproductive when the need to avoid corruption takes priority over achieving the aims and objectives of the organization. Some reformers have more limited ambitions and reject the holistic approach in favour of targeting the most vulnerable parts of state activity; for example, customs services and procurement procedures.

The debate on corruption and anti-corruption strategies continues because it is a complex, multi-faceted phenomenon. Few reforms to date have been completely successful and some have been counterproductive. Anti-corruption strategies are beset by problems of transferability, sustainability, cost effectiveness, sequencing and intent. The choice of strategy has implications for different elements of the government. A focus on investigating corruption has obvious implications for the criminal justice system, its resourcing and independence. If the focus is on prevention rather than retribution, or on attacking the causes rather than the consequences of corruption, different considerations apply. All require state resources, and decisions have to be made about whether the concern is the loss of state income or the diversion of state expenditure into unnecessary and expensive projects. Where low level, 'petty' corruption is concerned, anti-corruption strategies sometimes focus on empowering the public through information and access in order to hold local officials to account. If grand and petty corruption both flourish best in secrecy, openness and transparency are often seen as key elements in anti-corruption strategies. The contributions assembled here do not definitively resolve the above issues but rather offer a range of perspectives and approaches which illustrate the scale and difficulty of the task.

Taken together, the four volumes offer a representative, up-to-date and authoritative guide to the literature on corruption. They do not purport to be comprehensive because the literature has expanded so rapidly in the past ten years. Hard choices had to be made about what to exclude and what the balance should be between academic and policy-related literature and between theoretical and empirical work. The result is four volumes which contain, in the editor's judgement, the most informative, important and influential articles written on corruption in the last third of the twentieth century. The intention is to provide students of corruption with a substantial body of material which shows how the subject has developed and how it is currently understood and explained. Volumes 2 and 3 illustrate and explain the scope, incidence and consequences of corruption in a variety of political settings in the developed and developing worlds. The decision was made to place Russia in the developed world although, sadly, it is recognized that there is now a case for locating it in the developing world.

Corruption differs from many other subjects in that those who study it are often committed to combat it. Volume 4 is therefore dedicated to illustrating the variety of prescriptions that have been presented as ways of controlling corruption. Although the problems which bedevil anti-corruption strategies are, as *Controlling Corruption* shows, considerable, that should not deter reformers. Academics may be content to define, conceptualize, theorize, interpret and explain but detachment is difficult when the pernicious effects of corruption are felt across the globe. Perhaps Karl Marx had corruption as well as class struggle in mind when he wrote that 'philosophers have only interpreted the world, the point is to change it'. But we first need to recognize and understand the enemy before it can be overcome. These volumes are offered as a contribution to that vital process.

Acknowledgement to the Department for International Development (DFID)

All the members of the editorial team worked together on a two year research project funded by DFID on corruption and anti-corruption strategies. We would like to record our appreciation to DFID for its recognition of the seriousness of the global problem of corruption and for its financial and other support for our research. I would like to emphasize that the Introduction and the final selection of articles are the editors' responsibility and do not represent the views or policies of DFID.

Other Acknowledgements

The task of the editorial team was made more manageable by the development of corruption databases and by the establishment of a unique library of articles and reports. Our research colleague, Stephanie McIvor, was largely responsible for this work and, on behalf of the editorial team, I would like to record our thanks to her. I would also like to thank my editorial colleagues, Alan Doig, Robin Theobald, Rachel Flanary and Jonathan Moran, for their invaluable assistance in the editorial process. They do not bear responsibility for the Introduction or the final difficult choice of articles, and the blame for any important omissions is mine.

In Durham, I would like to thank Jean Richardson and Heather Marquette for their timely and crucial help and, last but not least, I would like to thank Edward Elgar for suggesting this collection to me. We first discussed the possibility of publishing a book on corruption almost twenty years ago and, while this is a totally different project, I hope he is as pleased as I am that our conversations have finally borne fruit.

[1]

A THEORY OF CORRUPTION

Based on a Consideration of Corruption in the Public Services and Governments of British Colonies and ex-Colonies in West Africa.

M. McMullan

There is some corruption in all governments and in the public services of all countries. Some countries, however, suffer from a greater degree of corruption than others. Only very recently and in only a handful of countries has such corruption been so far reduced as to be practically negligible, that is to say so far reduced that it does not normally enter into a citizen's relations with his government. In most countries throughout most of their known history such corruption has been an accepted feature of life. In extreme cases today it can be a major obstacle to economic development and a major cause of political instability. It deserves attention for its intrinsic interest as part of the 'pathology' of bureaucracy, for its practical importance for the political and economic development of the poorer nations of the world, and for the contribution that an analysis can make to sympathetic understanding of what may otherwise be a repulsive feature of some societies. In this paper I try to relate the corruption observed in the British Colonies and ex-colonies of West Africa to the social conditions and histories of those countries and to make some tentative generalisations from a comparison of conditions there and in other parts of the world.

I am not asserting that these West African territories are peculiarly given to corruption; there are many countries in the world where the governments are more corrupt and many more where they were equally corrupt in the recent past; the choice of these countries is dictated only by the accident of the writer's own experience.

The Effects of Corruption

Understanding is desirable, but it is wrong to underrate the evil consequences of widespread corruption. People sympathetic to African and other nationalist movements are sometimes tempted to brush aside corruption as being a 'passing phase' of no real political

M. McMullan

or social importance. Whether it is a 'passing phase' or not in West
Africa I do not know, though I shall give reasons for thinking that
it is at least not a phase that will pass quickly; but I am certain
that it is of real political and social importance. Some of the evils
which widespread corruption may be expected to bring are:—

1. Injustice. This needs no explanation.

2. Inefficiency. In countries where the general standard of technology is low this is a serious matter. Railway accidents are caused
by Station Masters corruptly agreeing to load logs that are too heavy
for the wagons. Patients in hospitals may be denied treatment they
require or bribe nurses to give them treatment they want (in West
Africa usually injections), but which may be unsuitable for their
condition. Corruption in making appointments may be relatively
unimportant in a country where the general standard of competence
is high, but in West Africa, where professional and technical competence is still rare, corruption results in the appointment of unsuitable
people and the waste and frustration of the right man.

3. Mistrust of the government by the citizen. This is peculiarly
serious where the government is anxious to carry out a programme
of economic development for which the enthusiasm of the population
needs to be enlisted. It also increases the difficulties of enforcing
criminal, revenue, and other laws.

4. Waste of public resources. Corruption in the government
involves the ultimate transfer of public funds to the pockets of politicians or officials. The businessman who has to bribe to get a
government contract ultimately charges the bribe to public funds.

5. Discouragement of enterprise, particularly foreign enterprise.
Corruption adds an incalculable hazard to the normal thickets of
bureaucratic procedure. The final bribe is never paid. Investors
and entrepreneurs are dismayed and frustrated, and may find that the
unofficial cost of starting an enterprise is too great for it to be
profitable.

6. Political instability. In a country where there is a great deal
of corruption, political attacks on people in positions of power are
easy to mount and easy to get popular support for. Much of the
political history of some unfortunate countries could be told as the
'ins' being accused, correctly, by the 'outs' of corruption; popular
indignation at the corruption causing the replacement of the 'ins' by
the 'outs', who in turn become corrupt and are attacked by a new
group of 'outs'. This process could be demonstrated in detail from

A Theory of Corruption

the history of some local government bodies in West Africa during the past ten years.   At the national level it can lead either to political chaos, or

7.   Repressive measures. It may be easier to deal with the accusations of corruption than with the corruption itself.

8.   Restrictions on government policy. I recall a conversation with an American doctor who was an admirer of the British National Health Service. 'No such service would at the moment be possible in my home State', he said, naming the State, 'the civil service is too inefficient and corrupt to be capable of running it'. A corrupt civil service and police force restricts the range of policies available to a government.

Evidence

There is one preliminary problem which must be faced but cannot be solved; the problem of evidence. Arguments and statements about corruption cannot be demonstrated by factual or statistical evidence of the type normally acceptable as a basis for political or sociological generalisation.   There are plenty of reports, histories and trial records[1] exemplifying corruption in different countries, but corruption is not a subject which can be investigated openly by means of questionnaires and interviews. Even if it were, in principle, possible to quantify the phenomenon, there would be no practical possibility of doing so.   The reader is asked to accept as a premise of the argument of this paper that there is more corruption in these West African countries than in, for instance, the United Kingdom. This is a view based on my own observations over a decade, broadly shared by other well placed observers and supported by public expressions of concern by indigenous political and religious leaders in West Africa.[2] But it cannot, nor can many of the other statements in this paper be proved in the ways in which statements about less disreputable aspects of society can be proved. Corruption still awaits its Kinsey report. This difficulty must be recognised but we cannot refuse to discuss important topics simply because the best type of evidence is not available.

Definition

I shall not attempt a comprehensive or legally precise definition of corruption,[3] and will content myself with the common understanding that a public official is corrupt if he accepts money or

M. McMullan

money's worth for doing something that he is under a duty to do anyway, that he is under a duty not to do, or to exercise a legitimate discretion for improper reasons. Institutions have official aims, the human beings that work them have personal aims. The ideal relation between the individual and the institution is that the individual should be able to satisfy his personal aims in harmony with, and while forwarding, the official aims of the institution. It is nothing to the Home Office that the prison warder has six children to feed, but the prison warder is acting legitimately in working as a prison warder so that he can feed his six children with his salary. Should he find his salary insufficient, however, and take money from the prisoners for doing them favours, he will be described as corrupt. He will be using his position in the prison to forward his personal aims in a way which conflicts with the official aim of the institution. There is a conflict between the attitudes and aims of a corrupt official and those of the service, and an equally important divergence between the attitudes and aims of the member of the public who induces the corruption of the official, and the aims and attitudes of the society as a whole. These divergencies may be defined by reference to the laws and regulations in which the official aims and attitudes are set out.

The Argument

The corruption discussed here is, by definition, illegal. People break laws because they do not accept them, or because they have other interests or desires which they prefer or are impelled to follow. Some laws in a society find almost universal acceptance, other laws are broken by large numbers of people. Head-hunting, for instance, is illegal in New Guinea and in France, but the laws against it are more often broken in New Guinea than in France. Obviously the law against head-hunting in New Guinea is further from the popular attitude towards that activity in New Guinea than is the similar law in France from the popular attitude there. If there is greater corruption in West Africa than in Denmark the popular attitude towards corruption in West Africa must be different from that in Denmark.

Thus far is tautology. The problem is to identify the reasons for the popular attitude. The argument of this paper is that a high level of corruption is the result of a wide divergence between the attitudes, aims and methods of the government of a country and those of the society in which they operate, in particular of the procedures and aims of the government which put particular groups of

A Theory of Corruption

the population at a special disadvantage: that therefore the different levels of corruption in different countries depend on the extent to which government and society are homogeneous.

Pre-Colonial Society

The question of how far corruption can be said to have existed in pre-colonial times in West Africa, and how far present corruption is the result of the persistence of attitudes from that time, is an extremely difficult one. To discuss it adequately would require far greater knowledge of those societies than I can pretend to, and a great deal of space if due regard was to be had to the variety of social and political structures which existed. I shall, therefore, make only three points about pre-colonial society: points which are possibly obvious, but which are too important to be taken for granted.

1. Pre-colonial West African societies were familiar with conflicts between personal aims and official or social aims, hence their laws and customs and the punishments and other sanctions by which they were enforced, *but* although men wielded political power, judged causes, led armies, and collected taxes, their functions were less precisely defined in relation to those activities than they are in the bureaucratic governments of colonial and post-colonial times. The judicial functions of a chief were not sharply distinguished from his familial function as arbitrator and peacemaker, or his political function as a leader concerned with the manipulation of power, so that impropriety in the exercise of his judicial function, such as favouritism, could less easily be attributed to him as corruption than in the case of a modern magistrate whose sole function is to judge. To say this is to come near to saying that, as there was no public service in pre-colonial West Africa, there could be no corruption of it, but this is not quite accurate. In fact, examples could be given of behaviour clearly recognisable as corrupt (and recognised as such in the pre-colonial society) from the histories and legends of the peoples concerned. Such examples might be expected to be most common among the larger and more articulated political systems such as those of Northern Nigeria[4], which had evolved many bureaucratic features long before the advent of the colonial bureaucracy.

2. A man may, of course, be bribed with a horse, a woman, or a gun as effectively as with a roll of notes, but the possibilities and utility of bribery obviously increases with the growth of a money economy. In pre-colonial West Africa, money played a relatively

M. McMullan

minor part, though its importance varied from place to place. To take an extreme instance: in an area where the people lived at subsistence level and, as would be likely, had a political structure almost without full-time professionals, there would be neither the need for, nor the means of, bribery. Even more important perhaps, is the availability of the sort of goods and opportunities on which to spend money, that makes money of greater value than any other single commodity. This is relevant to the claim that the Communist Government of China has greatly reduced corruption in that country, once notorious for it. Obviously, corruption must lose much of its attraction if there is little on which to spend the proceeds, and the acquisition of wealth is in itself (quite apart from the question of punishment for law-breaking) looked on with disfavour. Only in a money economy and a society which allows a good deal of freedom to individuals in disposing of their property, loosely speaking a capitalist economy, will the types of corruption we are dealing with be widespread.

3. In considering the relationship between corruption and traditional society in West Africa, observers often isolate the customary exchanges of gifts as the element in traditional life which has led to the growth of corruption in modern times. While not denying the relevance of customary gift exchange to bribery, the facility with which a bribe may be disguised as a customary gift, and, indeed, the genuine ambiguity of customary gifts in some traditional contexts, it is, in my opinion, wrong to isolate one feature of traditional life in this way. There were and are many features of the traditional way of life which, in the context of colonial and post-colonial society, contribute to the prevalence of corruption. My argument is that it is this clash of old customs, attitudes, etc., with the new forms of government that gives rise to corruption. The customary gifts are just one example. Other examples are easily found; the extended family system which leads to the overburdening of an official with family responsibilities so that his pay is insufficient, his family and tribal loyalties which obscure his devotion to the national community, the absence of an established class system which makes it hard for the official to cultivate the aloofness which perhaps must, for most people, be the accompaniment of official integrity.

Corruption in Colonial and Post-Colonial Times

In modern times my thesis concerns the disharmony between the

186

A Theory of Corruption

government and the traditional society on which it is imposed and which it seeks to change. Specifically, of course, this modern government was in West Africa the colonial bureaucratic government. It was alien to West Africa in obvious ways: it was controlled from a distant land, and the controllers were subject to pressures and had aims often quite unrelated to the situation in West Africa; its key men were foreigners, often with little understanding of West African society, usually with no understanding of the indigenous languages, while its junior officials recruited from the indigenous peoples struggled to find a balance between their alien masters and the demands of their own people. The disharmonies were innumerable, and I shall consider only two of the most important; the first typical of an economically underdeveloped country, second of a type found universally but which can be seen particularly clearly in West Africa. Before dealing with these, however, there is one important general topic.

The Climate of Corruption

Some years ago, I was escorting an African judge from the court in which he had just sentenced a murderer to death, to his car. The large crowd which had assembled to hear the case lined the path, cheering and dancing to express their pleasure at the verdict. One phrase was shouted over and over again, and was eventually taken up by the whole crowd and chanted in chorus. The judge asked me if I understood what it meant, and I said that I could catch the first words, 'You're a good judge . . . ' but could not understand the rest. 'What they are shouting', said the judge, 'is "You're a good judge, we thought you had been bribed, but you haven't" '. With that he got into his car and was driven away.

No one there was surprised. A wryness of tone was the judge's only comment on the compliment that he was being offered. No one in the crowd saw any reason to disguise the implication that there would have been nothing surprising if the judge had been bribed. We were all living in a country where corruption was a very normal part of the scene and the assumption of corruption was part of everyone's equipment for his daily business.

Such a climate of corruption is in itself an important factor. There is a continuous interaction between the willingness of people to pay bribes and the willingness of officials to receive them. People normally behave in the way that the people they live with behave. In a

M. McMullan

society with a high level of corruption, hardly any citizen can carry
out his business, avoid trouble with the government, and generally
get through life comfortably, without acquiescing to some extent at
least in the prevailing corruption. There are not a few such societies
in the world, and persons from more fortunate countries must, when
visiting them or doing business with them, conform (or at least
acquiesce), unless they prefer empty gestures which will inconvenience themselves to no useful purpose. At the other extreme, in an
ideally uncorrupt society, the single corrupt man would offer to give
or receive bribes in vain.

Divergencies Between Government and Society

The two examples of divergence between governments and West
African society in Colonial and post-colonial times which I shall
discuss are : —
    (a) that between a literate government and an illiterate society, and
    (b) that arising from laws in conflict with popular attitudes.

(a) *Literate Government in an Illiterate Society*

Colonial rule in West Africa was and is the rule of an illiterate
society by a literate government. The government operates in accordance with and by means of written rules and regulations. No one
who cannot read and write can hope to occupy effectively any position in the public service. Entry into even the lowest grades is only
for those who can read and write. Not only is reading and writing
essential, but reading and writing *in English,* a foreign tongue. The
majority of the population is illiterate and has little or no understanding of English. (Literacy and understanding English, are in
these countries, almost synonymous). Friction between the literate
public servant and the illiterate population is inevitable, and is, of
course, greatest at the base of the public service pyramid, where
functionaries and contacts with the public are most numerous, and
it is at this level that the greatest *volume* of corruption occurs (the
amount of damage done and money involved may well be greater
at higher levels). Between the public and the functionaries with
whom they most often deal, there is a constant flow of presents and
bribes, given willingly or unwillingly, pressed on the official or
extorted from the public.

Many examples of this process could be given (and it should
be borne in mind that the public service in economically under-

A Theory of Corruption

developed and colonial territories is of infinitely greater importance as the main channel of social initiative and the main route of personal advancement than it is in countries like Britain), but as an example of literate government operating in an illiterate society and how it differs from the same situation in an almost wholly literate society like our own, consider the confrontation of a police constable and a farmer. The farmer is barefoot, and the policeman is wearing a pair of large, shiny boots, and this difference may stand as a symbol of their relative ability to protect themselves in modern West Africa. The police constable is literate, he has learnt (at some pain perhaps) not only to adapt himself to a specific set of rules and regulations, but to wield them against others; he is an authority on the law, at least at his own level; he can arrest the farmer, or report him, and he has, again at his own level, innumerable official and semi-official contacts with officers of other branches of government service. The farmer is relatively a child. He is uncertain of the exact contents of the various laws that affect him, and uncertain how he stands in relation to them. He knows he should have a licence for his shotgun but cannot be sure that the one he has is still valid, or if the clerk who issued it cheated him with a worthless piece of paper. He knows he should have paid his taxes, but he has lost his receipt, and anyway there is something called a tax year, different from a calendar year, which 'they' keep on changing, so perhaps he should have paid some more anyway. Even if he feels sure that he has committed no crime, he cannot defend himself against the policeman. To complain to the constable's superior would not be much good in the face of the *esprit de corps* of the police. He can defend himself only by going to some other member of the literate class, a letter writer perhaps, or if the case is really serious, a lawyer, but has none of the skills necessary to choose a competent practitioner, and he may be so misunderstood that his real case is never put. Even if he has a good case and wins, it may not do him much good. All the policeman's colleagues will know about it and sooner or later, of course, he *will* break a law. Much better give the policeman what he is asking for, or if he is not asking for anything, better give him something anyway so that when something does go wrong, he will be more likely to be nice about it. *A man does not,* says the Ashanti proverb, *rub bottoms with a porcupine.*

Consider for a moment a similar scene in, say, the prosperous county of Sussex. In Sussex the farmer would be as well if not better

189

M. McMullan

educated than the policeman, and will know those parts of the
law which affect him better than does the policeman. The farmer
may be himself a magistrate or a local government councillor, or
know magistrates and councillors and perhaps the Chief Constable
socially. For *this* policeman to demand money from *this* farmer for
doing him a favour or not doing him a disfavour would be a
laughable miscalculation.

This contrast may be overdrawn, but serves to make the point.
The illiterate man entangled in the toils of a literate government
is under a disadvantage for which practically nothing can compensate
him, but wealth can help[5]. Sometimes the West African farmer, in
addition to his other disabilities, would be poorer than the policeman, though the pay of a police constable in West Africa is not high;
but if he were a cocoa farmer, a rubber farmer, a coffee farmer, or
not a farmer at all, but one of the large number of persons who,
although illiterate, make more money than a police constable, then
the temptation for the farmer to compensate himself for his lack of
power and knowledge by use of his money becomes clear. Equally
clear are the opportunities for an ill-paid policeman to turn his
power over wealthy illiterates into a supplement to his pay. This
exchange of wealth for power, and power for wealth, is, of course,
the typical pattern of corruption.

The phenomenon of a literate government in an illiterate society
arose in West Africa with the imposition of colonial rule, but it does
not, of course, pass with the coming of independence. The independent governments in Nigeria and Ghana are quite as much committed to literate government as was the colonial regime, indeed,
since independence, departments, officials, laws and regulations have
multiplied at a great rate. The removal of this particular disharmony
cannot be achieved by the abolition of literate government, but only
by the abolition of illiteracy in the society.

(b) *The Operation of the Law*

My second example of persons and groups put under a disadvantage by official policy and thereby becoming a source of corruption is
the operation of certain laws. All laws put certain persons under a
disadvantage, i.e., those who do or wish to do what the laws forbid.
Such persons are a source of corruption in every country.
But laws differ:—
    (i) in the extent to which public opinion supports them;

A Theory of Corruption

(ii) in the ease with which their breach can be detected;

(iii) in the profits to be made by breaking them.

(ii) and (iii), of course, stem to some extent from (i).

If a man tries to land an aeroplane in a suburban garden he will find: —

(i) that all the neighbours are anxious to assist the police;

(ii) that his transgression has become instantly notorious;

(iii) that the financial rewards are not impressive.

If he tries to sell alcoholic drinks after hours he will find: —

(i) that many members of the public will be very pleased;

(ii) that it can often be done without the police getting to hear of it;

(iii) that it is a source of financial profit.

Obviously, it is breaches of the law of the second sort which are most likely to be a source of corruption. Laws regulating gambling and drinking, for instance, usually have little general support from the population, will be broken by otherwise law-abiding citizens, are difficult to enforce, and frequently broken. They tend to bring all laws into disrepute, and, by the creation of a large class of persons vulnerable to legal action at the hands of the petty officers of the law, they encourage corruption. An extreme example of this type of law was, of course, prohibition in the United States. Post-war rationing in the United Kingdom had similar consequences, fortunately on a smaller scale, but will remind us that such laws are occasionally necessary whatever the price that must be paid for them.

Let us return for a moment to our Sussex policeman. Is there any group of people with whom his relations are similar to the relations of his West African confrere with the West African farmer? The answer is Yes. There are, first of all, the professional criminals, those who habitually break the law. Such people he can harrass, and they find it very hard to strike back at him, however unjustly he may beset them. Criminals are a notorious source of corruption in any police force. Next, and perhaps more important, as they usually have more money than the criminal classes proper, are people who engage in trade and activities where the line between legality and illegality is so fine, and the regulations so complex, that they are always in danger of unwittingly committing an offence, nearly always being tempted to commit one, and can therefore plausibly be accused of an offence at almost any time. Notable examples are public-house keepers, bookmakers and motorists.[6] Any

191

M. McMullan

government must, and does, put some activities out of bounds; each time it does so, however, it puts some of the population at a disadvantage and anxious to defend themselves by corrupting those whose duty it is to enforce the laws.

For obvious historical reasons, these West African territories have an unusually large number of laws which, by the criteria I have suggested, are likely to give rise to corruption. A colonial regime, especially one like the British, responsible to a representative government in the metropolitan country, is bound, and indeed most people in the metropolitan country regard it as duty bound, to frame its laws with more regard to British than West African standards of desirable behaviour. Particularly during the early years of colonial rule, the colonial governments were more responsive to British than to West African pressure groups. For instance, the abolition of slavery was brought about by a popular agitation in Britain, but brought the British Government's representatives in West Africa into conflict with powerful and traditionally respectable elements of African society. Another example is the rules which arose from the British Government's adherence to the Geneva Convention restricting the sale of spirits to the inhabitants of protectorates. These may have been excellent, but did not spring from West African conditions or West African demands, and were consequently a source of conflict and alienation between rulers and ruled. The enforcement of these laws was, of course, sporadic and uncertain, so lightly were the territories administered and policed. Many of the difficulties that might have arisen from the imposition of alien laws were avoided by the sheer impossibility of enforcing them, and the wide discretion given to District Officers to adjust the intentions of the Statute Book to the realities of the local situation. But not all conflict could be avoided. The Second World War, for instance, produced a great many laws intended to regulate economic activity. Without adequate means to enforce such regulation, and without any understanding by the population of why such regulation was desirable, laws of this sort served mainly to corrupt the officers charged with their enforcement. An excellent example is the Exchange Control laws. Introduced during the war, when the Imperial Government understandably required all sterling territories to have approximately similar laws concerning the import and export of currency, etc., they were practically unenforceable against the indigenous merchants who crossed and recrossed the unpatrolled and often undefined land

A Theory of Corruption

frontiers of West Africa. At the same time, 'smuggling' of currency was, and still is, profitable and completely devoid of any 'criminal' stigma; after all, the evasion of currency regulations was widely practised in the United Kingdom, where the population had much more reason to appreciate the need for them. Still, the law was there, and was, through honest zeal, malice, or with intent to extort, spasmodically enforced, so that many who regarded themselves as honest merchants were vulnerable to attacks from officers of the law, and under the necessity of buying them off. Trade across the frontier in West Africa is often extremely profitable, and these laws became a serious focus of corruption for enforcement officers. At some customs stations a *pro rata* tariff was extracted by the officials from those travellers who wished to import foreign currency, but were too lazy to walk through the bush with it.

Once again, this type of conflict between the government and society first arose with colonialism, but it does not disappear with the coming of independence. President Nkrumah's government, for instance, is more strongly committed to the transformation of Ghanaian society than the colonial regime ever was, and this transformation is bound to involve acute strains between the laws and the behaviour of the ordinary Ghanaians. This is particularly true, of course, of laws controlling economic behaviour in one way or another, inevitable when a government is committed to developing the country as rapidly as possible. High taxation, for instance, will enrol many normally honest people into the semi-criminal ranks of the tax evaders. Any form of direct control of rare resources has the same effect.[7] No society can be transformed without laws that go against the interests and accepted behaviour of some people in it; these laws will set up the sort of conflicts which give rise to corruption. A wise government might be expected, while recognising this regrettable fact, to limit such laws to what it regards as absolute essentials. Such attractive possibilities as the prohibition of nudity, polygamy, or football pools might be thought to be unnecessary additions to the strains and frictions which will be imposed by a nationalist government's essential programme.

The Subjective Element

As I said earlier, there is a constant interaction between the willingness of officials to receive bribes and the willingness of the public to give them. It is part of the general conflict between the aims and

M. McMullan

methods of the government and the society which is being governed
that the subjective attitude of many officials in these countries should
not be in harmony with their objective rôles. The official rôle is
not one indigenous to West Africa, but an import from another
society where it has grown up flanked and buttressed by many attitudes and social forces missing in its new environment. Many West
African officials have successfully adopted and internalised the qualities required for their rôle, but it is not surprising that many have
not been completely successful. The West African official, subject
to pressures of which his British colleague knows nothing,⁸ is caught
and squeezed precisely at the point of conflict between the colonial
(or post-colonial) government and the indigenous society. The British
official in West Africa is an overseas projection of a well established
and understood mode of metropolitan behaviour, protected by traditions of aloofness and difference, and the approval of those that
matter most to him (other British officials) from the alien pressures
of West African society. This subjective aspect of the question, the
question of the individual morality, is of great importance, and I
shall touch on it again when I discuss possible remedies for
corruption.

High Level Corruption

I have so far been dealing mainly with corruption at the lower
levels of the government, the level at which hundreds of petty
officials enforce the laws on the general public. Corruption at a high
level, corrupt behaviour by Cabinet Ministers, Judges, Ambassadors,
presents different though related problems. A Cabinet Minister who
accepts bribes is trading his power for money just as surely as is the
police constable, but we are here moving out of the realm where
sociological generalisation is *necessarily* useful. A Cabinet Minister
may be corrupt in any society, but this may have much more to do
with his individual circumstances than any generalisation that can
be made about the society. Yet most informed people would agree
that these West African territories are more troubled by corruption
among Cabinet Ministers or their like than is, say, Denmark. This
fact can be related to certain features of these societies.

(a) A climate of corruption in a society will affect Ministers as
well as policemen, and, perhaps more important, will lead to public
condonation of corruption by Cabinet Ministers. It is a most dis-
concerting feature of these societies that ordinary citizens will believe,

A Theory of Corruption

and recount, the most fantastic stories, some of them palpably untrue, of corruption among their leaders, with no or very little sense of indignation. Even when official enquiries have disclosed instances of undoubted corruption, this has often had no effect on the political careers of the persons involved.

(b) Politicians in West Africa do not come from an established patrician class. Most of them are 'new men' and have therefore had no opportunity to develop standards different from the rest of society, such as can develop in a particular class or group, and are not personally wealthy (at the beginning of their careers at least). Elevation to Cabinet rank therefore presents them at once with new needs for money (see (c) below), and new opportuities for acquiring it by trading their power for the wealth of others.

(c) As Ministers in a British-type parliamentary regime, they are playing rôles not well suited to their own education or to the society in which they are expected to play them. I will give two examples:—

(i) The sharp distinction that has grown up in Britain between the purposes for which public funds can and cannot be used creates special difficulties in a West African context. In England in Henry VII's day the King's money was the King's money, and was used for forwarding the interest of his government in every way. Subsequently there grew up a constitutionally important but by no means wholly logical distinction between those functions of the government on which public money could be spent, and those functions (e.g., the organisation of public support) for which politicians organising themselves in parties were expected to find finance elsewhere. In England, money for political parties is available from the large funds accumulated by businesses or Trade Unions, but in West Africa such sources are not available. As in most other parts of the world, standard subscriptions from ordinary party members are not sufficient to finance this important aspect of government. Governmental corruption, 'kick-backs' on profitable contracts, the sale of profitable or prestige-giving appointments, are an obvious source of party funds. A great deal of the corruption at ministerial level in West Africa is to be explained along these lines, and in these cases really amounts to a transfer of public funds from one type of political expenditure (i.e., legitimate by British criteria), to the other type, i.e., party political expenditure.

(ii) In Britain, the distinction between the official and private

195

M. McMullan

capacities of the holders of high office is widely understood and accepted. As a private person, a Minister of the Crown is not expected to be particularly hospitable or lavish in his hospitality. In West Africa, if a man holds high office, he is often expected to entertain his relations, tribesmen, political supporters, for such generosity may be a condition of continued political eminence.

(d) The desire for wealth, for whatever purpose, is reinforced in many cases by a sense of the impermanence of the new status. It is not easy for a man who has risen from poverty to eminence and riches in a few years, as many African leaders have done, to feel confident that the present affluence will continue. The widespread stories of secret bank accounts in Switzerland and other foreign countries are, if true, to be accounted for by the desire to hoard against possible lean years ahead.

The Function of Corruption

What is the social function of corruption in West Africa? Although damaging to official ideals and aims, it is clearly not a subversive or revolutionary phenomenon. It is rather an emollient, softening conflict and reducing friction. At a high level it throws a bridge between those who hold political power and those who control wealth, enabling the two classes, markedly apart during the initial stages of African nationalist governments, to assimilate each other. At the lower level it is not an attack on the government or its instruments by the groups discriminated against, but an attempt by them to reach an accommodation by which they accept their inferior status but avoid some of its consequences. In spite of the damage it does to a government and its policies, it may be of assistance in reducing resentments which might otherwise cause political difficulties. This useful role can be demonstrated by the semi-official recognition given by the British colonial regime to a practice which in the United Kingdom would be classified as corrupt—the acceptance of gifts from local chiefs by District Officers. This well-established, well-known, but never, for obvious reasons, officially recognised practice, grew from the traditional custom of presenting gifts to chiefs when approaching them with requests for favours. It was tolerated by the colonial regime, albeit in a limited form, because of its value for that regime. The colonial District Officer was, to most of the chiefs of his district, an unpredictable alien, wielding wide, undefined, powers according to incomprehensible criteria, whose arrival in the local

196

A Theory of Corruption

rest house was often a cause of alarm. The courtesies of the offer and acceptance of gifts of eggs and chickens brought this alarming official some way into the chief's familiar world, threw some bridge across the gulf which separated the two men, and created a relationship in which the inevitable frictions were softened by a personal familiarity and a traditional context. This was, of course, of great value to the District Officer in doing his job, and was therefore tolerated by the colonial authorities. A similar softening of what might otherwise be an intolerable relationship between the official and the people he deals with can result from more heinous dealings. Indeed, the greater the corruption the greater the harmony between corruptor and corruptee.

Application and Development of the Argument

I cannot attempt a detailed application of my tentative thesis to other societies, but on a superficial view it seems to have much to recommend it. Countries such as the Scandinavian States, with a marked homogeneity of society, are, it is generally agreed, fairly free from corruption. The shortcomings in this respect of the U.S.A. can be related to its large immigrant populations and its second class races. The rôle of immigrants in the corruption of big city politics is a commonplace of American political science.[9] The corruption in Spain, Portugal and some Middle Eastern countries might be explicable in terms of the wide divergence between the very wealthy classes, who have a considerable voice in government, and the general poor. Despotic and dictatorial government might be found to be more likely to produce and indeed to protect corruption than forms of government more responsible to the views of the ruled. A theoretically interesting limiting case is that of slavery. Slaves are a group under an extreme disability, with an obvious need to protect themselves. Under many forms of slavery, however, they have no money or other means to corrupt their overseers. The extreme degrees of disability therefore may not result in corruption, as they remove the means of protection. The optimum conditions for corruption, according to this theory, surround a group under a harsh disability but still possessed of considerable wealth—a Jewish money-lender in a 19th century Polish ghetto, for instance—a Negro book-maker in an Arkansas town—a wealthy brothel-owner in London. These conclusions do not seem to be contradicted by what we know of the facts.

197

M. McMullan

Remedies for Corruption

Responsible leaders in West Africa often make statements denouncing the prevalence and the dangers of corruption and not infrequently launch campaigns to 'root it out'.[10] I am unaware of any such campaign which has had any lasting effect, or indeed has even led to many prosecutions. Various remedies from prayer to flogging have been suggested, but none has been seriously tried.

Draconian programmes for combating corruption are sometimes elaborated. These involve extremely heavy punishments together with a highly-trained, well-paid corps of *agents provocateurs*. The combination of the two is supposed to alarm all potential corruptors or corruptees so much that they are frightened ever to offer or accept a bribe for fear of being denounced. Unfortunately, such violent police pressure unsupported by public opinion would be quite likely to result in an *increase* of corruption and of blackmail. The *agents provocateurs* themselves would have to be members of the society in which they were operating and it is hard to imagine that such a job would attract persons whose integrity would be beyond doubt. Frequent change of personnel would be required so that large numbers of such *agents* would be needed, making it even more difficult to ensure a high standard. Their opportunities for blackmail would be immense, and it is easy to see that such a campaign could only lead to unpleasantness far outweighing any possible beneficial result.

Given the continued desire by the governments of the West African countries for rapid economic development and general modernisation, conflicts fruitful of corruption will continue and are indeed almost certain to increase so that no immediate improvement is at all likely. It will be a long time before the societies are remoulded and homogeneous with the government; even total literacy will take considerably more than a generation. Does this mean that there is nothing useful that can be done except to wait for the slow evolution of the society?

The answer is, I think, that a great many useful things can be done, but none which will have dramatically rapid results. To achieve anything at all, of course, the leadership of the country concerned must regard the problem as really important, and be prepared on occasion to sacrifice political advantage by, for instance, making an example of a corrupt Minister even though he has a

A Theory of Corruption

politically useful following in the country. Given such leadership, and it cannot be taken for granted that it is always available, the following measures suggest themselves:—

(a) Exemplary proceedings against Ministers or other important functionaries to publicise the government's determination;

(b) A slight increase of police pressure against corruption at all levels;

(c) A fairly low-pitched but steady and continuous educational effort in schools, colleges, and in the newspapers, and by other means of publicity. Not just a short and violent campaign, but one continuing over years and becoming a normal part of all educational processes.

(d) Most important of all, a special effort with the public service. This is the most hopeful line of approach and might produce relatively quick results. If I am right about the effect that development and modernisation will have on these societies, there is no hope of removing the public servant's opportunities for corruption. It may, however, be possible to train him not to take advantage of his opportunities. Small groups of people can be trained to have different standards in some respects from those of the generality of people, and in any society this is a normal feature of specialisation; each specialised group has special standards in respect of its own work. By educational pressure and disciplinary measures it should be possible to raise the standard of the public service. Such a policy could only succeed, however, if service conditions and salaries were good and the status of the service high.

(e) Careful scrutiny of existing and projected laws to eliminate those that tend to increase the opportunities for corruption unnecessarily.

It will be seen that I have not included in this programme any reference to religious or social emotions sweeping through the population. Such events are, however efficacious, not usually to be invoked by statesmen.

Conclusion

In conclusion, I should like to emphasise two points.

1. In the West African countries under consideration, the colonial regime is the obvious historical source of the conflict between the government and the society. It is not suggested that similar conflicts cannot arise without colonialism, or that colonialism is exceptionally

M. McMullan

potent as a cause of corruption. There are countries which have never been colonies in the sense in which the word is used of West Africa, where corruption is much greater than it is in these countries. Moreover, as I have indicated, the succession regimes there are committed to a far more thoroughgoing programme of change than their colonial predecessors, so that the conflicts productive of corruption may be intensified after independence. Moreover, corruption under the colonial regime was limited by the presence of colonial service officials whose standards were those of the British public service. It is not yet certain how far an indigeneous civil service can have the same effect.

2. Corruption is an evil, but the avoidance of corruption cannot be more than a subsidiary aim of government policy. If my thesis is correct, colonialism and the modernising westernising policy of succession governments give rise to corruption—but this, in itself, is not a condemnation of colonialism or a modernising policy. Governments must frequently act in ways which result in conflicts fruitful of corruption. The means of control, forced purchase and rationing necessary to deal with a local famine, for instance, are always productive of corruption, but no one would hesitate to pay this inevitable price when people are threatened with starvation. What one may, however, hope, is that a consciousness among policy makers that corruption is a phenomenon with causes that can be understood, will lead to a choice of methods designed to minimise corruption, and to an understanding of the need to strengthen factors working against it—the most important of which is the subjective integrity of the public service.

London.

---

[1] In West Africa, the Nigerian Governments have published some very useful reports of Enquiries into allegations of corruption, e.g. *The Report of the Commission of Enquiry into Port Harcourt Town Council*, Government Printer Enugu 1953; *The Report of the Enquiry into the Allocation of Market Stalls at Aba by P. F. Grant*, G.P. Enugu 1955; dealing with activities at a higher level there is the *Report of the Tribunal Appointed to Enquire into Allegations of Improper Conduct by the Premier of Eastern Nigeria in Connection with the Affairs of the African Continental Bank Ltd.*, G.P. Lagos 1957. From Ghana there is the *Report of the Commission of Enquiry into Mr. Braimah's resignation and the Allegations Arising therefrom*, G.P. Accra 1954. For similar phenomena in another colonial territory, see *Commission of Enquiry into Matters Affecting the Public Service*, G.P. Kuala Lumpur 1955.

A Theory of Corruption

[2] E.g. President Nkrumah's announcement that the Ghana Government would set up a permanent Commission to investigate all forms of corruption and to receive complaints about it (*Ghana Today*, 22 June, 1960).

[3] In England there are a large number of laws against corruption. The most comprehensive definition is that in Section 1(1) of the Prevention of Corruption Act 1906, which includes not only corruption by public officials, but also similar behaviour by any agent or employee. Of course the type of behaviour which is the subject of this paper is not in West Africa or anywhere else confined to public officials. Similar behaviour is common among the employees of private companies, educational institutions, etc.

[4] I can claim no direct acquaintance with Hausa Histories or folk-tales but Hausa friends assure me that bribery is a not uncommon theme or incident in them. It seems to figure much less in Akan legends and tales.

[5] It is worth mentioning here that in many countries with a largely illiterate population the defence of the unlettered man against government officials is often an important function of political parties. Here the illiterate is buying protection in exchange for his vote or his general support for the party.

[6] In West Africa lorry drivers are always complaining about extortion by the police. It is often alleged that the police on road patrol simply collect a toll from all passing lorry drivers. If the driver refuses to pay it is, of course, never difficult for the police to accuse them of some driving offence or to find some detail of their lorry that does not conform to the, inevitably, complex regulations.

[7] The allocation of Market Stalls by Local Government Councils in West Africa is a regular cause of scandals. The trouble is that these exceedingly valuable properties are usually let at rents greatly below what they are worth. The difference inevitably transforms itself into bribes. The simple device of charging as much rent as the traders would be prepared to pay does not, perhaps understandably, commend itself to the Councillors and officials.

[8] See Chinua Achebe's novel *No Longer at Ease*, William Heinemann Ltd. 1960, for an excellent description of these problems.

[9] The classic statement is, of course, in Lincoln Steffen's *The Shame of the Cities* and his autobiography.

[10] After this paper was written, President Nkrumah announced (see *Sunday Times* of April 19th, 1961, for a report by Mary Dorkenoo) new measures directed particularly against corruption among M.P.s and party officials. The tone of the announcement would seem to indicate that this new campaign will be conducted with some vigour.

[2]

Economic Development
Through Bureaucratic Corruption

by Nathaniel H. Leff

Among scholars the subject of corruption is nearly taboo. Placing it in a model of developing economy as a developing factor is even worse in some eyes. No doubt, Nathaniel H. Leff's analysis will be misunderstood. So be it. It still bids us to understand an important area of social behavior, and tells us why public policies will fail. The author is at Harvard University.

THE BUREAUCRATIC CORRUPTION of many underdeveloped countries has been widely condemned both by domestic and foreign observers. Apart from the criticism based on moral grounds, and the technocratic impatience with inefficiency, corruption is usually assumed to have important prejudicial effects on the economic growth of these societies.[1]

Corruption is an extra-legal institution used by individuals or groups to gain influence over the actions of the bureaucracy. As such, the existence of corruption *per se* indicates only that these groups participate in the decision-making process to a greater extent than would otherwise be the case. This provides information about the effective—as opposed to the formal—political system, but in itself, tells us nothing about the content and development effects of the policies so determined. These depend on the specific orientation and interests of the groups which have gained political access. As we shall see, in the context of many underdeveloped countries, this point can be crucial. For example, if business groups are otherwise at a disadvantage in articulating their interests to the government, and if these groups are more likely to promote growth than is the government, then their enhanced participation in policy formulation can help development.

Furthermore, our discussion is limited to corruption of a particular type: namely, the practice of buying favors from the bureaucrats responsible for formulating and administering the government's economic policies. Typical examples are bribery to obtain foreign exchange, import, export, investment or production licenses, or to avoid paying taxes. Such bribes are in the nature of a tax levied on economic activity. These payments have not been legitimized by the correct political process, they are appropriated by the bureaucrat rather than the state, and they involve the subversion of the government's economic policies—hence the stigma that attaches to them. The question for us to decide is whether the net effects caused by such payments and policy redirection are likely to favor or hinder economic development.

We should also distinguish between bureaucratic corruption and bureaucratic inefficiency. Corruption refers to extra-legal influence on policy formulation or implementation. Inefficiency, on the other hand, has to do with the success or failure, or the economy of means

used by the bureaucracy in attaining given goals, whether those of its political directors, or those of the grafters. Empirically, inefficiency and corruption may appear together, and may blend into each other. Both as a policy problem and for analytical purposes, however, it is important to distinguish between two essentially different things.

Who Condemns Corruption?

Before proceeding to our analysis of the economic effects of bureaucratic corruption, it may be useful to make a brief detour. Any discussion of corruption must contend with the fact that the institution is almost universally condemned. Insofar as this criticism is based on moralizing—explicit or latent—self-interest, or ideology, it can be a formidable obstacle to rational analysis. Consequently, in order to gain a degree of perspective on the subject, I would like to consider the sources of the widespread prejudice against corruption. Identifying the specific sources of bias, and breaking down generalized censure to its component parts should help us to evaluate each argument on its own merits. For this purpose, let us consider the origins of the critical attitude held by such groups as foreign observers, government officials, and entrepreneurs, and by intellectuals, politicians, and businessmen in the underdeveloped countries themselves.

Foreigners living in the underdeveloped countries have been persistent critics of corruption. First, they have resented the payments of graft to which they are often subjected in the normal course of their business. Secondly, they have condemned corruption on moral grounds, and criticized it as both a cause and a characteristic of the backwardness of these countries.

A more sophisticated, and recent version of this argument derives from the new interest in promoting economic development. As economists and observers of economic development have grown aware of the enormous obstacles to spontaneous growth, they have come to assign an increasingly important role to the governments of the underdeveloped countries.

First, there has been an emphasis on the need for entrepreneurs, coupled with the fear that the underdeveloped countries may lack indigenous sources of entrepreneurship. Secondly, recent economic theory stressed the importance of indivisibilities, externalities, and other structural features that may prevent an underdeveloped economy from breaking out of a low-income equilibrium trap. In addition, there was the realization that the flow of private capital and technical skills was insufficient for promoting large-scale growth. With the ensuing flow of inter-governmental transfers, came the need for the governments of the underdeveloped countries to assume responsibility for the resources they were receiving.

Because of these reasons and political pressures, the governments of the underdeveloped countries have come to occupy a very prominent place in most visions of economic development. In a sense, economists have collected their problems, placed them in a box labelled "public policy", and turned them over to the governments of the underdeveloped countries.

In order for the governmental policies to be effective, however, the bureaucracies must actually implement them. Hence it becomes crucial that officials not be influenced, through graft, to deviate from their appointed tasks. The logic of this argument goes as follows: development—bureaucracy—efficiency—probity. This chain of reasoning is central to the whole critique of corruption, and we shall examine it carefully in the next section. Before going further, however, let us note a few important points about this argument.

First, it confuses bureaucratic inefficiency and bureaucratic redirection through dishonesty and graft. Secondly, transferring these problems to the governments and bureaucracies is hardly enough to solve them, for these institutions may not be at all likely to promote growth. Rather than leading the development process, the governments and bureaucracies may be lagging sectors. Finally, the argument implies that because the bureaucracy is so strategic an institution, an attack on bureaucratic corruption deserves high policy priority, offering relatively cheap and easy gains.

Foreign aid missions seem to have been particularly prone to draw such conclusions, for understandable reasons. The bureaucracy's performance will determine the success or failure of many other projects. Moreover, in contrast with some of the other problems facing foreign development specialists, reform of the civil service may seem a relatively straightforward matter. Furthermore, whereas in other development efforts foreign specialists may feel hampered by the lack of well tested doctrine and procedures, in restructuring the bureaucracy, they can rely on the expertise of public administration and management science. Therefore, it is not surprising that so much foreign development attention and activity have been directed toward the reform of the bureaucracies of underdeveloped countries.

In the underdeveloped countries themselves, much of the condemnation of graft has also come from interest in economic development, and from the apparent cogency of the development/bureaucracy/efficiency/probity logic.

Here, moreover, the special ideological perspectives and interests of powerful and articulate groups have reinforced the criticism. Let us consider the specific perspectives that intellectuals, politicians, and businessmen in the underdeveloped countries possess.

The attitudes of intellectuals and of politicians toward corruption overlap to a certain degree. As members of the same rising elite, they condemn corruption because of the idealistic streak which often pervades radicals and reformers. Contemporary intellectuals in underdeveloped countries often emulate the Jacobins in their seeking after virtue. Moreover, as Shils has pointed out,[2] they frequently attribute sacral value to the governmental sphere: hence their hostility to the venality that would corrupt it. More generally, they may see graft as an integral part of the political culture and system of the *ancien regime* which they want to destroy.

Furthermore, they also have a direct interest in discrediting and eliminating corruption because of its functional effects. In most underdeveloped countries, interest groups are weak, and political parties rarely permit the participation of elements outside the contending cliques. Consequently, graft may be the only institution allowing other interests to achieve articulation and representation in the political process. Therefore, if the ruling elite is to maintain its exclusive control of the bureaucracy, it must cut off or control this channel of influence.[3] Such considerations apply especially when the politically disadvantaged group consists of an ethnic minority or of foreign entrepreneurs over whom the elite would like to maintain its dominance.

Entrepreneurs in underdeveloped countries have also condemned bureaucratic corruption. This is understandable, for they must pay the bribes. Moreover, because of certain economic characteristics of graft, the discontent that it arouses probably goes far beyond the cost of the bribe alone.

It is important to realize that most of the objects of corruption are available only in fixed and limited supply. For example, at any point in time, there is only a given amount of foreign exchange or a given number of investment licenses to be allocated. Consequently, when the number of favors is small relative to the number of aspirants, entrepreneurs must bid against each other in what amounts to a clandestine and imperfect auction. With competition forcing prices up, the favors will tend to be allocated to those who can pay the highest prices. In the long run, the favors will go to the most efficient producers, for they will be able to make the highest bids which are compatible with remaining in the industry.

Marginal firms, on the other hand, will face severe pressures. Either they accept sub-normal profits, or they must make the effort to increase efficiency, so as to muster the resources necessary to bid successfully. If they drop out of the contest, they are placed in a weakened position *vis-a-vis* the other firms, which are now even more intra-marginal because of the advantages given by the bureaucratic favor.

This sort of situation, where the efficient are able to out-do the inefficient, is not generally appreciated by businessmen. It is likely to be the less popular in under-developed countries where—in deference to the prevalence of inefficiency, and to local ideas of equity—the more usual practice is to tax efficient producers in order to subsidize the inefficient. Moreover, as we have seen, corruption may introduce an element of competition into what is otherwise a comfortably monopolistic industry.

Furthermore, in their bidding for bureaucratic favors, businessmen may have to give up a substantial part of the profits from the favor. The economic value of the favor is equal to the return expected from the favored position it makes possible. This value constitutes the upper limit to the bids made by entrepreneurs. The actual amount paid is indeterminate, and depends on the relative bargaining skills of the bureaucrats and the businessmen. The competitive bidding between businessmen, however, may force the price to approach the upper limit. In such a case, the bureaucrat captures the lion's share of the profits expected from the favor. Competitive selling by different bureaucrats may strengthen the bargaining position of the businessmen, but in general they are probably forced to pay out a relatively large portion of their expected gains. Hence, it is not surprising that they dislike an institution which deprives them of the fruits of their enterprise.[4]

The foregoing discussion suggests that many of the negative attitudes toward corruption are based upon special viewpoints and interests. We should also realize that the background material available on the subject is both scanty and one-sided. Those who engage in corruption maintain secrecy about their operations, so that the little data available comes from declared opponents of the institution. Moreover, those who profit from corruption may themselves have no idea of the socially beneficial effects of their activities.

The widespread condemnation of corruption has come to constitute a serious obstacle to any reexamination of the subject. Indeed, the criticism has become something of a ritual and symbol-laden preamble accompanying policy discussion and statements in the underdeveloped countries. As such, it is cherished for the modicum of consensus it provides to otherwise antagonistic groups.

Positive Effects of Corruption

The critique of bureaucratic corruption often seems to have in mind a picture in which the government and civil service of underdeveloped countries are working intelligently and actively to promote economic development, only to be thwarted by the efforts of grafters. Once the validity of this interpretation is disputed, the effects of corruption must also be reevaluated. This is the case if the government consists of a traditional elite which is indifferent if not hostile to development, or of

a revolutionary group of intellectuals and politicians, who are primarily interested in other goals. At the same time, the propensity for investment and economic innovation may be higher outside the government than within it.

Indifference and hostility of government

In the first instance, the government and bureaucracy may simply be indifferent to the desires of entrepreneurs wanting to initiate or carry on economic activities. Such a situation is quite likely in the absence of effective popular pressure for economic development, or in the absence of effective participation of business interests in the policy-making process. This is especially the case when entrepreneurs are marginal groups or aliens. More generally, when the government does not attribute much value to economic pursuits or innovation, it may well be reluctant to move actively in the support of economic activity.

Even more important, the bureaucracy may be hostile to entrepreneurs, for it dislikes the emergence of a competing center of power. This is especially the case in colonial economies, where a large domestic middle class has not emerged to challenge traditional power-holders.

Governments have other priorities

The foregoing relates to societies where although lip-service may be paid to the importance of economic development, the government and bureaucracy are oriented primarily to maintaining the *status quo*. It is also relevant in countries where a successful revolution against the *ancien regime* has occurred. There, the government may be proceeding dynamically, but not toward the promotion of economic development. Other goals, such as an increase in the military power available to the elite, or expansion of its control over society, may be justified in terms of economic development, however "ultimate". At the same time, the immediate effect of such policies is to impede growth.

Typically the bureaucracy plays an extensive interventionist role in the economy, and its consent or support is a *sine qua non* for the conduct of most economic enterprise. In such a situation, graft can have beneficial effects. First, it can induce the government to take a more favorable view of activities that would further economic growth. The policies or freedom sought by the entrepreneurs would help development, while those they subvert are keyed to other goals. Secondly, graft can provide the direct incentive necessary to mobilize the bureaucracy for more energetic action on behalf of the entrepreneurs. This is all the more important because of the necessity for bureaucratic help in so many areas—e.g., licenses, credit, and foreign exchange allocation—in order to get anything done.

Corruption reduces uncertainty and increases investment

Corruption can also help economic development by making possible a higher rate of investment than would otherwise be the case.

The investment decision always takes place in the midst of risk and uncertainty. As Aubrey has pointed out,[5] however, these difficulties are very much compounded in the economic and political environment of underdeveloped countries. The basic estimates of future demand and supply conditions are harder because of the lack of data and of the sharp shifts that can occur during a period of economic change. The dangers of misjudging the market are all the more serious because of the lower elasticities of substitution at low income levels.

Aside from the problems of making such economic estimates, the potential investor also faces a major political unknown—the behavior of the government. The possible dangers arising from the government's extensive role in the economy are increased because of the failure of representative government to put an effective check on arbitrary action. The personalist and irrational style of decision-making, and the frequent changes in government personnel and policies add to the risks. Consequently, if entrepreneurs are to make investments, they must have some assurance that the future will not bring harmful intervention in their affairs. We can see an illustration of these difficulties in the fact that in periods of political uncertainty and crisis, investment shrinks, and economic stagnation occurs. By enabling entrepreneurs to control and render predictable this important influence on their environment, corruption can increase the rate of investment.

Corruption and innovation

The would-be innovator in an underdeveloped society must contend with serious opposition from existing economic interests. Unable to compete economically with the new processes or products, they will usually turn to the government for protection of their investments and future returns. If the bureaucracy supports innovation and refuses to intervene, the innovation can establish itself in the economy. In the more usual case, however, existing economic interests can depend on their longstanding associations with bureaucratic and political compadres for protection.

In this situation, graft may enable an economic innovator to introduce his innovations before he has had time to establish himself politically.[6] Economic innovators in underdeveloped countries have often supported oppositional political cliques or parties. Corruption is another, less radical way of adjusting to the same pressures and goals.

Corruption, competition, and efficiency

As we have seen in the previous section, bureaucratic corruption also brings an element of competition, with its attendant pressure for efficiency, to an underdeveloped economy. Since the licenses and favors available to the bureaucrats are in limited supply, they are allocated by competitive bidding among entrepreneurs. Because payment of the highest bribes is one of the principal criteria for allocation, the ability to muster revenue,

either from reserves or from current operations, is put at a premium. In the long run, both of these sources are heavily dependent on efficiency in production. Hence, a tendency toward competition and efficiency is introduced into the system.

Such a pressure is all the more important in underdeveloped countries, where competition is usually absent from many sectors of the economy. In the product market, a high degree of monopoly often prevails. International competition is usually kept out by quotas, tariffs, and overvalued exchange rates. In the factor market, frictions and imperfections are common. Consequently, we can appreciate the value of introducing an element of competition, if only through the back-door.

Corruption as a hedge against bad policy

Corruption also performs the valuable function of a "hedge" and a safeguard against the full losses of bad economic policy. Even when the government of an underdeveloped country is proceeding actively and intelligently to promote growth, there is no assurance that its policies are well-conceived to attain its goals. In effect, it may be taking a vigorous step in the wrong direction. Corruption can reduce the losses from such mistakes, for while the government is implementing one policy, the entrepreneurs, with their sabotage, are implementing another. Like all insurance, this involves a cost—if the government's policy is correct. On the other hand, like all insurance, it is sometimes very welcome.

An underdeveloped country often stands in special need of such a safeguard. First, even when policy goals are clearly specified, competent counsel may well be divided as to the best means of achieving them. For example, the experts may differ among themselves on such basic issues as export promotion vs. import substitution, or other inter-sectoral priorities. Consequently, if the government has erred in its decision, the course made possible by corruption may well be the better one, supported by a dissenting segment of expert opinion. Moreover, the pervasive effects of government policy in an etatistic economy compound the effects of poor decisions, and increase the advantages of having some kind of safeguard against the potential consequences of a serious policy mistake. Corruption provides the insurance that if the government decides to steam full-speed in the wrong direction, all will not be lost.

Some illustrations may help clarify this point. For example, the agricultural producers whose graft sabotaged Peron's economic policies were later thanked for having maintained Argentina's capacity to import. Another example shows in more detail how this process can operate. An important element in the recent Latin American inflations has been the stagnation of food production, and the rise in food prices. In both Chile and Brazil, the governments reacted by freezing food prices, and ordering the bureaucracy to enforce these controls.

In Chile, the bureaucracy acted loyally to maintain price controls, and food supplies were relatively stagnant. Inflation rose faster, supported in part by the failure of food production to increase. In Brazil, however, the bureaucracy's ineffectiveness sabotaged the enforcement of price controls, and prices received by producers were allowed to rise. Responding to this price rise, food production also increased somewhat, partially limiting the course of the inflation.[7]

In this case, we see the success of entrepreneurs and corrupted officials in producing a more effective policy than the government. Moreover, subsequent economic analysis justified this "decision", by emphasizing the price elasticity of agricultural supply, and the consequent need to allow the terms of trade to turn in favor of rural producers.

These points are perhaps strengthened when viewed with some historical perspective. As John Neff has remarked, the honesty and efficiency of the French bureaucracy were in great measure responsible for the stifling of economic innovation and progress during the 18th century.[8] By way of contrast, the laxity of the British administration permitted the subversion of Colbertism, and allowed new economic processes and activities to flourish.

Alleged Negative Effects of Corruption

Most of the arguments concerning the negative effects of corruption are based on the assumption that development can best proceed through the policies of an uncorrupted government and bureaucracy. As noted in the previous section, this assumes that the government really wants economic development, and that its policies would favor growth more than the activities of an unregulated private sector. Actually, the economic policies of the governments of many underdeveloped countries may be predicated on priorities other than global economic development. Even in countries where there has been a successful revolution against the colonial *ancien régime*, policy may aim primarily at advancing the economic interests of the ruling clique or of the political group on which it bases its dominance. Although the economic policies of some countries may be foolish or catastrophic from the viewpoint of development, they may be well conceived for implementing these other goals.[9]

Impeding taxation

One version of this argument focuses on taxation. Specifically, it asserts that bureaucratic corruption may hamper development by preventing the government from obtaining the tax revenues necessary for developmental policies.

This argument probably attributes to the government an unrealistically high propensity to spend for development purposes. Economic development usually has a less compelling priority among the elites of these societies than among the westerners who observe them. Even if the dominant groups are aware and sensitive to the situation of the lower classes, they may be reluctant to bear the costs of development. Hence, the actual level of taxes collected, and their allocation in the budget may represent the decision of the ruling group as to how hard they want to press forward with economic development. In these circumstances, it is misleading to criticize the bureaucracy for the effects of its ineffective tax collection on economic growth. Of the revenues they might have collected, only a part would have gone for development rather than for the many forms of non-developmental expenditure. Moreover, when the entrepreneurs' propensity to invest is higher than the government's, the money saved from the tax collector may be a gain rather than a loss for development.

Usefulness of government spending

Furthermore, there is no reason to assume that the government has a high *marginal* propensity to spend for development purposes, based on a high income elasticity of demand for development. Without changes in the factors determining the average allocational propensities, increases in governmental revenue may well go for more lavish satisfaction of the same appetites. For example, as budgetary receipts rise, the military may be supplied with jet aircraft rather than with less expensive weapons.

Cynicism

Another argument has emphasized the social effects of corruption as an impediment to development. For example, it has been claimed that immorality and self-seeking of bureaucratic corruption may cause widespread cynicism and social disunity, and thus reduce the willingness to make sacrifices for the society's economic development.

This argument can be criticized on several points.

First, insofar as the disillusion is engendered among the *lower* social orders, the effects on development may not be as important as assumed. Because of economic and social conditions, these people are probably being squeezed as much as is possible, so that with all good will, they could not sacrifice any more.

Secondly, if the cynicism caused by bureaucratic corruption leads to increased self-seeking in the rest of the society, this may not be a completely bad thing for economic development. Many of the wealth-creating activities which make up economic growth depend on such atomistic egoism for their stimulus. Consequently, if cynicism acts as a solvent on traditional inhibitions, and increased self-seeking leads to new ambitions, economic development may be furthered.

Moreover, this argument also exaggerates the extent to which economic growth depends on a popular rallying-around rather than on many individual selfish activities. The implicit picture seems to be that of an "all-together" social effort, perhaps under etatistic direction. Once stated explicitly, such a model appears more like a fantasy of intellectuals rather than an accurate guide to how economic development takes place.

More generally, we should recognize that there are very good reasons for the incivism and unwillingness to make sacrifices that are often characteristic of under-developed societies. Mutual distrust and hostility usually have much deeper roots in cultural gaps, inequitable income distribution, and long experience of mistreatment. Rapid change, dislocating existing institutions and values, also disrupts social solidarity. In such circumstances, reduced bureaucratic corruption would make only a marginal contribution to improved public morale.

Corruption as a Policy Problem

The foregoing analysis and perspective may also be helpful in dealing with bureaucratic corruption as a policy problem.

First, we should be clear as to the nature of "the problem" that policy is attempting to solve. As we have seen, much of the criticism of corruption derives from the political, economic, and ideological interests of particular groups. Presumably the elimination of corruption is a problem only insofar as we share their specific concerns.

Aside from these special interests, however, let us consider corruption from the point of view of its effects on economic development. As we have seen, under certain conditions, the consequences of corruption for development are not as serious as is usually assumed. At the same time, it may have important positive effects that are often overlooked. Consequently, to the extent that reality approaches the conditions of our model, corruption of the type discussed in this paper may not be a problem at all. This will depend on specific conditions, and will vary between countries and between sectors.

When the conditions of our model do not obtain, however, corruption will be an important barrier to development. To the extent that corruption exists as a policy problem, it is probably wise to accept it as a particularly intractable part of an underdeveloped country. On a superficial level, we should recognize that corruption creates its own political and economic interests that will resist efforts at its eradication. More important, corruption is deeply rooted in the psychological and social structure of the countries where it exists. On the psycho-cultural plane, corruption will persist until universalistic norms predominate over particularistic attitudes. Socially, the elimination of corruption probably requires the emergence of new centers of power outside the bureaucracy, and the development of competitive politics. Such changes will come, if at all, only as the result of a long period of economic and social development.

Bureaucracy the lagging sector

Two conclusions emerge from this discussion. First, we should realize how illusory is the expectation that bureaucratic policy can intervene as a *deus ex machina*

to overcome the other barriers to economic growth. In many underdeveloped countries, the bureaucracy may be a lagging rather than a leading sector. Secondly, it should be clear that direct policy efforts against such deeply rooted psychological and social conditions cannot hope for much short-term success. As Braibanti concludes,[10] powerful investigatory commissions may have a limited success, but one should expect the problem to be improved "more by time than by effort".

Despite the pessimistic prospects for the usual direct-action policies against corruption, certain possibilities do exist for dealing with it indirectly. The problem is perhaps best conceptualized in terms of the need to economize in the use of a particularly scarce and important resource—honest and capable administrators. Indeed, for several reasons, this shortage may be more serious than others more often cited, e.g., the lack of capital. Because of political reasons, this input into the development process cannot be imported on a large scale. Furthermore as we have noted, available domestic supplies cannot be expected to increase for a long time in most underdeveloped countries. Finally, this input is all the more crucial because of its importance for the successful deployment of other resources. If we view corruption as a problem in the allocation of scarce administrative resources, two solutions are immediately suggested.

Two techniques

First, the available resources should be concentrated in areas where their productivity in promoting development would be greatest. Such budgeting of administrators would avoid dispersion of honest and able personnel, and make them available only for tasks of the highest priority.

A second way of economizing in the use of this scarce resource would be the use of alternative production techniques to achieve the same development results. In our context, this would mean employing measures to achieve the goals of policy without reliance on direct administration and bureaucratic regulation of the economy.

In many cases, the desired effects could be achieved either by market forces, or by indirect measures creating the necessary incentives or disincentives—i.e., with much less direct government intervention, and the consequent need to rely on the bureaucracy. For example, a government which wants to keep down the domestic price level can either institute a cumbersome system of price regulation, or it can permit a measure of competition from imports. Similarly, a straightforward currency devaluation can have many of the beneficial effects achieved by an administration-intensive regime of differential exchange rates. Admittedly, such policies may have some undesired consequences and side-effects that ideally would be avoided by more sophisticated government management of the economy. The point is, however, that when policy alternatives are evaluated, it would be better to take explicit account of how bureaucratic corruption will affect the direct management policies contemplated. This would lead to a more realistic choice between the means which can accomplish similar goals. Perhaps the best procedure would be to select a mixture of direct and of indirect management policies, taking account of the bureaucratic resources available.

By way of contrast, the more usual practice is to choose the policies that would be best *if* the whole bureaucracy were dependable, and then to deplore its corruption, and condemn it for the failure of the policies chosen. Following the procedure suggested here, however, governments would accept corruption as an aspect of their societies, and try to optimize policy-making within this framework.

Finally, we should note that preoccupation with corruption can itself become an impediment to development. This occurs if the focus on corruption diverts attention from other political and economic deficiencies in the society, and from the measures that can be taken despite corruption. To avoid the losses from such misdirection. re-thinking of the sort suggested here may be helpful.

REFERENCES

I am grateful to Richard Eckaus, John Plank, Lucien Pye, and Myron Weiner for their comments on an earlier draft of this paper. They bear no responsibility for the remaining deficiencies.

[1] But see V. O. Key, *The Techniques of Political Graft in the United States*, privately printed, 1936. Robert K. Merton, *Social Theory and Social Structure*, New York, 1959, pp. 19-85. Harold Lasswell, "Bribery," in *The Encyclopedia of the Social Sciences*, vol. 2, New York, 1930. Cf. especially, F. W. Riggs, "Bureaucrats and Political Development: A Paradoxical View," paper prepared for the Social Science Research Council Committee on Comparative Politics, Conference, January 29–February 2, 1962, to be published in a forthcoming volume edited by J. LaPalombara.

[2] Edward Shils, "Political Development in the New States," *Comparative Studies in Society and History*, 1960, p. 279.

[3] Cf. Riggs, *op. cit.*, pp. 28-30.

[4] These processes are nicely brought out in Alexandre Kafka, "The Brazilian Exchange Auction," *The Review of Economics and Statistics*, October, 1956.

[5] H. C. Aubrey, "Investment Decisions in Underdeveloped Countries" in *Capital Formation and Economic Growth*, National Bureau of Economic Research. Princeton, 1955, pp. 404-415. Also cf. the finding of Y. Sayigh (*Entrepreneurs of Lebanon*, Cambridge, Mass. 1962, p. 117) that political conditions constituted the greatest unknown facing the entrepreneurs surveyed.

[6] Cf. Lasswell, *op. cit.*, p. 671.

[7] I am indebted to an eminent expert in Latin American economic development for this observation.

[8] *Industry and Government in France and England: 1540–1640*. Cf. also, J. J. Spengler, "The State and Economic Growth—Summary and Interpretations," p. 368, in H. Aitken, editor, *The State and Economic Growth*, N. Y. 1959.

[9] Cf. Frank Golay, "Commercial Policy and Economic Nationalism," *Quarterly Journal of Economics*, 1958, and B. Glassburner, "Economic Policy-Making in Indonesia, 1950–1957," *Economic Development and Cultural Change*, January 1962.

[10] Ralph Braibanti, "Reflections on Bureaucratic Corruption," *Public Administration*, Winter, 1962, p. 370, and p. 372.

[3]

The Journal of Modern African Studies, 3, 2 (1965), pp. 215–30

What is the Problem About Corruption?

by COLIN LEYS*

THE 'MORALISTIC APPROACH'

THE systematic investigation of corruption is overdue. There are three main types of literature in English on the subject: historical studies of corrupt practice in Britain; inquisitional studies, mainly of the U.S.A. and the English-speaking West African and Asian countries; and sociological studies which deal with corruption incidentally. So far as I know no general study in English has appeared.[1] One reason for this seems to be a widespread feeling that the facts cannot be discovered, or that if they can, they cannot be proved, or that if they can be proved, the proof cannot be published. All these notions seem dubious. There are nearly always sources of information, some of them—such as court records—systematic in their way, and some of them very circumstantial (like privileged parliamentary debates). Many of the people involved are quite willing to talk. And commissions of enquiry have published large amounts of evidence, obtained by unusual powers of compulsion.

I doubt if it would really be as hard to discover the facts about corruption in most countries as it would be to find out the facts about some legitimate political matters which those involved really want to keep secret. One could even find ways of measuring, within broad limits, the scale and economic effects of some forms of corruption. Publishing the results might present difficulties, but these would only be acute if naming persons were essential to the object of publishing, which is not ordinarily the case in scientific enquiry, even in the social sciences. As anyone who has written on contemporary issues is aware, there are adequate con-

---

* Professor of Politics, School of Social Studies, University of Sussex, Brighton.

[1] The best known English study is perhaps Norman Gash's *Politics in the Age of Peel* (London, 1953). Much of the American literature is reviewed in V. O. Key, *Politics, Parties and Pressure Groups* (New York, 1955), ch. 13, 'Party Machine as Interest Group'. See also *The Annals of the American Academy of Political and Social Science* (Philadelphia), March 1952, special number on 'Ethical Standards in American Public Life'. The wide range of reports of commissions of enquiry into colonial malpractice is indicated in the footnotes to Ronald Wraith and Edgar Simpkins' recent work *Corruption in Developing Countries* (London, 1963). While the bulk of this material is from West Africa and deals with local government, there are valuable reports from East Africa, and also from India and Malaya and elsewhere. Unfortunately I have not had an opportunity to study Professor Van Klaveren's series of articles in *Vierteljahrschrift für Sozial und Wirtschaftsgeschichte* since 1957, referred to in his comments on M. G. Smith's 'Historical and Cultural Conditions of Political Corruption Among the Hausa', in *Comparative Studies in Society and History* (The Hague), January 1964, pp. 164–98.

ventions which enable events and incidents to be described anonymously
or obliquely without reducing their credibility or value as evidence.

But so far very few people have approached the subject of corruption
in this spirit, aiming to describe, measure, analyse, and explain the
phenomena involved.[1] This is curious when one considers the word
itself (corruption=to change from good to bad; to debase; to pervert);
it denotes patterns of action which derive their significance from the role
of value-systems in social behaviour. Similar phenomena, such as
suicide, crime, or religious fanaticism, have intrigued sociologists greatly.
However, the question of corruption in the contemporary world has so
far been taken up almost solely by moralists.

The recent book by Ronald Wraith and Edgar Simpkins on *Corruption
in Developing Countries* is of this *genre*. They are concerned with 'the
scarlet thread of bribery and corruption', with corruption which

flourishes as luxuriantly as the bush and weeds which it so much resembles,
taking the goodness from the soil and suffocating the growth of plants which
have been carefully, and expensively, bred and tended.

It is a 'jungle of nepotism and temptation', a 'dangerous and tragic
situation' in which the enthusiasm of the young African civil servant
turns to cynicism, and where there are 'not the attitudes of progress and
development'.[2]

They are aware that the 'moralising approach' (their own term) involves a difficulty, namely that their standpoint may differ from that of
those who do the things which they regard as corrupt. For instance, they
can see that since any African who is so fortunately placed as to be able to
get jobs for his relatives is felt (by the relatives at least) to be under an
obligation to do so, it is peculiar to call this corrupt:

an act is presumably only corrupt if society condemns it as such, and if the
doer is afflicted with a sense of guilt when he does it; neither of these apply
to a great deal of African nepotism.[3]

However, they are convinced (no evidence is adduced) that the results
of nepotism and all other forms of what they call corruption ('in the
strict sense . . . in the context of the *mores* of Great Britain') are serious
and bad; and they take courage from the fact that a small minority in
most developing countries shares their ethical viewpoint. Consequently

[1] An interesting and ably-written exception is M. McMullen, 'A Theory of Corruption',
in *Sociological Review* (Keele), July 1961, pp. 181–201. The author has, however, a rather
restricted conception of what corruption is, and a number of unwarrantable assumptions about
the results.

[2] Wraith and Simpkins, op. cit. pp. 12–13 and 172.   [3] Ibid. p. 35.

they conceive the problem as one of seeking in British history the causes which led to the triumph in Britain of this point of view, with its attendant advantages, in the hope that African and other developing countries might profit from the experience of Britain. (Over half the book is devoted to this enquiry.)

The results are, as they recognise, inconclusive, which is not surprising when one considers that this formulation of the problem ('Why does the public morality of African states not conform to the British?') contains an obvious enough answer: because they have a different social, economic and political system, and a different historical experience. The approach is not as bad as it sounds, for Mr Wraith and Mr Simpkins have observed the Nigerian scene with discrimination and sympathy. But the basis of the whole book is a simple faith, that corruption is what it is, namely what has been known as corruption in Britain for a long time; and it has at bottom a 'simple cause'—avarice:

the wrong that is done is done in the full knowledge that it is wrong, for the concept of theft does not vary as between Christian and Muslim, African and European, or primitive man and Minister of the Crown.[1]

Emotionally and intellectually, this seems to be in a direct line of descent from the viewpoint of those missionaries who were dedicated to the suppression of native dancing. The subject seems to deserve a more systematic and open-minded approach.[2]

WHAT IS CORRUPTION?

Under what circumstances are actions called corrupt? It seems best to start from some examples.

(1) In the spring of 1964 the (Republican) Secretary of State of Illinois died. Under the State constitution the (Democratic) Governor temporarily filled his place by appointing a young (Democratic) official to the office. Within a few weeks a substantial number of State civil

[1] Ibid. p. 45.

[2] The authors display a militant ignorance of sociological theory and research, which may be partly a consequence of their reluctance to abandon their ethical absolutism, but seems more a part of the settled philistinism on this matter which is still so depressingly common in Britain. 'It is always unwise' (they write of social anthropology) 'to argue with exponents of this formidable science, since they have their own vocabulary, which differs from that of the ordinary man, and their own concepts, which are not readily understood' (p. 172), and they proceed to represent the main burden of the social anthropologist's contribution on the subject as being to the effect that all corruption in their sense is the African's idea of a customary gift. One is provoked to echo Campbell-Bannerman's exasperated reply to the outmoded dialectics of Balfour: 'Enough of this foolery.'

servants appointed by the late Secretary of State were dismissed, and their jobs were filled by Democratic Party supporters.

(2) In Chicago about the same time a controversy was taking place concerning school desegregation. Active desegregationists alleged that they were prevented from attending in force a meeting of the City Council as part of their campaign, because all the public seating was filled by council employees who had for this purpose been given a holiday by the city administration.

(3) In Kampala, Uganda, in August 1963 the City Council decided to award a petrol station site to a majority-party member of the Council, who offered the lowest price, £4,000; the highest offer was for £11,000. It was alleged in the National Assembly that the successful purchaser resold the plot to an oil company at a profit of £8,000.[1]

(4) In Port Harcourt, Nigeria, in 1955, there were people in the Town Hall drawing labourers' salaries not provided for in the estimates; they were employed on the personal recommendation of individual councillors.[2]

(5) In New York City, in 1951, it was estimated that over $1 million per annum was paid to policemen (for overlooking illegalities) by a bookmaking syndicate.[3]

(6) In Lagos, Nigeria, in 1952, the practice of giving an unofficial cash gift or a fee for services rendered was fairly authoritatively stated to be found

in hospitals where the nurses require a fee from every in-patient before the prescribed medicine is given, and even the ward servants must have their 'dash' before bringing the bed-pan; it is known to be rife in the Police Motor Traffic Unit, which has unrivalled opportunities on account of the common practice of overloading vehicles; pay clerks make a deduction from the wages of daily paid staff; produce examiners exact a fee from the produce buyer for every bag that is graded and sealed; domestic servants pay a proportion of their wages to the senior of them, besides often having paid a lump sum to buy the job.[4]

One thing which all these events have in common is that someone regards each of them as a bad thing. Equally, however, it is clear that

[1] *Uganda Parliamentary Debates*, 27 September 1963, pp. 179–200, and 3 October 1963, pp. 411–21. The Uganda Government subsequently denied that any such sale had taken place.

[2] *Report of the Commission of Enquiry into the Working of Port Harcourt Town Council, 1955;* quoted in Wraith and Simpkins, op. cit. p. 22.

[3] *Third Interim Report of the Senate Committee to Investigate Organised Crime in Interstate Commerce, 1951* (Kefauver Committee), quoted in H. A. Turner, *Politics in the United States* (New York, 1955), p. 412.

[4] From the Storey Report, *Commission of Inquiry into the Administration of Lagos Town Council, 1953* (Lagos, 1954).

WHAT IS THE PROBLEM ABOUT CORRUPTION?   219

at least someone else—i.e. those involved in the acts in question—regards each of them as a good thing. Writers of the moralist school accept this, but they are convinced that such behaviour is always against the 'public interest'. But what is the 'public interest'? Some substantial arguments have been put forward to suggest that the public interest may sometimes *require* some of these practices. The most famous of these is probably the American defence of patronage, as in case (1) above, and 'honest graft'.[1] This argument turns essentially on the view that democratic politics in 'mass' societies can only be ensured by the integration of a multitude of interests and groups into political parties, capable of furnishing leadership and coherent policies;[2] this involves organisation and inducements, both of which cost money; therefore politics must be made to pay. From this point of view the political role of money is to serve as a cement—'a *hyphen* which joins, a *buckle* which fastens' the otherwise separate and conflicting elements of a society into a body politic; 'the greater the corruption, the greater the harmony between corruptor and corruptee', as one candid critic recognised.[3] And Professor Hoselitz has argued that the early years of the life of a nation are dominated by these 'persistent integrative needs of the society', and that

> Much of the alleged corruption that Western technical advisers on administrative services of Asian and African stages encounter, and against which they inveigh in their technical reports with so little genuine success, is nothing but the prevalence of these non-rational norms on the basis of which these administrations operate.[4]

This can be taken a stage further. The moralist school of thought may recognise that some of the activities recorded above indirectly serve these

[1] See William Turner, 'In Defence of Patronage', in *The Annals of the American Academy of Political and Social Science*, January 1937, pp. 22–8, and William J. Riordan, *Plunkitt of Tammany Hall* (New York, 1958). Plunkitt coined the phrase 'honest graft' in a famous passage:

> There's an honest graft, and I'm example of how it works. I might sum up the whole thing by sayin': 'I seen my opportunities and I took 'em.' Just let me explain by examples. My party's in power in the city and it's goin' to undertake a lot of public improvements. Well, I'm tipped off, say, that they're going to lay out a new park at a certain place. I see my opportunity and I take it. I go to that place and I buy up all the land I can in the neighbourhood. Then the board of this or that makes its plan public and there is a rush to get that land which nobody cared particular for before. Ain't it perfectly honest to charge a good profit and make a profit on my investment and foresight? Of course it is. Well, that's honest graft.

[2] See V. O. Key, op. cit. pp. 395–8.
[3] M. McMullen, op. cit. p. 197.
[4] Bert F. Hoselitz, 'Levels of Economic Performance and Bureaucratic Structures', in La Palombara (ed.), *Bureaucracy and Political Development* (Princeton, 1963), p. 190.

broadly beneficial purposes. But they generally assume that the economic price paid is a heavy one. For instance:

The sums involved in some of the proved cases of corruption in Africa would have brought considerable benefits to people for whom 'under-privileged' is too mild a word, if they had been properly spent.[1]

But spending public money properly does not guarantee that it will benefit the poor.[2] The Uganda Minister of Information was much criticised for giving a lucrative and unusual monopoly of television set sales to an American contractor, in return for building a transmission station at cut rates: even had corruption been involved the policy did produce a television station much more quickly and cheaply than the policy adopted in neighbouring Kenya.[3] To take another example, one may ask whether the Russian consumer would be better off without the operations of the illegal contact men who derive illegal incomes in return for their aid in overcoming bottlenecks in the supply of materials for production.[4] Even in the case of petty bribery or extortion, it is relevant to ask, What is the alternative? Could an equally efficient and socially useful administration be carried on if effective means of eliminating perquisites were found and all concerned were required to live on their salaries? Would the pressure for higher salaries be no greater? Could it be resisted? If it could not, would increased taxation fall on those most able to pay and would this, or reduced services, be in the public interest? To ask these questions is to realise that the answers call for research and analysis which is seldom undertaken, and that they are likely to vary according to circumstances. One also becomes aware that near the heart of the moralists' concern is the idea that the public interest is opposed to anything that heightens *inequality*. But we also have to ask how far equality and development are themselves compatible ideals. The régime most committed to both of them—the U.S.S.R.—found it necessary to postpone its concern with equality in order to achieve development.[5] This is not to say that all kinds of inequality promoted by all

---

[1] Wraith and Simpkins, op. cit. p. 172; although previously they do say 'The economic effects of all this [corruption] on a country may not be very considerable.' McMullen also believes the economic costs are high, but his definition of economic cost appears to be somewhat Gladstonian; op. cit. p. 182.

[2] For an interesting discussion of the general question, see C. C. Wrigley, *Crops and Wealth in Uganda* (Kampala, 1959), pp. 70–3.

[3] *Uganda Parliamentary Debates*, 8 November 1963, pp. 108–112, and 11 November 1963, pp. 137–142. Corruption was alleged by the opposition.

[4] M. Fainsod, *How Russia is Ruled* (Cambridge, Mass., 1958), p. 437.

[5] For a brief but penetrating comment on this see W. Arthur Lewis, *The Theory of Economic Growth* (London, 1955), pp. 428–9.

kinds of corruption are beneficial from the point of view of development; it is merely to challenge the assumption that they are invariably bad.

But we still have not answered the question, Under what circumstances are actions called corrupt? What is at issue in all the cases cited above is the existence of a standard of behaviour according to which the action in question breaks some rule, written or unwritten, about the proper purposes to which a public office or a public institution may be put. The moralist has his own idea of what the rule should be. The actors in the situations concerned have theirs. It may be the same as the moralists' (they may regard themselves as corrupt); or quite different (they may regard themselves as behaving honourably according to their standards, and regard their critics' standards as irrelevant); or they may be 'men of two worlds', partly adhering to two standards which are incompatible, and ending up exasperated and indifferent (they may recognise no particular moral implications of the acts in question at all—this is fairly obviously quite common). And in addition to the actors there are the other members—more or less directly affected—of their own society; all these positions are possible for them too.[1]

THE ANALYSIS OF CORRUPTION

The following questions suggest themselves as a reasonable basis for the analysis of any case in which corruption is alleged:

(1) What is being called corrupt and does it really happen? In the case of the African Continental Bank it became clear that no one was able to formulate a clear enough allegation against Dr N. Azikiwe showing precisely what was the rule which he had broken.[2] A precise statement is required of the rule and the sense in which it is said to have been perverted. It may turn out, as in the case of the African Continental Bank, that there is really no clear idea of what the rule is; or that there is a clear rule but that it has not clearly been broken (this was Lord Denning's verdict on the Profumo case).[3]

(2) Who regards the purpose which is being perverted as the proper or 'official' purpose? It may be so regarded by most people in the society, including those who pervert it; or it may be so regarded by only a few

---

[1] Chinua Achebe provides a fascinating selection in *No Longer at Ease* (London, 1960), pp. 5–6 and 87–8. See also E. C. Banfield, *The Moral Basis of a Backward Society* (Chicago, 1958), ch. 5.

[2] See *Report of the Tribunal appointed to inquire into allegations reflecting on the Official Conduct of the Premier of, and certain persons holding Ministerial and other Public Offices in, the Eastern Region of Nigeria* (London, 1957).

[3] *Lord Denning's Report* (London, 1963).

people (e.g. state political patronage is regarded as corrupt by only a relatively small group of American reformers).[1]

(3) Who regards the allegedly corrupt action as perverting the official purpose? This is not necessarily the same question as question (2) above. For example, in a subsequent debate in the Uganda National Assembly on the petrol station site mentioned above, the Minister of Regional Administrations accepted the principle that the Council ought not to accept offers lower than the official valuer's valuation of the property, but held that they were by no means obliged to accept the highest offer and that the Council were justified in preferring to give a 'stake' in the city to a poor man rather than to a rich one.[2] The opposition took the view that it was the man's politics rather than his poverty which actuated the majority on the Council, and that the loss to the public revenue was too high a price to pay for assisting one individual member of the public. They also took the view that the official object should be to accept the highest bid, unless circumstances of public importance not present in this case dictated otherwise. Thus the nature of the rule was also a matter of controversy, but both sides to the dispute to some extent made the distinction between the rule on the one hand, and the question of what amounted to breaking it on the other.

(4) What are the short-term and long-term consequences of the behaviour in question, both of each particular case and of such behaviour generally? The answer might usefully, if roughly, be broken into two parts: (a) objective consequences, and (b) subjective consequences. Under (a) will come such questions as, What resources are directed from what applications to what other applications? What are the real as opposed to the theoretical opportunity costs of the alleged corruption? What are the effects for income distribution? And what consequential effects are there on the pattern of loyalties, the scope of party activities, the incentives to economic activity? etc. etc. Under (b) will come such questions as e.g., What effect does behaving in this way have on the work of civil servants who regard themselves as behaving corruptly? and, What effect does observing such behaviour have on the attitudes and/or behaviour of others? etc. etc.

It is natural but wrong to assume that the results of corruption are always both bad and important. For instance it is usually assumed that

---

[1] Wraith and Simpkins ally themselves with the analogous minority in West Africa whom they identify as 'the most eminent and responsible citizens' of these countries; op. cit. p. 173. It appears that Chinua Achebe should be included among these, and to this extent it is permissible to wonder how typical are the reactions of his hero in *No Longer at Ease*, who has an ultimate and profound revulsion against his own acceptance of bribes.

[2] *Uganda Parliamentary Debates*, 27 September 1963, p. 187.

a corrupt civil service is an impediment to the establishment of foreign private enterprise, which has enough difficulties to contend with without in addition having to pay bribes. This may be clearly the case, but sometimes also the reverse appears to be true. Where bureaucracy is both elaborate and inefficient, the provision of strong personal incentives to bureaucrats to cut red tape may be the only way of speeding the establishment of the new firm. In such a case it is certainly reasonable to wish that the bureaucracy were simpler and more efficient, but not to argue that bribery *per se* is an obstacle to private economic initiative.[1] On the other hand the results may be unimportant from any practical standpoint, even if they are not particularly nice.

From such questions one may go on to pose another which is clearly the central one for the scientific study of the problem: In any society, under what conditions is behaviour most likely to occur which a significant section of the population will regard as corrupt? Some obviously relevant points are:

(1) *The 'standing' of the 'official purpose' of each public office or institution in the society.* This involves the diffusion of understanding of the idea generally, and within particular relevant groups (e.g. civil servants or police); how strongly supported this conception is, generally, and within particular groups; and what effect distance and scale have on both these dimensions. For example, ordinary people in England did not immediately condemn the Ferranti company for wanting to keep over £4 million windfall profits on a defence contract, because it was an incomprehensibly vast sum gained in highly unfamiliar circumstances; but the same people would instantly condemn a local contractor who made a windfall profit of £40,000 on laying a drainpipe for the Rural District Council. And the 'standing' of the 'official purpose' of anything is also affected by the 'standing' of other rival conceptions of its purpose, e.g. the competing moral claims of relatives on a civil servant who is making junior appointments.

(2) *The extent to which action which perverts or contravenes such official purposes is seen as doing so*—another complex problem of research into attitudes.

(3) *The incentives and disincentives to corrupt the official purposes of an office or institution.* For instance, the size of the profits to be made by bribery,

---

[1] McMullen, op. cit. p. 182, takes the orthodox view: 'Investors and entrepreneurs are frustrated and dismayed and may find that the unofficial cost of starting an enterprise is too great for it to be profitable.' Another view is that this is one method of reducing excess profits. In the case of extractive industries this has some plausibility. McMullen points out (p. 197) that 'a group under harsh disability but still possessed of considerable wealth' provides the 'optimum conditions for corruption' and that it is perhaps another 'useful' function of corruption to enable economically energetic ethnic minorities to protect themselves.

or the losses liable to be incurred by refraining from it, compared with the penalties attached to being caught and exposed.

(4) *The ease with which corruption (once defined) can be carried on.* This involves such things as the ease of a particular type of corruption, and the extent to which ordinary people are exposed to opportunities for it (which is among other things affected very much by the range of the activities of the state).[1]

All these aspects clearly interact with each other.

NEW STATES AND THE CONCEPT OF CORRUPTION

It is clear that new states are very likely to be the scene of a great deal of behaviour that will be called corrupt. Neither attitudes nor material conditions in these countries are focused on the support of a single concept of the national interest or of the official purposes of state and local officers and institutions which would promote that interest. We can consider this under the headings outlined above:

(1) The idea of the national interest is weak because the idea of a nation is new. And the institutions and offices of the state are, for most people, remote and perplexing. Even to the civil servants and politicians directly involved in them they are new; they are aware of the 'official purposes' which are attached to them by importation, but they scarcely regard them as 'hallowed' and hence they do not necessarily regard them as sacrosanct.[2] On the contrary their western origin makes them suspect. To many people the 'state' and its organs were identified with alien rule and were proper objects of plunder,[3] and they have not yet been re-identified fully as instruments for the promotion of common interests. Meanwhile to the illiterate peasant the 'state' and its organs continue to be the source of a web of largely unknowable and complicated regulations, and hence of a permanent threat of punishment; against this threat

---

[1] An official study of civil service corruption in Malaya in the 1950's found much more corruption in those departments of government which provide extensive services than in those which do not.

[2] Dr Lucy Mair has put this excellently: 'they have been cast for a play in which the *dramatis personae* are enumerated but the lines are not written. The new African governments are recruited from new men...The relationship of the leader with his followers, of ministers with their colleagues, with bureaucrats, with the general public, are new relationships.' *The New Nations* (London, 1963), p. 123.

[3] Cf. Senator Kefauver's comment on the attitude of Americans to colonial administration before the American Revolution: 'In a sense the whole populace engaged in the profitable process of mulcting the government—which was after all a hated tyrant—of every possible penny'; *The Annals of the American Academy of Political and Social Science*, March 1952, p. 2. M. G. Smith (op. cit. pp. 191–3) reported some reduction in bribery and extortion in the Zaria area of Northern Nigeria as a result of internal self-government.

WHAT IS THE PROBLEM ABOUT CORRUPTION? 225

it is very reasonable to take any available precaution, such as offering bribes.[1] Some official purposes of public office are challenged by strongly supported counter-conceptions, especially the strong obligations of family, tribe, and district in the matter of awarding jobs, scholarships, or other scarce commodities in the gift of the state. Neither politicians nor civil servants are usually drawn from a class brought up for public service from an early age, or insulated from corrupting pressures by the established aloofness of a mandarin class. And to the extent that the rules of public morality lean ultimately on the strength of the rules of private morality, they are weakened by the hammer blows delivered to all moral rules by rapid social and economic change.

(2) The incentive to corrupt whatever official purposes public institutions are agreed to have is especially great in conditions of extreme inequality and considerable absolute poverty. The benefits of holding an office—any office—are relatively enormous; by comparison the penalties for attempting to obtain one by bribery are fairly modest, in relation to the low standard of living of the would-be office holder, or in relation to the pressure of relatives' claims on his existing standard of living. Generally, corruption seems likely to be inseparable from great inequality.

(3) Corruption is relatively easy to conceal in the new states. Partly this is because people are generally not too clear about what the official rules are, or what (*really*) constitutes breaking them; or if they are clear, it may be because they do not greatly resent their being broken, and so are not zealous to prevent corruption. Partly it is because the law is ineffectively enforced and the police themselves may not be immune from corruption. And while traditional gift-giving can be distinguished from a bribe of money, it is quite obvious that from the point of view of the giver the one has shaded into the other, so that although the practice has taken on a new significance, as the open gift of a chicken is replaced by a more furtive gift of a pound note, it is nevertheless an established fact of life, in which the precise nature of the rule-infringement is partially concealed by continuity with an older custom.[2]

---

[1] McMullen (op. cit. p. 189) puts this point forcefully: 'The farmer . . . is uncertain of the exact contents of the various laws that affect him, and uncertain how he stands in relation to them. He knows that he should have a licence for his shotgun but cannot be sure that the one he has is still valid, or if the clerk who issued it cheated him with a worthless piece of paper. He knows he should have paid his taxes, but he has lost his receipt, and anyway there is something called a 'tax year', different from a calendar year, which 'they' keep on changing . . . much better give the policeman what he is asking for, or if he is not asking for anything, better give him something anyway . . . *A man does not*, says the Ashanti proverb, *rub bottoms with a porcupine.*'

[2] See the interesting and detailed discussion of this in A. W. Southall and P. C. W. Gutkind, *Townsmen in the Making* (Kampala, 1957), p. 189–94.

To say all this is only to explain, however, why there is likely to be much behaviour in new states that will be called corrupt. It is not to say anything about the 'level' of morality of the citizens of these countries. It is only to say that, poised as they are between the inherited public morality of the western nation-state and the disappearing public morality of the tribe, they are subject to very considerable cross-pressures which make it unlikely that the western state morality, at least in its refined and detailed forms, will emerge as the new public morality of these countries; meantime, however, the criteria of the west have sufficient standing in some quarters to ensure that the accusation of corruption is freely levelled against all behaviour which does not conform to them. To go much beyond this is, in the apt words of Lucy Mair, to ignore

the kind of social pressure that is in fact responsible for the practice of the virtues that are cherished in any given society. Good men do not practise . . . industry in circumstances where this would lead to a reduction in piece-rates.[1]

What is the Problem in New States?

Of course there are ample grounds for *concern*, if not for moralising, about corruption in new states. The most important of them can probably be best isolated by making the comparison with Britain again, but from a different point of view.

Wraith and Simpkins tend to present a picture of Britain, for instance, as having been—around 1800—the scene of great corruption, which was then quite remarkably eliminated. However, the prevalence and the robustness, so to speak, of the practices which they, following the Victorian reformers, regard as corrupt, suggests a rather different interpretation; namely that according to the previously obtaining moral code many of these practices were not corrupt, but either had no moral significance, or indeed were actually quite right and desirable. For instance, the average landlord thought it quite natural, and to that extent desirable, that his tenants should use their votes on behalf of his favoured candidate and did not hesitate to put pressure on them to this end. Jobbery, sinecures, rotten boroughs, treating, and other colourful political practices of the period were practised with an openness that shows that they were not regarded as improper by those whose opinions mattered.[2] What is really remarkable is the rapidity and completeness of the reformers' victory during the nineteenth century.

---

[1] Lucy Mair, op. cit. pp. 124–5.

[2] 'In the latter half of the eighteenth century *it was taken for granted* that the purpose for going into Parliament or holding any public office was to make or repair a man's personal fortune.' R. M. Jackson, *The Machinery of Local Government* (London, 1958), p. 345. (Italics mine.) It seems clear that during this period there was a tendency for this attitude to become more

What seems to have happened is that the ruling classes were induced to accept an altered perception of the nature of the public interest and so to redefine the purposes of the public offices and state institutions which remained, during most of this period, still under their control. It was precisely because they already had a clear notion of the public interest that the assertion of the new notion was established with such completeness. What was involved was not the establishment for the first time of a set of ideas about how public offices and institutions were to serve the public interest, but the adaptation of an established set. Britain did not, in other words, pass from a corrupt condition to a very pure one; rather it passed from one set of standards to another, *through* a period in which behaviour patterns which were acceptable by the old standards came to be regarded as corrupt according to the new. It is arguable that, at the height of this experience, public life in Britain was not much less 'pure' than it is today. Certainly the records of so-called corruption in the early nineteenth century have about them an air of innocence which is largely lacking in the literature on the same subject in the U.S.A.

Such innocence is also absent from the portrait of corruption in modern Nigeria drawn in the novels of, for instance, Chinua Achebe and Cyprian Ekwensi, and no doubt this partly explains the compulsive moralism of so many commentators on it. In Britain the corruption of public office was by a ruling class who *had* had a clear conception, even if in the end it was rather tenuous, of the public interest and the duty they owed to it by their use of the public offices and institutions under their control, a conception which complemented their frank exploitation of those offices and institutions for personal gain. In the era of reform they eventually accepted a redefinition of the principles governing the use of those offices and institutions and this, together with the other adaptations on their part, in large measure ensured their survival as a ruling class.

By contrast the ruling classes of Africa are new classes, exercising a new rule. Only a minority have been brought up in ruling-class circles. The idea contained in the phrase, *noblesse oblige*, scarcely applies. There is no previous experience, and so no prior ideology, of the roles of public offices and institutions in relation to the public interest, in terms of which the private exploitation of public office could be rationalised. There *is* a prevailing conception of the national interest and dedication to popular welfare. But it is precisely this idea that may be called into question by

widespread and the consequences more extensive and expensive, and that this in turn aided the development of the reform movement. However, the use of public office for private gain was a recognised public practice going back to a period in English history when these distinctions were still imperfectly worked out.

the way in which public office is actually exploited by those who occupy it. They have publicly accepted, at least by implication, the official purposes officially attached to public offices and institutions by the colonial powers. If their practice is indefensible by any standards which they are publicly prepared to defend, it robs the whole business of any air of innocence, and this is what provoked Dumont's reluctant protest against the creation in Africa of 'a bourgeoisie of a new type, which Karl Marx could scarcely have foreseen, a bourgeoisie of the public service'.[1]

The contrast between this contemporary phenomenon and the English scene in the early nineteenth century can be exaggerated. But it would not be hard to sharpen it further. Before the era of reform there were, as well as sinecures worth thousands of pounds, exacting civil service jobs which were not paid enough to induce anyone competent to occupy them, and which consequently were made attractive only by perquisites. Government-provided services, too, tended to be needed primarily by the relatively affluent sections of the population. And the idea was broadly accepted that well-born young men had some sort of entitlement to be maintained in one capacity or another in the public service. By contrast, in contemporary Africa public service is not merely paid well, in relation to local income levels, but lavishly;[2] government services affect the ordinary citizen in numerous ways, not as a luxury but as a conventional (or even an actual) necessity; and there is no accepted 'natural' ruling élite. In any case, these eighteenth-century ideas do not seem to have been invoked in defence of 'corruption' by those engaged in it today.

This is, perhaps, the main reason for the automatic condemnation of these widespread behaviour patterns by most contemporary commentators, and it seems rather reasonable. For to the extent that the official public morality of a society is more or less systematically subverted, especially if the leadership is involved in it, it becomes useless as a tool for getting things done, and this is expensive in any society where other resources are scarce. What is involved here is the idea of a 'corrupted society'.

It seems impossible to declare that a society without an effective public morality *cannot* develop economically. On the other hand, there do seem to be reasons for doubting whether in African conditions this is likely to happen. In the first place, most African states are extremely dependent

[1] R. Dumont, *L'Afrique noire est mal partie* (Paris, 1962), p. 66.

[2] Cf. Dumont's notorious comparison: 'A deputy works (?) for three months a year, but receives from 120,000 to 165,000 CFA per month. In six months of salary—i.e. in one and a half months' work—he makes as much as the average African peasant in 36 years, in a whole life of hard labour.' Ibid.

upon government action for their development. Their development prospects largely depend on attaining the targets chartered in development plans, and by very fine margins. This requires single-minded hard work from all holders of public office. If the top political élite of a country consumes its time and energy in trying to get rich by corrupt means, it is not likely that the development plans will be fulfilled.

Secondly, if this is the pattern of behaviour of the élite and if this is fairly well known, it is likely to rob them of much of their authority both with subordinates in the government and with political followers in the countryside. The country will be apt to forfeit whatever benefits can be derived by the output of effort not solely motivated by the hope of personal gain.

Thirdly, the wealth improperly accumulated by the top élite may be modest by world standards, but still large in relation to the level of investment on which the economic development of the country depends. In this case much will turn on how such wealth is redeployed. If political leaders try to buy security by depositing their wealth in numbered accounts in Swiss banks it represents a wholly negative drain on the economy.[1] (But perhaps they will buy farms and make them very productive.) Fourthly, if the top élite flout the public moral code which is cherished by 'donor' nations the supply of foreign aid may diminish.

The likelihood of the last two developments seems remote. The possibility which seems most solid and even obvious is the first; there are perfectly plain differences to be seen between one developing nation and another in terms of the amount of public spirit and devotion to duty shown by their élites, and the idea of a society economically stagnating in the grip of a self-seeking and corrupt élite is not a pure fantasy. The line of escape from such a situation is also fairly clear. Typically, a nucleus of 'puritans'—drawn from groups such as an independent business class, professional groups, or small farmers—begins to exercise effective pressure to apply the official but disregarded public code of ethics.

By and large this was the experience of the reform movement in the U.S.A. The moral vulnerability of the ruling groups was very great, and so piecemeal advance was possible. Distinctions were gradually insisted upon which narrowed the area of operation of self-interest and widened that of the public interest; it came to be held, for instance, that 'private profit by public servants at the expense of the public welfare was corrupt; but private profit by public servants obtained as a *concomitant* to service in the general welfare was quite proper.'[2] (A similar

[1] See, e.g., Frantz Fanon, *Les Damnés de la terre*, quoted by Dumont, op. cit. pp. 67–8.
[2] Kefauver, op. cit. p. 3.

distinction was drawn by Achebe's hero when he took to accepting bribes: 'But Obi stoutly refused to countenance anyone who did not possess the minimum educational and other requirements. On that he was unshakeable'.)[1] The result in the U.S.A. is a patchwork: the scope of political patronage has been greatly reduced and the cash bribery of higher public servants largely eliminated. At the same time, large areas of public life have so far remained more or less immune to reform, and practices that in one sphere would be regarded as corrupt are almost taken for granted in another.

The question is where the puritans are to come from in the new states, with their prevailing lack of economically independent professional and middle classes and the corresponding weakness of the puritan ethos; and whether the puritans in new states can succeed by gradualist means, rather than by revolution.

[1] Achebe, op. cit. p. 169.

[4]

CORRUPTION AND POLITICAL DEVELOPMENT:
A COST-BENEFIT ANALYSIS*

J. S. NYE
Harvard University

"Private Vices by the dextrous Management of a skillful Politician may be turned into Publick Benefits."

—Bernard Mandeville, 1714

I. THE STUDY OF CORRUPTION IN LESS DEVELOPED COUNTRIES

Corruption, some say, is endemic in all governments.[1] Yet it has received remarkably little attention from students of government. Not only is the study of corruption prone to moralism, but it involves one of those aspects of government in which the interests of the politician and the political scientist are likely to conflict. It would probably be rather difficult to obtain (by honest means) a visa to a developing country which is to be the subject of a corruption study.

One of the first charges levelled at the previous regime by the leaders of the coup in the less developed country is "corruption." And generally the charge is accurate. One type of reaction to this among observers is highly moralistic and tends to see corruption as evil. "Throughout the fabric of public life in newly independent States," we are told in a recent work on the subject, "runs the scarlet thread of bribery and corruption . . ." which is like a weed suffocating better plants. Another description of new states informs us that "corruption and nepotism rot good intentions and retard progressive policies."[2]

Others have reacted against this moralistic approach and warn us that we must beware of basing our beliefs about the cause of coups on post-coup rationalizations, and also of judging the social consequences of an act from the motives of the individuals performing it.[3] Under some circumstances Mandeville is right that private vice can cause public benefit. Corruption has probably been, on balance, a positive factor in both Russian and American economic development. At least two very important aspects of British and American political development—the establishment of the cabinet system in the 18th century and the national integration of millions of immigrants in the 19th century—were based in part on corruption. As for corruption and stability, an anthropologist has suggested that periodic scandals can sometimes "lead to the affirmation of general principles about how the country should be run, as if there were not posed impossible reconciliations of different interests. These inquiries may not alter what actually happens, but they affirm an ideal condition of unity and justice."[4] However, the "revisionists" who echo Mandeville's aphorism often underestimate tastes for moralism—concern for worthiness of causes as well as utilitarian consequences of behavior. There is always the danger for a corrupt system that someone will question what it profits to gain the world at the price of a soul. The purpose of this paper is less to settle the difference between "moralists" and "revisionists" about the general effect of corruption on development (although a tentative conclusion is presented) than to suggest a means to make the debate more fruitful. After discussing the problem in the usual general

* The author is indebted to Samuel P. Huntington, Leon Lindberg and Robert Erwin for reading an earlier version of this paper.

[1] C. J. Friedrich, *Man and His Government* (New York, 1963), p. 167. See also "Political Pathology," *The Political Quarterly*, 37 (January–March, 1966), 70–85.

[2] Ronald Wraith and Edgar Simpkins, *Corruption in Developing Countries* (London, 1963), pp. 11, 12. K. T. Young, Jr., "New Politics in New States," *Foreign Affairs*, 39 (April, 1961), at p. 498.

[3] See, for example: Nathaniel Leff, "Economic Development Through Bureaucratic Corruption," *The American Behavioral Scientist*, 8 (November, 1964), 8–14; David H. Bayley, "The Effects of Corruption in a Developing Nation," *The Western Political Quarterly*, 19 (December, 1966), 719–732; J. J. Van Klaveren in a "Comment" in *Comparative Studies in Society and History*, 6 (January, 1964), at p. 195, even argues that "recent experience in the so-called underdeveloped countries has most vividly brought home the fact that corruption is not a mass of incoherent phenomena, but a political system, capable of being steered with tolerable precision by those in power."

[4] Max Gluckman, *Custom and Conflict in Africa* (Oxford, 1955), p. 135.

terms of possibility, we shall turn to more specific hypotheses about probability.

This paper is concerned with the *effects* of corruption, but a word should be said about causes to dispel any impression that corruption is a uniquely Afro-Asian-Latin American problem. I assume no European or American monopoly of morals. After all, Lord Bryce saw corruption as a major American flaw and noted its outbreak in "virulent form" in the new states in Europe.[5] Yet behavior that will be considered corrupt is likely to be more prominent in less developed countries because of a variety of conditions involved in their under-development—great inequality in distribution of wealth; political office as the primary means of gaining access to wealth; conflict between changing moral codes; the weakness of social and governmental enforcement mechanisms; and the absence of a strong sense of national community.[6] The weakness of the legitimacy of governmental institutions is also a contributing factor, though to attribute this entirely to the prevalence of a cash nexus or the divergence of moral codes under previous colonial governments or to the mere newness of the states concerned may be inadequate in light of the experience with corruption of older, non-colonial less developed states such as Thailand or Liberia. Regardless of causes, however, the conditions of less developed countries are such that corruption is likely to have different effects than in more developed countries.

Most researchers on developing areas gather some information on corruption, and this paper will suggest hypotheses about the costs and benefits of corruption for development that may lure some of this information into the open. However, in view of the fact that generalizations about corruption and development tend to be disguised descriptions of a particular area in which the generalizer has done field work, I will state at the outset that generalizations in this paper are unevenly based on field work in East Africa and Central America and on secondary sources for other areas.

Definitions pose a problem. Indeed, if we define political development as "rational, modern, honest government," then it cannot

coexist with corruption in the same time period; and if corruption is endemic in government, a politically developed society cannot exist. "Political development" is not an entirely satisfactory term since it has an evaluative as well as a descriptive content. At least in the case of economic development, there is general agreement on the units and scale by which to measure (growth of per capita income). In politics, however, there is agreement neither on the units nor on a single scale to measure development.[7] Emphasis on some scales rather than others tends to reflect an author's interests.

In this author's view, the term "political development" is best used to refer to the recurring problem of relating governmental structures and processes to social change. It seems useful to use one term to refer to the type of change which seems to be occurring in our age ("modernization") and another to refer to capacity of political structures and processes to cope with social change, to the extent it exists, in any period.[8] We generally assume that this means structures and processes which are regarded as legitimate by relevant sectors of the population and effective in producing outputs desired by relevant sectors of the population. I assume that legitimacy and effectiveness are linked in the "long run" but can compensate for each other in the "short run."[9] What constitutes a relevant sector of the population will vary with the period and with social changes within a period. In the modern period we tend to assume that at least a veneer of broad participation is essential for establishing or maintaining legitimacy. In other words, in the current period, political development and political modernization may come close to involving the same things.

In this paper, political development (or decay) will mean growth (or decline) in the

[5] James Bryce, *Modern Democracies* (New York, 1921), Vol. II, p. 509.

[6] Colin Leys, "What is the Problem About Corruption?" *Journal of Modern African Studies*, 3, 2 (1965), 224–225; Ralph Braibanti, "Reflections on Bureaucratic Corruption," *Public Administration*, 40 (Winter, 1962), 365–371.

[7] Nor, by the nature of the subject, is there likely to be. In Pye's words, "no single scale can be used for measuring political development": Lucian Pye (ed.), *Communications and Political Development* (Princeton, 1963). See also Lucian Pye, "The Concept of Political Development," *The Annals*, 358 (March 1965), 1–19; Samuel Huntington, "Political Development and Political Decay," *World Politics*, 17 (April, 1965), 386–430; Robert Packenham, "Political Development Doctrines in the American Foreign Aid Program," *World Politics*, 18 (January, 1966), 194–235.

[8] See Huntington, *op. cit.*, 389.

[9] S. M. Lipset, *Political Man* (Garden City, 1959), 72–75.

capacity of a society's governmental structures and processes to maintain their legitimacy over time (i.e., presumably in the face of social change). This allows us to see development as a moving equilibrium and avoid some of the limitations of equating development and modernization. Of course, this definition does not solve all the concept's problems. Unless we treat development entirely ex post facto, there will still be differences over evaluation (legitimate in whose eyes?) and measurement (national integration, administrative capacity, institutionalization?) as well as what constitutes a "long" and "short" run. Thus we will find that forms of corruption which have beneficial effects on economic development may be detrimental for political development; or may promote one form of political development (i.e., defined one way or measured along one scale) but be detrimental to another. We shall have to continue to beware of variations in what we mean by political development. (Alternatively, those who reject the term "political development" can still read the paper as relating corruption to three problems of change discussed below.)

The definition of corruption also poses serious problems. Broadly defined as perversion or a change from good to bad, it covers a wide range of behavior from venality to ideological erosion. For instance, we might describe the revolutionary student who returns from Paris to a former French African country and accepts a (perfectly legal) overpaid civil service post as "corrupted." But used this broadly the term is more relevant to moral evaluation than political analysis. I will use a narrower definition which can be made operational. Corruption is behavior which deviates from the formal duties of a public role because of private-regarding (personal, close family, private clique) pecuniary or status gains; or violates rules against the exercise of certain types of private-regarding influence.[10] This includes such behavior as bribery (use of a reward to pervert the judgment of a person in a position of trust); nepotism (bestowal of patronage by reason of ascriptive relationship rather than merit); and misappropriation (illegal appropriation of public resources for private-regarding uses). This definition does not include much behavior that might nonetheless be regarded as offensive to moral standards. It also excludes any consideration of whether the behavior is in the public interest, since building the study of

the effects of the behavior into the definition makes analysis of the relationship between corruption and development difficult. Similarly, it avoids the question of whether non-Western societies regard the behavior as corrupt, preferring to treat that also as a separate variable. To build such relativism into the definition is to make specific behavior which can be compared between countries hard to identify. Moreover, in most less developed countries, there are two standards regarding such behavior, one indigenous and one more or less Western, and the formal duties and rules concerning most public roles tend to be expressed in terms of the latter.[11] In short, while this definition of corruption is not entirely satisfactory in terms of inclusiveness of behavior and the handling of relativity of standards, it has the merit of denoting specific behavior generally called corrupt by Western standards (which are at least partly relevant in most developing countries) and thus allowing us to ask what effects this specific behavior has under differing conditions.

II. POSSIBLE BENEFITS AND COSTS

Discussion of the relation of corruption to development tends to be phrased in general terms. Usually the argument between moralists and revisionists tends to be about the possibility that corruption (type unspecified) *can* be beneficial for development. Leaving aside questions of probability, one can argue that corruption can be beneficial to political development, as here defined, by contributing to the solution of three major problems involved: economic development, national integration, and governmental capacity.

1. *Economic Development.* If corruption helps promote economic development which is generally necessary to maintain a capacity to preserve legitimacy in the face of social change, then (by definition) it is beneficial for political development.

There seem to be at least three major ways in which some kinds of corruption might promote economic development.

a. Capital formation. Where private capital is scarce and government lacks a capacity to tax a surplus out of peasants or workers openly, corruption may be an important source of

[10] The second part of the definition is taken from Edward C. Banfield, *Political Influence* (Glencoe, Ill.: Free Press, 1961), p. 315.

[11] See, for example: M. G. Smith, "Historical and Cultural Conditions of Political Corruption Among the Hausa," *Comparative Studies in Society and History*, 6 (January, 1964), at p. 194; Lloyd Fallers, "The Predicament of the Modern African Chief: An Instance from Uganda," *American Anthropologist*, 57 (1955), 290-305. I agree with Bayley on this point: *op. cit.*, 720-722.

capital formation. There seems to be little question about the effectiveness of this form of taxation—Trujillo reputedly accumulated $500 million and Nkrumah and relatives probably more than $10 million.[12] The real question is whether the accumulated capital is then put to uses which promote economic development or winds up in Swiss banks.

b. Cutting red tape. In many new countries the association of profit with imperialism has led to a systematic bias against the market mechanism. Given inadequate administrative resources in most new states, it can be argued that corruption helps to mitigate the consequences of ideologically determined economic devices which may not be wholly appropriate for the countries concerned.[13] Even where the quality of bureaucrats is high, as in India, some observers believe that "too much checking on corruption can delay development. Trying to run a development economy with triple checking is impossible."[14] Corruption on the part of factory managers in the Soviet Union is sometimes credited with providing a flexibility that makes central planning more effective.

c. Entrepreneurship and incentives. If Schumpeter is correct that the entrepreneur is a vital factor in economic growth and if there is an ideological bias against private incentives in a country, then corruption may provide one of the major means by which a developing country can make use of this factor. This becomes even more true if, as is often the case, the personal characteristics associated with entrepreneurship have a higher incidence among minority groups. Corruption may provide the means of overcoming discrimination against members of a minority group, and allow the entrepreneur from a minority to gain access to the political decisions necessary for him to provide his skills. In East Africa, for instance, corruption may be prolonging the effective life of an important economic asset—

the Asian minority entrepreneur—beyond what political conditions would otherwise allow.

2. _National Integration._ It seems fair to assume that a society's political structures will be better able to cope with change and preserve their legitimacy if the members share a sense of community. Indeed, integration is sometimes used as one of the main scales for measuring political development.

a. Elite integration. Corruption may help overcome divisions in a ruling elite that might otherwise result in destructive conflict. One observer believes that it helped bridge the gap between the groups based on power and those based on wealth that appeared in the early nationalist period in West Africa and allowed the groups to "assimilate each other." Certainly in Central America, corruption has been a major factor in the succession mechanism by integrating the leaders of the new coup into the existing upper class. Whether this is beneficial for political development or not is another question involving particular circumstances, different evaluation of the importance of continuity, and the question of the relevant period for measurement.

b. Integration of non-elites. Corruption may help to ease the transition from traditional life to modern. It can be argued that the man who has lived under "ascriptive, particularistic and diffuse" conditions cares far less about the rational impartiality of the government and its laws than he does about its awesomeness and seeming inhumanity. The vast gap between literate official and illiterate peasant which is often characteristic of the countryside may be bridged if the peasant approaches the official bearing traditional gifts or their (marginally corrupt) money equivalent. For the new urban resident, a political machine based on corruption may provide a comprehensible point at which to relate to government by other than purely ethnic or tribal means. In McMullan's words, a degree of low-level corruption can "soften relations of officials and people" or in Shils' words it "humanizes government and makes it less awesome."[15]

However, what is integrative for one group may be disintegrative for another. The "traditional" or "transitional" man may care far more that he has a means to get _his_ son out of jail than that the system as a whole be incorruptible, but for "modern" groups such as

[12] A. Terry Rambo, "The Dominican Republic," in Martin Needler (ed.), _Political Systems of Latin America_ (Princeton, 1964), p. 172; _New York Times_, March 5, 1966. Ayeh Kumi's quoted statement has almost certainly greatly underestimated his own assets.

[13] On the economic problems of "African socialism," see Elliot Berg, "Socialism and Economic Development in Tropical Africa," _Quarterly Journal of Economics_, 78 (November, 1964), 549–573.

[14] Barbara Ward, addressing the Harvard Center for International Affairs, Cambridge, Mass., March 3, 1966.

[15] M. McMullan, "A Theory of Corruption," _The Sociological Review_ (Keele), 9 (July, 1961), at p. 196; Edward Shils, _Political Development in the New States_ (The Hague, 1962), p. 385.

students and middle classes (who have profited from achievement and universalism) the absence of honesty may destroy the legitimacy of the system. Finally, it is worth noting again Gluckman's statement that the scandals associated with corruption can sometimes have the effect of strengthening a value system as a whole.

3. *Governmental Capacity.* The capacity of the political structures of many new states to cope with change is frequently limited by the weakness of their new institutions and (often despite apparent centralization) the fragmentation of power in a country. Moreover, there is little "elasticity of power"—i.e., power does not expand or contract easily with a change of man or situation.[16]

To use a somewhat simplified scheme of motivations, one could say that the leaders in such a country have to rely (in various combinations) on ideal, coercive or material incentives to aggregate enough power to govern. Legal material incentives may have to be augmented by corrupt ones. Those who place great faith in ideal incentives (such as Wraith and Simpkins) see the use of corrupt material incentives as destructive ("these countries depend considerably on enthusiasm and on youthful pride of achievement . . .")[17] of governmental capacity. With a lower evaluation of the role of ideal incentives, however, corrupt material incentives may become a functional equivalent for violence. In Mexico, for instance, Needler has described the important role which corruption played in the transition from the violent phases of the revolution to its institutionalized form.[18] At the local level, Greenstone notes that while patronage and corruption was one factor contributing to an initial decline in governmental capacity in East Africa, corrupt material incentives may provide the glue for reassembling sufficient power to govern.[19]

Governmental capacity can be increased by the creation of supporting institutions such as political parties. Financing political parties

tends to be a problem in developed as well as less developed countries, but it is a particular problem in poor countries. Broad-based mass financing is difficult to maintain after independence.[20] In some cases the major alternatives to corrupt proceeds as a means of party finance are party decay or reliance on outside funds. Needless to say, not all such investments are successful. The nearly $12 million diverted from Nigeria's Western Region Marketing Board into Action Group coffers from 1959–1962 (and probably equivalent amounts in other regions)[21] seem to have been wasted in terms of institution-building; but on the other hand, investment in India's Congress Party or Mexico's *Partido Revolucionario Institucional* has been more profitable for political development.

Those who dispute the possible benefits of corruption could argue that it involves countervailing costs that interfere with the solution of each of the three problems. They could argue that corruption is economically wasteful, politically destabilizing, and destructive of governmental capacity.

1. *Waste of Resources.* Although corruption may help promote economic development, it can also hinder it or direct it in socially less desirable directions.

a. Capital outflow. As we mentioned above, capital accumulated by corruption that winds up in Swiss banks is a net loss for the developing country. These costs can be considerable. For instance, one source estimates that from 1954–1959, three Latin American dictators (Peron, Perez Jimenez, and Batista) removed a total of $1.15 billion from their countries.[22] It is no wonder that another source believes that economic development in some Latin American countries has been "checked" by corruption.[23]

b. Investment distortions. Investment may be channeled into sectors such as construction not because of economic profitability, but because they are more susceptible to hiding corrupt fees through cost-plus contracts and use

[16] See Herbert Werlin, "The Nairobi City Council: A Study in Comparative Local Government," *Comparative Studies in Society and History,* 7 (January, 1966), at p. 185.

[17] Wraith and Simpkins, *op. cit.,* p. 172.

[18] Martin Needler, "The Political Development of Mexico," this REVIEW, 55 (June, 1961), at pp. 310–311.

[19] J. David Greenstone, "Corruption and Self Interest in Kampala and Nairobi," *Comparative Studies in Society and History,* 7 (January, 1966), 199–210.

[20] See J. S. Nye, "The Impact of Independence on Two African Nationalist Parties," in J. Butler and A. Castagno (eds.), *Boston University Papers on Africa* (New York, 1967), 224–245.

[21] Richard L. Sklar, "Contradictions in the Nigerian Political System," *Journal of Modern African Studies,* 3, 2 (1965), at p. 206.

[22] Edwin Lieuwen, *Arms and Politics in Latin America* (New York, 1960), p. 149.

[23] F. Benham and H. A. Holley, *A Short Introduction to the Economy of Latin America* (London, 1960), p. 10.

of suppliers' credits. This was the case, for instance, in Venezuela under Perez Jimenez and in Ghana under Nkrumah.

c. Waste of skills. "If the top political elite of a country consumes its time and energy in trying to get rich by corrupt means, it is not likely that the development plans will be fulfilled."[24] Moreover, the costs in terms of time and energy spent attempting to set some limits to corruption can also be expensive. For instance, in Burma, U Nu's creation of a Bureau of Special Investigation to check corruption actually reduced administrative efficiency.[25]

d. Aid foregone. Another possible wastage, the opportunity costs of aid foregone or withdrawn by outside donors because of disgust with corruption in a developing country could be a serious cost in the sense that developing countries are highly dependent on external sources of capital. Thus far, however, there has not been a marked correlation between honesty of governments and their per capita receipt of aid. If corruption is a consideration with donors (presumably it weighs more heavily with multilateral institutions), it is not yet a primary one.

2. *Instability.* By destroying the legitimacy of political structures in the eyes of those who have power to do something about the situation, corruption can contribute to instability and possible national disintegration. But it is not clear that instability is always inimical to political development.

a. Social revolution. An argument can be made that a full social revolution (whatever its short-run costs) can speed the development of new political structures better able to preserve their legitimacy in the face of social change. Thus, in this view if corruption led to social revolution, this might be a beneficial effect for political development. But it is not clear that corruption of the old regime is a primary cause of social revolution. Such revolutions are comparatively rare and often depend heavily on catalytic events (such as external wars).

b. Military takeovers. If corruption causes a loss of legitimacy in the eyes of those with guns, it may be a direct cause of instability and the disintegration of existing political institutions. But the consequences for political development are again ambiguous. Much depends on differing evaluations of the ability of military regimes (which tend to comprise people and procedures oriented toward moder-

nity) to maintain legitimacy in a democratic age either by self-transformation into political regimes or by being willing and able to foster new political institutions to which power can be returned. To the extent that this tends to be difficult, then if corruption leads to military takeover, it has hindered political development.[26]

The degree to which corruption is itself a major cause of military takeovers is, however, open to some question. Despite its prominence in post-coup rationalizations, one might suspect that it is only a secondary cause in most cases. Perhaps more significant is military leaders' total distaste for the messiness of politics—whether honest or not—and a tendency to blame civilian politicians for failures to meet overly optimistic popular aspirations which would be impossible of fulfillment even by a government of angels.[27] Indeed, to the extent that corruption contributes to governmental effectiveness in meeting these aspirations, it may enhance stability.

Crozier sees "revulsion against civilian incompetence and corruption" as a major cause of coups in several Asian countries including Burma, but he also states that the main cause of Ne Win's return to power was the Shan demand for a federal rather than unitary state.[28] Similarly, corruption is sometimes blamed for the first coup in Nigeria, but the post-electoral crisis in the Western region and the fear of permanent Northern domination was probably a more important and direct cause. In Ghana, corruption may have played a more important role in causing the coup, but not so much because of revulsion at dishonesty, as the fact that corruption had reached an extent where it contributed to an economic situation in which real wages had fallen. Nonetheless, its impact in relation to other factors should not be overestimated.[29]

c. Upsetting ethnic balances. Corruption

---

[26] In Pye's words, the military "can contribute to only a limited part of national development," *Aspects of Political Development* (Boston, 1966), p. 187.

[27] "Have no fear," General Mobutu told the Congo people, "My Government is not composed of politicians." Mobutu alleged that political corruption cost the Congo $43 million: *East Africa and Rhodesia*, January 13, 1966; *Africa Report*, January 1966, 23.

[28] Crozier, *op. cit.*, pp. 62, 74.

[29] For two interpretations, see Martin Kilson, "Behind Nigeria's Revolts"; Immanuel Wallerstein, "Autopsy of Nkrumah's Ghana," *New Leader*, January 31, 9–12; March 14, 1966, 3–5.

[24] Leys, *op. cit.*, at p. 229.

[25] Brian Crozier, *The Morning After: A Study of Independence* (London, 1963), p. 82.

can sometimes exacerbate problems of national integration in developing countries. If a corrupt leader must be fired, it may upset ethnic arithmetic as happened in both Kenya and Zambia in 1966. Of course this can be manipulated as a deliberate political weapon. In Western Nigeria in 1959, an anti-corruption officer was appointed but his jurisdiction was subject to approval by the cabinet, which meant that no case could be investigated "unless the party leader decided that a man needed to be challenged."[30] But as a weapon, charging corruption is a risky device. Efforts by southern politicans in Uganda to use it in 1966 precipitated a pre-emptive coup by the northern Prime Minister in alliance with the predominantly northern army.

3. *Reduction of Governmental Capacity.* While it may not be the sole or major cause, corruption can contribute to the loss of governmental capacity in developing countries.

a. Reduction of administrative capacity. Corruption may alienate modern-oriented civil servants (a scarce resource) and cause them to leave a country or withdraw or reduce their efforts. In addition to the obvious costs, this may involve considerable opportunity costs in the form of restriction of government programs because of fears that a new program (for instance, administration of new taxes) might be ineffective in practice. While this is a real cost, it is worth noting that efficient bureaucracy is not always a necessary condition for economic or political development (at least in the early stages), and in some cases can even hinder it.[31]

b. Loss of legitimacy. It is often alleged that corruption squanders the most important asset a new country has—the legitimacy of its government. This is a serious cost but it must be analysed in terms of groups. As we have seen, what may enhance legitimacy for the student or civil servant may not enhance it for the tradition-oriented man. It is interesting, for instance, that there is some evidence that in Tanganyika petty corruption at low levels seems to have increased during the year following the replacement of an "illegitimate" colonial regime by a "legitimate" nationalist one.[32] Loss of legitimacy as a cost must be coupled with assessment of the power or importance of the group in whose eyes legitimacy is lost. If they are young army officers, it can be important indeed.

III. PROBABILITIES

Thus far I have been discussing *possible* benefits and costs. I have established that under some circumstances corruption can have beneficial effects on at least three major development problems. I have evaluated the importance of a number of frequently alleged countervailing costs. It remains to offer hypotheses about the *probabilities* of benefits outweighing costs. In general terms, such probabilities will vary with at least three conditions: (1) a tolerant culture and dominant groups; (2) a degree of security on the part of the members of the elite being corrupted; (3) the existence of societal and institutional checks and restraints on corrupt behavior.

(1) Attitudes toward corruption vary greatly. In certain West African countries, observers have reported little widespread sense of indignation about corruption.[33] The Philippines, with its American colonial heritage of corruption. and appreciation of the politics of compromise, seems able to tolerate a higher level of corruption than formerly-Dutch Indonesia. According to Higgins, the Indonesian attitude to corruption (which began on a large scale only in 1954) is that it is sinful. He attributes the civil war of 1958 to corruption and argues that in the Philippines, "anomalies" are taken more for granted.[34] Not only is the general level of tolerance of corruption relevant; variations of attitude within a country can be as important (or more so) than differences between countries. Very often, traditional sectors of the populace are likely to be more tolerant of corruption than some of the modern sectors (students, army, civil service). Thus the hypothesis must take into account not only the tolerant nature of the culture, but also the relative power of groups representing more and less tolerant sub-cultures in a country. In Nigeria, tolerance was by many accounts considerable among the population at large, but not among the young army officers who overthrew the old regime.

(2) Another condition which increases the probability that the benefits of corruption will outweigh the costs is a degree of security (and perception thereof) by the members of the elites indulging in corrupt practices. Too great

[30] Henry Bretton, *Power and Stability in Nigeria* (New York, 1962), p. 79.
[31] Bert Hoselitz, "Levels of Economic Performance and Bureaucratic Structures," in Joseph LaPalombara (ed.), *Bureaucracy and Political Development* (Princeton, 1963), 193–195. See also Nathaniel Leff, *loc. cit.,* 8–14.
[32] See *Tanganyika Standard,* May 15, 1963.

[33] McMullan, *op. cit.,* p. 195.
[34] Benjamin Higgins, *Economic Development* (New York, 1959), p. 62.

TABLE 1. CORRUPTION COST-BENEFIT MATRIX

Types of Corruption	Political Conditions	Development Problems							General Probability that Costs Outweigh Benefits
		1. Economic development			2. National integration		3. Governmental capacity		
		a. capital	b. bureaucracy	c. skills	d. elite	e. non-elite	f. effectiveness	g. legitimacy	
1. Level									
top, bottom	F	low	uncertain	uncertain/low	low	uncertain	low	low	low/uncertain
bottom	F	high	uncertain	uncertain/high	uncertain	low	high	low	high
top, bottom	U	high	uncertain	uncertain/high	high	high	low	high	high
2. Inducements									
modern	F	low	uncertain	uncertain/low	low	low	low/uncertain	uncertain	low/uncertain
traditional	F	high/uncertain	uncertain	high	high	uncertain	high	uncertain	high
modern, traditional	U	high/uncertain	uncertain	uncertain/low, high	high, little relevance	high, uncertain	low/uncertain	high	high
traditional				high		uncertain	high	high	high
3. Deviation									
extensive, marginal	F	uncertain	high	uncertain/low	uncertain	low	uncertain/low	uncertain/high	high
marginal	F	uncertain	low	uncertain/low	low	low	uncertain	low	low
extensive, marginal	U	uncertain	high	uncertain/low	high	high	low	high	high

Norms:
F   favorable political conditions (cultural tolerance, elite security, checks).
U   unfavorable political conditions
High   high probability that costs exceed benefits
Low   low probability that costs exceed benefits
Uncertain   little relationship or ambiguous relationship

insecurity means that any capital formed by corruption will tend to be exported rather than invested at home. In Nicaragua, for instance, it is argued that the sense of security of the Somoza family encouraged them in internal investments in economic projects and the strengthening of their political party, which led to impressive economic growth and diminished direct reliance on the army. In contrast are the numerous cases of capital outflow mentioned above. One might add that this sense of security, including the whole capitalist ethic, which is rare in less developed countries today, makes comparison with capital formation by the "robber barons" of the American 19th century of dubious relevance to less developed countries today.

(3) It is probable that for the benefits of corruption to outweigh the costs depends on its being limited in various ways, much as the beneficial effects of inflation for economic growth tends to depend on limits. These limits depend upon the existence of societal or institutional restraints on corruption. These can be external to the leaders, e.g., the existence of an independent press, and honest elections; or internalized conceptions of public interest by a ruling group such as Leys argues that 18th-century English aristocrats held.[35] In Mandeville's words, "Vice is beneficial found when it's by Justice lopt and bound."[36]

Given the characteristics of less developed countries, one can see that the general probability of the presence of one or more of these conditions (and thus of benefits outweighing costs) is not high. But to conclude merely that the moralists are more right than wrong (though for the wrong reasons) is insufficient because the whole issue remains unsatisfactory if left in these general terms. Though corruption may not prove beneficial for resolution of development problems in general, it may prove to be the only means to solution of a particular problem. If a country has some overriding problem, some "obstacle to development"—for instance, if capital can be formed by no other means, or ethnic hatred threatens all legal activities aimed at its alleviation—then it is possible that corruption is beneficial for development despite the high costs and risks involved.)While there are dangers in identifying

[35] Leys, *op. cit.*, p. 227. See also Eric McKitrick, "The Study of Corruption," *Political Science Quarterly*, 72 (December, 1957), 502–514, for limits on corruption in urban America.

[36] Bernard Mandeville, *The Fable of the Bees*, Vol. I (Oxford: Clarendon Press, by F. B. Kaye, 1924), 37.

"obstacles to development,"[37] and while the corruption that is beneficial to the solution of one problem may be detrimental to another, we need to get away from general statements which are difficult to test and which provide us with no means of ordering the vast number of variables involved. We are more likely to advance this argument if we distinguish the roles of different types of corruption in relation to different types of development problems.

The matrix in Table 1 relates three types of corruption to three types of development problems, first assuming favorable and then assuming unfavorable conditions described above. Favorable conditions (F) means a tolerant culture or dominance of more tolerant groups, relative security of the elite corrupted, and societal/institutional checks. Unfavorable conditions (U) means intolerant culture or groups, insecure elite, and few societal/institutional checks. The development problems are those discussed above: economic development, national integration, and governmental capacity. The scores are a priori judgments that the costs of a particular type of corruption are likely to outweigh the benefits for a particular development problem or sub-problem. They represent a series of tentative hypotheses to be clarified or refuted by data. Under economic development, the specific sub-problems discussed are whether capital accumulation is promoted (benefit) without capital flight (cost); whether cutting bureaucratic red tape (benefit) outweighs distortion of rational criteria (cost); whether the attraction of unused scarce skills such as entrepreneurship (benefit) is greater than the wastage of scarce skills of, say, politicians and civil servants (cost).

Under the problem of national integration are the sub-problems of whether a particular type of corruption tends to make the elite more cohesive (benefit) or seriously splits them (cost); and whether it tends to humanise government and make national identification easier for the non-elites (benefit) or alienates them (cost). Under the problem of governmental capacity are the sub-problems of whether the additional power aggregated by corruption (benefit) outweighs possible damage to administrative efficiency (cost); and whether it enhances (benefit) or seriously weakens the governmental legitimacy (cost).

1. *Level of Beneficiary.* Shils argues that "freedom from corruption at the highest levels

is a necessity for the maintenance of public respect of Government . . ." whereas a modicum of corruption at lower levels is probably not too injurious.[38] On the other hand, McMullan reports that West Africans show little sense of indignation about often fantastic stories of corruption by leaders, and impressions from Mexico indicate that petty corruption most saps morale.[39] In India, Bayley notes that "although corruption at the top attracts the most attention in public forums, and involves the largest amount of money in separate transactions, corruption at the very bottom levels is the more apparent and obvious and in total amounts of money involved may very well rival corruption at the top."[40]

The matrix in Table I suggests that under unfavorable conditions neither type of corruption is likely to be beneficial in general, although top level corruption may enhance governmental power more than it weakens administrative efficiency. It also suggests that under favorable conditions, top level corruption may be beneficial but bottom level corruption probably is not (except for non-elite integration). If these judgments are accurate, it suggests that countries with favorable conditions, like India, which have considerable bottom level corruption but pride themselves on the relative honesty of the higher levels may be falling between two stools.

The rationale of the scoring is as follows: (A) Capital. Bottom level corruption with smaller size of each inducement will probably increase consumption more than capital formation. While top level corruption may represent the latter, whether it is invested productively rather than sent overseas depends on favorable political conditions. (B) Bureaucracy. Other factors seem more important in determining whether expediting is more important than distortion; except that those with the power of the top levels will probably distort investment criteria considerably in conditions of uncertainty—witness the alleged selling of investment licenses under a previous government in Guatemala. (C) Skills. Whether top level corruption permits the use of more skills than it wastes depends upon their supply. Where they exist, as with Asians in East Africa or "Turcos" in Honduras, it is probably beneficial. Corruption of those at lower levels of power may be more likely to waste energies than to be im-

[37] See Albert O. Hirschman, "Obstacles to Development: A Classification and a Quasi-Vanishing Act," *Economic Development and Cultural Change*, 13 (July 1965), 385–393.

[38] Shils, *op. cit.*, p. 385.
[39] McMullan, *op. cit.*, 195; Oscar Lewis, *The Children of Sanchez* (New York, 1961).
[40] Bayley, *op. cit.*, p. 724.

portant in permission of use of new skills simply because their power is limited.

(D) Elite Integration. It is difficult to see a clear relation between bottom level corruption and elite integration. At the higher levels under unfavorable conditions, e.g., a powerful intolerant part of the elite such as students or army, corruption would probably have a more divisive than cohesive effect. Under favorable conditions it might be more cohesive. (E) Non-elite integration. Under unfavorable conditions it seems likely that both types of corruption would tend to alienate more than enhance identification, whereas under favorable conditions corruption by the lower levels that the populace deals with most frequently might have the humanizing effect mentioned above, and alienation would be slight in the tolerant culture. Top level corruption might have the same effect though the connection is less clear because of the lesser degree of direct contact.

(F) Effectiveness. Bottom level corruption is more likely to disperse rather than aggregate power by making governmental machinery less responsive than otherwise might be the case; whereas at top levels the ability to change the behavior of important power holders by corrupt inducements is likely to outweigh the loss of efficiency, even under unfavorable conditions. (G) Legitimacy. Whether corruption enhances or reduces governmental legitimacy depends more on favorable conditions than on level of corruption. Much depends on another factor, visibility of corrupt behavior, which does not always have a clear relationship to level of corruption.

2. *Inducements*. Another distinction which can be made between types of corruption is the nature of the inducement used, for instance the extent to which they reflect the values of the traditional society or the values of the modern sector. A traditional inducement such as status in one's clan or tribe may be more tolerable to those who share the ascriptive affinity, but others outside the ascriptive relationship would prefer the use of money which would give them equality of access to the corruptee. Weiner writes of India that "from a political point of view, equal opportunity to corrupt is often more important than the amount of corruption, and therefore ... an increase in *bakshish* is in the long run less serious than an increase in corruption by ascriptive criteria."[41]

[41] Myron Weiner, *The Politics of Scarcity* (Chicago: University of Chicago Press, 1962), p. 236.

As scored here, our matrix suggests that under favorable political conditions (e.g., India?) Weiner's hypothesis is probably correct but would not be correct under unfavorable conditions. (A) Capital. Modern inducements (i.e., money) probably lead to capital formation (at top levels) which may be invested under favorable conditions or be sent abroad under unfavorable conditions. Traditional inducements (kin status) do not promote capital formation (and may even interfere with it) but probably have little effect on capital flight. (B) Bureaucracy. What edge modern inducements may have in expediting procedure may be offset by distortion of criteria, so the relation between type of inducement and this problem is scored as uncertain. (C) Skills. Assuming the existence of untapped skills (as above), modern inducements increase the access to power while traditional ones decrease it. (D) Elite Integration. Under favorable conditions modern inducements are unlikely to divide elites more than make them cohere, but traditional inducements tend to preserve and emphasize ethnic divisions in the elites. Under unfavorable conditions, both types of inducements tend to be divisive. (E) Non-elite integration. Whether modern inducements promote identification or alienation varies with political conditions in the expected way, but the effect of traditional inducements is more ambiguous and probably varies from positive to negative according to the prevalence of traditional as against modern values in the particular country in question. (F) Effectiveness. Modern inducements probably give the government greater range to aggregate more sources of power than traditional inducements do. The probabilities will vary not only with political conditions but also by the opportunity costs—whether there is an efficient administrative machine to be damaged or not. (G) Legitimacy. Under favorable conditions whether traditional or modern inducements will decrease legitimacy more than they enhance it remains uncertain because it will vary with the (above mentioned) degree of existence of modern and traditional values in a society. Under unfavorable conditions, both will likely have higher costs than benefits.

3. *Deviation*. We can also distinguish types of corruption by whether the corrupt behavior involves extensive deviation from the formal duties of a public role or marginal deviation. This is not the same thing as a scale of corrupt inducements, since the size of the inducements may bear little relation to the degree of deviation. For instance, it is alleged that in one Central American country under an insecure recent

regime, a business could get the government to reverse a decision for as little as $2000, whereas in a neighboring country the mere expediting of a decision cost $50,000. Such a distinction between types of corruption by extent of deviation is not uncommon among practitioners who use terms like "speed-up money" or "honest graft" in their rationalizations.[42]

(A) Capital. It is difficult to see that the extensiveness of the deviation (except insofar as it affects the scale of inducement) has much to do with the probabilities of capital formation or flight. (B) Bureaucracy. On the other hand, marginal deviations (by definition) are unlikely to involve high costs in distortion of criteria and even under unfavorable conditions may help expedite matters. Extensive deviations are likely to have high costs in terms of rational criteria regardless of conditions. (C) Skills. It is not clear that extensive deviations call forth more unused skills than they waste administrative skills; nor is the matter completely clear with marginal deviations, though the costs of administrative skills wasted may be lower because the tasks are simpler. (D) Elite Integration. Under unfavorable conditions, the effects of corruption on elite cohesiveness are likely to be negative regardless of the extent of deviations, though they might be less negative for marginal deviations. Under favorable conditions, marginal deviations are likely to have low costs, but the effect of extensive deviations will be uncertain, varying with other factors such as existing cohesiveness of the elite and the nature of the extensive deviations. (E) Non-elite integration. Under unfavorable conditions, corruption is likely to have more alienative than identification effects regardless of the nature of the deviations. Under favorable conditions, marginal deviation will not have high costs in terms of alienation, and extensive deviation may have special appeal to those who are seeking human and "reversible" government more than impartial or "rational" government. (F) Effectiveness. It is difficult to see that extensive deviations alone would increase governmental power more than weaken administrative efficiency, but with marginal deviation, the extent of the latter would be sufficiently small that the benefits would probably outweigh the costs. (G) Legitimacy. Under unfavorable conditions either type of corruption would be more likely to weaken than to enhance legiti-

macy, but under favorable conditions the lesser challenge to rationality might make marginal corruption less detrimental than extensive—though this would depend on the proportion and dominance of groups in society placing emphasis on modern values.

IV. CONCLUSION

The scoring of the matrix suggests that we can refine the general statements about corruption and political development to read "it is probable that the costs of corruption in less developed countries will exceed its benefits except for top level corruption involving modern inducements and marginal deviations and except for situations where corruption provides the only solution to an important obstacle to development." As our matrix shows, corruption can provide the solution to several of the more limited problems of development. Whether this is beneficial to development as a whole depends on how important the problems are and what alternatives exist. It is also interesting to note that while the three conditions we have identified seem to be necessary for corruption to be beneficial in general terms, they are not necessary for it to be beneficial in the solution of a number of particular problems.

At this point, however, not enough information is at hand to justify great confidence in the exact conclusions reached here. More important is the suggestion of the use of this or a similar matrix to advance the discussion of the relationship between corruption and development. The matrix can be expanded or elaborated in a number of ways if the data seem to justify it. Additional development problems can be added, as can additional types of corruption (e.g., by scale, visibility, income effects, and so forth). The above categories can be made more precise by adding possibilities; for instance intermediate as well as top and bottom levels of corruption, or distinctions between politicians and civil servants at top, bottom, and intermediate levels.

Despite the problems of systematic field research on corruption in developing countries mentioned above, there is probably much more data on corruption and development gleaned during field work on other topics than we realize. What we need to advance the study of the problem is to refute and replace *specific* a priori hypotheses with propositions based on such data rather than with the generalities of the moralists. Corruption in developing countries is too important a phenomenon to be left to moralists.

[42] Cf. William Riordan, *Plunkitt of Tammany Hall* (New York, 1948), p. 4.

[5]

The Analysis of Corruption in Developing Nations

JAMES C. SCOTT

University of Wisconsin

Those who think of trading with Siam should bring three ships: One loaded with presents for the king and his ministers, another loaded with merchandise and a third loaded with patience.[1]

> Msgr. Denis-Jean Baptiste Pallegoix, 1854

The business of a servant of the [East India] Company was simply to wring out of the natives a hundred or two hundred pounds as speedily as possible, that he might return home before his constitution has suffered from the heat, to marry a peer's daughter, buy rotten boroughs in Cornwall and give balls in St. James' Square.[2]

> Macaulay, *circa* 1850

By way of introducing so charged a subject as corruption we do well to remind ourselves that if the traditional rulers of the colonized areas left much to be desired in terms of present standards of public office-holding, the colonizers themselves could scarcely be regarded as models of probity. Colonial office until the twentieth century was regarded more often than not as an investment in an exclusive franchise that was expected to yield a good return to the political entrepreneur who acquired it. In Spain this conception was reflected in the practice of selling certain colonial posts at public auction. Dutch practice in Batavia, although not identical, signified a similar notion of office. Here the colonial administrator owed his superiors a regular charge that could be described as a 'license to hold office' in return for which he could anticipate, in addition to his small salary and a share of the district crop yield, more or less open payments from the Dutch business interests he had assisted in the course of his duties.[3]

Lest the franchise conception of colonial office seem merely a quality attributable to the fact that most colonial ventures in Asia began as licensed business enterprises, it should be stressed that the view of public office as private property was common in much of Western Europe till at least the mid-nineteenth century. There were, of course, always traditional norms that set some limits on how much could be squeezed from the

---

[1] Quoted in *New York Times*, April 22, 1968, p. 28.
[2] Quoted in John B. Monteiro, *Corruption: Control of Maladministration* (Bombay: Manaktalas, 1966), p. 20.
[3] W. F. Wertheim, *East–West Parallels: Sociological Approaches to Modern Asia* (Chicago: Quadrangle Books, 1965), pp. 116–19.

316   JAMES C. SCOTT

populace. Nevertheless, the control of administration we know today would have been impossible without the development in the late nineteenth century of government accountability to broadly representative legislative bodies.[1] Prior to that time many state offices had become hereditary—*de facto* if not *de jure*—and virtually identical with private property. They could be mortgaged, given as a dowry, or sold at auction to the highest bidder. So stable and secure had the proprietorship of these revenue-yielding offices become in France as a result of the Decree of Paulet that the crown came to rely on a parallel system of salaried *intendants* to restore some measure of central control.[2]

Until less than a century ago, therefore, European practices at home and abroad were not so radically different from indigenous practices in colonial territories that the debarking European would have had much trouble appreciating the local pattern. Whether office was conferred by virtue of status, kinship ties, purchase or any combination of the three, it was largely a personal possession that was expected by its holder to provide at least a steady flow of revenue and perhaps even a handsome profit if astutely managed. Nor was *elected* office in Europe any exception to this rule.[3] The starting point of an analysis of corruption in new nations is thus an avoidance of the ahistorical treatment that mars much of the popular writing on this subject. The often exaggerated but real changes that have occurred both in the standards of behavior expected of public officials and in the means of enforcing those standards should not obscure the fact that the practices of the pre-industrial and industrializing West resemble rather closely the practices of the pre-industrial and industrializing non-West.

A number of Western social scientists—profiting at last, perhaps, from their own nations' long experience in this area—have recently begun to re-examine the role of corruption in a more systematic, dispassionate, and comparative fashion than was common a decade ago.[4] In this new spirit

[1] W. F. Wertheim, *op. cit.*, p. 115.
[2] Between 1610 and 1640 roughly one-half of the total royal revenue came from the sale of offices. For a thorough discussion of such administrative patterns in Europe see: K. W. Swart, *Sale of Offices in the Seventeenth Century* (The Hague: Martinus Nijhoff, 1949).
[3] In England, for example, parliamentary seats could be purchased by bribing small borough electorates until the Redistribution Act of 1885 and thereafter through large contributions to a political party. 'Many of the merchants who had gone out to India from Manchester found bribery to be just as useful in the Commons as in Calcutta, and sometimes they combined to purchase a borough.' Ronald Wraith and Edgar Simpkins, *Corruption in Developing Countries* (London: Allen and Unwin, 1963), p. 67. The office was of course expected to yield a profit.
[4] The most detailed but not entirely dispassionate effort thus far is Wraith and Simkins, *op. cit.* See also M. McMullan, 'A Theory of Corruption', *The Sociological Review* (Keele), 9 (July 1961), 132–52; W. F. Wertheim, *op. cit.*, pp. 103–31; J. David Greenstone, 'Corruption and Self Interest in Kampala and Nairobi', *Comparative Studies in Society and History*, VIII (January 1966), 199–210; Colin Leys, 'What is the Problem About Corruption?', *Journal of Modern African Studies*, 3, 2 (1965), 215–30; J. S. Nye, 'Corruption and Political Development: A Cost-Benefit Analysis', *American Political Science Review*, LXI, 2 (June 1967), 417–27. Portions of Myron Weiner, *The Politics of Scarcity* (Chicago: University of Chicago Press, 1962) are also relevant.

an attempt is made here to (1) indicate the nature of the obstacles that make comparisons of the extent of corruption between nations and between time periods all but impossible—or, if possible, often meaningless; (2) propose that corruption may be viewed as a process of political influence such that similar practices may violate community norms at one place and time and not at another; (3) outline a model of informal political influence by which the effects of corruption on governmental policy might be gauged; and (4) suggest what empirical relationships might be found between types of political systems and the distribution of benefits from corruption. Wherever it seems appropriate I have introduced illustrative data both from the industrialized nations and from the less developed (mostly India and Southeast Asia) nations. Given the secrecy which generally surrounds corruption, the necessarily suggestive character of the data presented hardly bears reiteration.

I

Much of the recent speculation about corruption in developing nations has focused on its social context in an explicit attempt to pinpoint those social situations that make corruption more likely. This change in perspective away from accusation and toward analysis was in some measure a product of a reassessment of the American urban political machine that flourished in the late nineteenth and early twentieth centuries.[1] The rapid influx of new populations for whom family and ethnicity were the central identifications, when coupled with the award of important monopoly privileges (traction, electricity, etc.) and the universal franchise, seemed to provide the ideal soil for the emergence of corrupt 'bosses'. Developing nations could be viewed as offering a social context with many of the same nutrients. New governments had in many cases only recently acquired control over the disposal of lucrative posts and privileges, and they faced electorates that included many poor, newly urbanized villagers with particularistic loyalties who could be easily swayed by concrete, material incentives.

Viewed from this vantage point, the way seemed open to comparisons of the extent of corruption at different times in different nations. Since the presumption often was that corruption is in fact more severe in presently underdeveloped nations than say in England during the eighteenth and early nineteenth centuries, the greater severity of the facilitating conditions we have noted were adduced to explain this disparity. The rate of change in developing nations is more rapid, the clash of new and old values more

---

[1] Some of the more prominent examples include: V. O. Key, *The Techniques of Political Graft in the United States* (Chicago: University of Chicago Libraries, 1936); Richard Hofstadter, *The Age of Reform* (New York: Random House, 1955); and Edward C. Banfield and James Q. Wilson, *City Politics* (Cambridge, Mass.: Harvard University Press, 1965).

318   JAMES C. SCOTT

grinding and therefore, so the reasoning goes, corruption will in all likelihood be more rampant.[1]

Apart from other objections one might wish to raise about this line of analysis, it leaves a central dilemma of the comparison unexamined. It fails to state precisely what behavior is being compared, with the result that the comparative findings are essentially the artifact of a definition of corruption, implicit or explicit, the biases of which have been overlooked. Specifically, the biases are introduced by the common definition of corruption that is limited to *illegal* private-regarding behavior in a *public* role,[2] excluding acts which are either not covered by law or are legally ambiguous, and focusing on the public sector. On *a priori* grounds the strict definition has much to recommend it since the illegality of the behavior has become a part of the contemporary notion of corruption, not to mention the very real effect of the legal environment on the nature, extent, and consequences of such behavior. While there are very good reasons for not considering corruption independently of the legal environment, I am suggesting that to do so determines, in advance, the outcome of comparisons between the earlier experiences of developed nations and the less developed nations today.

The distortions for comparative analysis created by the conventional definition of corruption will, as I hope to show, leave one with the impression that 'much the same thing is going on' and he is only comparing changes in the formal status of similar behavior. At least two factors account for this distortion: (1) the varying gap between social practice and legal norms; and (2) the difference between private sector standards and public sector standards.

1. *Social practice and legal norms.* The legal standards now in force in developing nations offer the civil servant or politician much less scope for maneuver than his counterpart in Europe a century before. Application of the legal criterion often means calling the receipt of 'side-payments' on government supply contracts in Rangoon in 1955 'corruption' while withholding that label from quite similar practices in nineteenth-century England. This difficulty afflicts comparisons of an exclusively temporal kind as well. The 'rise of corruption' in the Dutch East Indies, for example, was entirely a function of the change in how Dutchmen at home viewed certain behavior rather than of any actual change in practices.[3]

For most Western nations, after all, the development of legal standards in the conduct of public office in the eighteenth and nineteenth centuries was

---

[1] This perspective is most obvious in M. McMullan, *op. cit.*, and Wraith and Simkins, *op. cit.*

[2] A careful statement of this narrower definition is contained in J. S. Nye, *op. cit.*, p. 419. 'Corruption is behavior which deviates from the *formal* duties of a public role because of private-regarding (personal, close family, private clique) pecuniary or status gains; or violates *rules* against the exercise of certain types of private-regarding influence.'

[3] Wertheim, *op. cit.*, p. 111.

largely an internal affair. A host of common practices by office-holders throughout that period, which today would unquestionably contravene the law, were either quite within the law or at least legally ambiguous. In England, before civil service reforms eventually eliminated the practice, a tremendous number of sinecures ('offices without employment') and pensions were regularly distributed or sold by the crown with an eye to gaining allies and/or revenue. Although contemporary observers had begun to object to this custom,[1] such patronage did not violate any existing law until the Whigs found it to their political advantage to pass one.

The developing nations, by contrast, have for the most part adopted the full panoply of laws and regulations that evolved from, and gave expression to, the long political struggle for reform in the West. In trying to assess the severity of corruption in public office, an official Indian report explicitly recognized the difficulty of comparisons with England at an earlier date because, for India, the entire legal framework was already in place.[2] Considering only the matter of political patronage, for example, the Indian, Malaysian, or Nigerian politician finds himself denied by law many of the spoils that aided the building of strong parties in England and the United States. Patronage in India and in early Victorian England may seem to serve much the same purpose but, from the legal perspective, the former is corruption; the latter is not.

The legality criterion brings about misleading results in comparative research for still another, related reason. Most developing nations have not only taken over Western legal forms; they have often adopted the most restrictive and demanding forms available. Whereas regulations governing public office in the United States make some allowance for political criteria in appointments—most notably in the selection of postmasters— ex-British colonies are saddled with a set of laws that offer much less latitude in filling government posts.[3] That is, the United States has institutionalized, legalized, if you will, practices that violate the law in many new nations. The difficulty in devising a useful comparison, then, is not limited to comparisons across time but extends as well to contemporary cross-national comparisons.

In the case of the patronage practices we have explored by way of illustration, it should be apparent that a comparison of such patterns across space or time will be greatly affected by the criterion of legality. One may still wish to retain this criterion in the definition of 'patronage corruption' but it is likely he will actually be measuring changes in the legal

[1] See John Wade, *The Black Book* (London: 1820), cited in J. F. C. Harrison, ed., *Society and Politics in England: 1780–1960* (New York: Harper, 1965), pp. 93–8.

[2] *Report of the Committee on Prevention of Corruption*, K. Santhanam, Chairman (Delhi: Government of India, Ministry of Home Affairs, 1964), p. 6.

[3] Those who are familiar with American practices in this respect will find recognizable similar patterns in the Philippines. It would not be easy, I might add, to convince an Indian or Malaysian civil servant that such patterns are not 'corrupt'.

320   JAMES C. SCOTT

environment rather than any shift in the rate of placing friends and allies in public office.

2. *Private standards and public standards.* Ever since the distinction between acting in a public capacity and acting in a private capacity—without which corruption in the legal sense is difficult to imagine—became widely accepted in the nineteenth century, the legal standards of behavior for the public sector have been more puritanical than those for the private sector. The president of a business firm may appoint his inept son-in-law assistant vice-president and, although he may regret the appointment from a financial point of view and be accused of poor taste, he remains quite within the law. Similarly, if he lets an overpriced supply contract to a close friend in return for a percentage of the excess profit, the market may punish him, but not the law.[1] Should a politician or bureaucrat feel similarly inclined, however, he might well, if caught, find himself without office or perhaps the object of a criminal suit brought by the state.

Whether a given act takes place within the public sector or outside it thus makes a substantial difference in whether it meets the legal definition of corruption. Restraints in the case of the public sector are the responsibility of law enforcement agencies while, outside the public sector, it is largely the discipline of the market that checks such behavior. Because of this distinction it follows that the larger the relative size and scope of the public sector, the greater is the proportion of certain acts that will legally be considered corrupt. As the role of the public sector is comparatively more important in many new states than it was historically in the West, this fact alone is responsible for the appearance of more corruption, legally speaking, in these nations.[2] Once again, acts which in other respects are strikingly similar are called corruption when they occur in one context but not in another. That the context of behavior is important cannot be denied; for some analytical purposes, knowing whether the person who received a side-payment for letting a contract was employed in the public or private sector might be of great importance. Nonetheless, comparisons that are based on the legal distinction between the two will often actually be measuring the relative size and scope of the public sector between

[1] With the separation of ownership and operation in the modern corporation, stockholders are entitled to bring stockholders' suits in such instances. Nevertheless, 'corruption' in private business became an enormous problem in the West after the introduction of limited liability.

[2] The private sector also averts much corruption by the use of the price system. The relative scarcity of a good or service in the private sector generally raises its price while public sector standards of allocation often assign values to such things as licenses and franchises that are well below what they would bring on the open market. In such circumstances a part of the difference between market value and official value is occasionally offered to public officials in the form of bribes. Thus corruption is often evidence that the market has penetrated areas from which it is officially excluded. For an analysis along these lines see Robert Tilman, 'Administration, Development, and Corruption: The Emergence of Black-Market Bureaucracy', a paper presented to the Southern Political Science Association annual meeting, November 1967.

nations rather than rates of private-regarding violations of official roles in large organizations.

For the reasons outlined above, the comparative study of corruption across national frontiers and through time presents imposing conceptual obstacles. Usage of the customary legal perspective not only restricts the behavior considered to quite narrow limits; it also biases the comparison against developing nations in ways that have generally been overlooked. How corruption is conceptualized depends, of course, on the focus of the inquiry. If attention is centered on the violation of legal norms, the legal perspective is surely necessary, although such a focus virtually excludes pre-nineteenth-century Europe by definition and must struggle with differences in legal norms and economic systems.

Attempting to transcend this limitation and still focus on the violation of community norms, Tilman and Brasz have proposed that the criterion of *secrecy* be added to the definition.[1] The attempt at secrecy is taken as a sure sign that the standards of conduct of the community are being violated. While no doubt this is an improvement on the strict legal perspective, it ignores the central fact that the amount of secrecy in which an act is clothed is itself strongly affected by that act's legal standing. A civil servant openly willing to risk opprobrium in receiving bribes may resort to secrecy when a law is passed that threatens his freedom as palpably as his good name.

II

The usual approach to the study of corruption has, by virtue of its concern with the legal or normative standing of such practices, all too often simply disregarded their political significance. Much of what we call corruption can be appraised as a transaction[2] in which one party exchanges wealth— or trades on more durable assets such as kinship ties—for a measure of influence over the authoritative decisions of government. Whether the 'buyer' seeks an honorary title (status), a post of some authority (power), a large supply contract (wealth), or some combination of these three, the essential characteristics of the transaction involved fit this general pattern. The role of inducements is important to the corrupt transaction. Positive inducements may be material (e.g., bribery) or may involve simply bonds of friendship or kinship. Negative inducements (e.g., the threat to withdraw a benefit, to impose a penalty) are often involved too, but, beyond a certain point, negative inducements must be considered coercion rather than corruption. Corruption thus frequently represents an

---

[1] H. A. Brasz, 'Some Notes on the Sociology of Corruption', *Sociologia Neerlandica*, 1, 2 (Autumn 1963), 111–28, and Robert Tilman, *op. cit.*

[2] While most corruption involves two parties, there are situations in which a public official lets a contract, say, to himself in his private capacity while violating regulations. Here one individual enacts both roles. Key calls this 'auto-corruption', *op. cit.*, p. 391.

F

alternative to coercion as a means of influence; one likely to be employed where each party to the transaction is powerful enough to make coercion very costly.

Although not all acts that might be considered corrupt can be interpreted in this fashion, an analysis of some forms of corruption as a process of political influence allows for the grouping of events that would be separated by a framework based on the violation of community norms (formal or informal). In other words, this approach highlights the functional equivalence of a variety of acts of political influence, some of which violate all standards of community ethics and some of which are totally beyond reproach. Seen from the vantage point of political influence rather than societal norms, many forms of corruption become part of a broader framework of analysis.

Three instances of the ways in which wealth may be used to influence decisions of the state will provide an illustration of the expressly political perspective. Each case exemplifies in a different manner the tendencies that are at work in a society where the preponderance of wealth is in different hands from the preponderance of political power. In one instance the permeability of power by wealth was achieved through corruption, in another by quite unexceptionable means, and in still another by devices that are questionable but not illegal.

In England throughout the seventeenth and eighteenth centuries the lower, wealthy gentry and the growing commercial elites were able to buy positions of political authority either through the purchase of peerages from the crown or, especially later, through the purchase of 'rotten' parliamentary boroughs.[1] Although the traditional landed classes were naturally distressed at the dilution of their ranks, the new classes and their economic interests began to replace the older nobility in the affairs of state.

In contemporary Thailand the business elite is largely Chinese, not Thai, and thus formal positions of authority are not open to it. Instead, members of the Chinese business community have established fairly stable relations with individual clique leaders in the Thai military and bureaucracy in order to protect and advance their entrepreneurial concerns.[2] The relationships are, of course, enormously rewarding for members of the Thai bureaucratic elite who oversee the licensing and taxing of enterprises, and many of the transactions that provide the cement for such

[1] See Swart, *op. cit.*, Chapter 3, and Charles R. Mayes, 'The Sale of Peerages in Early Stuart England', *The Journal of Modern History*, XXIX, 1 (March 1957), 21–35. Wraith and Simkins, *op. cit.*, pp. 55–86, also provide a brief account. The assumption that during this period wealth had first to be translated into status before it could beget political authority was not necessarily the case.

[2] A full account of this pattern can be found in G. William Skinner, *Leadership and Power in the Chinese Community of Thailand* (Ithaca: Cornell University Press, 1958), *passim*. For an abbreviated account see Fred W. Riggs, *Thailand: The Modernization of a Bureaucratic Polity* (Honolulu: East–West Center Press, 1966), pp. 245–54.

relationships are quite illegal. Deprived of formal office-holding, Chinese businessmen in Thailand have nevertheless managed well—albeit through 'corruption'—to share fulsomely in the decisions which affect them.

Wealthy business elites in Japan, operating in a very different fashion from Thai entrepreneurs, have also managed to wield great political influence. Working through the factions, particularly the 'main current' factions, of the Liberal Democratic Party that has dominated elections in the post-war era, businessmen have provided the lion's share of this party's huge electoral war chest.[1] Rather than for each firm to work out its own arrangements, as in the Thai case, Japanese businessmen functioned collectively through peak associations that assessed member firms according to their assets and annual profits and passed on these funds to factions of the LDP.[2] Japanese entrepreneurs have thus had a large, and quite legal, hand both in determining which clique would prevail within the LDP and in assisting the party's electoral campaign afterward. The legislative program of the LDP has of course consistently reflected the support it has received from large business concerns.

The three illustrations cited are all cases in which wealth elites attempt, more or less successfully, to influence government actions. In the Thai case, much of what occurs meets the common definition of corruption, while the English case would require a quite broad definition of corruption to encompass it, and the Japanese case would be difficult to construe as corruption in any sense. The point is not that the consequences of each of these processes are identical. The point is rather that the routes by which wealth as a political resource influences government policies—and whether such routes are 'corrupt' or not—depend largely on the nature of the political system. Drawing only from the instances at hand, the English case suggests that the prevalence of a patrimonial view of office makes the direct pursuit of office by new wealth elites a common pattern; the Thai case suggests that the social background of wealth elites may circumscribe the alternatives for acquiring political influence; the Japanese case suggests that the existence of a party system and organized interest groups greatly affect the channels and style by which wealth elites seek political influence. Salient characteristics of the political system, by setting parameters on the modes available to wealth elites in influencing formal power holders, thereby affect both the incidence and style of corruption. The analysis tends to indicate that in many presently underdeveloped nations, represented here by Thailand, the 'legitimate' avenues for wealth to permeate political power may be severely circumscribed.

One further illustration of the perspective advocated here will serve

[1] James R. Soukup, 'Japan', pp. 737–56 in Richard Rose and Arnold J. Heidenheimer, eds., *Comparative Studies in Political Finance: A Symposium*, *Journal of Politics*, 25, 4 (November 1963).
[2] *Ibid.*, pp. 749–50.

to highlight the effect of political change on the phenomenon of corruption.[1] In a competitive party system, the party that controls the government quite naturally wishes to influence voters to prefer it to its competitors. There are a host of ways in which the government can offer concrete, material inducements to voters with this end in view; some methods are proper (e.g., raising social welfare payments, building a new school for a village) while others are considered corrupt (e.g., bribing individual voters with cash). The kind of inducements a party will offer, other things being equal, depends on the character of the electorate. If most voters have strong loyalties to class or occupational groups and at least a middle-run view of political rewards, the party's purpose will be served quite well by 'sectoral inducements' such as changes in tax laws, welfare payments, etc. If, however, the electorate is attached most closely to region or village, some kind of 'pork-barrel' legislation (also legal, albeit somewhat less tasteful) will probably prove most useful. Finally, if only family or small-group loyalties count, and if short-run incentives are most prized, inducements that are effective are likely to run afoul of the law.

Given a competitive party system, then, the level of corruption (excluding fraud and force) in electoral campaigns will be influenced by the nature of loyalties and time horizons among the electorate.[2] It is obvious that broad, sectoral loyalties have developed most in the industrial nations whereas the rapid social change and disorganization experienced by underdeveloped countries in recent decades has produced an electorate most easily 'moved' by more immediate and particularistic incentives.[3] Confronted with such an electorate, governing parties in many new nations have often enlarged the civil service to meet patronage needs, resorted to illegal inducements, or else dismantled the electoral system altogether. To the extent that symbolic rewards such as ideology proved inadequate cement for the party organization, these governing parties have come to resemble the urban political machine in the United States around the turn of the century.[4] Corruption surrounding elections, both in the urban machine and in many new states, is thus a reflection of the shared qualities of the electorate that is being mobilized.

I have suggested that corruption can often be more profitably seen as

[1] A further article, in preparation, will deal more elaborately with corruption and political development.

[2] One need hardly point out that the opposition party operates at a substantial disadvantage in trying to sway a skeptical electorate oriented to short-term material gain. It can only offer promises of later rewards.

[3] The 'pork-barrel' variant is also widespread in developing nations, particularly in rural areas. Many rural development programs in new nations are more accurately analyzed as organizations geared to provide patronage and electoral inducements rather than to raise rural productivity.

[4] For an excellent discussion along these lines see Aristide R. Zolberg, *Creating Political Order: The Party States of West Africa* (Chicago: Rand McNally, 1966), pp. 160–61. See also Banfield and Wilson, *op. cit.*, pp. 337–40.

one of many processes of political influence than as simply the misuse of office in violation of community norms. By way of illustration, the influence of wealth elites on government action and the efforts of governing parties to secure electoral support were each examined from this perspective. Under some conditions these patterns of influence occurred in an institutionalized, legitimate fashion while in others the pattern was characterized by the frequent violation of formal standards of official conduct. The cases examined thus far tend to indicate that conditions in most developing nations are such as to restrict many legitimate avenues of influence and thereby divert it along illegitimate paths. A more elaborate and systematic effort to place corruption in the context of political influence can, I feel, be of particular value in three major analytical tasks: (1) grasping how the pattern of political influence is changed by corruption; (2) specifying the effect of major political system variables on the pattern of corruption and its level; and (3) delineating more precisely the relationship of corruption (by type and level) to the process of political development. Segments of the two initial tasks are examined below while the third must await more extensive treatment.

III

Political scientists are by now well acquainted with a growing body of theoretical and empirical literature that examines the process by which interest groups influence legislation. The strategies of influence, the relationship between elected officials and pressure groups, and the effects of the legislative process itself on patterns of influence are aspects of interest-group politics that have received close scrutiny. To use the conceptual distinction between the input and the output functions of a political system, the studies referred to are concerned with the input function.

In contrast to the well-developed structures for expressing and combining important political interests found in industrialized Western nations, students of the less developed nations have encountered slim pickings indeed. The picture that has emerged from such studies most often emphasizes (1) a low level of feelings of political efficacy among citizens, thereby inhibiting the expression of demands; (2) the weakness or absence of interest structures that might organize and expound previously inchoate interests; (3) the relative absence of widely accepted institutional forms through which demands might be communicated to political decision-makers. Coupled with the largely personal character of political loyalty, the weakness of interest structures allows national leaders in developing nations to formulate policy free from most of the restraints imposed by parties and pressure groups in the West.

The effect of feeble interest structures, even where competitive elections occur, is that political demands originating outside elite circles will have

326   JAMES C. SCOTT

far less influence on legislation than they have in older, more highly organized political systems. As a statement about the legislative process such a conclusion is accurate, but it would be a grave mistake to assume that, merely because the legislative atmosphere is free from the din of pressure groups, the public has little or no effect on the eventual 'output' of government. Between the passage of legislation and its actual implementation lies an entirely different political arena that, in spite of its informality and particularism, has a great effect on the execution of policy.

Much of the expression of political interests in the new states has been disregarded because Western scholars, accustomed to their own polities, have been looking in the wrong place. A sizable number of individual, and occasionally group, demands in less developed nations reach the political system, not before laws are passed, but rather at the enforcement stage. Influence before legislation is passed is generally called 'pressure-group politics' and receives great attention from political scientists; and influence at the enforcement stage often involves 'corruption' and has seldom been treated as an alternative means of interest articulation, which in fact it is.

The peasants who avoid their land taxes by making a smaller and illegal contribution to the disposable income of the Assistant District Officer are as surely influencing the outcome of government policy as if they formed a peasant union and agitated for the reduction of land taxes. In a similar fashion, businessmen who protect their black-market sales by buying protection from the appropriate civil servants are changing the outcome of policy as effectively as they might by working collectively through chambers of commerce for an end to government price controls. A strong case can be made, in fact, that in certain circumstances it may be more 'efficient' (and here the term efficient is used in the sense of minimizing the costs involved in attaining a given objective) to advance one's interests when policy is being implemented rather than when it is still being debated in cabinet or parliament. Three examples of situations in which corruption may minimize costs are suggested below.

1. Where the narrowness of loyalties or the scarcity of organizational skills inhibit the formation of political interest groups, the corruption of law enforcement may be a more efficient means of affecting changes in *de facto* policy.[1] The divisive loyalties of many peasants to their kin, ethnic, village, religious, or caste grouping, create enormous barriers that all but preclude their induction into a common association that would advance their interests *qua* peasants. Given this fact, it is more efficient for the

---

[1] Here we are assuming, of course, that there are no compunctions about corruption and no costs attached to such an act—e.g., probability of arrest. Whether the bureaucrat 'sells' influence, given a fixed reward, depends as well on the probability of being caught, the penalty if caught, and his moral scruples.

individual peasant, or for say the peasants of one village, to influence laws that may disadvantage them by bribing local government officials.

2. Where legislative acts tend to be formalistic, that is, where the administration of law is so loose and erratic that existing law bears little relation to administrative behavior, it may be more efficient to make demands known at the enforcement stage than at the legislative stage. Even though interest structures may exist, businessmen in developing nations may realize that the administration of even the most favorable tax laws will have little or no resemblance to what is called for in the statutes. That is, they may have to bribe as much to secure enforcement of a favorable law as to escape the provisions of an unfavorable one. Under the circumstances, it may make more sense for each enterprise to quietly 'buy' precisely what it needs in terms of enforcement or non-enforcement rather than to finance an open campaign for a new law that would be as formalistic as the existing one.[1]

3. Where a minority is discriminated against and its political demands are regarded as illegitimate by the governing elite and the general population, its members may feel that open pressure group action would destroy what little political credit they enjoy. They may therefore turn to the corruption of politicians and/or bureaucrats to safeguard their interests and avoid damaging political attacks from more powerful groups. The case of the Chinese community in Thailand that was cited earlier is not unique in this respect. Throughout much of Southeast Asia and East Africa, a large portion of commerce and industry is in the hands of groups which, even if they have acquired local citizenship, are considered aliens by much of the local population. It would be foolish, even suicidal in some instances, for these so-called 'pariah' capitalists to seek influence openly as an organized pressure group. A healthy regard for their property and skin alike impels them to rely upon payments to strategically placed power-holders.[2]

Each of the three situations described in which influence at the enforcement stage minimizes costs are frequently cited characteristics of the less developed nations. The weakness of interest structures, the attenuated links between legislation and implementation, and the existence of minority groups that are virtually excluded from the political community all occupy a prominent place in the literature about underdeveloped nations.

---

[1] Politicians may occasionally even pass legislation that restricts the private sector so as to retain the proper ideological stance while, at the same time, private firms continue operation almost unimpeded through corruption in which politicians may share.

[2] For a brief discussion of the East African pattern see J. David Greenstone, 'Corruption and Self-interest in Kampala and Nairobi', *Comparative Studies in Society and History*, VIII, 2 (January 1966), 199–210. For contrasting Southeast Asian patterns, Riggs, *op. cit.*, and Virginia F. Baterina, 'A Study of Money in Elections in the Philippines', Part I, *Philippine Social Sciences and Humanities Review*, XX, 1 (March 1955), 39–86; Part II, XX, 2 (June, 1955), pp. 137–212, provide descriptions of Thai and Philippine practices.

One further situation deserves special emphasis in this context. All three circumstances just outlined are designed to illustrate how potential political demands on the government might rationally be channeled along corrupt paths even in a functioning parliamentary system. For the vast majority of Afro-Asian nations, however, parliamentary alternatives are no longer available and, in the absence of such open, fixed procedures for influence, informal channels have become all the more decisive. To be sure, some informal channels of influence are not improper, but many others would meet even the most restrictive definition of corruption. Informal paths of influence also enjoy, in a real sense, the sanction of tradition; they brought together power-holders and would-be influencers in both pre-colonial and colonial periods.

Seen as a process of informal political influence, then, corruption might be expected to flourish most in a period when the formal political system, for whatever reasons, is unable to cope with the scale or nature of demands being made on it. Samuel Huntington, in his analysis of what he calls 'political decay' in the new states, sees corruption from virtually the same vantage-point.[1] Rapid social mobilization—urbanization, politicization, and so forth—he argues, has placed an impossible burden on their frail political institutions, thereby leading to the decline of political competition, to political instability, institutional decay, and corruption. But corruption, in this sense, is not only a reflection of the failure of the formal political system to organize and meet the demands of important sectors; it represents as well a kind of subversive effort by a host of individuals and groups to bend the political system to their wishes. Those who feel that their essential interests are ignored or considered illegitimate in the formal political system will gravitate to the informal channel of influence represented by corruption. As in the case of the American urban machine, while the formal political process may seem restrictive and rigid, corruption and other informal arrangements may add substantial openness and flexibility to ultimate policies. Important political interests that seem unrepresented may enter unobtrusively through the back door.

An empirical assessment of the interests served by ultimate policy 'outputs' would be inadequate, then, if it stopped at the content of laws or decrees and failed to ask in what direction and to what extent corruption in fact altered the implementation of policy. The table below represents an effort to distinguish between those groups that usually achieve direct access to the formal political system and those groups that, for a variety of reasons, must enter the political competition at a more informal level (see Table 1).

This categorization is a rather sketchy composite and will not do com-

---

[1] Samuel P. Huntington, 'Political Development and Political Decay', in Claude E. Welch, Jr., ed., *Political Modernization: A Reader in Comparative Political Change*, pp. 207–41.

plete justice to any single developing nation; it is however sufficiently descriptive of the situation in enough cases to alert one to the variety of interests that may gain a hearing, albeit surreptitiously. Aside from those groups that are blocked from formal participation for ideological reasons —for they are frequently modern and well organized—the formal political system is *par excellence* the domain, virtually the monopoly, of the modern

TABLE 1

Groups and Their Means of Access to the Political System in Less Developed Nations

Generally easy access to formal political system	Groups often securing access primarily by means of corruption because denied formal access by virtue of:		
	Ideological Reasons	*Parochial Reasons*	*Lack of Organization*
1. Political elite	1. Indigenous commercial and industrial groups	1. Minority ethnic or religious groups	1. Unorganized peasants
2. Cadre, branches of ruling party	2. Foreign business interests		2. Unorganized urban lower classes
3. Civil servants' associations	3. Political opposition		
4. Professional associations			
5. Trade unions			

social sector. The very nature of the formal political system places minorities and the unorganized at such a disadvantage that they are seldom represented at the policy-making stage. Although modern sector groups have access to informal means of influence too, corruption may serve as an important corrective to the comparative advantage such groups enjoy in a modern political system designed to accommodate them.

IV

Who benefits from corruption in developing nations? Determining what groups benefit most from corruption in different circumstances is a task of great complexity. As definitive conclusions are clearly out of the question, it is more appropriate, at this point, to suggest what the important factors are and how such factors might influence the distribution of benefits. Three factors that seem of special note in this context are: (1) the openness or restrictiveness of access to corruption; (2) the presence or absence of a competitive electoral system; and (3) the stability and security

330   JAMES C. SCOTT

of the political elite. Each factor and its probable consequences for the pattern of corruption is explored in turn.

1. *'Parochial-vs.-Market' Corruption*

As ideal types, 'parochial' corruption represents a situation where only ties of kinship, affection, caste, and so forth[1] determine access to the favors of power-holders while 'market' corruption signifies a virtually impersonal process in which influence is accorded those who can 'pay'[2] the most, regardless of who they are. The real world, of course, rarely if ever contains such pure cases; one is more likely to encounter mixed cases in which, say, a politician will do illegal favors only for members of his ethnic group but nonetheless extracts from them what he can in cash, goods, or services. To the extent that parochial considerations predominate, however, the beneficiaries will be those with 'connections' such as kinship, friendship, and ethnicity. Where market considerations prevail, on the other hand, wealth elites will most likely benefit more since they are in a position to make the most lucrative bids.

The proportion of market to parochial corruption, and hence the pattern of beneficiaries, varies widely among developing nations. In Southeast Asia, for example, corruption in the Philippines seems to involve a high component of straightforward bidding procedures (or 'side payments') that are fixed for all who seek an identical favor. The Diem period in Vietnam, by contrast, was characterized by a marked preference in access accorded Catholic ex-northerners, although market corruption was by no means absent.

Inasmuch as parochial corruption represents an ascriptive and particularistic arrangement while market corruption stresses universalistic achievement patterns, it might be supposed that long-run trends would favor the more 'modern' market form. In the late eighteenth century, for example, the role of status in securing a rotten borough became negligible, and auction techniques grew; the electors of Shoreham in 1771 actually formed a 'Christian Society' that 'sold the seat to the highest bidder and then distributed the proceeds among the electorate'.[3] Such trend statements, however, go well beyond our present knowledge and ignore the real possibility that influence through corruption may remain the arena of particularistic ties *because* such ties are not accorded a legitimate place in the formal, modern political system.

---

[1] The term 'parochial' is one of convenience for underdeveloped nations. It is conceivable that favors could be done on the basis of working-class ties, for example, that one could hardly call parochial, but the unlikelihood of this occurring warrants ignoring such complications.

[2] The term 'pay' is not entirely accurate since market corruption is not confined exclusively to cash transactions. Payment in kind—extending, say, even to army commanders bidding for patronage by offering to supply some army trucks to take voters to the polls—is intended to fall within its meaning.

[3] Wraith and Simkins, *op. cit.*, p. 66.

In any event, the different patterns of access to influence created by each type of corruption may have quite divergent political consequences. Commenting on the Indian case, Myron Weiner writes:

> . . . from a political point of view, equal opportunity to corrupt is often more important than the amount of corruption, and therefore that an increase in backshish is in the long-run less serious than an increase in corruption by ascriptive criteria. So long as the businessman and the peasant can obtain what they want from local administrators through the payment of money, there is less likely to be popular discontent than if those who can and wish to make payments discover that caste and family connections are more decisive. For in that case, those of lower status backgrounds but rising economic success will find themselves blocked and political disaffection is likely to increase. . . .[1]

If indeed market corruption, as exemplified by minutely calculated amounts *every* sub-contractor for Indian Railways must pay to at least a half-dozen officials,[2] is less disturbing to the public than caste or ethnic favoritism, this is surely a reflection of the predominant cleavages in Indian society. Corrupt practices which favor the wealthy, regardless of who the wealthy may be, are less disturbing to a nation divided along ethnic or religious fissures than such practices would be in a community divided along economic class lines. The test, then, is whether the predominant form of corruption cuts across or reinforces existing cleavages; ethnic-based corruption would accordingly be less politically disruptive in a class-oriented community than in an ethnic-oriented one. Finally, for the developing nations, one must not ignore the frequent coincidence of wealth and ethnicity. Where this is the case, market corruption will consistently favor one ethnic group at the expense of others simply because one ethnic group controls most of the community's wealth. In practice, access by virtue of wealth may thus have the same impact as parochial corruption.

2. *Electoral Competition*

The most striking consequence, for this analysis, of electoral competition by political parties, is that it widens the arena of political influence. Ordinary voters come to control a valuable political resource; the giving or withholding of their vote now makes a difference in the affairs of those who seek to manage the state. Provided members of the electorate are not motivated wholly by traditional bonds of loyalty, one may expect that they will use their franchise to secure some gain from the contestants for power.

The inducements that power-holders and power-seekers in an electoral system can offer voters may or may not fall within the bounds of corruption. If class consciousness and ideological concerns are of importance

---

[1] Myron Weiner, *op. cit.*, p. 236.
[2] *Report of the Railway Corruption Enquiry Committee, 1953–55,* 'Kripalani Committee' (Delhi: Government of India, Ministry of Railways, 1956), p. 48.

332   JAMES C. SCOTT

to the electorate, promises of satisfactory policies may be all that is required in the way of inducements. But if, as in most developing nations, the desire for immediate, particularistic gains predominates, leaders of political parties will find it more difficult to provide appropriate inducements without violating formal standards of public probity. In the short run, at least, competitive political parties are more likely to respond to the incentives that motivate their clientele than to transform the nature of these incentives.

It is not astonishing, then, that the growth of corruption surrounding elections in developing nations may in fact indicate the growing effectiveness of popular democracy. The decline of terrorism and outright fraud in Philippine elections was accompanied by a quite noticeable increase in vote-buying by candidates.[1] Some of the material inducements needed to attract votes could be supplied through legal patronage and pork-barrel legislation but more irregular channels become an indispensable part of any campaign. No longer able physically to threaten voters or stuff ballot boxes, candidates and parties were obliged to proffer material rewards as a means of persuasion. The decisiveness of material incentives in the absence of force or fraud at certain points in political development can also be seen in the case of urban political machines in the United States. In the course of his vivid portraits of city politics at the turn of the century, Lincoln Steffens shows that the material rewards at the disposal of the Philadelphia machine were distributed less widely than in other cities owing to the ability of its leaders to 'fix' electoral results through fraud.[2] The Tammany Machine in New York, by contrast, 'had government founded on the suffrages of the people' that Steffens called 'democratic corruption', commenting that '. . . its grafting system is one in which more individuals share than any I have studied'.[3] Its voting power not diluted by fraud, the New York City electorate seemed to share more fulsomely in the distribution of rewards.

To the extent that an effective, competitive party system changes the locus of significant political decisions from the administrative to the legislative level, corruption is affected in still other important ways. First, since politicians (policy-makers) are now more powerful than administrators (enforcers), those individuals and groups that previously sought to protect and advance their interests at the enforcement level will establish ties instead with politicians. Regardless of the precise nature of these ties between interests and parties/politicians, the change in the locus of power benefits party elites; the more dominant the party elite, the more it potentially benefits. Important commercial interests in India, for example, which

[1] David Wurfel, 'The Philippines', pp. 757–73 in Rose and Heidenheimer, eds., *op. cit.*, pp. 770–1. Wurfel gives an excellent account of the role of money in Philippine elections.
[2] Lincoln Steffens, *The Shame of the Cities* (New York: Hill and Wang, 1963), p. 139.
[3] *Ibid.*, pp. 203, 205.

provided illegal salary supplements for a number of civil servants prior to independence, now divert a portion of those funds to the Congress Party and its politicians who make many of the crucial decisions.[1] Dutch business enterprises with concerns in Indonesia made a similar transition in the inter-war period when they discovered that their interests could be advanced more easily, and legally as well, by campaign contributions in the Hague than by particularistic ties to colonial civil servants in Batavia.[2] These examples, and many similar transitions that could be cited, underscore a second fact about influence over decisions where political parties are powerful; in such systems non-corrupt channels of influence are created that do not exist in bureaucratic systems. For a businessman to give money to a civil servant is generally illegal, whereas the same amount given to a politician's campaign fund may 'buy' just as much influence over government decisions, but is quite proper. The party system not only provides a legitimate way for interest groups to give decision-makers money, but also provides legitimate ways for decision-makers to influence voters by means of more or less particularistic rewards; e.g., legal patronage, pork-barrel legislation. This is not to say that the overall level of corruption (legally defined) is lower in party systems. In fact, the pressures of electoral competition may make massive resort to illegal measures quite common. The point is rather that the party system generally legitimizes certain patterns of influence that could only occur corruptly in a (non-traditional) bureaucratic system.

At this point in the analysis, it is appropriate to try to summarize a number of the proposed relationships between the political system and the pattern of beneficiaries from corruption. Table 2 below, though limited in scope and suggesting only rough comparisons, offers a convenient summary of a portion of my analysis.

It is assumed realistically in the table that those persons and groups most closely connected with members of the ruling elite will always profit to some extent from corruption. If corruption exists at all, it will be difficult to deny the persuasive claims of family and friends. The further patterning of rewards for each political system is explained briefly below.

(a) Where parties are either weak or non-existent and where administrators, perhaps in league with the military, dominate the political system, bureaucrats (military or civil) and wealth elites will be the chief beneficiaries of corruption.

This pattern finds clear expression in Thailand where the reigning military/bureaucratic elite is relieved of electoral anxieties and where non-parochial corruption consequently centers largely around payments made

---

[1] See A. H. and G. Somjee, 'India', in Rose and Heidenheimer, *op. cit.*, pp. 686–702.
[2] Wertheim, *op. cit.*, p. 122.

334   JAMES C. SCOTT

TABLE 2

Pattern of Beneficiaries from Corruption by Group and Type of Political System in Less Developed Nations

Type of political system	Individuals and groups with parochial ties to power-holders	Wealth elites	Bureaucrats/ military	Party leaders and cadre	Voters and vote brokers
			Recipients of benefits*		
A. Bureaucratic/military polity [e.g. Thailand]	x	X	X		
B. Party-dominated polity— non-competitive [e.g. Guinea]	x	x	x	X	
C. Party-dominated polity— competitive [e.g. Philippines]	x	X	x	X	X

* Large X's indicate the probable major beneficiaries of corruption in each type of political system, while small x's indicate minor beneficiaries. The overall level of corruption is not a factor in this table; only the distribution of benefits from whatever level exists. Thus, it is conceivable that a minor beneficiary in one system might, because the overall level was quite high, actually receive more benefits than a major beneficiary in another system with less corruption.

by local and foreign business concerns to secure licenses, tax relief, government contracts, etc. Given the nature of the system, the major political resource within the government is control over coercive force, not control over votes. What distribution takes place is intended to cement the ties that bind particular military–civil cliques together and prevent defection to other potential 'coup-groups'.[1] There being no elections, the important clientele narrows to those who control force and special skills; there is no need to pass on the proceeds realized from the business community to cement electoral coalitions, nor is broad pork-barrel legislation a decisive factor.

The bureaucracy/military dominated polity and the pattern of corruption that characterizes it are becoming, if anything, increasingly common as the decline of political parties coupled with restive officer-corps and a strong central bureaucracy conspire to create them. To mention but a few, new nations such as Pakistan, Indonesia, Ghana, Burma, and Dahomey presently fall into this classification. In a few of these states, notably Burma, extensive nationalization has virtually eliminated the independent wealth elite thereby making much corruption a purely intramural affair.

(b) As an intermediate case, party-dominated regimes without electoral competition have fewer and fewer empirical referents. Tunisia, Tanzania, Guinea, and pre-coup Ghana come to mind as examples, although the demise of many similar regimes over the past decade may make the category itself rather ephemeral.[2]

The central role of the party and the effort to strengthen it that characterizes such regimes are likely to mean that party leaders and cadre are likely to share significantly in whatever corruption exists. Not only has the party generally politicized many decisions that might otherwise be administrative questions, but the party often needs a large stock of rewards that may be used to weld the party together and overcome the centrifugal forces of ethnicity, family, region, and so forth. Many such rewards can be provided legitimately; many cannot. To the extent that the regime approximates a personal political machine (e.g., pre-coup Ghana), such corruption is more likely to be widespread than if ideology (e.g., Tunisia) also furnishes some organizational cement.

A further distinction between such regimes that affects corruption is the degree to which they are plebecitarian. One would expect that the rewards of corruption would be more widely distributed where the desire for broad

---

[1] Changes of a substantial nature in the personnel who run the Thai government occur when a successful 'coup-group' ousts the previous ruling coalition. For a discussion of this pattern see James A. Wilson, *Politics in Thailand* (Ithaca: Cornell University Press, 1966), pp. 254–9. The National Assembly has occasionally wielded some power but never for long.

[2] For a careful assessment of the strengths and weaknesses of such regimes in Africa see Zolberg, *op. cit.*, *passim*.

336 JAMES C. SCOTT

public support necessitated satisfying particularistic demands from all quarters than if such support were neither needed nor prized.

Finally, I have indicated that wealth elites will probably benefit less in this regime than in the other two types. This assessment is based less on *a priori* grounds than on the fact that such regimes have generally shown marked preference for the expansion of the public sector at the expense of the private sector. Where this is so, both the size and influence of extra-governmental wealth elites is diminished.

(c) The power-holder (or contender) in a competitive electoral situation is, as mentioned earlier, in a very different position from the power-holder in a bureaucratic polity. Whereas the latter has no special reason to disburse rewards beyond what suffices to maintain his ties to a few powerful groups, the former has great incentives to disburse rewards to those who control the votes that may be decisive in the outcome of elections. Rewards may, and often do, take the form of local development programs, pork-barrel legislation, and legal patronage,[1] but the resort to more irregular inducements is also common. This is especially so in less developed nations where particularistic rewards are likely to be especially persuasive.

The more hotly contested the elections, the greater the distributive effort is likely to be.[2] Elections are generally all or nothing affairs and uncertainty over the outcome will raise costs; when the race is close the marginal utility of the additional dollar is all the greater.[3] The access of wealth elites to influence—both corrupt and legitimate—is all but assured in such a situation as parties and candidates must have funds for campaign purposes. In the three-cornered relationship that is thus created, one can view the politician as a broker who, in return for financial assistance from wealth elites, promotes their policy interests while in office but who must pass along some of his assets to a particularistic electorate from whom he 'rents' his authority. These transactions may or may not assume corrupt forms.[4]

The outstanding example of corruption in a competitive electoral con-

[1] Many development programs, particularly community development programs, in new nations serve important electoral functions for governing parties. Many of the anomalies that confound the observer when they are analyzed as rational economic efforts to raise productivity disappear once they are seen as, above all, an effort to build an effective electoral machine on a particularistic base. One perceptive analyst of Indonesia's nationalization program when parties flourished concluded, 'On the whole, their measures of Indonesianization failed to bring about any major increase in the *power* of Indonesian nationals within the economy, a fact which suggests that the patronage function of these measures may have been more important than their policy aspect'. Herbert Feith, *The Decline of Constitutional Democracy in Indonesia* (Ithaca: Cornell University Press, 1962), p. 557.

[2] A proportional representation system, of course, lessens the distributive pressure.

[3] Alexander Heard, *The Costs of Democracy* (Chapel Hill, North Carolina: University of North Carolina Press, 1960), p. 68.

[4] The party in power has a tremendous advantage in that it can use state funds to reward some of the electorate and can often do this quite legally. 'Out' parties, even if they can secure the financial backing, will ordinarily have to resort to simple bribery, since promises are seldom adequate.

text is of course the Philippines. Per capita, direct campaign expenditures are the highest in the world as a proportion (1.6%—1961) of average per capita national income and are equal to 13 per cent of the national budget.[1] A realistic accounting would also have to include the immense pork-barrel funds (400,000 pesos per senator; 200,000 per congressman) used for electoral purposes and the cash given to the 10–20 per cent of the electorate that actually sells its vote.[2] Wurfel offers a vivid description of the redistributive process.

> For presidential, vice-presidential and senatorial candidates, an increasing percent, now probably almost half of all expenses are payments to local groups and individuals and to the candidates' 'leaders', i.e. loyal congressmen, governors, and mayors. For the congressmen, governors, and mayors, however, more than two thirds of total outlay is to *their* lieutenants, i.e. mayors, municipal councilmen, barrio or village heads, friends, relatives, and other potential followers.[3]

One can appreciate the significance of this filtering effect by the fact that a common laborer will often receive the equivalent of an entire month's salary in exchange for his vote.[4] Wealth elites provide (openly and covertly) a large share of the campaign funds in the knowledge that the satisfaction of a host of short-run, material claims by a poor electorate is the price for a continuation of policies that allow their commercial interests to thrive. The conjunction of highly competitive elections, powerful wealth elites outside government, and an electorate that is no longer automatically loyal to its superiors but has not yet developed strong, horizontal, class or occupational loyalties has conspired to make the Philippines something of a model of electoral-based corruption.[5]

3. *Elite Cohesion and Security*

The relationship between security of tenure and the exploitation of an official post has long been recognized. The outright sale of offices in the seventeenth century was deemed more prudent than their rental since the buyer of office thereby acquired a stake in the long-run profitability of his post. The renter, on the other hand, would often squeeze as much as possible from his office in the limited time granted him regardless of the long-run effects. Urban political machines in the United States at the turn of the century admit of similar distinctions in the use of office. At one point, the disorganization and tenuous foothold of the Chicago machine had produced such rapacious chaos that, according to Steffens, businessmen 'went into the City Council to reduce the festival of blackmail to decent and systematic bribery'.[6] Clearly the chaos had reached such

---

[1] Wurfel, *op. cit.*, p. 761.
[2] *Ibid.*, p. 763.
[3] *Ibid.*, pp. 761–2.
[4] *Ibid.*, p. 769.
[5] Other nations that exhibit some of the same characteristics are: Lebanon, Malaysia, Ceylon, Chile, Uruguay, and parts of India. The differences are due, for the most part, either to less intense electoral competition or to stronger ideological concerns among the electorate.
[6] Steffens, *op. cit.*, p. 165.

G

338   JAMES C. SCOTT

proportions that it threatened 'the goose that laid the golden egg'. The Ashbridge Machine in Philadelphia, however, was such an entrenched, centralized, efficient machine that it could effectively control and direct corruption so as to safeguard its own long-run interests.[1] Having a broader time horizon, the Ashbridge Machine had some concern for the goose's state of health.

The implicit analogy with a business enterprise is not amiss in this context. Urban political machines in the U.S. have been analyzed as a business operation,[2] and, in the Philippines, a party leader once likened the liberal party to a corporation where all members are stockholders and dividends are paid in accordance with what has been invested.[3] One would not expect a prudent businessman to pursue long-run gains where instability and uncertainty abound, but rather to invest in short-term commercial transactions and maintain high liquidity, precisely what many do in developing nations. Political entrepreneurs behave in much the same manner. When their tenure in office is likely to be brief and insecure, they are likely to emphasize quick returns; when their tenure is relatively stable and long, it makes more sense for them to preserve their economic base so as to maximize gains over the long haul.[4] Attention to longer-run gains is also strongly influenced by the cohesion or centralization of the political elite. Corruption is likely to be more severe and chaotic where uncontrolled coalition parties or bureaucratic factions share power in an unstable environment than where the political elite is more effectively hierarchical.

The combined impact of elite cohesion and security and of electoral competition on patterns of corruption in developing nations can be illustrated in Table 3 below. Although important variations are lost in examining only two dichotomous variables, the features emphasized do approximate some salient empirical patterns in many developing nations.

The stability and cohesion of the elite seems important quite apart from whether or not there is electoral competition. In Indonesia the coalition character of pre-1958 cabinets and the tenuous nature of the parliamentary system itself contributed to rather anarchic patterns of corruption. Within such cabinets, moreover, the smaller parties—particularly those who had reason to think that this might be their last time in power—were 'the most opportunistic of all'.[5] The long-term effects of such conditions can be appreciated in this typical tale of the period:

[1] Steffens, *op. cit.*, p. 152. See also Eric L. McKitrick, 'The Study of Corruption', *Political Science Quarterly*, 72, 4 (October 1957), 502–14.

[2] Banfield and Wilson, *op. cit.*, p. 115.

[3] Former Liberal Party leader Jose Avelino, *The Manila Chronicle*, January 18, 1949, cited in Baterina, *op. cit.*, p. 79.

[4] One should be aware, of course, that the stable machine, due to its moderation and concern for the long run, may actually make corrupt arrangements more durable.

[5] Feith, *op. cit.*, p. 422.

In 1957 I heard the following story: A Chinese trader from Menado (Northern Celebes) told a friend in Jakarta of his intention to return to Menado. 'But why, I thought you left there after the Revolution because you could do better business over here?' 'Yes, in those days. But you know how it is. . . . Here in Jakarta I have to tip five high officials to get a license, but in Menado I only have to bribe one lieutenant.'[1]

Until recently, by contrast, the relatively stable electoral majority of the Congress Party in India seems to have resulted in more moderate and orderly corruption.[2] A similar distinction between chaotic corruption and

TABLE 3

Variation of Patterns of Corruption with Characteristics of Political System in Developing Nations[3]

	Electoral competition	Little or no electoral competition
Political elite relatively stable and cohesive	moderate levels of corruption relatively highly organized and predictable some downward distribution, e.g. India, Malaysia	moderate levels of corruption relatively highly organized and predictable little downward distribution, e.g. Pakistan
Political elite relatively unstable and divided	high levels of corruption relatively atomized and unpredictable some downward distribution, e.g. (pre-1958) Indonesia, Philippines	high levels of corruption relatively atomized and unpredictable little downward distribution, e.g. (post-Diem) South Vietnam

more predictable arrangements, but in a setting where there is little or no electoral competition, is provided by South Vietnam and Pakistan respectively. The relative stability of General Ayub Khan's regime had prevented the anarchic corruption that has come to characterize the weak, factionalized military regimes in Saigon.[4]

[1] Wertheim, *op. cit.*, p. 127.
[2] See for example *Report of the Commission of Inquiry* [into allegations against S. Partap Singh Kairon, Chief Minister of the Punjab] (New Delhi: Home Ministry, June 11, 1964) for an account of a well-oiled political machine.
[3] If, instead of four cells, the table were to be conceived of as continua along two dimensions, more precise distinctions would be possible; e.g., between the greater electoral competition in the Philippines than in Malaysia or even pre-1958 Indonesia, for that matter. The table also assumes that elections *per se* have no appreciable effect on levels of corruption. For a particularistic electorate in which the distribution of rewards is of more concern than standards of probity, this seems a safe assumption.
[4] One hesitates to use South Vietnam here since the vast amounts of military aid and social disorganization resulting from the war make it a very special case. Nonetheless, the instability of the regime has an independent effect over and above these factors. The Diem regime in the more stable days of, say, 1956 had imposed a degree of predictability, limited though it was, that present-day military cliques cannot achieve.

340 JAMES C. SCOTT

In conclusion, one must ask of corruption the same questions one asks of any other political process: who gets what, when, how? For the less developed nations especially, the analysis of corruption as a process of political influence promises to recast not only the study of corruption, but also the study of policy 'outcomes'.

Whether or not certain kinds of political influence involve corruption depends, as we have seen, on many of the structural and legal features of a political system. The adoption of restrictive administrative codes, the growth of the public sector, and the central role frequently played by bureaucratic elites in making crucial decisions all serve to narrow the legitimate avenues open to those who wish to influence policy. Patterns of influence that would probably find legitimate means of expression in, say, a working party system are, in most developing nations, relegated to channels that violate formal standards of public conduct. A more detailed inquiry into the kinds of political influence that are legitimized or forbidden over time by virtue of changes in community norms and political structures can place the study of corruption more firmly in the context of political development.

Corruption, representing as it does an important means for influencing policy at the enforcement stage, can work important changes in government policy. An analysis of political influence that focuses on the legislative process alone will thus risk seriously distorting the actual pattern of influence in settings where enforcement-level influence has assumed significant proportions. In the less developed nations a number of groups, excluded from overt influence for various reasons, are nevertheless represented in ultimate policy results by means of corruption. Any effort to accurately assess the distribution of influence within a political system will thus necessarily have to consider pressure during implementation as well as during the legislative process.

Determining empirically who gets what from corruption depends in large part on the nature of both the political system and the political elite. In this context we have examined three of the more significant variables (the proportion of 'market' to 'parochial' corruption; the degree of stability and security of the political elite; and the presence or absence of electoral competition) and suggested what their probable impact on the nature, level, and distribution of benefits might be. Quite clearly, it is impossible to ascertain the effects of corruption on political integration, income distribution, or economic growth without first asking who benefits in what ways from what kinds of corruption. And since the pattern of benefits varies in turn with the nature of the political system, a careful inquiry must begin there.

The frequent replacement of party-based electoral machines by military/bureaucratic regimes over the past decade in the new states indicates that the pattern of corruption is changing accordingly. The new regimes, unlike those they replaced, have little need to distribute the rewards of office widely. Facing no electoral pressures, most corruption centers around the consolidation of clique groups at whose core are the commanders of armed force. In some instances the secure position of one ruling clique may impose some order and limits to this corruption, while in less secure situations more Hobbesian patterns may prevail. The military/bureaucratic pattern of corruption, however, whether in its stable or unstable variant, seems to have become the modal type.*

* I am very grateful to Edward Friedman, Fred Hayward, and Crawford Young for their searching comments on an earlier version of this paper.

[6]

ENDEMIC AND PLANNED CORRUPTION IN A MONARCHICAL REGIME

By JOHN WATERBURY*

Recent experience in the so-called underdeveloped countries has most vividly brought home the fact that corruption is not a mass of incoherent phenomena, but a political system, capable of being steered with tolerable precision by those in power.

—*J. J. Van Klaveren*[1]

Even if the sovereign was willing to relax the links of personal dependence, he would never go so far as to renounce the riches which, in his view, are but a part of his own, just as their possessors are but a part of all those who belong to the dynasty: the possessor, in effect, acquired his riches thanks only to the dynasty and in the shadow of its authority.

—*Ibn Khaldoun*[2]

CORRUPTION may be defined in a legal or normative sense, and in some societies the two definitions may be coincident. In the legal sense, corruption is self-regarding behavior on the part of public functionaries that directly violates legal restrictions on such behavior. Normatively, a public functionary may be considered corrupt whether or not a law is being violated in the process. A legally corrupt person may arouse no normative reprobation; a person judged corrupt by normative standards may be legally clean. What is common to both definitions is the notion of the abuse of public power and influence for private ends. It can safely be assumed that any society or political system manifests some level of one or the other, or both of these forms of corruption.

We may consider this level (while begging the question of how to measure it) as the amount of free-floating, endemic corruption in a system. In general, analysts of corruption have portrayed it as mostly unwanted (although sometimes convenient), and most often un-

---

* This study was stimulated by two periods of field research in Morocco. The first, from 1965 to 1968, resulted in my book, *The Commander of the Faithful: The Moroccan Political Elite—A Study in Segmented Politics* (New York and London 1970). The second period, winter and spring 1970, was devoted to an interview-study of ninety high-ranking bureaucrats, in conjunction with a cross-national study of bureaucratic and political elite cultures under the supervision of S. J. Eldersveld of the Department of Political Science of the University of Michigan.

[1] From a "Comment," *Comparative Studies in Society and History*, VI (January 1964), 195, as cited in J. S. Nye, "Corruption and Political Development: A Cost-Benefit Analysis," *American Political Science Review*, LXI (June 1967), 417.

[2] G.-A. Bousquet, *Ibn Khaldoun: les textes sociologiques et économiques de la Mouqaddima* (Paris 1965), 171.

planned. It has been seen as a concomitant phenomenon accompanying the politico-administrative process, but only marginally instrumental in the maintenance and vitality of that process. The real or perceived saliency of corruption in the developing countries has generated some rethinking of the functions of corruption in both political and economic development. Again, because of the difficulty of measuring something that may be legally and morally condemned, we cannot be sure if the degree or level of corruption in various developing countries is really higher than in economically advanced nations. Perhaps, because in many developing countries cultural norms are more tolerant of corruption as legally defined, and because the laws themselves are so out of touch with cultural expectations and actual administrative practice, corrupt behavior, as judged by the outsider, is far more open than in advanced nations where such behavior is masked by legal subterfuge and the complexity of the deals.

Whatever the difficulties of measuring and comparing levels of corruption, the contemporary experience of the developing countries has provoked considerable speculation as to whether or not corruption may ultimately prove beneficial to economic growth and political development. Three authors, who will receive greater attention further on, have pointed out that corruption may promote national integration, capitalist efficiency, capital formation, administrative flexibility, and a shift toward popular democracy.[3] Those speculations must be tested against empiric evidence, and in this essay evidence will be drawn from contemporary Morocco.

Beyond that, the analysis will be carried a step further. Not only must we consider the possibility that corruption may have certain beneficial effects on the development process, but, however we appraise these effects, it may be that corruption is far more than an accompanying phenomenon of the political process. It may be seen as a planned, cultivated, and vital element in assuring the survival of a regime. As the case of Morocco would tend to demonstrate, corruption is not simply an aspect of politics but has displaced and dwarfed all other forms of politics.

Thus, in Morocco, free-floating corruption is manipulated, guided, planned, and desired by the regime itself. Although the terms may not

---

[3] Nye (fn. 1); Nathaniel Leff, "Economic Development through Bureaucratic Corruption," *American Behavioral Scientist*, viii (November 1964), 8-15; James C. Scott, "The Analysis of Corruption in Developing Nations," *Comparative Studies in Society and History*, xi (June 1969), 315-41. I regret that in the preparation of this article I was unable to consult James Scott's recent *Comparative Political Corruption* (Englewood Cliffs, N.J. 1972).

CORRUPTION IN A MONARCHICAL REGIME 535

fit with precision, the Moroccan monarchy can be seen as a patrimonial regime with strong rationalizing tendencies. The elements of rationalization manifest themselves in at least two ways. First, the growing central bureaucracy is increasingly subject to rational criteria of organization, recruitment, and training. Bureaucrats, in terms of education, exposure to outside currents of thought, mental outlook, and career expectations, are *somewhat* removed from the traditionalistic, clientelistic, and particularistic ethos of the patrimonial regime.[4] Moroccan bureaucrats tend to identify with an exogenous cultural referent that leads them to condemn morally corrupt behavior which, for the rest of society, may be corrupt in the legal sense only. Second, although they condemn corrupt practices, a very substantial part (again the phenomenon defies precise measurement) of the bureaucrats are involved in them. But because of their outlook and their skills, they have brought about some rationalization of the system of patronage and of corruption itself. They are willing participants in a particular regime's system, and are in some ways its accomplices. Their participation has a price which comes in the form of illicit rewards. There is, then, a notion of contract at play here, one that is defined almost entirely in terms of participation on the one hand and payoffs on the other. This represents a straightforward, rational transaction.

The patrimonial aspects of the regime[5] are quite obvious and will be dealt with in detail further on. Suffice it to say for the moment that the monarchy underscores its supremacy within the system by constantly spawning new relations of dependency between itself and various sectors of the society. Dependency is maintained by manipulating access to various kinds of administrative prebends. These may, of course, be seen as part of the distribution system, but they are not subject to criteria of state planning, rational development priorities, or organizational performance. Instead, they are subject to bargaining, threats, influence-trading, and, above all, the judgment and sometimes the whim of the man who has his hand on the tap.

The fact that the Moroccan regime is a monarchy highlights the patrimonial characteristics of the regime, but guided or planned corruption need in no way be confined to monarchies. Keeping in mind that manipulation of a spoils system may be not only useful to a regime but crucial to its survival, we may refer to Ann Ruth Willner's portrayal of Sukarno.

[4] Cf. James Bill, "Modernization and Reform from Above: The Case of Iran," *Journal of Politics*, xxxii (February 1970), 19-40.

[5] See Max Weber, *Theory of Social and Economic Organization*, trans. by Talcott Parsons (Glencoe, Ill. 1947), 313-29.

President Sukarno successfully assumed lifetime tenure, an impressive array of titles, and a style of life that included the entourage, regalia, and rituals customarily maintained by traditional Javanese monarchs. . . . Significantly, he did not maintain his position of supremacy by direct control of a tightly organized and disciplined political, bureaucratic, or military apparatus, commanding either overt or implicit instruments of coercive pressure at his direction. Rather, his strength derived from his adroit command of various strategies of manipulation, negotiation, and bargaining; from bestowal and withdrawal of approval; from appointments and emoluments, and from psychological exploitation of his knowledge of the probable responses of his chief lieutenants and subordinates, their lieutenants and subordinates, and other leaders and contenders for power and position.[6]

It may be that any head of state who wishes to remain in power indefinitely, i.e., permanently, is pushed towards the elaboration of a neo-feudal patronage system. In Mexico, the PRI has avoided one-man rule, but has nonetheless created the problem of the dynastic survival of what James Wilkie calls the "Revolutionary Family." Regime maintenance has come to be founded on an elaborate system of state patronage, the benefits of which are disbursed under the budget heading *erogaciones adicionales*; in any year these may account for 15-23 per cent of all budgeted expenditures.[7] It must be emphasized that the phenomenon under examination goes beyond mere pork-barrelism and is essential to the maintenance of the regime. In the context of United States politics, the closest analogies are to be found in the city-boss systems where, again, relations of dependency are created and maintained through the discriminatory use of the power and privileges of public office. The vote is simply a convenient way to reaffirm these ties and to measure their extent as well as their cost within the boss's arena.[8]

CHARACTERISTICS OF ENDEMIC CORRUPTION IN DEVELOPING COUNTRIES

To reiterate an earlier point: Any political system, regardless of the nature of its regime, manifests some level of corruption; in turn, this may be incorporated into the lifeblood of those regimes that predicate their survival upon its use. It has already been intimated that corrup-

[6] Ann Ruth Willner, "Neotraditional Accommodation to Political Independence: The Case of Indonesia," in Lucian Pye, ed., *Cases in Comparative Politics: Asia* (Boston 1970), 249. Cf. Marvin Zonis, *The Political Elite of Iran* (Princeton 1971), esp. 100-102. The systemic parallels between Morocco and Iran are extraordinarily, although not coincidentally, close.

[7] James W. Wilkie, *The Mexican Revolution: Federal Expenditure and Social Change since 1910* (Berkeley and Los Angeles 1967), 5-9.

[8] For a relevant analysis, see James C. Scott, "Corruption, Machine Politics, and Political Change," *American Political Science Review*, LXIII (December 1969), 1142-58.

CORRUPTION IN A MONARCHICAL REGIME 537

tion may best be seen as a variant of the broader phenomenon of patronage. Patronage is founded upon asymmetrical relations between a powerful person or group of persons and their clients, who seek protection, favors, and rewards from the patrons. At the same time, to an important extent the patron is powerful as a result of the size or nature of his clientele, and is able to protect and reward his supporters because he uses them to strengthen his hand in bargaining for scarce resources.[9] A patron, of course, need not be a public official; he can attract clientele on the basis of his wealth or his control of or access to scarce resources such as jobs, or land, or arms. However, when a patron occupies a public position or extracts favors from those in public positions, patronage and corruption overlap.[10]

In developing societies, which are characterized by material scarcity, both real and perceived, the asymmetry in relations between the powerful and the less powerful is particularly pronounced. Scarce resources are relatively more scarce, and the power derived from controlling them is more extensive and inescapable. The few resources at the disposal of the poor and the powerless can be easily lost or destroyed, and awareness of this fact heightens a general sense of vulnerability and potential disaster, and sets in motion myriads of clients in search of patrons. There is no real escape from the quest until and unless the contextual scarcity is overcome. Networks of dependency, or what Andreski more vividly calls "relations of parasitism," are continually regenerated: "Once a society is pervaded by parasitic exploitation, the

[9] For some excellent discussions of what has become the subject of a great deal of study among anthropologists, sociologists, and political scientists, see Jeremy Boissevain, "Patronage in Sicily," *Man: Journal of the Royal Anthropological Institute*, I (March 1966), 18-33; René Lemarchand and Keith Legg, "Political Clientelism and Development: A Preliminary Analysis," *Comparative Politics*, IV (January 1972), 149-78; Lemarchand, "Clientelism and Ethnicity in Tropical Africa: Competing Solidarities in Nation-building," *American Political Science Review*, LXVI (March 1972), 68-90; Alex Weingrod, "Patrons, Patronage, and Political Parties," *Comparative Studies in Society and History*, X (July 1969), 376-400; James C. Scott, "Patron-Client Politics and Political Change in Southeast Asia," *American Political Science Review*, LXVI (March 1972), 91-113; Richard Sandbrook, "Patrons, Clients, and Factions: New Dimensions of Conflict Analysis in Africa," *Canadian Journal of Political Science*, V (March 1972), 104-19.

[10] For a useful discussion of the overlap between patronage and corruption, see Edward Van Roy, "On the Theory of Corruption," *Economic Development and Cultural Change*, XIX (October 1970), 86-110. Scott calls attention to the same overlap when he proposes ". . . that corruption may be viewed as a process of political influence such that similar practices may violate community norms at one place and time and not at another" (fn. 3), 317. I do not concur in the relevance of the distinction between "patron," a person who controls resources, and "broker," a person who controls *access* to resources—a distinction made by both Scott (fn. 9), 96-98, and Lemarchand (fn. 9), throughout. It would seem to me unlikely that any given patron would fail to combine some aspects of both functions, and, after all, connections are resources, as is the number of clients.

choice is only to skin or be skinned. A man may combine the two
roles in varying measure but he cannot avoid them: he cannot follow
Candide's example and till his garden, relying on hard work for his
well-being, because he will not be left alone: the wielders of power
will pounce upon him and seize the fruits and tools of his labour."[11]

It has often been observed that the search for protection from nature,
violence, and the exactions of arbitrary and predatory governments
was a constant theme of social life in so-called traditional societies.
Although today the vagaries of nature and the extent of communal
violence may be more subject to technological control than they
were in the past, the application of technology has become a quasi-
monopoly of new state systems. The poor of the Third World may
have exchanged one kind of vulnerability for another. The introduction of Mexican wheat may lead to increased yields, but the peasant
must somehow obtain credit from the state agricultural credit bank
and hope for the best in a market pricing system partially or totally
determined by the state. The need for intercessors, protectors, and patrons is no less great now than it was in the past. Moreover, the contemporary power and penetration of the modern state apparatus has
in many instances been achieved without any modification of the
degree of real or perceived material scarcity. Competition for privileged access to state services or relief from impositions has come to
dominate political life; the scope for corrupt patronage has expanded
with the state itself.[12]

It has frequently been the case that in polities where class structures
range from fragile to nonexistent, access to political power has been
the surest means to wealth (rather than the reverse which, according
to Marx, was characteristic of the development of capitalist structures).
The very notion of a prebend presupposes the use of office as a means
to acquire property. In patrimonial and neo-patrimonial systems, passing on access to public office (if not the office itself) from generation
to generation has been a more dominant and rational motive than

---

[11] Stanislav Andreski, *Parasitism and Subversion: The Case of Latin America* (New
York 1969), 11; see also Lemarchand (fn. 9), 75, n. 27, citing Ronald Cohen; Scott
(fn. 9), 101.

[12] Boissevain (fn. 9), develops this theme with reference to Sicily, suggesting that
Catholicism, a saint-oriented religion, gives an other-worldly impetus to the quest for
intercession. It may be that saints are part and parcel of belief systems emerging out
of situations of real material scarcity. Islam, while hostile to saints, has been forced
to tolerate saintly cults most everywhere it has spread. For more on the interrelation
of scarcity, state power, and patronage, see Lemarchand and Legg (fn. 8); A. Vingradov
and J. Waterbury, "Situations of Contested Legitimacy in Morocco: An Alternative
Framework," *Comparative Studies in Society and History*, XIII (January 1971), 32-59.

CORRUPTION IN A MONARCHICAL REGIME 539

acquiring wealth; in such systems, wealth has usually been subject to the destruction, confiscation, or other predatory actions of the state.

In the contemporary period that motive has been reinforced in many ways. Frequently the governments of the developing countries maintain arbitrary and predatory practices that involve the destruction of resources of real or imagined enemies. Moreover, the technological and administrative means to achieve these ends have been greatly expanded in the twentieth century. At the same time, relatively well-organized and penetrative state bureaucracies have come to intervene in and control large areas of the economic life of their societies. Not only do these bureaucracies regulate and sanction ever wider spheres of social and economic behavior, but they influence and determine the allocation of desired resources on a hitherto unprecedented scale. It is little wonder then that, for the ambitious, access to public power has become more than ever the key to material success as well as to the formation of clientelistic support.[13] For the average citizen, reaching some sort of *modus vivendi* with a state system that affects nearly all aspects of one's life has become a daily chore.

In brief, historical precedent and conditions, combined with the logic of contemporary bureaucratic expansion in the developing countries, have fostered the growth of extensive amounts of systemic corruption.

For the most part it is corruption in the legal sense only, for while the politics and abuses of patronage may be disliked by the masses, they are not regarded as illicit; in effect, they are seen as a fact of life that one cannot avoid and that had best be mastered. "Corruption," Huntington posits, "is behavior of public officials which deviates from accepted norms in order to serve private ends."[14] But self-regarding or client-regarding activities of public officials do not deviate from accepted norms. Something of the attitudinal ambivalence involved here is revealed by certain findings of a recent mass survey in India. Forty-two per cent of an urban and 48 per cent of a rural sample thought that the majority of civil servants was corrupt. At the same time, 76 and 89 per cent, respectively, of the same samples stated that they would prefer to work for the government as compared with the private sector: "The expectation of dishonesty and corruption in government is high in

[13] William J. Siffin emphasizes this process with regard to Thailand. See his "Personnel Processes of the Thai Bureaucracy," in Heady and Stokes, eds., *Papers in Comparative Administration* (Ann Arbor 1962), 207-28.

[14] Samuel P. Huntington, *Political Order in Changing Societies* (New Haven 1968), 60.

Explaining Corruption

India and, paradoxically, for the same people who see government service as prestigeful. Government service is apparently seen in two separate images, from two distinct value positions. It is both corrupt and prestigeful."[15] On the basis of this statement, I would suggest that the paradox is more apparent than real, and that the corrupt and prestigeful images of the bureaucracy are in fact reconciled within an ethos founded on asymmetrical relations of dependency and vulnerability.[16] Power and privilege are simultaneously resented and coveted by those who do not have them.

The tolerance of corruption at all levels is predicated upon the basic cynicism of the people with regard to their government. No one is dupe in this game where services and influence are marketable commodities and where buyers and sellers use all their wiles to strike a bargain.

> When, as a supplicant, the peasant tries to bribe a clerk, or to establish a dependent relationship with an official in the idiom of a family relationship or of a courtier at the king's palace, he is in fact trying to coerce the clerk or the official by including him within his own moral community. He is trying to transform the transaction, which he knows is one of exploitation, into a moral relationship, *because it is in his interest to do so.* In just the same way, when the campaigning politician addresses him as "brother," the peasant sees this as an act of hypocrisy, and looks behind the facade of symbolic friendliness for the hidden interest.[17]

As regards transactions inherent in administrative corruption, we are dealing with the distribution of and payment for services and dispensations. For the masses of supplicants, paying for the service (brib-

[15] See S. J. Eldersveld and others, *The Citizen and the Administrator in a Developing Democracy* (New Delhi 1968), 31-33 (citation from p. 33).

[16] It may be hypothesized, although I have seen no systematic test of the hypothesis, that in many developing countries corruption fails to arouse mass moral indignation because the notions of public and private spheres are not highly developed. That is, when we speak of the use of public power for private ends, it is assumed that we can define what is private, and that public power is subject to universalistic criteria. It is also assumed that there is a kind of multiple role specialization whereby a bureaucrat is a "public" figure for eight hours a day and a "private" citizen the rest. In fact, it is common for bureaucrats in developing countries to carry role-playing to extremes by insulating themselves rigidly in the impartiality and rule-conscious role of the public official in order to stave off the importunities of clients who want to force them into the role of dispenser of particularistic favors. Variations on this theme are explored in Fred Riggs, *Administration in Developing Countries: The Theory of Prismatic Society* (Boston 1964); Hahn-Bee Lee, "Developmentalist Time and Leadership in Developing Countries," *CAG Occasional Papers* (Bloomington 1966); and José A. Silva Michelena, "The Venezuelan Bureaucrat," in *A Strategy for Research on Social Policy* (The Politics of Change in Venezuela), I (Boston 1967), 86-119.

[17] F. G. Bailey, "The Peasant View of the Bad Life," *Science and Culture* (Calcutta), xxxiii (February 1967), 31-40 (emphasis in original).

ing) is not reprehensible in itself; but when the market value of services becomes too high, moral indignation is aroused. In Morocco, for instance, some evidence suggests that the inflation in the price of corruption has become onerous and resented. Passports and work permits are too highly priced, price-control brigades shake down retailers too often and for too much, entrance "fees" for state examinations have been greatly inflated, and so forth. It is at this point that the indignation of the masses over the excessive prices of needed services may mesh with the professed indignation of the educated elites who condemn corruption regardless of its costs.

Finally, we may note that pervasive administrative corruption at the lower echelons of the bureaucracy is particularly favored by the low level of literacy in many developing countries, as well as by the personalized rendering of administrative services. Where literacy is at a premium, there are very few routine operations that can be performed anonymously between the citizen and the functionary. One must line up, find someone to fill out the forms, locate the intermediary who knows the right office, and then bargain one's way to some sort of solution. The process is on a face-to-face basis, with several possible services to be purchased along the way.[18]

THE COSTS AND BENEFITS OF CORRUPTION IN MOROCCO

With virtually no exceptions, the kinds of endemic corruption set forth in the preceding pages are to be found in Morocco. Is it possible to establish some sort of balance sheet as to their costs and benefits to the Moroccan polity and society?

Both Leff and Nye have suggested a number of possible benefits resulting from corruption. Regarding economic development, Nye argues that corruption may encourage capital formation where taxation would inhibit it. Further, illegal purchases of administrative favors may help cut red tape and overcome the rigidity of administrative practices. Finally, corruption may promote efficient entrepreneurial behavior. Leff joins Nye in emphasizing this point. In situations of what he calls "market corruption," the highest bribe wins the contract or favor, and it may be that the most efficient capitalist is the one who can muster the highest bribe; ergo, corruption rewards efficiency.[19]

We may summarize some of the other advantages, particularly as

---

[18] See the graphic description of one such process in Richard Patch, "The La Paz Census of 1970," *American Universities Field Staff Report* (West Coast Latin American Series, Hanover, N.H., 1970), 7-10.

[19] Leff (fn. 3); Nye (fn. 1).

presented by Nye, as follows: corruption (implicitly on a broad scale) may tend to overcome elite cleavages by means of the unobtrusive and clandestine redistribution of spoils. It is perhaps this "function" that Scott has in mind in his remarks about Thailand: "What distribution [of corruption] takes place is intended to cement the ties that bind particular military-civil cliques together and prevent defection to other potential 'coup-groups.' "[20]

In addition, corruption permits access to the distribution system to groups and minorities that might otherwise be frozen out. Ironically, corruption is thus seen as overcoming certain discriminatory practices and as promoting national integration. Along these same lines, corruption—particularly when viewed as a facet of broader patronage networks—may mitigate potential ethnic or class conflict by diverting the attention of spokesmen from the exploitation of grievances to the distribution of spoils.[21] A third political and integrative benefit may derive from the use of corruption to create supporting institutions such as political parties, and to grease the wheels of electoral politics. Moreover, it may be, as Scott argues, that electoral corruption indicates a real spread of popular democracy when a regime can no longer control elections through violence, threat, or fraud, and must pay for votes rather than extract them by force.

We may now try to determine how Morocco scores on some of these dimensions, but a preliminary remark is in order. It is illusory to think that we can actually measure the costs and benefits of corruption in Morocco or in any other country. The reason is simple. Either one is dealing with a country in which some level of corruption is apparent or with a country in which, at least for the sake of argument, no corruption is apparent. On the one hand, a discussion of the benefits of corruption would oblige the observer to make a purely hypothetical guess as to how the system would function without corruption, and on the other, how a noncorrupt system would function with corruption. One can convincingly and legitimately analyze only what actually is going on and what the costs and benefits seem to be. It is very difficult to suggest what the costs and benefits of some hypothetical process might be. The only way out of this bind would be to find (or simulate) two or more governmental systems sharing the same cultural environment and basic socioeconomic configurations

---

[20] Scott (fn. 3), 335; see also Weingrod (fn. 9).

[21] Boissevain (fn. 9) sustains this point with regard to Sicily; see also Ernest Gellner, "Patterns of Rural Rebellion in Morocco: Tribes as Minorities," *European Journal of Sociology*, III, No. 2 (1962); Lemarchand (fn. 9), 68.

and political regimes, one of which is "corrupt" and the other "clean," and then compare the functioning of the two systems in terms of costs and benefits. Unfortunately, no two such comparable units come to mind.

MARKET CORRUPTION ENCOURAGES CAPITAL FORMATION AND ENTREPRENEURIAL EFFICIENCY

Leff's hypothesis regarding the positive effect of corruption upon capital formation is too simplistic and naive. The amount of capital the bidder is able to offer depends on far more than efficiency. The highest bidder may be—and in the Moroccan context frequently is— a talented speculator who made a killing in urban real estate or in import-export. In general, the indigenous native bourgeoisie has accepted and cultivated relations of dependency with the state bureaucracy and semipublic authorities. It is a parasitic bourgeoisie that lives off privileged access to state-controlled resources or the differential application of state regulations. At the same time, individual entrepreneurs may specialize in serving as intermediaries between the Moroccan State and various foreign private investors. Whatever deal they are able to arrange entitles them to a percentage of the investment: As brokers they take a "commission" but invest nothing except their time and influence.[22]

It is true that the biggest bribes in Morocco can be and probably are offered by the French industrial establishment (*patronat*) of Casablanca and other Moroccan cities. It is also true that the *patronat* represents the most efficient industrial and commercial enterprises in the country. Their payoffs, in the form of protection money to avoid discriminatory application of regulations, and in placing influential Moroccans on their boards of directors with high salaries, may be seen as promoting efficient capitalist endeavor. But the relationship is blurred by the existence of protected markets or industries, and the fact that various enterprises (banks, vehicle assemblies, breweries, cement factories, sugar refineries) are branch operations of metropolitan enterprises rather than independent establishments that must sink or swim on their own.

[22] Many Moroccan entrepreneurs combine elements of the Marxist notion of "comprador" as well as the more graphic expletive of "Lumpen-bourgeoisie" used by André Gunder Frank in *Lumpen-bourgeoisie et lumpen-développement*, Maspéro, Cahiers Libres 205-206 (Paris 1971). Omar Ben Messaoud, former attaché in the Royal Cabinet and go-between between Pan American and the Moroccan Ministry of Finance, is exemplary of the Moroccan bourgeoisie, although his arrest indicates that he overplayed his hand. See Waterbury, "The Coup Manqué," *American Universities Field Staff Report*, North African Series, xv, No. 1 (1971).

A not unusual scenario involving some of the themes mentioned above might unfold as follows. *X, Y,* and *Z* are prominent Moroccan businessmen with connections in the Palace and, more often than not, close relations or friends in the Ministry of Finance. They approach a thriving French textile plant and propose that they be allowed to acquire a certain proportion of the company's stock, let us say 15 per cent of all outstanding shares. It is understood that they will pay nothing for the shares, but that dividends will accrue in their names until they are equivalent to the value of the shares on the day of "purchase." The company can use those dividends as they accumulate, and, depending on the bargain, include interest in the purchase price. In the meantime, *X, Y, Z* will have been "elected" to the board of directors with salary. Without investing a penny, the three entrepreneurs can each pick up a salary and eventually a share of the company's assets. The more influential they appear to be, the more often they can repeat this gambit. In return for what is essentially protection money, they do favors for the company, such as arranging duty-free importation of machinery or keeping the labor inspector from closing the place down for violation of safety regulations.

It should also be noted that Leff's analysis of market corruption does not take into account the use of illegal payments in an ongoing process that Fred Riggs has called "strategic spending."[23] To summarize Riggs's argument, an individual's surplus earnings—be he public official or private entrepreneur—are disbursed in tributes and gifts to safeguard his power position and to maintain his ability to extract tributes and gifts in turn. Wealth is not power; rather, it is spent in the quest for power. As a result, Riggs concludes, strategic spending keeps surplus resources from productive investment and hence leads to "negative development."

In Morocco, and elsewhere, strategic spending may be perfectly legal, but more than likely it will involve trading in privileges and favors dependent upon persons in public office. Private groups may pay protection, good will, or access money as a strategic device, and hope for administrative favors in return. In addition, considerable strategic spending goes on within the administration, including falsified accounts, manipulation of personnel and promotion, differential application of watch-dog and auditing procedures, cost-plus contracting where the work is performed by a public agency, and so forth. All these operations may be carried out as tributes and loans among bureaucratic clans and political power-holders.

[23] Riggs (fn. 16), 141-42.

CORRUPTION IN A MONARCHICAL REGIME 545

This kind of trading, rather than constituting market corruption, seems designed to insulate the participants in a protective web of obligations and expected services that makes every man at once a creditor and a debtor. In an administration whose upper reaches are subject to the whims of the ruler, the unpredictable redistribution of prebends, and the vagaries of clan-infighting, strategic spending leads to some minimal degree of predictability of social security. No one really has much incentive to break away from the web, for, while he may escape his debts, he will also abandon his claims to what is owed him. Investments in this web bear no interest, and some degree of stability is bought at the price of productivity. Finally, flight into the private sector solves nothing: to the extent that it is dependent on the administration, the refugee's web of obligations will follow him.

The notion of protection payments warrants further attention, for it bears directly upon entrepreneurial activity and capital formation. The kind of corruption that is under discussion is a negative transaction between some branch of the administration (and by implication, the regime itself) as one party and any designated interest as the other. In return for political loyalty or apoliticism, the regime offers *not* to apply discriminatory practices. In 1966, for example, an important sugar importer and newspaper owner received word that his connections with a leftist party were well known and unfavorably viewed in higher circles. It was suggested that these connections be terminated lest his warehouses be closed for various violations or his applications for import licenses be turned down. In such a transaction nothing is exchanged; both parties agree to conditions guaranteeing that neither will engage in activities harmful to the other.[24]

Because there is some tendency in Morocco's political system for the Palace to view any successful entrepreneur as politically dangerous (he could buy clientele, influence, and a political power base) there is also a tendency to break or domesticate such men, to reassert the links of dependency essential to the regime's survival. Most actors are aware of the possibility of discriminatory sanctions, and this awareness or general expectation is more important than the actual frequency with which sanctions are applied. Anticipatory reaction to this threat motivates entrepreneurs to make short-term speculation and protection payments

---

[24] In this instance, sanctions were applied. The businessman's newspaper was temporarily closed down by order of the Minister of Interior, just long enough for the shipping companies that published their schedules in it to transfer their advertising and notices to another newspaper. The "leftist" newspaper went out of business. Its publisher, after having mulled over his fate for a while, was put at the head of an important state investment body.

and to shun strategies of long-term investments. In conclusion: corruption in the Moroccan system does little to contribute to entrepreneurial efficiency or capital formation.

CORRUPTION PROMOTES ADMINISTRATIVE FLEXIBILITY

In one respect, the flexibility hypothesis would seem to apply in Morocco. Corruption does, to some extent, promote flexibility in *intra-administrative* procedures. These involve skirting, manipulating, or violating civil-service rules for all matters regarding living, promotion, salaries, benefits, expense accounts, and so forth. One quasi-legal device is the contract system (*contrat fonctionnel*). Access to various levels of the civil service is nominally determined by educational and training qualifications. When Morocco first became independent, there was a severe shortage of Moroccans who could meet French educational standards for various posts. To overcome this, ministries were allowed to negotiate bilateral contracts to meet staffing needs. The same kind of contract could be renegotiated to promote the contractee to a higher post. However, even after the initial shortages were overcome, the practice of using discretionary contracts continued, for they provided a means by which a minister or *directeur* could reward his clientele with coveted posts. In this way the *contrat fonctionnel* became an integral part of the patronage system while at the same time eroding some of the rigidity inherent in the civil service code.

It could be argued that the possibility to milk an office or market administrative services helps attract talented personnel to the administration—personnel that might otherwise be discouraged by the very low salaries paid at all levels. This judgment would apply particularly to the middle and upper reaches of the civil service. Each ministry or agency may contain an internal prebendary system by which service payments at one level are disbursed to the personnel involved while a certain percentage is passed on to the next level. In addition, some ministries or directors within them may be particularly well placed to extract large-scale tributes: Public Works, contracting for road and dam construction; Education, contracting for school construction; and Commerce, contracting for licensing, market inspection, weights and measures, import permits, and so forth. All of these ministries offer a vast potential for kickbacks and protection money. The administrative "entrepreneurs" who seek out appointments as ministers or in key directions all know the relative ranking of these agencies. The prebend is known in the trade (with no offense to David Easton) as the *caisse noire* or "black box." The biggest and most coveted black box is that of the Ministry of Finance which extracts tribute from all other ministries and agencies through the budget and auditing process and the control of the civil-service payroll, *and* from the non-governmental sector through fiscal control. The Minister of Finance and his clients have a finger in every pie and can exact a heavy price for their vital services.[25]

To an important degree, a parallel, non-official, and illegal system of payments and incentives has developed, providing a possibility for high material rewards that the official salary structure precludes. Perhaps talented Moroccans would shun administrative careers without the parallel system. Corruption, it could be argued, serves in this instance to maintain a façade of austerity while at the same time attracting quality personnel to the administration. Yet to the extent that this is true, the benefit is cancelled by at least two major costs. First, budget austerity was originally designed to stabilize the salary structure in the public sector and free state resources for productive investment. For all intents and purposes that objective has been abandoned. Second, the civil-service code was designed to bring stability and predictability to administrative careers, an element notably lacking to date. Moreover, talented personnel is wasted by immersion in the game of manipulating the quasi-illicit procedures that have developed to improve career prospects and earnings. Without reallocating state resources, civil-service salaries could probably be raised across the board and promotion practices standardized without reallocating state resources. But for reasons of political control, the King has been reluctant (at least until July 1971) to put an end to these civil-service games precisely because the ambitious civil servant becomes so preoccupied with them that he has little time left over to think about the "system" as a whole.

The flexibility hypothesis seems misplaced as regards corruption arising between civil servants and the citizenry. In fact, corruption in the form of taking and offering bribes is directly linked to the maintenance of red tape. A service charge is to be expected in every instance that an administrative regulation is applied. The service charge does not permit the payee to *avoid* the regulation, but rather guarantees —sometimes—that the civil servant will expedite the payee's case. The Royal Gendarmerie inspects trucks and cars for faulty headlights or

[25] There are so many operations going on within the Ministry of Finance that it is hard to know which are the most profitable. One steady source of income to the Ministry's black box comes from the processing of all governmental claims for overtime payments. A fixed percentage of whatever total is approved by Finance for a given agency is retained for Finance's black box. A threat that Finance can always use vis-à-vis other ministries is to refuse to budget their unfilled slots; as much as 25 per cent of all funded slots in the civil service may go unfilled, allowing one man to draw two salaries. Finance holds the key to this practice.

tires: a flat fee is charged whether or not there is a violation; Moroccans who work in Europe need passports and renewals: a service charge is required before the wheels grind. Virtually any piece of paper issued by local authorities requires a fee or the promise of further services: birth certificates, work permits, death and marriage documents, affidavits that one is destitute, that one has a sick child requiring medical attention, that one has school-age children, that one is an army veteran entitled to a pension, that one is a cripple—all of these have a price. Add to these building permits, trading licenses, property deeds, water rights, zoning regulations, taxes, building and work inspection, and price controls, and it is clear that administrative corruption touches all aspects of the citizen's life, whether rich or poor. The underpaid civil servant renders his career somewhat more palatable, but he is being bribed to perform his normal duties rather than to cut through red tape.

CORRUPTION MITIGATES ETHNIC OR CLASS CONFLICT BY DIVERTING ATTENTION TO THE SPOILS SYSTEM

The mitigation of class conflict is indeed a consciously sought-after objective of the Moroccan spoils system. However, the notion of level is important here. Corruption runs throughout the administration, and the most humble Moroccan can nourish the hope that his son may someday, with a modicum of education, accede to the lower echelons of the civil service. Thus, the opportunity of social mobility may operate against alienation from the system along class lines. Yet, to the extent that this is true, spoils and corruption are not the key elements. The status and salary associated with civil-service employment would be sufficient in themselves to attract the offspring of the poor.

But if it is implied that entire classes or segments thereof can be co-opted through systems of corruption, the situation is far different. On the one hand, the regime has actually been creating a dependent *kulak* class through the illegal sale of land taken over by the state from the French. The sales have gone on since 1956, linking the material well-being of officials of the Ministry of Interior, army officers, and the rural nobility to the survival of the regime. To some extent, the formation of this quasi-class may serve as a buffer between the growing numbers of landless peasants and the traditional rural land-owning groups. At the same time there is little the regime can do to avert the increase of the landless peasantry and its derivative, the urban unemployed. If there are remedies to the growth of these groups, they do not lie in the

CORRUPTION IN A MONARCHICAL REGIME 549

expansion of the spoils system. Co-optation through spoils on a class basis may be possible, if at all, only in those developing societies that have exceptional resource bases, such as Iran.

While conventional class cleavages can be partially bridged by corruption, this same phenomenon contributes to the development of an administrative class. In Morocco, the state is by far the largest employer in the country. Civil servants at all levels are relatively privileged and relatively resented. There is a strong tendency for the citizenry to talk in terms of "us and them." While administrative corruption is regarded as normal, it is nonetheless disagreeable and serves to reinforce the cleavage between the masses and the administration.

At the uppermost levels of the civil service, where corruption takes place on a major scale, ethnicity, class, and participation in the spoils system tend to overlap. The merchant-bourgeois elite, drawn disproportionately from families from the city of Fez (hence the appellation *Fassi* for this group) represented, before 1912, a relatively well educated and skilled group that had an initial edge in acceding to privileged positions in the administration and the market economy developed by the French during the Protectorate (1912–1956).[26] The essential point here is that a particularist elite category—the Fassi—overlaps with a nascent class category, the indigenous *haute bourgeoisie*. These groups have taken over the lion's share of high-level administrative posts. At the same time they dominate the private and semi-private sectors of the economy (if one leaves aside the French *patronat*) which depend on the favors and protection of the state. They have, to say the least, privileged access to those public officials who can grease the wheels. Thus, administrative and entrepreneurial elites are really wings of the same group. Not only is there much back-scratching and evidence of joint ventures between the two wings, but also a constant coming and going of personnel. A civil servant, let us say in the Ministry of Industry and Mines, can facilitate the success of an enterprise whose directorship may subsequently be his reward. Of course, these kinds of transactions also take place with regard to the French *patronat*, but there, relations are not so chummy and room to maneuver is somewhat more restricted. After the attempted coup d'état of July 1971, there was much talk that the rebel officers had wanted to clean up the "Fassi Mafia"; to view this group in such terms does not distort reality.

The conclusion that can be drawn here is that high-level corruption

[26] See Waterbury, *The Commander of the Faithful: The Moroccan Political Elite—A Study in Segmented Politics* (New York 1970), chaps. 5 and 6.

has taken place to some extent in a socially closed circuit. Market corruption may allow outsiders to buy their way into the circuit, but it is no easy task. In sum, corruption in Morocco may have contributed to the stratification of resources within a particularist bourgeois elite.

CORRUPTION AFFORDS ACCESS TO THE ADMINISTRATION FOR MINORITIES
    THAT MIGHT OTHERWISE BE EXCLUDED

The French *patronat*, either by numbers or by nationality, is a minority that has bought its way into the system. The most obvious, although dwindling, Moroccan minority is that of the Jews. Despite the fact that the Six-Day War of 1967 and the attempted coup d'état of July 1971 accelerated the rate of Jewish emigration, we can make some generalizations about Jewish integration in the system since 1956. Like the Fassi, the Jews enjoyed educational advantages not shared by most of the Moroccans. Under the Protectorate they had become prominent in commerce, manufacturing, insurance and banking, the free professions, and the administration. Several Jews have been, and still are, highly placed civil servants (although only one ever rose to ministerial rank). Quite clearly they traffic in influence and favors as much as anybody, but they must be more careful than the Muslims. A Jewish businessman may have to be more circumspect in offering a bribe, or perhaps pay a higher price. When on the receiving end, the Jewish civil servant may find that he cannot refuse a bribe. Either way, he must play the game while running a higher risk of discriminatory denunciation.

The reason is simple and reflects the peculiar dependency relationships that have long defined the Jews' room for maneuver within the dominant community. Jewish patronage networks are always partially interwoven with Muslim networks, and any Jewish participant must have his Muslim umbrella. In a very real sense, "the umbrella of umbrellas" for the Jews is the King himself who has made efficient use of this protected minority, holding them in thrall by the fear of what his removal would mean to them.

Still, it is impossible to say whether or not the Jews have better access to the system through corruption than they would have without it. Their integration is founded on traditional dependency, supplemented by the modern business, technical, and managerial skills they are able to offer their protectors. What is clear, however, is that the weighing of costs and benefits in this respect is irrelevant because in the coming years the Jewish minority will have *dis*-integrated itself from the system and moved elsewhere.

CORRUPTION IN A MONARCHICAL REGIME 551

CORRUPTION IN ELECTORAL POLITICS MAY INDICATE THE SPREAD OF
POPULAR DEMOCRACY

Constitutionally, Morocco is a multi-party system. Up to 1965, when King Hassan suspended Morocco's first elected parliament, there was at least an outside chance that a competitive multi-party system might actually emerge. But during the 1960's the Palace made a concerted and successful effort to drain all important sources of patronage and spoils away from the parties. By 1970, with a quasi-monopoly on patronage sources, the Palace had achieved its objective of keeping up a "liberal" multi-party regime in which the parties could not really compete but only participate. Since 1963 various rounds of local and parliamentary elections and referendums have demonstrated, if anything, only that the carrot may be cheaper than the stick: It is probably less expensive to buy votes than to extract them by force. In Morocco's noncompetitive electoral process, material inducements such as distributing PL 480 American wheat can buy an election for the regime without its having to stuff the ballot box.[27] The incidence of electoral corruption in Morocco says nothing one way or another about the vitality of popular democracy in that country.

PLANNED CORRUPTION IN MOROCCO

The elements of corruption in the Moroccan system that have so far been described are to be found in all political systems. But only under some regimes are they the ingredients of regime survival and an essential source of its cohesion. Several of the strategies of the utilization of corruption and patronage by the monarchy have been alluded to in the preceding pages. It is now time to try to pull them together.

All systems must provide rewards for those who agree to participate in them. Participation implies something less than the acceptance of the legitimacy of the regime on the part of the participants. Whether or not they actually believe in its legitimacy is not essential to its survival; what is essential is that they continue to play the game. In this sense participation is equivalent to acquiescence; the regime can maintain control of the political arena if strategic groups acquiesce.

The rewards of acquiescence vary from regime to regime. Prestige, power, high salaries, and the satisfaction of serving national or ideo-

[27] At the time of writing, Morocco was awaiting new parliamentary elections in the wake of the attempted coup of July 1971. It may be that the opposition parties will participate in the elections, and, because the King needs their participation, the elections may be relatively unrigged. But the parties do not have many material rewards to attract voters; they must rely on the appeal of their programs and the rewards they can offer *if* they win a majority of Parliament.

logical goals may all be involved. But Morocco, as a monarchy, cannot easily handle rewards in the same way as non-monarchist nation-states. To the extent that Morocco is a partrimonial system and the King is ruler for life, rewards, promotions, and demotions within the administrative and military spheres are dependent upon the will of the monarch. Only in this way can he assure his relevance to the system. In general, the King's degree of political control varies directly with the level of fragmentation and factionalization within the system, and inversely with the level of institutionalization among political parties and administrative agencies. The King must always maintain the initiative through the systematic inculcation of an atmosphere of unpredictability and provisionality among all elites and the maximization of their vulnerability relative to his mastery of the situation. With their political and material fortunes always in doubt, he is in a position to exert and maintain the asymmetrical lines of dependency and protection that the elites seek to establish. If at any time (as when the rebel officers struck) the King's mastery is questioned, then the asymmetry of the relations disappears, and his relevance to the system is immediately called into question.

With specific regard to the civil service, what the King has sought to avoid is a psychological disposition among strategic elites that would lead to the notion of a meritocracy. High-ranking bureaucrats must not believe that they have earned their positions; there must always be the recognition that were it not for H.M.'s favor, they might never have made it.[28] Conversely, they must always be aware that they may rapidly fall from grace despite their professional qualifications. In successfully nurturing this disposition, the King has maintained the initiative; all elites are preoccupied with trying to anticipate or trying to react to the King's moves. Seldom do they have the confidence, and almost never the resources, to take initiatives themselves. They are constantly reminded of their vulnerability by the unpredictable and sometimes arbitrary interventions of the King into the administrative sphere. Rapid and unexplained demotions and promotions and inscrutable policy decisions leave any high-ranking bureaucrat fearful for his future. The participants in this system are thus reduced as much as pos-

---

[28] So too, senior army officers, most of whom served in the French army at the time King Hassan's father, Mohammed V, was sent into exile by the French authorities in 1953. That these officers wound up in command of the Moroccan armed forces after 1956, rather than being tried as traitors, is attributable only to the will of the Moroccan monarchs. Both Mohammed V and Hassan II never let them forget that fact—which is all the more testimony to their desperation in trying to overthrow Hassan II in July 1971 and again in August 1972.

CORRUPTION IN A MONARCHICAL REGIME 553

sible to the role of competent (rational) and obedient (patrimonial) executors of the Royal Will. If they find this too demeaning, they can try to find another game. The King once remarked in an interview, "If one day all my ministers resigned, I would say to my chauffeur, be minister."[29]

Quite clearly, inculcating the mental disposition among the elite that maximizes royal control of the game limits the kinds of rewards the King can offer to his clients. He cannot offer them career stability; nor can he offer them significant influence over the policy-making process. He cannot offer them the satisfaction of devoting themselves to a coherent doctrine of government or of development. Finally, he cannot offer them even the satisfaction of developing and implementing specific programs. Career instability and policy impotence go hand in hand, and Moroccan bureaucrats are aware of this pairing. Even though they may have a sincere interest in the programs of their agencies, there are no institutional guarantees that they will be around long enough to have any effect upon them.[30] Personnel turnover may be no more rapid in the Moroccan administration than in any other,[31] but Moroccan civil servants are aware that, in their case, turnover *could* be extremely rapid. Most of them, at the level of *chef de service* and above, feel at the mercy of the discretionary powers of promotion and transfer vested in the minister and, by derivation, in the King—against which there are no institutional defenses.

The compensation offered to the Moroccan participant is access to the spoils system. Above all else, access is subject to the arbitrary manipulation of the Palace, and hence is supportive of patrimonial ties. At whatever level—the policeman who takes a bribe or the minister who builds a chateau on $13,000 a year—access is a privilege which is *not earned* or *merited*. It is a privilege whose ultimate source is always known and which can easily be revoked. Finally, it is a privilege which is always to some degree illicit. The participant runs the risk of exposure by rivals or superiors, of scandals, and of the confiscation of the fruits of his acquiescence and participation. Moreover, it is somewhat degrading to compete for material reward in this way, and success in the competition is not something of which the participant can feel

[29] From an interview in *Réalités*, No. 250 (November 1966).

[30] Interviews with ninety high-ranking bureaucrats revealed that only a few ventured to predict what job they would have a year hence. It is not pure hyperbole to note that one of those who did predict was shot and killed at Skhirat a year later. It is also important to note that the rebel officers were allegedly partially motivated by their unhappiness with unstable careers and political marginality.

[31] Over a period of twelve months, 25 per cent of an initial sample of 160 high-ranking bureaucrats changed posts at least once, some of them three times.

proud. The participant becomes the accomplice of the system. What holds it together is not necessarily loyalty to its master; rather it is the commensal sharing of its spoils. Everyone the master deems of strategic importance is invited or cajoled to join the feast. When the privileges are revoked, the erstwhile participant has no recourse. He must simply keep his silence, for what he knows of the system's corruption he learned through participation in it. The strategy is not foolproof, as the attempted coup of 1971 indicated. The King published the inventory of the rebel officers' ill-gotten gains within forty-eight hours of the coup attempt. It was a hollow gesture, because fear of exposure was supposed to have kept the officers from acting in the first place. But even if the temple had crashed down upon the King's head, he would have had the last word: Few Moroccans would ever have accepted the rebel officers as undefiled builders of a new order; they would still have been seen as self-seeking accomplices of the *ancien régime*.

The preoccupation of all sectors of the elite with governmental spoils has made competition for access to the administration the major form of politics in the country. From the point of view of the Palace this development is not only desirable but planned; the politics of patronage are essentially non-ideological. The competition is not among "isms" or programs, a realm in which the monarch is relatively weak and vulnerable, but among patronage groups who vie for material advantage, a process in which the monarch-boss is indeed supreme. De-politicization of the administration (for it was highly politicized from 1956 to 1961) is bought in this manner. Individuals and groups can re-politicize the system only at the risk of police repression ("leftist" plots and subsequent trials were staged in 1963 and 1971; in-between, Mehdi Ben Barka was kidnapped and assassinated) and in face of the artfully manipulated threat that the army would intervene if the politicians became too active. Much to the King's surprise the army did intervene, apparently out of disgust for the patronage system and its own inglorious role in it; but, having survived the intervention, the King is still able to argue that if civilians do not like his game, they will like the army's even less.

In the absence of some major breakdown in the system, the old rules still obtain. Administrative patrons, rotating in and out of various offices, build their own nest eggs in terms of material resources or favors and obligations that they can cash in on later. The politico-administrative ethos that has emerged in the 1960's is strikingly similar to that of the old Sultanate before 1912. The Sultan turns over a prebend to a "trusted servant" who then farms it as intensely as possible, gaining

CORRUPTION IN A MONARCHICAL REGIME 555

title to the usufruct but not to the farm itself. An atmosphere of every man for himself and every clan for itself emerges that precludes large-scale coalition-building or politicking in the bureaucracy. Various clans, to the extent that they have any political coloring at all, represent only marginal policy options: X is pro-American, Y pro-French; Z wants six dams instead of eight, and Y wants to introduce hybrid corn, etc.

Whatever the participant amasses he is permitted to keep; but that too is a privilege, not a rule. The artful administrative patron can accumulate, through his office and strategic spending, enough resources to sustain him through thick and thin. The fall from grace is seldom draconian, for the King does not want to alienate ex-participants.[32] Inasmuch as there has been a tendency to maximize the numbers of participants (accomplices) by encouraging the rotation of personnel in and out of the administration, the regime might, by employing harsher methods, risk creating a large class of disgruntled ex-participants. Therefore, title to usufruct is seldom revoked.

Very few Moroccans have any illusions about the game: certainly not the King or the participants, nor, for the most part, the masses. It is for this reason that, although the term "patrimonial" has been used, it is somewhat misplaced: loyalty is not a crucial element in the Moroccan system. There is a general level of cynicism running throughout—the cynicism of the non-participant masses who fall back on the traditional reflex, "government has ever been thus"; the cynicism of the participants who partake of the system individually while refusing any responsibility for it; and the cynicism of the King who plays on the weakness and greed of his subjects.

In this system, corruption serves only one "positive" function—that of the survival of the regime. Resources are absorbed in patronage and are drained away from rational productive investment. Morocco remains fixed in a system of scarcity in which the vulnerable seek protection and thus regenerate the links of dependency and patronage that perpetuate the system. The dilemma for the ruler in such a system is whether, in the short term, his survival can be made compatible with rational administration and economic development, or whether, in the long term, it can be made compatible with planned corruption.

[32] Since the attempted coup, some ministers have been actually been put on trial for corruption—up to then an unheard-of punishment. At the same time, a minister who was fired in the fall of 1970 amid rumors of malfeasance has been made Minister of Interior.

[7]

CORRUPTION AS A FEATURE OF GOVERNMENTAL ORGANIZATION*

EDWARD C. BANFIELD
Harvard University

T HIS is an exploratory paper the purposes of which are to identify the principal variables having to do with corruption in governmental organizations in the United States and to point out some significant relationships among them. The paper begins by setting forth a conceptual scheme for the description and analysis of corruption in all sorts of organizational settings. This is applied first to the "typical" business and then to the "typical" governmental organization. (The reason for introducing the business organization into the discussion is to create a contrast that will highlight the characteristic features of governmental organization.) In the concluding section some dynamic factors are noted.

THE CONCEPTUAL SCHEME

The frame of reference is one in which an *agent* serves (or fails to serve) the *interest* of a *principal*. The agent is a person who has accepted an obligation (as in an employment contract) to act on behalf of his principal in some range of matters and, in doing so, to serve the principal's interest as if it were his own. The principal may be a person or an entity such as an organization or public. In acting on behalf of his principal an agent must exercise some *discretion*; the wider the range (measured in terms of effects on the principal's interest) among which he may choose, the broader is his discretion. The situation includes *third parties* (persons or abstract entities) who stand to gain or lose by the action of the agent. There are *rules* (both laws and generally accepted standards of right conduct) violation of which entails some probability of a penalty (cost) being imposed upon the violator. A rule may be more or less indefinite (vague, ambiguous or both), and there is more or less uncertainty as to whether it will be enforced.

An agent is *personally corrupt* if he knowingly sacrifices his principal's interest to his own, that is, if he betrays his trust. He is *officially corrupt* if, in

* The writer is grateful for the encouragement and suggestions given by his colleague, Julius Margolis, and for criticisms by Susan Rose-Ackerman and Barry M. Mitnick. He has also benefited greatly from reading Mitnick's The Theory of Agency: The Concept of Fiduciary Rationality and Some Consequences (unpublished Ph.D. dissertation, Univ. of Pa., Dep't Pol. Sci., 1974).

serving his principal's interest, he knowingly violates a rule, that is, acts illegally or unethically albeit in his principal's interest.

Agents are in varying degrees *dependable*. The more dependable an agent, the larger the psychic costs to him of a corrupt act and accordingly the higher his reservation price for the performance of the act.

MINIMIZING CORRUPTION: CONSTRAINTS

As a means of showing the relationships among these and other variables it will be useful to imagine a situation every feature of which tends to minimize corruption. In such a situation agents are selected after an elaborate search on the basis of their exceptional dependability and law-abidingness, all of their other qualities being deemed of no importance as compared to these. The agents are given whatever kinds and amounts of incentives will motivate them to loyal service and whatever disincentives (for example, high risk of discovery followed by dismissal with loss of pension rights) will deter them from disloyalty. The principal's interest (ends, objectives, goals, purposes, etc.) is fully explicated, and agents are given discretion no broader than is judged necessary to fully serve that interest. Rules are definite (that is, neither vague nor ambiguous) and it is known whether or not they will be enforced. If an agent's duty requires him to try to attain mutually exclusive or competing ends his dilemma is resolved by his principal. An agent's performance is carefully monitored; if there is any doubt about his loyalty, he is dismissed forthwith. Monitors are themselves carefully monitored.

Obviously all of this implies centralized control: there must be an authority (that of a chief executive or "top management") capable of selecting dependable agents, establishing an effective incentive system, explicating the principal's interest, monitoring monitors, and so on.

It will be seen that the situation just described—one in which everything possible is done to minimize corruption—is in many respects highly unrealistic. The principal may be an abstract entity such as a corporation, labor union, or public, in which case some surrogate—a board of directors or chief executive—must explicate its interest and be a monitor-in-chief who cannot himself (or themselves) be monitored.[1] There may be no central authority capable of doing the things necessary to minimize corruption—for example, to dismiss agents whose loyalty is questionable. The rules may be indefinite,[2] and there may be much uncertainty as to whether they will be enforced.[3]

---

[1] "[U]nfortunately," writes Frederick Andrews, "no one has devised a way to impose effective [internal] controls on the very top officers, those whose rank enables them to over-ride controls." Wall Street Journal, June 12, 1975, at 1, col. 5.

[2] The recently enacted Federal pension law "requires that fiduciaries follow the 'prudent man rule' which requires them to act 'with the care, skill, prudence and diligence' that a prudent man 'acting in a like capacity and familiar with such matters would use in the conduct of an enterprise of a like character and with like aims'." Wall Street Journal, Feb. 14, 1975, at 28, col. 1.

Perhaps the least realistic feature of the "ideal" situation is the implicit assumption that there exists only one objective—viz. to minimize corruption. In the real world there are always competing objectives, a condition that makes it necessary to give up something in terms of one in order to get more in terms of another. Each of the measures that might be taken to reduce corruption entails costs. Getting the information upon which an estimate of the dependability of a prospective agent can be based is costly, and to secure the services of one who has this scarce, and hence valuable, quality is also costly—costly not only in money and other resources that are paid out but also, and perhaps chiefly, in terms of opportunities foregone, it being highly unlikely that the candidates standing highest in dependability will also stand highest in all other qualities (for example, intelligence, energy, willingness to take risks, etc.) which may be of value to the organization.[4] Similarly supplying the incentives and the disincentives necessary to secure loyalty is costly in resources and in opportunities foregone.[5] So is the explica-

---

The bribery conviction of former Senator Daniel B. Brewster was overturned by a U.S. Court of Appeals because the "trial court's instructions did not set forth a clear and comprehensive standard for the jury to make the distinction between receiving bribery payment in return for being influenced in the performance of an official act, receiving illegal gratuities and receiving legal, normal campaign contributions." Philadelphia Evening Bulletin, Aug. 2, 1974, at p. 1.

[3] The uncertainties regarding enforcement of some rules may be seen from the following: "If the Public Officers Law [of New York state] were enforced, and those who accepted or promised a reward in return for a vote were actually incarcerated, few of the state's legislators would remain outside prison bars."

". . . the act of paying for a judgeship is, after all, an indictable offense, though never enforced."

"To survive politically, most congressmen must overlook the Corrupt Practices Act, which places a ceiling on campaign expenditures, and pretend ignorance on the subject of where their money originates." Martin & Susan Tolchin, To the Victor—Political Patronage from the Clubhouse to the White House, 94, 146, 246 (1971).

[4] Ancient Athens provides an interesting exception. There magistrates, whether chosen by lot or elected, were subjected to an examination not to prove capacity or talent but "concerning the probity of the man." Fustel de Coulanges, The Ancient City 330 (1956). For a close analysis of the costs of policing the agent see Barry Mitnick, The Theory of Agency: The Concept of Fiduciary Rationality and Some Consequences (unpublished Ph.D. dissertation, Univ. of Pa., Dep't Pol. Sci., 1974). With regard to "indirect" costs of such policing, see his The Theory of Agency: The Policing "Paradox" and Regulatory Behavior, Public Choice (forthcoming, Spring 1976).

[5] Gary S. Becker & George J. Stigler, Law Enforcement, Malfeasance, and Compensation of Enforcers, in Capitalism and Freedom, Problems and Prospects 242 (Richard T. Selden ed. 1975). This article first appeared in 3 J. Leg. Studies 1 (1974). One of the methods proposed by Becker and Stigler to deter malfeasance or nonfeasance is "to raise the salaries of enforcers [agents] above what they could get elsewhere, by an amount that is inversely related to the probability of detection and directly related to the size of bribes and other benefits from malfeasance." However, malfeasance, Becker and Stigler say, can be eliminated without paying the enforcers lifetime salaries exceeding what they could get elsewhere by requiring them to post a bond which they would forfeit if fired for malfeasance. *Id.* at 237.

In some jurisdictions an official who resigns before charges are brought may retain his pension rights. The Knapp Commission remarked on this and another practical difficulty in the way of making the threat of pension rights effective. "The result of the present [New York] forfeiture rule," it said, "has been that the courts on appeal have directed the reinstatement of patently unfit officers because they could not tolerate the injustice involved in the forfeiture of

tion of the principal's objective and the negotiation of an agreement between a principal and an agent.[6] So also is monitoring: it entails not only direct costs, such as the salaries of monitors,[7] but also indirect ones such as the lowering of morale that may occur when agents feel "spied upon." The same may be said of narrowing agents' discretion: it is costly to form an estimate of the amount of the corruption that would be prevented by setting this or that limit; moreover, narrowing discretion may injure morale (the exercise of discretion being for many an important non-monetary reward) and, while preventing the agent from doing (corrupt) things that are slightly injurious to the principal it may at the same time prevent him from doing (non-corrupt) ones that would be very beneficial to him. If simply to prevent corruption an agent is given a narrower discretion than would be optimal if there were no possibility of corruption, whatever losses are occasioned by his having a sub-optimal breadth of discretion must be counted as costs of preventing corruption.[8]

It is evident that the costs of eliminating, or controlling, corruption may on occasion be greater than the gains from doing so. One can imagine a firm's spending itself into bankruptcy in an effort to end corruption or a labor union's sacrificing the advantage of its monopoly position by employing an honest but incompetent business agent.[9]

This being so, one might expect the management of an organization to try to discover: a) what level of corruption is optimal for it—that is, the level at which the marginal cost of anti-corruption measures equals the gain from them, and b) what trade-offs among the variously "priced" anti-corruption measures will yield an optimal set, that is, one in which the marginal return from each measure is the same.

Because of technological factors the substitution possibilities may be severely limited. For example, in certain circumstances it may be impossible to substitute monitoring for dependability (the agent's work may have to be

vested pension rights." New York City, The Knapp Commission Report on Police Corruption, 228-29, 26 (1972) [hereinafter cited as Knapp Commission].

[6] "With some recent exceptions, police agencies have tended to keep the policies under which they act ambiguous and unwritten. The reasons may include the fear of articulating clear guidelines because of possible controversy and the difficulties in formulating rules for the varied situations police encounter." Police Foundation, Toward a New Potential (1974).

For a homely example see William A. Niskanen's account of his difficulties in including a selling agent to maximize his (N's) returns from the sale of a house, in Capitalism and Freedom, Problems and Prospects 26 (Richard T. Selden ed. 1975).

[7] " 'If we examined every item over $100,000—which really isn't much for a huge corporation—that would drive our fees sky-high. There's a real cost-benefit problem here,' says . . . a top partner at . . . the largest audit firm." Wall Street Journal, June 12, 1975.

[8] For example, the cost to New York City of prohibiting a uniformed patrolman from making a gambling arrest unless a superior officer is present. Knapp Commission 90.

[9] Cf. Simon Rottenberg, A Theory of Corruption in Labor Unions, in Am. Ass'n for the Advancement of Sci., Symposia Studies Series No. 3, at 4 (Nat'l Inst. of Soc. & Behav. Sci., June 1960) reprinted in Univ. of Chicago, Industrial Relations Center, Reprint Series, No. 96.

done in absolute secrecy); similarly, in certain circumstances it may be impossible to substitute a narrowing or discretion for dependability (the work may require the exercise of a very broad discretion).[10]

It should be noted also that the nature of corruption puts special difficulties in the way of getting information on the basis of which to make a rational allocation of resources. Thus, for example, a principal cannot know how much a third party may bid to secure a corrupt action from an agent and therefore he cannot know how much it will pay him (the principal) to invest in agent loyalty.

INSTITUTIONAL FORMS: BUSINESS

The concepts and relationships that have been set forth in the abstract will be useful in describing some of the main structural features of a concrete form of organization: the "typical" business (more precisely, the competitive corporation). The reason for discussing the business organization here is to provide a contrasting background, so to say, against which the characteristic features of governmental organization can be more readily seen.

1. In a business organization the principal's interest consists of one—or of a very few—objectives the parameters of which—for example, a satisfactory level of profit and beyond that the maximization of emoluments (including staff and expenses) to managers—are easily ascertained. The goods and services produced by the organization can generally be brought under the measuring rod of money and can be distributed via market competition, thus reducing, and to some extent eliminating, the need to exercise discretion. If over time the revenues of the firm do not cover its costs it must go out of business.

2. The incentive system of a business organization is based very largely upon personal, material incentives, especially money. Although the employee may find his work intrinsically interesting and may get satisfaction from "associational benefits," money rewards, or the expectation of them, are in the usual case by far the most significant of the inducements which motivate him. Business executives whose attachment to the organization they serve is almost purely pecuniary are probably not at all uncommon.

3. There exists a highly integrated system of control through which a chief executive (sometimes a team: "top management") can: a) reduce the objectives of the organization to lower levels of generality by defining "targets," b) select agents, c) fix limits on their discretion, d) give or withhold rewards and punishments, e) arrange for monitoring the performance of agents (and also of monitors). The chief executive may himself be chosen and monitored by a

---

[10] Gary S. Becker & George J. Stigler, *supra* note 5, at 243, remark that the role of trust in an employment contract is larger: the less easily and quickly the quality of performance can be ascertained, the more diverse the activities of the enterprise, the more rapidly it is growing or declining, and the more unstable the industries in which it is operating in each case.

board of directors.[11] So long as profits are satisfactory he is not likely to be disciplined or removed by his board. Frequently its monitoring of him is *pro forma* since it must depend largely upon him for information (although some boards have independent auditing committees) and he is likely to have selected most of its membership.

4. Since there exists in a business organization an ultimate authority (the chief executive or, in some matters, the board of directors), it is possible, in principle at least, for agents to get authoritative rulings as to the terms on which conflicts among ends should be settled. Questions which lie outside an agent's discretion—for example, which of two mutually exclusive criteria of choice should be invoked in a concrete situation—are passed up the hierarchy to one who *has* discretion in the matter.

5. The chief executive of a business organization normally continues in office if profits are "satisfactory" until he reaches retirement age. That is, the one condition he must normally meet in order to maintain his control of the organization is business success.[12] Apart from a poor showing on the balance sheet, the principal danger to his tenure is from a hostile take-over or a merger; this danger exists only as outsiders believe they could operate the corporation enough more profitably to yield them a net gain over the costs of acquiring control—costs which the incumbent chief executive is usually in a position to make discouragingly high.[13]

6. The business organization may do whatever is not prohibited by law or government regulation. (Technically a corporation may do only what its charter allows, but as a practical matter it is usually possible to obtain a charter that allows almost anything lawful.) Within the limits set by law and regulation, the business organization may withdraw from one line of activity and enter upon another; it may hire and fire, reward and punish as it sees fit, and it may purchase what it pleases (including the services of consultants of all sorts) at whatever price it is able and willing to pay. Except as it must make disclosures in accordance with government regulations, its affairs are secret.

SOME IMPLICATIONS

These features of business organization have several implications relevant to a discussion of corruption:

[11] On the changing role of the corporate director see the article by John V. Conti, Wall Street Journal, Sept. 17, 1974, at 1, col. 6.

[12] Union members not uncommonly tolerate corruption on the part of agents who win them advantageous contracts. Philip Taft, Corruption and Racketeering in the Labor Movement 6, 28 (N.Y. St. Sch. Ind. & Labor Rel. Bull. 38, 1958). Similarly, voters sometimes prefer candidates whom they have reason to believe corrupt. Of a sample of 1,059 Boston homeowners (taken in 1966), 41% agreed that "a mayor who gets things done but takes a little graft is better than a mayor who doesn't get much done but doesn't take any graft." Unpublished data gathered by James Q. Wilson and the writer.

[13] See Henry G. Manne, Mergers and the Market for Corporate Control, 73 J. Pol. Econ. 110 (1965). Also, Company Executives Shore Up Defenses Against Take-Overs, Wall Street Journal, Oct. 21, 1974, at 1, col. 6.

CORRUPTION AND GOVERNMENTAL ORGANIZATION   593

a) Its principal—perhaps its only—object being profit, the business organization will incur costs to prevent corruption insofar—but *only* insofar—as
it expects them to yield marginal returns equal to those that could be had
from other investments. Similarly, it will incur costs in order to corrupt (that
is, to induce the agents of others to betray their trust) insofar—but again *only*
insofar—as it expects them to contribute to profit.

b) The business organization will invest heavily in search costs and in
incentives to assure that its chief executive: 1) will not be personally corrupt,
and 2) will be officially corrupt insofar as may be necessary to secure the
success, or at least avoid the failure, of the business. These qualities, although obviously not sufficient conditions of a good chief executive (ability is
probably much more important), are surely necessary ones and in the effort
to secure them the board of directors may choose someone who has close
family or friendship ties with a principal (large stockholder) or who has
"come up through the organization"—that is, whose "loyalty" has been
tested over a long period in positions of successively greater responsibility. In
order to identify the interest of the chief executive even more closely with
that of his principal the board may give him not only a high salary and
generous pension rights but also bonuses in the form of stock or stock options.

c) The task of the business executive being to optimize rather than to
minimize corruption, he may follow a policy of "leniency" in dealing with
certain types of personal corruption (for example, petty pilfering of supplies)
because to do otherwise might create disaffection among employees who
object to being "checked up on." What Dalton calls "unofficial rewards"—in
plain language, petty graft—is sometimes a significant element in an incentive system.[14]

d) In dealing with personal corruption at a high level of hierarchy the
chief executive is likely to shun publicity; rather than prosecute an offender
he may transfer him, force him to resign, or if there is no other way, arrange
for his early retirement. To acknowledge that there was personal corruption
in a high place would be "bad for the organization": it might produce unfavorable publicity and, worse, encourage a take-over bid, that sort of corruption being widely regarded as indicative of poor management. (Insofar as
the chief executive chooses to ignore or "cover up" such corruption because
the revelation of it would reflect on his own work he is of course personally
corrupt.) On the other hand, personal corruption at the bottom of the hierarchy in excess of the permitted limit may be dealt with harshly, for the
exposure of such corruption is generally taken as a sign of good management.

e) Obviously to be effective a monitoring system in a business organization must operate selectively; its mission is: a) to keep corruption at the lower

[14] Melville Dalton, Men Who Manage, ch. 6 (1959). See also Alvin W. Gouldner, Patterns of
Industrial Bureaucracy 87, 159-62, 176 (1954).

levels within permitted levels and, b) to inform the chief executive about corruption at the higher levels but in a manner that does not oblige him to let its existence become generally known.

f) Although the structure of the business organization makes possible the resolution of the dilemma faced by an agent who is required to attain mutually exclusive objectives, in practice it may fail to do so. When "top management" insists—presumably unwittingly—that agents do what they cannot possibly do without violating rules (that is, without being officially corrupt) the monitoring system is likely to be by-passed, or if it is not, to adapt itself to the situation by "turning a blind eye" on all except the most flagrant rule violations. There will be a tendency also for colleague-groups and perhaps monitors as well to define the situation so as to reduce the psychic costs of rule violations (for example, it was "against the rules" but "not really wrong or unethical").[15]

g) Arrangements which allow for the by-passing of monitors or for selective monitoring may easily become dysfunctional by withholding, sometimes for a monitor's own corrupt purposes, information that a chief executive wants and expects to have. A situation which produces rule-violation in the line of duty (that is, official corruption) in effect taxes dependable agents (that is, those for whom rule-violation entails psychic costs) and subsidizes the undependable. One would expect that under these circumstances the undependable would eventually replace the dependable.

h) If its sole purpose is the maximization of profit, the business organization may have an incentive to corrupt the agents of other organizations—competitors, labor unions, government agencies, etc.[16] Its only disincentives are in the nature of business risks—for example loss of reputation within the trade, unfavorable publicity, and fines and other legal penalties (until recently criminal sanctions have rarely been imposed upon officers of corporations which violated the law). The expected disutility of these will presumably be weighed against the expected gain of successful corruption.

i) One would expect the tendency to corrupt other organizations to be the

---

[15] For an account of a business organization (GE) in which "disjointed authority" led to men being required to do what was illegal see Richard Austin Smith, Corporations in Crisis ch. 5-6 (1963). Striking parallels are to be found in Joseph S. Berliner, Factory and Manager in the USSR, chs. 11 & 12 (1957).

[16] Taft found that racketeering in labor unions tends to appear in industries that are highly competitive and have a highly mobile labor force, and that when these conditions coexist some corruption is "almost inevitable." Philip Taft, *supra* note 12, at 33. The Knapp Commission found the second largest source of police corruption in New York City (the first was organized crime) to be "legitimate business seeking to ease its way through the maze of City ordinances and regulations. Major offenders are construction contractors and subcontractors, liquor licensees, and managers of businesses like trucking firms and parking lots, which are likely to park large numbers of vehicles illegally. If the police were completely honest, it is likely that members of these groups would seek to corrupt them, since most seem to feel that *paying off the police is easier and cheaper than obeying the laws or paying fines and answering summonses* . . . ." (Italics added.) Knapp Commission 68.

strongest among those profit-maximizing businesses which must depend upon a small number of customers or suppliers (whether of capital, labor, or materials) and whose profit margin in the absence of corruption would be non-existent or nearly so. These might fail if they indulged in any form of "social responsibility."[17] Oligopolistic businesses, having ample "slack," although avoiding the vulgar *quid-pro-quo* forms of corruption, probably tend to be lavish in entertainment, consultants' fees, and other expenditures intended to "create goodwill," "maintain good working relations," and "make friends." Insofar as such expenditures cause corruption, it is likely to be of a kind difficult or impossible to identify clearly as such.

INSTITUTIONAL FORMS: GOVERNMENT

The structural features of "typical" American governmental organization differ strikingly from those of business.

1. Fragmentation of authority both within and among Federal, state and local jurisdictions, a conspicuous and distinctive feature of the American political system, gives incentive to the formation and energetic activity of a multitude of pressure groups. Accordingly American governmental organizations characteristically have objectives that are numerous, unordered, vague and ambiguous, and mutually antagonistic if not downright contradictory.[18] The product (services generally) of a governmental organization is frequently of such a nature as not to be susceptible to being priced in a market or perhaps to quantitative measurement of any kind. Almost all government regulation is of this character.[19] Governmental products that might be priced usually are not, and if they are, the price is usually set so low as to subsidize the consumer and (if the supply is short) to create a rationing problem which necessitates exercises of discretion on the part of governmental agents.[20] As Robert C. Brooks wrote early in the present century, ". . . as soon as regulation is undertaken by the state a motive is supplied . . . to break the law or bribe its executors."[21] When, as is often the case, the

[17] Arrow has remarked that an ethical code "may be of value to the running of the system as a whole, it may be of advantage to all firms if all firms maintain it, and yet it will be to the advantage of any one firm to cheat—in fact the more so, the more other firms are sticking to it." But he concludes that the value of maintaining the system "may well" be apparent to all and that "no doubt" ways will be found to make ethical codes a positive asset in attracting consumers and workers. Kenneth J. Arrow, Social Responsibility and Economic Efficiency, 21 Public Policy, 330, 315-16 (1973).

[18] These points are elaborated in Edward C. Banfield, Political Influence (1961), esp. pt. 2.

[19] These features of governmental organization are illustrated and analyzed by James Q. Wilson, Varieties of Police Behavior (1968).

[20] See Arnold J. Meltsner, The Politics of City Revenue 33-35 (1971).

[21] Robert C. Brooks, Corruption in American Politics and Life 166 (1910). The construction industry provides a case in point. New York City has a 843-page building code; a builder is required to get at least 40-50 permits and licenses (for a very large project as many as 130) from a maze of city departments. "Each stage," John Darnton writes in the New York Times, July 13, 1975, sec. 4, at 5, col. 3, ". . . is an invitation to a payoff. By withholding approval, or

governmental organization has a monopoly a strong incentive exists for third parties to seek to influence the agent's exercise of discretion by offering a bribe—that is, to pay a monopoly price, the money going not to the government but to the agent.

The governmental organization's existence is not jeopardized by selling its products at prices that are below the cost of production since typically it gets some or all of its revenue by taxation. If there is any threat to its existence, it is likely to arise from its having failed to distribute enough in subsidies to get the support it needs in the legislature or at the polls.

2. Although the incentive system of the governmental organization is based mainly on money and other personal material incentives, other types of incentives usually bulk larger in it than in the incentive system of business organization. At the lower levels of government hierarchy job security is an important incentive. At the middle levels the satisfactions of participating in large affairs, "serving in a good cause," and of sharing (albeit perhaps vicariously) in the charisma that attaches to an elite corps (for example, the F.B.I.) or to a leader (for example, J. Edgar Hoover or Robert Moses) are also of importance. At the top level power and glory are among the principal incentives (for example, Hoover and Moses). It would probably be hard to find in government a very high level official whose attachment to his job is purely pecuniary.[22]

3. From a legal-formal standpoint and often in fact, control of a governmental agency is in many more hands than is control of a business. Normally a chief executive or a small team ("top management") has authority over all of the operations of a business. A governmental agency, by contrast, is usually run by a loose and unstable coalition of individuals each of whom has independent legal-formal authority over some of its operations. Not only is there separation among legislative, judicial and executive functions, but the executive function is itself divided. In the Federal government, for example, there are numerous independent bodies (for example, the Federal Reserve System) which exercise an authority independent of the Presi-

---

concentrating on a minor infraction, or simply not showing up at all, an inspector can cost a builder dearly or delay his recouping a multi-million-dollar investment." In practice, the Knapp Commission found, "most builders don't bother to get all the permits required by law. Instead, they apply for a handful of the more important ones (often making a payoff to personnel at the appropriate agency to insure prompt issuance of the permit). Payments to the police and inspectors from other departments insure that builders won't be hounded for not having other permits." Knapp Commission 125. Recently two-thirds of the construction inspectors in Manhattan were suspended without pay on bribery charges. None of the charges seems to have resulted from a builder's effort to get around the requirements of the building code. What was being bought and sold, an official said, was time. Robert E. Tomasson in the New York Times, July 18, 1975, at 5.

[22] Moses, Caro writes, found "a hundred ways around" civil service pay and promotion rules. But his men were mainly attached to him because they were "caught up in his sense of purpose" and because they "admired and respected" him. Moses himself, Caro asserts, came to be motivated solely by an insatiable lust for power and glory. Robert A. Caro, The Power Broker, Robert Moses and the Fall of New York 273 (1974).

dent's. In state and local government, executive authority is much more widely distributed.[23] The mayor of a moderate-sized city, for example, has no control whatever over at least a dozen bodies whose collaboration is indispensable. The comptroller and district attorney, for example, are usually independently elected, and there are numerous bodies, notably the civil service commission, in which the mayor has little or no voice. The governmental chief executive appoints his principal subordinates (subject usually however to their confirmation by a separate authority), but the incentive system is fixed by law and regulation and is as a rule of such a nature as to preclude competition with business organizations for executive talent. Moreover the governmental chief executive and his principal subordinates, having no control over the tenure or pay of lesser ("career") executives, have not much more than nominal authority over the lower levels of bureaucracy. For example, the mayor of New York, according to Sayre, has few levers to move the several hundred bureau chiefs; he works "at the margins of bureau autonomy" by creating and staffing new bureaus and by praising or attacking those who are or are not responsive to him but "his victories are temporary and touch only a few bureaus."[24]

4. Whereas the business organization may hire, promote or demote, and dismiss salaried employees at will (subject to civil rights and other such laws), the governmental one is severely restricted by civil service regulations. The governmental executive cannot dismiss a career civil servant whom he considers untrustworthy; instead he may prefer formal charges supported by evidence before a trial board from the decision of which the employee may usually appeal. The procedure is so time-consuming and dismissals so hard to get that it is invoked only in cases so flagrant as to make it unavoidable.[25]

5. The fragmentation of formal authority in government is overcome to a greater or lesser degree by informal arrangements: officials exchange favors (for example, voting support, jobs, opportunities to make money by legal or other means) with other officials and with interest groups and voters in order to assemble the authority they require to maintain and if possible increase their power.[26] In the extreme case the result is a stable structure in which

---

[23] See Edward C. Banfield & James Q. Wilson, City Politics, ch. 6 (1963).

[24] Wallace S. Sayre, in Agenda for a City 576 (Lyle C. Fitch & Annmarie Hauek eds. 1970).

[25] General Motors' procedure in dismissing salaried employees is in sharp contrast to that of the New York Police Department. When there was reason to believe that some of them were accepting favors and "kickbacks," GM marched salaried employees, some of whom had been with the company for more than 25 years, through an "assembly line" for questioning by two company investigators. Forty-three who admitted taking gifts of more than nominal value were fired on the spot. Wall Street Journal, April 24, 1975, at 1, col. 6 and New York Times, June 15, 1975, at 1, col. 6.

In the New York Police Department, on the other hand, an officer under indictment for a felony may not be suspended; instead he is placed on "modified assignment," retaining his salary, fringe benefits, and gun until final disposition of his case, which may take three or four years. New York Times, July 19, 1974, at 39, col. 1.

[26] For an account of the patronage, favors, and "honest graft" distributed in a relatively

THE JOURNAL OF LAW AND ECONOMICS

control is as highly integrated as in the business organization; this is the "machine," the chief executive of which (who may or may not be the chief executive of a governmental organization) is the "boss."[27] One difference between the machine and the business organization requires particular notice: the business executive's control, resting as it does on a solid legal-formal base, is stable as compared to that of the boss, which arises from extra-legal, if not illegal, arrangements, is *ad hoc,* and must be continually renewed by "deals" in order to prevent it from collapsing.

6. The agent of a governmental organization is both likely to be required to serve objectives that compete or are mutually exclusive (this is because, as noted, the objective function of a government organization is characteristically vague, ambiguous, and unordered) and unlikely to get the dilemma that he faces resolved by passing it up the hierarchy: there is hardly ever a chief executive with authority over all the matters involved in the conflict and, if there is and if the conflict is passed up the hierarchy to him, the answer that will come back to the agent will probably be: "Maximize *all* objectives."[28] The fundamental fact of the situation is that the electorate or some set of interest groups (that is the principal) *demands* states of affairs that are mutually exclusive.

7. The chief executive of a governmental organization normally serves a two- or a four-year term after which he must face "take-over" bids first in a primary and then in a general election; in many jurisdictions he may not succeed himself more than once or twice. As compared to his opposite number in business his tenure is uncertain and brief.[29] Although as an incumbent he has a decided advantage, much of what he does or fails to do in office is with a view to increasing the probability of his reelection.

8. Unlike the shareholder, the citizen cannot easily disassociate himself from a corrupt organization: to escape it he must incur the costs of moving to another city, state, or country. Nevertheless, in the usual case he will have no incentive to invest in its reduction because it, or rather the absence of it, is a "public good" the benefits of which will accrue as much to "free riders" as to others.[30] There are, however, institutions, notably the media and the

---

"clean" medium-sized city (New Haven) see Raymond E. Wolfinger, The Politics of Progress, ch. 4 (1974).

[27] On the machine, see Edward C. Banfield & James Q. Wilson, *supra* note 23, at ch. 9.

[28] In the Federal bureaucracy, Kaufman writes, subordinates may have to pick and choose among many directives for justification. "This obligation may be thrust upon them by the inescapable ambiguities as well as inconsistencies of the instructions to them." Herbert Kaufman [with the collaboration of Michael Couzens], Administrative Feedback: Monitoring Subordinates' Behavior 2 (Brookings Inst. 1973).

In Oakland, California, the city manager sends a guidance letter to officials involved in the budget process. "The important thing to understand about the manager's letter is that it contains nonoperational guidance, or decision rules that are not decision rules." Arnold J. Meltsner, *supra* note 20, at 165 & 271.

[29] On turn-over of mayors, see Raymond E. Wolfinger, *supra* note 26, at 394-95.

[30] See Mancur Olson, The Logic of Collective Action (1965).

ambitious district attorney, that stand to gain by searching out and making much of corruption, whether real or seeming.

9. From a formal standpoint, a governmental organization may do *only* what the law expressly authorizes and it *must* do what the law expressly requires. In fact, when public opinion permits, it sometimes withdraws from tasks assigned by law which expose it to corruption.[31] Its freedom to avoid exposure to corrupting influences is small as compared to that of the business organization however.

10. A governmental organization may have few secrets. To a large and increasing extent, its affairs (for example, the salaries of employees, the number of widgets bought and the price paid, etc.) are matters of public record. Generally public hearings must be held and public participation secured before a governmental undertaking may get under way. Sometimes there must be a referendum. Meetings at which decisions are to be made must often be open to the public. In many instances officials are required to disclose their property holdings and business connections. As "public figures" they are for all practical purposes unprotected by laws against slander and libel.

Consequences of These Differences

Obviously the structural differences between business and governmental organizations have consequences affecting corruption:

a) In governmental organization the costs of preventing or reducing corruption are not balanced against gains with a view to finding an optimal investment. Instead corruption is thought of (when it comes under notice) as something that must be eliminated "no matter what the cost." Even when no deterrent effect could be expected, a governmental organization—the IRS, for example—would not act uncharacteristically in spending, say, $50,000 to uncover and punish a misdeed which could not possibly have cost the government more than, say, $500.

b) In the absence of central control there is no real (as opposed to nominal) chief executive or "top management" which can make substitutions among anti-corruption measures (for example, more investment in dependability and less in monitoring) in an effort to "balance the margins."

c) In the absence of central control, an agent whose duties are mutually incompatible cannot get a resolution of his dilemma by administrative action; therefore—unless he resigns—he must act corruptly. As Rubinstein remarks in *City Police*, "a policeman cannot escape the contradictions imposed on him by his obligations."[32]

---

[31] The New York Police Department announced that as an anti-corruption measure it would not arrest low-level figures in gambling combines or enforce the Sabbath laws (except upon complaint) or the laws pertaining to construction sites (unless pedestrians are endangered or traffic impeded). New York Times, Aug. 19, 1972, at 1.

[32] Jonathan Rubinstein, City Police (1973).

d) Where authority is highly fragmented there is no centralized system of monitoring or, more generally, of control. Under these circumstances corruption is likely to occur "because the potential corrupter needs to influence only a segment of the government, and because in a fragmented system there are fewer centralized forces and agencies to enforce honesty."[33] Although there may be officials in roles specialized to perform monitoring or other anti-corruption functions—typically an independently elected district attorney—these frequently fail to perform vigorously when doing so would be contrary to their political or other interests; in any case no chief executive can *require* them to—that is, there is no effective provision for monitoring the monitors.

e) Because of the inflexibility of government pay scales and promotion rules a government executive is often unable to offer an agent incentives (monetary and nonmonetary) equal to those he could earn elsewhere. One consequence is that the government agent is likely to be less dependable and less able than his business organization counterpart. Of more importance, perhaps, the government agent has less to lose from dismissal.[34]

f) The nature of governmental activity often precludes precisely stating or narrowly limiting the breadth of an agent's discretion.[35] If the objective is no more definite than to "improve the quality of life," the agent's decisions must necessarily be on grounds that are highly subjective. The monitoring of such decisions presents obvious difficulties: almost any can be given a plausible rationale.

g) When output standards cannot be made definite, the organization may try to compensate by making input specifications very detailed. The effect of this, however, is to reduce the number of competitive suppliers, thereby making collusion easier between sellers and corrupt purchasing agents. Sometimes an agent establishes specifications that only one supplier can meet.

h) Both because of the relatively open (not secret) nature of most government activities and because of the fragmentation of control, monitoring agents from *outside* the organization is probably more common in government than in business. "Unplanned feedback" (that is, information and clues

---

[33] Raymond E. Wolfinger, *supra* note 26, at 114.

[34] As Becker and Stigler remark, *supra* note 5, at 242, "Trust calls for a salary premium not necessarily because better-quality persons are thereby attracted, but because higher salaries impose a cost on violations of trust." The principle was applied by New York Police Commissioner Murphy who limited the "exposure [to temptations offered by gambling and narcotics interests] to officers of higher rank who presumably have a greater stake in maintaining their reputations." Knapp Commission 238.

[35] Recently the General Services administrator took steps to monitor some of his own necessarily subjective decisions by delegating the choice of architects to a panel of career civil servants which will rate candidates in writing on the basis of published criteria. Final decisions remain the administrator's responsibility. Wall Street Journal, June 11, 1974, at 7, col. 1. For an account of the difficulties police administrators have in managing the discretion of policemen see James Q. Wilson, *supra* note 19, at 64-65 and *passim*.

that come to the organization from clients, competitive agencies, the mass media, public prosecutors, civic groups, etc.) may be of special importance in governmental organizations because of the lack (due to fragmentation) of *planned* feedback.[36] Selective monitoring (that is, the filtering out of information damaging to certain "higher ups" or posing a threat to the successful functioning of the organization) is difficult to manage when there is much "unplanned feedback."

i) Governmental organizations are much less likely than business ones to be permissive about petty corruption ("unofficial rewards"). For one thing, the governmental organization, which is not seeking to maximize profit, is willing to accept whatever loss of productivity may result from employee's disaffection at being closely watched. For another, no one in the organization has authority to permit "stealing from the government." Such petty corruption as exists within a governmental organization reflects a failure of management, not, as it might in a business organization, a cost deliberately incurred to avoid a still larger one.

j) Insofar as government executives are motivated more by non-pecuniary values (for example, power, participation in large affairs, "serving in a good cause," etc.) than are business executives, they are probably less susceptible to pecuniary inducements to corruption. By the same token, they are probably *more* susceptible to non-pecuniary inducements such as "the good of the organization."[37]

k) Because the opportunity to exercise wide discretion in important matters (that is, to wield power) normally comprises a larger part of the "package" of incentives offered to government executives than of that offered to business executives, close monitoring is probably more disruptive of management in government than in business.

l) The existence of governmental organizations in which authority is highly fragmented presents an opportunity for a political entrepreneur to "purchase" pieces of authority (that is, to bribe or otherwise influence the possessors of authority to use it as the "purchaser" requires) and thus to create a highly integrated system of control (machine).

[36] Herbert Kaufman, *supra* note 28, at 10, writing about the Federal bureaucracy, describes the sources of "unplanned feedback" as follows: "Clientele or customer objections, the normal interactions of organizations with each other, for example, staff agencies such as budget, personnel, administrative management, audit, legal counsel, and public relations can be expected to turn up some information for line executives about the behavior of line subordinates. Competitive agencies may reveal a good deal about each other's field activities. Some individuals and organizations thrive on exposing shortcomings in public agencies employing sensational publicity, reporters from the mass media, public prosecutors, grand juries, civic groups, public investigatory commissions. Subordinates themselves give clues about their own activities when they seek clarification of policy announcements, overlapping circles of acquaintances, membership in clubs and community groups, gossip and humor." See also, *id.* at 35, 41 & 74.

[37] Barnard believed corrupt acts such as falsifying books "for the good of the organization" to be rare in industrial organizations "but undoubtedly have occurred not infrequently in political, governmental, and religious organizations." Chester I. Barnard, The Functions of the Executive 277 (1938).

m) Where the formal decentralization is not overcome by an informal centralization (that is, a machine) corruption is likely to be widespread, there being no mechanism capable of regulating it. "Prudential considerations restraining corruption," Brooks wrote early in the present century, "are apt to be much more keenly felt by a thoroughly organized machine than in cases where corruption is practiced by disorganized groups and individuals each seeking its own or his own advantage regardless of any common interest.[38]

n) To the extent that there is a machine, that is, to the extent that the formal fragmentation of authority has been replaced by an informal centralization, the governmental organization will resemble the typical business organization. Its chief executive ("boss") will have reasonably secure tenure, a well-defined objective function (to maintain and enhance the organization), and the ability to exercise control.[39] He will invest heavily in the dependability of his principal subordinates (one "comes up through" a machine by demonstrating loyalty over time),[40] regulate their breadth of their discretion, maintain an incentive system that motivates machine workers (especially job patronage, legal fees, the purchase of insurance, construction contracts, etc.), and monitor them to check unauthorized corruption.

SOME DYNAMIC FACTORS

In the nature of the case it is impossible to know how much corruption there is at any given time. On theoretical grounds, however, it seems safe to say that for several decades corruption has been increasing in the United States and that it will continue to do so.

[38] Robert C. Brooks, *supra* note 21, at 107. See also Raymond E. Wolfinger, who writes, *supra* note 26, at 114: "John A. Gardiner's study of the notoriously corrupt city of Wincanton provides evidence for the proposition that decentralized political systems are *more* corruptible, because the potential corrupter needs to influence only a segment of the government, and because in a fragmented system there are fewer centralized forces and agencies to enforce honesty. The Wincanton political system is formally and informally fragmented; neither parties nor interest groups (including the criminal syndicate) exercise overall coordination. The ample patronage and outright graft in Wincanton are not used as a means of centralization. Indeed, governmental coordination clearly would not be in the interests of the private citizens there who benefit from corruption, nor of the officials who take bribes. Attempts by reformers to stop graft or patronage founder on the cities commission form of government, which is both the apotheosis of local governmental fragmentation and a hospitable environment for machine politics."

[39] Early in the present century an observer found New York state's formal administration "a drifting, amorphous mass, as helpless as a field of seaweed in the ocean" with power dispersed among nearly 170 units and "no head, no manager, no directing will *legally committed* to preside." At the same time the extra-legal side—that is, the political parties—had "no loose ends, no irresponsible agents—that is, "authority is clearly defined, obedience is punctiliously exacted; the hierarchy is closely interlinked, complete, effective." Quoted in Clifton K. Yearley, The Money Machines 254 (1970).

[40] Writing of James Marcus, a high official of the Lindsay administration who was convicted of bribery, Moscow remarks: "Marcus could not have happened in a Tammany administration, in which a man of loose morals might have been appointed, but not without full knowledge of his weaknesses." Warren Moscow, The Last of the Big-Time Bosses 202-03 (1971).

Adam Smith remarked that those who trade often with each other find that honesty is the best policy.[41] For traders, mutual adherence to rules constitutes a public good. If the traders are fewer than some critical number, each will find it to his advantage to abide by the rule and even to contribute to its enforcement upon others. But if they exceed the critical number, each may find it to his advantage to violate the rule and none will voluntarily contribute to its enforcement because each will know that the situation will be essentially the same no matter what he does and that therefore it will pay him to be a "free rider."[42]

It is easy to point out instances in which honesty is still the best policy (the Chicago grain pit is one example and the Chicago political "machine" another). Nevertheless, it seems likely that for several decades the proportion of situations of the large-number type, in which dishonesty is likely to be the best (that is, most profitable) policy, has been increasing. Certainly there are relatively few executives who think of their organization as an entity (for example, a "house") that will exist in essentially the same environment for generations to come. This being so, there is now relatively little incentive to invest in acquiring reputation ("character," to use Smith's word), something which, unlike an "image," can only be had by consistent adherence to the rules over a long period of time.

A second factor tending to increase corruption in the United States has been the dramatic enlargement of the scope and scale of government, local, state and national. Doubtless this enlargement has been to some extent a response to problems that have arisen because of the inability of traders who interact in large numbers and over short periods to maintain the rules that could be taken for granted when most traders interacted frequently and over long periods of time. As honesty gradually ceased to be the best policy, there were more demands that government offer incentives and disincentives to make it so once again. Moreover, the American passion for equality has always encouraged the replacement of the invisible hand of competition by the visible—and supposedly fairer—one of bureaucracy. (As Tocqueville remarked, "equality singularly facilitates, extends, and secures the influence of a central power" and every central power "worships uniformity [because] it relieves it from inquiry into an infinity of details. . . .").[43] But uniformity was bound to leave many individuals dissatisfied—the infinity of details could not be ignored without cost—, and thus to create pressures for special treatment.

Whatever their causes, every extension of government authority has

---

[41] Quoted from Adam Smith's Lectures by Edwin Cannan in his introduction to The Wealth of Nations, at xxxii (Mod. Libr. ed. 1937).

[42] For a general discussion see James M. Buchanan, Ethical Rules, Expected Values, and Large Numbers, 76 Ethics, Oct. 1965, at 1-13 and his further remarks on The Samaritan's Dilemma, in Altruism, Morality and Economic Theory 71 (Edmund S. Phelps ed. 1975).

[43] 2 Alexis de Tocqueville, Democracy in America 295 (Knopf ed. 1945).

created new opportunities and incentives for corruption. Over the long run this has helped to make it appear normal, tolerable, and even laudable.[44]

Had the growth of government been accompanied by the centralization of control and certain other structural changes, the increase in corruption would doubtless have been less. But the structural changes that occurred were mainly in the "wrong" direction: executive control has been reduced by merit system practices, recognition of public employee unions, civil rights legislation, laws requiring "citizen participation," "sunshine" laws, and the like. At the same time, the extra-legal arrangements through which control was informally centralized in a "machine" which, sometimes at least, found it advantageous to moderate and limit corruption have in most instances been wiped out or rendered less effectual by "good government" reforms.

A third factor, closely related to the second, has been the imposition upon business organizations of constraints much like those under which government operates. Public opinion (including often that of businessmen!) more or less obliges the business organization to subordinate the profit criterion to other objectives—ones which, as in government, are vague and conflicting. Like government organizations, businesses are more and more expected to tolerate, even to encourage, participation in their affairs by outsiders ("public interest groups") and to give the public details of dealings the success of which requires secrecy. Frequently courts and regulatory agencies play leading roles in making business decisions.[45]

If these are indeed the trends, one may well ponder what their outcomes will be. Presumably the culture that is being formed today contains a much smaller stock of dependability than did that formed a generation, or two, or three ago. Substitutes (for example, monitoring) can take the place of much dependability, but they will surely be relatively costly and there is doubtless some "technological" limit to the amount of substitution that is feasible: it is hard to believe that complex social organizations can exist in the complete absence of dependability.[46] In any case there are more important questions.

---

[44] Indeed, as has been frequently noted, corruption frequently serves socially desirable functions—for example, it may make a grossly unfair tax more nearly equitable, it may keep the government going in a time of hyperinflation, it may deter a policeman from beating an innocent person, etc.

[45] Consider, for example, the ruling by an administrative law judge of the National Labor Relations Board that a newspaper may not prohibit its reporters and editors from accepting gifts ("freebies") from news sources. New York Times, Jan. 17, 1975, at 43, col. 4. Weidenbaum has written recently of a "second managerial revolution" involving a shift ". . . from the professional management selected by the corporation's board of directors to the vast cadre of government regulators that influences and often controls the key decisions of the typical business firm." Murray L. Weidenbaum, Government-Mandated Price Increases 98 (Am. Enterprise Inst. for Public Policy Res., 1975).

[46] Cf. J. S. Mill: "There are countries in Europe, of first-rate industrial capabilities, where the most serious impediment to conducting business concerns on a large scale, is the rarity of persons who are supposed fit to be trusted with the receipt and expenditure of large sums of

In a society in which *dishonesty* is the best policy, will not the individual feel
contempt for himself and for his fellows and will he not conclude—rightly
perhaps—that he and they are "not worth saving"?

---

money." 1 Principles of Political Economy 151 (5th ed.). See also Edward C. Banfield, The
Moral Basis of a Backward Society (1958).

[8]

THE PROBLEM OF CORRUPTION:
A CONCEPTUAL AND COMPARATIVE ANALYSIS*

Robert J. Williams
University of Durham

Corruption, like beauty, is in the eye of the beholder. Unlike beauty, it is widely believed to be more than just skin deep. This paper is concerned to demonstrate that most observations of the phenomenon are hindered by myopia or astigmatism. Such defects contribute to the oversimplified and distorted view of corruption present in most contemporary literature. Myopia is responsible for what might be termed the iceberg complex in that attention is almost exclusively concentrated on the small part of corruption that is most visible and prominent, while its true scope and underlying causes go unnoticed. Astigmatism is merely another consequence of the modern academic division of labour. Thus economists, lawyers, public administration specialists, sociologists, anthropologists and political scientists all have interesting things to say about corruption, but the overall picture is blurred and lacks coherence. In essence, we have astigmatic views of corruption in that structural defects in the academic community appear to prevent the partial rays of light shed by different disciplines from being brought to a common focus.

This paper does not pretend to offer a new understanding of corruption but merely points to factors which seriously challenge the existing conventional wisdom. While the primary emphasis of the paper is on methodological difficulties, they are discussed with particular reference to the problem of corruption in developing countries. The first part of the paper is devoted to a preliminary discussion of the meaning and significance of corruption.

The study of corruption is like a jungle and, if we are unable to bring it to a state of orderly cultivation, we at least require a guide to the flora and fauna. This need has impelled many writers to find a precise definition which will accurately characterise the phenomenon. While it is not necessary at this stage to examine any particular definition, it is important to note that there are nearly as many definitions of corruption as there are species of tropical plants and they vary as much in their appearance, character and resilience. The point is that the search for the true definition of corruption is, like the pursuit of the Holy Grail, endless, exhausting and ultimately futile.

Too few writers on the subject seem to recognise that definitions, despite the lexicographers, are neither true nor false. A definition of corruption, or anything else, is like a proposal of marriage; it may be accepted or rejected but the proposal itself cannot, in any meaningful sense, be said to be true or false. Definitions are not statements of fact and should not be treated as such. They are, in fact, more like rules which "can be accepted or rejected, complied with or violated"[1]. The important point is not that definitions themselves are true or false, but that statements about whether a particular definition expresses accepted conventional usage are either true or false. This is merely to emphasise that statements about a definition are of a different order from the definition itself. It has proved only too easy for writers on corruption to get bogged down in reformulating definitions and it may prove salutory to remember that

---

*Paper to the 1976 PAC Conference, University of York.

"Definitions are only conventions, and apply only because of agreement that they should apply"[2].

It may be that, like beauty, we feel unable to define corruption, but are nevertheless confident of our ability to recognise it when we see it. Unfortunately, the visibility of corruption is largely dependent on the nature of its environment and this, of course, differs from place to place and from time to time. A lack of awareness of the varying ecology of corruption bedevils much current writing on the subject.

Although scholars disagree about the effects of corruption, they seem united as to its importance. But this is more often assumed than explained and its is worthwhile to elaborate on the significance of corruption for public order and political activity. It is a fundamental premise of this paper that corrupt acts, or violent ones, directly contravene legal rules, and it is on such rules that the existence of society ultimately depends. Law is not a synonym for order, it is a necessary though not sufficient condition for its existence. Without public order it becomes impossible for civilised life to continue as there is no recognition of rights to be enjoyed or duties to be fulfilled. Such a situation constitutes a break-down of society in that it is only in society that there exists procedures by means of which change is accomplished in a settled and orderly manner.

It seems axiomatic that no society can exist without the shared acceptance of conventions about the manner in which the activity of citizens and officials is to be regulated. Rules are complied with not for pecuniary advantage but because citizens recognise that they have a mutual interest in the maintenance of that order whose existence is provided for by those rules. Corruption weakens public confidence in the integrity of officials and destroys the fabric of mutual expectation. The apparently most blatant examples of corruption in developing countries are perhaps the most misleading because they occur in environments which are insensitive to the above requirements for public order and political activity. In many developing countries there are no accepted rules or standards by which political and administrative activity is conducted. There may not even be an awareness of the need for such rules as politics is often a minority game where the rules are altered to fit the needs of the elite participants and not those of the passive majority.

In societies where there is a shared understanding of the rules necessary to maintain public order and confidence, corruption not only threatens those rules but also other principles and moral standards which help to define the current forms of human co-existence and interaction. Corruption is not merely then a threat to legal rules but to the principles which govern the way men should act in society. Legal rules embody moral principles and are interpreted and created in accordance with them. Thus the significance of corruption is a consequence not only of the type of society in which it occurs but is dependent on there being at least a rudimentary acceptance and comprehension of the pre-requisites, procedures and principles of political and public life. Discussions of corruption which attempt quantitative analysis neglect the qualitative difference in the forms of society under scrutiny. Where there are few rules, inadequately articulated and only partly shared principles and standards to regulate the behaviour of public officials, then it is inappropriate to employ concepts whose accepted usage is dependent on conditions relevant to a radically different context. It is the failure to make this distinction which distorts much of the contemporary literature on corruption.

42

Writers on corruption have not confined their attention to any one country or area of the world, rather they have studied the problem in many differing situations. But the diversity of the resulting empirical data is not matched by a similar eclecticism of approach. Methodologically, nearly all the work on corruption employs one of two distinct approaches. First, there is what is normally termed the moralistic approach which compares potentially corrupt behaviour with an absolute moral standard, or at least it is assumed that the moral standard is absolute. The other major approach, which includes several variants, if the functionalist one. Functionalists claim to be value free and are concerned to understand how corruption contributes to the maintenance and balance of whichever political, social or administrative system has been selected for study. The next part of this paper is largely concerned with an evaluation and assessment of these approaches as aids to understanding corruption in both developed and developing countries.

The paradigm of the moralistic approach is that employed by Wraith and Simpkins[3] in their study of corruption in contemporary West Africa and in eighteenth and nineteenth century Britain. They assert that "Corruption is above all a moral problem, immeasurable and imponderable"[4]. There seems little doubt in this analysis that corruption is an evil and the authors proclaim that, "In Africa corruption flourishes as luxuriously as the bush and the weeds it so much resembles, taking the goodness from the soil and suffocating the growth of plants which have been carefully and expensively bred and tended"[5]. The authors find significant the fact that examples of corrupt behaviour found in contemporary Africa were once also prevalent in Britain.

These writers find this apparent similarity significant because they relate it to a broader concept which sees corruption as part of a worldwide development process. In their view, the fact that Britain has seemingly passed through a period of virulent corruption suggests that the major problem is one of seeking the factors which helped eliminate corruption at home in the expectation that Africa can learn from our experience. The assumption apparently is that corruption is a transitory feature of societies which have not reaped the full benefits of the modernisation process.

The underlying theme of the moralistic approach is that corruption is 'bad' and is defined for all places and times by the current understanding of corruption in Britain and Western Europe. The moralists do not seem greatly concerned to explore the different character of the African historical experience, nor do they appear very interested in the consequences of variegated social, economic and political systems for public morality. The simple cause of corruption is avarice and greed and, while the special circumstances of African life may partially mitigate the moral delinquency of these countries, they do not and can not excuse or condone corruption.

The moralist approach is one which defines corruption as an immoral deviant form of behaviour which has serious and detrimental effects on a whole range of political and economic activities. Corruption is blamed for a lowering of national respect, for reducing administrative efficiency, hindering economic development and for undermining political stability. It is, in this view, a cancer on the society which must be removed if the patient is to survive.

Almost every writer on the subject of corruption has his own set of remedies which, like proverbs, are often inconsistent and contradictory. Some of the suggested remedies clearly indicate their country of origin and form part of a larger cultural export trade. In this respect, prescription rather than explanation is the order of the day and the prescriptions are invaribaly vague and difficult to operationalise.

Some writers place their faith in time and economic progress as necessary and sufficient conditions for the cure[6]. Others point to the need to cultivate a common acceptance of Western standards of governmental morality[7], while still others, stress the importance of strengthening the idea of the national interest and reducing economic inequalities[8].

There may well be much to be said for such remedies but the major difficulty is that they merely contrast the ideal with the real without offering any practical guide to action. However regrettable it may be, it remains true that in most African countries the sense of national identity is embryonic, that Western standards of official morality are not practised and accepted, that their economic position is weak and vulnerable and that substantial inequalities are prevalent. More importantly, it seems certain that these conditions will continue in the forseeable future.

The second approach to the study of corruption, the functionalist approach, merits a more extensive treatment. The anthropoligcal version of functionalism is thought to explain corrupt activities as expressions of traditional pre-colonial values and practices which serve both to reflect and strengthen social and political ties. Anthropologists reject the disapproving approach of the moralists and are inclined to see gift giving and nepotism in a more sympathetic light. Attempts to eradicate corruption would, in such a view, threaten to destroy the delicate social fabric of traditional societies which are already undergoing the stresses of rapid social and economic change.

This view explains nepotism in terms of the persistence of family, tribe and ethnic loyalties which conflict with official standards of bureaucratic conduct. Using this perspective, attempts to organise a Weberian form of bureaucracy, which is impersonal and legalistic in character, are held to be inappropriate to the kinds of social relationships which pertain in Africa. The concept of the public interest is not widely shared or understood and hence is quite unable to resist the pressures exerted through more primary loyalties. In this view, corruption is suggestive not of the moral degeneracy of public officials, but evidence that traditional social obligations place African officials at the mercy of their kinfolk.

Political scientists and sociologists are more interested in examining how corruption is functional to the political and administrative systems. Functionalists are concerned primarily with the utilitarian qualities of corruption. While acknowledging the influence of both custom and traditional values, they tend to classify corruption as a phenomenon which compensates for the deficiencies of existing political and administrative arrangements. It may be seen to offer a way of overcoming institutional obstacles, of cutting through 'red tape' and generally accelerating administrative performance. Corrupt practices are sometimes seen as helping to bridge divisions based on tradition and ideology, as assisting in reducing political and administrative friction, as providing linkages between the political elite and economic or cultural outsiders and as creating mutual interests between potential or real antagonistic forces. Corruption can then be seen not as an illegitimate or subversive activity but as a necessary and

44

efficient alternative method of making demands on political and administrative systems.

Functionalists are not interested in moralising but they seem to assume that if the consequences of corruption were not beneficial, if it did not lubricate or compensate for the deficiencies of formal channels, it would not exist. At its simplest, this view suggests that "because corruption exists, it is assumed to be culturally integrative: survival is prima facie proof of functionality"[9]. If functionalism constitutes an advance on the more extreme versions of the moralistic approach, it is still open to fundamental criticism. It is not self evident as to how or why corruption is 'culturally integrative', nor is it obvious how one could decide whether a particular corrupt act was functional or dysfunctional. Murder, arson and rape survive in all societies, are they too to be regarded as functional?

Logically, it is hard to see how functionalists can avoid regarding every element in the status quo as functional just because it is a part of the status quo, and in a tautological sense necessary to it. The inability to produce appropriate criteria for distinguishing between functional and dysfunctional compels the functionalist to adopt a form of determinism whereby any and all phenomena are interpreted as being functionally necessary to the system.

It may be both necessary and desirable to discard the term functionalism as positively misleading. The meaning and superficiality of the term function is clarified when it is translated as intended and unintended useful consequences[10]. Once the jargon has been eliminated, the essentially normative characteristic of much allegedly scientific inquiry becomes evident. Unless the analysis includes assumptions concerning a desired social or political condition then it is logically impossible to judge the consequences of any activity as being useful or harmful. It should thus be clear that functionalism is unable to offer general causal propositions about corruption which might persuade the sceptic that a value free social science is a real possibility.

This analysis has demonstrated that the students of corruption are in a state of considerable disagreement and confusion. They differ both in methodology and in their substantive conclusions. There is no common agreement concerning what corruption is, what its causes are, or whether its consequences are, in any specific sense, beneficial or harmful. To some it is an unacceptable form of deviance from the ethical standards of the modern British Civil Services, while to others it is a mere chimera produced by the misapplication of irrelevant moral and ethical criteria to states which fundamentally differ from our own.

The evil effects of corruption were obvious to Edmund Burke who colourfully asserted that "Corrupt influence is itself the perenial spring of all prodigality and and of all disorder; it loads us with more than millions of debts; takes vigour from our arms, wisdom from our councils, and every shadow of authority and credit from the most venerable parts of the constitution"[11]. Some modern observers take a more sympathetic view and one has gone so far as to describe corruption as a substitute for political and administrative reform[12]. In this view, just as actual reform may reduce class pressures for structural changes, so corruption serves to reduce group pressures for policy changes. Instead of attempting to get rigid or outmoded laws changed, individuals and groups often use corrupt methods to circumvent their provisions. The value of such activity is held in great esteem by one leading scholar who suggests perhaps paradoxically that corruption may actually contribute to, rather than undermine, political stability and economic development[13].

The mystery of corruption goes ever deeper as its causes are confidently attributed to the universal and timeless sins of greed and avarice or to the matrix of loyalties and customs which bind traditional society and even to what Huntington has characterised as "political decay"[14]. The deficiencies of the methodologies used in the study of corruption are equalled by the discrepancies and inconsistencies in the conclusions which derive from them.

The next part of this paper is concerned to examine some of the problems an explicitly comparative analysis of corruption presents. One basic difficulty is that the pattern or incidence of corruption in a particular nation at a given point in time is unique. This excludes the possibility of ever formulating laws of corruption. Thus only limited and qualified generalisations are possible and even within these modest limits there are bound to be inconsistencies and exceptions. In this case the exceptions do not prove the rule because there are no actual, well established or accepted rules. It may be that the pattern of corruption in a particular place at a given time reflects a configuration of institutions, values, circumstances and conditions which are to be found in other societies in greater or lesser degree, but this has yet to be proven.

Spatio-temporal considerations severely handicap many attempts at comparative analysis. Not only do some scholars exhibit a barely disguised ethnocentrism but they often lack sensitivity in assessing the impact of historical change. This only compounds the problem of judging as corrupt the kinds of behaviour which deviate from accepted norms. The unanswered questions are, of course, what standards and accepted by whom? The way in which spatio-temporal considerations shape the answer to such questions when applied to corruption in developing countries can be summarised as follows, "modernisation involves a change in the basic values of the society . . . , and behaviour which was acceptable and legitimate according to traditional norms becomes unacceptable and corrupt when viewed through 'modern' eyes. Corruption in a modernising society is thus in part not so much the result of the deviance of behaviour from accepted norms as it is the deviance of norms from the established pattern of behaviour"[15].

Once this perspective is adopted the view advanced by some scholars[16] that during the nineteenth century Britain passed from a corrupt condition to a pure one can be seen to be mistaken. What actually occurred in the nineteenth century was that Britain passed through a period in which behaviour patterns which were acceptable by the old standards came to be regarded as corrupt by the new ones[17]. If it is illegitimate to judge corruption in Africa by British standards, it is equally invidious to use twentieth century criteria to characterise nineteenth century behaviour. Corruption has a spatio-temporal referent which is the only legitimate yardstick for analysis.

Comparative studies are bedevilled by other intractable difficulties. It seems somewhat ludicrous to compare the incidence of corruption in nations whose formal norms of office holding are quite different. The 'spoils' system is an integral and recognised part of the American political and administrative process but similar practices carried on in countries with a less generous conception of the discretions of public office might well be deemed corrupt. Clearly, comparative analysis is problematical in such circumstances, but, even where actual behaviour rather than formal provisions are compared, we should not assume that similar behaviour patterns necessarily enjoy the same significance in different societies.

One major weakness of comparative analysis is that little empirical research has been done on the consequences of corruption. Too many scholars have found themselves trapped in a definitional and conceptual impasse. Attempts to overcome ethnocentrism have only led to excessive vagueness and abstraction. Under what circumstances are actions judged as corrupt? What is at issue is the existence of a standard of behaviour according to which the standard in question breaks some rule, written or unwritten, about the proper purpose to which a public office may be put. It may be that in some cases there is really no clear idea what the rule is, or there may be a rule but it has not been clearly broken.

Dissatisfaction with the generality of such a concept of corruption has made a more explicitly legalistic view of the problem more attractive to many scholars. Although legal codes do delineate the parameters of legitimate official behaviour, the inadequacies of the legal understanding of corruption have long been clear. As early as 1910, it was obvious that "definitions of corrupt practices found in every highly developed legal code are scarcely broad enough to cover the whole concept . . . The sanctions of positive law are applied only to those more flagrant practices which past experience has shown to be so pernicious that sentiment has crystallized into statutory prohibitions . . . Even within this comparatively limited circle clearness and precision are but imperfectly attained"[18].

An awareness of the limitations of the legal approach frequently directs students to the concept of the public interest. Corruption is then simply defined as the subversion of the public interest for private ends. But some American scholars have asserted that there is no incompatibility between the public interest and apparently corrupt practices and they have gone on to defend patronage and "honest" graft. In this view, political activity requires the dedication of individuals and the efficiency provided by party organisations, thus where ideological or religious motivation is weak or absent then material inducements are necessary to produce cooperation and cohesion. Politics in such systems must be made to pay and "the political role of money is to serve as a cement — 'a hyphen which joins a buckle which fastens' the otherwise separate and conflicting elements of a society into a body politic"[19].

Without necessarily accepting this view of American government and politics, it seems obvious that the concept of the public interest poses more problems than it resolves in understanding corruption. It is an elusive, amorphous concept which is susceptible to conflicting interpretation by different groups in a society. It is most frequently defined in favour of the dominant group or strata and is really no more than "an attempt to solve an essentially normative or ideological question by definition"[20].

One popular alternative has been to invoke the weight of public opinion in the judgment of what is to be called corrupt and there is little doubt that it plays an influential part in determining the effectiveness of anti-corruption measures. But public opinion is not monolithic and often proves divided, ambiguous and inconsistent, even assuming that it is possible to gauge it accurately. One American study[21] suggests that poor city residents had a tolerant attitude to corruption in local government, while the more affluent residents only became indignant when the malpractices reached the more respectable parts of the city.

In such cases, it is unclear whether majority or elite opinions should act as the yardstick and it leaves unresolved the problem of how to monitor changing attitudes and opinions.

Although legalistic definitions only address a part of the problem, they do offer certain attractions in that the illegality of behaviour is already one aspect of contemporary notions of corruption and because of the impact of legal codes and procedures on the nature, extent and consequences of such behaviour. But this attraction is misleading when such an approach is applied to historical and comparative studies. Law also enshrines the distinction between private interest and public duty beloved of organisational theorists from Weber to the present. This involves assumptions concerning the depersonalisation of public office which is still as much an aspiration for the future or an echo of the past as an actual reality in many societies. Favouritism for Kikuyus in Kenya, for Irish in Boston or for party members in the Soviet Union are all evidence that the public/private dichotomy is scarcely adequate to contain the various shades and nuances of what is sometimes called corruption.

This paper has, in part, considered the defects in methodology of some of those who have studied corruption and it has indicated the inadequacies and weaknesses of some popular contemporary concepts and definitions. The final section of this paper is concerned to explore still further difficulties in discussing corruption and to suggest a redirection of interest and emphasis to potentially more fruitful lines of inquiry.

One important, obvious but neglected factor is the distortion introduced to analysis when scholars try to compare corruption in countries which differ greatly in the size and scope of governmental responsibilities and activities. Is it merely coincidental that most writers on corruption originate from societies where there is a large, even dominant role for private economic interests?

The size and the role of the public sector greatly affects the nature, incidence and type of corrupt behaviour found in a particular society. Behaviour which is accepted and even highly valued in private business is frequently seen as illegitimate or illegal in the public service. After all, the traditional family business is but the most common form of nepotism. In the public service, appointments are formally made on achievement rather than ascriptive criteria but it is widely believed that many developing countries only pay lip service to this principle. But it would be a mistake to believe that developed nations are free from nepotism as the invasion of government by the Kennedy clan testifies.

In categorizing an act as corrupt it is clearly critical, whether it takes place within or outside the public sector. It seem obvious that the larger the relative size and scope of the public sector, the greater will be the proportion of certain acts that meet legalistic criteria of corruption. It may be that the public sector is comparatively more important in most new states than in the West and this fact alone could be responsible for the appearance of a greater incidence of corruption in such nations[22]. In a laissez-faire state there is little scope except for electoral malpractice and the sale of offices, but with the growth of the positive, interventionist state the rich pickings of the 'pork barrel' become available.

Without denying the significance of individual greed or the importance of traditional values, it is clear to the present writer that much corruption in the third world is related to structural and institutional factors. The most important feature is the paramount role of the government in most developing countries as a source of goods, services and employment. In many African countries, politics and administration are the most important, if not the only, sources of status, wealth, prestige and security. The pressure on public employment, for example, is so great that inevitably appointments are subject to considerable intrigue. As the government is often a monopoly employer, it is easy to practice favouritism by ensuring unequal access to employment opportunities. Furthermore, to use Schaffer's[23] terms, there are rarely channels through which disappointed applicants can 'voice' their grievances and there are few 'exits' from the situation except corrupt ones.

Where a private entrepreneurial class does exist in the third world, it is often denied access to formal political and administrative processes. This is especially so where "Its members are drawn from a marginal group — racially, ethnically, religiously — or of alien origin"[24]. Riggs suggests that a symbiotic relationship develops whereby bureaucrats supplement their incomes by extracting bribes in return for overlooking commercial transgressions. But, as the recent history of Uganda shows, the comfortable accommodation between bureaucrats and 'pariah capitalists' is susceptible to swift and drastic change. Where a large and growing proportion of national income and development capital passes through the hands of politicians and administrators, then the possibilities and opportunities for corruption increase correspondingly. It sometimes appears that the bureaucratic elite devote more attention to siphoning off development funds than they do to accomplishing development goals.

In his attempts to explain corruption in developing countries, Riggs has interestingly noted that insofar as colonial regimes were administrative states, they encouraged the growth of an elitist bureaucracy which was aloof from other potential power centres [25]. He argues that the relative weakness of political parties, interest groups and other potential competitors has meant that the administrative apparatus is dominant and uncontrolled[26]. In this view, corruption is encouraged because no extra-bureaucratic agency is strong enough to control it or make it accountable.

This vision of a rampant bureaucracy has been elaborated by other scholars who suggest that, "In the absence of agencies that could enforce performance standards, bureaucratic factions blossom luxuriantly and each division of the apparatus becomes a virtual feudal domain that may parasitically exploit its clientele or the portion of the economy over which it wields power"[27]. Some empirical studies support the thesis that uncontrolled bureaucracy is responsible for endemic corruption. One student of Ghanaian affairs has concluded that, "It was the weakness of the Nkrumah regime in its inability to control what went on rather than its totalitarian facade which facilitated corruption"[28].

Popular control of bureaucrats is made more difficult by the gulf in status and education which exists between citizens and officials. The impact of this on what might be termed consumer expectations is that, "Instead of expecting services and benefits as of right, most citizens feel that they are asking for a personal favour"[29]. This sort of attitude not only encourages the offering of bribes but increases the propensity of officials to demand them. Where bureaucracy is viewed as remote and potentially hostile, it is frequently thought advantageous to placate the official to avoid possible delay or harassment. Bureaucrats are to be treated with deference for, as the Ashanti proverb has it, "A man does not rub bottoms with a porcupine."

49

In the search for appropriate comparative models, one scholar has sought to draw a parallel between the activities of parties such as the Convention Peoples Party in Ghana and the famous urban party machines of the United States[30]. The American party machine was, and is, a non-ideological organisation interested in securing and retaining political office for its leaders and distributing income to those who run it and work for it. It represents a distinctive and possibly unique way of mobilizing voters and hence is found only in systems where getting out the vote is essential to gaining control of the government. Its reputation as a corrupt organisation stems from its reliance on material rewards to maintain and extend its control over the electorate. It depends on money and favours not charisma, coercion, loyalty or ideology to maintain its support.

The argument is that the conditions which gave rise to and supported the urban machine in the United States are broadly similar to those prevailing in Africa today and which encourage corruption[31]. The population was poor and particularly susceptible to material incentives, political power was fragmented and ethnic division and social disorganisation was prevalent. According to this analysis, the leaders of many developing nations have similar problems to the old style city bosses[32]. They also face a highly differentiated population, divided along ethnic, religious, linguistic or regional lines, but also representing various stages of incorporation into the 'modern' sector and varying degrees of loyalty and hostility to the nation state.

The machine has largely disappeared from the United States, despite the dinosaur figure of Mayor Daley, because the economic progress of immigrants made the machine and its services redundant. In developing countries, attempts to develop 'machine style' politics have been hindered by a lack of resources and have frequently been aborted by military coups. One distinguished scholar even suggests that the corruption associated with such a political style has been the main justification for the coup d'etat[33].

But generalisations valid for the American historical experience are unlikely, or only coincidentally, to make much sense when discussing the contemporary situation in the third world. The United States differs so greatly and in so many ways from the states of tropical Africa, that any attempt to construct an explanation based on their superficial similarities rests on very flimsy foundations. One important difference which is often neglected concerns the relationship of politics to economics in the different cultures. Broadly speaking, privately acquired economic wealth is used, directly or indirectly, to purchase political influence in the United States, whereas in most African states, it is the pursuit and possession of political power which enables its wielders to acquire private wealth. Where there is only a limited role for private entrepreneurs, the government and administration becomes the major tool for the accumulation of capital by individuals[34].

This paper has tried to examine different ways of approaching and understanding the problem of corruption. In the course of this analysis, certain deficiencies and omissions in the methodologies employed have been noted. The most striking gap in the literature on corruption is the scant attention paid to political systems where corruption has been effectively curbed. Despite the almost total lack of 'hard' evidence, there appears to be a consensus amongst Western observers that the communist regimes found in the developing countries of Asia are noticeably free of corruption compared to their non-communist neighbours. Even allowing for the obvious research difficulties, there appears to be a noticeable lack of analysis attempting to explain the situation.

It may be less than mischievous to suggest that perhaps some Western writers have fought shy of embarking on studies which may produce unacceptable and unpalatable political and administrative conclusions. Time and again, the contemporary literature shows Western writers, consciously and unconsciously, using a model of government and administration which bears an uncanny resemblance to that found in Britain or, more especially, the United States. The reality of American government is transformed into an ideal which then acts as a measure by which to judge the performance of developing countries. Having rightly pointed out the important role played by bureaucracy in the developing countries, Riggs goes on to assert that there exists a lack of balance between politics and administration[35]. What Professor Riggs appears to mean is that the role of bureaucrats is larger than it is in the United States and he seems to regard any such deviations as regrettable.

The weakness of such studies is one of associating the possibilities of reform to reduce corruption exclusively with the institutions and standards of Western democratic politics. The Western model is becoming increasingly irrelevant to an understanding of the developing countries. Generalisations about corruption derived from electorally oriented multi-party systems with impartial bureaucracies can only have a tenuous and contingent relationship to the problems of societies which lack all these features. The wearing of rose-tinted democratic spectacles not only distorts the view of corruption, but it ensures that radical political and administrative solutions are overlooked.

Writers on corruption have generally failed to place corruption in a wide social, political and economic context. Not only is there a tendency to abstract corruption from its environment for special study, but the academic division of labour ensures that each discipline or subject only concerns itself with a small part of the problem. Corruption can only be understood in relation to particular kinds of political and economic system and the totality of the problem is difficult to appreciate when scholars try to compartmentalize the phenomenon.

A preliminary glance at the experience of the developing communist states reveals approaches to the problem which are largely ignored by Western writers. There appears to be no literature devoted to the role of political education in eliminating corruption and nor is much attention devoted to the role of foreign capital in many African states. In the communist regimes the role of the market is much diminished, but this decline has been coupled with the growth of the party organisation which parallels the bureaucratic one. Control of the bureaucracy is therefore exercised, not by the electorate or their representatives, but by another breed of functionary, the party bureaucrat. This coupling of party organisations with ideological conviction appears to have a striking effect on the incidence of corruption. The apparent lack of interest in such solutions, by Western writers busily engaged in preparing more congenial remedies for the developing states, is evidence that they regard certain cures as worse than the disease itself. The suggestion that, in the African context at least, a politically indoctrinated bureaucracy may be a better safeguard against corruption than an allegedly impartial one, is calculated to cause some disquiet to those who are proud of the ethical standards of the British public service.

This paper has been concerned to argue that current understandings of corruption are inadequate and misconceived. It has tried to indicate the nature

51

and sources of the methodological errors and confusions found in too much of the contemporary literature. The final part of the paper has stressed the need for a fuller appreciation of the ecology of corruption as an antidote to the excessive specialisation of many modern studies. The conclusion to the paper calls for an end to prescription and the restoration of explanation as the goal for students of social science. Unless and until the political and academic blinkers are removed and the methodological sterility is overcome there can be little hope that we can make any substantial advance in understanding the perennially interesting problem of corruption.

REFERENCES

1. W.C. Salmon, *Logic*, Prentice-Hall, 1963, p. 90.
2. A. Ryan, *The Philosophy of the Social Sciences*, Macmillan, 1971 p. 5.
3. R. Wraith and E. Simpkins, *Corruption in Developing Countries,* Allen and Unwin, 1963.
4. Ibid p. 17.
5. Ibid p. 12–13.
6. Ibid p. 208.
7. R. Braibanti, "Reflections on Bureaucratic Corruption", *Public Administration*, Autumn, 1962, p. 365.
8. C. Leys, "What is the Problem about Corruption", *Journal of Modern African Studies*, 3, 2, 1965, p. 224–5.
9. H. Werlin, "The Roots of Corruption: the Ghanaian Inquiry," *Journal of Modern African Studies*, 1972, p. 250.
10. Ryan, op. cit. p. 190.
11. Speech on Economical Reform, 1780.
12. S. P. Huntington, *Political Order in Changing Societies*, Yale U.P., 1968, p. 64.
13. Ibid p. 68–9.
14. Ibid p. 86.
15. Ibid p. 59–60.
16. Wraith and Simpkins op. cit. p. 55–106.
17. Leys op. cit. p. 227.
18. R. C. Brooks, quoted in A. J. Heidenheimer (ed.) *Political Corruption*, Holt, Rinehart and Wilson, 1970, p. 7.
19. Leys op. cit. p. 219.
20. J. C. Scott, *Comparative Political Corruption*, Prentice-Hall, 1972 p. 3.
21. See R. E. Lane, *Political Ideology*, Free Press, 1962, p. 335.
22. Scott op. cit. p. 13–14.
23. B. B. Schaffer and G. B. Lamb, "Exit, voice and access", *Social Science Information*, 13 (b) pp. 73–90.
24. F. W. Riggs in *Bureaucracy and Political Development*, (ed) J. La Palombara, Princeton U.P., 1963, p. 142.

25. Ibid p. 120–167.

26. Ibid

27. Scott, op. cit. p. 15.

28. Werlin, op. cit. p. 261.

29. J. V. Abueva, quoted in Scott op. cit. p. 15.

30. Scott op. cit. p. 113–123.

31. Ibid p. 114–115.

32. Ibid p. 116.

33. J. Myrdal, *Asian Drama*, Twentieth Century, 1968, p. 937.

34. See R. First, *The Barrel of a Gun,* Penguin, 1970, p. 100–104.

35. Riggs op. cit. p. 120.

[9]

The Corruption of a State*

J. PATRICK DOBEL

University of Michigan, Dearborn

This article presents a theory of corruption which unifies the moral, political, economic and social causes and patterns of corruption in one theoretical framework. The theory is constructed from the scattered insights about the "corruption of the body politic," building in particular upon the work of five theorists–Thucydides, Plato, Aristotle, Machiavelli and Rousseau. Corruption is defined as the moral incapacity of citizens to make reasonably disinterested commitments to actions, symbols and institutions which benefit the substantive common welfare. This extensive demise of loyalty to the commonwealth comes from the interaction of human nature with systematic inequality of wealth, power and status. The corruption of the polity results in certain identifiable patterns of political conflict and competition. The central feature of these patterns is the emergence of quasi-governmental factions and an increasingly polarized class system. The politics of the factions leads to an undermining of the efficacy of the basic political structures of the society and the emergence of systematic corruption in all aspects of political life. The theory advanced in this article identifies several crucial prescriptions to stave off the tendency towards corruption. Among these are an extension of maximum substantive participation by all citizens in all aspects of political life and a stringent control over all sources of great or permanent inequality in the polity.

The disintegration of ordered arrangements of life is a central problem of politics. When the daily interactions among people and institutions no longer provide normal opportunities for the exercise of integrity, personal right, or fulfillment, political theorists can no longer ignore the decay. As people proclaim the "twilight," "decline," or "crisis" of every major aspect of our culture, we must try to comprehend the nature of political disintegration.

The explanations for the increased disordering of human lives have tended to divide along three lines—institutional, moral, and economic. The institutional approach argues that outmoded social and political structures can no longer provide for a population whose size, values and expectations have radically changed since they were instituted. The moral explanation sees certain undesirable moral changes result in a collapse of traditional moral disci-

*An earlier version of this paper was presented at the American Political Science Association convention at Chicago in 1976. Since then, the paper has benefited immensely from the help of many individuals, notable among them are Donald Anderson, Dennis Dutton, Jamieson Doig, Fritz Kratochwil, Arlene Saxonhouse, Lea Vaughn and Frank Wayman. I owe a special debt of gratitude to the anonymous referees whose invaluable help enabled me to rectify many of the original shortcomings. For the weaknesses that remain, the responsibility is mine.

plines, and sees people without self-discipline or altruism placing unwarranted demands upon institutions. Finally, the economic interpretation argues that unequal economic and power distributions have generated forces which have alienated the people and lead to the social breakdowns. In this paper I will present the theory of corruption as an alternative account of the decay of trust, loyalty and concern among citizens of a state.

While in contemporary usage "corruption"[1] usually means the betrayal of public trust for individual or group gain, the technical notion of the "corruption of the body politic" has a long and impressive history in both political philoso- [958] phy and polemics.[2] The decay of the moral and the political orders are phenomena which political theorists have constantly had to confront. In this article I assume that, while historical situations change, there is a continuous tradition of rational reflection upon such problems and that the results of this reflection need not be limited to the comprehension of a particular era. I further assume that the decay of political orders are not incommensurable events.[3]

The arguments about corruption are scattered throughout the western political tradition but a coherent theory of corruption has never been fully articulated. "Standing on the shoul-

[1] *The Oxford English Dictionary, Compact Edition* (1971, Vol. 1, pp. 566–67) cites a number of definitions which are relevant to the theory and reflect the older Latin and French usage. The first definition of "to corrupt" is "to turn from a sound into a unsound impure condition." The fourth definition specifies another aspect, "to destroy or pervert the integrity or fidelity of a person to his discharge or duty; to induce to act dishonestly or unfaithfully; to make venal; to bribe." The notions of decomposition and degeneration apply to many areas but the most prominent is the corruption of the customs, habits and morals of individuals and societies. The second basic category of meaning under the word "corruption" is "moral." Moral corruption can apply to "agents, practices, institutions, natures, customs, officials" and almost every aspect of human activity where moral choice involves the possibility of acting in one's own interests or being loyal to a public trust, law or another's welfare.

[2] A detailed analysis of the various forms of the theory can be found in Pocock (1975). Bailyn (1967) and Wood (1969) analyze its form and importance in the period of the American Revolution.

[3] Wolin (1960, pp. 1–28).

ders of giants," I have found the insights of five theorists—Thucydides, Plato, Aristotle, Machiavelli and Rousseau—fruitful enough to enable me to construct an independent theoretical account of the decay of a political order.[4] This theory of corruption is worthy of serious consideration and further study because it makes a number of significant contributions to our understanding of politics.

First, the theory establishes a clear link between the moral and social prerequisites of a just and stable state and structural inequality. While taking "conservative" moral concerns seriously, it does not divide them from more structural concerns. In this, it provides a non-Marxist framework to comprehend the relations among inequality, classes, civic morals, interest group/factions and the structures of government. *Second*, the theory presents a suggestive critique of "liberalism" by arguing that several of liberalism's normative and psychological assumptions are insufficient either to justify or sustain a just, equal and stable state. *Third*, the theory complements and enriches many of the existing critiques of pluralism. By identifying certain types of interest groups as factions, it provides a set of moral and social insights about the limits of pluralism and gives an overarching moral coherence to the whole critique of

---

[4]This article is *not* an historical survey of particular theorists. Nor is it an explication of the theory of corruption which might underlie all the various theorists. Rather, my formulation of the theoretical model draws upon, but is not necessarily identical to, the insights culled from them. Even with this caveat, one may ask why I selected these five theorists upon which to base my theory. Quite simply, I found that these five provided all of the initial historical and theoretical analysis necessary to develop the full theory.

Because I base my theory on these theorists, it is necessary to note the following. While the theorists' views of the just state may vary depending upon assumptions about equality, property and human nature, their portrayal of corruption is almost uniformly the same. But underlying their notions of corruption, one will find two basic differences. These concern their differing notions of a philosophy of history and human equality. The cyclic theory of history, found in Plato and Machiavelli, or more modern progressive notions of history are not addressed in this paper. I do not believe such historical theories are necessary to the theoretical model, and the analysis, as I develop it, may actually count against holding a theory of history. The nature of equality will be discussed under "The Cause of Corruption."

pluralism. *Fourth*, the theory provides a suggestive and comprehensive model which explains certain prevalent patterns of politics and synthesizes a wide variety of insight and empirical work. It is especially relevant in its redefinition of political decay and stability and its presentation of alternative policies to build a stable polity. Some of the relevant empirical work encompasses the function of co-optation, the role of the military in a civilian state, the political powerlessness of the poor, the effects of political participation, the role of political socialization, and the importance of political symbols and acquiescence. *Finally*, without resorting to either reaction or revolution, the theory provides limited and realistic prescriptions for ameliorating one of the recurring problems of politics—the corruption of a state.

At this point I will briefly summarize the theory and then examine its tenets in more detail. The theory of corruption involves the following propositions:

1. Certain patterns of moral loyalty and civic virtue are necessary to maintain a just, equal and stable political order. The privatization of moral concerns and the accompanying breakdown of civic loyalty and virtue are the cardinal attributes of a corrupt state.

2. Extensive inequality in wealth, power and status, spawned by the human capacity for selfishness and pride, generates the systematic corruption of the state. Members of the upper classes sacrifice their basic civic loyalty to gain and maintain their positions and the established inequality undermines the loyalty and substantive welfare of the general citizenry.

3. This change in the moral quality of life of the citizen, coupled with inequality, generates factions. Factions are objective centers of wealth, power, police and policy which, by their own dynamics, usurp vital governmental and political functions. Factional politics involves the systematic attempt to corrupt public agency and law. Membership and practice in the factions changes the moral character of persons, undermines their loyalty to the community and [959] encourages radical selfishness or limited loyalty to factions.

4. The factional conflict and continued inequality extend corruption across the entire citizenry. Violence increasingly becomes the dominant substratum of all relations, and political discourse is reduced to transparent rationali-

zation. Public office, law and adjudication
become tools of faction and class. The disen-
franchised populace and the upper classes become increasingly polarized. Demagogic factional politics, sporadic uprisings and co-
optation mark political relations as the society
moves in a restless cycle from aborted attempts
at "restoration" and "reform" to increasing
alienation, violence and institutional anarchy.

5. The socialization of education, family
life, religion and the military also sustains
communal values and loyalty, sometimes even
after the corruption of the political process.
The final corruption of the state involves the
failure of the citizenry to support these primary
structures voluntarily.

The Corruption of the State

Moral corruption is the loss of a capacity for
loyalty. Individual moral life becomes progressively privatized and self-interest becomes the
normal motive for most actions. The privatization of moral concerns changes the moral
calculus of the society. The self-interested
contract becomes the normal social relation,
and any arrangement becomes rational through
which an individual gains more from another
than is given. The primary attitude among
citizens is wary competition to preserve what
one possesses and to gain more if possible.

Societal or state corruption involves the
moral incapacity of citizens to make disinterested moral commitments to actions, symbols
and institutions which benefit the common
welfare. A slightly weaker definition is that
citizens are unable or unwilling to do anything
which does not bring them sensual gratification,
money or security. Corruption leaches the trust
and fraternity from the social life of the state.
Acceptable communal answers to problems
such as marriage or property defense become
problematic. Mistrust and latent competition
among individuals change the everyday moral
universe and citizens no longer can or wish to
sustain, at some cost to themselves, certain
patterns of committed relations to other citizens.

Loyalty is the focus of this theory because it
is the constitutive moral and psychological
attribute of the minimum civic virtue necessary
to sustain the symbols, laws and institutions of

the state. Josiah Royce in *The Philosophy of Loyalty* defines loyalty as

> *the willing and practical and thoroughgoing devotion of a person to a cause.* A man is loyal when, first, he has some *cause* to which he is loyal; when, secondly, he *willingly* and *thoroughly* devotes himself to this cause; and when, thirdly, he expresses his devotion in some *sustained and practical way*, by acting steadily in the service of his cause.[5]

The importance of loyalty flows from its central role in moral autonomy. Moral autonomy requires a self-conscious capacity to rationally and emotionally affirm impersonal values, concrete relations and symbols which embody these relations and values. Without a capacity for loyalty to these "causes," people could not exercise the self-discipline necessary to override self-interested desires or work for other people's or even their own welfare. The exercise of duty to ourselves and others flows from the capacity for loyalty. Royce argues that people cannot really be loyal to their own desires; while these desires might form a random or Hobbesian hierarchy of impulses, they do not form an impersonal coherent whole, a personal character. Desires of themselves define the content of selfishness, not selfhood. The capacity for loyalty enables people to order their beliefs and their lives and create selfhood and virtue in their strict sense.[6] Thus, loyalty constitutes the absolutely necessary, but by no means sufficient, moral and psychological prerequisite of moral autonomy and civic virtue.

Civic virtue is the dutiful activity which arises from a reasonably disinterested commitment to the well-being of other citizens and the institutions which provide for the basic

[5]Royce (1969, Pt. 2, p. 861). Royce goes on the claim that loyalty to loyalty is sufficient to provide the content of a strong humanistic ethic. While not wishing to defend Royce's derivation of ethics from loyalty, I do agree that a person cannot be moral or virtuous in any meaningful sense without the exercise of loyalty.

[6]Royce (1969, Pt. 2, Chs. 1, 5, esp. p. 886 ff.). This impersonality of self resides in the laws, personal rules of conduct and relations which exist independent of an individual's personal desires and needs and form a coherent and predictable moral personality.

needs and integrity of all citizens. Unlike simple consensus or opinions, the moral beliefs and actions of civic virtue are exceptionally stable and possess a degree of psychological autonomy as opposed to interests and inclinations. Civic virtue leads to actions not merely intended to maintain stability but also to achieve justice [960] even if this goal involves some sacrifice. The capacity for disciplined sacrifice which flows from this type of moral commitment enables any real-life state to resolve its myriad conflicts with a minimum of violence and a maximum of justice.

A classic case of this sort centers upon citizens' willingness to risk their lives in political situations. A litmus test of corruption has always been the ability of a country to mobilize its citizenry and militia to defend itself effectively against tyrants and foreigners.[7] The willingness of citizens actively to support the laws as opposed to their willingness to reject them, drastically affects the overall stability of the society. The resolution to resist the law, although made in the crucible of economic and social flux, is, in the end, a personal moral decision. In his analysis of the Florentine conspiracies against the usurption of the Duke of Athens, Machiavelli recounts, "Many citizens, of every sort, determined to lose their lives or to have their liberty again."[8]

Civic virtue requires not only loyalty but also disinterestedness and personal allegiance to the common good. Consequently totally selfish persons are totally corrupt in that they possess no loyalty, no disinterestedness and no commitment to the common good. Loyalty, however, is prior, for without it a person could be neither disinterested nor committed to the community.

Civic virtue depends upon the extension of loyalty to the communal structures of the society. Habits, customs and spontaneous empathy with other citizens give daily content to active loyalty. This active civic loyalty is not simply emotion-dominated patriotism. Rather, all true loyalty requires reasoned reflection

---

[7]Machiavelli (1965, *Discourses*, Bk. 1, Chs. 4, 43; Bk. 2, Chs. 10, 12); Rousseau (1964, *Du contrat social*, Bk. 3, Ch. 15).

[8]Machiavelli (1965, *History of Florence*, Bk. 2, Ch. 36).

before the beliefs are affirmed. Loyalty also underlies committed actions for the disinterested welfare of people in the family, church or fraternal organizations.

Loyalty of itself, however, has never been a sufficient barrier against corruption. The classic problem arises with people who are loyal to morally hideous values or a reprobate group—a loyal Nazi or Mafia member. Insofar as such individuals are reflective and disinterested in commitment and dedicated in belief, they cannot be said to be corrupt. Insofar as the policies of the faction to which they are loyal undermine the substantive welfare of the citizenry, they are corrupt, but only in this more limited sense.

The Cause of Corruption

It is often a temptation to dismiss corruption as a fact of life rooted in flaws of human nature and to analyze most acts of corruption as isolated individual acts. However, there is unanimous agreement among the theorists that the source of systematic corruption lies in certain patterns of inequality.[9] In a limited sense most corruption requires individual moral choices and depends upon the human capacity for avarice and evil; nevertheless, the corruption of a state results from the consequences of individual human nature interacting with systematic and enduring inequality in wealth, power and status. Under such inequality certain groups of individuals have de facto or legally sanctioned priority of access to wealth, power and status.[10]

It should be clear that not all corruption

[9]Plato (1957, 421d–422b; 547a–53e); Aristotle (1962, Bk. 2, Ch. 7; Bk. 5, Ch. 2); Machiavelli (1965, *The Prince*, Ch. 9; *Discourses*, Bk. 1, Chs. 2–5); Rousseau (1964, *Discours sur l'inégalité*, pp. 171, 174–86, esp. pp. 187–91; *Discours sur l'economie*, p. 258).

[10]All the theorists acknowledge the innate capacity of human beings for selfishness and evil. Rousseau designates it in his distinction between "amour de soi" and "amour propre" (1964, *Discours sur l'inégalité*, p. 164 ff.). For Machiavelli even the best of individuals can be "bribed" by a "little ambition" and "avarice" (1965, *Discourses*, Bk. 1, Chs. 3, 42). He also points out that "moreover, human wants are insatiable, since man has from nature the power and wish to desire everything" (1965, *Discourses*, Bk. 2, Preface) and

necessarily occurs as a result of inequality. Nor
will the end of all systematic inequality result
in the elimination of all corruption. Corruption,
however, can be viewed on a spectrum ranging
from random individual acts through increasingly widespread corruption to the point where
the citizenry, both in and out of government,
engage in politics permeated by corruption.
Certain patterns of inequality are the main   [961]
generators of such increasing corruption, as
opposed to random individual acts.

The focus is upon equality because of its
relation to the common good. As the words
imply, the common good at least partially
entails goods which are equally common to all
citizens. Given human selfishness and the normal conflicts of a state, maintaining the common good requires some loyalty to other
people and to the policies and institutions
which guarantee the common good. Loyalty
declines under the pressure of inequality as
individuals pursue purely selfish activities or act
from limited loyalties to factions. Both these
types of activities seek to benefit individuals or
groups unequally, regardless of the consequences for the equal distribution of common
goods. The methods of seeking such benefits
extend the corruption of the people and undermine the structures designed to provide for the
common good.

The theory, however, never assumes that all
inequality is unjust and corrupting. The practical requirements of a society necessitate some
inequality in the economic and political realms.
The theory distinguishes just and reasonable
inequality from that which generates corruption. The non-corrupt state guarantees certain
basic forms of substantive economic, juridical
and political equality, but it does not require
absolute equality in all aspects of life. Any
reasonable inequality can be justified as long as

"republics go to pieces" when men "climb from one
ambition to another" (1965, *Discourses*, Bk. 1, Ch.
46). Plato identifies the avaricious element of the soul
as the most dangerous element in the triad of human
nature. The corruption of the city and of human
nature is defined by the increasing dominance of the
avaricious and selfish part of the soul (1957, 444a–
445d, 547b–587d, esp. 577d–587d); Aristotle argues
that "men are always wanting something more and are
never contented until they get to infinity" (1962, Bk.
2, Chs. 7, 8).

it contributes to the substantive commonweal or at least does not endanger citizens' substantive freedoms.

Practical inequality in the ownership or control of wealth can be justified on two grounds: (1) the limited but legitimate claims of distributive justice, (2) the need to generate surplus wealth to finance the government and the common good. The functional specialization necessary for the maintenance of a society above the subsistence level, the natural unequal distribution of talents and interests, as well as the exigencies of a money economy, generate some economic inequality. In turn, the inequality generates the surplus necessary to finance the state.[11] Economic inequality, however, must never develop to the extent where it threatens the integrity of law or government. Hereditary sources of great wealth cannot be tolerated and any significant wealth must be controlled by law. All citizens must have their economic integrity guaranteed. Redistributing property to provide all citizens with a livelihood, progressive taxation, inheritance taxes, sumptuary laws, excise taxes, and minimization of foreign trade have all been proposed as means of warding off the dangers of wealth in a state. Machiavelli argues that it was the relative economic equality of the German city republics which gave them the strength to maintain their freedoms against superior forces.[12]

Political and social subordination and the accompanying inequality in power are the preeminent forms of inequality necessary for the state. The laws must be legislated, promulgated, enforced and administered, and these activities require that unequal power and respect be given to some individuals. Spontaneous obedience is the heart of a just, equal and stable state. Yet without qualifications, obedience to the laws may bring stability but certainly not justice or equality. Consequently there are two sets of qualifications about the quality of laws and officials in a non-corrupt state.

First, the laws must apply equally to all

[11]Plato (1957, 369b–374e); Aristotle (1962, Bk. 2, Chs. 2–7); Machiavelli (1965, *Discourses*, Bk. 1, Ch. 1); Rousseau (1964, *Du contrat social*, Bk. 3, Ch. 8).

[12]Machiavelli (1965, *Discourses*, Bk. 1, Chs. 37, 55); Rousseau (1964, *Du contrat social*, Bk. 2, Ch. 11; *Projet pour la Corse*, pp. 904–06, 930–37; *Considérations sur le Pologne*, pp. 972–75, 1003–12).

citizens and be fairly administered. The laws must be designed to benefit all citizens equally and not one particular group. Finally, those who make and administer the laws must be equally subject to them.[13]

Second, the spontaneous acceptance of government assumes that government officials are loyal to the common welfare. It also assumes that their dedication is augmented by talent and competence. The destruction of the Athenian forces at Syracuse under the well-meaning incompetence of Nicias and the unprincipled ambition of Alcibiades, demonstrates the dangers of one set of qualifications without the other.[14] Justified hierarchical inequality presumes talent, dedication and virtue in those to whom office is entrusted.

In the real world of politics it is extremely difficult to maintain any equality or to maintain both competent and virtuous individuals in office. The realm of politics tends to attract talented and ambitious citizens regardless of their civic virtue; the weaknesses of human nature combined with the temptations to abuse official authority necessitate some more substantive limits upon political power.[15] Substantive citizen participation is the best way to accomplish this. Such participation allows all citizens in office and offsets inequalities in wealth and status, and it maximizes the responsibility and virtue of the majority of citizens while limiting the opportunities for misuse of power. There are a number of political strategies to ensure limits upon inequality and corruption. These are: maximum citizen participation in elections, offices, and the armed forces; constant rotation of representative and bureaucratic governmental offices; a citizen army; a maximum number of elected officials; open civilian juries; the minimization of the

[962]

[13]Rousseau (1964, *Du contrat social*, Bk. 2, Chs. 3–6, 11, 12; Bk. 3, Ch. 10; *Discours sur l'economie*, pp. 247–60, esp. pp. 252–53); Machiavelli (1965, *Discourses*, Bk. 1, Chs. 7, 8, 24, 58; *History of Florence*, Bk. 3, Ch. 5).

[14]Thucydides (1934, Bk. 6, Chs. 18, 19; Bk. 7, Chs. 22, 23); Machiavelli (1965, *Prince*, Chs. 14–16; *History of Florence*, Bk. 3, Ch. 23).

[15]Thucydides (1934, Bk. 3, Ch. 10); Plato (1957, 521a); Aristotle (1962, Bk. 5, Ch. 8).

hereditary element in any positions; and extension of the meritocratic award of office.[16]

At this point in the formulation of the theory I side with Aristotle, Machiavelli and Rousseau in their insistence that just equality demands open and meaningful participation by the widest possible body of citizens. This is probably the most relevant difference among the sources of the theory. For Plato, the stasis of corruption derives from the failure to match the specialized jobs of government with the innate, invariant and hierarchical distribution of talent and knowledge in the society. Rousseau, and to a lesser extent, Aristotle and Machiavelli argue that most citizens both are capable of participating in the political realm and must participate to adequately achieve virtue and guard against the onslaught of corruption. Although this difference sets the theorists apart on most issues, it does not affect the moral and political consequences of corruption. The essence of corruption remains the same: the decline in the ability and willingness of the citizens to act spontaneously or disinterestedly to support other citizens or communal institutions.

The relation between inequality and corruption centers upon the moral relations of people in an unequal state and the patterns of politics which they engender. There are two types of inequality which corrupt the state: permanent or massive inequality in wealth, and exclusionary inequality in political power and authority.

The corruption stemming from economic inequality is the most insidious and pervasive. It begins with the moral life of the seeker of great riches. To expend time and energy in amassing wealth not only requires talent but also a peculiar moral perspective in which most emotions and talents are honed exclusively towards the satisfaction of personal desires. The attainment of great wealth also requires the use and organization of people and resources. Other citizens must be viewed primarily as a means to a private end. This instrumentalization of hu-

[16]The classic statement of most of these ideals resides in Rousseau's *Considérations sur le Pologne*. This underrated work, along with *Projet de constitution pour la Corse*, represents Rousseau's final synthesis of his Platonic, democratic and republican heritage. They provide a systematic statement of the classical republican ideal with a strong democratic tinge.

man relations and the habit of using citizens for one's own ends slowly erode the individual's disinterested commitment to their welfare. Even their shared community of aims begins to change. It becomes rational for the rich person to worry more about fellow citizens' envy rather than their lack of equality. It becomes morally rational to subvert the government to protect one's position and ensure that no one else can use the government against one's wealth.[17]

Selfish individuals do not of themselves destroy the state and can actually help if their pursuit is tied to the public glory and aggrandizement. Machiavelli's chronicle of Lorenzo and Cosimo de Medici's success at holding Florence together with corruption, talent and prosperity shows the accomplishments and the limits of this idea. At their death, as was the case with Pericles in Athens, the corrupt system fell apart without their singular personal strengths to hold it together. In the long run such a system destroys the remnants of loyalty and will collapse.[18]

The other corruption-generating inequality begins once citizens are denied participation in government and authority except on the basis of exclusive criteria such as land, title, or party. All governments tend to act as dangerous self-interested factions, and members of the government try to assert their long-term prerogative to rule regardless of the initial form of government. All corrupt governments move toward hereditary power. The result might be a simple heriditary nobility or a de facto hereditary state such as a self-perpetuating one-party state or a merchant oligarchy as in Venice. Even elected officials of a democratic republic will move in this direction, as Machiavelli shows in [963] his study of the Decemvirate in the Roman Republic.[19]

Once a group gains exclusionary control of the government and authority—or, at least, has

[17]Plato (1957, 550c–556e); Machiavelli (1965, *Discourses*, Bk. 1, Chs. 2, 5, 46; *History of Florence*, Bk. 3, Chs. 5, 8–11); Rousseau (1964, *Discours sur l'inégalité*, pp. 171–74, 177–82, 202–04).

[18]Thucydides (1934, Bk. 2, Ch. 7); Machiavelli (1965, *History of Florence*, Bk. 7, Chs. 1–6); Rousseau (1964, *Discours sur l'economie*, pp. 252–62).

[19]Rousseau (1964, *Du contrat social*, Bk. 3, Ch. 10); Machiavelli (1965, *Discourses*, Bk. 1, Chs. 40–44).

first priority in access—it becomes morally rational to try to maintain this power position. A diverse variety of claims are used to justify this control. Among these claims are: a group has a greater interest in the state and more time because of its wealth; a group is better trained and more experienced as in a hereditary nobility; a group has more talent and commitment as in a one-party state. Over time these claims reduce to nothing more than rationalizations to maintain power. It is feasible that with strong socialization, discipline and tradition an exclusionary group would not unduly tyrannize the population and might rule in the common interests of all the citizens. Yet, even when the elite performs well, the people's perception of permanent inequality will undermine their loyalty.[20] More likely, the elite socialization will slip and the scions of the ruling group will ultimately use the government for their own aggrandizement or act to maintain their own prerogatives whenever they feel threatened by the claims of the citizenry. Only significant and guaranteed participation by the citizenry can ward off these tendencies.

Factions

One of the root meanings of corruption is literally "to break into many pieces." This is the fate of a corrupted state. The community was never expected to be homogeneous, but a just, equal and stable society needs a minimum set of rational and emotional commitments to the common welfare and the sustaining structures of the state. These social commitments enable the rifts and conflicts over inequality and human mischievousness to be reconciled peacefully and enable a community to defend itself, to provide social answers to basic human problems and to encourage gradual reform of injustice. The factions into which the community breaks destroy the loyalties which sustain this community.

These are not the simple factions of Madison's or economists' dreams. Neither Madison nor ersatz Madisonians account for the dangers wrought in the community by a true faction. *The History of Florence, The Discourses on the First Decade of Titus Livy* and *The Peloponnesian War* are, if anything, historical rejections

[20]Aristotle (1962, Bk. 5).

of the naive Madisonian and pluralist thesis that the conflict among factions will result in the prevention of tyranny or the long-term maximization of all citizens' welfare.

The factions are objective centers of power; they encompass families, corporations, unions, governmental bureaucracies and similar associations; their hallmarks are autonomous power and internal cohesion sufficient to distort government and to provide semigovernmental services for their dependents. They are capable of directing people and resources for the pursuit of their own goals against opposition, legal or otherwise. Their membership can possess loyalties, traditions and goals of their own and literally become "laws unto themselves" with quasi-official private police forces to rule their domains and resist the state if necessary.[21]

Commanding power, money and security, the factions develop dependents who rely upon them for welfare and services. In some ways the factions develop their own laws for their members. To protect and earn members' trust, they must often suborn government officials and gain privileges from the law. It becomes rational to work systematically to corrupt the government in order to maintain the faction's own basis of power.

As moral phenomena, factions put limited private interests before the public responsibilities of the citizens and the government, and they socialize the citizens into this framework. They engender citizens whose economic need and dependency are turned into quasi-self-interested loyalty to the faction, not to the community. Broken from basic loyalties to others in the community, the member of a faction begins to view law as a tool to further factional interests. Although little loyalty exists among atomized selfish people, factions try to engender some loyalty in their members simply to strengthen themselves. Since "very rarely do men understand how to be altogether bad or altogether good," the totally corrupt individual is a rarity.[22] Often the "love of a party," or ties of friendship or affection for a leader will create some tenuous loyalty among partisans. Rousseau suggests that although the "individual

[21]Machiavelli (1965, *History of Florence*, Bk. 3, Ch. 5; Bk. 7, Chs. 1, 2, 23; *Discourses*, Bk. 1, Ch. 46); Rousseau (1964, *Du contrat social*, Bk. 3, Chs. 10, 11, 15).

[22]Machiavelli (1965, *Discourses*, Bk. 1, Ch. 27).

will" supplants "the communal self" in a corrupted person, these "small societies" will act as sort of a pseudo "general will" for the [964] individual.[23] A person might even come to internalize the goals of a faction and become loyal in the fuller emotional and moral sense. At this point the loyalty has been narrowed to the concerns of the faction, not the common good. Civic loyalty is undermined and either destroyed or transferred to lesser associations. By narrowing the focus of loyalty, the faction also undermines disinterestedness by limiting the morally significant individuals to the faction's membership.

In gauging the loyalty which exists in such factions, a distinction can be made between groups which evolve from primary emotional and ethical loyalties, such as clans, families and churches, and those which develop from more institutionalized corporate groupings. This second set of corporate groups might be further divided into consciously self-interested factions such as corporations and unions or more public or governmental factions such as rogue bureaucracies, secret liberation societies or political parties. In both cases, but especially that of the public groups, there might exist a complex mix of private, organizational and public interest motives in each participant. Thus official vigilantism might involve individuals seemingly committed to communal loyalties but using the corrupted methods of factions. This last situation is the most complex and dangerous because individuals with authentic loyalty to the common good utilize factional methods which only further contribute to the corrupted political practices. In spite of relatively sincere beginnings, a public interest faction maximizes the long-term dangers of the faction by quite unconsciously asserting its own prerogatives while the members still believe they are serving the community.

The crucial factor in the unstable competition among factions is the possession of the government. The government can be regarded as a complex of symbols, office, institutions, laws and personnel to make, administer and enforce concrete policies. This complex confers

[23]Machiavelli (1965, *History of Florence*, Bk. 4, Ch. 27; Bk. 5, Ch. 31; Bk. 7, Ch. 1); Rousseau (1964, *Du contrat social*, Bk. 4, Ch. 1; *Discours sur l'economie*, pp. 245–47, 252–54).

the mantle of legitimate concern for the common good and can still command some residual loyalties among all citizens. Since it is systematically and constantly financed, the government exists independently as a set of resources which can be "captured" by any faction.

In theory, the government is the institution open to maximum participation by all citizens. It passes and administers laws which guarantee the economic and moral integrity of *all* citizens. By the mobilization of overarching loyalties, it provides the means of reconciling conflict, maximizing communal cooperation, and maintaining common defense. Politics ought to be the arena in which the greatest amount of human virtue and care is exercised. In reality, the government becomes a factional tool used by individual factions to protect and aggrandize themselves while limiting the power of other factions. The government might begin to act as a faction and thus encourage even greater and easier penetration of the government by self-interested factions. Once the dynamics of competition and factionalization begin, they extend to all sections of the state. Only by aligning with or forming a faction can citizens hope to influence policy effectively. Even virtuous and loyal citizens are reduced to the expediency of so-called "public interest" factions.

The relations between quasi-autonomous factions and the government are quite complex. The dominant factions need to maintain an effective government which can resist or control the poor.[24] The government will either repress the poor or confuse them with illusions of efficacy, while the factions ensure their own power and penetrate the government by subversion of office or party. This permits the government to control the masses while neutralizing its threat to the dominant factions.

When a number of fairly coequal factions compete, government can also serve some important functions. A "balance of power" politics might emerge where the government performs a referee function. Overall it would legitimize the power and wealth distribution, perform effective police and defense functions and prevent the factions from tearing each other apart and upsetting the balance. As a

---

[24]Aristotle (1962, Bk. 5, Ch. 6); Rousseau (1964, *Discours sur l'inégalité,* pp. 176–78).

regulator of the poor or a referee, the government enforces "the rules of the game" to minimize violence and regularize relations among factions.

The moral and political relations of factions to the community are primarily those of convenience, not loyalty. Contractual arrangements and bargaining do not reflect a moral consensus. The dynamics of factions are towards dominance and control, not simple competitive co-existence. While this dominance may often be indirect, the domination of all or part of the state by a family, corporate entity or other faction is a constant tendency of the politics of faction. Even war will not dampen [965] the competition among factions to control the state—it may make the competition worse. Thucydides' narration of the history of Cleon or Alcibiades and their factions in Athens demonstrates the type of conflict involved. In his analysis of Genoa, Machiavelli explores a totally corrupt state where a private corporation of merchants, the Bank of San Giorgio, achieved such a degree of control and discipline that it performed all the effective functions of rule; the government and the rest of the state were totally without effective control.[25]

Patterns of a Corrupt Politics

Inequality combined with the decline of civic virtue and factional competition produces several characteristic patterns of politics. These are: (1) the disintegration of effective public law and fair adjudication, (2) the decline of a meaningful political discourse, (3) the emergence of violence as the dominant substratum of legal and political relations, (4) the constant tendency towards demogoguery and class war, and (5) an increasing unlikelihood of successful reform or revolution.

1. *Law and Adjudication.* Human beings are loyal to internalized laws which they accept and which embody their beliefs and emotional commitments. When people are loyal, even to themselves, it is almost always to impersonal rules of conduct embodied in an individual's character.[26] Political laws are the medium by

[25]Machiavelli (1965, *History of Florence*, Bk. 8, Ch. 29). The story of Cleon is narrated in Thucydides (1934), Bks. 3–5, and the story of Alcibiades in Bks. 6–7.

[26]Royce (1969, Pt. 2, Chs. 1, 5, esp. 866 ff.).

which politics and personal morality interrelate. They are embedded in the education, the customs, the habits, and the social pressures of daily life and form the bases of concrete moral loyalties. The legal and judicial systems give substance to the moral and economic integrity of the citizens and assure reasonably impartial treatment for all citizens.

The effectiveness of laws depends upon a complex of factors. Only when the vast majority of citizens spontaneously accept the laws even when they disagree with them, can law be a tool for community direction and reform. In a healthy state coercive enforcement is peripheral to the law. This loyalty is reinforced by constitutional limits, political participation and reliable and fair methods of adjudication and conflict resolution.

Once certain groups can unduly influence legislation, buy immunity from judgment and punishment, or use the judicial system against their opponents, citizens will lose faith in the state and join factions for their own protection.[27] The fractious populace views law as privately legislated, selectively enforced and administered on the basis of privilege, not equity. Law loses the trust which it needs for practical effectiveness, and obedience even to good laws must be forced or bribed.[28] This cynical rejection of law, except when necessary or convenient, saps the vitality of law for political direction.

Another litmus test of a corrupt polity occurs when even reform laws are futile and sometimes precipitate far more harm than good. The rich dominant factions will ignore them with virtual impunity; the administrators will sabotage them; the citizens whom they are designed to benefit will mistrust them or use them as a pretext for violence. For example, when the Gracchi attempted to resurrect the egalitarian Agrarian Laws in the late Roman Republic, the laws were unenforceable against the upper classes and the Gracchi's efforts precipitated uncontrollable violence and the Marian civil wars.[29]

While the dominant factions might use the

[27]Machiavelli (1965, *Discourses*, Bk. 1, Chs. 7, 8, 24; *History of Florence*, Bk. 3, Ch. 5; Bk. 4, Ch. 28).

[28]Machiavelli (1965, *Discourses*, Bk. 1, Ch. 55); Rousseau (1966, Ch. 20).

[29]Machiavelli (1965, *Discourses*, Bk. 1, Ch. 37).

legal system for conflict resolution among themselves, the law is unable to control most factions for the common good. This corruption of fair conflict resolution leaves violence and subversion as the methods of redress. The lack of "normal" access engenders more apathy and violence especially among minor factions and atomized masses.

2. *Political Discourse.* The transformation of law into a symbol of oppression rather than equality or equity reflects the destruction of a viable political discourse.[30] An effective political discourse depends upon the ability of traditional political symbols and rhetoric to evoke spontaneous emotions of affirmation for the possessors of the symbols. It also assumes that the structures covered by the symbols are capable of rational evaluation and discussion to complement and deepen the emotional affirmation. In non-corrupt discourse the symbols not only evoke trust and loyalty in citizens but call forth a deep sense of responsibility from those in authority. "The office makes the man." Oaths, laws and the moral goals of the community are rationally known and emotionally compelling to both citizen and ruler.

[966]

In a healthy state the meanings of the basic political symbols are firmly established. The political battles are over the possession of those symbols and the policies which they justify, but do not involve fundamental ideological conflicts. Political activity is removed from simple coercive power relations. Reason is delimited by points of authoritative reference and a degree of peace and consent exists which enables people to persuade one another rather than resort to force. An authentic political discourse establishes a realm of ordered coherence where

---

[30]Wolin (1960, Ch. 1) mentions certain classical themes which identify both political philosophy and politics as human activity. Pocock (1973, Chs. 1, 2, 7) argues that these themes and countless others are embedded in languages, customs and symbols of peculiar historical eras. They carry significant power to explain, justify and persuade individuals of those eras. Pitkin (1972, Chs. 3, 5–7, 9) provides part of the epistemological bases for the linguistic aspects of the theory of political discourse. The study of the symbolic, as opposed to purely linguistic, aspects of the theory has been carried out by authors too numerous to mention; notable among them are Ernst Cassirer and George Herbert Mead. Edelman (1964) summarizes them.

nonoppressive patterns of authority can exist and evolve.

This orderly realm may escape the stigma of corruption for a long time. Constant efforts will be made under its aegis to remedy injustice and inequality. All classes, particularly the upper classes, will be recalled to symbolic adherence to the common good. Reformers in Florence and the Roman republic constantly tried to use the institutions and laws to "restore" the state.[31] However, the solutions in a corrupt state are usually incomplete and cosmetic. The basic inequality will still remain and citizens will finally recognize the futility of attempts to "restore" or "renew" the commonwealth. The recognition of the hypocritical manipulations of the government by the upper classes, gives the *coup de grace* to any rational or emotional loyalties which cut across class or faction.

Thus corruption destroys the coherence of the political discourse. Exercising little emotional or rational power, symbols are used to rationalize gain. Political controversy now often focuses on the very meaning or existence of the symbols. When symbols do command the loyalty of some citizens, they confuse and oppress the people by giving them false hope.[32] Thucydides relates how oaths, promises and treaties were violated whenever "calculation" suggested to a Greek faction that it might gain some advantage from treachery. Such sophistication becomes equated with "superior intelligence." Calumny becomes a normal rhetorical tool and good advice is often ignored because of impugned motives. With no "language of persuasion," almost any incident from a slander to sexual infidelity can unleash violence in the tinder box of a corrupt state. Political rhetoric degenerates to a politics of noise.[33]

3. Violence. With the greater inequality and the decline of the legal system and political discourse, normal political relations in the state

[31]Machiavelli (1965, *Discourses*, Bk. 1, Ch. 7; Bk. 3, Ch. 1 and passim; *History of Florence*, passim).

[32]Rousseau (1964, *Discours sur les sciences*, pp. 5–26; *Discours sur l'inégalité*, pp. 176–84).

[33]Thucydides (1934, Bk. 3, Chs. 9–11; Bk. 4, Ch. 14; Bk. 6, Chs. 18, 19; Bk. 8, Ch. 25); Aristotle (1962, Bk. 5, Chs. 4, 5); Machiavelli (1965, *Discourses*, Bk. 1, Chs. 7, 8, 40–44; Bk. 3, Ch. 26; *Prince*, Chs. 15–19; *History of Florence*, Bk. 3, Ch. 5; Bk. 4, Ch. 28; Bk. 6, Ch. 23).

are increasingly undergirded by violence. There is no longer the requisite consensual trust or loyalty to generate sufficient patience and compromise for workable and peaceful solutions to political problems. Crime increases in all orders of society and, although unable to deal effectively with upper-class crime, the government increasingly resorts to imprisonment and repression of citizen criminals. Respect for law declines and ruling requires greater emphasis upon coercion or social bribery.[34]

While physical violence is largely confined to relations between the rulers and masses, competition among factions involves increasing levels of deception, treachery, bribery and covert violence or assassination. Balance of power politics and the hope of economic gain may often lead to somewhat stable arrangements among the dominant factions, but the alliances become more brittle and disintegrate if any of the partners see a chance of significant gain. The "rules of the game" are increasingly violated and as they decline in efficacy, non-integrative violence increases. Machiavelli recounts how in the early Roman republic violence in the state identified weaknesses and enabled the republic to reintegrate and develop enduring solutions to the problems. But as factions became more polarized, the violence led to civil war and disintegration.[35]

Political solutions rest on a foundation of predatory violence and fear, not internalized acceptance. Coalition building becomes so unstable that even long-term interest and familial [967] ties cannot hold together factional alliances.[36] As the conflict becomes more acute, factions resort increasingly to imprisonment, exile and indirect punishments or segregation of other factions. Fair proposals for compromise are usually ignored and promises are soon broken. Fearing reprisals from the other side and having no confidence in the integrity of the government, more factions resort more quickly to violence or treachery. The moral bankruptcy of

[34]Machiavelli (1965, *Prince,* passim; *History of Florence,* Bks. 6, 7).

[35]Machiavelli (1965, *Discourses,* Bk. 1, Chs. 4, 17).

[36]Machiavelli (1965, *History of Florence,* Preface; Bk. 4, Ch. 2; Bk. 6, Ch. 9; Bk. 7, Ch. 1).

communal loyalty reaches its epitome when factions call in foreign intervention on their behalf even at the jeopardy of the state. Thucydides recounts how factional bitterness in Corcyra, Mytilene and Megara brought Athenians and Spartans into the cities and resulted in the end of effective freedom. For Thucydides one of the main causes of the extension of the Peloponnesian War was the tendency of corrupted factions to invite the dominant powers in to destroy their enemies. Machiavelli remonstrates about this same danger when he recounts the history of the Guelfs and Ghibellines in Florence and Italy.[37]

4. *Class War and Co-optation*. The rise of a permanent wealthy class and factions with quasi-governmental independence signals the existence of a permanent class of poor people. The poor have no independent means of economic subsistence and therefore depend upon the community, corporate groups, and the rich. The inequality is so great that "two societies" might be said to coexist.[38]

There will be endemic conflict in a state where poverty breeds "the courage of necessity" and riches breed "ambition, insolence and pride."[39] This conflict and violence, however, can result in just and enduring solutions if there is sufficient trust and loyalty among all citizens. Both classes must be willing to compromise and not push the other side to violence. In early Rome, Athens and Florence, constant class war was mitigated with compromise solutions such as the Roman Tribunate.[40] But a just and reasonable politics depends upon the willingness of factions to set limits upon their demands and to honor compromises with fellow citizens. Once the broad consensus breaks, loyal

---

[37]Thucydides (1934, Bk. 1, Chs. 4, 5; Bk. 2, Ch. 6; Bk. 3, Chs. 9–11; Bk. 4, Chs. 13, 14); Machiavelli (1965, *History of Florence*, Bk. 1, Ch. 4; *Discourses*, Bk. 2, Ch. 25; *Prince*, Ch. 11).

[38]Machiavelli (1965, *Discourses*, Bk. 1, Ch. 4); Rousseau (1964, *Du contrat social*, Bk. 4, Ch. 2).

[39]Thucydides (1934, Bk. 3, Ch. 9); Plato (1957, 421d–423b).

[40]Aristotle (1962, Bk. 5, Chs. 8, 9; Bk. 6, Ch. 5); Machiavelli (1965, *Discourses*, Bk. 1, Chs. 4, 17; *History of Florence*, Preface); Rousseau (1964, *Du contrat social*, Bk. 3, Ch. 9).

care will not temper vicious self-interest; the demands will escalate and the two classes and factions will participate in increasingly intractable conflict with no possibility of just compromises. In Plato's terms, the state becomes "two cities" locked in irreconcilable war.[41]

Corruption also extends to the poor. The inherent degradation of utter dependence provides no social or economic basis for a sense of self. Human relations break down under the constant competition for scarce jobs and resources. The desperate economic plight of the poor inculcates avarice merely for survival. They slowly lose a sense of loyalty to a community which cannot provide dignity or freedom for them. Laws which can be manipulated at will by the wealthy lose their spontaneous acceptance. Their work relations, families, religion and even friendly associations break down and leave the poor distrustful, envious, competitive and cynical. They become easy prey for the co-optative enticements of money or volunteer as recruits for mercenary or professional armies. In the army, at least, they gain the status and money denied them as citizens.

The poor are usually characterized by political inertia; they may periodically rebel, but without leaders and organization they fail. Although atomized, the corrupt state is vulnerable to damagogues such as Cleon, Marius or Alcibiades who can lead popular uprisings and expropriation attempts.[42] The fragmentation and ineffectiveness of the under class is accentuated by a number of political patterns: the elites recruit mercenaries to quell violence; a dole is established to take the edge off of desperate poverty; and finally the political myths of a united citizenry with equality before the law are perpetuated by external wars and periodic, highly publicized legal successes.

The emphasis upon the politics of factions and class is theoretically consistent. Most effective factions are products of the upper classes.

[41]Plato (1957, 423a).

[42]Thucydides (1934, Bk. 2, Ch. 7; Bk. 5, Chs. 14–17; Bk. 8, Chs. 25, 26); Aristotle (1962, Bk. 5, Chs. 4–6); Machiavelli (1965, *Discourses*, Bk. 1, Chs. 40, 57; *History of Florence*, Bk. 3, Chs. 13, 15–19); Plato, 565a–580e).

The maintenance of a power base and the capacity to suborn government require either wealth and organization or the internal cohesion of the kind found in an aristocratic family of the ruling class. The corrupted poor are notoriously deficient in all of the above. Factional competition is confined to the dominant classes and their allies with two great exceptions. [968]

In the first, a member of the elite or one of the dominant factions might try to provide the poor with leadership and mobilize them as a power base. The Duke of Athens in Florence and various Athenian aristocrats resorted to this policy with varying degrees of success.[43] A leader might also gain control of the army, which is largely recruited from the poor, and use it to gain power. When the poor are armed and effectively led, class war erupts. The danger is so real that the upper classes in a corrupt polity often fear to arm their lower classes except in last-ditch defense.[44]

The second exception might be called the politics of liberation and co-optation. The seething dissatisfaction of the oppressed generates factions of a different order. These are liberation factions which have the dual goals of freeing both their own members and the entire society from inequality and injustice.

The initial mobilization usually depends upon an attack upon the regime and its symbolic panoply. The liberation attack simultaneously weakens general respect for the communal values and institutions and seeks to either "renew" or "overthrow" the state, often in the name of the very values which it attacks. Most revolutionary attempts, unless part of a general class war, will probably be repressed. In a less ambitious strategy, however, the factions might gradually win access and power and bring about some concrete changes.

[43]Thucydides (1934, Bk. 2, Ch. 7; Bk. 8, Chs. 24–26); Machiavelli (1965, *History of Florence*, Bk. 2, Chs. 34–36).

[44]Thucydides (1934, Bk. 2, Ch. 8; Bk. 3, Ch. 9; Bk. 8, Chs. 24–26); Plato (1957, 551d–552a); Aristotle (1962, Bk. 5, Ch. 6; Bk. 6, Ch. 7). To overcome this problem the Spartan elite developed a stratagem to identify the 200 best helots and then arranged for their destruction. Having eliminated all the potential leaders among the helots, the Spartans could then arm them for defense (Thucydides, 1934, Bk. 5, Ch. 14).

The claim to serve all citizens coupled with its factional nature creates serious weakness in the liberation strategy. Success suddenly makes the maintenance of the faction's power critical. Over the long run the insurgent faction ends up imitating the dominant factions and often supports the power distribution in order to preserve its own ability to influence policy. The whole policy is assisted by the faction's ambivalent disrespect for the goals and institutions which it both attacks and exploits. This encourages its use of informal power politics rather than open participatory procedures. Ironically the faction's initial polemics often make it more difficult to resuscitate active community commitment, and as long as they accomplish something under the "reformed" system, they often do not try. One of the most common examples of this is the fate of workers' organizations. Machiavelli describes how the Florentine guilds were initially designed to gain economic and political power for workers. However, they became stratified into two different levels and one level became a part of the ruling elite while many of their own members and nonorganized workers were squeezed out.[45]

5. *The Unlikelihood of Reform and Revolution.* Once corruption becomes widespread, there is very little possibility of successful, significant reform of injustice in the state—even a successful violent revolution becomes almost an impossibility. Since the theory emphasizes the moral as well as the economic and institutional requirements of a just state, any significant legal, political or even economic changes will be quite irrelevant since the citizens will either frustrate the goals or use the new arrangements for their own radically self-interested benefit. Without the consensual loyalty and trust of the citizenry, the new reforms will simply be shams to rationalize the continuation of corrupt practices. Citing the failure of Solon's laws at Athens and the policy of equal division of land at Leucas and elsewhere, Aristotle argues that the radical redistribution of wealth will accomplish little unless the education and mores also changes. For Machiavelli, the corruption of the mores of the citizens

[45]Machiavelli (1965, *History of Florence*, Bk. 3, Chs. 11, 12).

in Florence and Rome was the final limit on all
government reform.[46] This pessimism accounts
for a paradox in thinkers like Plato and
Rousseau who provide deep and ruthless indict-
ments of their society but whose practical
politics are fairly conservative and only ameli-
orative.

Revolutionary attempts at reform usually
engender far more harm and tyranny than
good. Any revolution is dangerous and violent
and has tyrannical tendencies. When the people   [969]
do not have the habits, customs and willingness
to compromise and make the sacrifices for the
revolutionary institutions, then the revolution
usually requires a maximum of long-term violence and elite leadership to gain adherence to
"reforms."[47]

There is, however, a very limited possibility
of a great and revolutionary "renewal" of the
country. The praxis of a violent revolution, a
great religious crusade or awakening, a desperate war, or a combination of any of these are all
historically verified manners of regenerating
communal loyalty and concerted action to
overcome class and factional barriers. Machiavelli cannot help but remark that Florence is
usually most harmonious when it is engaged in
war.

None of these approaches is particularly
recommended. Violent revolutions rarely happen and even more rarely succeed. Religious
revolutions, while more likely to succeed, are
even more quickly corrupted and destroyed
than secular revolutions. Wars may temporarily
reintegrate the society, but the class and factional competition is only repressed. As the war
goes on and the poor bear a disproportionate
burden of its cost, foreign intervention becomes
more likely or a dominant military leader may
take over. The war will wreck the state. Only
consistent good leadership, real participation
and abolition of massive inequalities will "re-

[46]Aristotle (1962, Bk. 2, Chs. 6, 7; Bk. 5);
Machiavelli (1965, *Discourses*, Bk. 1, Chs. 17, 18;
History of Florence, Bk. 3, Ch. 5; Bk. 4, Ch. 1);
Rousseau (1964, *Discours sur l'inégalité*, pp. 191–93;
Du contrat social, Bk. 2, Ch. 8; *Discours sur
l'economie*, pp. 252–53).

[47]Machiavelli (1965, *Discourses*, Bk. 1, Chs.
16–18); Rousseau (1964, *Du contrat social*, Bk. 2,
Chs. 8–10).

store" the state to its original principles of justice, fraternity and equality.[48]   [970]

Education:
Formal, Family, Religion and Militia

Inequality dominates the causes of systematic corruption, but human nature must also be addressed. Education and socialization must inculcate disciplined commitment to other citizens and loyalty to the commonweal.[49] Customs, habits and mores can sometimes be strong enough to sustain institutional integrity and loyalty among citizens even after great inequality exists. Education and socialization, however, fight a rear-guard action. Neither equality without education nor education without equality can sustain a just, stable and equal state. Corruption spreads beyond the political realm and cripples the structures which generate reasonably disinterested loyalty and civic virtue. As relations become instrumentalized under the pressure of inequality, citizens lose the capacity for piety, dutifulness and affectionate loyalty. Four vital areas of political socialization are undermined: formal education, the family, organized religion and mutual self-defense.

The society's civic educational system is corrupted by several onslaughts. As the corruption of values in government and the wider society becomes more apparent, it becomes harder to find teachers who can seriously teach these values. Teaching, itself, becomes an undervalued occupation in a world of great economic and social disparities, and fewer talented people enter it. Additionally the teachers and schools come under constant attack from various factions for teaching a set of values which might lead a student to question a particular faction's place in society or damage a faction's future recruitment. The schools also

[48]Thucydides (1934, Bk. 2, Ch. 7; Bk. 6, Chs. 18, 19; Bk. 8, Chs. 24–26); Aristotle (1962, Bk. 5, Ch. 7); Machiavelli (1965, *History of Florence*, Preface; Bk. 2, Ch. 27; Bk. 3, Ch. 11; Bk. 4, Ch. 28; *Discourses*, Bk. 1, Ch. 25; Bk. 3, Ch. 1); Rousseau (1964, *Du contrat social*, Bk. 2, Ch. 8).

[49]Plato (1957, 386a–416c; 423e–424c); Aristotle (1962, Bk. 2, Chs. 7, 8; Bks. 7, 8); Rousseau (1964, *Du contrat social*, Bk. 2, Chs. 6, 12; *Discours sur l'economie*, pp. 260–61).

confront students and parents who see that the "older" concern with rational and humane mores and loyalty are counterproductive in a world of atomized selfishness and factional competition. The schools are slowly transformed into nothing more than occupational training for the factions and become devoid of any independent values linked to loyalty to the common good and other citizens.

The incapacity for loyalty also wrecks the social stability of the family. The loyalty of husband and wife lasts only as long as it is convenient; adultery and divorce become normal and justifiable whenever duties of fidelity interfere with immediate pleasures. As the parents liberate themselves, the children are neglected or shunted off because they seem unrewarding.

The lack of loyalty and care in the family destroys the family as a socializing agent. In families citizens acquire basic moral beliefs and learn rudimentary forms of justice, cooperation and affirmation of authority.[50] As parents betray one another and lose confidence in their authority, children learn to ignore parental authority and pursue their own interests. Individuals learn to perceive all law and morality as oppression.[51] If children have no respect for rules given by parents, they will never accept laws which impinge upon them for the benefit of others.

The corruption of organized religion destroys another voluntary organization which sustains moral commitments to others.[52] The change is not so much one of religiosity as of piety. The moral claims of religion to limit avarice or encourage charity lose their force. Fear of God wanes and the self-sacrifice of piety is outweighed by love of gain.

[195]

The decay of religion occurs on two levels. First, citizens slowly leave the churches or transform them into purely social or private activities. Second, the church itself becomes a faction. To maintain its institutional power it might ally itself with the elite and then act as

---

[50]Machiavelli (1965, *Discourses*, Bk. 1, Chs. 11–15; Bk. 2, Ch. 2; Bk. 3, Ch. 33); Rousseau (1964, *Discours sur l'economie*, pp. 261–62).

[51]Plato (1957, 553a–553e; 562e–565e).

[52]Machiavelli (1965, *Discourses*, Bk. 1, Chs. 11–15; Bk. 2, Ch. 2; Bk. 3, Ch. 33); Rousseau (1964, *Du contrat social*, Bk. 2, Ch. 7; Bk. 4, Ch. 8).

an agent of control rather than one of grace and worship. The constant vacillation of the Delphic oracle among the various Greek factions reflects such bankruptcy. The religion might also follow the strategy of the Roman Catholic Church of Machiavelli's or Rousseau's time and use its spiritual authority to gain riches, land and power for itself while sacrificing the moral integrity of its leaders and the spiritual welfare of its members.[53]

Religion's inherently mysterious and evocative relation with people gives it the constant potential to renew the moral life of the community. Its clergy can be corrupted, its membership thinned, but the possibility of prophecy and regeneration remain. The resurrection of Florence under its unarmed prophet, Savonarola, and Geneva's transformation by its armed prophet, Calvin, were classic examples of religion's "restorative" powers.[54]

The increasing dissolution of the citizens' bonds of loyalty ends the state's ability to generate its own militia. In a just and stable state a voluntary citizen army served three purposes. First, it was a counterweight to the rich and powerful. As long as the citizens controlled the main source of legitimate coercion and defense, the loyalty of the elites was reinforced by fear of arms. Second, loyal and committed citizens made better and less ambitious soldiers. Third, a participatory militia was a great equalizer. It pulled all classes of society together and made it more democratic in its values and reinforced the loyalty of citizens for one another.[55]

In an unequal and corrupted state the bulk of the citizenry have little reason to defend a state which gives them so little. The elites care too much for themselves and possess their own means of protection. They also fear to see the poorer citizens armed. The state is reduced to

[53]Thucydides (1934, Bk. 1, Chs. 5, 6); Machiavelli (1965, *Discourses*, Bk. 1, Ch. 12; *History of Florence*, Bk. 8, Ch. 17; *Prince*, Chs. 7, 11, 12); Rousseau (1964, *Du contrat social*, Bk. 4, Ch. 8).

[54]Rousseau (1964, *Du contrat social*, Bk. 2, Ch. 7); Machiavelli (1965, *Prince*, Ch. 6; *Discourses*, Bk. 2, Ch. 16; Bk. 3, Chs. 1, 24; Letter 3, Vol. 2, pp. 886–89).

[55]Machiavelli (1965, *Discourses*, Bk. 2, Ch. 10; *Art of War*, Preface; Bk. 1); Rousseau (1964, *Considérations sur le Pologne*, pp. 1012–20).

expedients for defense: payoffs to enemies, mercenary soldiers, wars by proxy and a professional army. The bribery scheme works in the short run, but it is too dangerous in the long run and often generates internal unrest because of the humiliation and cost involved.[56] Mercenaries, like Francisco Sforza, The Duke of Milan, are inefficient, expensive, often disloyal and liable to turn on the country and conquer it.[57] Proxy wars, as the Athenians discovered in trying to rule their empire indirectly, are extremely costly and they usually involve unreliable allies and pull the state into increasingly larger and costlier intervention.[58] The last solution, the professional army, is much more militarily efficacious, but it poses a great threat to internal freedom. The army is loyal to those who pay it and can easily become an adjunct to the ruling classes. The maintenance of a standing army involves larger budgets and creates many opportunities for corrupt alliances between the military and various economic factions which supply it. Finally, if the army should develop its own inner cohesion, the army can become the most powerful faction in the state. The state can either buy it off with great sums of money or the military faction may sell itself to a political entrepreneur or simply take over the government.[59]   [196]

Conclusion

The corruption of a state encompasses the changes in the aggregate social and political relations which in turn reflect the changes in the basic moral constitution of the citizens. While this theory provides a model of the relations among inequality, mores, factions and politics; it makes no pretense of neutrality. It explicates the decay of a socio-political unit into a world where right, fulfillment and

[56]Machiavelli (1965, *Discourses*, Bk. 2, Chs. 10, 30).

[57]Machiavelli (1965, *Prince*, Chs. 12, 13; *History of Florence*, Bks. 1–6, passim, esp. Bk. 1, Ch. 39; Bk. 4, Ch. 24; Bk. 5, Ch. 34; Bk. 6, Chs. 1, 20).

[58]Thucydides (1934, Bks. 3–8, passim, esp. Bk. 3, Chs. 10, 11; Bk. 5, Ch. 16; Bk. 7, Ch. 21; Bk. 8, Chs. 24–25; Bk. 1, Ch. 4).

[59]Machiavelli (1965, *Art of War*, pp. 566–76; *Prince*, Chs. 6, 12; *Discourses*, Bk. 2, Ch. 12); Rousseau (1964, *Discours sur l'economie*, p. 269).

happiness are systematically unattainable in normal relations among citizens. This recognition of the sadness and evil of the phenomenon makes most of the analysis a prelude to prescriptions. The theory is militantly non-utopian and recognizes that no social or political system will ever "transform" human beings into spontaneously altruistic and caring individuals with sufficient strength to transcend the temptations of selfishness and arrogance. It also manifests an abiding pessimism about the success of significant reforms once corruption becomes widespread; it does, however, offer a number of positive prescriptions for struggling states.

First, corruption is a part of the human condition, and practical honest politics requires structures designed to limit, discourage, and channel these tendencies. Day-to-day politics must be conditioned by a concrete evaluation of the moral beliefs of citizens and their willingness to obey laws. There are times when even good and well-intentioned laws would create nothing but social unrest and actually undermine the goal for which they were designed.

Second, any viable polity must concentrate upon education to inculcate loyalty towards fellow citizens and create an initial willingness to sacrifice self-interest to the common welfare. The need for universal political education is the most important aspect of politics. Primary institutions which lay the foundations of a just and stable authority must have strong legal and structural supports.

Third, political participation continues the process of political education and contributes to the stability of the regime. Massive substantive participation by all citizens in public office and public service can offset the unequal classes and factions. It also democratizes and reinforces the loyalty of all citizens. This openness and participation also encourages the maximum use of the political processes to accommodate conflict and violence. In the long run, open participation through limited terms in office, widespread elections, and rotation of all bureaucratic offices will prevent governmental agencies from turning into isolated non-responsible factions.

Finally, it is absolutely necessary that severe limits be placed upon great accumulations of wealth and hereditary privilege. The entire dialectic of injustice and corruption begins with

such inequality. A healthy polity must prevent
any effective derogation of its power to private
governments and destroy any factions which
gain enough power to consistently subvert the
law. The theory insists upon the absolute
danger of a permanently impoverished class.
Politics must insure the economic integrity of
all citizens in terms of basic needs and work or
run the risk of complete corruption and class
war.

The corruption of states and the corruption
of people proceed hand-in-hand. It has been the
dream of diverse ideologies that one problem
could be solved without the other—my analysis
suggests otherwise. To take corruption seriously
is to take civic virtue seriously; to take civic
virtue seriously is to demand not just moral
education but to demand substantive participation, and economic and political equality.

References

Aristotle (1962). *Politics*. Edited and translated by
    Ernest Barker. New York: Oxford University Press:
    Galaxy Books.
Bailyn, Bernard (1967). *The Ideological Origins of the
    American Revolution*. Cambridge, Mass.: Harvard
    University Press, Belknap Press.
Edelman, Murray (1964). *Symbolic Uses of Politics*.
    Urbana and Chicago: University of Illinois Press.
Machiavelli, Niccolò (1965). *The Art of War*. In Allan
    Gilbert (ed. and trans.), *Machiavelli: The Chief
    Works and Others*, Vol. 2. Durham, N.C.: Duke
    University Press, pp. 561–726.
———— *Discourses on the First Decade of Titus
    Livius. Chief Works*, Vol. 1, pp. 174–529.
———— *The History of Florence. Chief Works*, Vol. 3,
    pp. 1025–1435.
———— *The Prince. Chief Works*, Vol. 1, pp. 5–96.
Oxford English Dictionary, Compact Edition. (1971).
    New York: Oxford University Press.
Pitkin, Hanna (1972). *Wittgenstein and Justice*. Berke-
    ley: University of California Press.
Plato (1957). *The Republic*. Translated by A. D.
    Lindsay. New York: Dutton.
Pocock, J. G. A. (1973). *Politics, Language and Time*.
    New York: Atheneum, Studies in Political Theory.
———— (1975). *The Machiavellian Moment*. Princeton:
    Princeton University Press.
Rousseau, Jean-Jacques (1964). *Considérations sur le
    gouvernement de Pologne*. In Bernard Gagnebin
    and Marcel Raymond (eds.), *Oeuvres complètes de
    Jean-Jacques Rousseau*, Vol. 3. Paris: Bibliothèque
    de la Pléiade, pp. 953–1041.
———— *Du contrat social. Oeuvres complètes*, Vol. 3,
    pp. 349–470.

_____ *Discours sur l'economie politique. Oeuvres complètes*, Vol. 3, pp. 241–78.   [972]

_____ *Discours sur l'origine et les fondemens de l'inégalité parmi les hommes. Oeuvres complètes*, Vol. 3, pp. 111–223.

_____ *Discours sur les sciences et les arts. Oeuvres complètes*, Vol. 3, pp. 1–30.

_____ *Projet de constitution pour la Corse. Oeuvres complètes*, Vol. 3, pp. 901–39.

_____ (1966). *Essay on the Origin of Language Which Treats of Melody and Musical Imitation*. In John H. Moran and Alexander Gode (trans.), *On the Origins of Language*. New York: Ungar.

Royce, Josiah (1969). *The Philosophy of Loyalty*. In John J. McDermott (ed.), *Basic Writings*, Vol. 2. Chicago: University of Chicago Press.

Thucydides (1934). *The Peloponnesian War*. In Robert Crawley (trans.), *The Complete Works of Thucydides*. New York: Random House, Modern Library.

Wolin, Sheldon S. (1960). *Politics and Vision*. Boston: Little, Brown.

Wood, Gordon S. (1969). *The Creation of the American Republic, 1776–1787*. New York: Norton.   [973]

[10]

Graeme C. Moodie

On Political Scandals and Corruption

SCANDAL AND CORRUPTION ARE CUSTOMARILY THOUGHT OF
in much the same ways as pigs and whistles; they go together.
Strangely, however, academic studies of corruption seem to pay
little attention to scandal.[1] It is strange if only because in societies like this corruption tends to be obscure, a condition in
which its participants wish it to remain, and it is to the occasional scandal that we are indebted for what knowledge is
generally accessible. This is particularly true in Britain where
the major scandals have usually been followed (sometimes
illuminated) by official inquiries; certainly that has been the
practice in this century from the Marconi shares scandal in 1913
to the Poulson scandal sixty years later which spawned both a
committee and a Royal Commission.[2] A closer look at the incidence of political scandal, this article will suggest, is an additional tool for the study of corruption and perhaps particularly
so for comparative studies. A more fundamental (and more
widely canvassed) problem, however, is so to define corruption
as to facilitate reliable comparisons across temporal and cultural
boundaries. We will first discuss that problem.

Current writing about political corruption tends to leave aside
that wide notion of corruption as deterioration or decay which,
for example, preoccupied Plato and Machiavelli; it is concerned
more commonly with a narrower range of transgressions by
holders of office. Heidenheimer suggests that virtually all the

---

[1] For example, I have noticed very few mentions and no discussion of it in that
invaluable pioneering compendium, Arnold J. Heidenheimer (ed.), *Political Corruption. Readings in Comparative Analysis*, Holt, Rinehart & Winston, 1970.

[2] The Radcliffe-Maud Committee on Local Government Rules of Conduct which
reported in 1974 and the Salmon Commission on Standards of Conduct in Public
Life which reported in 1976.

definitions encountered in the modern literature can be grouped under one or other of three headings: public-office-centred, market-centred and public-interest centred. The emphasis is behavioural in all cases, and there seems to be a near consensus round the public-office kind of definition. One example is the definition put forward by J. S. Nye as: 'behaviour which deviates from the normal duties of a public role because of private regarding . . . , pecuniary or status gains; or violates rules against the exercise of certain types of private-regarding influence. This includes such behaviour as bribery . . . ; nepotism . . . ; and misappropriation . . .'.[3] Similar, but incorporating an allusion to the public interest, is Friedrich's usage. In discussing the core meaning of the term he says that corruption occurs 'whenever a power holder who is charged with doing certain things, that is a responsible functionary or office holder, is by monetary or other rewards, . . . induced to take actions which favour whoever provides the reward and thereby damage the group or organization to which the functionary belongs'.[4] Despite the proper warning that 'the search for the true definition of corruption is, like the pursuit of the Holy Grail, endless, exhausting and ultimately futile'[5] it is still necessary to devote more space to the pursuit of a serviceable one.

The main problem is that definitions like Nye's seem to be too culture-bound to permit comparative studies either across time (Britain today and in the eighteenth century, for example, when many of the practices he instances were not considered corrupt) or across cultures (in particular, Western and many developing countries where, for example, 'nepotism' is an obligation or a small bribe is no more corrupt than a tip is thought to be in the average European restaurant). There is much to be said for operating only with local standards — defining corruption as what is thought to be so in any given society. But this option seems to impede comparative studies of corruption and it is evidently difficult to eschew evaluations of some of the practices encountered or to avoid intruding a more constant element

[3] Heidenheimer, *op. cit.*, pp. 1—10. See too the brief survey in S. Riley, 'Teaching Political Corruption', *Teaching Politics*, 8, 1979, pp. 71—8.

[4] C. J. Friedrich, *The Pathology of Politics*, Harper & Row, 1972, p. 128.

[5] Robert J. Williams, 'The Problems of Corruption: A Conceptual and Comparative Analysis', a paper delivered to a Public Administration Committee Conference in York, 1976, p. 2.

in ideas of corruption. Thus, in a well-known article,[6] Colin
Leys stresses the relativity of norms, but also suggests that 'the
idea of a society economically stagnating in the grip of a self-
seeking and *corrupt* elite is not a pure fantasy' (emphasis not in
the original), which seems to imply a more universal meaning to
the term. Somewhat similarly, R. J. Williams, in the article from
which I have already quoted, first suggests that, in contradistinc-
tion to the United States, 'in most African states, it is the pursuit and possession of political power which enables its wielders
to acquire private wealth', an activity he seems to hold is not
corrupt (i.e. by the relevant local standards), and then proceeds
to suggest that 'in the African context at least, a politically
indoctrinated bureaucracy may be a better safeguard against
corruption than an allegedly impartial one'. Whether to use
'corruption' in a completely relative sense or in a more stable
and transcendent one is, it seems, a very sharp dilemma.

The problem exists, of course, within societies as well as between them. Samuel Plunkitt's distinction between honest and
dishonest graft is well known.[7] The key to his distinction may
thus be paraphrased (somewhat euphemistically): any public
worker, contract, or real estate development will provide some
private individuals and groups with jobs, windfall profits or other
accidental benefits. 'Honest graft' ensures that such inevitable
private benefit is deliberately and not accidentally channelled
in particular directions. Dishonest graft would also involve
cheating, short-changing, stealing, adulteration of service or
such other conventionally immoral behaviour. One does not
need to go all the way with Plunkitt to agree that corruption is
not always particularly immoral any more than it is always
illegal. 'One does not condemn a Jew for bribing his way out of
a concentration camp' to take a particularly clear example.[8]

Motive, intention and context thus enter into our judgments
even about domestic corruption. Generally, too, they seem to

[6] 'What is the Problem of Corruption?' *Journal of Modern African Studies*, 3(2),
1965, pp. 215–30. Most is reprinted in Heidenheimer, *op. cit.* pp. 31–7 and 341–5.
In my view insufficient attention has been paid to his recommendations about how
to study corruption.

[7] See William L. Riordon, *Plunkitt of Tammany Hall* (1st ed., 1905). In the Dutton,
1963, edition see, in particular, pp. xxii, 4–5, 30–32, and 37–40.

[8] Susan Rose-Ackerman, *Corruption. A Study in Political Economy*, Academic
Press, 1978, p. 9. This is a particularly valuable study for anyone interested in the
conditions favourable to corruption and thus with its 'cure'.

affect the ease or difficulty with which we draw the line of acceptability between various practices: between (say) contributing to Nixon's secret campaign funds in 1972 in return for the dropping of an anti-trust law case and a British trade union's increased contribution to the Labour Party's election fund in 1974 because it agreed with Labour policy towards industrial relations legislation; between filling civil service posts with one's kith and kin in West Africa, appointing other former pupils of one's exclusive school to positions in a British cabinet, and using one's children as aides-de-camp (as Churchill and F. D. Roosevelt did) or as roving presidential ambassadors (as Carter does); or between giving a statesman the pen with which he signs a treaty, giving a standard discount to all buyers,[9] and winning a contract for the sale of aircraft by massive and selective bribery at the highest levels of government and public office.

The problem of relativity can, however, be over-stated. It need not vitiate comparative studies provided only that care is taken with the terms of the comparison. One approach, suggested by David H. Bayley,[10] is to stick to the customary denotations of the term as used in the West, namely, bribery, nepotism and misappropriation. He defends this usage because many Third World elites tend to think of corruption in the same terms and because, unlike purely relative definitions, this does not muddy communication. Unfortunately he still is culture bound in continuing to regard all these practices as examples of corruption. One relatively simple solution for the comparative student is to drop that assumption and to inquire into the incidence and significance of nepotism, 'bribery' or other specific *practices*, and only consequently into whether they ought to be or are judged corrupt (and by whom).[11] Another possible tack is adopted by Friedrich, and that is to retain the conventional Western tests,

---

[9] According to Martin Woollacott, *The Guardian*, 22 September 1973, 'leading European buyers routinely take cuts from the manufacturing houses [in Hong Kong, 1973] . . . to whom they give their orders. The normal rate is half per cent of the value, paid into a Swiss bank annually.'

[10] In his 'The Effects of Corruption in a Developing Nation', *Western Political Quarterly*, December 1966; reprinted in Heidenheimer, *op. cit.*, pp. 523–33.

[11] I take this to be part of what Leys meant by his 'central question' for the study of corruption: 'In any society, under what conditions is behaviour most likely to occur which a significant section of the population will regard as corrupt?'. See the article cited above.

but to acknowledge that the crucial question may be whether
corruption, in any particular setting, is functional (i.e. tends to
serve some public end) or is disfunctional and therefore reprehensible.[12] The effects of certain practices are clearly relevant
to one's attitude to them, but this does not solve the difficulties
of deciding which functional or disfunctional practices can usefully be labelled 'corrupt' in a variety of settings. The basic
issue remains that of finding criteria or tests by which to decide
whether some act should be deemed corrupt.

Let us therefore return to the public-office type of definition
with its suggestion that the core meaning is the abuse or misuse
of an office of trust for private gain (not necessarily of a monetary kind). On consideration, there seem to be certain key
conditions, analytical or empirical, for corruption of this kind
to take place. It is worth listing them and noting the relationship
of those conditions to the problem of corruption in developing
countries. But first we must dispose of one red herring. Nye
refers to 'rule-breaking' in his definition and Lord Bryce tied his
discussion of corruption to illegality. In this country and
America much of what is deemed corrupt has been made illegal
and it is common to encounter arguments that the law should at
least seek to encompass all corrupt acts,[13] but few pretend it
always does. In much of the Third World illegality may be even
less useful as a test of corruption. The same activities as here
may be illegal, but in much of Africa and Asia the law will often
reflect alien, i.e. colonial power, conceptions of what is corrupt
or lack force for having been part of an alien package of ideas
and rules. Legal prohibition is thus not a necessary condition
for the existence of corruption, though any relevant legal rules
must clearly form part of its study. The first positive, and
obvious, requirement is that some official or ruler has room to
manoeuvre. Formal discretion and lax supervision or control are
among the sources of that space, just as low penalties or a low
probability of discovery are encouragements to make use of it.
The extent of that space obviously varies with the nature of
the government, the checks on its powers, the openness of its

[12] See his whole discussion of political corruption in *op. cit.* pp. 127–41.

[13] See, for example, Michael Roberts's discussion of the place of interested individuals who may attend local authority party group meetings that make policy for a
council of which they are not members and who thus need not declare their interest.
'Conduct in Local Government – Situating the Redcliffe Maud Report', *Public Administration Bulletin*, 18 June 1975, pp. 39–48, at p. 43.

activities, the range of its jurisdiction and the availability of alternative rulers, but so might it vary with the kind of loyalties that politicians are obliged to hold while in office — to kin in West Africa or to party in the USA for example. (It is worth noting that nepotism can limit scope for the sale of offices and that some limit is set to both by a rigorous 'spoils system' especially if it is operated by a doctrinaire or messianic political party.) There must, secondly, be some accepted distinction between a ruler's public and private personality, a version of the 'Becket rule'[14] which separates role from occupant. If office and power are part of the man (his own private property), money-grabbing or the use of office for profit is no more corrupt than taxation, however immoral it might be.[15] This crucial distinction is not generally or clearly established in all parts of the Third World. Associated with it, thirdly, there must be some concept of the role (of ruler, official, etc.) as constituting an 'office of trust', and criteria for recognizing perversions, lapses, breaches, or abuses. In virtually all societies there seem to be some expectations and norms about ruling behaviour; but those expectations differ not only in content but also in, for example, the detail in which expectations are specified or in the ambiguity of the language. The lack of a clear and precise definition of an official role, it may be noted, is both a factor blurring any concept of corruption and, according to Waterbury, one element in a package of circumstances favourable to the maintainance of patronage between strong and weak.[16] The expectations do not, moreover, relate only to the absence of 'corruption' unless that term is extended to cover every kind of error or short-coming.[17] There must therefore, finally, be evidence that any particular lapse was for the reasons, with the purposes, or under the circumstances that put it under the sub-heading of a corrupt lapse.[18]

[14] It was the absence of this at Henry II's dinner-table, so legend has it, that misled his knights into thinking it was the King, and not merely the temporarily irate and frustrated individual, who wished to be rid of Thomas à Becket.

[15] See, for example, Heidenheimer, *op. cit.*, chap. 2.

[16] See John Waterbury, 'An Attempt to Put Patrons and Clients in their Place', in Ernest Gellner and John Waterbury (eds.), *Patrons and Clients in Mediterranean Societies*, Duckworth, 1977, p. 329—42.

[17] There is, of course, biblical precedent for regarding all lapses as evidence of human corruption since the Fall, but it is surely politics itself that results from the Fall, with political corruption a perverted or at least special sub-category thereof.

[18] John G. Peters and Susan Welch (see their 'Political Corruption in America: A Search for Definitions and a Theory', *American Political Science Review*, 72 (3),

If we are to attempt comparative studies of corruption, this breakdown of the formal conditions for its existence may help make the project manageable. For if an investigator looks at each of them he can leave room both for the recognition of cultural variety, for the relativity of 'corruption' and, without recourse to a mere list of activities stipulated as corrupt, yet preserve a central notion round which to organize discussion. This is to say that the conditions listed also constitute categories or factors which lend themselves to comparison across time and space. Only if one attempts to compare societies by reference to a single general category of 'corruption', it may be suggested, does confusion normally arise, and it arises largely, one suspects, because writers have been loathe to sacrifice the element of moral disapproval inseparable from the word itself.

Two other approaches also promise escape from a purely relative concept. The first of these 'stable' notions (as they might be labelled) derives from consideration of the effects of an extensive practice of bribery, nepotism and misappropriation. *The Economist* insists that, in the end, 'Trains really do not run to time' and refers to 'the impotence of a corrupt regime'; and Gunnar Myrdal points out that 'where corruption is widespread, inertia and inefficiency, as well as irrationality, impede the process of decision-making'; and a member of the Singapore government warned (in 1968) that a society unscandalised by corruption (a 'kleptocracy') 'will steer itself into more and more corruption, and finally into economic and political chaos'.[19] Regardless of the standards prevalent in a particular society, the effect of what we in Britain would label corrupt behaviour is real and far from relative — something between economic stagnation and general chaos. Extending this argument it might then be suggested that any practice which frustrated government might be labelled 'corrupt' — a test that is in principle capable of general application. This is tempting, but there seems no reason to use the label 'corrupt', for governments can be

September 1978, pp. 958–73) offer an interesting analysis of the components of corrupt acts and the use of those components for a comparison of various acts and the degreees to which they are corrupt. This analysis is conducted explicitly within the American context, but is a good example of how a detailed breakdown can help analysis.

[19] See the relevant excerpts in Heidenheimer, *op. cit.*, at, respectively, pp. 489–91, 540–5, and 564–8. See, too, the comment by Colin Leys quoted earlier in this article (see above, fn. 6).

frustrated, economies stagnate and societies collapse for many reasons other than bribery and corruption as we conventionally understand the terms; as we have already suggested, there is more than one way of being 'disfunctional'.

The second stable conception takes us into that 'wider' meaning of the term mentioned at the start of this article and involving the ideas of disintegration and decay or, specifically, the idea of a corrupt society. Dobel has suggested recently[20] that the crucial element is the breakdown of civic virtue and the disappearance of the capacity for loyalty to the common welfare or common ends of the state. This condition is followed by factionalism (the existence of 'objective centres of power and loyalty' that are laws unto themselves and are related to the community only by negotiation and for the sake of convenience); and it is the product of, above all, permanent and massive inequality. This is not the place to enter into a full discussion of a theory which is claimed by its author to derive from Thucydides, Plato, Aristotle, Machiavelli and Rousseau. But one must note the resemblance of Dobel's picture not only to certain aspects of contemporary British and American[21] society but, above all, to those developing countries whose 'corruption' (in the narrow sense) has most struck Western European observers. On the other hand it might well be argued that 'corruption' (in this wider sense) is an inappropriate term to apply to a Third World state which, so far from decaying, suffers from the weakness consequent upon novelty, artificiality, or (to use the older phrase) underdevelopment. Nevertheless, if it be accepted that to talk of political corruption at all is to use the term metaphorically or by reference to some ideal or goal and not to an actual historical past, then it may be acceptable to use the term to refer to a condition analogous to 'decay' or 'perversion' regardless of whether a particular state is passing through it, so to speak, on the way up or the way down. Although one might expect 'corrupt practices' in the narrow sense to form part of this condition, they are not a necessary part (if there is no agreed conception of public purpose, for example). This is therefore best regarded as a use of the term quite distinct from any of the others we have been considering.

20 J. Patrick Dobel, 'The Corruption of a State', *American Political Science Review*, 72 (3), September 1978, pp. 958–73.

21 Cf. Theodore J. Lowi's analysis in his *The End of Liberalism*, New York, W. W. Norton, 1979.

Returning, therefore, to my suggestion that comparative studies might usefully attend more to the conditions for corruption, it may readily be granted that to do so would not obviate the need also to look at the relevant details in whatever society or societies are under discussion. One must still deal with uncertainties about the local criteria of corruption, and about the nuances of conduct and circumstance associated with any particular activity. Gifts may be taken as an illustration. Clearly a gift to an official may be a token of personal friendship, a ritual courtesy, an expression of unsolicited and spontaneous gratitude, a bribe, or a contribution extorted by the official, to list a number of possibilities ranging, in order, from the innocent to the tainted. But where should the line between innocence and taint be drawn and, for example, regardless of its degree of innocence, into which category should a tip be placed, and how big a sum can change hands and still be a tip? More generally, what distinguishes a privilege from a perquisite and the latter from misappropriation? In many societies there may be fairly stable and consistent answers obtainable from any reasonably sophisticated group of citizens — from 'the man-of-the-world on the Clapham omnibus' as it were. But there may not always be a consensus about a particular activity, or the existence of the activity may not be widely enough known. It is at this point that scandals can sometimes provide answers — both about the incidence of a practice and about its acceptability. In any event, part of the story of corruption in any society is the story of how, unless it is all-pervasive and obvious to all, it becomes known and how that knowledge is received. Scandal may once again provide the answer. In itself and for students scandal may therefore be valuable, and not least because looking at scandal involves looking also at much else in any given society.

In referring to scandal here I have in mind not so much the ordinary and enjoyable retailing of scurrilous stories about colleagues and notables but rather those complexes of deviant behaviour, revelation and public reaction that together make up a historical event like 'Watergate'. For such a scandal to occur there must be more than mere wrongdoing. There are at least three major requirements: an exposer or informer, channels through which to communicate the message and an audience or public which finds the information to be scandalous. Each deserves comment, if only to indicate where the study of scandal can lead.

First, then, there has to be an 'informer': someone has to 'grass' or 'sneak' to some appropriate 'outsider' (journalist, policeman, or MP for example) except in those cases where wrongdoing is epidemic and blatant. The slang terms are deliberately used as a reminder that the proverbial 'honour among thieves' often extends much more widely. Part of the full history of any scandal is why and how the disclosure came about, and often why, especially, it was for so long delayed. In the north east of England, for example, the Labour Party seemed to have the support of the National Executive in trying to avoid a public inquiry or even much serious public discussion of the allegations of corruption widespread in the 1960s and early 1970s — as Eddie Milne, the Member for Blyth, discovered to his ultimate cost. In Glasgow local politics, too, the old hands used to say that it was impossible to persuade the City Labour Party to institute its own 'house-cleaning' operations. In both cases the argument commonly put forward was that even to admit that there might be a problem was to play into the hands of other parties. To take a very different example: Martin Woollacott, writing about Hong Kong (in *The Guardian* of 22 September 1973) said that 'it is the classic case of the corrupt city: at one end of the scale those few who talk are afraid that their livelihoods and even their lives might be in danger. And at the other, among affluent British and Chinese professionals, while they may not fear physical attack, they are reluctant to upset the modus vivendi that even honest men have arrived at with the system'. There, as in New York City before the Knapp Commission (which reported in 1972) or in parts of Scotland Yard before Sir Robert Mark took over, information was probably also withheld because of the general belief that the police themselves were so deeply involved that to tell them was at best a waste of time.[22] Sheer administrative failure must also be listed. Thus in the Profumo case it seems that ample information had been available in different parts of the Whitehall machine but had neither been brought together nor reported to a relevant Minister at an early enough stage to avert the security risks and political disruption that ensued.

[22] For the reference to the Knapp Commission I am indebted to Michael Pinto-Duschinsky, 'Corruption in Britain', *Political Studies*, XXV, 2, June 1977, pp. 274–84. In this review of the *Report of the Royal Commission on Standards of Conduct in Public Life*, Cmnd. 6524 of 1976, a strong case is made for setting up some permanent civil inspectorate to assist in obtaining information about corruption.

Conversely, it is sometimes worthwhile noting why certain scandals did 'break' at all. In this country accident seems typically to be the explanation. In 1948 a lender pressed Sidney Stanley for the repayment of a loan – and by October the Lynskey Tribunal was set up to investigate gifts of whisky and holidays to a member of the government and other more lurid allegations.[23] 'Watergate' owed much, not only to such general factors as the American tradition of investigative journalism and distrust of authority and to the relative freedom of comment on public persons and events, but also to such specific factors as the already flourishing vendetta between Nixon and the press and the resentment of Congress at the exceptionally bullying methods of Nixon's White House staff. Other factors include the existence of political conflict so that some groups have a strong positive interest in uncovering scandalous matter about, for example, the 'Gang of Four' in China, or dealings in Marconi shares in Britain before the First World War, let alone alleged dealings in land by close associates of Harold Wilson. Money for certain kinds of story from certain kinds of newspaper is another obvious link between scandal and particular social institutions.

The second pre-condition for the existence of a scandal, access to effective channels for public communication, requires less comment. Obviously the more famous scandals have been those publicized in the press, novels, pamphlets, wall-newspapers, or 'underground' broadsheets, and nowadays by broadcasting. The so-called 'Muldergate' scandal was a testimony to some remaining freedom in South Africa as well as to that country's desperate need to 'win friends and influence people'. All channels are in some degree selective and it is often suggested that British law would have muzzled any local equivalent to the *Washington Post*'s 'Watergate' revelations. In war-time Britain, too, no publicity was given to the refusal, in 1941, of Zenith to 'complicate post-war business' by altering its contract with Bendix of the USA and Siemens of Germany so as to permit the British Air Ministry to manufacture increased numbers of aircraft carburettors.[24] Even in peacetime one expected few scandals in the Colonels' Greece or Franco's Spain. On the other hand, a private press avid for circulation may also serve to create

[23] See M. R. Robinson, 'The Lynskey Tribunal', *Political Science Quarterly*, March 1953, reprinted in Heidenheimer, *op. cit.*, pp. 249–58.

[24] See James Stewart Martin, *All Honorable Men*, Little, Brown, 1950, p. 11.

a market for scandalous information almost without reference to its reliability, as Lord Denning emphasized on the final page of his report on the Profumo affair[25] — a state of affairs that can lead all too easily to possibly unfounded contempt for politicians or an erosion in the standards of behaviour expected of public men.[26]

For there to be a scandal, finally, there must be a public ready to be shocked or scandalized and not merely entertained or titillated by political sensationalism. This requirement is not such a straightforward one. To begin with, it is a compound of, first, the events as reported (the reports may or may not be reliable) and, secondly, a censorious judgment passed upon them by, thirdly, a relevant public (those in a position to do something about the events or actions in question).[27] Further complications arise from the mutual dependence of the elements involved. If the events described or known about are sufficiently outrageous, for example, they can mobilize new groups into political activity and thus transform the nature of the relevant public — which seems to have been one factor in the recent revolution in Iran. Similarly, as we have already suggested, it may only be as a result of a hostile and shocked response that a particular type of behaviour is recognized to be scandalous or, if appropriate, corrupt. Clearly, however, the revelation of what behaviour is considered to be offensive and by whom is a necessary aspect of any scandal and may also be a key to identifying corruption.

An essential function of scandal (in the sense of 'defamatory talk'), it has been argued, is precisely to strip off the impersonal masks donned by those in authority as part of their role.[28] It is concerned, that is, with revealing the humanity and especially the human frailty of others — and in politics that means mainly of rulers, representatives and administrators. This may, in Bailey's

25 'True or false, actual or invented, it can be sold. The greater the scandal the higher the price it commands. If supported by photographs or letters, real or imaginary, all the better.' Lord Denning's *Report*, Cmnd. 2152 of 1963, p. 114.

26 See the comments on the situation in early twentieth-century America in Robert C. Brooks, 'The Nature of Political Corruption', in Heidenheimer, *op. cit.*, pp. 56–61.

27 See Heidenheimer's interesting distinctions between 'black', 'gray' and 'white' corruption depending on whether a practice is condemned or condoned by one or both the elite and the masses in a particular society, *op. cit.*, pp. 26–28.

28 See F. G. Bailey, *Gifts and Poison, the Politics of Reputation*, Blackwell, 1971, for a social anthropological discussion.

phrase, be both a gift and a poison: it may serve to liberate or
at least to constitute salutory criticism, but it may also serve
merely to make a given society virtually ungovernable. And there
are other respects in which scandal may be only a limited blessing either to a society or to the academic student of corruption.

An obvious limit is that political scandals do not deal exclusively with corruption; they may well centre rather on inefficiency, incompetence, or mere carelessness which owes little or
nothing to the pursuit of private gain or any other private
purpose. (The Crichel Down scandal may well be a case in
point.) In extreme cases, too, either of oppression or of a
populace that universally participates in a corrupt state, widespread corruption may be accompanied by a complete absence
of scandal — but in an oppressive regime, it may be noted,
scandal (followed by some remedial action) might well benefit
ruler and ruled alike. In other situations scandal is limited,
often, by being so much at the mercy of chance and accident
(as we have already noted about Britain). It may also serve to
divert public attention from issues that, to the moralist or
political activist, are of greater importance.[29] But none of these
limitations affect the positive attributes for which this article
has argued.

To note the multiple sources of scandal may provide a useful
reminder that the purposes of public office may be betrayed for
a variety of different reasons and that at least some people would
not wish to label them all as corrupt (in any of the normal
meanings of that term). 'Betrayal' thus can stem from arrogance,
self-righteousness[30] and other motives which should perhaps be
considered as corrupt in some very wide sense of the term, but
conscience, treason for purely ideological reasons, fear, or
stupidity must surely fall outside any useful category of corruption. In some situations of conflicting loyalties or trusts, it may
not be clear which should be given preference. Democrats,
moreover, rely on officials to disobey orders that, for example,
put democratic government itself in peril for partisan advantage

[29] See Rose-Ackerman's observation that the fragmentation of authority to deal
with corruption (venality) may lead merely to 'a strategy of "following the scandals"
rather than a broader look at the range of alternatives available'; *op. cit.*, p. 225n.

[30] Self-righteousness, one of the motives that seems to have informed aspects of the
Watergate cover-up, for example, has the great advantage that it brings a continuous
'pay-off' in self-satisfaction.

— and if disobedience were encouraged by bribery, many would regard that as only 'technically' corrupt (or, in other language, as being 'functional' corruption). Scandals, including any associated debate or inquiry, again may help to sort out the ambiguities and uncertainties.

Much of the interest in corruption, even academic interest, seems morally inspired, which, as already suggested, is the source of some at least of the confusion to which I have referred. In this article I have tried to detach the argument from moral preferences, but it is by no means morally irrelevant. For one thing, the approach here advocated makes it easier to accept the fact that corruption in politics is not necessarily the worst of conditions or evils and, by insisting on a distinction between particular practices and the core meaning of 'corruption', to recognize the positive value of venality in some circumstances. Thus for those with something to give (money, sexual favours, or whatever) such corruption may be the only way to blunt the edges of tyranny or introduce an element of control into an otherwise completely arbitrary and hostile system.[31] To the moralist, too, my analysis may suggest that scandal should not be shunned — to encourage it should, indeed, be the moralist's aim. The important point, however, is that moral judgments about particular actions or situations should form the conclusion and not the premiss of the argument.

This article has, for the most part, been couched in somewhat general, abstract and possibly academic (in the pejorative sense) terms. In conclusion, therefore, I will indicate, briefly and somewhat abruptly, certain concrete and practical proposals for dealing with political corruption, in the conventional and rather narrow sense, to which my arguments lend support (as distinct from either proving or inventing). The requirements for there to be corruption point, for example, to the importance of that 'wider loyalty (to the community), backed by firm rules and punitive measures' which forms 'the necessary foundation for the modern Western and Communist mores by which certain behaviour reactions are kept apart from considerations of personal benefit', to quote from Myrdal.[32] The pre-conditions for

---

[31] Compare Friedrich, *op. cit.*, p. 129: 'Corruption is a corrective of coercive power and its abuse, when it is functional'.

[32] See his *Asian Drama. An Inquiry into the Poverty of Nations*, Penguin, 1968, Vol. II, pp. 949–50.

222   GOVERNMENT AND OPPOSITION

scandal suggest not only that more open government, organized opposition and a free press are desirable but also that more heed should be given to the case for a permanent investigating body independent of both government and police.[33] To stress the dependence of corruption on context and intention and to recognize that it is only one category of shortcoming is both to suggest that it be seen as only a special case of the general problems involved in securing good and efficient administration, and to leave one sympathetic to Plunkitt's view that 'Higher salaries is the cryin' need of the day . . . You can't be patriotic on a salary that just keeps the wolf from the door . . . But, when a man has a good fat salary, he finds himself hummin' 'Hail Columbia' . . .'.[34] In so far, however, as the approach acknowledges a variety of impulses to corrupt and of forms of corruption, it tends to be pessimistic about the likelihood that to abolish capitalism, or Communism, or any other system would do much more in the long run than change the nature, not the existence, of the problem.[35] There will thus always be a need for scandal, whatever may be the case about the opportunities for it.

[33] See the case made in Pinto-Duschinsky, *op. cit.*, pp. 281–4.

[34] *Op. cit.*, p. 56; and see Rose-Ackerman's infinitely more sophisticated analysis of the political economy of corruption cited above.

[35] See Friedrich again, at p. 141: 'Corruption in the historical perspective appears to be ever present where power is wielded'.

[11]

New Directions in the Study of Administrative Corruption

Simcha B. Werner, University of Manitoba

Administrative corruption was long a neglected area of research in American public administration. This neglect was due primarily to the axiomatic belief of earlier scholars that American public administration was inherently moral. Given the scientific origin of the discipline of public administration, and given Woodrow Wilson's division of politics and administration, this is not surprising. But developments after the Second World War not only made Wilson's dichotomy obsolete, but also led to new ethical dilemmas. Nevertheless, while dealing with these dilemmas,[1] the discipline of public administration continued with its *a priori* premise that public administrators remained "philosopher-kings."[2]

During the 1960s, the ethos of public administration was affected by the advent of policy analysis and by the developmental and structural-functional approaches in political science. These approaches were responsible, as will be demonstrated, for the existing gap between corruption in American social institutions and scientific knowledge about the various causes of, and remedies for, corruption. Mark Lilla commented in his essay on the ethics of policy analysis:

The year 1960 proved to be a turning point for the field of public administration and the democratic ethos it embodied. The . . . "whiz-kid" in the Kennedy Administration . . . was prepared to apply the latest 'scientific' management and analytic tools to the problems of public policy. . . . Professors, with their bulging analytic tool-kits in hand over-ran Washington attempting to 'rationalize' everything from defense procurement to government budgeting. . . . However inadequate the old public administration was in analytic sophistication, it did embody an ethos which prepared the student, through an informal moral education, to take his place within a democratic government. Public policy has no such ethos. . . . Students flocked to public policy programs . . . (and) found out that they would simply be taught analytic techniques. And the techniques themselves, it was claimed, were 'biased' in favor of those in power and had led to inhumane policies at home and abroad. In short, policy analysis was immoral.[3]

In building up "applied ethics," policy analysis, according to Lilla, became a new form of medieval casuistry,[4] a "political ethic" developed during the 17th century and adopted by the Jesuits as a science, art, or reasoning to resolve cases of conscience by applying the general rules of religion and morality to particular instances in which there appears to be a conflict of duties.

■ The paper presents a succinct review of the points of contention between the functionalist school of corruption of the 1960s and the post-functionalist approach that emerged in the 1970s. The "new" literature draws attention to the systemic revitalization of corruption in the developed countries, as well as describing its dysfunctional aspects. While the functionalists argued that corruption is doomed to self-destruction with the national maturation process, post-functionalists argue that corruption feeds on a variety of causes, and that it is self-perpetuating. This ultimate dysfunctionality is enhanced by the "spillover effect." Three types of spillover effect are examined: leader-follower spillover, the dimensions of corruption spillover, and institutional spillover. In assuming that corruption is individual, functional and above all, doomed to self-destruction, the functionalists displayed a fatal ennui. Post-functionalists demonstrate anxiety about the problem and subsequently, suggest a multi-dimensional strategy to cope with the threat. The potential importation of a "community justice" strategy is *inter-alia* discussed.

While domestically, American policy analysts rationalized the need for applied ethics, students of the structural-functional approach shifted attention to the developing countries, pointing to the functional contributions of political and bureaucratic corruption to political and economic development. The functionalists came to regard corruption as an inherent aspect of the normal growth-decay life cycle, and challenged the moralist school which deemed corruption to be ultimately pathological and, therefore, destructive. Corruption received a "sympathetic understanding"[5] and, instead, was classified as a "functional dysfunction." According to Nye,[6] the functionalists echoed Bernard Mandevill's aphorism: "Private vices, by the dextrous Management of a skillful politician, may be turned into Publick Benefits." This is to say that corruption is merely the price to be paid for certain advantages. However, as Nye argued, whether ". . . the benefits of corruption . . . outweigh the costs depends on its (corruption's) being limited. . . ."[7] This, in turn, suggested the following theoretical tenets: (1) Corruption as an inseparable byproduct of modernization and development; (2) corruption as a functional influence in political and economic development; (3) corruption as a self-destructive process; and (4) corruption as an individual action committed by the occasional immoral official for personal benefit.

The author wishes to thank the Institute of Governmental Studies at U.C. Berkeley, where he stayed on sabbatical leave (1980-81), for partly supporting this paper. The author owes a special debt of gratitude to Stephan Zatuchni, Norman Frohlich, Howard Harmatz, and anonymous referees for their invaluable comments.

Simcha B. Werner was a 1981-82 fellow of the Canada-Israel Foundation for Academic Exchange and is continuing to teach in the Department of Public Policy at the University of Manitoba. He has published articles in Israeli and English professional journals in the areas of public enterprise, administrative reform, and bureaucratic ethics.

These tenets stifled investigation of the apparently ubiquitous phenomenon of corruption by unconsciously introducing a fatal ennui. If, for example, corruption was associated with political development and apparently withered away with political maturation, then, since western nations are mature, corruption is by now restricted to non-western nations. Moreover, as it assists them in developing it concomitantly destroys itself. Its "transitory" nature obviated the need for study.

During the 1970s, as a result of American scandals, public administration and political science research was characterized by a rather prolific growth in the literature of corruption in developed countries, particularly in the United States. This new literature is coalescing into a distinctive "post-functional" approach to the study of administrative and political corruption. At present, this emerging approach can be best identified by a growing body of descriptive studies that: (a) point to the reckless generalizations and intellectual inconsistencies of the functionalists; (b) contradict the theoretical tenets and premises of the functionalists; (c) warn that academia, state, and society must rouse themselves from the auto-narcotic effects of the "functional corruption" myth, and develop multi-dimensional strategies to defeat corruption; and (d) fail to offer a new deductive theory of corruption.

The Definition of Corruption

Kirkegaard, the stern moralist of the 19th century, has argued that "aesthetics" is the true ethics. Similarly, Peter Drucker calls our attention to the replacement of ethics by "ethical chic," because the latter describes a media event rather than a moral or philosophical absolute.[8] Both "aesthetics" and "ethical chic" are, as terms relative, for beauty (or corruption, in this case) lies in the eyes of the beholder. Also, corruption is determined in large part by prevalent cultural norms.

Despite the obscurity of relevant concepts, definitions of corruption have been categorized[9] into three groups: (1) public office-centered definitions which involve the deviation from legal and public duty norms for the sake of private benefits, be it for pecuniary or status gains, or influence; (2) market-centered definitions which view corruption as a "maximizing unit," a special type of stock-in-trade, by which public officials maximize pecuniary gains according to the supply and demand that exist in the marketplace of their official domains; (3) public interest-centered definitions which emphasize the betrayal of public interests by preference of particular to common interests.

Peters and Welch[10] classified corruption according to its legal, public interest, and public opinion bases. While the first two bases are not unique, the third deserves scrutiny because it does not so much define corruption as asks who determines what is corrupt. This was based upon Heidenheimer's "litmus test," which deemed corruption to be black, gray, or white, depending upon the commonality of perception by the public and its officials. If the public and its officials agreed that a specific "bad" action was to be either condemned

or condoned, then that act would be an example of, respectively, either black or white corruption. A lack of accord produced a gray area.

Peters and Welch, then, took the next logical step in categorizing a corrupt act in accord with its four components: the donor, the recipient, the favor, and the payoff. They wrote that corruption would be perceived as "limited" when: the recipient public official acts as a private citizen; a constituent pays a public official as opposed to the official "putting his hand in the till"; the favor is a routine part of the public official's job or benefits the public interest; and the payoff is small, long-range, general (e.g., an unspecified, future electoral consideration), or in the form of support rather than money. In the final analysis, then, a "bad" political act is deemed less corrupt if it is performed for the "good" of the constituency.

Also, in 1978, Dobel published his essay on "The Corruption of a State," in which he discusses the relative nature of corruption. Dobel defines corruption as, essentially, a factor of specific cultural attitudes regarding loyalty, morality and the usurpation of the public good.[11] This definition assumes that there are levels of loyalty and interest, such as can be found by differentiating between the welfare of the state and the welfare of the individual. It also assumes that corruption is, therefore, more venal as it is more avaricious, and less corrupt as it is less individual.

Thus, for example, the news of Lockheed bribing overseas buyers need not have been regarded as evidence of corruption, because Lockheed, in developing and increasing its markets, was working for the benefit of a large constituency, the company, its employees, and their families, and, more implicitly, for the benefit of the United States' economy, business, and political community.

This concept of "noble" or "patriotic" corruption contradicts traditional definitions of corruption as betrayal of the public trust for private gain. Lilla[12] and Drucker[13] noted the revitalization of such "casuistry" in government and business, and deemed it to be ultimately dysfunctional. As Schwartz observed in his study of Soviet public enterprises:

> Not infrequently an evasion of the law begins with expediency and is allegedly dictated by 'business interests,' and gradually, almost imperceptibly, is transformed into common thefts where the 'noble objectives' serve as cover for private gain. . . . If one must falsify for the good of the cause, then why not add a little more for one's self.[14]

Vulnerability to Corruption

Influenced by the developmental approach of the 1960s, corruption was associated with the process of modernization. Every modernizing system was regarded as being susceptible to corruption, as was the case in Western societies which evidenced peak levels of corruption as they experienced socio-political development. Developing countries, therefore, were assumed to allow corruption to become a usual and expected part of the national maturation process.

It, thus, became simplistic to attribute corruption in developing countries to cultural heritages which produced "supportive values." In these countries, where citizens have negative attitudes toward public authority, "gift-giving" practices have been transformed into corruption only by the imposition of western values.[15] In these countries, "there exists a gap between law (as imposed by western and alien standards) and accepted informal social norms (sanctioned by prevailing social ethics). . . ."[16] In sum, these countries demonstrate a "folklore,"[17] a "climate,"[18] and a "way of life"[19] with regard to corruption.

However, in rebuttal to the "self-destructive nature" theory of corruption, common wisdom in the United States indicates that corruption has now become part of the national lifestyle. A growing body of literature suggests that corruption may well be endemic to United States politics,[20] businesses, and social institutions.[21] Similarly, corruption as a *modus operandi* has been observed throughout most of the world.[22] This implies a lack of boundaries to corruption imposed by political ideology or development. Corruption, for example, is a feature of communist countries[23] and nations now in the final stages of political development.[24]

Therefore, the theoretical tenet that corruption is a dependent variable of development is false. Corruption is universal. It can thrive and propagate itself in any level of political and bureaucratic development. More contemporary research suggests that:

1. Patron-client networks which border on corruption can thrive at any level of political development or institutionalization;[25]
2. Socio-economic or political inequalities stimulate corruption;[26]
3. A consumer-oriented society and the gap between desire and the means of fulfillment is now becoming universal;[27]
4. Too little or too much government control tends to enhance corruption;[28]
5. Too little or too much institutionalization tends to enhance corruption;[29]
6. Expanded governmental functions in less-developed countries, and extensive welfare programs in more-developed countries (e.g., food stamps) provide open invitation to major corruption;[30]
7. Economic scarcity and inflation can turn ordinary citizens to relatively minor crimes, such as the view of England as "a nation of petty thieves";[31]
8. American politicians are susceptible to foreign bribery (as demonstrated in Abscam), and to organized crime;[32] and
9. Weak administrative detection and control mechanisms combine with leadership apathy and limited knowledge of corruption to produce cross-cultural, cross-developmental corruption.

Given the prevalence of corruption, perhaps even its inevitability, it is necessary to determine whether it has beneficial aspects.

Dysfunctional versus Functional Corruption

The functionalists identified the following functional propositions:

Economic Market Propositions: Corruption brings with it a wider range of economic choices by encouraging foreign investment and strengthening the private vis-à-vis the public sector. It is, therefore, a means of bypassing cumbersome, genuinely hampering, governmental economic regulations.[33] Bayley argued that corruption is an "accommodating device" a " 'must' for successful development."[34]

The Integrative Function: Corruption allows citizens access to public officials and thereby fosters the integration of immigrant or parochial groups.[35]

Institutionalization Initiative: Either corruption encourages institutionalization and party-building,[36] or an honest, merit-oriented and incorruptible bureaucracy hampers the rise of political leadership.[37]

Administrative Advocacy: Corruption brings elasticity and humanity to rigid bureaucracies.[38] It may also serve to increase the caliber of public servants because corruption brings with it opportunities for supplemental income which may compete with co-optive forces arriving from the non-governmental job market.[39]

Pacifistic Corruption: In the absence of structural reform, violence as the other alternative to corruption threatens the stability of already unstable systems: "He who corrupts a system's police officer is more likely to identify with the system than he who storms the system's police station."[40]

By the end of the 1960s, functionalism came under attack. A scathing condemnation of the supposed morality of the functionalists was sounded by Singapore's Minister of Foreign Affairs and Labor, S. Rajaratnam:

I think it is monstrous for these well-intentioned and largely misguided scholars to suggest corruption as a practical and efficient instrument for rapid development in Asia and Africa. Once upon a time, Westerners tried to subjugate Asia . . . by selling opium. The current defense of Kleptocracy is a new kind of opium by some Western intellectuals, devised to perpetuate Asian backwardness and degradation. I think the only people . . . pleased with the contributions of these scholars are the Asian Kleptocrats.[41]

Academics, too, began to criticize openly the "opportunistic rationalization of corruption,"[42] and the tendency of the functionalists toward ". . . shallow research, reckless generalizations and loosely formulated plans of action."[43] This sloppy reasoning of the functionalist school became the focus of post-functionalist research.

Even assuming that corruption is functional, the question arose: ". . . at what point does the 'least developed' country develop to the point where such corruption is no longer functional."[44] If corruption indeed enhances the opportunities for modernization, then there should be some element in the functionalist theory ". . . which should explain the actual dynamics whereby the new norms evolve, and what kind of norms these will be."[45]

Studies were performed, and the claims of the functionalists for the benefits of corruption to developing systems were shattered. Tilman[46] pointed out that in the Philippines under the Marcos regime, martial law had to be enforced as a means to recover a decaying economy long tainted by institutionalized corruption. McHenry[47] demonstrated that food donated to Bangladesh is politically controlled. Only 10 percent of U.S. aid reached those in the rural areas who needed it most. The rest was used to keep the Bengali government in power by rationing it out to the political constituency in urban areas. The dysfunctional results are smuggling, a black market economy, and disincentive effect on domestic agriculture, not to mention mass starvation. Goodman[48] proved that political corruption in Yucatan, Mexico, inhibited evolution toward universalistic norms by protecting incompetence rather than by rewarding the efficient producer.

Studies on bureaucratic and political corruption in India[49] indicated that corruption is so rampant that government reform policies based upon law were inadequate for their task. Instead of assisting in the development of a functional party system, corruption generally aided in strengthening the dominance of one party, weakened the economy and fostered national disintegration. Eventually, concerned Indians came to regard corruption as a "multi-faced monster" against which "war" must be declared, a war which could be won only if India underwent a "moral revolution."[50] Developed countries and those nearing the final stages of development also failed to provide proof of the assertions of the functionalists.

Mamoru and Auerbach[51] have shown that venality is still intrinsic in the contemporary Japanese political system. The culturally rooted concepts of *takari* (to be a hanger-on) and *nareai* (illicit collusion) explain why corrupt officials are condoned. In the Japanese system, then, while "patronism" can lead to the trivialization of corruption, the intrinsic system of bribery can lead to the actual purchase of votes. Ben-Dor's study[52] of the Israeli case demonstrates that corruption serves only itself. After Israel was established as an independent state, it absorbed immigrants from diverse cultures and countries. Corruption did not foster the integration of those immigrants into the political system. Instead, "opportunities" for corruption were selective. The mass of immigrants could not find the channels to the centers of influence.

In the fully-developed countries of the West, corruption manifests dysfunctional aspects almost entirely. The growth of pilfering and related "minor" examples of corruption in England constitute an entire "hidden economy."[53] Pilfering is known as "larceny by servants" and is, according to Henry, an everyday phenomenon in factories, shops, and offices. It became a method of survival, a response to rapid inflation, high prices, scarce money, restrained income, crippling taxation, and a government policy which offered "equality of sacrifice."[54]

Comprehensive studies[55] of political and administrative corruption in the United States also carry the seeds of a post-functionalist thesis. As corruption becomes in-

stitutionalized and systemic, it "involves the loss of moral authority, weakens efficiency of government operations, increases opportunities for organized crime, encourages police brutality, adds to (the) taxpayers' burden . . . undermines political decisions, leads to inefficient use of resources, and benefits the unscrupulous at the cost of the law abiding."[56]

These observations led to a rather contradictory confluence of views between the functionalists and the post-functionalists. The premise of the functionalists that corruption is a "self-extinguishing catalyzer," brought with the corollary that political development and corruption are interlocked in a "moving equilibrium."[57] The more corruption fosters development, the more it undermines the conditions of its own existence.

However, in arguing that corruption is dysfunctional, the post-functionalists made an argument for its self-perpetuating nature. Corruption feeds upon itself, blocking organizational change and societal reform. As reform is blocked, it becomes increasingly onerous to achieve, and more corruption is fostered as a remedy to existing corruption. Demonstration of a dynamic corruptive mechanism will lay the foundations for further empirical research and subsequent change. Such a corruptive mechanism is the "spillover effect."

The Spillover Effect

If left to itself, corruption will grow, "spilling over" and affecting increasing portions of a given organization or society. This effect is abetted by complacency, naiveté and lethargy on the part of the functionalists and the new casuists. However, three specific spillover mechanisms can be demonstrated, and the knowledge derived can be used as a beginning of a formulation of a strategy to reverse the multiplicative tendency of corruption. These three spillover mechanisms are:

I. Leader-Follower Spillover

The spillover effect is evidenced to the greatest extent by the leaders of a given entity. Leaders, by definition, play a large role in shaping public opinion and societal behavior. Therefore, the corruption of leaders tends to affect the trust, loyalty, and personal integrity of their followers.

Machiavelli observed that "what the prince does the many will also soon do—for in their eyes the prince is ever in view." Corruption of leaders is dangerous because leaders are the paradigms of the body politic. Equally important, the leaders are usually those individuals charged with rooting out corruption.

Halayya[58] has pointed out a gap between verbal condemnation of corruption and action to thwart it. For example, Pandit J. Nehru, Prime Minister of India, announced that the corrupt "should be hanged from the nearest lamp post," but did nothing to combat corruption and even shielded some of his corrupt ministers. In the United States, the Commission on Law Enforcement and Administration observed: "Derelictions of corporations and their managers, who usually occupy leadership positions in their communities, establish an example which tends to erode the moral base of law and provide an opportunity for other kinds of offenders to rationalize their conduct."[59] Also, white-collar crime has a definite spillover effect on blue-collar workers.[60]

The failure to condemn corruption will result in the administrative equivalent of a permeable membrane through which corruption is diffused in an osmotic manner. Consider, for example, the effects of Stalin's slogan for the first Soviet Five Year Plan: "Victors of production are not judged."[61] Levi Eshkol, the late Prime Minister of Israel, when questioned about a corrupt official, replied with a quote from Deuteronomy 25:4: "Thou shalt not muzzle the ox when he treadeth out the corn."

Rationalization of corruption enhances the negative effects of the leader-follower spillover effect. This occurs in three distinct ways:

1. By the leaders designating themselves as the only ones capable of differentiating between "honest" and "dishonest" graft. Also, by support of the proposition that leaders who act for the good of the organization are "entitled" to compensation beyond their salaries.
2. By arguing, as the casuists did, that certain circumstances require "alteration of the rules," and that it is the responsibility, even the loyal duty, of leaders to commit corruption for the "good" of their organization. As Peter Drucker observed, rulers think they "have to strike a balance between ordinary demands of ethics which apply to them as individuals and their social responsibility' to their subjects, their kingdom or their company;"[62]
3. By the legitimization technique which occurs after corruption becomes prevalent. Those who are caught will blame the system rather than find guilt in themselves.

In sum, the corrupt behavior of leaders—whether by excessive use of perquisites or by massive abuse of the system—is certain to be emulated by members of the leaders' organization. This is the essential truth of the Latin proverb: *"corruptio optimi pessima*—the corruption of the best is the worst."

II. The Dimensions of Corruption Spillover Effect

The previously-mentioned classifications of corruption are useful, but they are also too static, failing to elucidate the mechanism(s) by which corrupt acts change in intensity. Heidenheimer,[63] argued that gray corruption is the most destructive, because it is the most difficult to define, detect, and punish. This paper proposes that white corruption best evidences the spillover effect and, therefore, is the most destructive.

The salient characteristic of white corruption is its being a petty and borderline type, which neither the public nor public officials regard as being punishable. Often, white corruption does not clearly violate the law. While every code of law does define corruption, it also "carries the seeds of its own neutralization,"[64] because it does not account for extenuating circumstances. White corruption is psychologically condoned or rationalized because it is so prevalent. By attributing little or no importance to a corrupt act, trivialization and rationalization function as a self-perpetuating mechanism.

Schwartz observed that, in the Soviet Union, minor types of corruption are regarded by the government as truisms in social life. The press, on the other hand, complains that official tolerance of petty violations leads to "a general sense of impunity, and that this encourages more serious types of corruption."[65] In the United States, McGee and Anzelmi[66] have shown in a case study that "there is no such thing as a free ride," in that "friendship" between a police service professional and a businessman can turn subtly into a pitfall.

The rationalization of white corruption, as well as the failure of the system to determine when corruption becomes destructive, cause the formulation and subsequent enforcement of control strategies to be severely constrained. Unchecked, white corruption is a growth industry. When a corrupt act is regarded as being innocuous, that act is removed from previous definitions of corruption. The acceptance of white corruption as being "legitimate" tends to contribute to the legitimization of other types of corruption. The gray and black shades become progressively lighter, and a further momentum of spilling over is established.

III. Institutional Spillover

The influence of specific behavior patterns of different organizations, or groups within the same organization, has not been well documented. However, it is reasonable to deduce that effective institutional corruption will reproduce itself. If, for example, aircraft manufacturer A consistently loses contracts to aircraft manufacturer B, who has an unwritten policy of providing "sales commissions" to influential governmental officials, then aircraft manufacturer A will be induced or compelled to follow suit. Furthermore, there is evidence of a coalition of corrupt politicians, law enforcement officers, businessmen, and labor officials in the United States[67] and, in the underdeveloped countries, coalitions of businessmen, politicians, and administrators.[68]

Whatever the arrangement, corrupt leaders allow their corruption to spread from one institution to another. This spread is either desirable, for corruption has been seen to produce benefits without substantive cost, or is imperative, a means of successfully competing. Dobel has observed that corruption spreads beyond the political realm and cripples the structures "which generate reasonably disinterested loyalty and civic virtues."[69] Also, corruption spreads from family to school, and from organized religion to other voluntary social organizations. Finally, even the army can become loyal to those who pay it.

The Diffusion of Corruption: Systemic versus Individual

A basic area of contention between the functionalists and their successors is that of the diffusion of corruption. Gerald and Naomi Caiden correctly point out that, although advocates of functional corruption of the 1960s "deal with social variables, they still think of corrupt behavior in individual terms without recognizing the existence of systemic corruption."[70] The corollary of this functionalist premise comes from their definition of corruption as a legal deviation, optical illusion, and intellectual inconsistency. "If corruption is illegal, it tends to appear as occasional acts of dishonesty on the part of civil servants. . . . The root of corruption lies exclusively in the *appetitus divitarum infinitus,* the insatiable avarice that is one of the human weaknesses. . . ."[71]

The Caidens suggest that within an organization, systemic corruption implies the existence of an external code of ethics which is contradicted by internal practices.[72] These internal practices encourage and conceal violations of the external code.

Violators of the external code are protected, although non-violators are penalized, particularly in the case of "whistle-blowers." Systemic corruption thus prevents policy change and blocks administrative reform. From the perspective of the spillover effect, it is perhaps the most significant type of corruption because of its thorough permeation of an organization.

According to the post-functionalist view, systemic corruption occurs primarily because a series of isolated incidents—accidental or intentional—have proven their value. The organization, therefore, follows the path of least resistance, and will continue to do so until an insurmountable barrier or an unacceptable cost is placed in its path. Furthermore, when corruption becomes systemic within an organization, spilling over and affecting an increasing portion of that organization, a corrupt code of conduct will replace the legal code, and institutionalization of corruption will become a *modus operandi* for subsequent organizational goals. Two possible examples of this later case include the corruption of entire United States police departments,[73] and the built-in corruption in land-use and building regulation statutes throughout the United States.[74]

More cynical observers of the American scene have come to accept that, even if corrupt officials are removed from office, they will be replaced by equally corrupt officials who have benefitted from the mistake of their predecessors. This is perhaps the ultimate dysfunction of corruption.

In assuming that any given political system is vulnerable to corruption, one is forced to assume that the system does not reflect the will of the people in the intended manner. In other words, corruption becomes the unofficial but actual political or administrative order. Such a situation demands violent reform as a corollary of citizen frustration. In lieu of reform, the morality and loyalty of the citizens may become further factionalized.

Control Policies: Toward Multi-Dimensional Control Strategy

In assuming that corruption is individual, functional, and self-destructive, the functionalists deny the need for remedy. If there is no diagnosis of sickness, then there can be no attempt to provide a cure. The post-functionalists have, on the other hand, demonstrated anxiety about the problem and subsequently proposed a number of remedies.

If, as political economists have argued, corruption is a variant of economic choice, then the remedy is to reduce the benefits while increasing the costs of corruption.[75] One means of accomplishing this is to increase organizational accountability. Another remedy might mandate payment of exorbitant sums, multiples of the original payoff, for individuals caught in a corrupt act. However, these sanctions will be to no avail without increased efforts to detect corruption.[76] However, when corruption of state and society reflects the privatization of morality and a loss of loyalty to communal institutions, reducing opportunities and incentives will not change the motive for corruption. It will instead force the corrupted person to adapt and to make his technique for bypassing administrative and legal barriers more sophisticated. Those who corrupt will raise the bid to make the sale of public officials' "stewardship power" once again worthwhile.

When corruption is institutionalized, systemic, or an intrinsic part of everyday life, the traditional wisdom that corruption can be effectively contained or eliminated only by legal and police measures is disproved. Not only is every law limited by its definition, but also, the punishments prescribed neither reform nor deter "unless the punished respects both the punishers and the norms underlying the penalty."[77] Dobel observed ". . . that only when the vast majority of citizens spontaneously accept the laws even when they disagree with them can law be a tool for community direction and reform."[78] Others point to the dysfunctional utility of prohibitory regulations because—as in the case of trade, customs, gambling, liquor, drug, and prostitution laws —the prohibitory regulations themselves can become an incentive for corruption.[79] Therefore, "the objective should be to create an atmosphere of reform which the law will serve to consolidate."[80]

During the past decade, the "whistle-blowing movement"[81] grew out of this concern for the deterioration of morality. Although the strategy is, at present, to incorporate whistle-blowing into policies designed to improve overall accountability of public agencies, it involves a conflict of "loyalty to conscience" and "loyalty to team." Drucker[83] pointed out the destructive import of whistle-blowing. Similarly, students of criminology and white collar crime have argued that people, not laws, make things work.[84] It is not the police and the law which prevent crime, it is the community. Studying the anemic "hidden economy" in England, Henry has argued that only by community justice, can we ever hope to "liberate" society from the hypocrisy of its attitudes toward crime and only then will be capable of controlling it.[85]

Community justice, according to Henry, enables us to understand the perspectives of all parties to a corrupt or criminal offense, as well as the context of the crime and allows for the involvement of all parties it affects. Decentralized, popular community tribunals are used successfully in socialist countries, primarily in the Soviet Union and China. In Great Britain, where borderline crime and corruption is rampant, the Schweppes Company is experimenting with factory tribunals where management and labor representatives act as judges. Although community justice seems a return to the old pre-development commonplace of justice, it may be a potential productive means to supplement the inadequacy of formal legal systems in dealing with contemporary systemic corruption. As the corrupted tend to rationalize their offenses by blaming an impersonal system rather than themselves and so neutralizing or mitigating the effects of their offenses upon otherwise unidentified individuals, community, informal justice may be more effective, because of its internalization of peer pressure.

The post-functionalists have not yet articulated a "community justice strategy." They have, however, set forth the necessity of developing a "communal and societal strategy" to combat corruption by consciously endeavoring to achieve and sustain public concern and scrutiny. In a recent provocative essay on corruption in the contemporary American presidency and administration, Theodore Lowi has observed: "In the age of large and growing government, we had better cultivate the art of political criticism, or we will have to learn the science of revolution."[86]

Conclusions

In the study of corruption, research of the 1970s has pointed to the reckless generalizations and logical inconsistencies which the functionalist school of the 1960s displayed. This new research, however, can best be described as a growing but nevertheless inconsistent body of descriptive studies which loosely attempts to theorize on the general phenomenon. It is premature to even attempt to articulate a new deductive theory of corruption. The articulation of such a theory requires that, in the next period of research, greater attention must be given to the following areas of corruption that are under-represented in extant empirical work:

a) The scope, nature, and dynamics of systemic corruption.
b) The causes and values of corruption. If, for example, case studies on mature systems yield insufficient data about how corruption changes in intensity, then the focus should be shifted to those countries now making the final stages toward development. These countries provide sufficient institutionalization so that the battle between dysfunctional corruption and functional growth can be more clearly observed.
c) The scope, nature, and dynamics of patriotic corrup-

tion, or what Peter Drucker and Mark Lilla referred to as the new casuistry.

If the field of administrative corruption is to become more theoretical and less descriptive, it must develop a framework and methodology that will permit comparative analysis. Also, it cannot ignore asking questions on the rather amorphous problems of corruption, such as whether corruption is a learned behavior, where values are diffused through a process, and by agents, of socialization. In this sense, the concept of the spillover effect, while lacking sufficient theoretical depth, does serve as a transitional phase between the inadequacies of past research and the need for more theoretical research. While post-functionalists point to the need for articulating a multi-dimensional strategy to control corruption, the newly introduced concept of "community control," has not yet sparked noticeable academic enthusiasm. It seems, however, that it deserves more theoretical elaboration and experimentation to learn about its potential importation into social institutions in western democracies. The need for these studies is both imperative and immediate, for corruption threatens the very pillars of the democratic experience.

Notes

1. See, for example, H. P. Appleby, *Morality and Administration in Democratic Government* (Baton Rouge: Louisiana State University Press, 1952); K. S. Bailey, "Ethics and the Public Service," *Public Administration Review*, Vol. 24 (November-December 1974), pp. 234-243; H. Cleveland and H. D. Lasswell (eds.), *Ethics and Bigness: Scientific, Academic, Religious, Political and Military* (New York: Harper and Brothers, 1962); T. R. Golembiewski, *Men, Management and Morality: Toward a New Organizational Ethics* (New York: McGraw-Hill, 1965); D. Waldo, "Development of Theory of Democratic Administration," *American Political Science Review*, Vol. 64 (March 1982), pp. 81-103.
2. M. E. Gunn, "Ethics and the Public Service: An Annotated Bibliography and Overview Essay," *Public Personnel Management*, Vol. 10, No. 1 (1981), pp. 172-178.
3. T. M. Lilla, "Ethics, and Public Service," *The Public Interest*, Vol. 63 (Spring 1981), pp. 7-9.
4. *Ibid.*, pp. 11-13.
5. M. McMullan, "A Theory of Corruption," *Sociological Review*, Vol. 9, No. 2 (July 1961), pp. 181-201.
6. J. S. Nye, "Corruption and Political Development: A Cost-Benefit Analysis," *American Political Science Review*, Vol. 61 (June 1967), p. 417.
7. *Ibid.*, p. 424.
8. F. P. Drucker, "What Is Business Ethics?" *The Public Interest*, Vol. 63 (Spring 1981), pp. 18-36.
9. A. J. Heidenheimer (ed.), *Political Corruption: Readings in Comparative Analysis* (New York: Holt, 1970).
10. J. G. Peters and S. Welch, "Political Corruption in America. A Search for Definition and Theory; Or, If Political Corruption Is in the Mainstream of American Politics, Why Is It Not the Mainstream of American Politics Research?," *American Political Science Review*, Vol. 72, No. 3 (September 1978), pp. 974-984.
11. J. P. Dobel, *"The Corruption of a State," American Political Science Review*, Vol. 72, No. 3 (September 1978), p. 960.
12. Lilla, *op. cit.*
13. Drucker, *op. cit.*

14. A. C. Schwartz, "Corruption and Political Development in the USSR," *Comparative Politics,* Vol. 11, No. 9 (July 1979), pp. 431-432.

15. J. C. Scott, *Comparative Political Corruption* (Englewood Cliffs, N.J.: Prentice-Hall, Inc., 1972), p. 11.

16. E. G. Caiden and N. Caiden, "Administrative Corruption," *Public Administration Review,* Vol. 37, No. 3 (May-June 1977), p. 303.

17. G. Myrdal, *Asian Drama* (New York: Twentieth Century Fund, 1968).

18. McMullen, *op. cit.*

19. V. T. LeVine, *Political Corruption: The Ghana Case* (Stanford: Hoover Institution Press, 1975).

20. See, for example, G. Benson, *Political Corruption in America* (Lexington: Lexington Books, 1978); L. L. Berg, H. Hann and J. R. Schmidauser, *Corruption in the American Political System* (Morristown, N.J.: General Learning Press, 1976); S. Rose-Ackerman, *Corruption: A Study in Political Economy* (New York: Academic Press, 1978).

21. L. Sherman, *Scandal and Reform: Controlling Police Corruption* (Berkeley: University of California Press, 1978); G. Amic, *The American Way of Graft* (Princeton, N.J.: The Center for the Analysis of Public Issues, 1976).

22. LeVine, *op. cit.*

23. Schwartz, *op. cit.*; J. M. Kramer, "Political Corruption in the U.S.S.R.," *Western Political Quarterly,* Vol. 30, No. 2 (June 1977), pp. 213-224.

24. See, On Israel, G. Ben-Dor, "Schitut, Misud Ve'itpatchut Politit," *Rivon Le'Mechkar Chevrati* (August 1973), pp. 5-21 (Hebrew); On Japan, S. Mamoru and H. Auerbach, "Political Corruption and Social Structure in Japan," *Asian Survey,* Vol. 17 (June 1977), pp. 556-564; On Mexico, M. Goodman, "Does Political Corruption Really Help Economic Development: Yucatan, Mexico," *Polity,* Vol. 7, No. 2 (Winter 1974), pp. 143-162.

25. Ben Dor, 1973, *op. cit.*

26. Dobell, *op. cit.*; S. Dasgupta, "Corruption," Seminar 185 (January 1975), pp. 35-38.

27. Dasgupta, *idem;* Schwartz, *op. cit.*

28. S. P. Varma, "Corruption and Political Development in India," *Political Science Review,* Vol. 13, Nos. 1-4 (January-December 1974), pp. 157-179.

29. G. Ben Dor, "Corruption, Institutionalization, and Political Development: The Revisionist Thesis Revisited," *Comparative Political Studies,* Vol. 7 (1974), pp. 63-83.

30. A. Wildavsky, *Speaking Truth to Power: The Art and Craft of Policy Analysis* (Boston: Little, Brown and Company, 1979), p. 118.

31. *The Baltimore Sun,* "We All Pay," August 9, 1976, p. 2.

32. J. W. Chambliss, *On the Take: From Petty Crooks to Presidents* (Bloomington: Indiana University Press, 1978).

33. H. D. Bayley, "The Effects of Corruption in a Developing Nation," *Western Political Quarterly,* Vol. 19, No. 4 (December 1966), pp.719-732; N. H. Leff, "Economic Development Through Bureaucratic Corruption," *American Behavioral Scientist,* Vol. 8 (November 1964), pp. 10-12; Nye, *op. cit.*

34. Bayley, *ibid.,* p. 719.

35. Bayley, *idem.;* Scott, *op. cit.*

36. J. V. Abueva, "The Contribution of Nepotism, Spoils, and Graft to Political Development," *East-West Center Review,* Vol. 3 (June 1966), pp. 45-54; S. I. Huntington, *Political Order in Changing Societies* (New Haven, Conn.: Yale University Press, 1968); R. K. Merton, "Some Functions of the Political Machine," pp. 72-82, in R. K. Merton, *Social Theory and Social Structure* (New York: Free Press, 1957).

37. R. Braibanti, "Public Bureaucracy and Judiciary in Pakistan," in J. LaPalombara (ed.), *Bureaucracy and Political Develop-*

ment (Princeton: Princeton University Press, 1963); W. F. Riggs (1963), "Bureaucrats and Political Development: A Paradoxical View" in J. LaPalombara (ed.), *idem.*

38. Nye, *op. cit.;* Bayley, *op. cit.*

39. Bayley, *op. cit.*

40. Huntington, *op. cit.*

41. Manuscript of speech given at the Second Public Service International Asian Regional Conference in Singapore, Nov. 14, 1968. Reproduced in Heidenheimer (ed.), *op. cit.,* p. 54.

42. Myrdal, *op. cit.*

43. R. O. Tilman, "Emergency of Black Market Bureaucracy: Administration, Development and Corruption in the New States," *Public Administration Review,* Vol. 28, No. 5 (September/October 1968), pp. 437-444.

44. Ben-Dor, 1974, *op. cit.,* p. 68.

45. Caiden and Caiden, *op. cit.,* p. 305.

46. R. O. Tilman, "The Philippines Under Martial Law," *Current History,* Vol. 71, No. 422 (December 1976), pp. 201-204.

47. F. McHenry, "Food Bungle in Bangladesh," *Foreign Policy,* Vol. 27 (Summer 1977), p. 72-88.

48. Goodman, *op. cit.*

49. L. M. Hager, "Bureaucratic Corruption in India: Legal Control of Maladministration," *Comparative Political Studies,* Vol. 6, No. 2 (July 1973), pp. 179-219; M. Halaya, *Emergency: A War on Corruption* (New Delhi: Chand and Co. Ltd., 1975); Varma, *op. cit.*

50. Halayya, *ibid.,* pp. 134-135.

51. Mamoru and Auerbach, *op. cit.*

52. Ben-Dor, 1974, *op. cit.*

53. Henry, *op. cit.*

54. *Ibid.,* p. 11.

55. Benson, *op. cit.*; J. Gardiner and T. Lyman, *Decisions for Sale: Corruption and Reform in Land-Use and Building Regulation* (New York: Praeger, 1978); Rose-Ackerman, *op. cit.*; Sherman, *op. cit.*

56. N. Caiden, "Shortchanging the Public," *Public Administration Review,* Vol. 39, No. 3 (May-June 1979), p. 295.

57. Nye, *op. cit.,* p. 419.

58. Halayya, *op. cit.,* p. 128.

59. Quoted in R. D. Cressey, "White Collar Subversives," *The Center Magazine,* Vol. 11, No. 6 (November/December 1978), p. 48.

60. *Idem.*

61. Quoted in Schwartz, *op. cit.,* p. 430.

62. Drucker, *op. cit.,* p. 22.

63. Heidenheimer, *op. cit.*

64. D. Matza, *Delinquency and Drift* (New York: John Wiley and Sons, 1964), p. 60.

65. Schwartz, *op. cit.,* p. 440.

66. P. F. McGee and F. J. Anzelmi, "There Is No Such Thing as a Free Ride," *Public Personnel Management,* Vol. 10, No. 1 (1981), pp. 161-164.

67. Chambliss, *op. cit.*

68. A. H. Somjee, "Social Perspectives on Corruption in India," *Political Science Review,* Vol. 13, Nos. 1-4 (January-December 1974), pp. 180-186.

69. Dobel, *op. cit.,* p. 970.

70. Caiden and Caiden, *op. cit.,* p. 301.

71. Van Klaveren, "Corruption as a Historical Phenomenon," in Heidenheimer (ed.), *op. cit.,* pp. 67-75.

72. Caiden and Caiden, *op. cit.,* pp. 306-307.

73. Sherman, *op. cit.*

74. J. Darton, "Construction Industry: The Graft Is Built In," *New York Times,* July 13, 1975; *Corruption in Land Use and Building Regulation: An Integrated Report and Conclusions* (Washington, D.C.: U.S. Department of Justice, 1979).

75. Sherman, *op. cit.*

76. Amick, *op. cit.;* Corruption in Land Use, *op. cit.*
77. Cressey, *op. cit.,* p. 45.
78. Dobel, *op. cit.,* p. 971.
79. Varma, *op. cit.,* p. 164.
80. Hager, *op. cit.,* p. 217.
81. J. Bowman, "Dissent in Government: A Bibliography and Resource Guide on Whistle-Blowing." *Paper presented at the annual convention of the American Society for Public Administration, San Francisco, April 1980.*
82. E. Weisband and T. M. Frank, *Resignation in Protest: Political and Ethical Choices Between Loyalty to Team and Loyalty to Conscience in American Public Life* (New York: Grossman, 1975).
83. Drucker, *op. cit.*
84. M. Frome, "Blowing the Whistle," *The Center Magazine,* Vol. 11, No. 6 (November-December 1978), pp. 50-58.
85. Henry, *op. cit.,* p. 173.
86. T. J. Lowi, "The Intelligent Person's Guide to Political Corruption," *Public Affairs,* Vol. 82 (September 1981), p. 6.

[12]

Anatomy of Corruption:

An Approach to the Political Economy of Underdevelopment

By M. SHAHID ALAM*

ABSTRACT. An examination and critique of the functionalist literature on *corruption* in the *political administration* of *Less Developed Countries* (LDCs) indicate that its claims are without empirical foundation. Its theses with regard to the *political, economic* and administrative effects in most LDCs contrast with the facts. No benefits for *development* from corruption are found; *market corruption,* for example, does not appear to improve *allocative efficiency.* The erosion in a government's capacity to formulate and implement policies making for *economic growth* is an obstacle to *economic progress.*

I

Introduction

ALTHOUGH THE PUBLIC'S PERCEPTIONS about corruption in developing countries are likely to be wholly negative, much of the existing scholarly literature on the subject tends to take the opposite view. Corruption, in this literature, is seen as resulting from the clash of indigenous values and the alien norms of a modern bureaucracy.[1] It is, therefore, thought to be unavoidable—but more, its implications for political and economic development are on balance considered to be beneficial. According to one such functionalist view,[2] corruption in developing countries plays a "role which is sufficiently important that if it was not played by this device must be played by another or the consequences might severely undermine the pace, but more importantly the character of the development effort."

This functionalist perspective on corruption, we hope to show, stems from two sources: the failure to perceive its often systemic character[3] and an unwillingness to examine its effects in a dynamic perspective. It is maintained here that the phenomenon of corruption in developing countries cannot be understood unless we recognize its instrumentality in appropriating wealth for the rulers and their clients; in other words, corruption tends to become the end of power and not only a means towards its continuance. Further, we also undertake to analyze more carefully than before some of the claims made about the economic effects of corruption, *i.e.,* whether it improves allocative efficiency or

* [M. Shahid Alam, Ph.D., is assistant professor of economics at Northeastern University, 301 Lake Hall, Boston, MA 02115.]

American Journal of Economics and Sociology, Vol. 48, No. 4 (October, 1989).
© 1989 American Journal of Economics and Sociology, Inc.

makes a net contribution to capital formation. These claims are shown to be improbable. But before we take up these issues, there follows a discussion on the definition and taxonomy of corruption.

II

Definition and Taxonomy

CORRUPTION IS POTENTIALLY an attribute of all agent-principal relationships[4] and as such may be defined as (1) the sacrifice of the principal's interest for the agent's, or (2) the violation of norms defining the agent's behavior. In their definition of bureaucratic or political corruption, functionalists avoid the first approach since it hinges on being able to define public interest: a matter of controversy. Corruption is, therefore, more often defined as a departure from the norms of a modern bureaucracy,[5] *e.g.,* rationality, achievement-orientation, universalism, etc. While this approach is open to charges of ethnocentrism, we will take the view that it is worth examining whether economic and political development is possible in the absence of modern bureaucratic norms.

Any comprehensive study of corruption must begin with a taxonomy of corrupt activities. While no taxonomy can aspire to completeness in a field so diffuse as that of corruption, a fairly comprehensive taxonomy may be constructed by examining the different ways in which officials—in their private interest—distort the correspondences established by law and policy between an agent's attributes and its rights (claim to benefits) and obligations (costs it must occur). Corrupt activities may now be seen as falling into one of four classes.

(1) *Cost-reducing corruption.* This arises when officials seek to lower the agent's costs in some given situation below the established level. Most commonly this takes the form of tax reductions or laxity in the enforcement of some regulation; the cost saving may be shared between the official and the agent.

(2) *Cost-enhancing corruption.* The opportunities for this type of corruption present themselves in three situations. Where excess demand exists for an officially supplied good or service—including the official's time—at fixed prices, the bureaucrat may seek to appropriate the implicit rent by charging what the market will bear. This *market* corruption is the favorite of economists analyzing corruption.[6] Occasions for raising costs may also arise when officials enjoy monopoly power *via* their control over licensing procedures. Here the official's objective is to acquire at least a part of the premium associated with the license. Finally, opportunities for raising costs arise from the misuse of an official's coercive power, *e.g.,* in illicit tax-collection.

(3) *Benefit-enhancing corruption.* This arises whenever an official seeks to transfer benefits to an agent in excess of what is legally established, *e.g.,* excess

payments made by over-reporting work done. This may be motivated by a collusive sharing of gains, nepotism or political patronage.

(4) *Benefit-reducing corruption.* In this case officials directly appropriate benefits intended for agents, *e.g.,* delaying payment of pension funds and appropriating the interest thereon or stealing supplies from a hospital. This form of corruption may occur whenever agents are not aware of their entitlements; and officials can reduce benefits also by employing coercion.

The preceding categories of corrupt activities arise during the *implementation* of laws and policies, but corruption may also enter into their *formulation* by threatening to legislate higher costs (or lower benefits) or promising to legislate lower costs (or higher benefits). Generally, these two broad genres may be taken to correspond to bureaucratic and political corruption. But it is not difficult to see that this division will not hold under the conditions of systemic corruption that we hypothesize for many developing countries. In such a situation, politicians may seek to obtain for themselves a share of the corruption revenue collected by bureaucracy.[7] The relation between politicians and the bureaucracy may well be a symbiotic one, with politicians creating or maintaining opportunities for earning corruption revenue on the assurance of receiving some agreed share in the proceeds.

III

Facts of Corruption

EMPIRICAL ACCOUNTS OF CORRUPTION are more difficult to come by than theoretical analyses of the phenomenon. Some writers maintain that this is due to the clandestine nature of the activity; this is said to prevent its study with the aid of interviews and questionnaires.[8] While the difficulties of obtaining systematic data on corruption cannot be slighted, with some perseverance the conventional tools of research may still be employed to advantage. For example, if one wishes to investigate corruption in the customs department, the interviews may be directed to importers or retired officials of the department; officials in active service, unless honest, are less likely to volunteer information. That such studies have been so rare attests less to their difficulties than the lack of demand for them in the ruling circles of developing societies.

The accounts that we do have of corruption, therefore, are in most instances less than systematic, consisting mostly of anecdotal evidence available from news reports and, occasionally, official enquiries, case studies and results of surveys. The evidence that may be culled from such sources point, in several countries, to the presence of systemic corruption, *i.e.,* it is both pervasive and organized, affecting different levels of government, and practiced by bureaucrats and politicians alike in nearly all government departments. Included in this category would be countries like Ghana, Zaire, Nigeria, the Philippines, India, Bangladesh, Indonesia (Sukarno era), Thailand, Mexico, and Haiti:[9] this list is so short because information on most other countries is generally unavailable. Countries in which such systemic corruption does not exist would include South Korea, Taiwan, Singapore and Tunisia.[10]

While we cannot examine the evidence on corruption in all the countries listed above, its systemic character may well be illustrated with respect to one of these countries, *viz.* India. The pervasiveness of corruption across nearly all government departments in India is attested to by an official commission which published its findings in 1964; but the problem was thought to be most serious in customs, revenue collection, public works, purchasing agencies, railways and all offices issuing licenses, permits and the like.[11] The report also attests to the organized nature of this corruption in some areas: on "all contracts of construction, purchase, sales and other regular business on behalf of the government, a regular percentage is paid by the parties to the transaction, and this is shared in agreed proportions among the various officials concerned."[12] An earlier report on corruption in the railways also gives evidence of organized corruption with fixed shares of the illicit revenue going to officials of different ranks.[13] More recently, Wade has provided a systematic account of organized corruption in the irrigation system of a South Indian state. He provides evidence of a fairly active internal labor market as a means of channelling corruption revenue upwards. Evidence of such illicit internal labor markets are also found in the departments of labor, forestry, agriculture, public health, police, revenue, etc.[14]

From the above account, it would appear that the substitution of private interests for the formal objectives of bureaucracy may well be endemic in Indian government. On this subject, Wade writes that the "essential business of a state minister is not to make policy. It is to modify the application of rules and regulations on a particularist basis, in return for money and/or loyalty."[15] But if systemic corruption appears roughly to characterize the conduct of government in India, it would hold *a fortiori* for the governments in several other developing countries where the illicit revenue—as a proportion of national income—that is appropriated by officials or conferred by them on others may well exceed that in India by a wide margin. Thus, in Zaire two-thirds of its civil servants in 1979 were discovered to be fictitious, representing an annual drain of more than 300 million dollars from the budget[16]; three Latin American dictators (Peron, Perez Jimenez and Batista) removed, between 1954 and 1959, 1.5 billion dollars from their countries[17]; a presidential commission appointed in the Philippines estimated Swiss bank accounts held by Marcos at 5 billion dollars and had by

February 1987 frozen Marcos' assets in the Philippines estimated at 1.5 billion dollars;[18] international loans worth 500 million dollars were used by the government in Bangladesh for buying political patronage,[19] etc. Corruption on this scale is on the best evidence unknown to India and would appear to be unlikely under the institutional arrangements she has managed to sustain.

IV

Causes of Corruption

FUNCTIONALISTS EMPHASIZE both attitudinal and structural determinants of corruption in developing countries.[20] An attempt will be made here to integrate all these disparate factors within a single unifying framework. It will also be pointed out that several factors which are identified only as causes of corruption are also its effects: in this way we hope to take a dynamic view of our subject.

Our unifying framework proceeds from an examination of the inducements to corruption as perceived by a public official. This may be defined as consisting of the expected net illicit benefits (ENIB) from corruption: the benefits need not be monetary but may be thought of as having monetary equivalences and include both benefits received by the official or his kin and cronies. It will be maintained that

$$\text{ENIB} = B(1 - \Theta_t) - (\Theta_t - \Theta_{tp}) C_t - \Theta_{tp} C_p \qquad [1]$$

where: B is the monetary value or the monetary equivalent of the illicit benefits; C_t is the cost of being transferred to a hardship post upon detection of corrupt behavior; C_p is the cost of dismissal and other punishment upon detection of corrupt behavior; Θ_t is the probability of detection; Θ_{tp} is the probability of dismissal contingent upon detection; and $(\Theta_t - \Theta_{tp})$ is the probability of transfer.

Our analysis of the causes of corruption may now be organized into two sets of factors (not mutually exclusive): those that lower the official's aversion to corruption, what Johnson[20] described as the value placed on an extra dollar from illicit activities compared to an extra dollar from legal activities; and those factors that raise the value of ENIB by raising the value of B or lowering the values of Θ_t, Θ_{tp}, C_p and C_t.

Among the first set of factors, the strength of particularist attachments to one's kinship, ethnic and religious group is most often cited as the cause of corruption in developing societies.[21] The pressures of particularist attachments is probably strongest—as in most countries of tropical Africa—where the successful members of a kinship group are often under obligation to pass the benefits of their position to their kinfolk. But these pressures are present in varying degrees in most developing societies where values of political modernization are not yet widely accepted.

There are other factors, too, whose presence may be seen as reducing the public official's aversion to corruption. The willingness to engage in corruption, especially at the lower levels of bureaucracy, frequently receives an impetus from low and often declining real value of public salaries. In the higher echelons, on the other hand, officials may be under social pressure to emulate the material conditions of a European life style, which may have become unaffordable because of inflation and higher import duties on consumer goods.[22] Officials in developing societies will have a weaker aversion to corruption also because in most cases they have been catapulted from the lower ranks into positions of power and, therefore, lack both a sense of mission and social distance from those they deal with.[23] The absence of a national bourgeoisie too creates strong temptations for public officials to use their position to fill this vacuum.[24] Finally, the aversion to corruption may be influenced by what Myrdal[25] describes as the folklore of corruption, *i.e.,* people's beliefs about corruption and government's policy towards it. He argues, for instance, that beliefs "that known offenders can continue their corrupt practices with little risk of punishment, are apt to reinforce the conviction that this type of cynical asocial behaviour is widely practiced."

The factors which increase the value of ENIB are often the same which we have seen to influence the public official's aversion to corruption, though their influence on the former variable acts through new channels. In any society, some amount of corruption will be unavoidable because of the difficulties inherent in tracking corruption, *i.e.,* the Θ's cannot be equal to unity.[26] But our concern is not with this residual corruption; we want to explain why the Θ's in most developing countries are so close to zero,[27] as they must be if we are to understand the phenomenon of systemic corruption. The near zero values of the Θ's cannot be explained unless we recognize the manner in which corruption fits into the objectives of government and politics of developing countries. At least three such fits will be described here, although much of the political science literature fixes its attention on the first.

Given the particularist direction of loyalties in such societies, it has been argued that political parties in a competitive political system will take on the character of "political machines" in order to meet the demands of particularist interests. Scott[28] argues that since legislation is couched in universalistic terms, parochial demands are more conveniently accommodated by using corruption at the enforcement level to create benefits for particular groups of people. But the premise of this argument appears scarcely credible: legislation can be, and frequently is, designed to benefit specific ethnic, regional or other groups. Moreover, benefits can be, and are, directed towards specific groups by means of investment projects designed to concentrate their benefits on such groups. What factors then account for the widespread use of corruption as an instrument of redistribution when these legal instruments are available? Some of the reasons we can think of tend to weaken the functionalist argument about corruption.

First, the individual recipients of corrupt benefits can be more easily determined than in the case of particularist legislation or investment projects. Corruption at the enforcement level also carries the advantage of making transfers that are frequently hidden from public scrutiny, *i.e.,* corruption represents what Leroy Jones[29] described as politically efficient reallocation which makes "someone better off without making anyone else *aware* that he is worse off." But most importantly, corruption is an instrument whose main function is to transfer benefits *to* public officials whereas the hitherto mentioned instruments are employed by government officials to transfer benefits to their constituencies. To the extent that these three considerations are valid, they suggest that systemic corruption is less the "political machine" that it is credited to be and much more a convenient tool for the enrichment of particular ruling cliques or ethnic and other groups at the cost of all others.

It is not difficult to imagine that instead of seeking to mollify a clutter of particularist demands, a dominant ethnic or religious group because of its ascendancy in the army or bureaucracy, may decide instead to monopolize the benefits of corruption by taking measures to eliminate rival groups from positions of power. The situation in several developing countries, especially in tropical Africa, comes nearer to being described by this model.[30] One other variant of systemic corruption is also conceivable, and may be observed in some developing countries. In this case, the State apparatus is seized—in conditions where the dominant power groups are divided—by a clique which then proceeds to consolidate its power by channeling some of the illicit benefits from corruption to recruit clients solely because of their ability to coerce the population.[31]

While it is well known that the developmental, enterprise and regulatory functions assumed by governments in developing countries contribute to corruption by increasing the potential value of illicit benefits, the government's political dependence on such benefits often tends to perpetuate and magnify them. Thus, developmental functions assume forms which lend themselves more easily to corruption; or having once taken such forms, their reform militates against the government's interests. Naturally, the same tendencies also afflict the administrative functions of government. All this, however, results in an intermingling of cause and effect—an issue that is taken up in the next section.

V

Effects of Corruption

ONCE IT IS RECOGNIZED that systemic corruption is primarily a political phenomenon, *i.e.,* those in power use the government to transfer illicit benefits to themselves or their clients, it follows, as pointed out in the preceding paragraph,
that the governing elite will seek to expand the flow of illicit benefits through
official channels—*via* extension in its fiscal, regulatory, market and enterprise
functions and also by seeking to eliminate or weaken all political competition.
This further implies that at least some of the factors earlier identified as causing
corruption may also be its effects. Thus, the indiscriminate use of direct interventions in the economy, the persistence and proliferation of discretionary instruments, the sluggishness of bureaucratic procedures hampered by layers of
decision-making, the wasteful uncertainties surrounding government policies,
the often unchecked expansion of public employment, the interminable delays
in administration of justice and similar pathologies of life in many developing
countries must now be seen at least in part as creations of corrupt governing
elites.

With the advantage of this dynamic perspective on corruption, several of the
advantages that are claimed to follow from corruption, *e.g.,* the speeding of
bureaucracy by bribes, will be seen to be illusory because the problems they
overcome exist so that they may induce corruption. We shall see more of this
as we examine some of the functionalist claims regarding the economic and
political benefits of corruption.

VI

Economic Effects of Corruption

THREE PURPORTED BENEFITS flowing from corruption will be examined here: improvements in allocative efficiency, promotion of capital formation and substitution for a public works program. It will be shown that most of these benefits
are far from real.

Allocative Efficiency: Whenever governments take over market functions—
which is very often the case in developing countries—it is often claimed that
bribery will improve allocative efficiency because it substitutes market prices
for the mandatory prices set by bureaucracy. As Leff[32] argues, in the long run
the favors handed out by government officials must go "to the most efficient
producers, for they will be able to make the highest bids which are compatible
with remaining in the industry." Such arguments, while apparently convincing,
are really quite simplistic because of several complications that they leave out:

risks of detection, risk-hedging, aversion to corruption, induced uncertainties in the supply of goods and services, etc. These complications are explored with respect to five different situations commonly encountered in developing countries: rationing of inputs, contracts, licenses, utility connections and the bureaucrat's time. Only some of the complications are taken up here.

Most importantly, where risks of detection arise from the complaints of unsuccessful bidders (*i.e.,* bribers), the official will regulate entry into the auction only to those he can trust. And since trust is unrelated to the production efficiency of aspirants, such entry restrictions may be enough to prevent favors from going to the most efficient producers. But there may be deadweight losses too from resources devoted by the official and the aspirant to cover up or legalize the bribe; an example of such bribery-legalizing activity would be the opening of several trading firms to conceal excess allocation of foreign exchange to an aspirant. Alternatively, where the controlled input (or output) lends itself to adulteration, corruption may well take the form of supply stretching, *i.e.,* the selling of adulterated input (or output) at official prices. Adulteration will arise from risk-aversion on the official's part whenever the risks of detection from bribery are greater than those from selling adulterated output. The direct costs of such adulteration, say, in the case of a new agricultural input will be the loss of productivity from adulteration. The eventual costs may be much greater because of the nonadoption of the new input by farmers. Finally, the failure of bribery to improve allocative efficiency may also arise from its crowding out effect on entrepreneurs who are efficient but honest or find the risks of detection unacceptable.

In some situations, bribery may impose costs because of the official's efforts to maximize the offers of bribes. Officials may seek to do this by introducing uncertainty into the supply of inputs (or outputs) where none need have existed. Such behavior has been observed by Wade[33] among irrigation officials in a district of India. Or, officials may slow down bureaucratic processes in an effort to induce or lengthen queues and, thereby, invite bribes from those eager to jump the queue.

While Leff and others assume implicitly that bribery will lead to clandestine auctioning of the *available supply* of the controlled good, it is not realized that the maximization of bribe-revenue (*i.e.,* the excess of "auction" over official price multiplied by quantity sold) may well induce a reduction in the amount available for auction; the loss in utility or output from such a reduction in supply must clearly be offset against any gains in efficiency from bribery. Also, the attempt by successive groups of officials in the utilities departments (*e.g.,* water, telephone, electricity, etc.) to extract bribes may lead them to offer utility connections beyond their installed capacity. This will lead to uncertainties, discontinuities and decline in the quality of the utilities supplied. The loss in productivity resulting from such a decline could easily exceed the gain in output from the additional utility connections that result from corruption.

We may consider the economic effects of bribery in two other spheres of government activity: the award of contracts for capital projects or supplies, and taxation. In the first case, while the highest bidder wins the contract this may have nothing to do with his/her greater efficiency; the higher bribe may be financed by cheating on the terms of the contract—with or without the connivance (*i.e.,* bribery) of the monitoring agencies. The costs to society from this kind of bribery arise not merely from the loss of allocative efficiency. The more considerable costs in this case are likely to stem from the underfulfillment of the contract. Generally, the decline in the economic value of the project will be far greater than the saving from deterioration in its quality. For instance a saving of 10 percent on the cost of a construction project—made possible, say, by a twenty percent cut in its cement content—could reduce the useful life of a project by half or even more.

Let us now turn to the bribery of tax officials. It may be thought that the reduction in tax revenue—corresponding to given tax base and tax rates—may be offset by the corrupt officials' interest in expanding the tax base. But the augmentation of the tax base will not be sought until the potential for illicit revenue from the already known sources has been tapped. More importantly however, the tax officials may for a higher bribe decide to keep the tax-dodgers they uncover off their tax list. If corruption, therefore, reduces tax revenue, the government will counter it with higher tax rates. The argument that bribing of tax officials stimulates economic activity by reducing taxes then may not be valid in a dynamic context if the higher tax rates too were caused by leakages of revenue due to corruption.

Finally, is there any presumption that it is efficient producers who will succeed more often than others in getting their taxes reduced? It would appear that the more efficient producers would feel less constrained by competitive pressures to engage in such activity. It is the less efficient and dishonest entrepreneurs who seem more likely to seek such reduction through bribery. Once again, corruption appears to be frustrating an important advantage of market forces, *i.e.,* weeding out inefficient producers.

In focusing our analysis on market corruption (*i.e.,* bribery), we do not wish to imply that corruption in developing countries most commonly takes the form of bribery. On the contrary, given the widespread use of corruption as an instrument of statecraft, it may be argued that access to government favors is often a matter of political patronage. Kinship and other ties may also be important influences. But where corruption assumes such non-market forms, there could scarcely be any presumption regarding their allocative efficiency.

Capital Formation: While it is often believed that corruption is an important source of capital formation in many developing economies, the logic of this claim has rarely received careful consideration. It appears from the few recorded remarks that illicit funds acquired by entrepreneurs or officials make a *net* contribution to capital formation.[34] But do they? To answer this question, we must proceed by first identifying some of the major sources of corruption revenue to the officials and favored aspirants alike. These include the illicit transfer of funds allocated for investment; bribes resulting from reduction in tax liabilities; illicit benefits from the corrupt allocation of controlled goods and services. We take these up in turn.

There are several ways in which funds earmarked for investment may be converted into corruption revenue. Often, such funds which are ostensibly meant to be allocated for making loans to tested private entrepreneurs, are instead diverted to political favorites or shared out between officials and phony investors. In such cases, since there exists no real obligation to repay the loans, they are more than likely to be diverted to consumption. A second leakage of investment funds into corruption revenue occurs, as mentioned earlier, when bribes are used to influence the award of public contracts for investment projects. In such cases, the bribe is generally paid out of savings from cheating on the terms of the contract. There can be little question of a net contribution to investment from the corruption revenue since the loss in the economic value of the project from milking the contract will generally exceed the savings therefrom.

Where corruption results in net reduction of tax liabilities, its effect upon net capital formation must depend on a comparison of the government's marginal propensity to spend on consumption against the same propensity amongst bribe-receiving officials and those benefitting from tax-reductions. Whether any net addition to saving takes place, therefore, cannot be determined *a priori;* it will depend, for instance, on who receives the tax reductions, or whether public officials can freely live beyond their means.

The probability of a net contribution to capital formation out of the corrupt transfer of premia attached to controlled goods and services would appear to be very small. Where such allocations are motivated politically, often the premia is diverted from the legitimate users to political favorites who then sell their quotas to the former at market prices. A decline in capital formation is almost certain in this case. The same result may be thought to hold where such rent accrues to officials rather than to their legitimate users. It seems unlikely that public officials would have a higher marginal propensity to save than producers using such controlled inputs as cement, steel, fertilizers, foreign exchange, etc.

One final point about the impact of corruption on net capital formation remains to be made. We have earlier examined and rejected the claim that corruption improves allocative efficiency. If corruption then reduces current output below what it would be in its absence, one must also take into account the loss of savings from this reduction in national income. The magnitude of this loss would depend on the marginal propensity to save and the loss of income from allocative inefficiencies attendant upon corruption.

Substitute for Public Works: The expansion of public employment often constitutes an important mechanism for buying public support. And expansion of public employment resulting from nepotism and political patronage is regarded by some functionalists[35] as a welcome substitute for a public works system, especially in situations where unemployment threatens to boil over into open discontent. In confronting the merit of such an argument, one must point to the opportunities for creating productive employment that are foregone because of the politically motivated and unproductive expansion in public employment. In Egypt where official guarantees of employment for college graduates and demobilized military conscripts may have led to 20 percent excess employment in non-financial public enterprises, a redirection of wages paid to this surplus staff would under reasonable assumptions according to one article create productive jobs for the surplus staff in six years and also raise the public enterprise sector's value-added by 11 percent.[36]

VII

Political Effects of Corruption

DISCUSSIONS IN THE LITERATURE on the political effects of corruption follow from analyses of its causes. Under the most common scenario, the material inducements of corruption are seen to be substituting for the missing ideological bond, class interests and national commitment that motivates people to aggregate into political parties or throw their support behind governments engaged in national construction.[37] The third world countries are seen as divided by primary loyalties to family, clan and ethnic groups. Their demands, therefore, must be particularistic and can only be met by corruption at the enforcement stage of policies. In the words of Bayley, "Where potential schisms based upon the claims of caste, tribe, region, religion or language are manifold, common interest in spoils may provide cement or effective political unity, especially within a single dominant party."[38]

It was earlier suggested by us, in opposition to Scott,[39] that legislation need not be universalistic; it can be designed to benefit particular regions, groups and even individuals. And such legislation exists aplenty in most developing countries. Benefits of a particularist nature can be, and are created by appropriate timing and location of public projects. Should the widespread presence of corruption then lead us to conclude that the above legal means are inadequate for satisfying the excessive volume of particularist demands? Our suggestion is that corruption exists instead primarily to enrich the dominant ruling elite and has much less to do with the attempts of otherwise clean rulers forced to employ corruption as a nation-building tool.

Instead of performing a politically integrative function, such corruption seems more likely to do the opposite.[40] The very existence of revenues to be made out of corruption is likely to intensify the competition amongst various ethnic groups and cliques for its control. Where the corruption revenue comes to be monopolized by one ethnic group, this will generate discontent and political instability; and to counter such opposition there may well emerge a repressive State apparatus. But there also exists the possibility that the corruption revenue may come to be monopolized by a small clique which is then able to use a part of this revenue to buy out opponents or eliminate them if they turn out to be incorruptible. We then have a government which may give the appearance of a political machine, even though its internal dynamic is very different.

VIII

Concluding Remarks

THE ANALYSIS PRESENTED in this paper, we hope, has succeeded in undermining the functionalist theses regarding the political, economic and administrative effects of corruption in most developing countries. We have shown that the benefits of corruption are not apparent even where they are most confidently expected, *i.e.* market corruption does not appear to improve allocative efficiency. Nor does corruption appear likely to generate net additions to capital formation; rather a reduction in investment is more to be expected. What these results suggest is that the erosion in a government's capacity to formulate and implement economic policies—as a result of corruption—cannot be a blessing in disguise. But corruption does not appear either to generate the political benefits claimed for it: rather than helping to bind disparate ethnic groups, regions, clans and families with narrow loyalties, it is more likely to exacerbate these divisions. To sum up then: corruption appears not to be beneficial for economic development, nor is it indispensable as a tool of political integration.

454   *American Journal of Economics and Sociology*

Notes

1. See the survey by G. E. Caiden and N. J. Caiden, "Administrative Corruption," *Public Administration Review* 37, 3 (May–June 1977):301–9.

2. See D. H. Bayley, "The Effects of Corruption in a Developing Nation," *Western Political Quarterly* 19, 3 (December 1966):719–32, reprinted in *Political Corruption: Readings in Comparative Analysis*, ed., A. Heidenheimer (New York: Holt, Rhinehart and Winston, 1970):533.

3. This point is also made by Caiden and Caiden. It may be noted that the urban political machine to which the functionalist perspective was originally applied represented corruption that was limited to the elected officials of some city administrations in the U.S. See R. K. Merton, "Some Functions of the Political Machine," in: *Social Theory and Social Structure* (New York: Free Press, 1957):78–82.

4. See E. C. Banfield, "Corruption as a Feature of Governmental Organization," *Journal of Law and Economics*, 18 (1975):587–605.

5. See J. S. Nye, "Corruption and Political Development: A Cost-Benefit Analysis," *American Political Science Review* 61, 2 (1967):419; S. P. Huntington, "Modernization and Corruption," *Political Order in Changing Societies* (New Haven, Conn.: Yale University Press, 1968):59; and Bayley: 526.

6. See N. H. Leff, "Economic Development through Bureaucratic Corruption,: *American Behavioral Scientist*, 8, 3 (November 1964):8–14, reprinted in Heidenheimer: 510–20; A. Blomqvist and S. Mohammad, "Controls, Corruption and Competitive Rent-Seeking in LDCs," *Journal of Development Economics* 21 (1986):161–80; S. Rashid, "Public Utilities in Egalitarian LDCs: The Role of Bribery in Achieving Pareto Efficiency," *Kyklos* 34, 3 (1981):448–60; and R. O. Tilman, "The Emergence of Black-Market Bureaucracy: Administration, Development and Corruption in the New States," *Public Administration Review* (September/October 1968):437–44.

7. This may be done by placing party officials into lucrative positions generally reserved for career bureaucrats; also, they may engage in sale of appointments and transfers; or, arrangements may exist to transfer corruption revenue collected by bureaucracy to party coffers or powerful politicians.

8. See G. Myrdal, *Asian Drama*, Vol. 2 (New York: Pantheon: 1968):947; M. McMullan, "Corruption in the Public Services of British Colonies and Ex-Colonies in West Africa," *Sociological Review* 9, 2 (June 1961):181–200, reprinted in Heidenheimer: 318–19; and S. Andreski, "Kleptocracy or Corruption as a System of Government," in: *The African Predicament* (New York: Atherton, 1968):93.

9. For Ghana, see H. H. Werlin, "The Roots of Corruption: The Ghanaian Case," *Journal of Modern African Studies*, 10, 2 (1972):247–66; R. M. Price, *Society and Bureaucracy in Contemporary Ghana* (Berkeley, CA.: University of California Press, 1975); R. B. Seidman, "Why Do People Obey the Law? The Case of Corruption in Developing Countries," *British Journal of Law and Society*, 5, 1 (Summer 1978):49–50; and V. T. LeVine, *Political Corruption: The Ghana Case* (Stanford, CA.: Hoover Institution Press, 1975). For Zaire, see D. J. Gould, *Bureaucratic Corruption and Underdevelopment in the Third World: The Case of Zaire* (New York: Pergamon Press, 1980). For Nigeria, see R. Wraith and E. Simpkins, *Corruption in Developing Countries*, (W. W. Norton and Co., 1963); V. Eker, "On the Origins of Corruption: Irregular Incentives in Nigeria," *The Journal of Modern African Studies*, 19, 1 (1981):173–82; and C. Leys, "What Is the Problem About Corruption?" *Journal of Modern African Studies*, 3, 2 (1965):215–24. For Philippines, see J. V. Abueva, "What Are We in Power for? The Sociology of Graft and Corruption," *Philippine Sociological Review*, 18, 3 & 4 (July–October 1970):203–8. For India, see Myrdal: 943–46; R. Wade, "The System of Administrative and Political Corruption: Canal Irrigation in South India," *Journal of Development Studies*, 18, 3 (April 1982):287–328; R. Wade, "The Market for Public

Office: Why the Indian State Is Not Better at Development," *World Development*, 13, 4 (April 1985):480; and S. Kohli, ed., *Corruption in India* (New Delhi: Chetana Publications, 1975). For Bangladesh, see *The Economist* (London), Oct. 18, 1968:23–26. For Mexico, see J. W. Wilkie, *The Mexican Revolution: Federal Expenditure and Social Change* (Berkeley: 1967). For Indonesia, Thailand and Haiti, see J. C. Scott, *Comparative Political Corruption* (Englewood Cliffs, N.J.: Prentice-Hall, 1972):56–91.

10. See Scott: 16 and M. S. Alam, "The South Korean Miracle: Economics, Politics and Beyond" (Department of Economics, Concordia University: Discussion Paper No. 10, 1986).

11. See, *Report of the Committee on the Prevention of Corruption* (New Delhi: Government of India, 1964):10, 18, 108–9.

12. *Ibid.:* 10.

13. See, *Report of the Railway Corruption Enquiry Committee* (Delhi: Government of India, Ministry of Railways, 1955), quoted in R. Wade, "The Market for Public Office": 480.

14. See Wade, "The Market for Public Office."

15. *Ibid.:* 480.

16. See Gould: XIV.

17. See E. Lieuwen, *Arms and Politics in Latin America* (New York, 1960):149.

18. See S. Mydans, "Manila's No. 1 Conglomerate: Panel Seizing Marcos Wealth," *New York Times* (Feb. 9, 1987):1.

19. *The Economist:* 24.

20. O. Johnson, "An Economic Analysis of Corrupt Government, with Special Application to Less Developed Countries," *Kyklos* 28, 1 (1975):48.

21. These particularist tendencies are emphasized by nearly all writers. See, McMullan: 321; Myrdal: 947; W. F. Werthiem, "Sociological Aspects of Corruption in Southeast Asia," *Sociologica Neerlandica*, 1, 2 (Autumn 1963):129–52, reprinted in: Heidenheimer: 210–11; J. V. Abueva, "The Contributions of Nepotism, Spoils and Graft to Political Development," *East-West Center Review*, 3 (1966):45–54, reprinted in: Heidenheimer: 535; Price: 148; O. P. Dwivedi, "Bureaucratic Corruption in Developing Countries," *Asian Survey*, 12, 4 (April 1967):247; Eker: 175; Andreski: 352, etc.

22. See Price: 150–1.

23. See Leys: 341 and S. P. Huntington, "Modernization and Corruption," *Political Order in Changing Societies* (New Haven, Conn.: Yale Univ. Press, 1968):59–71, reprinted in: Heidenheimer: 496.

24. See M. Szeftel, "Political Graft and the Spoils System in Zambia: The State as a Resource in Itself," *Review of African Political Economy*, 24 (1982):4.

25. Myrdal: 940–42.

26. See Banfield.

27. The proportion of officials charged with corruption in most developing countries is miniscule. Moreover, this also amounts to tokenism in most cases: most of the recorded charges are laid against petty officials.

28. J. C. Scott, "Corruption, Machine Politics and Political Change," *American Political Science Review*, 63, 4 (1969):1142–1159.

29. L. P. Jones, "Public Enterprise for Whom? Perverse Distributional Consequences of Public Operational Decisions," *Economic Development and Cultural Change*, 33, 2 (Jan. 1985):333.

30. See R. Sandbrook, "The State and Economic Stagnation in Tropical Africa," *World Development*, 14, 3 (March 1986):319–32.

31. Haiti under "Papa Doc" and "Baby Doc" Duvalier easily fits this description. See Scott, *Comparative Political Corruption:* 84–86.

32. Leff: 513 and 515.

33. Wade, "The Market for Public Office": 485.

34. See Nye: 419 and J. Abueva, "The Contribution of Nepotism, Spoils, and Graft to Political Development,": 538.

35. See Bayley: 531.

36. See Jones: 340–41.

37. See Abueva, "What Are We in Power for"; Abueva, "The Contribution of Nepotism, Spoils and Graft to Political Development"; Bayley; and M. Weiner, *The Politics of Scarcity* (Chicago: Chicago Univ. Press, 1962).

38. Bayley: 530–31.

39. Scott, "Corruption, Machine Politics and Political Change."

40. See R. Lemarchand and K. Legg, "Political Clientilism and Development: A Preliminary Analysis," *Comparative Politics*, 4, 2 (January 1972):173.

[13]

CORRUPTION*

ANDREI SHLEIFER AND ROBERT W. VISHNY

This paper presents two propositions about corruption. First, the structure of government institutions and of the political process are very important determinants of the level of corruption. In particular, weak governments that do not control their agencies experience very high corruption levels. Second, the illegality of corruption and the need for secrecy make it much more distortionary and costly than its sister activity, taxation. These results may explain why, in some less developed countries, corruption is so high and so costly to development.

I. INTRODUCTION

We define government corruption as the sale by government officials of government property for personal gain. For example, government officials often collect bribes for providing permits and licenses, for giving passage through customs, or for prohibiting the entry of competitors. In these cases they charge personally for goods that the state officially owns. In most cases the goods that the government officials sell are not demanded for their own sake, but rather enable private agents to pursue economic activity they could not pursue otherwise. Licenses, permits, passports, and visas are needed to comply with laws and regulations that restrict private economic activity. Insofar as government officials have discretion over the provision of these goods, they can collect bribes from private agents.

Corruption is both pervasive and significant around the world. In some developing countries, such as Zaire and Kenya, it probably amounts to a large fraction of the Gross National Product. Corruption is also common in the developed countries: defense officials sometimes sell contracts for personal gain, and local zoning officials are bribed to rezone. Still, economic studies of corruption are rather limited. Following Becker and Stigler [1974], most studies (e.g., Banfield [1975], Rose-Ackerman [1975, 1978], and Klitgaard [1988, 1991]), focus on the principal-agent model of corruption. This model focuses on the relationship between the principal, i.e., the top level of government, and the agent, i.e., an official, who takes the bribes from the private individuals interested in some government-produced good. These studies examine ways of motivating the agent to be honest, ranging from efficiency

*We are grateful to Lawrence Katz and two anonymous referees for comments, and to the Bradley Foundation for financial support.

wages [Becker and Stigler, 1974] to indoctrination [Klitgaard, 1991]. In this paper we take the principal-agent problem as given—the corrupt official has some effective property rights over the government good he is allocating—and focus on *consequences* of corruption for resource allocation.

In particular, we address two issues. First, we discuss the implications of how the corruption network is organized. In some economies, such as Korea today and Russia under Communists, while corruption is pervasive, the person paying the bribe is assured that he gets the government good that he is paying for, and does not need to pay further bribes in the future. In other economies many government goods can be obtained without bribes altogether. For example, a citizen can get a passport in the United States without paying a bribe. In yet other economies, such as many African countries and post-Communist Russia, numerous bureaucrats need to be bribed to get a government permit, and bribing one does not guarantee that some other bureaucrat or even the first one does not demand another bribe. We examine the implications of these three regimes for the level of corruption and for the effects of corruption on economic activity.

Second, we ask why even well-organized corruption appears to be more distortionary than taxation. Several authors have pointed out that some corruption might be desirable [Leff, 1964]. First, it works like a piece rate for government employees (a bureaucrat might be more helpful when paid directly). Second, it enables entrepreneurs to overcome cumbersome regulations. Yet most studies conclude that corruption slows down development [Gould and Amaro-Reyes, 1983; United Nations, 1989; and Klitgaard, 1991]. We ask why bribery might be much more costly than its sister activity, taxation, and argue that the imperative of *secrecy* makes bribes more distortionary than taxes.

The next section sets out our basic model of corruption, and briefly addresses the question of why corruption spreads. Section III looks at the market structure of the supply of government goods as a determinant of the level and consequences of corruption. Section IV examines the costs of corruption focusing on secrecy. Section V concludes.

II. BASIC MODEL

To fix ideas, we consider the simplest model of one government-produced good, such as a passport, or a right to use a government road, or an import license. We assume that this good is homogeneous, and that there is a demand curve for this good, $D(p)$, from the private agents. We assume that this good is sold for the government by an official, *who has the opportunity to restrict the quantity of the good that is sold.* Specifically, he can deny a private agent the passport, access to a road, or an import license. In practice, this denial might mean a long delay or an imposition of many requirements. But it is easier to assume for now that the official can simply refuse to provide the good. An important reason why many of these permits and regulations exist is probably to give officials the power to deny them and to collect bribes in return for providing the permits [De Soto, 1989].

We also assume that the official can in fact restrict supply without any risk of detection or punishment from above. Corrupt officials go unpunished because their bosses often share in the proceeds and because public pressure to stop corruption in most countries is weak. We shall also discuss the case in which corruption is penalized. But for now, the government official is a monopolist selling the good. His objective is to maximize the value of the bribes he collects from selling this government good.

Let the official government price of this good be p. We assume that the cost of producing this good is completely immaterial to the official since the government is paying this cost. This assumption is a bit restrictive. While it covers the sale of an import license, a passport, or a passage on a government road, a policeman who sells his services that he is supposed to provide for free does exert personal effort and so does care about its cost. For simplicity, we focus on government goods that cost the official nothing personally to provide, so that he has no interest in how much it costs the government to produce these goods.

What then is the marginal cost to the official of providing this good? We distinguish two cases. First, in the case *without theft,* the official actually turns over the official price of the good to the government. In this case, the marginal cost of providing the good to the official is this government price p. For example, when an official sells a license for a government price plus a bribe, he keeps the bribe but the amount p stays with the government; hence p is his marginal cost. In contrast, in the case *with theft,* the official does not turn over anything to the government at all, and simply hides the sale. In this case, the price that the buyer pays is only equal to the bribe, and might be even lower than the official price. For example, customs officials often let goods through the border for less than the official duty, but then give nothing at all to the government. In this case, the marginal cost to the official is zero. While conceptually the two cases are similar—they differ only in the level of the marginal cost to the official—in the first case corruption always raises the total price of the good, whereas in the second case it might reduce it. Corruption with theft is obviously more attractive to the buyers.

If the official cannot price discriminate between buyers, then as a monopolist, he will simply set the marginal revenue equal to the marginal cost. In the case without theft, the total price with the bribe always exceeds the government price. It pays the official to create a shortage at the official price, and then to collect bribes as a way to clear the market for the government-supplied good [Shleifer and Vishny, 1992]. In the case with theft, the total price might be below the government price. Figures Ia and Ib present the solutions to this problem for the cases without and with theft, respectively.

This analysis suggests a similarity between bribes and commodity taxes. In the case without theft, the bribe is exactly equal to the revenue-maximizing commodity tax when marginal cost is equal to the state price p. Of course, taxes need not be set to maximize revenue. More importantly, taxes are typically kept by the government rather than the bureaucrats. In monarchal regimes, the

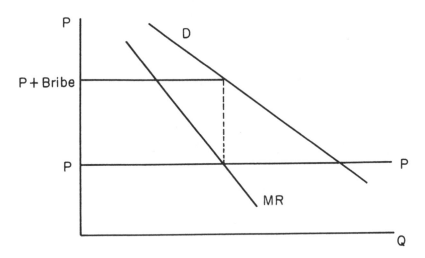

FIGURE Ia
Corruption without Theft

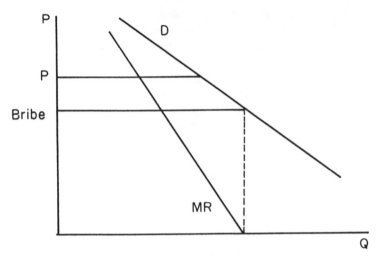

FIGURE Ib
Corruption with Theft

distinction between taxes and bribes is blurred by the fact that the treasury is indistinguishable from the sovereign's pocket. Yet for most governments, the distinction is material and shows how corruption substitutes for taxation.

Penalizing the official for corruption changes the level of the bribe he demands, but does not change the essence of the problem. If the probability of detection and the penalty are independent of the bribe and of the number of people who pay it, the official will charge the same bribe provided that the penalties are not so high that corruption is no longer profitable. If the expected penalty increases with the level of the bribe, he might reduce the bribe and raise output. On the other hand, if the expected penalty rises in the number of people he charges a bribe (for example, because of the higher probability of a complaint), then he will reduce the supply and raise the bribe. The official trades off the benefits given in Figures Ia and Ib against the expected penalties. For our purposes, we do not need to focus on this aspect of the problem (see Becker and Stigler [1974], Rose-Ackerman [1978], and Klitgaard [1988]).

This simple analysis suggests that corruption spreads because of competition both between the officials and between the consumers. If jobs are distributed among officials through an auction mechanism, whereby those who pay the most for a job get it, then the prospective officials who do not collect bribes simply cannot afford jobs. Conversely, those who will collect more (perhaps through more effective price discrimination), will offer the higher officials more for the jobs, and so will be able to get them. Competition between officials will assure that maximal bribes are collected.

Even more important for the spread of corruption is competition between the buyers in the case with theft. If buyer A can buy the government service more cheaply than buyer B can, then he can outcompete buyer B in the product market. So if buyer A bribes an official to reduce his costs, his competitors must do so also. If all real estate owners in a city can bribe their way out of paying taxes, then those who pay them will not survive. If some trucks carry goods across a border after paying a small bribe instead of the official customs duty, the importers who pay the duty will not survive. Competition between buyers of government services assures the spread of cost-reducing corruption. Interestingly, such competition does not help the spread of corruption *without* theft.

Corruption with theft spreads because observance of law does not survive in a competitive environment. In addition, the buyer in this case has no incentive to inform on the official, and hence the likelihood that corruption is detected is much smaller. This creates a further incentive for corruption with theft to rise. Because corruption with theft aligns the interests of the buyers and sellers, it will be more persistent than corruption without theft, which pits buyers against sellers. This result suggests that the first step to reduce corruption should be to create an accounting system that prevents theft from the government. In the collection of taxes and customs duties, such accounting systems might well reduce corruption because without theft bribes raise the buyer's cost and hence give him the incentive to expose the corrupt official.

III. The Industrial Organization of Corruption

The model above makes two strong assumptions. First, a buyer needs only one government good to conduct his business. Second, the official is a monopolist in the supply of this good. Yet some critical issues in corruption arise when these assumptions do not hold. In many cases, a private agent needs several *complementary* government goods to conduct business. For example, an importer might need several government licenses and permits, to be obtained from several agencies, to bring in, unload, transport, and sell an imported good. A builder might need several permits from different departments, such as fire, water, and police. With multiple goods, the market structure in their provision becomes important. The different agencies that supply the complementary goods might collude, sell the different goods independently, or even compete in the provision of some goods. The focus on market structure in the provision of complementary government goods sheds light on the consequences of corruption.

The model of the previous section is most appropriate for understanding corruption in monarchies, such as the Bourbons in France or Marcos' Philippines, in the old-time Communist regimes, and in regions dominated by a single mafia. In such places, it is always clear who needs to be bribed and by how much. The bribe is then divided between all the relevant government bureaucrats, who agree not to demand further bribes from the buyer of the package of government goods, such as permits. In Russia, for example, bribes were channeled through local Communist party offices. Any deviation from the agreed-upon pattern of corruption would be penalized by the party bureaucracy, so few deviations occurred. Once a bribe was paid, the buyer got full property rights over the set of government goods that he bought. Carino [1986] and Klitgaard [1988] describe similar monopolistic corruption structures in the Philippines.

There are two extreme alternatives to this monopoly corruption scheme. The first alternative is corruption in some African countries, in India, and in post-Communist Russia. Here the sellers of the complementary government goods, such as permits and licenses, act independently. Different ministries, agencies, and levels of local government all set their own bribes independently in an attempt to maximize their own revenue, rather than the combined revenue of all the bribe collectors. In Russia in 1991, for example, getting a business started often required bribing the local legislature, the central ministry, the local executive branch, the fire authorities, the water authorities etc. In some African countries, many quasi-independent government agencies have the power to stop a project, and use it to set bribes without collusion with other agencies [Klitgaard, 1990]. The army and the police also often demand a cut for protection—another needed government input. Unlike the single monopoly model, here complementary government goods are sold by independent monopolists.

Formally, consider first a joint monopolist agency that sets the cum bribe prices p_1 and p_2 of two government goods. Let x_1 and x_2 be the quantities of these goods sold. Let the official prices, equal to the monopolist's marginal costs, be denoted by MC_1 and MC_2. The per unit bribes then are $p_1 - MC_1$ and $p_2 - MC_2$. The joint monopolist agency sets p_1 at which

$$(1) \qquad MR_1 + MR_2 \frac{dx_2}{dx_1} = MC_1,$$

where MR_1 and MR_2 denote marginal revenues from the sale of goods 1 and 2, respectively. When the two goods are complements, as government permits for the same project are, then $dx_2/dx_1 > 0$, and so at the optimum, $MR_1 < MC_1$. The monopolist agency keeps the bribe on good 1 down to expand the demand for the complementary good 2 and thus to raise its profits from bribes on good 2. For the same reason, this agency keeps down the price of good 2.

Suppose alternatively that permits 1 and 2 are allocated by independent agencies. Each agency then takes the other's output as given, and in particular, in equation (1), dx_2/dx_1 is set to zero. At the independent agency's optimum, $MR_1 = MC_1$. Hence the per unit bribe is higher, and the output lower, than at the joint monopolist optimum. Because the independent agency ignores the effect of its raising its bribe on demand for the complementary permits and hence the bribes to the other agency, it sets a higher bribe, which results in a lower output and a lower aggregate level of bribes. By acting independently, the two agencies actually hurt each other, as well as the private buyers of the permits.

This problem is made much worse in many countries by free entry into the collection of bribes. New government organizations and officials often have the opportunity to create laws and regulations that enable them to become providers of additional required permits and licenses and charge for them accordingly. Having paid three bribes, the buyer of these inputs learns that he must buy yet another one if he wants his project to proceed. In some cases, the officials who have collected the bribe previously come back to demand more (see Klitgaard [1990] for striking examples). In these cases, the property rights to his project are not really transferred to the buyer when he pays the bribe. The point is that even the list of the complementary inputs is not fixed, and tends to expand when profitable corruption opportunities stimulate entry. When entry is completely free, the total bribe rises to infinity and the sales of the package of government goods, as well as bribe revenues, fall to zero.

In the third scenario, *each one* of the several complementary government goods can be supplied by at least two government agencies. For simplicity, begin with the case of one such good, such as a United States passport or a driver's license. A citizen can obtain a U. S. passport without paying a bribe. The likely reason for this is that if an official asks him for a bribe, he will go to another window or another city. Because collusion between several agents is difficult, bribe competition between the providers will drive the level of bribes down to zero. This example can be extended to the case of multiple complementary goods. If a builder needs several permits to erect a building, but any one of them can be obtained from one of several noncolluding government agents, Bertrand competition in bribes will force the equilibrium bribe on each permit down to zero. Unlike the first model, where a unified monopoly provides all the goods, and the second model, in which monopoly suppliers of different goods act independently, here the market for each government-supplied good is competitive.

As in other industrial organization contexts, even having two competitors is not necessary if the market is subject to potential competition or entry [Demsetz, 1968]. Consider, for example, a single government employee in a small U. S. city, who controls building permits, dog permits, permits to dispose of old appliances, etc. If this employee attempts to charge a bribe, or to price his services above marginal cost, another individual would offer the public the same service at a lower price, and the corrupt official will be recalled or fail to get reelected. The threat of such competition would then keep corruption down to zero, assuming that the official price covers the marginal cost of providing the permits.

The level of bribes is the lowest in the third case, intermediate in the first, and the highest in the second. But the total amount of revenues collected is higher in the first case than in the second, since the independent monopolist suppliers drive the quantity sold so far down that the total revenues from corruption fall. This result is obvious: in the first case the suppliers of the complementary inputs collude to maximize the total value of bribes, but in the second they do not.

This problem is formally identical to a standard problem in industrial organization. Suppose that a carmaker needs two complementary inputs, glass and steel. If both are provided by one monopolist, he will realize that raising the price of glass reduces the demand for his own steel, and hence his profits on the steel sales, and similarly with raising the price of steel. Accordingly, he will price steel and glass taking account of the demand complementarities. In contrast, if glass and steel are sold by two independent monopolists, each will ignore the effect of his raising his price on the demand for the product of the other. As a result, each would charge a higher price than a joint monopolist would, and both the quantity of steel and glass sold, and the combined profits from these sales would be lower. In the last scenario, if each of these independent monopolists can sell both steel and glass, and they compete on price, they will drive the price of both steel and glass down to the marginal cost. The profits will be the lowest, and output the highest, of the three cases. Competition is the best; joint monopoly is the second best; and independent monopoly is the worst for efficiency. Moreover, the more inputs car production requires, the lower is output with independent monopolists.

Another helpful analogy is to tollbooths on a road. The joint monopoly solution corresponds to the case of one toll that gives the payer the right to use the entire road. The independent monopolists solution means that different towns through which the road passes independently erect their own tollbooths and charge their own tolls. The volume of traffic and aggregate toll collections fall. In fact, they fall to zero when *any* party can erect its own tollbooth on this road. The competitive case corresponds to multiple booths competing with each other for the right to collect the toll, or alternatively to the case of multiple roads. In this case, the volume of traffic is obviously the highest, and toll collections are the lowest.

This, in fact, is a very close analogy. In India, taking a road between two towns indeed requires paying a bribe in every village through which the road passes. Taking goods inland in Zaire is more expensive because of corruption than bringing them from Europe by ship to a port. In 1400 there were 60 independently run tolls along the Rhine. Along the Seine there were so many tolls that to ship a good twenty miles cost as much as its price. In contrast, rivers in England were free of such tolls, which in part explains the ability of England to develop specialized, commercial agriculture feeding London, the world's center of commerce [Heilbroner, 1962]. These examples suggest how costly free entry into bribe collection might be to development.

This industrial organization perspective on corruption sheds light on the consequences of corruption in different countries and places. It also raises the far deeper question: what determines the industrial organization of the different corruption markets? How did Brezhnev and Marcos manage to enforce joint profit maximization? Why has this system fallen apart in Russia, and never existed in Africa? How has the U. S. government managed to eradicate corruption in the provision of at least some, though by no means all, government goods?

Enforcement of joint profit maximization in bribe collection is closely related to the problem of enforcing collusion in oligopoly. Stigler [1964] shows that collusion is more likely to be enforced when price-cutting can be easily detected, and punishment for price-cutting can be severe. In the corruption context the parallel argument is that collusive bribe maximization can be enforced more easily when bribe *increases* can be more easily detected and more severely punished.

Bribe increases can be easily detected in several circumstances. First, when the government has an effective policing machine to monitor the actions of the bureaucrats, such as the KGB in the Soviet Union or Mayor Daley's Democratic Party machine in Chicago, it is hard to charge excessive bribes without being found out. Second, when the ruling elite is small, as in the Philippines or in Communist Russia, deviations from normal bribes will be easy to see. Third, when the society is homogeneous and closely knit, as in East Asia, deviations from normal bribes are likely to become known to friends and family, and such knowledge is likely to spread. Police states, small oligarchies, and homogeneous societies are thus likely to come closer to joint bribe maximization than more open, less tightly governed and more heterogeneous societies.

The ability of the cartel to punish those who charge excessive bribes is also essential to enforcing collusion. The ability of the leadership to exclude deviators from the rents associated with being an insider is essential. When large rents come from being a communist in Russia, a democratic politician in Chicago, a part of the ruling clique, or a member of the military elite, and when the sovereign can take these rents away from the deviators, deviations are unlikely. On the other hand, if the rents are small, and, more importantly, the sovereign is in no position to take them away, joint bribe maximization cannot be sustained. For example, in feudal Europe, in post-Communist Russia, and in many African countries, the central government is so weak that it cannot fire or penalize officials in the provinces, or even bureaucrats sitting in the capital, for running their own corruption rackets. In this situation the "independent monopolists" model, with its devastating economic consequences, describes reality best.

Huntington [1968] observes that political modernization, defined as a transition from an autocratic to a more democratic government, is usually accompanied by increases in corruption. He attributes this problem to underdeveloped institutions under the newly formed governments. If underdeveloped institutions mean a weak state machine, then Huntington's story fits well with our model. New governments lose monopoly over bribe collection, and as a result, multiple agencies take bribes where only one did before, leading to a much less efficient allocation. In the Philippines under Marcos, all corruption flowed to the top; since his demise, the number of independent bribe takers has increased, and so the efficiency of resource allocation has probably declined. Russia under Communists had a monolithic bribe collection system. With Communists gone, central government officials, local officials, ministry officials, and many others are taking bribes, leading to much higher bribes in equilibrium though perhaps lower corruption revenues, just as the model predicts. Similar stories are told about Africa after independence, when the colonial corruption machines disintegrated [Ekpo, 1979]. The evidence is strikingly consistent in showing the superiority of monopolistic bribe taking over that by independent monopolists.

The two cases we examined share basically authoritarian governments with little responsiveness to public pressure against corruption. As a result, both produce high levels of corruption, although they differ in how inefficient this corruption is. Countries with more political competition have stronger public pressure against corruption—through laws, democratic elections, and even the independent press—and so are more likely to use government organizations that contain rather than maximize corruption proceeds. It is implausible to think, for example, that the U. S. president maximizes corruption proceeds, since such a president is likely to be exposed and thrown out of office. Even in Japan and Korea, where corruption is very common, the level of bribes tends to be significantly lower than in Russia or the Philippines. The likely reason for this is political competition within the ruling parties as well as from the opposition parties in these countries. Because low bribes keep potential competitors out, political competition keeps corruption down (see Demsetz [1968]).

Our industrial organization perspective suggests that the best arrangement to reduce corruption *without theft* is to produce competition between bureaucrats in the provision of government goods, which will drive bribes down to zero. The passport office, and many other agencies of the U. S. government, have actually introduced such arrangements. The Pentagon has not, and it is probably more corrupt. The general idea behind federalism is precisely such competition in the provision of public goods, although it is usually stated in terms of taxes rather than bribes. Of course, in the case of corruption *with theft*, competitive pressure might increase theft from the government at the same time as it reduces bribes. The appropriate policy, then, is to create competition in the provision of government goods while intensively monitoring theft.

IV. CORRUPTION AND SECRECY

Although some political scientists have argued that the optimal level of corruption is positive [Leff, 1964; Huntington, 1968], most studies suggest that existing corruption levels are detrimental to development [Gould and Amaro-Reyes, 1983; United Nations, 1989; Klitgaard, 1991]. Africa is reputed to be a very corrupt continent; it is also the poorest one. Central and South America are also known for the extreme corruption and poverty. In contrast, developed countries appear to be less corrupt.

Mauro [1993] presents the first systematic empirical analysis of corruption by focusing on the relationship between investment and corruption. Mauro uses an index of corruption from *Business International* [1984], a publication of *Economist Intelligence Unit*, which supplies subjective assessments of 56 risk factors for 68 countries to private investors. The corruption variable is defined as "the degree to which business transactions involve corruption and questionable payments," and is used for 1980. The average ratio of total and private investment to GDP for the period between 1970 and 1985 is drawn from Barro [1991], as is real GDP per capita for 1980. Mauro finds that, holding 1980 real GDP constant, countries with higher corruption have a lower ratio of both total and private investment to GDP. The estimates are statistically significant. These results are consistent with the view that corruption is bad for development.

The independent monopolists model, which shows that under free entry of bribe takers supplying complementary inputs the total bribe rises to infinity and productive output falls to zero, may help explain why the most corrupt countries are so poor. Yet even more modest corruption seems to have detrimental effects. In this section we discuss these detrimental effects of corruption.

In the case of an economywide bribe-collecting monopolist, such as Marcos, corruption is similar to revenue-maximizing taxation. Like the sovereign who optimally taxes different goods and activities, the monopolist will set bribes to maximize revenue. In this world it is difficult to distinguish between bribes and taxes. Taxes are the markup on the price that goes into the treasury, and bribes are the markup that goes into the pocket of the monopolist. When the treasury and the pocket are one and the same, as in the case of kings and Marcos, taxes and bribes are exactly the same. With multiple monopolists, bribes are also similar to taxes, except that tax rates on different activities are set by independent agencies. In setting tax rates in this way, the agencies maximize their own tax revenues rather than the aggregate tax revenue. Because they ignore the cross elasticities of demand, the aggregate tax revenues are lower in this case. Finally, the case of competing monopolists corresponds to the federalist ideal of competing juris-dictions. In this case as well, bribes are similar to taxes.[1]

Despite these similarities, bribes differ from taxes in one crucial way, namely, unlike taxation, corruption is usually illegal and must be kept secret. Efforts to avoid detection and punishment cause corruption to be more distortionary than taxation. On some goods, taking bribes without being detected is much easier than on others. Government officials will then use their powers to induce substitution into the goods on which bribes can be more easily collected without detection. For example, officials might ban some imports to induce substitution into others. Or they might prohibit entry of some firms to raise bribe revenue from existing monopo-lies. Historically, sovereigns used such mercantilist policies to increase tax collections because monopoly profits are easier to tax than income [Ekelund and Tollison, 1981]. But such policies can also be used to increase bribes. Using our roadblock analogy, bureaucrats shut down some roads to increase the tolls on the passage through others, especially if the tolls on the shut-down roads are more difficult to collect.

A very simple numerical example may clarify this point. Suppose that a country can import either green or red cars, and that the border price of either car is 5. Suppose that consumers demand only ten cars total and that the valuation of a red car is 15 for each consumer but of a green car it is only 10. In a free market the country will import only red cars at the price of 5, and end up with a consumer surplus of $10 \times (15 - 5) = 100$. If the ministry

---

1. Importantly, if corruption with theft *replaces* taxes, then the corrupt state might have to replace the lost revenue through very distortionary taxation.

could tax car imports, it would charge an import duty of 10 per car, which would result in the importation of ten red cars, no consumer surplus, and the government revenue of 100. In this case, taxes lead to no efficiency losses but a redistribution from consumers to the government. Suppose alternatively that the trade ministry bureaucrats want to raise revenue through bribes rather than taxes. However, they cannot undetectably collect bribes at the border for importing *red* cars (which are too bright and noticeable), but can collect bribes for importing green cars. The ministry then bans red car imports altogether, and demands a bribe of $10 - 5 = 5$ on each imported green car. In equilibrium, no red cars are imported, the consumer surplus falls to zero, and bureaucrats collect $10 \times 5 = 50$ on the import of green cars. Social surplus falls from 100 in the case of taxation to 50 in the case of corruption.

The surplus is even lower if resources are spent by the bureaucrats on securing their positions, and by them and importers on avoiding detection and punishment. These rent-seeking activities consume resources and dissipate gains from bribes [Tullock, 1967; Krueger, 1974]. In the extreme case, the cost of such rent-seeking activities adds up to the whole remaining bribe surplus of 50. In this case, corruption eliminates the social surplus from imports completely.

A real-world example of a bottle-making factory in Mozambique illustrates these distortions from corruption. In 1991 that factory had modern Western equipment for making bottles, but used a traditional process for putting paper labels on these bottles. Three old machines were used: one cut the labels from paper; one then glued the white label on the bottle; and finally one printed a red picture on the label. The bottles were moved manually between these machines. In roughly 30 percent of the cases, the picture was not centered on the label. When this happened, the bottles were handed over to approximately twelve women who sat on the floor near the machines and scraped off the labels with knives, so that the bottles could be put through this process again.

Apparently, the process of labeling bottles could be mechanized with a fairly simple machine that cost about $10,000 and could be readily bought with aid money from any of a number of western or even Third World suppliers. The manager of the factory, however, did not want to buy such a machine, but instead wanted to have a $100,000 machine, that not only mechanized the existing process, but also printed labels in sixteen colors and different shapes, and put them on different types of bottles. Only one producer in the world made that machine, and the Mozambiquan government applied to the producer's home country for an aid package to buy it. Since that aid was not immediately forthcoming, the factory kept using the traditional technology.

The demand for equipment much fancier than the factory appeared to need seems irrational until one realizes that buying a fancier machine offered the manager (and the ministry officials) much better opportunities for corruption. If the factory bought a generic machine, the manager would probably have to use international donors' guidelines and consider several offers. There would be very little in this deal for him personally. On the other hand, if he got a unique machine, he would not have to solicit alternative bids. The supplier in turn would be happy to overinvoice for the machine, and kick back some of the profits to the manager (and his ministerial counterpart). The corruption opportunities on buying a unique and expensive machine are much better than such opportunities on buying cheaper generic products.

The social cost of corruption in this example may be large. If the social value of the $100,000 machine is only $20,000, and the bribe that the manager can collect from overinvoicing is $3000, then the social cost of corruption is $80,000. In other words, social costs of misdirection of resources toward activities that offer better corruption opportunities can vastly exceed bribe revenues.

Western observers often wonder about the preference for unnecessarily advanced rather than "appropriate" technology by Third World governments. Overinvoicing provides the obvious explanation for this preference for advanced technology. The rational managers and bureaucrats in poor countries want to import goods on which bribes are the easiest to take, not the goods that are most profitable for the state firms. To do that, they basically discourage or even prohibit the importation of appropriate technology, and encourage the importation of unique goods on which overpayment and overinvoicing are more difficult to detect. As a result, very poor countries end up with equipment way beyond their needs.

This example fits neatly into our framework. To maximize the value of their personal revenues, bureaucrats prohibit imports of goods on which bribes cannot be collected without detection, and encourage imports of goods on which they can collect bribes. As a consequence, the menu of both consumer and producer goods available in the country is determined by corruption opportunities rather than tastes or technological needs. This argument might suggest why so many poor countries would rather spend their limited resources on infrastructure projects and defense, where corruption opportunities are abundant, than on education and health, where they are much more limited. In light of the enormous returns on these forgone health and education projects, the social costs of corruption might be enormous. Without the need to keep corruption secret, officials could collect their bounty in much less distortionary ways.

The imperative of secrecy entails another potentially important cost of corruption, namely its hostility to change and innovation. Keeping corruption secret requires keeping down the number of people involved in giving and receiving bribes. The elite must then include only a small oligarchy of politicians and businessmen, and refuse entry to newcomers. This situation may well describe the Philippines under Marcos, Russia under Communists, or some African dictatorships. But innovation and change are often precipitated by outsiders. To the extent that the elite prevents them from entering, to maintain their profits or simply to keep down its numbers to preserve secrecy, growth will suffer. It remains an interesting puzzle how small ruling elites in Korea have managed to keep up innovation and growth despite the effective exclusion of outsiders from both economic and political participation.

V. CONCLUSION

This paper has explored two broad reasons why corruption may be costly to economic development. The first reason is the weakness of central government, which allows various governmental agencies and bureaucracies to impose independent bribes on private agents seeking complementary permits from these agencies. When the entry of these agencies into regulation is free, they will drive the cumulative bribe burden on private agents to infinity. A good illustration of this problem is foreign investment in post-Communist Russia. To invest in a Russian company, a foreigner must bribe every agency involved in foreign investment, including the foreign investment office, the relevant industrial ministry, the finance ministry, the executive branch of the local government, the legislative branch, the central bank, the state property bureau, and so on. The obvious result is that foreigners do not invest in Russia. Such competing bureaucracies, each of which can stop a project from proceeding, hamper investment and

616   *QUARTERLY JOURNAL OF ECONOMICS*

growth around the world, but especially in countries with weak governments.

Downs [1967] calls the expansion of bureaucracies into new regulations "territoriality," but does not elaborate on its consequences for resource allocation. We showed how costly territoriality can be when different agencies are neither kept honest nor controlled by a central authority. We have explored the effects of territoriality when agencies impose regulations independently to maximize their individual bribe revenues. But even if bureaucrats are kept honest and introduce regulations only to expand their own domains without coordination from above, compliance with these regulations can be very costly to private agents.

The second broad reason that corruption is costly is the distortions entailed by the necessary secrecy of corruption. The demands of secrecy can shift a country's investments away from the highest value projects, such as health and education, into potentially useless projects, such as defense and infrastructure, if the latter offer better opportunities for secret corruption. The demands of secrecy can also cause leaders of a country to maintain monopolies, to prevent entry, and to discourage innovation by outsiders if expanding the ranks of the elite can expose existing corruption practices. Such distortions from corruption can discourage useful investment and growth.

Throughout the paper we have argued that economic and political competition can reduce the level of corruption and its adverse effects. If different agencies compete in the provision of the same services, corruption will be driven down provided that agents cannot simply steal. Similarly, political competition opens up the government, reduces secrecy, and so can reduce corruption provided that decentralization of power does not lead to agency fiefdom and anarchy.

HARVARD UNIVERSITY
UNIVERSITY OF CHICAGO

REFERENCES

Banfield, Edward, "Corruption as a Feature of Government Organization," *Journal of Law and Economics*, XVIII (1975), 587–605.
Barro, Robert J., "Economic Growth in a Cross Section of Countries," *Quarterly Journal of Economics*, CVI (1991), 407–44.
Becker, Gary S., and George J. Stigler, "Law Enforcement, Malfeasance, and the Compensation of Enforcers," *Journal of Legal Studies*, III, (1974), 1–19.
Business International Corporation, *Introduction to the Country Assessment Service* (New York: Business International Corporation, 1984).

Carino, Ledivina V., ed., *Bureaucratic Corruption in Asia: Causes, Consequences, and Controls* (Quezon City, The Philippines: JMC Press, 1986).

Demsetz, Harold, "Why Regulate Utilities?" *Journal of Law and Economics*, XI (1968), 55–66.

De Soto, Hernando, *The Other Path* (New York: Harper and Row, 1989).

Downs, Anthony, *Inside Bureaucracy* (Boston, MA: Little, Brown, 1967).

Ekelund, Robert B., and Robert D. Tollison, *Mercantilism as a Rent Seeking Society* (College Station, TX: Texas A&M University Press, 1981).

Ekpo, Monday, *Bureaucratic Corruption in Sub-Saharan Africa: Toward a Search of Causes and Consequences* (Washington, DC: University Press of America, 1979).

Gould, David J., and Jose A. Amaro-Reyes, *The Effects of Corruption on Administrative Performance*, World Bank Staff Working Paper No. 580 (Washington, DC: The World Bank, 1983).

Heilbroner, Robert, *The Making of Economic Society* (Englewood Cliffs, NJ: Prentice-Hall, 1962).

Huntington, Samuel P., *Political Order in Changing Societies* (New Haven, CT: Yale University Press, 1968).

Klitgaard, Robert, *Controlling Corruption* (Berkeley, CA: University of California Press, 1988).

——, *Tropical Gangsters* (New York: Basic Books, 1990).

——, "Gifts and Bribes," in Richard Zeckhauser, ed., *Strategy and Choice* (Cambridge, MA: MIT Press, 1991).

Krueger, Anne P., "The Political Economy of a Rent-Seeking Society," *American Economic Review*, LXIV (1974), 291–303.

Leff, Nathaniel, "Economic Development through Bureaucratic Corruption," *American Behavioral Scientist* (1964), 8–14.

Mauro, Paolo, "Country Risk and Growth," mimeo, 1993.

Rose-Ackerman, Susan, "The Economics of Corruption," *Journal of Public Economics*, IV (1975), 187–203.

——, *Corruption: A Study of Political Economy* (New York: Academic Press, 1978).

Shleifer, Andrei, and Robert W. Vishny, "Pervasive Shortages under Socialism," *Rand Journal of Economics*, XXIII (1992), 237–46.

Stigler, George J., "A Theory of Oligopoly," *Journal of Political Economy*, LXXII (1964), 44–61.

Tullock, Gordon, "The Welfare Cost of Tariffs, Monopoly and Theft," *Economic Inquiry*, V (1967), 224–32.

United Nations, *Corruption in Government* (New York: United Nations, 1989).

[14]

CORRUPTION AND GROWTH*

Paolo Mauro

This paper analyzes a newly assembled data set consisting of subjective indices of corruption, the amount of red tape, the efficiency of the judicial system, and various categories of political stability for a cross section of countries. Corruption is found to lower investment, thereby lowering economic growth. The results are robust to controlling for endogeneity by using an index of ethnolinguistic fractionalization as an instrument.

I. INTRODUCTION

Many economists argue that malfunctioning government institutions constitute a severe obstacle to investment, entrepreneurship, and innovation. North [1990] emphasizes the importance of an efficient judicial system to enforce contracts as a crucial determinant of economic performance. Low security of property rights over physical capital, profits, and patents may reduce incentives and opportunities to invest, innovate, and obtain foreign technology. Cumbersome and dishonest bureaucracies may delay the distribution of permits and licenses, thereby slowing down the process by which technological advances become embodied in new equipment or new productive processes.

The debate on the effects of corruption is particularly fervent. Beginning with Leff [1964] and Huntington [1968], some authors have suggested that corruption might *raise* economic growth, through two types of mechanisms. First, corrupt practices such as "speed money" would enable individuals to avoid bureaucratic delay. Second, government employees who are allowed to levy bribes would work harder, especially in the case where bribes act as a piece rate. While the first mechanism would increase the likelihood that corruption be beneficial to growth only in countries

*This is a revised version of the first chapter of my dissertation. I am grateful to Andrei Shleifer, Alberto Alesina, Robert Barro, Marianne Fay, Benjamin Friedman, Edward Glaeser, John Helliwell, Gregory Mankiw, Rebecca Menes, Enrico Spolaore, Aaron Tornell, the editor Lawrence Katz, an anonymous referee, and participants in seminars at Harvard University, the World Bank, the Eastern Economic Association Meeting, and the XIIIth Latin American Meeting of the Econometric Society for helpful comments and suggestions. I gratefully acknowledge financial assistance by Ente per gli studi monetari bancari e finanziari "Luigi Einaudi" and by the Harvard/MIT Positive Political Economy Group, which is supported by the National Science Foundation. The views expressed are my own and do not necessarily represent those of the International Monetary Fund. I do not necessarily agree with the Business International consultants' views and subjective indices relating to any individual country.

The Quarterly Journal of Economics, August 1995

where bureaucratic regulations are cumbersome, the second one would operate regardless of the level of red tape. In contrast, Shleifer and Vishny [1993] argue that corruption would tend to lower economic growth, and Rose-Ackerman [1978] warns of the difficulty of limiting corruption to areas in which it might be economically desirable.[1] Murphy, Shleifer, and Vishny [1991] provide evidence that countries where talented people are allocated to rent-seeking activities tend to grow more slowly.

Although most economists would probably agree that efficient government institutions foster economic growth, the magnitude of these effects has yet to be measured.[2] In order to fill this gap, I analyze a newly assembled data set, consisting of the *Business International* (BI) indices on corruption, red tape, and the efficiency of the judicial system for the period 1980–1983. The indices are based on standard questionnaires filled in by BI's correspondents stationed in about 70 countries. The purpose of this paper is to identify the channels through which corruption and other institutional factors affect economic growth and to quantify the magnitude of these effects.[3] To my knowledge, this is the first systematic cross-country empirical analysis that relates indicators of bureaucratic honesty and efficiency to economic growth.[4]

In attempting to measure the extent to which government institutions affect economic growth, one has to recognize that institutions and economic variables evolve jointly: not only do institutions affect economic performance, but also economic variables may affect institutions.[5] In order to address the issue of endogeneity, I use an index of ethnolinguistic fractionalization (which measures the probability that two persons drawn at

---

1. See Shleifer and Vishny [1993] for a more complete review of the literature on corruption.
2. However, there are authors who predict that there would be a *negative* correlation between good institutions and economic growth. For example, Olson [1963] argues that rapid economic growth would bring about political instability.
3. While the cross-country empirical literature on economic growth has so far devoted little attention to the efficiency and honesty of the bureaucratic and judicial systems, there is a considerable literature on the effects of political variables, which is surveyed in Levine and Renelt [1992].
4. The first systematic empirical analysis of bureaucratic efficiency is provided by Putnam [1993], who analyzes the regions of Italy and finds that "civicness"— both a century ago and today—is strongly associated with bureaucratic efficiency and income levels. He defines civicness as the extent to which citizens cooperate rather than free ride, and interact as equals rather than as patrons and clients. He measures civicness as a composite index of objective measures such as the number of recreational and cultural associations.
5. Tornell [1993] models the joint evolution of income and the system of property rights. Alesina, Ozler, Roubini, and Swagel [1992] empirically analyze the joint determination of political stability and economic growth.

random from a country's population will not belong to the same ethnolinguistic group) as an instrument. Ethnolinguistic fractionalization is highly correlated with corruption and other institutional variables. Yet it can be assumed to be exogenous both to economic variables and to institutional efficiency.

I find that corruption lowers private investment, thereby reducing economic growth, even in subsamples of countries in which bureaucratic regulations are very cumbersome. The negative association between corruption and investment, as well as growth, is significant, both in a statistical and in an economic sense. For example, if Bangladesh were to improve the integrity and efficiency of its bureaucracy to the level of that of Uruguay (this corresponds to a one-standard-deviation increase in the *bureaucratic efficiency* index introduced in the next section), its investment rate would rise by almost five percentage points, and its yearly GDP growth rate would rise by over half a percentage point. The magnitude of the estimated effects is even larger when instrumental variables are used.

The paper is organized as follows. The next section describes the data. Section III presents empirical evidence on the relationship between corruption, other institutional factors, and economic growth. Section IV concludes by suggesting possible interpretation of the results and directions for further research.

II. Description of the Data

II.1. The Business International Indices of Corruption and Institutional Efficiency

The indices proxying for corruption and various other institutional variables are drawn from Business International (BI), now incorporated into *The Economist Intelligence Unit*. BI is a private firm that sells these indices typically to banks, multinational companies, and other international investors. BI published indices on 56 "country risk" factors for 68 countries, for the period 1980–1983, and on 30 country risk factors for 57 countries, for the period 1971–1979. "Factor assessment reports" are filled in by BI's network of correspondents and analysts based in the countries covered. Assessment reports undergo further checks at BI's regional level, as well as BI's corporate headquarters, in order to ensure accuracy and consistency of the results. The indices reflect the analysts' perspectives on risk and efficiency factors, and may be taken to represent investors' assessments of conditions in the country in question. Evidence for the accuracy and relevance of the indices is provided by the considerable price that BI's clients are willing to pay in order to obtain them.[6]

In this paper I restrict my analysis to nine indicators of institutional efficiency. I choose these nine factors for two reasons: first, they are assessed independently of macroeconomic variables; second, they refer to the interests of *any* firm operating in the country in question, rather than specifically to foreign-owned multinational companies. The BI indices are integers between 0 and 10 and a high value of the index means that the country in question has "good" institutions. In Section III each indicator is the simple average for the country in question for the period 1980–1983.[7] BI's definitions of these indices are reported below.[8]

(1) *Political Change—institutional.* "Possibility that the institutional framework will be changed within the forecast period by elections or other means."

(2) *Political Stability—social.* "Conduct of political activity, both organized and individual, and the degree to which the orderly political process tends to disintegrate or become violent."

(3) *Probability of Opposition Group Takeover.* "Likelihood that the opposition will come to power during the forecast period."

(4) *Stability of Labor.* "Degree to which labor represents possible disruption for manufacturing and other business activity."

(5) *Relationship with Neighboring Countries.* "This includes political, economic and commercial relations with neighbors that may affect companies doing business in the country."

(6) *Terrorism.* "The degree to which individuals and businesses are subject to acts of terrorism."

(7) *Legal System, Judiciary.* "Efficiency and integrity of the legal environment as it affects business, particularly foreign firms."

(8) *Bureaucracy and Red Tape.* "The regulatory environment foreign firms must face when seeking approvals and permits. The degree to which it represents an obstacle to business."

(9) *Corruption.* "The degree to which business transactions involve corruption or questionable payments."

---

6. The data set I use would cost several thousand dollars if it were to be sold commercially.

7. The average over four years is a less noisy indicator of institutional variables, which we may expect to change only slowly.

8. The indices are described in more detail in Business International Corporation [1984].

In assigning a "grade" to the country in which they are based, BI correspondents follow general criteria which are outlined in the questionnaires they fill in. For example, for the bureaucracy and red tape index, a grade of 10 is given in the case of "smoothly functioning, efficient bureaucracy," while a grade of 4 means "constant need for government approvals and frequent delays." I collected the 1980–1983 data set by consulting the BI archives at their New York headquarters.[9] These indices were assembled by hand from hard copy. Descriptive statistics for all regression variables are provided in Appendix 1.

All BI indices are positively and significantly correlated, even controlling for GDP per capita. For example, the simple correlation between the corruption and red tape indices is 0.79 and the partial correlation—controlling for per capita GDP—is 0.66. The median of the simple correlations is 0.54, and the median of the partial correlations—controlling for per capita GDP—is 0.40 (p-value = 1 percent in both cases). Appendix 2 reports the correlation matrix for the BI indices. A number of mechanisms may contribute to explaining the positive correlation among all categories of institutional efficiency. Corruption may be expected to be more widespread in countries where red tape slows down bureaucratic procedures. In addition, the *Santhanam Committee Report* (quoted in Myrdal [1968, p. 952]) argues that corruption may even lead to more bureaucratic delay.[10] In fact, when individuals offer speed money to officials, they contribute to establishing a custom, so that the granting of, say, a license will be artificially delayed until a bribe is received. Corrupt practices such as speed money (which may actually avoid delay for an individual) may therefore increase red tape for the economy as a whole. The fact that all categories of country risk tend to move together is an interesting result.[11] At the

---

9. In Mauro [1993] I also analyze the 1971–1979 data set published in *Managing and Evaluating Country Risk* [1981]. The 1980–1983 indices refer to a larger number of different categories of country risk and are reported on a finer scale than the 1971–1979 ones, so they provide more information. In particular, the corruption index is available only from 1980. The results from the 1971–1979 data broadly confirm those presented in this paper.

10. Krueger [1993] and De Soto [1989] also argue that corrupt bureaucrats will intentionally introduce new regulations and red tape, in order to be able to extract more bribes by threatening to deny permits.

11. The finding that all indicators of bureaucratic efficiency and political stability tend to move together could not have been expected unambiguously, a priori. For example, in popular debate it is sometimes argued that corruption is more likely to become pervasive in countries where there are few changes in the elite running the country, that is, in stable countries. This argument is often made in connection with the corruption scandals in Italy and Japan in the early 1990s. One might also have expected that by allowing bureaucrats or other politically influen-

same time this multicollinearity makes it difficult to tell which of the several institutional factors examined is crucial for investment and growth.[12] As a consequence, it may be desirable to combine groups of variables into composite indices.

On the basis of the definitions of the variables, it seems that the judiciary system, red tape, and corruption indices represent closely related variables and that their simple average may be a reasonable proxy for what I will label bureaucratic efficiency. Part of the rationale for aggregating the indices into composite subindices is that there may be measurement error in each individual index, and averaging the individual indices may yield a better estimate of the determinants of investment and growth. Indeed, I consider the bureaucratic efficiency index to be a more precise measure of corruption than the corruption index on its own. Similarly, the simple average of the institutional change, social change, opposition takeover, stability of labor, relationship with neighboring countries, and terrorism indices may be a reasonable proxy for political stability. In addition to being closely related on a priori grounds, the indices that I choose to group together are more strongly correlated with each other. In some estimates I aggregate all nine indices into an average index of institutional efficiency, which I define as including bureaucratic efficiency, as well as political stability.

Table I is a frequency histogram of the bureaucratic efficiency index (BE) for 1980–1983. The country BI reported to have the best institutions is Singapore, which in 1980–1983 obtained grades of 10 out of ten for all the indices I use. It also had the highest investment rate over 1960–1985. Singapore experienced minimal corruption (and remarkable political stability) under the People's Action Party of Lee Kuan Yew. The ruling party is closely knit, and its younger members are gradually given more responsibilities. At the opposite extreme in 1980–1983, BI considered Zaire as having the worst institutions among the countries in the sample. According to BI's consultants, corruption was rampant. Zaire's investment rate has been extremely low. A casual glance at Table I shows

---

tial groups to collect bribes, the government may be able to achieve political stability, at least in the short run. For example, Business International [1984] has argued that Zaire's President Mobutu Sese Seko has been able to retain the support of the ruling *Mouvement Populaire de la Revolution* and of the military, by permitting large-scale corruption.

12. This is a common finding. Putnam [1993, p. 74] reports that all his indicators of bureaucratic efficiency for the Italian regions tend to move together to a remarkable extent, too.

CORRUPTION AND GROWTH 687

TABLE I
BUREAUCRATIC EFFICIENCY INDEX

1.5–4.5	4.5–5.5	5.5–6.5	6.5–7.5	7.5–9	9–10
Egypt	Algeria	Angola	Argentina	Austria	Australia
Ghana	Bangladesh	Dominican Rep.	Ivory Coast	Chile	Belgium
Haiti	Brazil	Ecuador	Kuwait	France	Canada
Indonesia	Colombia	Greece	Malaysia	Germany	Denmark
Iran	India	Iraq	Peru	Ireland	Finland
Liberia	Jamaica	Italy	South Africa	Israel	Japan
Nigeria	Kenya	Korea	Sri Lanka	Jordan	Hong Kong
Pakistan	Mexico	Morocco	Taiwan	Zimbabwe	Netherlands
Thailand	Philippines	Nicaragua	Uruguay		New Zealand
Zaire	Saudi Arabia	Panama			Norway
	Turkey	Portugal			Singapore
	Venezuela	Spain			Sweden
		Trinidad/Tobago			Switzerland
					United Kingdom
					United States

BE is the bureaucratic efficiency index, which I compute as the simple 1980–1983 average of three Business International indices: judiciary system, red tape, and corruption. A *high* value of the BE index means that the country's institutions are good.

that richer countries tend to have better institutions than poorer countries, and that fast-growers also tend to be among the countries with a higher bureaucratic efficiency index. Nevertheless, there are a few of surprises. In 1980 BI reported Thailand to be the most corrupt country, yet its economic performance has been relatively good. Korea has been a fast grower, in spite of the fact that it was reported to have relatively inefficient institutions. [13]

Figures I–III provide scatter plots of per capita GDP, the investment rate, and the per capita GDP growth rate versus the bureaucratic efficiency index for the 67 countries for which both Summers and Heston [1988] and BI data are available in 1980–1983. All these correlations are significant at the 1 percent level.

One of the most striking features of the data set is the strong association between bureaucratic efficiency and political stability.[14] Table II arranges the countries in the data set in a matrix, grouping them by quintiles depending on their bureaucratic efficiency and

13. The BI indices refer to the period immediately following the assassination of President Park Chung-hee.
14. Corruption may be more deleterious and thus reported as a more serious problem in politically unstable countries. Shleifer and Vishny [1993] argue that countries with weak (and, therefore, unstable) governments will experience a very deleterious type of corruption, in which an entrepreneur may have to bribe several public officials and still face the possibility that none of them really have the power to allow the project to proceed.

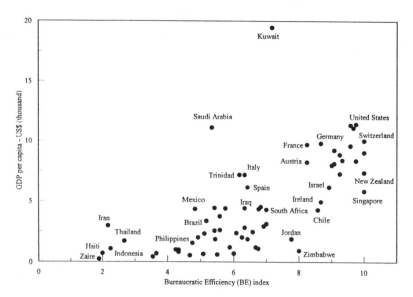

FIGURE I
Per Capita Income and Bureaucratic Efficiency

BE index is 1980–1983 average of BI indices of corruption, red tape, and judiciary.

Per capita GDP at PPP in 1980 is from Summers and Heston [1988].

67 countries, $r = 0.68$.

political stability indices. Most countries lie near or on the diagonal. The simple correlation coefficient between the bureaucratic efficiency index and the political stability index is 0.67, and the partial correlation coefficient controlling for per capita GDP in 1980 is 0.45, both significant at the 1 percent level. Yet, several relatively stable countries are reported to have relatively inefficient, corrupt bureaucracies. Conversely, several countries with relatively efficient, honest bureaucracies are relatively politically unstable. Based upon the 1980–1983 BI indices, Egypt, Greece, Indonesia, Saudi Arabia, and Turkey are at least two quintiles better on the grounds of political stability than on the grounds of bureaucratic efficiency. On the other hand, Angola, Chile, Iraq, Israel, Nicaragua, Peru, South Africa, and Zimbabwe score at least two quintiles better on bureaucratic efficiency than on political stability.[15] For example, Indonesia under President Suharto was

15. A similar matrix appears in Coplin and O'Leary [1982]. They classify 73 countries by political instability and restrictions of business. Their classification broadly confirms the one reported in Table II.

CORRUPTION AND GROWTH 689

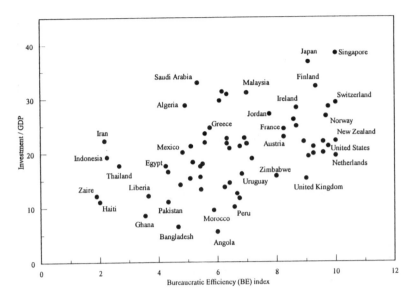

FIGURE II
Investment and Bureaucratic Efficiency
BE index is 1980–1983 average of BI indices of corruption, red tape, and judiciary.
Average investment 1980–1985 from Summers and Heston [1988].
67 countries, $r = 0.46$.

relatively politically stable, although BI reports that companies were hindered by a corrupt, cumbersome bureaucracy. According to BI's consultants, Peru's fragile democracy and its problems with social violence and terrorism and South Africa's racial tensions and active trade unions were in sharp contrast to their relatively efficient bureaucracies. Thus, even though bureaucratic efficiency and political stability are positively and significantly correlated, there is a wealth of information in the bureaucratic efficiency indices that can be used to analyze the determinants of investment and growth.

The fact that the indices reflect the *subjective* opinions of BI's correspondents presents both advantages and disadvantages. An advantage relates specifically to the political instability variables. Previous studies have used *objective* measures of political stability, such as the number of political assassinations or changes in government. Objective measures can often be misleading. For example, there have been over 50 changes of government in Italy since 1945, yet the country has been relatively politically stable. It

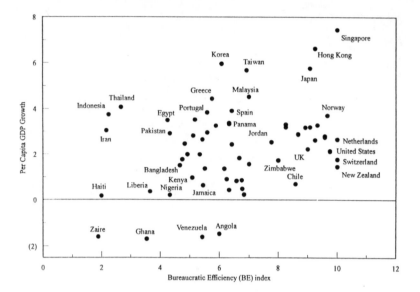

FIGURE III
Growth and Bureaucratic Efficiency
BE index is 1980–1983 average of BI indices of corruption, red tape, and judiciary.
Average GDP per capita growth 1960–1985 from Summers and Heston [1988]. 67 countries, $r = 0.32$.

may be argued that it is investors' *perceptions* of political uncertainty that determine the investment rate, and this is what subjective indices capture directly. A disadvantage is that it is unclear whether BI's attempts to ensure that the difference between a grade of 4 and 5 is the same as that between a 7 and an 8 are successful, which leads to difficulties in the interpretation of the coefficients. In order to address this concern, in one case I estimate the relationship between investment and dummies for "high," "medium," and "low" bureaucratic efficiency. An even more serious disadvantage is that one might suspect that the BI correspondents may be influenced by a country's economic performance when they evaluate its institutional efficiency.[16] In addition, good economic performance might increase institutional efficiency, regardless of how the latter is measured. In order to correct for such potential sources of endogeneity bias, I use an index of ethnolinguistic fractionalization as an instrument.

16. This would clearly be in conflict with the spirit of the questionnaires, and extensive interviews with BI personnel persuaded me that no macroeconomic

TABLE II
BUREAUCRATIC EFFICIENCY AND POLITICAL STABILITY

Bureaucratic efficiency (increasing ↓)		Political stability (increasing →)				
		5th quintile	4th quintile	3rd quintile	2nd quintile	1st quintile
	5th quintile	Ghana Iran Liberia Pakistan Philippines Thailand Zaire	Bangladesh Haiti Mexico Nigeria	INDONESIA	EGYPT	
	4th quintile	Colombia	Ecuador India Kenya Morocco	Algeria Brazil Jamaica Portugal Venezuela	GREECE SAUDI ARABIA TURKEY	

	3rd quintile	ANGOLA
		IRAQ
		NICARAGUA
		PERU
			Spain
			Sri Lanka
				Argentina
				Dominican
				  Republic
				Korea
				Panama
				Trinidad/
				  Tobago
					Italy
					Ivory Coast	

	2nd quintile	ISRAEL	CHILE SOUTH AFRICA ZIMBABWE	Ireland Jordan	Germany Kuwait Malaysia Taiwan	Austria France Uruguay

	1st quintile				Australia
					Belgium
					Denmark
					New
					  Zealand
					United
					  Kingdom
						Canada
						Finland
						Hong Kong
						Japan
						Netherlands
						Norway
						Singapore
						Sweden
						Switzerland
						United
						  States

The countries for which there is more than a one quintile discrepancy between the bureaucratic efficiency and the political stability indices are listed in small capital letters. The political stability index is the simple average of six Business International indices: institutional change, social change, opposition takeover, stability of labor, relationship with neighboring countries, and terrorism. The bureaucratic efficiency index is the simple average of three Business International indices: judiciary system, red tape, and corruption. There may not be exactly the same number of countries in each quintile.

II.2. The Index of Ethnolinguistic Fractionalization and Other Variables

The raw data from which the index of ethnolinguistic fraction-alization (ELF) is constructed refer to 1960 and come from the *Atlas Narodov Mira* [Department of Geodesy and Cartography of the State Geological Committee of the USSR 1964]. The latter is the result of a vast project whose goal was to provide an extremely accurate depiction of the ethnolinguistic composition of world population. The criteria for characterizing groups as ethnically separate related mainly to historical linguistic origin, and no economic or political variables were considered during the project. The ELF index is calculated by Taylor and Hudson [1972], who explicitly note that Soviet views did not bias the index. It is defined as

$$ELF = 1 - \sum_{i=1}^{I} \left(\frac{n_i}{N}\right)^2, \qquad i = 1, \ldots, I,$$

where n_i is the number of people in the ith group, N is total population, and I is the number of ethnolinguistic groups in the country.[17] *ELF* measures the probability that two randomly selected persons from a given country will not belong to the same ethnolinguistic group. Therefore, the higher the ELF index, the more fragmented the country. Table III groups the countries in the sample arranged by the ethnolinguistic fractionalization index for 1960.

I assume that the extent to which countries are fractionalized along ethnolinguistic lines is exogenous and unrelated to economic variables other than through its effects on institutional efficiency.[18]

---

variables are considered when constructing the BI indices. If this were the only source of endogeneity, it would be possible to correct for it simply by using the Barro [1991] objective variables as instruments. One could imagine a system of equations in which the number of assassinations, revolutions, and coups affects people's perceptions of country risk (the correlations are reported in Mauro [1993]), and the latter in turn affect investment and growth. The results of this estimation procedure are reported in Table V, row 7.

17. In 1960 Canada—the most fractionalized among industrialized countries—had 38.3 percent Anglo-Canadians, 30.1 percent French-Canadians, 5.7 percent Germans, 3.3 percent English, 2.6 percent Ukrainians, 2.5 percent Italians, 2.4 percent Dutch, 1.8 percent Poles, 1.7 percent Americans, 1.4 percent Jews, 1.2 percent Scots, 0.8 percent Irish, 0.8 percent Norwegians, 0.7 percent Swedes, 0.7 percent Russians, 0.5 percent Hungarians, 0.5 percent Athapaskans, 0.4 percent Algonquins, adding to a total of 95.3 percent, and yielding an ELF of 0.76.

18. Canning and Fay [1993] also assume that this homogeneity index is exogenous to both politics and economics. They use it as an independent variable in cross-country growth regressions. They show that homogeneity of the population

TABLE III
ETHNOLINGUISTIC FRACTIONALIZATION, 1960

100–75	75–55	55–35	35–15	15–5	5–0
Angola	Canada	Algeria	Argentina	Austria	Dominican
Bangladesh	Ghana	Belgium	Australia	Brazil	Rep.
India	Malaysia	Ecuador	Finland	Chile	Egypt
Indonesia	Pakistan	Iraq	France	Colombia	Germany
Iran	Peru	Morocco	Israel	Denmark	Haiti
Ivory Coast	Philippines	New Zealand	Kuwait	Greece	Hong Kong
Kenya	Thailand	Singapore	Mexico	Jamaica	Ireland
Liberia	Trinidad/	Spain	Nicaragua	Jordan	Italy
South Africa	Tobago	Sri Lanka	Panama	Netherlands	Japan
Zaire		Switzerland	Turkey	Saudi Arabia	Korea
		Taiwan	United	Sweden	Norway
		United	Kingdom	Venezuela	Portugal
		States	Uruguay		
		Zimbabwe			

The ethnolinguistic fractionalization index for 1960 is drawn from Taylor and Hudson [1972].

There is a negative and significant correlation between institutional efficiency and ethnolinguistic fractionalization, which makes the latter a good instrument.[19] The ELF index has a simple correlation coefficient equal to -0.38 with the institutional efficiency index, -0.41 with the political stability index, -0.28 with the bureaucratic efficiency index, and -0.31 with the corruption index, all significant at the 1 percent level. A number of mechanisms may explain this relationship. Ethnic conflict may lead to political instability and, in extreme cases, to civil war. The presence of many different ethnolinguistic groups is also significantly associated with worse corruption, as bureaucrats may favor members of their same group. Shleifer and Vishny [1993] suggest that more homogeneous societies are likely to come closer to joint bribe maximization, which is a less deleterious type of corruption than noncollusive bribe-setting. Strictly speaking, the ELF index is a

has a positive and significant effect on productivity growth. They also argue that it is a predetermined proxy for political stability. However, they do not use the homogeneity index as an *instrument* for political stability. Hibbs [1973] uses the index in a large system of simultaneous equations which is ultimately designed to explain mass political violence and other indicators of political instability.

19. Ethnolinguistic fractionalization is a valid instrument, while lags of the right-hand side variables such as beginning-of-period indicators of corruption and political instability would be unlikely to be valid instruments, because such institutional variables are highly autocorrelated.

valid instrument only for the institutional efficiency index, as fractionalization affects both corruption and political instability.

By consulting von der Mehden [1969], the *Encyclopaedia Britannica,* and the *World Handbook of Political and Social Indicators,* I also compiled a data set on the colonial history of the 118 countries in the Barro [1991] data set. It includes the date of independence and the last colonizer. In some estimates, I make use of dummies on whether the country ever was a colony (after 1776, following Taylor and Hudson [1972]), and on whether the country was still a colony in 1945, as additional instruments.[20] A country's colonial history may affect its ability to form a stable government, as well as the honesty and efficiency of its bureaucracy. Ekpo [1979] suggests that recently independent former colonies will have more decentralized bribe collection machines, so that they will be subject to more deleterious corruption. At the same time, a country's colonial history may be assumed to be exogenous, and to have no direct effect on the investment rate.

Even though formal specification tests (of the overidentifying instruments, reported in the next section) do not reject the joint null hypothesis that the ELF index and the colonial history dummies are valid instruments, a note of caution is needed on the very long-run exogeneity of the instruments. Countries whose economic performance is poor tend to be militarily weak and are therefore more likely to be colonized. In addition, when drawing the remarkably straight borders of some nations, colonizers often paid little attention to the ethnolinguistic composition of the population. Therefore, one might suspect that some unmeasurable factor affecting economic variables may also have affected not only a country's colonial history, but also its ethnolinguistic fractionalization.

The macroeconomic data are drawn from Summers and Heston [1988] and Barro [1991]; the objective data on political uncertainty from Barro [1991]; and the data on equipment investment from De Long and Summers [1991]. In the next section the sample of 58 countries is the intersection between the countries for which the BI data are available, the sample of countries analyzed by Levine and Renelt [1992], who do not include the major oil exporters—which experienced high growth thanks merely to one

---

20. Hibbs [1973] also uses a postwar independence dummy as an instrument in his system of equations relating economic performance and political stability. I found no significant evidence that a country's economic performance or its institutional efficiency were affected by *which* country colonized it. This result confirms earlier findings by von der Mehden [1969].

natural resource—and the Barro [1991] sample of 98 countries. Appendix 3 provides the indices of corruption, red tape, judiciary system, bureaucratic efficiency, and political stability from BI, and ethnolinguistic fractionalization from Taylor and Hudson [1972].

III. EMPIRICAL ESTIMATES

This section empirically analyzes the links between corruption, as well as other institutional factors, and economic growth. Subsection III.1 focuses on the relationship between corruption and the investment rate. I find that corruption is strongly negatively associated with the investment rate, regardless of the amount of red tape. In alternative model specifications, the corruption and bureaucratic efficiency indices are significantly and robustly negatively associated with investment even controlling for other determinants of investment, including the political stability index. There is evidence that institutional inefficiency *causes* low investment. Subsection III.2 analyzes the relationship between institutional efficiency and economic growth. The bureaucratic efficiency index is significantly and robustly associated with low growth, even controlling for other determinants of growth. Again, there is evidence that institutional inefficiency *causes* low growth. The main channel through which bad institutions affect the growth rate is by lowering the investment rate.

III.1. Corruption and Investment

Given the renewed debate in the literature on the effects of corruption, I provide some preliminary results using the corruption index. I find that there is a negative and significant association between corruption and the investment rate, both in OLS estimates and in 2SLS estimates using the ELF index as an instrument. The magnitude of the effect is considerable. A one-standard-deviation increase (an improvement) in the corruption index is associated with an increase in the investment rate by 2.9 percent of GDP. The magnitudes of the slope coefficients measuring the association between corruption and investment are far from being significantly different in low-red-tape and high-red-tape sub-samples of countries (Table IV).[21] Therefore, these results do not provide any support for the claim that, in the presence of a slow

21. For Table IV, I use the full sample of 67 countries, in order to have the maximum power to reject the hypothesis that corruption has the same effects regardless of red tape.

TABLE IV

INVESTMENT AND CORRUPTION

Dependent Variable: Total Investment/GDP, 1980–1985 Average

Constant	Corruption (slope coefficient)	R^2	Sample	N	p-value of restriction
0.125 (6.63)	0.0117 (4.41)	0.18	Whole BI sample	67	
0.018 (0.23)	0.0276 (2.56)	(*)	Whole BI sample Fractionalization as an instrument	66	
0.134 (3.52)	0.0105 (2.29)	0.09	Low red tape[1] (red tape index $\geq$ 5)	45	
0.116 (4.65)	0.0138 (2.63)	0.23	High red tape[1] (red tape index $<$ 5)	22	0.9
0.100 (1.30)	0.0152 (1.80)	0.11	Low red tape[2] (red tape index $>$ 7)	24	
0.140 (6.30)	0.0083 (2.04)	0.07	High red tape[2] (red tape index $\leq$ 7)	43	0.5

White-corrected t-statistics are reported in parentheses. A *high* value of the corruption (red tape) index means that the country does well in that respect, i.e., *low* corruption (red tape). The p-value of the restriction that the slope coefficients are the same in the two subsamples is calculated using a log-likelihood ratio test. [1]This Low red tape sample is defined as containing the countries that have a red tape index $\geq$ 5. [2]This Low red tape sample is defined as containing the countries that have a red tape index $<$ 7. (*) The R^2 is not an appropriate measure of goodness of fit with two-stage least squares.

bureaucracy, corruption would become beneficial, as suggested by Leff [1964] and Huntington [1968].

Table V analyzes the simple relationship between investment (or some of its components) and institutional variables in further detail.[22] A one-standard-deviation increase (an improvement) in the bureaucratic efficiency index is associated with an increase in the investment rate by 4.75 percent of GDP (obtained by multiplying 0.022, the slope coefficient, by 2.16, the standard deviation of the index). The estimated magnitude of the effects of bureaucratic efficiency on investment is even higher (and remains significant) when controlling for endogeneity by using 2SLS with the ELF index as an instrument than in the OLS estimates. The coefficient is still significant at the conventional levels (Table V, rows 3 and 4).

22. Further tests of robustness of this relationship are reported in Mauro [1993], where it is shown that the results are not driven by any particular group of countries (such as sub-Saharan Africa, Asian tigers, high income, or low income).

TABLE V
INVESTMENT AND BUREAUCRATIC EFFICIENCY

Row	Dependent variable	Constant	Corruption BI Index	Bureaucratic efficiency BI index	Institutional efficiency BI index	R^2	N
1	Total investment/GDP (1960–1985)	0.086 (4.14)	0.018 (6.43)			0.40	58
2	Total investment/GDP (1960–1985) Instrument: fractionalization	−0.021 (−0.27)	0.033 (3.04)			(*)	57
3	Total investment/GDP (1960–1985)	0.059 (2.74)		0.022 (7.47)		0.46	58
4	Total investment/GDP (1960–1985) Instrument: fractionalization	−0.082 (−0.78)		0.043 (2.84)		(*)	57
5	Total investment/GDP (1960–1985)	−0.023 (−0.65)			0.032 (6.73)	0.44	58
6	Total investment/GDP (1960–1985) Instrument: fractionalization	−0.133 (−1.28)			0.047 (3.37)	(*)	57
7	Total investment/GDP (1960–1985) Instruments: revcoup, assass	−0.014 (−0.25)			0.030 (4.00)	(*)	58
8	Total investment/GDP (1960/1985) Instruments: colonial dummies	−0.148 (−1.77)			0.049 (4.35)	(*)	58
9	Total investment/GDP (1960–1985) Instruments: fract., colonial dummies	−0.119 (−1.66)			0.045 (4.73)	(*)	57
10	Total investment/GDP (1970–1985)	0.066 (3.04)		0.021 (6.94)		0.42	58
11	Total investments/GDP (1970–1985) Instrument: fractionalization	−0.084 (−0.79)		0.043 (2.88)		(*)	57
12	Total investment/GDP (1980–1985)	0.075 (3.58)		0.019 (6.04)		0.33	58
13	Total investment/GDP (1980–1985) Instrument: fractionalization	−0.054 (−0.51)		0.037 (2.48)		(*)	57
14	Equipment investment/ GDP (1975–1985)	−0.072 (−0.64)		0.009 (5.44)		0.37	41
15	Nonequipment inv./ GDP (1975–1985)	0.011 (4.40)		0.007 (2.07)		0.07	41
16	Equip. inv./nonequip. inv. (1975–1985)	0.065 (0.87)		0.041 (3.94)		0.21	41
17	Private investment/ GDP (1970–1985)	0.052 (2.26)		0.020 (6.12)		0.40	50
18	Public investment/GDP (1970–1985)	0.022 (3.70)		0.002 (2.00)		0.06	50
19	Private inv./public inv. (1970–1985)	4.715 (2.76)		0.252 (1.17)		0.03	50

A *high* value of each index means the country has *good* institutions. One standard deviation equals 1.47 for the institutional efficiency index, 2.16 for the bureaucratic efficiency index, and 2.51 for the corruption index. White-corrected t-statistics are reported in parentheses. N is the number of observations. Revcoup and assass are the number of revolutions and coups, and assassinations, respectively, between 1960 and 1985, from Barro [1991]. Fractionalization is the index of ethnolinguistic fractionalization in 1960, from Taylor and Hudson [1972]. (*) The R^2 is not an appropriate measure of goodness fit with two-stage least squares.

It might be argued that ethnolinguistic fractionalization may affect investment not only by increasing corruption and political instability, but also via a direct channel. For example, it might slow down the diffusion of ideas and technological innovations within the country. In order to address that possibility, I run 2SLS regressions of the investment rate on the institutional efficiency index using as instruments not only the ELF index, but also dummies for whether the country ever was a colony and for whether it achieved independence after 1945. A test of the overidentifying restrictions fails to reject the null hypothesis that the only channel through which ethnolinguistic fractionalization affects investment is via its effects on institutional efficiency (Table V, row 9; p-value $= 0.25$).

The components of investment that have been found to be more closely associated with economic growth (see De Long and Summers [1991] for equipment investment and Barro [1991] for private investment) also seem to be more closely associated with bureaucratic efficiency. Equipment investment is significantly more closely associated with bureaucratic efficiency than nonequipment investment is (Table V, rows 14–16). There are some indications that private investment is more closely associated with bureaucratic efficiency than public investment is, although this is not significantly the case (Table V, rows 17–19).[23]

Table VI shows that both corruption and bureaucratic inefficiency are negatively associated with the investment rate even after controlling for a variety of other determinants of investment.[24] I adopt two types of specification that have become standard in the cross-country growth literature. The first one is that which Levine and Renelt ([p. 946, their expression 2, 1992] henceforth, the LR specification) use as the basis for their analysis of "robustness" of growth regressions. In some estimates I use the ELF index as an instrument. The second one is that adopted by Barro ([p. 426, his Table III, 1991] henceforth, the B specification). The rationale for the LR and B specifications is that a number of

---

23. It might be the case that the more corrupt countries report as "public investment" also projects that really represent consumption expenditure by the bureaucratic elite. Easterly [1993] models some types of public capital as complements (e.g., infrastructure), and others as substitutes (e.g., government enterprises in agriculture and tourism) for private capital. In Mauro [1993] I present results obtained by analyzing the Easterly and Rebelo [1993] data set on disaggregated public investment.

24. The dependent variable in Table VI is the 1960–1985 average of the total investment to GDP ratio. Results obtained using 1970–1985 or 1980–1985 averages are quite similar.

CORRUPTION AND GROWTH 699

TABLE VI

INVESTMENT ON CORRUPTION, BUREAUCRATIC EFFICIENCY
Dependent variable: investment/GDP (1960–1985 Average)

Independent variable	(1)	(2)	(3)	(4)	(5)	(6)	(7)
Constant	0.104	0.114	0.196	0.036	0.039	0.186	0.001
	(3.03)	(3.18)	(4.65)	(0.42)	(0.40)	(0.31)	(0.01)
GDP in 1960	−0.008	−0.006	−0.004	−0.026	−0.021	−0.015	−0.017
	(−1.31)	(−0.81)	(−0.60)	(−1.57)	(−1.41)	(−2.50)	(−2.73)
Secondary education in 1960	0.060	0.111	0.096	−0.078	0.017	0.082	0.115
	(0.97)	(1.68)	(1.40)	(−0.56)	(0.16)	(1.60)	(2.04)
Population growth	−1.373	−0.620	−0.913	−2.754	−1.144		
	(−1.38)	(−0.61)	(−0.82)	(−1.84)	(−1.12)		
Primary education in 1960						0.105	0.111
						(2.89)	(3.36)
Government expenditure						−0.166	−0.206
						(−1.06)	(−1.39)
Revolutions and coups						−0.009	−0.005
						(−0.22)	(−0.139)
Assassinations						−0.164	−0.276
						(−0.69)	(−1.03)
PPI60						−0.058	−0.061
						(−2.81)	(−2.79)
PPI60DEV						0.043	0.035
						(1.24)	(1.04)
Africa							0.036
							(1.92)
Latin America							0.017
							(0.88)
High Bureaucratic efficiency dummy			0.051				
			(2.26)				
Low Bureaucratic efficiency dummy			−0.014				
			(−0.77)				
Political stability index						0.013	0.014
						(1.64)	(1.79)
Bureaucratic efficiency index	0.019				0.004	0.010	0.009
	(4.04)				(1.76)	(2.19)	(1.76)
Corruption index		0.013			0.034		
		(2.94)			(1.56)		
Estimation method	OLS	OLS	OLS	2SLS	2SLS	OLS	OLS
R^2	0.51	0.47	0.44	(*)	(*)	0.65	0.66

A *high* value of a BI index means the country has *good* institutions. One standard deviation equals 2.16 for the bureaucratic efficiency (BE) index, 2.51 for the corruption index, and 1.29 for the political stability index. The high (low) BE dummy takes the value one when the BE index is above 8.33 (below 5.80); there are 19 high BE and 19 low BE countries. There are 58 observations in the case of OLS and 57 in the case of 2SLS. White-corrected t-statistics are reported in parentheses. The Barro [1991] regressors used are per capita GDP, primary education, secondary education, the purchasing-power parity value for the investment deflator (PPI60) and its deviation from the sample mean (PPI60DEV) in 1960, the 1960–1985 average of the ratio of government consumption expenditure (net of spending on defense and education) to GDP, population growth, the number of revolutions and coups, the number of assassinations, and dummies for Latin America and Sub-Saharan Africa where indicated. 2SLS indicates that the index of ethnolinguistic fractionalization in 1960, from Taylor and Hudson [1972], is used as an instrument. (*) The R^2 is not an appropriate measure of goodness of fit with two-stage least squares.

variables may affect the expected value and the variance of the marginal product of capital, thereby affecting the propensity to invest in the economy. These include initial per capita GDP; the educational level of the labor force, which may be a complement to physical capital in production processes; distortions, which may divert resources to less productive investment projects; and political uncertainty.

In the LR specification a one-standard-deviation improvement in the bureaucratic efficiency (corruption) index is significantly associated with an increase in the 1960–1985 average investment rate by 4.1 (3.3) percent of GDP (Table VI, columns 1 and 2). Application of the Levine and Renelt [1992] procedure (with their same control variables), which involves running a large number of regressions of investment on the variable of interest (in this case, the bureaucratic efficiency and corruption indices) and various conditioning sets shows that this relationship is robust. Using the ELF index as an instrument, the magnitudes of the coefficients remain considerable, although they become only marginally significant at the 10 percent level (Table VI, columns 4 and 5). When using dummies for high, medium, and low bureaucratic efficiency, the coefficients take the expected signs, although only the coefficient on high bureaucratic efficiency is significant at the conventional levels (Table VI, column 3).

Controlling for all the variables in the B specification and the political instability index, the bureaucratic efficiency index is always positively and significantly associated with the investment rate, although the level of significance is only 10 percent when dummies for Africa and Latin America are included in the list of independent variables (Table VI, columns 6 and 7). The magnitude of the coefficient on bureaucratic efficiency is in this case half as large as in Table V.

The finding that corruption is negatively and significantly associated with investment is consistent with the view that corruption lowers the private marginal product of capital (for example, by acting as a tax on the proceeds of the investment).

III.2. Corruption and Growth

Having provided evidence that corruption affects investment, and recalling that Levine and Renelt [1992] show that the investment rate is a robust determinant of economic growth, in this subsection I analyze the relationship between institutional efficiency and economic growth.

The corruption and the bureaucratic efficiency indices are both significantly associated with average per capita GDP growth over 1960–1985.[25] Again, I analyze the robustness of these simple relationships to alternative control variables, using the LR and B specifications as a model. A possible underlying rationale for these specifications is the neoclassical growth model. In that setting, population growth, education, and institutional variables (government expenditure, distortions, and corruption) contribute to determining steady-state per capita income levels. These variables and initial per capita income affect the speed with which the economy converges toward its steady state, thereby affecting the growth rate.

Controlling for the other determinants of growth included in the LR specification, the relationship is significant at the 5 percent level for the bureaucratic efficiency index, the more precise measure of corruption, though only at the 10 percent level for the corruption index. The magnitude of the effects is considerable: a one-standard-deviation improvement in the bureaucratic efficiency (corruption) index is associated with a 1.3 (0.8) percentage point (absolute) increase in the annual growth rate of GDP per capita (Table VII, columns 5 and 6). Application of the Levine and Renelt [1992] procedure (with their control variables), which involves running various regressions of per capita GDP growth on the bureaucratic efficiency or the corruption index and various conditioning sets, shows that this relationship is robust for bureaucratic efficiency, although not for corruption. The magnitude of the coefficients rises when the ELF index is used as an instrument (Table VII, columns 7 and 8). Controlling for all the Barro [1991] variables and the political stability index, the magnitude of the coefficient on bureaucratic efficiency becomes rather small and retains its significance at the 10 percent level only in some specifications (Table VII, columns 12 and 13).

The null hypothesis of no relationship between investment and corruption can be rejected at a level of significance higher than the null hypothesis of no relationship between growth and corruption can. This finding is consistent with the results reported by Levine and Renelt [1992], who find that indexes of revolutions and coups and civil liberties are not robustly correlated with growth, although they are robustly, negatively correlated with the investment rate.

25. Use of the 1970–1985 average per capita GDP growth as the dependent variable yields quite similar results in all specifications reported in Table VII.

TABLE VII
GROWTH ON CORRUPTION, BUREAUCRATIC EFFICIENCY
Dependent variable: Per Capita GDP growth (1960–1985 Average)

Independent variable	(1)	(2)	(3)	(4)	(5)	(6)	(7)	(8)	(9)	(10)	(11)	(12)	(13)	(14)	(15)
Constant	0.05	0.012	−0.049	−0.034	0.012	0.019	−0.011	−0.010	0.002	0.004	−0.006	0.006	0.013	0.001	0.007
	(0.63)	(1.63)	(−1.53)	(−1.33)	(1.26)	(1.86)	(−0.45)	(−0.32)	(0.23)	(0.47)	(−0.52)	(0.48)	(1.12)	(0.11)	(0.67)
GDP in 1960					−0.008	−0.007	−0.013	−0.012	−0.008	−0.006	−0.006	−0.008	−0.007	−0.008	−0.007
					(−4.87)	(−3.88)	(−2.91)	(−2.53)	(−4.55)	(−4.25)	(−3.97)	(−9.38)	(−8.02)	(−8.23)	(−5.95)
Secondary education in 1960					0.011	0.031	−0.031	−0.001	0.005	0.017	0.007	0.020	0.006	0.015	−0.005
					(0.81)	(2.40)	(−0.71)	(−0.03)	(0.37)	(1.42)	(0.351)	(2.62)	(0.95)	(1.78)	(−0.51)
Population growth					−0.654	−0.395	−1.077	−0.564	−0.519	−0.318	−0.246				
					(−2.85)	(−1.88)	(−2.04)	(−1.66)	(−2.35)	(−1.81)	(−1.24)				
Primary education in 1960												0.018	0.015	0.014	0.007
												(2.58)	(2.42)	(1.99)	(1.27)
Government expenditure												−0.114	−0.095	−0.108	−0.082
												(−3.66)	(−3.22)	(−3.76)	(−3.36)
Revolutions and coups												−0.008	−0.010	−0.008	−0.009
												(−1.25)	(−1.45)	(−1.24)	(−1.66)
Assassinations												−0.218	−0.190	−0.210	−0.173
												(−4.11)	(−3.57)	(−4.29)	(−3.98)
PPI60												0.001	0.003	0.003	0.009
												(0.06)	(0.64)	(0.73)	(1.86)
PPI60DEV												−0.018	−0.156	−0.019	−0.017
												(−2.88)	(−2.23)	(−3.14)	(−3.00)
Africa													−0.017		−0.021
													(−4.26)		(−5.21)
Latin America													−0.005		−0.006
													(−1.19)		(−1.70)

	OLS	OLS	2SLS	2SLS	OLS	OLS	2SLS	2SLS	OLS	OLS	2SLS (OI)	OLS	OLS	OLS	OLS
Political instability index												0.003 (2.35)	0.002 (1.95)	0.003 (2.34)	0.002 (1.82)
Investment 1960–1985									0.098 (2.82)	0.125 (3.64)	0.230 (3.14)			0.051 (2.16)	0.083 (3.60)
Bureaucratic efficiency index	0.003 (2.58)	0.011 (2.33)		0.006 (3.08)	0.014 (1.88)				0.004 (2.03)	0.002 (1.13)		0.001 (1.24)	0.002 (1.89)	0.001 (0.74)	0.001 (1.35)
Corruption index		0.002 (1.97)	0.008 (2.34)		0.003 (1.91)		0.011 (1.49)								
Estimation methods	OLS	OLS	2SLS	2SLS	OLS	OLS	2SLS	2SLS	OLS	OLS	2SLS (OI)	OLS	OLS	OLS	OLS
R^*	0.07	0.13	(*)	0.38	0.27	(*)	(*)		0.46	0.40	(*)	0.74	0.79	0.76	0.83

A *high* value of each index means the country has *good* institutions. One standard deviation equals 2.16 for the bureaucratic efficiency index, 2.51 for the corruption index, and 1.29 for the political stability index. White-corrected t-statistics are reported in parentheses. There are 58 observations in the case of OLS and 57 in the case of 2SLS. Initial GDP per capita, primary education, secondary education, population growth, the purchasing-power party value for the investment deflator (PPI60) in 1960, and its deviation from the sample mean (PPI60DEV) in 1960, the 1960–1985 average ratio of government consumption expenditure (net of spending on defense and education) to GDP, the number of revolutions and coups, and the number of assassinations are from Barro [1991]. 2SLS indicates that the index of ethnolinguistic fractionalization in 1960, from Taylor and Hudson [1972], is used as an instrument. 2SLS(OI) indicates that all 9 BI individual indices listed in Section II are used as instruments. The p-value of the test of the overidentifying restrictions is 7.5 percent. (*) The R^2 is not an appropriate measure of goodness of fit with two-stage least squares.

Having provided some evidence in favor of the claim that corruption lowers economic growth, I now turn to analyzing the channels through which this takes place. In the context of an endogenous growth model, bureaucratic inefficiency could affect growth indirectly (by lowering the investment rate) or directly (for example, by leading to misallocation of investment among sectors) [Easterly 1993]. Similarly, in neoclassical growth models, corruption could affect the steady-state level of income (for example, by leading to misallocation of production among sectors). Therefore, when the economy is below its steady-state income level, higher corruption could lead to lower growth, for a given level of income. In addition, bureaucratic inefficiency could also lower the private marginal product of capital, thus lowering the investment rate.

In order to assess the empirical relevance of these mechanisms, I adopt two approaches. First, I add investment to the list of independent variables in OLS growth regressions, and observe the magnitude and significance of the coefficients on the bureaucratic efficiency and corruption indices. The inclusion of the investment ratio in the LR specification of the growth regression leads the coefficient on the bureaucratic efficiency index to fall by about a third, although it remains significant at the conventional levels. On the other hand, the coefficient on the corruption index falls substantially and becomes insignificant (Table VII, columns 9 and 10). Inclusion of the investment rate in the B growth regression leads the coefficient on the bureaucratic efficiency index nearly to halve and to become insignificant (Table VII, columns 14 and 15). Second, I recognize that while the investment rate affects growth, it is also possible that growth in turn affects the investment rate (for example, through an accelerator mechanism). In order to avoid such endogeneity bias, I run 2SLS regressions using the nine BI indices as instruments. This procedure requires the testable assumption that institutional variables affect the investment rate, but do not affect growth directly. Using a test of the overidentifying instruments, the null hypothesis that the only channel through which institutions affect economic growth is through investment can be rejected, but only at the 10 percent level (Table VII, column 11).

Therefore, on the basis of this data set, there is only weak support for the hypothesis that corruption reduces growth by leading to inefficient investment choices. Overall, even though the evidence is mixed, it seems that a considerable portion of the effects of corruption on growth works through its effects on the total amount of investment.

IV. CONCLUDING REMARKS

This paper has used a newly assembled data set consisting of subjective indices of bureaucratic honesty and efficiency to provide empirical evidence on the effects of corruption on economic growth. The negative association between corruption and investment, as well as growth, is significant in both a statistical and an economic sense. For example, if Bangladesh were to improve the integrity and efficiency of its bureaucracy to the level of that of Uruguay (corresponding to a one-standard-deviation increase in the bureaucratic efficiency index), its investment rate would rise by almost five percentage points, and its yearly GDP growth rate would rise by over half a percentage point. As these relationships are robust to controlling for endogeneity by using an index of ethnolinguistic fractionalization as an instrument, there is evidence that bureaucratic efficiency actually *causes* high investment and growth. Furthermore—though some caution is needed, owing to data limitations—the paper has shown the extent to which the relationship is robust to controlling for standard determinants of investment and growth. In particular, there is evidence that bureaucratic efficiency may be at least as important a determinant of investment and growth as political stability. A number of issues remain unresolved. I briefly describe three areas for further research.

First, the positive and significant correlation between indices of bureaucratic efficiency and political stability requires explanation. A possible interpretation is that corruption and instability may be intrinsically linked, in the sense that they may result from the same coordination problem among members of the ruling elite.[26] In Mauro [1993] I suggest a new strategic complementarity that may be intuitively described as follows. Consider a game among the politicians that form the government. Each politician

26. The literature has already suggested that external effects and strategic complementarities may play an important role in determining institutional efficiency and economic performance. Putnam [1993] argues that a *tragedy of the commons* may explain the institutional and the economic failure of some Italian regions. Andvig and Moene [1990], Sah [1991], and Tirole [1993] derive models with multiple equilibria in corruption. Murphy, Shleifer, and Vishny [1993] derive a model of multiple equilibria in corruption and the *level* of income. Mauro [Ch. 2, 1993] derives a model of multiple equilibria in corruption and economic growth, which draws on the same *strategic complementarity* as in Murphy, Shleifer, and Vishny [1993].

has to decide whether to set up a private bribe collection system. If the individual politician decides to set a high bribe rate, economic performance will worsen and the whole government will be less likely to be able to stay in power. By doing so, the individual politician shortens the other politicians's horizons, thus making them also more willing to obtain a large slice of the cake today and to disregard the size of the cake tomorrow. This strategic complementarity yields multiple equilibria in corruption, political instability, and economic growth.

Second, it may be interesting to analyze how different types of government behave with respect to the composition of government expenditure. In Mauro [1993], using data from Barro [1991] and Easterly and Rebelo [1993], I find that—controlling for GDP per capita—corrupt, unstable governments spend less on education. This finding is consistent with the suggestion by Shleifer and Vishny [1993] that corruption opportunities may be less abundant on education than on other components of government expenditure.

Third, the empirical findings in this paper suggest a partial explanation for the stylized fact that poor countries tend to have corrupt, cumbersome bureaucracies and to be politically unstable. As institutional inefficiency persists over time, bad institutions in the past may have played a considerable role in bringing about low economic growth, thus leading to poverty today. At the same time this paper has not analyzed the reverse causal link from poverty to bad institutions, which may deserve further study.

APPENDIX 1:
DESCRIPTIVE STATISTICS OF REGRESSION VARIABLES

Series	Mean	Standard Deviation	Minimum	Maximum
Institutional efficiency index	7.37	1.47	1.89	10
Political stability index	7.61	1.29	5.00	10
Institutional change	8.13	1.68	3.00	10
Social change	7.43	1.71	4.33	10
Opposition takeover	8.66	1.28	5.00	10
Stability of labor	6.73	1.51	4.00	10
Neighboring countries	6.62	2.30	2.00	10
Terrorism	8.10	1.58	4.25	10
Bureaucratic efficiency index	6.90	2.16	1.89	10
Judiciary	7.33	2.17	2.00	10
Red tape	6.37	2.23	2.00	10
Corruption	6.99	2.51	1.00	10

CORRUPTION AND GROWTH   707

APPENDIX 1:

(CONTINUED)

Series	Mean	Standard Deviation	Minimum	Maximum
Ethnolinguistic fractionalization	34.6	29.0	0.0	90.0
Per capita GDP growth 1960–1985	0.025	0.017	−0.017	0.074
Investment/GDP 1960–1985	0.21	0.07	0.07	0.37
Per capita GDP in 1960	2.44	1.93	0.22	6.40
Primary education in 1960	0.90	0.25	0.30	1.44
Secondary education in 1960	0.30	0.22	0.02	0.86
Population growth 1960–1985	0.018	0.010	0.003	0.043
Government expenditure/GDP	0.092	0.048	0.001	0.209
Revolutions and coups	0.15	0.20	0.00	0.92
Assassinations	0.24	0.40	0.00	2.19
PPI60	0.73	0.34	0.26	2.57
PPI60DEV	−0.02	0.34	−0.49	1.83

There are 58 observations in the sample (57 for ethnolinguistic fractionalization). The Business International (BI) indices refer to the average of the 1980–1993 observations. The institutional efficiency index is the simple average of all nine individual indices. The political stability index is the simple average of the top six individual indices. The bureaucratic efficiency index is the simple average of the bottom three individual indices. A *high* value of a BI index means the country has *good* institutions. The index of ethnolinguistic fractionalization from 1960 is from Taylor and Hudson [1972]. The Barro [1991] regressors are per capita GDP, primary education, secondary education, the purchasing-power parity value for the investment deflator (PPI60) and its deviation from the sample mean (PPI60DEV) in 1960, the 1960–1985 average of the ratio of government consumption expenditure (net of spending on defense and education) to GDP, the number of revolutions and coups, and the number of assassinations.

APPENDIX 2:

CORRELATION MATRIX FOR BUSINESS INTERNATIONAL INDICES

	Institutional change	Social change	Opposition takeover	Stability of labor	Neighbors	Terrorism	Judiciary	Red tape	Corruption
Institutional change	1								
Social change	0.75	1							
Takeover	0.81	0.64	1						
Labor	0.40	0.52	0.42	1					
Neighbors	0.55	0.56	0.38	0.25	1				
Terrorism	0.54	0.75	0.45	0.39	0.60	1			
Judiciary	0.67	0.68	0.53	0.30	0.60	0.56	1		
Red tape	0.52	0.59	0.39	0.35	0.60	0.45	0.78	1	
Corruption	0.47	0.55	0.46	0.30	0.39	0.28	0.78	0.79	1

There are 67 observations in the sample. The Business International indices refer to the average of the 1980–1983 observations. A *high* value of a BI index means the country has good institutions.

APPENDIX 3:
BUSINESS INTERNATIONAL AND ELF INDICES

	Efficiency of the Judiciary System (1)	Red Tape (2)	Corruption (3)	Political stability (4)	Bureaucratic efficiency (average of 1–3) (5)	Ethno-linguistic fractionalization (6)
Algeria	7.25	2.5	5	7.71	4.92	43
Angola	4	5.33	8.66	4.61	6.00	78
Argentina	6	6.66	7.66	7.72	6.77	31
Australia	10	9.25	10	8.50	9.75	32
Austria	9.5	7.25	8	9.04	8.25	13
Bangladesh	6	4	4	6.50	4.67	NA
Barbados	NA	NA	NA	NA	NA	22
Belgium	9.5	8	9.75	8.00	9.08	55
Benin	NA	NA	NA	NA	NA	62
Bolivia	NA	NA	NA	NA	NA	68
Botswana	NA	NA	NA	NA	NA	51
Brazil	5.75	4	5.75	7.54	5.17	7
Burkina Faso	NA	NA	NA	NA	NA	68
Burma	NA	NA	NA	NA	NA	47
Burundi	NA	NA	NA	NA	NA	4
Cameroon	7	6	7	8.50	6.67	89
Canada	9.25	9.5	10	9.00	9.58	75
CAR	NA	NA	NA	NA	NA	83
Chad	NA	NA	NA	NA	NA	69
Chile	7.25	9.25	9.25	6.46	8.58	14
Colombia	7.25	4.5	4.5	6.00	5.42	6
Congo	NA	NA	NA	NA	NA	66
Costa Rica	NA	NA	NA	NA	NA	7
Cyprus	NA	NA	NA	NA	NA	35
Denmark	10	9.5	9.25	8.50	9.58	5
Dominican Rep.	6.75	6	6.5	7.58	6.42	4
Ecuador	6.25	5	5.5	6.63	5.58	53
Egypt	6.5	3	3.25	8.67	4.25	4
El Salvador	NA	NA	NA	NA	NA	17
Ethiopia	NA	NA	NA	NA	NA	69
Finland	10	8.5	9.5	8.79	9.33	16
France	8	6.75	10	8.92	8.25	26
Gabon	NA	NA	NA	NA	NA	69
Gambia	NA	NA	NA	NA	NA	73
Germany	9	7.5	9.5	8.21	8.67	3
Ghana	4.66	2.33	3.66	5.00	3.55	71
Greece	7	4	6.25	8.63	5.75	10
Guatemala	NA	NA	NA	NA	NA	64
Guinea	NA	NA	NA	NA	NA	75
Guyana	NA	NA	NA	NA	NA	58
Haiti	2	2	2	6.67	2.00	1

APPENDIX 3

(CONTINUED)

	Efficiency of the Judiciary System (1)	Red Tape (2)	Corrup- tion (3)	Political stability (4)	Bureaucratic efficiency (average of 1–3) (5)	Ethno- linguistic fractional- ization (6)
Honduras	NA	NA	NA	NA	NA	16
Hong Kong	10	9.75	8	9.50	9.25	2
Iceland	NA	NA	NA	NA	NA	5
India	8	3.25	5.25	7.00	5.50	89
Indonesia	2.5	2.75	1.5	7.46	2.25	76
Iran	2	1.25	3.25	3.25	2.17	76
Iraq	6	3	10	5.72	6.33	36
Ireland	8.75	7.5	9.75	7.67	8.67	4
Israel	10	7.5	9.25	6.25	8.92	20
Italy	6.75	4.75	7.5	7.92	6.33	4
Ivory Coast	6.5	7.75	6	8.33	6.75	86
Jamaica	7.33	4	5	7.50	5.44	5
Japan	10	8.5	8.75	9.42	9.08	1
Jordan	8.66	6.33	8.33	7.78	7.77	5
Kenya	5.75	5	4.5	6.96	5.08	83
Korea	6	6.5	5.75	7.50	6.08	0
Kuwait	7.5	6.25	7.75	8.33	7.17	18
Lesotho	NA	NA	NA	NA	NA	22
Liberia	3.33	5	2.66	5.00	3.66	83
Luxembourg	NA	NA	NA	NA	NA	15
Madagascar	NA	NA	NA	NA	NA	6
Malawi	NA	NA	NA	NA	NA	62
Malaysia	9	6	6	8.42	7.00	72
Mali	NA	NA	NA	NA	NA	78
Malta	NA	NA	NA	NA	NA	8
Mauritania	NA	NA	NA	NA	NA	33
Mauritius	NA	NA	NA	NA	NA	58
Mexico	6	5.25	3.25	6.88	4.83	30
Morocco	6.66	5.33	5.66	7.11	5.88	53
Mozambique	NA	NA	NA	NA	NA	65
Nepal	NA	NA	NA	NA	NA	70
Netherlands	10	10	10	8.83	10.00	10
New Zealand	10	10	10	8.50	10.00	37
Nicaragua	6	4	8.75	5.50	6.25	18
Niger	NA	NA	NA	NA	NA	73
Nigeria	7.25	2.75	3	7.29	4.33	87
Norway	10	9	10	9.50	9.67	4
Pakistan	5	4	4	5.33	4.33	64
Panama	6.75	7.25	5	7.54	6.33	28
Papua New G.	NA	NA	NA	NA	NA	42
Paraguay	NA	NA	NA	NA	NA	14

APPENDIX 3
(CONTINUED)

	Efficiency of the Judiciary System (1)	Red Tape (2)	Corruption (3)	Political stability (4)	Bureaucratic efficiency (average of 1–3) (5)	Ethno-linguistic fractionalization (6)
Peru	6.75	5.75	7.25	6.04	6.58	59
Philippines	4.75	5	4.5	6.08	4.75	74
Portugal	5.5	4.5	6.75	7.54	5.58	1
Rwanda	NA	NA	NA	NA	NA	14
Saudi Arabia	6	5.25	4.75	8.33	5.33	6
Senegal	NA	NA	NA	NA	NA	72
Sierra Leone	NA	NA	NA	NA	NA	77
Singapore	10	10	10	10.00	10.00	42
Somalia	NA	NA	NA	NA	NA	8
South Africa	6	7	8	6.50	7.00	88
Spain	6.25	6	7	6.67	6.42	44
Sri Lanka	7	6	7	7.22	6.67	47
Sudan	NA	NA	NA	NA	NA	73
Sweden	10	8.5	9.25	9.00	9.25	8
Switzerland	10	10	10	9.25	10.00	50
Syria	NA	NA	NA	NA	NA	22
Taiwan	6.75	7.25	6.75	8.58	6.92	42
Tanzania	NA	NA	NA	NA	NA	93
Thailand	3.25	3.25	1.5	5.63	2.67	66
Togo	NA	NA	NA	NA	NA	71
Trinidad/Tobago	8	4	6.5	7.79	6.17	56
Tunisia	NA	NA	NA	NA	NA	16
Turkey	4	5.33	6	8.17	5.11	25
Uganda	NA	NA	NA	NA	NA	90
United Kingdom	10	7.75	9.25	8.33	9.00	32
United States	10	9.25	10	9.33	9.75	50
Uruguay	6.5	6	8	9.00	6.83	20
Venezuela	6.5	4	5.75	7.71	5.42	11
Yemen	NA	NA	NA	NA	NA	2
Zaire	2	2.66	1	5.05	1.89	90
Zambia	NA	NA	NA	NA	NA	82
Zimbabwe	7.5	7.75	8.75	6.50	8.00	54

INTERNATIONAL MONETARY FUND

REFERENCES

Alesina, Alberto, Sule Ozler, Nouriel Roubini, and Phillip Swagel, "Political Instability and Economic Growth," NBER working paper No. 4173, September 1992.

Andvig, Jens Chr., and Karl Ove Moene, "How Corruption May Corrupt," *Journal of Economic Behavior and Organization*, XIII (1990), 63–76.

CORRUPTION AND GROWTH   711

Barro, Robert J., "Economic Growth in a Cross Section of Countries," *Quarterly Journal of Economics*, CVI (1991), 407–43.

Business International Corporation, *Managing and Evaluating Country Risk* (New York, NY: Business International Corporation, 1981).

Business International Corporation, *Introduction to the Country Assessment Service* (New York, NY: Business International Corporation, 1984).

Canning, David, and Marianne Fay, "The Effect of Transportation Networks on Economic Growth," Discussion Paper, Columbia University, May 1993.

Coplin, William D., and Michael K. O'Leary, *The 1983 Political Climate for International Business: A Forecast of Risk in 73 Countries* (New York, NY: Frost & Sullivan, 1982).

De Long, J. Bradford, and Lawrence Summers, "Equipment Investment and Growth," *Quarterly Journal of Economics*, CVI (1991), 455–502.

Department of Geodesy and Cartography of the State Geological Committee of the USSR, *Atlas Narodov Mira* (Moscow: 1964).

De Soto, Hernando, *The Other Path* (New York, NY: Harper and Row, 1989).

Easterly, William, "How Much Do Distortions Affect Growth?" *Journal of Monetary Economics*, XXXII (1993), 187–212.

Easterly, William, and Sergio Rebelo, "Fiscal Policy and Economic Growth: An Empirical Investigation," *Journal of Monetary Economics*, XXXII (1993), 417–58.

Ekpo, Monday, *Bureaucratic Corruption in Sub-Saharan Africa: Toward a Search of Causes and Consequences* (Washington, DC: University Press of America, 1979).

Heston, Alan, and Robert Summers, "What Have We Learned about Prices and Quantities from International Comparisons: 1987," *American Economic Review*, LXXVIII (1988), 467–73.

Hibbs, Douglas A., *Mass Political Violence: A Cross-National Causal Analysis* (New York, NY: John Wiley, & Sons, 1973).

Huntington, Samuel P., *Political Order in Changing Societies* (New Haven, CT: Yale University Press, 1968).

Krueger, Anne O., "Virtuous and Vicious Circles in Economic Development," *Papers and Proceedings of the American Economic Association*, LXXXIII (1993), 351–56.

Leff, Nathaniel, "Economic Development through Bureaucratic Corruption," *American Behavioral Scientist* (1964), 8–14.

Levine, Ross, and David Renelt, "A Sensitivity Analysis of Cross-Country Growth Regressions," *American Economic Review*, LXXXII (1992), 942–63.

Mauro, Paolo, "Essays on Country Risk, Asset Markets and Growth," Ph.D. thesis, Harvard University, Cambridge, MA, November 1993, Chapter 1.

Murphy, Kevin M., Andrei Shleifer, and Robert W. Vishny, "The Allocation of Talent: Implications for Growth," *Quarterly Journal of Economics*, CVI (1991), 503–30.

Murphy, Kevin M., Andrei Shleifer, and Robert W. Vishny, "Why Is Rent-Seeking so Costly to Growth?" *American Economic Review Papers and Proceedings*, LXXXIII (1993), 409–14.

Myrdal, Gunnar, *Asian Drama: An Enquiry in the Poverty of Nations*, Vol. II (New York, NY: The Twentieth Century Fund, 1968).

North, Douglass C., *Institutions, Institutional Change and Economic Performance* (New York, NY: Cambridge University Press, 1990).

Olson, Mancur, "Rapid Growth as a Destabilizing Force," *Journal of Economic History*, XXIII (1963), 529–52.

Putnam, Robert D., *Making Democracy Work: Civic Traditions in Modern Italy* (Princeton, NJ: Princeton University Press, 1993).

Rose-Ackerman, Susan, *Corruption: A Study in Political Economy* (New York, NY: Academic Press, 1978).

Sah, Raaj K., "Social Osmosis and Patterns of Crime," *Journal of Political Economy*, XCIX (1991), 1272–295.

Santhanam Committee, (New Delhi, *Report by the Committee on Prevention of Corruption* Government of India, Ministry of Home Affairs, 1964).

Shleifer, Andrei, and Robert Vishny, "Corruption," *Quarterly Journal of Economics*, CIX (1993), 599–617.

Summers, Robert, and Alan Heston, "A New Set of International Comparisons of
    Real Product and Price Levels Estimates for 130 Countries, 1950–1985,"
    Review of Income and Wealth, XXXIV (1988), 1–25.
Taylor, Charles L., and Michael C. Hudson, *World Handbook of Political and Social
    Indicators* (Ann Arbor, MI: ICSPR, 1972).
Tirole, Jean, "A Theory of Collective Reputations," mimeo, Toulouse, 1993.
Tornell, Aaron, "Economic Growth and Decline with Endogenous Property Rights,"
    NBER working paper No. 4354, May 1993.
Von der Mehden, Fred R., *Politics of the Developing Nations* (Englewood Cliffs, NJ:
    Prentice-Hall, 1969).

[15]

The Corruption Eruption

Moisés Naím

Senior Associate and Director of Latin American Studies
at the Carnegie Endowment for International Peace

W hy, in the 1990s, has corruption suddenly become such a political lightning rod? From India to Italy, from Japan to Brazil—why have societies which have traditionally tolerated corruption at the highest levels in government and the private sector suddenly lost their patience, their citizens willing to take to the streets to topple high officials accused of wrongdoing?

In the last few years, at least six heads of state, more than fifty cabinet ministers, scores of congressmen, and hundreds of businessmen throughout the world have lost their jobs, their liberty, and even their lives on account of allegations of corruption.[1] Indeed, suicides among powerful government officials and businessmen accused of corruption have become quite common. This veritable eruption of corruption scandals has affected every region of the world, regardless of cultural background or gross national product.

Even nations that pride themselves on their established democratic systems and rule of law have not been immune. In France, one ex-minister and a prominent senator have been jailed, a former treasury minister committed suicide after having been accused of improprieties, another minister was forced from office, and at least five additional ministers are under investigation on account of allegations of corruption. In Spain, popular support for the government of Felipe Gonzalez has been substantially eroded by repeated accusations

Kathleen Keller provided invaluable research assistance in the writing of this article. My thanks to Thomas Carothers and Christoph Bertram for their helpful comments on an earlier draft.

Moisés Naím

of corruption. In 1994, two British ministers resigned over a corruption scandal.[2] In the same year, Willy Claes, NATO's secretary general, became entangled in a scandal related to kickbacks that took place when he was the economic minister of Belgium. In Switzerland, a cabinet member was forced to resign after her husband was accused of using her position to advance his business interests.[3] In the United States, in 1994 alone, both a cabinet member and the powerful chairman of the House Ways and Means Committee were accused of unethical behavior—and subsequently lost their jobs—while a senior White House aide, who was also a close associate of President Clinton, committed suicide. In addition, a senior official at the Justice Department resigned, and pleaded guilty to wrongdoings in his previous activities as a lawyer in the private sector. In the 1994 presidential summit in Naples, the financial affairs of President Clinton and former prime ministers Hosokawa and Berlusconi received as much media attention as the deliberations of the heads of state. Even quiet Norway was dragged into the fray, as the director of the Oslo Stock Exchange was dismissed from his position and, some days later, found dead.

Countries with a long tacit acknowledgment of corruption have also been affected by the wave—what was once the norm has now become a cause for scandals. In Brazil and Venezuela, democratically elected presidents were impeached following accusations of corruption. In India, former prime minister V.P. Singh quit the ruling party and resigned from office, claiming that widespread corruption made governing impossible. Three ministers in the cabinet of P.V. Narashima Rao—Singh's successor—were accused of being involved in corruption scandals, and subsequently resigned after the ruling party suffered important losses in state elections; in those elections, in a break from the past, corruption became a central concern of the voters.[4] Japanese Prime Minister Morihiro Hosokawa resigned in April 1994, following charges that he had mismanaged funds and decimated his political support base.[5] In a four year period in Argentina, twenty ministers and senior presidential aides were forced to resign.[6] In Italy, where corrupt activities have long been the hallmark of the elite, twenty prominent politicians and businessmen have committed suicide over allegations of corruption. Prime Minister Berlusconi was toppled by a no-confidence vote after having been targeted by the famous Milan magistrates who, however, found themselves investigated shortly thereafter by the Ministry of Justice for their own alleged improprieties.[7]

> **Is not the daily disclosure of corruption a sign that democracy and markets are working?**

To some, this barrage of scandals is an unmistakable sign that corruption has reached unprecedented levels. It seems that the erosion of moral values and the excessive, almost anarchic, freedoms that accompany the present spread of democracy and capitalism are reinforcing each other, creating the conditions for corruption to soar. Yet, is not the daily disclosure of corruption a sign that democracy and markets are working? Indeed, more democratic regimes and freer markets are making government decisions more transparent, increasing the accountability of public officials, and reducing the impunity that has often accompanied the corruption of those in high places.

It is a paradox that corruption is perceived to be erupting just as new global, political, and economic circumstances are creating unprecedented conditions for the *decline* of corruption. Any discussion of corruption is constrained by the impossibility of arriving at reliable data with which to measure corruption's occurrence. Because corruption is, by design, covert, there is no real way of quantifying it; thus, there is no real way of knowing whether it is increasing or decreasing. However, there is no question that within the past five or ten years, the public's *perception* of corruption has greatly increased because of the great increase in publicity. This eruption of awareness stems from the increasing openness that accompanies democratic transition, and from changes in the nature of corruption, which, in many cases, make violations more visible. While constant media coverage on pervasive corruption may convey a sense of gloom over the current state of ethical behavior in the world, a deeper analysis of underlying trends shows that, instead, this is a time to be optimistic about the possibility of reducing corruption.

In addition to strong moral values, the best antidotes against corruption are an independent parliament and judiciary, a vigorous political opposition to the party in power, and a free and independent media. Moreover, the elimination of economic policies relying too heavily on the discretion of government officials to allocate resources and guide economic activities helps minimize the opportunities for corruption.

In recent years, the world has made unprecedented progress on these two fronts. According to Freedom House, an organization that tracks different measures of civil and political liberties, 114 countries had a political system classified as a democracy in 1994. This is the largest number in history—more than double the total of the early 1970s. The World Bank has the same opinion about the spread of free markets. The economic reforms that have swept the world during the last decade have created the freest economic landscape in recent memory. Democratization, decentralization, marketization, financial integration, and the globalization of business, the media, and even politics have surged with unprecedented force. Admittedly, some of these trends also create new forms of corruption and facilitate some of the old corrupt practices. However, in the long run the new global conditions will hinder, more than help, corruption.

Corruption has always existed, and will probably never be completely eradicated. But, if current global trends continue, it is possible to envision a world in which the scope for corruption is shrunk to its historical minimum. It will not be easy, and it will not occur spontaneously. Leaders in government, business, and the media will have to seize this emerging historical opportunity, and act together.

The effectiveness of such actions requires clear ideas about the nature of corruption and the way in which current international trends in politics, economics, and business are offering grounds for optimism in the fight against corruption.

Moisés Naím

Corruption's Multiple Meanings: A Conceptual Framework

Corruption, like cancer, has many manifestations. In the same way that different types of cancer require different treatments, fighting corruption requires different initiatives, tools, and institutions. For example, the money-laundering associated with the drug trade is a different phenomenon than the corruption that often distorts a government's procurement of large public works. Using the same approach and institutions to deal with both cases is surely less effective than targeting each with strategies that incorporate its relevant characteristics.

Nonetheless, corruption's multiple manifestations do share many commonalities. In principle, a conflict of interest underlies all acts of corruption. This conflict can often be open and brutal, such as when a government official extorts a payment in exchange for allowing imports to go through customs. Usually, however, the process is more subtle—perhaps a vendor's gift to the wife of a corporation's procurement manager, exchanged for his tolerance of higher prices. In fact, corruption can only exist when someone—the agent—is given authority to allocate the resources of others—the principals. All salaried managers in a private corporation act as the agents of the shareholders, who are the principals; all government officials are agents for their citizens. From this perspective, the potential for corruption exists every time a principal-agent relationship is present.

Every time an agent buys or sells on behalf of the principals, he can, in exchange for personal gain, conduct the transaction at prices above fair market value when buying, or under market value when selling. Moreover, in the case of governments, in addition to the buying and selling of properties on behalf of the community, officials can also sell their decisions for personal gain. From zoning rights that benefit a specific land developer, to health regulations that benefit specific pharmaceutical companies, government intervention offers a wide array of possibilities for the personal sale of public decisions. These decisions can be sold wholesale, as when government policies are distorted to benefit a specific interest group which has bribed policymakers. However, they can also be sold retail, as is the case when public employees personally collect a payment for the granting of a permit or a license. From this perspective, corruption in the public sector can only exist when the government buys goods and services, privatizes public assets, and regulates the activities of individuals and corporations.

The variety of corruption can lead to a complex system of classification, but for our purposes, we will focus on three specific categories, which together capture most of the instances of corruption more frequently denounced by the media and prosecuted by the courts: 1) competitive corporate corruption, 2) corruption instigated by organized crime, and 3) political corruption.

Competitive corporate corruption includes all the illegal activities that companies undertake to remain competitive. This is a form of institutional corporate corruption distinct from the individual corruption that occurs in corporations when employees benefit personally from their actions against the interest of the corporation. Competitive corporate corruption instead seeks to further the interests of the corporation. In some countries, it is impossible to win a bid for large public works projects without paying off government officials. In other countries, extensive government regulations make corporate survival overly dependent on the goodwill of public bureaucrats. Corporations challenged by competitors that are actively greasing the hands of eager government officials often find that they cannot compete unless they also relax their ethical standards. In some industries, these practices are widely accepted as part of the cost of doing business; some companies regretfully follow the practice, others do so enthusiastically, while still others rigorously and vehemently reject participating in corrupt practices, allowing competitors to take away their business. Often this ethical fortitude is supported by technological, financial, or other competitive advantages which make it affordable. Unfortunately, not all companies have the resources or the alternatives needed to withstand the consequences of losing business to rivals willing to break legal or ethical standards.

The point, however, is that the core business of companies involved in competitive corporate corruption is legal; they do not depend on systematically breaking the law to be profitable. Companies involved in *organized crime*, on the other hand, are purposefully created to break the law. While a legitimate private corporation may engage reluctantly in corrupt practices, occasionally, as a consequence of the competitive behavior of its rivals, or of the extortion of government officials, organized crime exists to break the law deliberately and constantly. As the profits of organized crime—especially the profits of narcotics trafficking—have soared, the natural path for these companies has been to diversify by investing in legitimate businesses whose survival and prosperity does not require illegal activities. Yet, because immoral and unethical acts are the basic business of these groups, they do not hesitate to—and actively seek to—corrupt government officials. Thus, the same group that keeps a Mexican drug enforcement official on its payroll will bribe a New York City official in order to keep its garbage-collecting cover operation in business. As organized crime groups increasingly operate across borders, they are becoming a critical element in international affairs.

Both categories are closely intertwined with *political corruption*, whose manifestations range from government officials stealing outright from the national treasury, to the illegal financing of political parties. The recent upheavals involving corruption in Italy and France, for example, can be traced to this category. In many countries, political parties customarily rely on the illegal payments of both private and state-owned corporations, which finance their activities and the posh lifestyles of the political elite. There is, of course, much overlap between the aforementioned three categories, as one form of corruption frequently spawns another.

There is little doubt that, in the last decade or so, some forms of corruption have greatly increased in scope and importance, and that such increases are related to changes in technology, as well as to changes in international politics and economics. Money laundering has been facilitated by the unprecedented

Moisés Naím

It is no coincidence that corruption has acquired its current political prominence just as democratic ideals are making their greatest progress.

level of international financial integration. The demand for illegal political financing has been boosted, as the spread of democracy has made elections more frequent, and the intense use of expensive media strategies has increased the cost of political campaigns. However, democracy and a free media are also increasing government accountability and lowering the impunity of corrupt politicians and businessmen. In addition, market reforms are decreasing the instances in which the profits of private firms depend on the signature of a government bureaucrat.

Beyond the Velvet Revolution

It is no coincidence that corruption has acquired its current political prominence just as democratic ideals are making their greatest progress. The type of political system is a determining factor in the behavior of civil servants and the transparency of business activities, especially those of large corporations.

In one of the best analyses of corruption, Robert Klitgaard argued that the level of corruption depends on three variables: the monopoly (M) on the supply of a given good or service, the discretion (D) enjoyed by the suppliers, and their accountability (A) to others that have the authority to reduce M or D, that is, the agents' monopolistic control of the supply or their discretion in administering their monopoly power. Klitgaard then suggested that the level of corruption (C) could be expressed as:

$$C = M + D - A$$

The more concentrated the supply of a good or service, the higher the discretionary power of those that control the supply; the lower their accountability to other authorities, the higher the corruption level will be.[8]

This equation would then predict that corruption is more probable in government agencies that have a monopoly on the supply of a specific good, service, or decision, than in a private corporation that sells goods and services in a highly contested market. Corruption will also be directly proportional to the degree of discretion accorded to those in charge of making the decision. A government agency that has to use some market-based benchmark to make its economic decisions has a narrower scope for corruption than one that relies only on the judgment of its officials. While competitive bidding among different suppliers does not necessarily eliminate the possibility for the distortionary effect of corruption on price and quality, it certainly limits its scope. In contrast, in a contract unilaterally awarded to a specific vendor in accord only with the judgment of the agents in charge, the room for corruption is obviously much larger.

In all cases, however, accountability has a significant inhibitory effect on corruption. From internal auditing processes to large scale congressional investigations, from organizational reporting procedures to media scrutiny, a wide array of mechanisms can be used to boost accountability and limit corruption.

Democracy and Corruption

A corollary of Klitgaard's equation is that the deepening of democratization should have corruption-curbing effects. Why, then, is there the perception that corruption is mounting, if democratic regimes are displacing authoritarian governments which are presumably more corrupt? Democracy provides opportunities for corruption which are necessarily more visible than those present under authoritarian rule. In a dictatorship, corruption can be more institutionalized, controlled, and predictable. A well-organized dictatorship allows for "one-stop shopping," where the right amount of money, given to the appropriate official, will take care of all of one's bribe-paying needs. The various bribe-takers, each of which has a monopoly on the service offered, work together to insure that the system continues to function, and the money continues to flow. This collusion can help insure that bribes stay both "reasonable" and out of the public view.[9] Democracy, on the other hand, is all about competition. If a government employee maintains his monopoly on a government service (such as, for instance, the one rubber stamp required to process a certain form), but is no longer in cooperation with his fellow bribe-takers, the bribe amount demanded can skyrocket, the employee caring little if he stifles demand for the various services, as long as he can continue to increase the amount of the graft. This sort of competition is inhibited in societies that are small, homogeneous, or controlled by a police state. However, when a society becomes more open, without eliminating the monopoly, the bribery problem becomes acute.

Elections, another crucial element of democracy, can affect corruption by increasing the need of politicians for two scarce resources: money and public affection. According to Transparency International—an international pressure group formed to fight corruption—the increased need for contributions has caused political parties to seek the support of business interests, increasing the potential for corrupt relations between the two.[10] This problem has recently become overt in France, where the national employers' federation, the *Patronat*, has urged a suspension of all corporate campaign contributions.[11] The problem has been blamed on French laws concerning campaign funding; these laws have undergone various changes in the past several years. As the old laws made legal fundraising difficult, a culture of corrupt campaigning developed; the laws remain ambiguous, furthering the problem. In Italy, the same problem was at the core of the scandals that have led to a fundamental restructuring of the country's political structure.

The increased competition for public affection engendered by elections encourages the revelation of corrupt acts. In a non-competitive system, the wolves travel in a pack, colluding and protecting each other. Only the insiders have the necessary evidence to convict the perpetrator. When a system is democratized, the wolves turn upon each other, offering up their knowledge in hopes of dashing their opponents and gaining a reputation as a reformer. The

Moisés Naím

danger here is evident: the anti-corruption crusade can easily be turned into a populist tool. While the accusations may be true, it does not necessarily follow that the accuser stands on higher moral ground. Brazilian President Fernando Collor de Mello won his presidency on an anti-corruption crusade, billing himself as a *cacador de marajás* ("hunter of overpaid bureaucrats"), only to be impeached two years later under accusations of corruption.[12] Ironically, many of the congressmen who actively sought President Collor's removal were later themselves accused of having embezzled huge amounts of funds through their influence in the Congressional Budget Appropriations Committee. For the non-insider, it is frequently difficult to know whom to believe. As power shifts from discredited politicians and bureaucrats accused of corruption, to journalists specializing in exposing graft in government, the latter soon become tempted to use their new-found power for their own personal gain. In Venezuela, the journalists who gained significant public acclaim through their aggressive denunciations of government officials were later found to have been paid by businessmen seeking to exert as corrupt an influence as that of the public bureaucrats exposed by the journalists themselves.

Democratization is frequently accompanied by the deliberate weakening of central state authority. In societies in transition from dictatorship, this is due to the bitter memory of abuses committed by states with absolute central authority. In other cases, decentralization is fed by the growing perception of corruption at the national level. The US, with its Congressional check-kiting and Savings and Loan scandals, is a good example. However, if corruption is already present, decentralization can frequently exacerbate an existing problem, giving local bureaucrats free reign to create new regulations that charge transaction fees. Moreover, as power devolves to regional authorities, operating nearer to the people, abuses of power also devolve downwards, becoming more evident to the people.

In addition, the dismantling of national institutions can lead to a regulatory and security vacuum which allows corruption to flourish. This is not to say that these old institutions should remain untouched—public agencies in developing nations are frequently bloated with non-productive personnel, and hobbled by unclear mandates. The devolution of power away from the center makes their effective reformation even more problematic.

As the ideological battlefield of the Cold War is vacated and the tenets of democracy take hold, government effectiveness is questioned both by citizens at home and by governments abroad. Corruption is becoming much more of a factor in political life in general, and in voter preferences in specific. The success of the democratization movement can be affected by the perceived level of government corruption. Just as citizens worldwide are discovering their ability to participate in and affect politics, they are also discovering how collusive and dirty politics can be. This tension threatens to drive a wedge between citizens and their governments. A poll of Brazilians conducted in 1993 showed a weakening commitment to democracy as the best system of government for Brazil, with "corruption/weak government" most often cited as a problem of democratic government.[13] Democracy requires some minimal amount of trust accorded to the government. While a lack of trust is evident even in nations with established democracies, for nations without a history of positive state-civil interaction, it is a critical hurdle which must be overcome.

The New Economic Order

In the last decade, not only has the political environment changed, but economic policy frameworks have been drastically altered, as government intervention and centralized planning have been increasingly displaced by market-oriented policies. These reforms are as good for the anti-corruption campaign as they are for macroeconomic stability. The less that economic decisions are made inside the state apparatus, the narrower the scope for corruption. State-owned industries, which have long enjoyed an unwarranted popularity in developing nations, generally provide fertile ground for bribe extortion or the utilization of company resources for the private use of their managers. It is now a well-established fact that while state-owned enterprises may, in principal, be owned by society at large, in practice, their "ownership" resides with the coterie of politicians, top managers, and union leaders that control the company's decisions. In state-owned enterprises, the benefits of ownership often accrue to an even smaller elite than that found in many privately owned companies.

Privatization eliminates the years of hidden, day-to-day corruption prevalent in state-owned companies. However, because privatization of a national firm is such a high-profile and high-profit event, it easily leads to corruption of a different sort. In one notable instance, when the Spanish airline Iberia acquired the Argentine national airline, Aerolineas Argentinas, it listed $80 million in expenses as "costs associated with the sale."[14] The Argentine privatization system came under so much criticism that it had to be entirely revised with help from the World Bank in 1991. Suspicion has now fallen upon the Eastern European privatization process. In Russia, where the process of *privatizatsia* ("privatization") has been nicknamed *prikhvatizatsia* ("grabitization"),[15] one study estimates that 61 percent of Russia's new rich are former Soviet managers who took advantage of privatization to make the industries their own.[16]

The process through which a state-owned firm is sold can, of course, be plagued by corruption. However, once the corporation is in private hands, the scope for corruption narrows. While there is no reason to assume that corruption will not also be found in a private corporation—especially those in which principals have inadequate control or information about their agents—it is safe to expect that market discipline will limit its extent, both in magnitude and in time.

In publicly listed companies, for example, investors demand greater transparency in corporate finances, with regular reports on expenditures. The common man provides an incentive for publicly-owned companies to keep their hands clean; when executives of French corporations Sant-Gobain and Alcatel were placed under investigation last fall, company stock fell immediately in

Moisés Naím

reaction to their foreseeable instability.[17]

While economic reforms decrease the opportunity for corruption, they also decrease public tolerance for corruption. As developing nations put a long-overdue end to decades of economic populism, and industrialized nations feel the pinch of economic slowdown, fiscal belts everywhere are being tightened. These changes do not go unnoticed by the population at large, which casts an ever-more-watchful eye on public accounts, as their own pet benefits and entitlements are slashed. The end result is closer monitoring of government officials, and greater public indignation over corruption. As one commentator, writing about the Japanese Recruit scandal of 1989, remarked, "public opinion only becomes critical when politicians are seen to be too greedy and start welshing on their obligation to deliver the appropriate share from Tokyo's bottomless pork barrel."[18] The reform process breaks the existing social contract wherein everyone got their cut: labor through higher wages and protected jobs, consumers through lower prices, and politicians through whatever they could skim off the public coffers.

The Globalization of Business and Corruption

Increased international trade and transnational business operations, stimulated by economic liberalization and marketization, have introduced new elements into what were once closed economies, causing old practices to be questioned. As competition among developing nations for international investment increases, companies have more options. In this context, corruption, or the lack thereof, has become one of the relevant factors in deciding where to invest. Macy's recently announced its withdrawal from the clothing industry in Myanmar, stating that it was "impossible to make money there," because corruption "makes normal operations impossible."[19] US businesses are forbidden by the 1977 Foreign Corrupt Practices Act from paying bribes in order to gain contracts.[20] As a result, US companies often feel they are at a disadvantage in a world where many of their international rivals do pay bribes and, in some cases, even declare payoffs a tax deduction. However, the ability to bribe is, at best, a costly advantage—last year, the French armament industry spent approximately 60 billion Belgian francs bribing foreign officials for contracts.[21] Businesses operating in China spend between 3 percent and 5 percent of their operating costs on "gifts" to officials; all this is frequently spent without any guarantee that results will be forthcoming. Moreover, a company which pays the big money quickly acquires a reputation as an easy mark, and, in this day of global gossip, this unwanted reputation frequently precedes its entry into new markets.

Corruption can be just as frustrating for the government concerned as it is for the corporation. For developing nations, the inefficiency and waste associated with corruption is often crippling. In Kenya last year, three banks failed as a result of corrupt practices involving campaign funds. In Ecuador, the cost to the state annually is estimated at $775 million, 9.5 percent of the GDP. It is estimated that bribes and blackmail add a 50 percent surtax onto Russian consumer goods. Even China, with its reputation as an economic powerhouse, has lost an estimated $50 billion due to the deliberate undervaluing of state assets by public employees. Moreover, countries desirous of foreign aid have a vested interest in proving themselves not to be corrupt "rat holes" which swallow up foreign aid, as Senator Helms has accused them of being.

The difficulties experienced by developing nations trying to reform themselves are often compounded by the outdated perceptions of foreign businessmen. Many companies operating in poor countries assume that corruption is pervasive, and that payoffs are an inevitable fact of doing business there. In a survey of American business leaders, more than half of the respondents affirmed that they would, under certain circumstances, bribe a foreign official in order to gain a desired contract—an act which is illegal under US law.[22] Their justifications were based on the ideas that business abroad could not be conducted without such bribes, that cultural differences made American business ethics inapplicable, and that such payments might not be illegal under foreign law. This attitude is itself a self-fulfilling prophesy, creating a vicious cycle of corruption in which foreigners continue to bribe because they think they have to, and officials continue to extort because they know they can. The incongruence of the resources involved—where the annual revenue of a large multinational can easily outweigh the GDP of a small developing nation—makes fighting corruption a daunting task for a government greatly in need of the jobs and goods provided by foreign firms.

However, small countries are beginning to make known their frustration with corrupt practices, acting independently to eliminate opportunities for the unethical. Last year, the Malaysian government declared several British firms found guilty of bribing officials ineligible to bid for government contracts.[23] Ecuador requires any company, foreign or domestic, which bids on government contracts to sign an agreement that it will not bribe officials, and to disclose all payments made to "consultants" or middlemen of any kind. By instituting open-bidding systems and mandating transparency in payments, a reforming government can make life much harder for the parasites in its own bureaucracy. A clear and transparent legal code is also necessary, as it prohibits bureaucrats from inventing their own regulations, thereby creating additional opportunities for graft, and allows the public to know when transgressions have been committed. Governments can remove some of the incentive to demand bribes by making sure that salaries are commensurate with responsibilities.

However, given the lack of international agreements concerning corruption, it is frequently difficult to enforce regulatory violations across borders. Governments are, in general, loathe to prosecute bribery when it is performed in another country, or by a foreign national. Legal jurisdiction in these cases—which are now among the most significant of bribery cases—is unclear, as laws differ among countries. International cooperation is needed to develop common standards of behavior and establish acceptable means of penalizing offenders. Unilateral action, such as the United States Foreign Corrupt Practices Act, can only go so far. The US example has failed to catch on; so far, only Sweden has instituted a similarly restrictive law.[24] As is the case with trade

Moisés Naím

liberalization, nations are understandably reluctant to act independently, since no one wants to feel that their companies are alone in operating at a disadvantage. Such a problem can best be solved by bilateral or multilateral agreements. In recognition of this fact, the OECD met in June 1994 to ratify the Recommendation on Bribery in International Business Transactions, the first multinational agreement to attack bribery in international trade.[25] A follow-up symposium was held in March 1995. Among the OECD's recommendations for its twenty-five member countries are: 1) to cease considering bribes as legitimate, deductible business expenses; 2) to extend national criminal law to acts committed by citizens in foreign countries where such acts are also illegal; 2) to treat payments made to foreign officials in the same way that payments to national officials are treated, at the request of the country involved; and 3) to extradite offenders to be prosecuted in the country involved.[26] The recommendations will be reviewed within three years and mandatory sanctions for noncompliance are being considered. The trend is catching on in the Western hemisphere as well; corruption was a major agenda item at the Summit of the Americas held last December in Miami.

The push is not limited to political leaders. Business leaders are also working on the problem. The World Economic Forum made corruption a major agenda item at its annual meeting last January, bringing together CEOs, politicians, social scientists, and law enforcement officials to discuss the topic. Out of the talks was born the Davos Group—named for the city in Switzerland where the meeting was held—which is working on an agenda to catalyze the adoption of international standards for business ethics and regulation.

The globalization of legitimate business practices, which has made it easier to transfer money between nations, has inadvertently aided the growth of international criminal groups. Organized crime has become truly global, and it has become apparent that it cannot be attacked from one country alone, as evidenced by the recent opening of a FBI branch office in Moscow. As authoritarian states disappear and market economies flourish, crime groups are making strongholds out of weak states, such as Russia, which still lack the framework and institutions for a market economy to function. The 26.5 percent surge in investment by the Cosa Nostra in the Italian manufacturing sector is attributed to their ties with the Russian mafia; the Italians export goods to the Russians, who enforce their distribution monopoly with an iron fist.[27] The vast sums of money controlled by these groups far outweigh the annual GDP of most countries, thus making it nearly impossible for nations acting individually to make much of an impact. Changes in the international finance system have made it increasingly more difficult to trace the source of this money. Every day, trillions of dollars are transferred electronically.[28] British intelligence estimates that around $500 billion may have been laundered through international finance channels last year.[29] A Financial Action Task Force, established in 1987 by the Group of Seven most industrialized nations and the European Community, issued forty recommendations, including making money-laundering a criminal offense, requiring banks to disclose more information, and extending some current regulations to cover firms other than banks; however, few member countries actually passed these directives into law.[30] Even this, though, would be less than adequate. If regulations are not truly international, dirty money will simply shift to safer havens, as it previously did when Switzerland tightened its regulations and money flowed into Luxembourg and the Netherlands Antilles.

A Shrinking World

Just as money flows across borders, political trends now spread from one nation to another. It is commonly suggested that the French magistrates have been inspired in their vigorous investigations by Italian magistrates. An American commentator, discussing the success of the magistrates in Southern Europe, concludes his commentary by noting "America does not have national magistrates, and our corruption takes a different form. But the mood is right for people with serious law enforcement backgrounds to have a serious national impact."[31] Allusions to the Italian magistrates frequently appear in Latin American newspapers as well. The hope exists that this marks the beginning of a trend towards imitation and transnational encouragement.

This global exchange is made possible by the increasingly international character of the mass media. Within the last few years, news has spread more quickly and farther than ever before. This is, in part, due to political changes, where increasingly open societies have led to a more numerous and independent press corps, and in part to technical advancements connected with the advent of satellite broadcasts and of CNN. The character of political journalism has also changed over the last two decades. Adam Gopnik has written that the journalistic profession has changed from an "access" culture into an "aggression" culture. Formerly, "in exchange for access, the reporter would show discretion."[32] If a reporter broke this gentlemen's code and published the seamier side of political life, he could suffer professional death. In the United States, this system ended with the Nixon era. In many other countries, however, the access system, which in a police state carried a penalty much greater than professional ostracism, has only recently ended. The burgeoning press of a newly opened society creates a stiff competition among journalists, accentuated worldwide by the growing importance of television news. Aggressive, investigative reporting, especially when it involves a scandal, sells papers and keeps independent newspapers solvent. Corruption has thus become the bread and butter of some journalists; Gopnick writes, "the reporter used to gain status by dining with his subjects, now he gains status by dining on them." It should also be remembered that journalistic power, like any other power, can be bought and sold. However, the new culture of aggression means that no one, be they politician, journalist or businessman, can be assured secrecy of action.

A Time for Action

Changes in the political, economic and social standards of the world have opened

Moisés Naím

a window of opportunity in the fight against corruption. However, while this time of upheaval provides unprecedented opportunities for corruption-fighting initiatives, it also provides an opening for the dishonest.

Money is pouring in and out of countries at a rate never before seen, while the globalization of business and communications systems has created a complex web of global interactions, making it increasingly difficult to discover, or even define, the criminal. Corruption has always existed, yet the problem is often dismissed as either an idiosyncratic inconvenience or an unavoidable cultural imperative. However, the stakes involved are growing, as is the scope of those affected. Now is not only an opportune moment to act, but, in fact, a critical moment. Vito Tanzi has posited that corruption stems from the failure to recognize the need for "arms-length" distance in government decision-making. This tendency is strongest in societies where communities are small and interactive, relationships are highly personal, and where the need to accumulate "social capital" is great.[33] The process of globalization destroys old-world patrimonialism, undermining the importance of social capital. Globalization, along with the economic pressure caused by years of governmental waste and the political pressure exerted by an increasingly informed populace, has made the old system of doing business simply untenable in today's world, leading to an eruption in the seams of

> The smoke-filled rooms and family politics of yesteryear are largely going the way of the dinosaur.

political life. The smoke-filled rooms and family politics of yesteryear are largely going the way of the dinosaur. The current challenge is to ensure that this old-style corruption is not replaced with a new-style corruption of international intimidation. Instead of denouncing corruption or moralizing about its ills, the time has come to address the issue head-on, creating incentives for businesses and government officials to stay clean, and the regulatory and penal frameworks to punish them when they do not.

It is important to strengthen the forces and trends that have lowered the tolerance for corruption, and to continue to heighten the consciousness of how these things pollute and endanger everyone's environment. Businesses, despite having a vested interest in cleaner politics, cannot act on their own. Politicians must cooperate internationally to generate frameworks that create behavioral inducements and disincentives. That will not happen until the politicians get strong signals from the political marketplace of voters. The solution is thus very dependent on the media and on public opinion. Corruption flourishes under public apathy. Happily, democracy and the free market are just the thing to reduce apathy by giving citizens a stake in how things are run. Perhaps the steady stream of discouraging stories is a consequence of a global renewal of political ethics. With the necessary pressure and encouragement, the recent eruption in the global perception of corruption could turn out to be the catharsis world politics needed.

Endnotes

[1] This includes Brazilian President Collor de Mello (impeached in 1992), Venezuelan president Perez (impeached in 1993), Japanese premiers Takeshita (1989) and Hosokawa (1994), Irish Prime Minister Haughey (1992), Pakistani Prime Minister Bhutto (dismissed in 1990, but later re-elected), and Italian Prime Minister Berlusconi (1995).

[2] "Hands Up all those hit by sleaze," *Economist*, 29 October 1994. *Financial Times*, 30 December 1994, 4.

[3] "Belgian Minister quits amid fraud claims," *Financial Times*, 9 December 1994.

[4] "Ex-Premier Quits Post in India Over Corruption," *New York Times*, 30 December 1994: A11. "Three Indian Ministers Quit," *Financial Times*, 23 December 1994.

[5] Bill Powell, "Tokyo Shock: Sayonara, 'Mr. Clean'," *Newsweek* 18 April 1994.

[6] Luigi Manzetti, "Economic Reform and Corruption in Latin America," *North-South Issues* 3, no. 1.

[7] "The Stain Spread in Italy," *New York Times*, 9 December 1994.

[8] Robert E. Klitgaard, *Controlling Corruption* (Berkeley: University of California Press, 1987).

[9] For a discussion on the idea of cooperative monopolies in bribe-taking as opposed to competitive monopolies, see Andrei Shleifer and Robert W. Vishny "Corruption," *Quarterly Journal of Economics* 108, no. 3 (August 1993).

[10] Peter Marsh, "More Potential for Corruption," *Financial Times*.

[11] John Ridding, "Halt to political funding urged," *Financial Times*.

[12] Luigi Manzetti, "Economic Reform and Corruption in Latin America," *North-South Issues* 3, no. 1 (1994).

[13] "Second Thoughts on Democracy in Brazil?" *USIA Opinion Research memorandum*, 22 February 1994.

[14] Luigi Manzetti, "Economic Reform and Corruption in Latin America," *North-South Issues* 3, no. 1 (1994).

[15] Peter Galuszka, "Red-Handed Russia." *Business Week*, 11 January 1993.

[16] Dorinda Elliot, "Lifestyles of Russia's Filthy New Rich," *Newsweek*, 19 December 1994, 42.

Moisés Naím

[17] Sharon Waxman, "Corruption Crackdown Shakes Europe's CEOs," *Washington Post*, 11 October 1994.

[18] Terry McCarthy, "The Sleaze Factor: It's not graft, just duty and obligation; Bribes in Japan form part of a system of gifts and incentives," *Independent*, 27 October 1994.

[19] G. Pascal Zachary "US Companies Back Out of Burma, Citing Human-Rights Concerns, Graft," *Wall Street Journal*, 13 April 1995: A10.

[20] The original impetus for this law was the scandal involving the Lockheed corporation's payment of some $25 million to Japanese officials in connection with aircraft sales. As a result of this scandal, Japanese Prime Minister Kankuie Tanaka was forced to resign, and US businesses lost considerable prestige overseas. The United States subsequently initiated an investigation by the Justice Department, the Securities Exchange Commission, and the Internal Revenue Service into overseas bribery payments. In the course of the investigation, 450 companies admitted to having made over $300 million worth of suspect payments. Public indignation led to the passage of the Foreign Corrupt Practices Act which forbids payments only to officials with discretionary powers, while allowing "facilitating payments," or "transaction" bribes, made to low-level officials in order to expedite paperwork or basic services. Opponents of the Act have claimed that the distinction is ambiguous, leading to unfair prosecution of American firms.

[21] "French Armament Industry Spent 60 Billion Franks on Bribes," *De Standaard*, 17 March 1995.

[22] Justin C. Longnecker, Joseph A. McKinney, and Carlos W. Moore, "The Ethical Issue of International Bribery: A Study of Attitudes Among US Business Professionals," *Journal of Business Ethics* 7 (1988).

[23] Barbara Ettore, "Why overseas bribery won't last," *Management Review* 83 (June 1994).

[24] Glenn A. Pitman and James P. Sanford, "The Foreign Corrupt Practices Act revisited." *International Journal of Purchasing and Materials* 30 (Summer 1994).

[25] Rosie Waterhouse, "War declared on corruption," *Independent*, 5 June 1994.

[26] Catherine Yannaca-Small, "Battling international bribery," *OECD Observer*, February-March 1995.

[27] "The Legitimate Assets Owned by the Crime Company," *Italian Federation of Public Enterprises*. Cited in FBIS-WEU-94-211-S, 1 November 1994: 2.

[28] "Crime Becoming Major Powerbroker," *Bangkok Post*, 14 January 1995: 5.

[29] "Money Launderers on the Line," *Economist Newspaper Ltd.*, 1994.

The Corruption Eruption

30 *US Department of State Dispatch*, 2 March 1992 3, no. 9: 163.

31 Jim Hoagland, "Revolt of the Magistrates," *Washington Post*, 11 October 1994.

32 Adam Gopnik, "A Critic at Large: Read All About It," *New Yorker*, 12 December 1994.

33 Vito Tanzi, *Corruption, Governmental Activities and Markets*, International Monetary Fund, Fiscal Affairs Department, August 1994.

[16]

The search for definitions: the vitality of politics and the issue of corruption

Michael Johnston

Introduction

The search for definitions has long been a feature of conceptual and political debates over corruption. Classical conceptions focusing on the moral vitality of whole societies have given way to modern 'behaviour classification' definitions in which specific actions are measured against a variety of standards. This modern meaning of the term is more specific, but has by no means settled the matter: the question of what constitutes 'corruption' still derails many a promising scholarly discussion and is central to many political disputes.

Not only are these modern definitions matters of dispute; at another level, they have come to seem incomplete, or even irrelevant to the episodes that spark public outcry. Corruption and scandal are not synonyms (Moodie, 1980) – we may find either in the absence of the other – and definitions need not necessarily suit public taste or further the cause of reform. But even in societies where legal and social conceptions of corruption are relatively settled and congruent, most analytical definitions omit a large penumbra of political actions that many perceive as corrupt, and that pose significant questions relating to fairness, justice, and the connections between wealth and power. In

Michael Johnston is Professor and Chair in the Department of Political Science, Colgate University, Hamilton, New York 13346 USA. For a number of years he co-edited the journal *Corruption and Reform*, merged in 1993 with *Crime, Law, and Social Change*, and he continues to co-edit the 'Corruption and Reform' issues of the merged journal. He is working on a book on corruption and political transitions in the UK, United States, Nigeria and China.

deeply divided or rapidly changing societies the ideas and distinctions on which most analytical definitions rest may be irrelevant to the realities of political life (Johnston and Hao, 1995). This is a problem not only for definitions, but also because corruption is often most pervasive and significant in those societies, both as specific syndromes and as a political issue conveying deeper grievances.

No one has ever devised a universally satisfying 'one-line' definition of corruption (Philp, 1987, p. 1). No more shall I. I do, however, hope to reconcile classical and modern ways of thinking about corruption by emphasizing the connections between the idea of corruption and the vitality of the political process. That corruption – or the widespread perception of corruption – threatens the vitality, openness and justice of politics is a familiar notion. But a vibrant political process is also critical to defining corruption in ways that are legitimate and meaningful in real situations. Thus, the search for definitions is a political as well as an analytical process. In societies with conceptions of corruption sufficiently settled and legitimate for the behaviour-classification approach to apply, notions of corruption embody settlements of politically contested issues, such as where distinctions between public and private roles and interests lie. Where matters are more unsettled,

ISSJ 149/1996 © UNESCO 1996. Published by Blackwell Publishers, 108 Cowley Road, Oxford OX4 1JF, UK and 238 Main Street, Cambridge, MA 02142, USA.

many of those same issues are matters of open conflict. In both settings, political contention helps mould and change the meaning of 'corruption'. While the concern to identify corrupt behaviour makes considerable sense in modern institutional settings, the overall political health of society – a central idea for classical thinkers – is still central to the meaning and significance of corruption.

Classical and modern notions of corruption

'Corruption' once had a much broader meaning than it does today. Plato (1957 edn, 421d–422b, 547a–553e), Aristotle (1962 edn, bk 2, ch. 7; bk 5, ch. 2), Thucydides (see Euben, 1978, and Dobel, 1978), and Machiavelli (1950 edn, bk I, ch. 2–7, pp. 211–30; see also Shumer, 1979) used the term to refer less to the actions of individuals than to the moral health of whole societies. This was judged in terms of distributions of wealth and power, relationships between leaders and followers, the sources of power and the moral right of rulers to rule; or of a people's 'love of liberty', 'the quality of . . . political leadership [and] the viability of . . . political values or style' (Shumer, pp. 7, 8), and for Machiavelli, *virtu* (Machiavelli, *op. cit.*; see also Shumer, 1979, p. 8). Politics was seen as a social process transcending the clash of specific interests, and emphasized the ends and justifications of political power as well as the means employed in its use or pursuit. For Thucydides (1954 edn, bk 5, ch. 7; see also Euben, 1978, and Dobel, 1978), the Athenian conquest of Melos sacrificed reason to a self-justifying claim of the necessity of conquest and signified the corruption of the state. Variations on classical themes remain with us today: Dobel (1978, 960) has defined corruption as 'the loss of a capacity for loyalty', and Shumer (1978, pp. 7–8, 13–16) suggests Machiavelli might have seen the disruptive American politics of the 1960s and 1970s as the vigorous disputation that fosters *virtu*.

Ironically, as the scope of politics has broadened, our conception of corruption has narrowed. Societies have become secularized and fragmented; many are seen more as arenas for contention among groups and interests than as embodying any coherent system of values; and ethical issues in politics revolve more around maintaining the fairness of that competition than around the pursuit of fundamental moral goals. The mass media have made politics widely (if superficially) accessible, and thereby often mundane. The institutions of government have become so elaborate, and social groups and their agendas so differentiated, that there now seems to be no way or reason to judge the corruptness of a whole political order. These generalizations may apply unevenly to democracies, and perhaps not at all to societies in transition. Still, for most analysts, judges, legislators, and participants in political life, 'corruption' now refers to specific actions by specific individuals – those holding public positions and (according to some definitions) those who seek to influence them. Defining corruption becomes a process of spelling out classifications of behaviour (Moodie, 1980, p. 209).

Behaviour-classifying definitions

Behaviour-focused definitions generally hold that corruption is the abuse of public office, powers, or resources for private benefit. By what standards do we identify 'abuse'? And what do 'public' and 'private' mean in practice, particularly when joined with the notion of 'benefit'?

Many scholars have sought 'objective' standards, arguing that answers to these questions can be found in the law or other formal regulations, or by making reference to the 'public interest'. Others propose 'subjective' or cultural definitions, pointing out that 'the public interest' is too vague or disputed to serve as a usable standard, and that laws and formal roles at times enjoy little legitimacy. Public opinion or cultural standards are also promoted as one way to assess the significance of corruption – that is, how much and why a corrupt act *matters* to the population, the elite, or to various segments of them. Not surprisingly, no universally applicable standard has been found.

While social or cultural perceptions of corruption have been the focus of several studies (for references to a number of studies, see Johnston, 1991), 'subjective' or explicitly cultural *definitions* are relatively uncommon. The argument from social standards more often appears as a critique or *caveat* with respect to the application of legalistic definitions. Moreover, such arguments often recognize that public opinion and cultural standards vary among segments of society. Smith (1964), while not proposing a general definition, did carefully compare the views of a number of status and communal groups in Nigeria in the 1960s. Senturia (1935, p. 449) proposed that 'Where the best opinion and morality of the time, examining the intent and setting of an act, judge it to represent a sacrifice of public for private benefit, then it must be held to be corrupt.' Peters and Welch (1978) conducted a survey of American state legislators, deriving intriguing categories and distinctions from their judgements. More recently, Gorta and Forell's ambitious survey of civil servants in New South Wales (1995) probed the sorts of considerations these officials might take into account in deciding whether or not to report instances of corruption. Gibbons' surveys of university students (1989) similarly illustrated the subtleties of perceived corruption, and Dolan, McKeown and Carlson (1988) conducted some of the most methodologically sophisticated work to date, employing a Q-method analysis. Heidenheimer (1989b) has outlined 'shades' of corruption, ranging from white through grey to black, delineated by similar or contrasting elite and mass opinion, in several kinds of societies. Still, while no one would advocate completely ignoring the cultural setting of politics, the subjectivity that is the source of richness and subtlety in such approaches can also make it difficult to build general definitions.

Most 'objective' definitions fall into Heidenheimer's enduring categories of 'public-office-centred', 'market-centred', and 'public-interest-centred' (Heidenheimer, 1989a, pp. 8–11). Nye provides the best-known example of the first kind:

[Corruption is] behaviour which deviates from the formal duties of a public role because of private-regarding (close family, personal, private clique) pecuniary or status gains; or violates rules against the exercise of certain types of private-regarding influence. (Nye, 1967, p. 417)

The potential advantage in this approach is one of relative precision. But – leaving aside the problems of deciding what is a public role

or a private benefit – laws can be vague or contradictory, and they do change; widely accepted behaviour becomes proscribed over time. Scott (1972, pp. 7–8) deals with the latter by calling it 'proto-corruption', a tempting solution but one that defines away, rather than illuminates, the ways in which a given kind of behaviour comes to be officially labelled corrupt. The last point is critical: some new legal delineations of corruption might reflect fundamental political changes, but Ferdinand Marcos, for example, rewrote sections of the Philippine Constitution to legalize his looting of the nation's wealth (Carbonell-Catilo, 1985, pp. 4–7, 18–19). Corruption can thus have moral meanings that may differ from, or extend well beyond, the letter of the law, while some illegal actions may be morally defensible. Marcos provides an example of the former sort; as for the latter, Rose-Ackerman (1978, p. 9) observes that 'One does not condemn a Jew for bribing his way out of a concentration camp.' Still, Nye's has been perhaps the most widely used definition over the years.

Heidenheimer (1989a, p. 9) offers Van Klaveren's definition as an example of the market-centred approach:

A corrupt civil servant regards his public office as a business, the income of which he will . . . seek to maximize. The office then becomes a 'maximizing unit'. The size of his income depends . . . upon the market situation and his talents for finding the point of maximal gain on the public's demand curve.

At one level, this is less a definition than a claim regarding the incentives that affect the *amount* and stakes of corruption taking place in a given situation, and that make corruption such an enduring phenomenon. It overlooks the intangible benefits (prestige, promises of political support) that can flow from the abuse of authority. Moreover, the 'market' for official favours can be complex and idiosyncratic: demand for official services may be inelastic, highly individualized (as in cases of cronyism), and far in excess of supply. In some cases – when, for example, several officials who perform identical services agree that all will charge the same under-the-table fees – corruption may involve collusion that undercuts the kind of market van Klaveren describes. Officials may contrive monopolies, delays, or shortages of goods, licences, and the like in order to raise the price of their discretion. Van Klaveren does, however, capture an important political and normative issue – that of the appropriate processes (market, or authoritative, or patrimonial) for allocating various goods. Much corruption does involve the intrusion of market or patrimonial processes into authoritative (and supposedly universalistic) decision-making, or of official power and discretion into market transactions.

Finally, public-interest-centred definitions address both the nature of the phenomenon and its consequences. Consider Friedrich:

> The pattern of corruption can be said to exist whenever a powerholder who is charged with doing certain things, i.e., who is a responsible functionary or officeholder, is by monetary or other rewards not legally provided for, induced to take actions which favor whoever provides the rewards and thereby does damage to the public and its interests. (Friedrich, 1966, p. 74)

To his credit, Friedrich seeks to retain an important moral aspect of corruption – harm to the public – while defining a category of behaviour. His approach might also offer a way to distinguish between trivial and harmful cases. But even if 'the public interest' could be shown to have a reasonably precise meaning, let alone one comparable from time to time and place to place, the *definition* of corruption and its *consequences* are distinct issues. Each is worthy of extended consideration in its own right, and the latter may well vary across different social settings and forms of corruption. Take the point about consequences away from Friedrich's definition, and – because of his reliance on the standards attendant on public office – we are left with the essentials of Nye's.

The definitions above do have one common element: they attempt to classify behaviour. They allow us to identify patterns of corruption, to consider institutional and political reforms, and to analyse the consequences of various corrupt actions. But while such definitions are defended on grounds of precision and objectivity, this claim is illusory, for the powers and limitations of official roles, and their relationships with private interests, are constantly being contested and reinterpreted, even in relatively settled systems. Indeed, Moodie argues that there are complexities inherent in official roles

that make a precise behavioural definition unlikely ever to be found. First, officials have a legitimate need for 'room to manoeuvre' (e.g., the working discretion accorded to police officers). Second, public roles entail working distinctions 'between a ruler's public and private personality, a version of the "Becket rule" which separates role from occupant (. . . the absence of this at Henry II's dinner-table, so legend has it, . . . misled his knights into thinking it was the King, and not merely the temporarily irate and frustrated individual, who wished to be rid of Thomas à Becket).' Third, an office necessarily requires a degree of trust because its mandate is usually a congeries of conflicting imperatives. Finally, Moodie contends that judgements of behaviour require 'evidence that any particular lapse was for the reasons, with the purposes, or under the circumstances that put it under the heading of a corrupt lapse' (Moodie, 1980, p. 213 text and note 14). (Later on we will consider Thompson's argument that corrupt motives may be beside the point.)

But there are problems with other terms and distinctions employed in behaviour-classifying definitions. Not only can it be difficult to agree on the meaning of 'abuse'; it may also be far from clear what constitutes a public role or resource, or a private benefit. The most explosive corruption issue in China, for example, involves *guandao* – profiteering and cosy relationships involving officials and entrepreneurs, with many individuals occupying *both* sorts of roles, in an economic setting neither wholly public nor private. Many deal in commodities bought at low official prices and then quickly resold in unrestricted non-plan transactions (Johnston and Hao, 1995). Even where public–private distinctions are clear, the conduct of private parties may or may not be a corruption issue: the debates over rules governing political contributions and lobbying in many nations demonstrate the pervasiveness of this question. Another issue is whether corruption can, and should, be seen as a matter of degree. Many behaviour-classification definitions – those, at least, that do not make reference to public opinion – do not help us resolve this question, nor lend themselves easily to judgements of degree should we decide they are appropriate. Even more complex, perhaps, is the question of what constitutes a 'private benefit'. Few would

Demonstration in Paris by victims of blood transfusions contaminated by the HIV retrovirus. Patrick Gely/Imapress

restrict the idea to cash and gifts accruing only to a public functionary, but once we extend that part of the definition, where does it end? If an official sponsors legislation, or uses her discretion to make administrative decisions, popular with a segment of the public, do the popularity and political support that may result constitute a 'private benefit'? Even where norms and roles are relatively settled, there will be substantial grey areas in any behaviour-classifying definition of corruption.

Principal-agent-client definitions

A somewhat different approach – still linked to official behaviour, but grounded in the analysis of interactions rather than spelling out a category of actions corrupt in and of themselves – draws upon the principal-agent-client ('PAC') framework. Instead of considering officials in

isolation, the PAC approach resolves the workings of public agencies into the relationships between a principal – that individual, say a department head, charged with carrying out a public function – his or her agent, who actually performs the operational functions of the agency – and the client, the private individual with whom the agent interacts (for a full presentation of this framework, see Rose-Ackerman, 1978, and Klitgaard, 1988). There are several basic forms of interaction among these three figures, but for Klitgaard 'this approach defines corruption in terms of the divergence between the principal's or the public's interests and those of the agent or civil servant: corruption occurs when an agent betrays the principal's interest in pursuit of her own' (Klitgaard, 1988, p. 24). Here he differs somewhat with Rose-Ackerman, who defined corruption more narrowly:

While superiors would like agents always to fulfill the superior's objectives, monitoring is costly, and agents will generally have some freedom to put their own interests ahead of their principals'. Here is where money enters. Some third person, who can benefit by the agent's action, seeks to influence the agent's decision by offering him a monetary payment which is not passed on to the principal. The existence of such a payment does not necessarily imply that the principal's goals have been subverted – indeed the payment may even increase the principal's satisfaction with the agent's performance. Both tips to waiters and bribes to low-level officials may often improve service beyond the level attained by employees paid only a regular salary. Thus my focus is not limited to payments that conflict with the principal's goals. Nor is it limited to payments that have been formally declared illegal. Rather it embraces all payments to agents that are not passed on to superiors. Nevertheless, many third-party payments *are* illegal, and it is only these which I shall call 'corrupt'. (Rose-Ackerman, 1978, pp. 6–7)

We need not resolve this debate here except to observe that even a simple PAC model places both officials and citizens in more realistic surroundings and complex incentive systems than do most behaviour-classifying definitions. It thus shifts the focus of analysis from individual actions judged against external (and at times, static) standards to the significance of officials' and clients' conduct within an institutional and political setting. For Klitgaard, this approach 'stresses that corruption is a matter of degree and tradeoffs' (Klitgaard, 1988, p. 24). Indeed, given limited resources and the often substantial costs of anti-corruption efforts, there will come a point at which the marginal costs of further reducing corruption will exceed the marginal benefits. An agency's 'optimal level' of corruption will thus be greater than zero (Klitgaard, 1988, pp. 24–27). This conclusion is not a definitional issue as such, nor is it logically precluded by a behaviour-classifying definition, but it is an insight we would be unlikely to reach via that latter route, and one that is important in judging the significance of corruption in real societies. Finally, the PAC approach makes room for a notion of the public interest in the form of the principal's interests. Even if it is, as Klitgaard (1988, p. 22) acknowledges, 'an unreasonable assumption' to equate the two, the PAC approach does focus more directly on the public interest and mechanisms of accountability as elements of the political and institutional setting, rather than attempting (as did Friedrich) to load those issues onto our assessment of individual actions themselves.

Thus the PAC approach offers real advantages, so long as it is reasonably clear which roles are and are not public, and what institutional linkages exist among them. Where public–private distinctions are weak, matters become more complex; and, as in the case of a dominant machine (or ideological) party that calls the shots from behind the scenes, it may be unclear in some cases just who is the principal, to whom the agent is accountable, and where (if anywhere) the public interest enters in. A more general problem is that while the PAC approach is well-suited to the analysis of bureaucratic corruption, other more broadly-based forms, such as market corruption and extended patronage networks, or intra-elite forms such as cronyism and nepotism, may fit the framework awkwardly or not at all.

For cases of political as opposed to bureaucratic corruption, we need to ask more questions. Where did the basic ideas that there are limits on official power, and that there are public–private boundaries, come from? How are those boundaries and limits drawn in practice, and how do they change? These are fundamentally political questions: even where 'public', 'private', and 'abuse' have agreed meanings, such agreement is in substantial measure a political settlement. Where such agreements do not exist, accepted and legitimate notions of corruption will require a political process open to (and capable of withstanding) contention over these terms and distinctions. Working settlements, accepted by a broad range of parties, are by no means a certain outcome of such contention, nor are they necessarily permanent once achieved. But the meaning of corruption and the search for definitions are both political *and* conceptual in nature, and while corruption can be a threat to the vitality of politics, a vital political process is also important in the creation of accepted notions of corruption.

The politics of propriety

Thus, while taking corruption out of politics may be a noble goal, taking politics out of our notions of corruption can be misleading. A focus on the political dimensions of corruption, and how its meanings are set and changed through political contention, will not yield up precise categories of behaviour. But it can reveal the interplay of formal institutions and social practices that together constitute a society's 'system of public order' (Rogow and Lasswell, 1963, p. 67ff), and in so doing reclaim classic questions of legitimacy, leadership and justice which are de-emphasized by the behaviour-classification approach.

Rules, roles, and conflict

Debates over political propriety once began and ended with 'the ancient rule that "the King can do no wrong"' (Friedrich, 1974, p. 102). As Theobald explains, 'If we go back to the pre-modern era . . . the state is not regarded as an impersonal legal entity but as the living embodiment of an inheritance which reached into the dim and distant past.' Under these circumstances, he adds, the state is 'personal property' – both in the sense of the royal claim to a territory, and in the sense of office as private property (Theobald, 1990, pp. 19–20). An absolute autocrat cannot be corrupt, in the modern sense of the concept, until some limitations are placed on his power. Thus, a modern notion of corruption will depend on the existence of countervailing or 'intermediary groups' (van Klaveren, 1989 edn, pp. 78–81), with significant political resources, who can confront those who rule. With them, the sovereign must at least take others' interests – and power – into account, and might eventually be made 'responsible' in a rudimentary sense (Friedrich, 1974, p. 13). The historic diffusion of political resources and a considerable amount of conflict were thus preconditions for the rise of distinctions between public and private sectors, personal and official powers and benefits, and the like.

Early intermediary groups were hardly moral innovators, or even advocates of any interests beyond their own. Even when their activities were channelled into formal political institutions, they did not necessarily revolve around questions of principle. Friedrich (*Ibid.*, p. 27) makes this point regarding 'government with estates':

Legislation played only a secondary role in the medieval governmental process. Laws were few and legislation rare, and medieval constitutionalism could thus concentrate its attention on the problem of the regulation of the abuse of the monarchic executive's power.

As we shall see, conflict often gave birth to new political ideals, but these often arose more as justification for various claims and grievances than as positive principles of good government. But eventually 'the Parliaments of the Middle Ages, which were primarily courts, found themselves confronted with the fact that the law had increasingly to be *made* rather than discovered and declared' (*Ibid.*, p. 31). With this came the task of devising explicit *rules* and standards.

Modern conceptions of corruption are based on the idea of explicitly public *roles* endowed with limited powers and bound by impersonal obligations. These ideas too have political roots. At one time, having 'a role in politics' meant being related to, or a crony of, powerful people, and having a personal share of power or favour. Public–private distinctions and notions of service or merit were non-existent; indeed, there were few obligations to anyone other than the sovereign or one's intermediate patrons. 'Politics' was the exercise and defence of personal power, its ends often little more than self-enrichment. But as the scale of society increased, and as intermediary groups developed and became more powerful, political roles began to change. Ruling elites grew beyond the size of personal retinues and extended households, and became increasingly factionalized. Wars, the acquisition of territory, and the emergence of 'proto-governments' with more elaborate structures and functions meant that sovereigns increasingly needed money, political support, and effective work by minions whom they could not easily oversee or coerce. Expanding regulatory activities – customs-collecting, various inspection functions, and the granting of patents for the manufacture and sale of goods – both increased the mutual contact between official power and social interests and created new, potentially lucrative roles which were useful as patronage (Peck, 1990). For Theobald this phase marks the difference between patriarchalism – in which 'the state is viewed as personal property', and the dominant family is the main arena of politics – and patrimonialism which, while still based on personal power, 'requires an administrative apparatus' (Theobald, 1990, pp. 19–20).

In time, extended personal or family networks became insufficient for the expanding scope of government. Administration became a full-time task, and functionaries had to be compensated if they were to remain loyal; as a result, various *benefices* – shares of grain, or title to the produce from a tract of land – and fees for services began to emerge (*Ibid.*, p. 21). So did tax- and customs-'farming' (Peck, 1990, pp. 38–44), whereby revenue-raising functions were franchised out to entrepreneurs who recouped their investments by keeping a share of the revenues. A related practice was the outright sale of such offices, as in Stuart England (Scott, 1972, ch. 3; Peck, 1990). No notions of merit were involved (though merit selection might well have recruited many of the same people who bought their way in), and citizens were still more exploited than served. But this emerging 'freehold conception of government office' was defended by Bentham and Montesquieu on grounds of efficiency, and by Burke as a legitimate property right (Scott, 1972, pp. 89–90, 93). Moreover, to argue that an office could be purchased was to acknowledge that at some point it had been distinct from the individual holding it, and might bear certain obligations, if only the revenue-collecting functions which were necessary to recoup one's investment. In France, Spain, England, and to a degree in China, feudalism gave way to an 'aristocratic bureaucracy' (Scott, 1972, pp. 89–94) or an 'early modern patrimonial bureaucratic state' (Peck, 1990, pp. 220–21) in which networks of 'freehold bureaucrats' supplied their patrons with revenue, political support, and an extended intelligence network.

Eventually, the rise of a money economy made regular taxation possible, and the growth of government made it necessary. Taxation, for Weber (in Gerth and Mills, 1946, pp. 204–209), was a 'presupposition of bureaucracy' allowing regular salaried compensation for officials and weakening the notion of personal service to patrons. These trends helped create the idea of a permanent civil service enforcing its own codes of behaviour, with salaries as an important means of control (Hurstfield, 1973, pp. 158–59). Enlightenment thinkers began to view officials as specialized parts of institutions and agendas much larger than themselves. The rise of political parties and expansion of mass electorates

likewise transformed elected positions, with the ideals of representation and service taking a place alongside the goal of winning power. As Scott (1972, p. 96) notes,

Finally, in the nineteenth century, when the more democratic form of government limited the aristocracy, and the modern idea of the State came into existence, the conception of public office as private property disappeared. The State became considered as a moral entity and the exercising of public authority as a duty.

New ideas about official power came into being as much through political contention, and as settlements among competing interests, as through moral or administrative innovation. Consider two cases. First, in 1583 the English essayist Phillip Stubbes, in *The Anatomie of Abuses*, described an illegitimate market in admissions to an Oxford College:

Except one be able to give the Regent or Provost of a House a piece of money, ten pounds, twenty pounds, yea a hundred pounds, a yoke of fat oxen, a couple of fine geldings, or the like, though he be never so toward a youth, nor have ever so much need of maintenances, yet he come not there I warrant you. (Stubbes, 1583, quoted in Wraith and Simpkins, 1963, p. 56)

Second, in 1641 a majority of the English House of Commons voiced the then novel argument that while the King could do no wrong, his counsellors were answerable to Parliament (Roberts, 1966, pp. 83, 89–91). This principle would become a cornerstone of the constitutional monarchy.

Stubbes made his lament at a time when the colleges of Oxford and Cambridge were turning out young men of ambition and high expectations in numbers greater than elite institutions could absorb them (Hurstfield, 1973, pp. 155–56), and when long accepted traditions of patronage and personal preferment in government, the church, and the universities were (not surprisingly) being decried by the excluded. Parliament's call for ministerial accountability surfaced in a bitter debate over its impeachment of the Earl of Stafford, who countered with an even more sweeping claim – that he enjoyed the consent of the governed, to whom he and Parliament were *both* subordinate (Roberts, 1966, pp. 89–91). This struggle, in turn, was part of Parliament's larger conflict with the King over funds, its desire to maintain autonomy in the face of Crown patronage, and fears of papist plots. In such a conflict, the idea of ministerial accountability was not so much a reform ideal as a political club useful for belabouring the King's inner circle. And as in many other settings – such as China today – when one could not legitimately make a fundamental challenge to those who rule, corruption issues were a useful way to take them to task for failing to uphold their own proclaimed policies and values. As Peck (1990, pp. 170, 163) points out, an old system based on reciprocity and royal prerogative was being challenged by new conceptions of duty and justice in a conflict between 'two systems of organizing obligation'; in the process, 'the language of corruption became a discourse of conflict capable of undermining governmental legitimacy, especially when it became tied to other critical issues'.

Several points can be drawn from these examples. First, conflict can produce new notions of political propriety as well as criticism of processes. Indeed, it may be *especially* in the course of conflict that contending parties will invoke higher values in their own cause, and as reasons to restrain each other. Second, where intermediary groups possess political resources and meaningful autonomy, rules will have to win acceptance and legitimacy if they are to be effective. Finally, these political settlements are by no means permanent. Customs-farming, once a welcome innovation, would today be denounced as hopelessly corrupt virtually everywhere – unless, perhaps, it was politically justified as 'privatization' – while the recent expansion of financial disclosure rules for elected and appointed officials in many nations reflects the presence of new advocacy groups and the rise of new ideas of accountability. The British House of Commons, which was proclaiming those kinds of ideas in the course of fighting for its independence in the seventeenth century, recently voted (again in the name of accountability) to subject its members to outside scrutiny on ethics issues for the first time ever.

At issue in these political processes is the creation of what Rogow and Lasswell (1963, p. 67) called a *system of public order*. This includes both 'the basic pattern of value distribution' and 'the fundamental institutions that receive protection from the legal system', thus embracing 'the "realities" as well as the "for-

malities" of a political system'. They explained this in an American context:

> The act of proclaiming stringent norms of rectitude is itself part of the established order; so too is disregard for many proclaimed norms in whole or in part . . . The constitution of the American commonwealth is reaffirmed every day whenever any established expectation or norm is adhered to; it is amended daily as new patterns gain credence on the basis of actual conduct. The conventional organs of government . . . are embedded in the social process. (*Ibid.*, p. 68)

More recently, Michael Reisman made a similar point in distinguishing between a society's 'myth system' – the norms expressed in the 'official picture' of the system – and the day-to-day realities of its 'operational code' (Reisman, 1979, pp. 15–16 and *passim*). These two kinds of standards are the contemporary manifestations of the developmental processes and conflicts discussed above. Social standards of political propriety are the present-day equivalent of the demands of 'intermediary groups' – made difficult to recognize, perhaps, by the greatly increased scope of political participation, and by the diffusion of universalistic terms of discourse. And legal standards reflect the current state of play in the evolution of official roles. Any definition of corruption raises the question of the stability of these sets of values, and of the degree of congruence or conflict between them. Where they exist in stable form, they embody settlements of political conflicts as well as ethical precepts. Where they are unclear or in conflict, differing outlooks over the meaning of corruption are not just 'noise', or a problem to be resolved by definition, but rather valuable clues to continuing political development.

'Neo-classical' approaches

If definitions that classify behaviour are too rigid to apply to all times and places, and if adapting them to those societies is likely to yield categories vague in content and soft at their boundaries, what then should a definition of corruption do? Perhaps definitions should identify a type of problem with politics – a problem that resides not in specific actions but rather in the broader processes through which consent is to be won, and influence and authority are to be used.[1] Such an approach might be termed

Reformation engraving showing a dealer in indulgences hanged by peasants. Kharbine collection/Edimedia

'neo-classical' because it seeks to reunite modern notions of corrupt politics with classical concerns about the moral health of whole societies.

In the course of introducing behaviour-classification definitions, I suggested that they share the general notion of the abuse of public roles or resources for private benefit. A 'neo-classical' approach might have it that corruption is the abuse, according to the legal *or* social standards constituting a society's system of public order, of a public role or resource for private benefit. Like others, this notion incorporates the basic idea of the abuse of public roles or resources for private benefit. Unlike them, it is not intended to specify a precise category of behaviour as corrupt, but rather is concerned with corruption as a political and moral issue. Where social and legal standards are reasonably congruent – a state of affairs similar to the mass/elite agreement making up part of Heidenheimer's schema – this definition would point to an agreed 'core meaning' of corruption not greatly different from many of the behaviour classifications already noted, while still making room for debate and change at the margins. Where the mass/elite or state/society gap is a wide one, or where consensus over social standards is weak, this kind of definition directs our attention to the forces contending over the meanings of concepts such as 'abuse', 'public role', and 'private benefit'. In all settings it encompasses both wrongful behaviour and the political processes that help define it as such and help shape its significance.

This approach could avoid both the charge of 'western bias' levelled at many legalistic definitions by making room for the many political forces shaping a society's system of public order, and the problems of relativism entailed by considering social norms alone. It invites us to consider not only how laws affect behaviour, but also how they might come to fit established customs. It links the study of corruption to the consideration of scandal via its emphasis on social values. And, as suggested above, it reintroduces some aspects of the classical outlook – the notion that politics can be a morally-charged *social* process addressing questions of morality, and the Machiavellian view that vigorous disputation can be a sign of political integrity in its broadest sense.

We do have some examples of this approach. Weber (in Gerth and Mills, 1946, pp. 127–30) recognized that the viability of formal rules rested in part upon 'social sanctions': 'relatively general and practically significant reaction[s] of disapproval'. Berg, Hahn, and Schmidhauser (1976) defined corruption as behaviour that 'violates and undermines the norms of the system of public order which is deemed indispensable for the maintenance of political democracy'. Jacek Tarkowski (1989, pp. 53–54), in an analysis of Poland and the USSR on the verge of their political transitions, proposed that:

> Corruption . . . is any activity motivated by interest, violating the binding rules of distribution, the application of which is within one's responsibility. Rules of distribution . . . refer not only to the letter of the law, but also to norms recognized as binding by society and/or to the system's 'official' norms and operational codes. Also 'corrupt' are those activities regarded by society as illegitimate or seen by the power elite as contradictory to the logic of the system.

Tarkowski found this broad definition useful in analysing the growth of 'hybrid' economic enterprises that were neither clearly public nor private, legal nor illicit, resembling in some ways *guandao* practices in China. And – a major point – he used his definition not primarily to classify certain kinds of behaviour as corrupt, but as a guide to the interplay between official institutions and the re-emerging forces of civil society, and to the 'grey areas' in which that process was taking place. In the end, he showed how corruption in the late 1980s, by creating new relationships between official and private interests, actually aided important aspects of reform – a provocative conclusion that, while eminently debatable as a proposition, would be very difficult to derive from more limited conceptions of corruption (*Ibid.*, pp. 55–61).

Dennis Thompson's intriguing notion of 'mediated corruption' is a different sort of attempt to revive classical notions of corruption as a property of a whole pattern of political action (Thompson, 1993).[2] Thompson does not redefine corruption as such, but rather posits mediated corruption as a category extending beyond 'conventional corruption' – outright bribery or extortion, presumably – to include actions that are corrupt because they damage the democratic process. He calls these 'mediated corruption'

> . . . because the corrupt acts are mediated by the political process. The public official's contribution to the corruption is filtered through various practices that are otherwise legitimate and may even be duties of office. As a result, both the official and citizens are less likely to recognize that the official has done anything wrong or that any serious harm has been done. (Thompson, 1993, p. 369)

To the extent that we are accustomed to defining corruption in terms of the characteristics of specific actions, this notion is not easy to grasp. It does not delineate sharp boundaries, either around corruption itself or between mediated and conventional corruption. It does, however, augment the core concept of corruption so as to connect academic analysis more closely to what much of the public has in mind when it complains of corruption, without making the concept merely a matter of public opinion. The focus is not on the status of specific actions or the specific goods being exchanged, but on the value of democratic politics itself:

> Mediated corruption . . . includes the three main elements of the general concept of corruption: a public official gains, a private citizen receives a benefit, and the connection between the gain and the benefit is improper. But mediated corruption differs from conventional corruption with respect to each of these three elements: (1) the gain that the politician receives is political, not personal and is not illegitimate in itself, as in conventional corruption; (2) *how* the public official provides the benefit is improper, not necessarily the benefit itself, or the fact that the particular citizen receives the benefit; (3) the connection between the gain and the benefit is improper because it damages the democratic process, not because the public official provides the benefit with a corrupt motive. In each of these elements, the concept of mediated corruption links the acts of individual officials to qualities of the democratic process. In this way, the concept provides a partial synthesis of conventional corruption (familiar in contemporary political science) and systematic corruption (found in traditional political theory). (Thompson, 1993, p. 369)

Thompson applies this concept to the *Keating Five* case (Thompson, 1993, pp. 369–74), involving dealings between the chairman of a failed Savings and Loan (similar to a British building society) and five members of the United States Senate. He argues that conventional notions of corruption lead to two equally unsatisfactory judgements of those events: either that corruption is endemic and all exchanges between citizens and politicians (in this case, campaign donations for the use of influence on regulators) are corrupt, or that such exchanges are necessary to the vitality of politics and therefore the vast majority are to be tolerated. For Thompson, both views miss the point of the *Keating Five* case. Corruption occurred there not because exchanges took place between politicians and a citizen, and not because of what was exchanged or the motives we might attribute to the participants. Rather, the transactions were corrupt because they avoided the democratic *process*, which is not to be regarded simply as the institutional formalities of politics but as embodying major values – representation, accountability, open debate, equality – in its own right. Thompson's is a subtle argument, but one that places the health and the core values of democratic institutions back at the centre of the corruption debate.

One problem with many behaviour-classifying definitions is that their authors sought somehow to treat corruption in a 'value-neutral' fashion, either with respect to generalizing about its effects or to the sensitivities involved in making judgements about times or societies other than one's own. The idea of mediated corruption, by contrast, is explicitly value-laden: not only is this kind of corruption a bad thing, but it is bad as judged against a definite conception of what constitutes *good* politics. Here the argument echoes Rose-Ackerman's observation that 'Normative statements about corruption . . . require a point of view, a standard of "goodness", and a model of how corruption works in particular instances' (Rose-Ackerman, 1978, p. 9). To be sure, we might question the precision of any list of democratic values as a standard of goodness. We might also ask how well the notion of mediated corruption might travel to transitional or deeply divided societies, not because of any reluctance to pass judgements on them but because the democratic values at stake have yet to be institutionalized in a legitimate political process. But analysts are free to reach conclusions about a political process, whether those conclusions would be accepted by participants or not. And as a practical matter, Chinese citizens, for example, have had little difficulty in judging *guandao* as undemocratic and corrupt, even though its legality and political status are in flux, and despite the fact that clear distinctions between public and private sectors of the economy have yet to emerge (Johnston and Hao, 1995). A different example is found in Britain, where MPs' conduct has long been regulated more by an unwritten, traditional gentlemanly code than by formal laws or ethical rules. There, the recent legislation imposing new disclosure and ethical scrutiny procedures was still justified in terms of preserving democratic values and processes of representation.

Thompson connects the modern and classical conceptions of corruption in ways that are useful to the analyst and which will also resonate with the disaffected citizens of many democracies. Moreover, he provides useful and politically realistic answers to the questions of what constitutes 'abuse' and 'personal gain': '. . . what is wrong is [not] personal gain, but a certain *kind* of personal gain; and it is wrong not because it is a *personal* gain at all but because of its effects on the system' (Thompson, 1993, p. 372). It is not necessarily corrupt for private parties to promote their agendas, or even to ask the support of public officials in doing so. Mediated corruption occurs when this is done by short-circuiting an open, accountable democratic process. At the very least, where boundaries and distinctions between public and private roles and interests are widely agreed upon, the concept of mediated corruption expands the modern conception of corruption in ways that recapture not only the classical outlook on politics but also the issue's contemporary political significance.

Conclusion

As conceded at the outset, this discussion has by no means settled the question of how best to define corruption. Perhaps the safest generalization is that in studying corruption we should remember why it is important, and be aware that our definitions may vary according to the questions we wish to ask and the settings within which we ask them. Where the major political conflicts underlying the notion of corruption have been largely settled – at least for a time – and where we wish to make comparisons that are limited in scope, we may well find a definition such as Nye's perfectly suitable, or

awkward only at the margins. But where our comparative agenda is more ambitious in terms of time, space, or cultural contrast, and/or where agreement over the meanings of 'public', 'private', 'abuse' and 'benefit' is weak, matters are more complex: it is an irony of corruption that where it is most important it can also be most difficult to define. There, we may wish to think of corruption as a politically contested or unresolved concept, and study the conflicts (real or potential) that may shape it as an issue.

These might include conflicts over: the boundaries between public and private roles, institutions, and resources; the boundaries between state and society; the distinction between individual and collective interests and rights; the distinction between politics and administration; and conflicts over the proper extent and limits of market, bureaucratic, and patrimonial processes of allocation. (An argument about corruption and the emergence of such boundaries and distinctions in contemporary China is offered in Johnston and Hao, 1995.) These are likely to be among the major issues in conflict – and bearing upon the meaning of corruption – in societies in transition. Where political divisions run beyond transitional issues – proper relationships between state and society, and principles of ownership and control in the economy – to deeper questions of fundamental order, another level of conflict regarding the 'ownership' of corruption issues may still be worth analysis. These might include conflicts over the extent and control of mass participation in politics, over the extent and the nature of elite accountability, and intra-elite conflicts over power and privilege. The issues here are literally those of who gets to make the rules of politics, and who shall and shall not have a say in the process.

In neither the transitional case nor in societies confronting deeper questions of order will these conflicts necessarily be the only ones on the agenda. Nor, of course, will they necessarily employ the specific ideas and concepts discussed here. In other cases we will encounter situations in which conflict has been stifled or pre-empted for a time – cases in which corruption concerns lack a public outlet, but are unlikely just to fade away. And in none of these cases are we likely to come up with categories of behaviour that are clear-cut *and* accepted by all the major forces in society. But a judicious analysis of political conflict may well shed light on the origins and uses of corruption as an issue – often, in fact, as an issue useful for raising a range of other grievances – and on the ways in which more coherent and accepted conceptions of corruption might, in time, emerge. It will also maintain a focus on the questions of the vitality of politics that have been matters of concern for a very long time, and that make corruption a concept worth our attention in the first place.

Notes

1. I am indebted to Dennis Thompson for his comments on this point.

2. In a recent book Thompson (1995) has elaborated on this concept, and has changed the term to 'institutional corruption'.

References

ARISTOTLE, 1962 edn. *The Politics* (tr. E. Barker). New York: Oxford University Press.

BERG, L. L.; HAHN, H.; SCHMIDHAUSER, J. R., 1976. *Corruption in the American Political System*. Morristown, N.J.: General Learning Press.

CARBONELL-CATILO, A., 1985. 'The Dynamics of Manipulation and Violence in Philippine Elections: A Case of Political Corruption'. XIII World Congress, International Political Science Association, Paris.

DOBEL, J. P., 1978. 'The Corruption of a State'. *American Political Science Review*, 72, pp. 958–73.

DOLAN, K.; McKEOWN, B.; CARLSON, J. M., 1988. 'Popular Conceptions of Political Corruption: Implications for the Empirical Study of Political Ethics'. *Corruption and Reform*, 3, pp. 3–24.

EUBEN, J. P., 1978. 'On Political Corruption'. *The Antioch Review*, 36, pp. 103–18.

FRIEDRICH, C. J., 1966. 'Political Pathology'. *The Political Quarterly*, 37, pp. 70–85.

FRIEDRICH, C. J., 1974. *Limited Government: A Comparison*. Englewood Cliffs, N.J.: Prentice-Hall.

GERTH, H. H.; MILLS, C. W., 1946. *From Max Weber: Essays in Sociology*. New York: Oxford University Press.

GIBBONS, K. M., 1989. 'Toward an Attitudinal Definition of Corruption'. In A. J. Heidenheimer, M. Johnston and V. Le Vine, *Political Corruption: A Handbook*, New Brunswick, N.J.: Transaction Publishers, pp. 165–71.

GORTA, A.; FORELL, S., 1995. 'Layers of Decision: Linking Social Definitions of Corruption and Willingness to Take Action'. *Crime, Law, and Social Change*, 23, pp. 315–43.

HEIDENHEIMER, A. J., 1989a. 'Perspectives on the Perception of Corruption'. In A. J. Heidenheimer, M. Johnston and V. Le Vine, *Political Corruption: A Handbook*, New Brunswick, N.J.: Transaction Publishers.

HEIDENHEIMER, A. J., 1989b. 'Terms, Concepts, and Definitions: An Introduction'. In A. J. Heidenheimer, M. Johnston and V. Le Vine, *Political Corruption: A Handbook*, New Brunswick, N.J.: Transaction Publishers.

HURSTFIELD, J., 1973. *Freedom, Corruption and Government in Elizabethan England*. Cambridge, Mass.: Harvard University Press.

JOHNSTON, M., 1991. 'Right and Wrong in British Politics: "Fits of Morality" in Comparative Perspective'. *Polity*, 24, pp. 1–25.

JOHNSTON, M.; HAO, Y., 1995. 'China's Surge of Corruption'. *Journal of Democracy*, 6, pp. 80–94.

Klitgaard, R. E., 1988. *Controlling Corruption*. Berkeley: University of California Press.

MACHIAVELLI, N., 1950 edn. *Discourses* (tr. and ed. L. J. Walker). New Haven: Yale University Press.

MOODIE, G. C., 1980. 'On Political Scandals and Corruption'. *Government and Opposition*, 15, pp. 208–22.

NYE, J. S., 1967. 'Corruption and Political Development: A Cost-Benefit Analysis'. *American Political Science Review*, 61, pp. 417–27.

PECK, L. L., 1990. *Court Patronage and Corruption in Early Stuart England*. Boston: Unwin Hyman.

PETERS, J. G.; WELCH, S., 1978. 'Political Corruption in America: A Search for Definitions and a Theory'. *American Political Science Review*, 72, pp. 974–84.

PHILP, M., 1987. 'Defining Corruption: An Analysis of the Republican Tradition'. International Political Science Association research roundtable on political finance and political corruption, Bellagio, Italy.

PLATO, 1957 edn. *The Republic* (tr. A. D. Lindsay). New York: E.P. Dutton.

REISMAN, M., 1979. *Folded Lies: Bribery, Crusades, and Reforms*. New York: Free Press.

ROBERTS, C., 1966. *The Growth of Responsible Government in Stuart England*. Cambridge: Cambridge University Press.

ROGOW, A.; LASSWELL, H. D., 1963. *Power, Corruption, and Rectitude*. Englewood Cliffs, N.J.: Prentice-Hall.

ROSE-ACKERMAN, S., 1978. *Corruption: A Study in Political Economy*. New York: Academic Press.

SCOTT, J. C., 1972. *Comparative Political Corruption*. Englewood Cliffs, N.J.: Prentice-Hall.

SENTURIA, J. A., 1935. 'Corruption, Political'. *Encyclopedia of the Social Sciences*, Vol. IV, New York: Crowell-Collier-Macmillan.

SHUMER, S. M., 1979. 'Machiavelli: Republican Politics and Its Corruption'. *Political Theory*, 7, pp. 5–34.

SMITH, M. G., 1964. 'Historical and Cultural Conditions of Political Corruption among the Hausa'. *Comparative Studies in Sociology and History*, 6, pp. 164–94.

STUBBES, P., 1583. *The Anatomie of Abuses*. Quoted in Wraith and Simpkins, 1963, *Corruption in Developing Countries*, London: George Allen and Unwin.

TARKOWSKI, J., 1989. 'Old and New Patterns of Corruption in Poland and the USSR'. *Telos*, 80, pp. 51–62.

THEOBALD, R., 1990. *Corruption, Development, and Underdevelopment*. Durham, NC: Duke University Press.

THOMPSON, D. F., 1993. 'Mediated corruption: the case of the Keating five'. *American Political Science Review*, 87, pp. 369–81.

THOMPSON, D. F., 1995. *Ethics in Congress: From Individual to Institutional Corruption*. Washington, DC: Brookings.

THUCYDIDES, 1954 edn. *History of the Peloponnesian War* (tr. Rex Warner). London: Penguin.

VAN KLAVEREN, J., 1989 edn. 'The Concept of Corruption'. In A. J. Heidenheimer, M. Johnston, and V. Le Vine, *Political Corruption: A Handbook*, New Brunswick, N.J.: Transaction Publishers.

WRAITH, R.; SIMPKINS, E., 1963. *Corruption in Developing Countries*. London: George Allen and Unwin.

[17]

Journal of International Development: Vol. 8, No. 5, 683–696 (1996)

THE EFFICIENCY IMPLICATIONS
OF CORRUPTION

MUSHTAQ H. KHAN
Department of Economics, SOAS, University of London, London, UK

Abstract: Corruption has different efficiency effects across countries. Conventional economic models of corruption are shown to be deficient in explaining these differences. Instead the article suggests that the distribution of power within the patron–client networks in which corruption is taking place is an important variable explaining the differences in the efficiency effects of corruption. Where patrons are powerful the range of rights transacted is limited and the allocation is likely to be efficiency maximizing. In contrast where patrons are weak the range of rights transacted is likely to be much wider with the rights allocated according to political calculations with large efficiency costs.

In late 1995 and early 1996 two parallel corruption scandals rocked India and South Korea. What is interesting is that although the sums of money involved in the Indian scandal were relatively small (some $20 million dollars spread over 30 or so politicians over two years) there was a general perception that poverty in India must have something to do with the corruption of its politicians. In contrast, in the South Korean scandal the sums of money involved were much larger. In late 1995 ex-president Roh Tae Woo admitted that he alone had accumulated a personal fortune of around $650 million over a five year period in office. While Roh's behaviour had equally serious political repercussions in South Korea, it was difficult to argue that economic performance had been seriously undermined as a result.

Does corruption have any effect on economic performance? If so, why did the presence of wide-spread corruption not have more damaging effects in countries like South Korea? These are the sorts of questions which the economic analysis of corruption seeks to answer. In this article we review the routes which contemporary economic theory has followed in providing models of the effects of corruption. We argue that in general these models are unsatisfactory because they ignore the distribution of power in the patron–client networks in which corrupt transactions are conducted. This distribution has an important effect on the efficiency of corruption by determining which rights are subject to corrupt transactions and the terms under which they are allocated.

CCC 0954–1748/96/050683–14

1 DEFINING CORRUPTION

Corruption has been defined in a number of ways in the literature. The basic distinction is between normative and positive definitions, summarized in Table 1. Two variants of normative definitions are provided in definitions 1 and 2 in Table 1. The first looks at acts and is clearly normative while the second looks at the consequences of acts. The second remains a normative definition because the definition of the public interest may differ across observers. It is also problematic to define corruption in terms of its consequences because this defines out of existence cases of beneficial corruption. Economic and sociological comparisons most often use the third, positive, definition using the standard of legal norms to identify deviations. Thus corruption is defined as deviations from the formal rules governing the allocative decisions of public officials in response to offers to them of financial gain or political support (based on Nye, 1967).

Table 1.   Definitions of corruption.

Normative definitions	Positive definitions
1. Deviations from Ethical Norms	3. Deviations from Legal Norms
2. Actions which Harm the Public Interest	

The stipulation that corrupt transactions should violate *formal* rules rather than simply ethical norms rules out any disagreements about the appropriate ethical standards. The additional stipulation that *public officials* are involved distinguishes corruption from *theft* which is illegal but which exclusively involves decisions by private individuals. The definition is still open to the problem that formal rules can vary across countries. A strict application of the definition could lead to different sets of practices being identified as corrupt. Fortunately, the corrupt practices which economists have wished to analyse would in fact violate formal rules in *most* countries.

The extent of corruption is difficult to objectively measure but it is widespread in many developing countries. Empirical evidence on corruption comes from journalistic and sociological case studies as well as cross-country indices of corruption such as those provided by Business International, Transparency International and the World Competitiveness Report. A number of empirical estimates of the effects of corruption have been based on such indices (Ades and Di Tella 1996). These provide a step forward but the subjectivity of local respondents in reporting the degree of corruption has to be kept in mind. It is likely that respondents in poorly performing economies will find even petty corruption more oppressive and therefore rank the extent of corruption higher. The case study based approach must therefore complement the index based one wherever possible.

The recent revelations of corruption in South Korea are interesting from this perspective. A major case which came to the surface in the 1990s was the decision of the Chun administration to disband the Kukje business group (chaebol) when its chairman refused to make large transfers to President Chun's chosen funds. In 1993 a South Korean court found the Kukje break-up illegal opening the way for further cases to be brought and indicating a shift in the overwhelming power of

the South Korean state. The Kukje case was only the tip of the iceberg. The revelations eventually led to the admission by ex-President Roh of his personal
involvement in the $650 million scandal.

The opposition leader Kim Dae Jung, one of the harshest critics of the corruption of the regime admitted to having received 2 1/2 million dollars from Roh. But
he pointed out that this was considerably less than his opponent, the conservative
victor for the presidency, Kim Young Sam, had received (*Financial Times* 28
October, 1995). In November 1995 24 of the country's chaebol were implicated
in the scandal including the big four: Hyundai, Samsung, Daewoo and Lucky
Goldstar. The other chaebol named included a 'roll-call of Korean industry'
(*Financial Times* 25 November, 1995). It would be difficult to argue that corruption was either small-scale in South Korea or limited to a few sectors or politicians. The figures are likely to turn out to be the tip of a much larger set of
redistributions which held the Korean industrial policy system together.

This kind of evidence challenges the conclusions of those who see a uniform
negative relationship between corruption and economic performance. The usual
response to the observation of corruption in dynamic countries has been to argue
that the extent of corruption and the presence of countervailing factors varied
across countries. According to this line of argument, the differential performance
is explained by saying that the practices identified as corrupt were (i) not equally
present everywhere, and/or (ii) that in the successful countries corruption was offset by countervailing factors. It is important to establish why this response is not
very satisfactory.

While it is virtually impossible to measure precisely the degree of corruption
with any precision, when we compare *specific* cases of corruption, such as examples of collusion between government and business it appears that similar practices have had very different outcomes. Moreover, the countervailing factors often
turn out to be precisely the details of the bargaining between government and
business rather than variables elsewhere in the economy. Thus the evidence suggests that the problem is not just the extent of corruption but also its type. We
should therefore try and see whether there are differences in the types of corruption which can account for the differences in observed effects.

2 CONVENTIONAL MODELS OF CORRUPTION

Economic models of corruption attempt to identify the efficiency implications of
changes in resource allocation brought about by corrupt transactions. The first
step in this exercise is to identify the *ex ante* allocation with which the effects of
corruption are to be compared. This is not as simple as it sounds and many of the
controversies in the literature can be traced to ill-defined benchmarks with which
the post-corruption allocation is being compared. Consider figure 1. Suppose we
are at the stage shown in box 5. Do we compare the efficiency implications of this
allocation with the allocations at stage 4, 3, 2 or 1?

The problem is solved in neoclassical models by choosing the perfectly competitive allocation as the benchmark. Suppose this is shown in box 1. Neoclassical theory tells us that welfare is optimized at this allocation and any intervention takes
us away from this optimal level of welfare. Consequently the welfare at stage 2 is

686   *M. H. Khan*

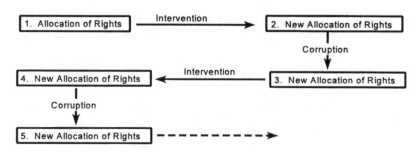

Figure 1.   The allocative effects of corruption: choosing benchmarks.

lower than at 1. The subsequent corruption which takes us to 3 can increase the
welfare loss, as in most rent-seeking models. On the other hand, it can undo some
of the misallocation by allowing resources to be bid back to higher valued uses,
though the level of welfare will still be lower than at stage 1. Thus even with the
neoclassical benchmark, our assessment of the effects of corruption will depend on
whether we compare the efficiency in box 3 with that in box 1 or 2.

Leff's (1964) argument that corruption had beneficial effects in sub-Saharan
Africa because it allowed some entrepreneurs to side-step restrictive monopolies
was effectively comparing a situation such as 3 with the even worse allocation at 2.
In contrast, Myrdal's (1968) argument took the opposite position, arguing that the
possibility of corruption would encourage state officials to deliberately introduce
restrictions which maximized their take. Here the comparison (anticipating subsequent rent-seeking arguments) is with a benchmark such as stage 1 which involves
neither the corruption nor the interventions which led to it.

In real-world comparisons where intervention of particular types and corruption
come as package deals, these problems are even more relevant. The perfectly
competitive benchmark may not be useful in such comparisons. Suppose the only
way to get efficiency-enhancing interventions which take us from stage 3 to stage 5
is to accept some of the efficiency loss brought about by corruption at stage 4. We
have to decide whether to choose 3 or 4 as our benchmark. If the corruption is
part of a package deal with particular kinds of intervention, so that stage 4 is not a
feasible benchmark, we should consider the corruption cost as a necessary cost for
attaining the improvement in welfare between 3 and 5. Comparing 5 with 3, corruption appears as a necessary cost of increasing welfare in the same way as labour
or input costs are necessary costs. If on the other hand it was feasible to attain the
allocation at 4, the corruption which took us to 5 would be an avoidable cost. Consequently by comparing 5 with 4, we would conclude that corruption reduced
welfare. The need to make this type of judgement about feasible benchmarks
makes the analysis of corruption difficult.

The next step in the economic analysis is to model how corruption at different
stages can explain the eventual allocation of rights. The aim is to explain the difference in welfare levels between the current level and that at some benchmark
allocation. The analysis of corruption has drawn most heavily on rent-seeking
models. These developed to answer the more general question of how the legal
and illegal expenditures on persuading activities affected welfare. While not all

rent-seeking is illegal and therefore corrupt, the general models can be amended to examine the effects of corruption. We argue that the models are indeterminate in terms of predicting both the *extent* of corruption as well as its likely *social cost*. In the next section we look at some of the factors which might make the analysis more determinate.

Rent-seeking theories have primarily looked at the determinants and effects of the *magnitude* of expenditures on rent-seeking. Rent-seeking describes the activities and expenditures of individuals who seek to change rights to earn the above normal profits described as rents. The theories of rent-seeking developed in response to the observation that measures of the deadweight losses associated with tariffs and other interventions were relatively small. Buchanan, Posner, Tullock, Krueger and others argued that the real efficiency cost of intervention was larger because the artificial rents would persuade other agents to spend resources trying to acquire rights to these rents till the rate of return had been equalized across activities (Buchanan *et al.*, 1980).

The first goal of the rent-seeking literature was to identify the magnitude of the rent-seeking expenditure. While some of this expenditure could be legal, in the form of lobbying, queueing and so on, much of it is likely to take the form of corruption in developing countries. The earliest models such as those of Krueger (1974) and Posner (1975) argued that the rent-seeking expenditure was going to be equal to the value of the rent being competed for. However, it was soon established that the aggregate expenditure is indeterminate in terms of conventional economic variables.

To some extent, the expenditure does depend on a number of conventional variables. These include the number of agents competing for rents and the number of state officials competing to supply the rights demanded. These factors can be modelled in a way familiar to economists. The structure of demand and supply in this 'market' partially but not fully determine total expenditures. However, total expenditure also depends on a number of other factors including the determinants of each individual's *probability* of getting the rent in response to expenditures on rent-seeking (Mueller 1989, pp. 231–235). This probability depends to some extent on the number of agents competing for the right but it also depends critically on other features of the political economy which determine the rules governing the allocation of rights in rent-seeking transactions.

For instance, if there are a small number of agents competing for the rents, they may end up spending far less than the total amount of the rent if some agents have a much higher probability of getting the rent. This could be the case if insiders have an advantage over outsiders (Rogerson, 1982). The outcome here depends not only on the small number of players but also critically on the enforceability of the rule determining the probabilities of different agents getting the rent. With the same number of agents the rent-seeking expenditure could be very large if there was a reasonable probability for outsiders to become insiders by spending large amounts of resources on rent-seeking. The analysis is therefore indeterminate without a description of the political economy which determines the distribution of probabilities of winning across groups and individuals.

Similarly, attempts to relate the magnitude of rent-seeking expenditures to the number of state officials offering the rights also proves to be indeterminate. One of the earliest models of how the agency structure of the bureaucracy can affect

688   *M. H. Khan*

the magnitude of corruption was provided by Rose-Ackerman. She considered a number of alternative bureaucratic structures: fragmented, sequential and hierarchical. In the fragmented structure each of a number of agencies provide part of the approval required, the sequential is similar except that approval is provided in sequence while the hierarchical corresponds to the command structure usually assumed in theories of bureaucracy. Rose-Ackerman's analysis established indeterminacy and showed that under particular conditions each of these structures may dominate in generating the greatest degree of corruption (1978, esp. pp. 176–88).

A similar indeterminacy exists in subsequent rent-seeking models which have attempted to model how the number of competing officials affects the magnitude of rent-seeking expenditures. Thus in Congleton's (1980) model, the competition amongst officials in a democracy could push the total bribe take down if each official was prepared to accept a low bribe. But if the minimum effective bribe was high, democracy may end up with a higher total bribe take than a dictatorship. Once again the total rent-seeking expenditure depends on features of the political economy of the society, here on the determinants of the bargaining power of bribe-givers and state officials.

While progress was made in pinning down at least some of the determinants of the *magnitude* of rent-seeking expenditures, less progress was made in identifying what part of this total expenditure was likely to be a true *social cost*. The problem here includes the one we discussed earlier of agreeing on a benchmark for comparing *ex post* outcomes. In the early rent-seeking models, the entire expenditure was assumed to be a waste. The justification for this was provided by Bhagwati (1982) who defined all expenditures on rent-seeking activities as *directly unproductive*. The basis for this definition was the assertion that the resources used up in rent-seeking activities do not produce an output which enters anyone's utility function.

However, in terms of neoclassical theory, this definition has the status of an assertion. It is clearly possible for expenditures, particularly if they are on pet political causes, to enter into the utility functions of the spenders as well as being rent-seeking expenditures. Moreover, as Bhagwati himself recognized, if the rent-seeking expenditures resulted in society moving from a less efficient to a more efficient position, it would be difficult to say that the expenditures were a waste from society's point of view. Recall that a move from stage 2 to stage 3 in figure 1 as a result of corruption could result in an improvement in welfare by reallocating resources to higher valued uses.

Thus an important source of confusion in the literature is the assertion that the *entire* rent-seeking expenditure was a social cost. This implicitly assumes that no welfare improvement comes about as a result of the reallocations of rights brought about by the expenditure. To properly identify the social cost associated with any given magnitude of rent-seeking expenditures, we would have to know the *particular* rights which were being reallocated or changed as a result. This is once again outside the ambit of rational choice models. In no society is every rent-yielding right up for reallocation or change through rent-seeking. A description of the political economy which determines *which* rights are up for negotiation is a critical precondition for analysing the waste implications of any particular level of rent-seeking expenditure. If the rights being reallocated result in welfare improvements, the rent-seeking expenditure may be a necessary cost and therefore no more a waste for society than the expenditure on fuel. If the rights being created or destroyed result in welfare losses, *any* level of expenditure on rent-seeking is a social waste.

A further source of confusion in the literature is a debate about whether bribes are a social cost if they are simply transferring resources between members of the same society rather than changing the level of output (Tullock, 1980, Browning, 1980). In theory, if bribes are pure transfers which change the distribution of income without affecting incentives, they have zero social cost apart from the transaction cost of organizing the bribes (Varian, 1989). In reality, bribes inevitably change incentives and therefore have effects on production. Like any other expenditures on rent-seeking, the efficiency losses due to acts of bribing have to be compared with the outcomes to assess their social cost.

The incentive effects of bribes have been modelled by Shleifer and Vishny (1993). Rose-Ackerman's early work had modelled the magnitude of bribes under different agency structures of the state. Shleifer and Vishny relate the agency structure to both the magnitude of bribes and their social cost in terms of lost output for society. Shleifer and Vishny's three-fold classification is quite similar to Rose-Ackerman's. Their first case is a centralized state where a *single* agency is the sole supplier of all relevant rights. The second case is a fragmented state where a *number* of agencies each provide one of a number of *complementary* rights. Each productive user requires a package of all these rights and therefore has to deal with all the agencies separately. The final case is one where there are a *number* of agencies but they can each supply *all* the relevant rights required by each productive user.

The outcome in terms of the effect on incentives for the productive sector is radically different between the three cases. The single agency case is equivalent to that of the monopoly case in industrial organization. State bureaucrats maximize their income from bribes by restricting the joint supply of the separate rights to their profit-maximizing level. Shleifer and Vishny argue that the total bribe collected will be the highest in this case as in a joint monopoly in industrial organization where the same firm supplies a number of complementary goods. Since the rights are over complementary inputs, the level of bribe demanded for *each* type of right will not necessarily be maximized.

The fragmented case is a version of the Cournot oligopoly case in industrial organization. Here a number of agencies each supply a right over a complementary input. One agency may supply the right to import raw materials, another may supply the right to set up the factory, and a third may supply access to credit. The different agencies face a prisoner's dilemma. In attempting to maximize rents for itself, each will raise the price of the particular right it supplies so high that overall activity shrinks and the *total bribe* collected by all agencies falls. The total bribe take falls because high individual bribes cause a fall in the level of activity and therefore in the demand for the rights sold by the state. Output and efficiency are lower than in the monopoly case.

The final case is a special case of fragmentation where each agency can supply a package deal to purchasers with all the complementary rights necessary to set up the business. This corresponds to the competitive case in industrial organization where a large number of suppliers are supplying the product. In this case the product is the *package* of rights necessary for productive activity. Competition between agencies will in theory push the price of the package of rights to zero and therefore the total bribe take to zero as well. The total bribe falls to zero not because the demand for rights has collapsed but rather because the price of each right has become zero. The absence of the bribe tax means that output and efficiency are now at their highest level.

The Shleifer–Vishny policy conclusion is straightforward. Corruption is best dealt with by increasing the competition between bureaucrats and allowing more agencies to supply similar rights. The aim is to approximate the third case: the competitive supply of rights. Total bribes are zero and output is highest. The worst case is that of competing agencies supplying complementary rights. Total bribes are not maximized but output is lowest because individual bribes are highest. The absolute monopoly case with the highest total bribe is in between, with a higher social output than the fragmented case.

Despite its apparent ability to model the consequences of state fracturing, the model does not actually fit a casual assessment of the costs of corruption across countries. As Shleifer and Vishny admit, most successful countries do not resemble the competitive agency structure of their theory. Indeed countries like South Korea appear to be closer to the monopolistic supply case rather than the competitive supply one. Equally, the classic cases of corruption-led sclerosis do not exhibit unqualified state fracturing. As the authors point out, countries such as the Philippines under Marcos were closer to the monopolistic supply case. A characteristic feature of such dictatorships has been that the strongman had a finger in every pie and could in principle have ensured that the total bribe was maximized for important packages of rights. On the other hand, Shleifer and Vishny point out that India approximates the fragmented case but it would be difficult to argue that the social costs of corruption were greater in India than, say, in the Philippines.

The model may therefore explain a *part* of the difference in the effects of corruption across countries in terms of these agency structure differences. But some of the most successful countries have monopolistic rather than competitive supply (South Korea, Taiwan). In this they are quite similar to some of the countries where the social costs of corruption were perceived to be the highest (Philippines under Marcos, Bangladesh under Ershad). On the other hand, some moderately successful countries (India) approximate the oligopoly case without collapsing in the way the model predicts.

One obvious shortcoming of the model is that it is silent about the packages of rights which are at issue. There is no description of the political economy of the society which determines *which* rights are being contested and the rules governing the resolution of these contests through the mediation of the state. We argue in the next section that differences across societies in these respects can explain why the social costs of rent-seeking can differ across institutionally similar state structures.

In summary, conventional models have limitations in determining both the magnitude of the expenditure on rent-seeking activities as well as in determining the social cost of these expenditures. The magnitude of expenditures does depend on some of the variables identified in rent-seeking models such as the number of competitors for rents and the number of agencies or officials supplying the rights to these rents. But the magnitude of the expenditure also depends on features of the society which determines how the probability of each individual getting the rent varies with the amount of expenditure she is willing to make. In the extreme case, the probability may have nothing to with expenditures but may instead be determined by other political or sociological variables. The models determining the social cost of these expenditures are even less determinate. To determine whether expenditures are a social cost or not we need to know *which* rights are being contested and the *rules determining success and failure* for individuals or organizations in these contests.

3 PATRON–CLIENT NETWORKS AND CORRUPTION

In this section we discuss what can be said in general terms about the factors which determine which rights are transacted between state and society and the terms of their exchange. Many of the determinants of these characteristics may be quite specific to societies but some relevant differences between societies can be identified at a general level. One of these determinants is the distribution of power between the state and the organizations in society which are demanding changes in rights.

Developing country states typically operate through patron–client relationships with key sections of society. State leaderships operate through these networks to *implement* their economic and political strategies and to *negotiate* changes in rights. A simple way of capturing the relevant differences in the balance of power across developing countries is to look at the power relationship between patrons and clients within such networks (Khan, 1996, and forthcoming).

A comparison of two ideal-typical cases will establish the importance of these differences. At one extreme we define the *patrimonial* patron–client network. The term patrimonial refers to the ability of the state to protect existing rights at low cost. This is actually implicit in much of economic theory where the state is assumed to have the power to enforce property rights at low cost. Underlying this is a distribution of power in society which allows the state to do this. This distribution of power between the state, right-holders and contestants of rights is in fact characteristic of a relatively narrow range of social structures in developing countries.

Patrimonial patron–client networks, where the state is able to protect the existing property right structure at low cost, are likely to be unusual in developing countries. This is because in developing countries current allocations of rights typically do not have a long history and civic institutions supporting such allocations are typically underdeveloped. Consequently, patrimonial patron–client relationships are only likely to develop in a relatively narrow range of developing countries where the distribution of power between the state and the coalitions contesting rights is tilted in favour of the state.

At the other end of the spectrum we define the *clientelist* patron-client network. State officials as patrons within these networks lack the power to enforce rights. Property rights within these networks are weakly-defined. Variants of the social distribution of power which produces this result are the norm in developing countries. Property rights over valuable resources are newly emerging and the groups or individuals getting access to these rights typically do not have a long history of possession. The degree of contestation over rights is consequently much higher.

692   *M. H. Khan*

In the clientelist case, state officials as patrons within patron–client networks are unable to monopolize the protection of rights. Mafia-like groups are likely to emerge engaged in private protection activities for patrons both in the private sector and in the state. In turn these 'clientelist' groups organize their own challenges on rights. This difference in the distribution of power within patron–client networks has important implications for the efficiency of corruption. On the one hand, the range of rights being contested varies greatly between clientelist and patrimonial networks. In addition, the factors determining success also differ between these networks with important allocative implications.

3.1 The Range of Contested Rights

The standard assumption in rent-seeking models is that the rent-seeking expenditures are being targeted towards a limited range of rights. This is consistent with the existence of patrimonial patron–client networks. It is assumed that rent-seeking does not affect the entire range of rights collectively. If all rights were being contested, the social allocation of rights would collapse without protection mechanisms (such as clientelist coalitions or mafias). In addition, the implicit assumption in conventional rent-seeking models is that while the state can limit the range of rights being negotiated, it only wishes to create (and trade in the creation of) socially harmful rights. It is not clear why the state should have such an objective function. One reason could be that only harmful rights have rents as in the standard neoclassical model. But most contributors to the rent-seeking literature would admit that in reality socially beneficial rents frequently exist (as when scarce resources or innovations have to be protected from free access).

Indeed, in developing countries, where capital, entrepreneurial skills and technical knowledge are in scarce supply, we would expect positive rents pervading the modern sector. If the distribution of power within patron–client networks was of the patrimonial type, state officials would be secure in their ability to allocate or protect such rents. This ability would enable them to capitalize (by appropriation) a share of the streams of future rents. The net present value of their streams of future income are maximized if productive rights are created and protected since over time productive rights are likely to create larger streams of appropriable income than redistributive rights. Corruption in this case may not be socially harmful because state officials have an incentive to create and protect productive rights.

The combination of economic dynamism and high levels of corruption in some East Asian countries can be explained in terms of the emergence of a distribution of social power which sustained patrimonial patron–client networks. Such a distribution of power emerged in South Korea under Park and under the KMT in Taiwan (Amsden, 1989; Wade, 1990). During their high-growth period, states in these societies could effectively enforce rights and could reallocate or change them at low cost. Long-run profit maximization by state officials dictated that productive rights were protected and changes were in efficiency-enhancing directions.

Under a clientelist political settlement, neither top state officials nor any other single group has the ability to define which rights will be protected and which changed. The range of rights which are being created or reallocated depends on the objective functions of a large number of clientelist groups and on their relative power. In a situation of instability no group is likely to have a long-term view and rights which maximize long-run profits are not likely to be created. Instead the rights which are likely to be created and reallocated are rights which generate rents over short time horizons. This does not mean that powerful individuals and groups within the state will not be getting very large benefits in the form of bribes. They will, but only by virtue of belonging to one or more of the clientelist organizations competing over rights.

It has often appeared to observers that dictators such as Ershad of Bangladesh or Marcos in the Philippines had the power to create productive rights but chose to create short-term rents instead. Their failure to create efficiency-enhancing rights is clear. The problem is to explain it. If we maintain the assumptions of the patrimonial system, we have to explain why a state which feels secure in its ability to selectively create rights will nevertheless choose to create and share socially damaging short run rents which do not maximize its profits. This can only be explained by persistent cognitive failure or a very short time horizon. It is interesting that new institutional economists have begun to stress differences in mental models and ideologies across countries (North, 1995; pp. 22–4). However, we would argue that it is possible to explain to a large extent the relative performance of states without recourse to cognitive problems by looking at differences in the distribution of power across countries (see also Khan, 1995).

The time horizon explanation is weak because these and other dictators *wanted* to be in power for very long. The cognitive failure explanation is also not satisfactory because dictators in these countries have occasionally tried to limit the effects of clientelist competition and failed. Marcos, for example, made an unsuccessful attempt in 1975 to crack down on the decentralized appropriation which we have described as clientelist contestation (Klitgaard, 1988; pp. 13–97).[*] A series of unsuccessful attempts by successive rulers in Pakistan and Bangladesh to combat clientelism is described in Khan (forthcoming). The problem lay not in the cognitive models of successive state leaderships but the social distribution of power which prevented them from defining *which* rights were to be created and protected.

Despite these occasional attempts at central control, a wide range of rights were being continuously contested by powerful clientelist groups with unplanned and unpredictable consequences. It was difficult in this context for the top state officials to create and allocate the rights which would maximize long-run rents. Given this constraint, the next best strategy was the one which was eventually followed. This was for the state leadership to organize the largest clientelist group, participate in the contestation of rights and use superior organizational power to grab most of what was available. This was a perfectly rational response and not the product of cognitive failure. The social consequences of such corruption were, however, large and negative.

3.2 The Allocation of Rights

Apart from the range of rights which are contested, the basis on which rights are *allocated* between agents is also likely to be different between these networks. The assumption in conventional rent-seeking models is that rights to rents are allocated in response to expenditures on rent-seeking. This assumption is more plausible in the patrimonial patron–client network. If the state officials acting as patrons can appropriate part of the rents, they are likely to allocate the right in response to bids being made by competing agents who wish to acquire the rent. This allocative procedure can be efficiency-enhancing because it favours the allocation of scarce resources to users who are most likely to maximize returns.

This is not necessarily the case in the clientelist patron–client network. Here the state officials who are patrons in particular transactions are themselves being challenged by state officials and private agents in competing clientelist coalitions. The allocative rule for patrons in this network is likely to be different. State officials are likely to look at a combination of economic and political rewards in making allocations. Rights will not be created or allocated to agents who are the highest bidders. Instead clients or clientelist groups with superior organizational power are likely to get payoffs for their support in the form of allocations of rights. This means that rights will not always (or indeed very rarely) go to individuals or groups who are the highest value adding users. This too contributes to the inefficiency generated by the clientelist system.

An important manifestation of a clientelist process is that while it may be relatively easy to create new rights, it is very difficult to change or transfer existing rights if this hurts powerful constituencies who already possess them. This means that even if some agents are higher value-adding users who are willing to bribe to change the structure of rights, the state may be *politically* unwilling to consider reallocations of rights. In contrast, in patrimonial networks or in the models considered in conventional economics, allocative decisions are based on calculations of economic gain by state officials.

If existing rights cannot be changed, competition results in the creation of new rights. One manifestation of this is excessive entry into new industries, excessive employment creation for powerful white collar workers and so on (Bhaskar and Khan, 1995). The proliferation of new rights dissipates rents even when their preservation is socially valuable. The multiple sources of power in the case of clientelist competition may give the appearance of the fragmented state machinery discussed by Rose-Ackerman and Shleifer and Vishny. But the causes are quite different. The problem is not that the *institutional* structure of the state is fragmented, preventing potential coordination. In fact in many countries with corrupt leadership, the supreme leader is nominally in a monopolistic position. Instead the problem is due to the proliferation of competing *clientelist organizations* many of which may include as key players powerful individuals within the state. The apparent similarity of clientelist competition with the disarticulated supply side structure of state agencies is misleading. The solution here is not further competition between bureaucrats. Competition between clientelist organizations which include important state bureaucrats and political elites is already high and is the source of the problem.

Let us return to our examples of the corruption scandals in India and South Korea. In both countries the magnitude of the transfers themselves should only be a starting point in an enquiry into the networks of patron–client exchanges. In South Korea our argument would be that the networks were patrimonial. The rights created and altered by the state were efficiency-enhancing. The profit maximizing strategy for state officials in patrimonial networks is usually to create the most productive rights and cream off as much of the rents created as possible. In the Indian case, the transfers were located within clientelist networks. Bribes paid by businessmen went into organizing political factions for their patrons who were clients of higher level patrons. What businessmen eventually get from their expenditures in clientelist networks depends very little on the rents they can potentially generate from productive enterprises created with state help. It depends rather more on the relative power which their chosen faction turns out to have relative to other clientelist factions. The cause of sclerosis is not the size of the expenditures on rent-seeking but rather the distribution of power between clientelist coalitions which prevents any group in society from pursuing long run profit maximization.

4 CONCLUSIONS

The efficiency effects associated with corruption depend on the way in which the rights to be transacted are selected and the terms under which the bargaining over their allocation happens. Conventional models analysing the efficiency implications of corruption are deficient because they ignore how rights are selected and the political constraints on their allocation process. We have argued that one of the important factors affecting these processes is the distribution of power between the state and the organizations competing over the creation or reallocation of rights. A number of mechanisms were suggested which would explain why corruption in countries with patrimonial patron–client networks may not be efficiency retarding. In contrast corruption in countries with clientelist patron–client networks may be associated with structural sclerosis, the proliferation of rights and slow growth. In each case performance is related not to the extent of corruption but rather to the political structures which sustain different processes through which rights are created and reallocated.

REFERENCES

Ades, A. and Di Tella, R. (1996). 'The causes and consequences of corruption: a review of recent empirical contributions', *IDS Bulletin* **27** (2).
Amsden, A. (1989). *Asia's Next Giant*. Oxford: Oxford University Press.
Bhagwati, J. (1982). 'Directly unproductive, profit-seeking (DUP) activities,' *Journal of Political Economy* **90** (5).
Bhaskar, V and Khan, M.H. (1995). 'Privatization and employment: a study of the jute industry in Bangladesh', *American Economic Review* **85** (1).
Browning, E. (1980). 'On the welfare cost of transfers'. In Buchanan, J. Tollison, R. D. and Tullock, G. (eds.) *Towards a Theory of the Rent-Seeking Society*. College Station: Texas A&M University Press.
Buchanan, J. Tollison, R. D. and Tullock, G. (1980). (eds) *Towards a Theory of the Rent-Seeking Society*. College Station: Texas A&M University Press.
Congleton, R. (1980). 'Competitive process, competitive waste and institutions. In Buchanan, J., Tollison, R.D. and Tullock, G. (eds.), *Towards a Theory of the Rent-Seeking Society*. College Station: Texas A&M University Press.
Khan, M. H. (forthcoming) *Clientelism, Corruption and Capitalist Development*.Oxford: Oxford University Press.

696   *M. H. Khan*

Khan, M.H. (1996). 'A typology of corrupt transactions in developing countries', *IDS Bulletin* **27** (2).

Khan, M. H. (1995). 'State failure in weak states: a critique of new institutionalist explanations'. In Harriss, J., Hunter, J. and Lewis, C. (eds) *The New Institutional Economics and Third World Development*. London: Routledge.

Klitgaard, R. (1988). *Controlling Corruption*. Berkeley: University of California Press.

Krueger, A. O. (1974). 'The political economy of the rent-seeking society', *American Economic Review* **64**.

Leff, N. (1964). 'Economic development through bureaucratic corruption', *American Behavioral Scientist*, (reprinted in Ekpo, M. U. (ed.) (1979). *Bureaucratic Corruption in Sub-Saharan Africa: Toward a Search for Causes and Consequences*. Washington: University Press of America).

Mueller, D. C. (1989). *Public Choice II: A Revised Edition of Public Choice*. Cambridge: Cambridge University Press.

Myrdal, G. (1968). *Asian Drama: An Inquiry into the Poverty of Nations*. New York: Pantheon.

North, D. (1995). 'The new institutional economics and Third World development'. In Harriss, J., Hunter, J. and Lewis, C. (eds) *The New Institutional Economics and Third World Development*. London: Routledge.

Nye, J. S. (1967). 'Corruption and political development: a cost–benefit analysis, *American Political Science Review*, **61** (2).

Posner, R. A. (1975). 'The social costs of monopoly and regulation', *Journal of Political Economy* **83**.

Rogerson, W. P. (1982). 'The social costs of monopoly and regulation: a game theoretic analysis, Bell Journal of Economics, **13**.

Rose-Ackerman, S. (1978). *Corruption: A Study in Political Economy*. New York: Academic Press.

Shleifer, A. and Vishny, R. W. (1993). 'Corruption', *Quarterly Journal of Economics*, **108** (3).

Tullock, G. (1980). 'The cost of transfers'. In Buchanan, J. Tollison R. D. and Tullock, G. (eds) *Towards a Theory of the Rent-Seeking Society*. College Station: Texas A&M University Press.

Varian, H. (1989). 'Measuring the deadweight costs of DUP and rent seeking activities', *Economics and Politics* **1** (1).

Wade, R. (1990). *Governing the Market: Economic Theory and the Role of Government in East Asian Industrialization*. Princeton: Princeton University Press.

[18]

'Fin de siècle' corruption: change, crisis and shifting values

Yves Mény

Corruption and its analysis: ambiguities, problems and divergences

For at least a decade, and more and more obtrusively in recent years, the problem of corruption has been at the centre of the political agenda. On this, all observers are agreed, and any divergent views merely concern minor points or subtle details. However, this unanimity on the acuteness of the problem as a political issue barely extends beyond such minimal agreement. On all the other aspects, divergences of opinion are numerous. They arise not only from the difficulty of grasping the issue, but also from its many modes of expression and the range of the participants in the debate. A quick glance at these diverging interpretations and judgements will give us an insight into the complexity of the problem.

The causes of corruption are sought in wholly different directions, depending on the ideological stance and preferences of the seeker. The neo-liberal school (which has contributed substantially to the analysis of the phenomenon) considers corruption to be one of the effects of the black market caused by excessive state interventionism. The more the state intervenes, the more it legislates, and the more it develops interfering bureaucracies, the greater the risks of parallel procedures

Yves Mény, Professor of Political Science at the Institut d'Etudes Politiques (Paris) is currently Director of the Robert Schuman Centre at the European University Institute. (Florence) CP 2330 Ferrovia, Italy. His research includes the reform of administration, regional questions, comparative politics and the French political system. His latest books are: *La corruption de la République* (1992), *Démocratie et corruption en Europe* (editor with D. della Porta) (1995). The Editor wishes to thank Professor Mény for his valuable assistance as editorial adviser for this issue of the ISSJ.

and markets spawning unlawful conduct. On the other hand, those who are not convinced of the state's intrinsic perversity or the market's unquestionable merits stress another aspect: the erosion of public ethics, the loss of the state's legitimate status as the incarnation of the general interest, and the dilution of communal values through the pursuit of profit and the defence of selfish private interests (Cartier-Bresson, 1993; Rose-Ackerman, 1978).

The newness of the phenomenon is also the subject of conflicting assessments. To those who maintain that corruption has never been as devastating as it is today, not only in the public sphere but also in that of private relations, other voices reply, sharply pointing out that corruption is as old as the hills, that it is inherent in all human action and that there is no cause for moral panic. For the former, the present era is marked by the fact that corruption has become widespread, that it affects more and more spheres of activity, and that it reflects a negative trend compared with the progress made in stamping it out, particularly in democracies. For the latter group – who do not deny that corruption exists – the extent of the degeneration of moral fibre or of public and private ethics is considerably exaggerated by the media. Some facts are blown up and amplified, while others only come to light because of passing interest in the problem, on a par with traffic offences. Such offences may remain almost constant, but they become increasingly obvious and questionable when a spectacular accident occurs, or when the government decides to carry out a policy of repression or prevention. According to this version of events, the new phenomenon is not so much corruption as the exploitation of corruption. More than the offence itself, it is the scandal and its political exploitation that warrant scrutiny (Sánchez, 1995).

The scale of corruption is a third aspect on which there is no general agreement. It is worthwhile noting in this connection that the debate on this point is almost bound to be inconclusive, given the very nature of the matter at issue. Corruption is, on the whole, a clandestine exchange (Claeys and Frognier, 1995) except where it has become systematic, and thus enjoys a quasi official status – that of an unwritten 'convention' which is nevertheless known and accepted by all. This secrecy accordingly has not facilitated the attempts to gauge the phenomenon which have been made on occasion, either through numbers of prosecutions and penal convictions or through reports in the press (Cazzola, 1988).

Any comparison therefore seems difficult, even impossible, from one period to another and one country to another, just as the factors governing repression are different and changeable (della Porta and Mény, 1995). To return to the example of traffic offences, it is obvious that the first effect of a crackdown on speeding is to make the statistics soar. All other things being equal, the scale of the offences will vary considerably, depending on the degree of leniency or harshness shown in defining the offences and in the application of the rules.

As a result, the real or assumed extent of corruption is as much a matter of perception and feeling as a mathematical measurement of the phenomenon. Given this uncertainty, discussion is inevitably inconclusive: optimists highlight the economic nature of the phenomenon, stressing journalists' fondness for the sensational and the over-zealousness of judges, who are often presented as radicals, bigots, or even as having repressed delinquent urges themselves. Pessimists, on the other hand, claim to be convinced that the facts which come to light are

merely the tip of the iceberg. They specifically draw attention to the fact that many 'scandals' are unmasked only by chance or unforeseen circumstances, such as an abandoned wife who denounces her husband, or a meticulous bookkeeper who keeps very accurate parallel accounts. The corruption brought to light and divulged to the public is therefore only a tiny fraction of the reality.

The same disagreements on the extent of corruption appear when an international comparison is attempted, even a comparison of viewpoints within the same society, let alone between different social groups. As the contributions to this issue show, the sensitivity of public opinion towards corruption varies considerably from one country and from one culture to another, not only between Europe and North America, or between Africa and Asia, but even within relatively homogeneous groups such as Western Europe (for instance, the contrast between Catholic countries with a Latin culture and Nordic, Protestant countries). Comparable variations are to be found in political systems between public opinion at large and social élites. Whereas the latter usually tend to minimize the scale of corruption (often after having ignored or denied it), public opinion has had a marked propensity in recent years to exaggerate its extent. Opinion polls in Italy, France and Japan specifically (but not only there) show that the vast majority of the people interviewed (sometimes more than 80 per cent!) are convinced that 'all politicians are corrupt'. Clearly, and whatever the real degree of corruption, *nothing* can be adduced as serious evidence for such a claim.

These disagreements also occur, of course, and are sometimes even greater, in attempts to define corruption. What is corruption? Is it only the misdemeanour identified as such by the criminal laws specific to each political system, or is there a need to give a definition that is less precise but based on a more realistic observation of the phenomenon. In other words, should we opt for a strictly legal definition, or should we take a more sociological approach?

The legal definition offers the advantage of safety and certainty, i.e. corruption is what the penal code defines as such, or what professional codes of ethics prohibit. By establishing what is allowed and what is prohibited, the law lays down in principle clear limits that should not be overstepped, and which enable the public and private individual, the citizen and the civil servant, to determine without too much uncertainty or hesitancy the line of conduct to adopt. In the absence of individual or collective ethics, the rule steps in as the arbiter of choice. Or, as Camus said, 'When there are no principles, rules are needed'. This positivistic and legally oriented approach nevertheless raises two problems, the first being strictly legal and the second ethical. To start with the legal aspect, the majority of jurists agree that this traditional approach entails limitations and constraints, because, in the first place, corrupt practices are seldom confined to the field defined by penal laws. Around the instance of corruption itself are clustered other related offences that make up a whole which is artificially segmented by legal qualifications. Some offences, such as the misappropriation of public funds or unlawful interference very often partake of corruption without being considered corruption proper. The slipperiness and the complexity of deviant practices cannot be made to fit the categories of the penal code, and the first to point out the obsolescence of the law have been the magistrates responsible for cracking down on corruption, especially the *Mani Pulite* ring in Italy. Similarly, the traditional pattern of corrupter and corruptee, the basis of many penal measures, no longer corresponds to the notion on which it was founded, namely that of a corrupter (a private individual) attempting to persuade the corruptee (a public servant) to violate the obligations of his or her office in exchange for personal gain. However, recent observation shows that more often than not the relation is reversed, owing to the fact that the offer of corruption no longer comes from the presumed 'corrupter' but from the person whom the codes consider to be the passive player, the corruptee: in other words, the politician or the civil servant. Increasingly, it is the public sector employee who actively corrupts (della Porta, 1992; Mény, 1992).

The strictly legalistic approach presents another shortcoming in that it tends to sidestep the ethical principles and values that are at the very root of repressive measures. Corruption is not an ordinary offence comparable to a violation of the highway code or fraud. It constitutes a violation of the duties of office and a negation of the values that should underlie the democratic political and administrative system founded on the rule of law, such as the distinction between private and public interests, equality of treatment for citizens, transparency of transactions, and so forth. By laying stress exclusively on the strictly penal definition of corruption, we may lose sight of the justification and purpose of these repressive measures. An illustration of this anomaly was the attitude of political parties in many countries (especially in Southern Europe, Spain, France, Italy and Greece), which claimed that there was in fact no corruption in circumstances where penally reprehensible practices were justified on the grounds of needing to help the parties which were essential for the smooth working of democracy. There was therefore personal corruption (deplorable) and corruption that worked for the well-being of the party (hence acceptable). This rather woolly attitude (which rests on the unacknowledged principle that 'the end justifies the means') goes to show that in such matters the ethical dimension cannot be passed over, and that the legal definition merely gives a partial, toned-down and at times inaccurate picture of what the problem entails.

Sociological analysis of behaviour may shed more light on the problem: what is the attitude of citizens and, more specifically, of the élite towards corruption? The different categories established by Heidenheimer (white corruption, grey corruption and black corruption) reveal still further how subjective and volatile the definition of corruption is (Heidenheimer *et al.*, 1989). White corruption would appear to cover practices that are not regarded as such either by public opinion or by the élite. In other words, 'corruption' is part and parcel of a culture that is not even aware of the problem. From this culture-oriented angle, what is corruption in one place (for example the United States) would not be in another (for example France). This cultural relativism (spatial, temporal and by class) may enable us to pick out the distinctive characteristics of one situation in comparison with another: Watergate, for example, was a major scandal whose repercussions lasted for many years, whereas the same kind of practices (the 'plumbers'' microphones made public in the *Canard enchaîné*) did not even cause a

Print of 1893 showing a scene from the trial of the 'Panama affair', a financial scandal that rocked French society.
Edimedia

hiccup in the career of the then Minister of the Interior. Black corruption meets with the same consensus, but the other way round, since all – élite and citizens alike – are agreed in disapproving of certain practices. The divergence of viewpoints emerges in the 'grey' alternative, inasmuch as what is defined as corruption by some is not considered to be such by others. It is this mismatch that may give rise to scandal – the clash between the perceptions of some and the practices of others, as happened, for instance, in the case of the funding of political parties. The unorthodox practices of the parties roused the indignation of the general public, while the former tried to justify themselves by referring to the necessities of life in a democracy. Incidentally, until the 1985–1990 crisis, few political leaders had really sought to improve moral standards since, in their opinion, certain practices were common to all and hence blameless.

In short, the definition (convergent or not) of corruption depends both on tolerance threshold (quantitative or symbolic) and on control over the system. Public opinion will not take umbrage at an underling's misdemeanour but, for the same amount of money embezzled, will be scandalized by the behaviour of a high-ranking civil servant or a politician. It will tolerate occasional corruption but may react strongly to regular and planned corruption. This blurring of definition shows how in some respects the general public's awareness and the emotion aroused by corruption depend on the coming together of highly diverse factors, such as the political actors involved, the nature of the offending behaviour, or the role of the press or the legal profession, for instance. The covert funding of parties was in fact merely an open secret for most observers of the French political system. It became a major scandal only under certain conditions: the revelation to the general public of facts that it had not suspected, the growing power of investigative journalism and a more independent judiciary and perhaps, above all, the glaring contrast between the moralizing rhetoric of the Socialist Party and its leader on the one hand and the surreptitious practices of the party on the other.

On the strength of these observations, we can therefore attempt to define corruption as a clandestine exchange between two markets – the political and/or administrative market and the economic and social market. This exchange is covert, since it violates the public rules of law and ethics, and sacrifices the general interest to private gain (personal, corporate, factional, etc.). Lastly, this transaction, which enables private actors to have access to public resources (contracts, financing, decisions) in a privileged and biased way (absence of transparency and competition), procures for corrupt public figures immediate or future material benefits for themselves or for the organization of which they are members.

The corruption which interests us here is therefore that which is expressed at the public and private interface and, in particular, in the sectors where the public decision-maker is not bound by totally restrictive rules. Corruption in a state where democratic law prevails has few opportunities to thrive if civil servants or public figures have no choice but to comply with the citizen's wishes provided that the requisite conditions are met: the issuing of a passport or the remittance of welfare payments are governed by strict rules that leave officials virtually no leeway. On the other hand, petty and large-scale corruption may creep in wherever the decision-maker has certain discretionary powers: for instance, assessing a physical disability that would give rise to a pension, choosing the 'best' contract or deciding on the allocation of investment funds are decisions which may be incorporated in procedures that are almost automatic, leaving considerable room for manoeuvre for the civil servants or politicians, specifically if the rules of procedure – which are supposed to guarantee the due process of law – are not observed to the letter or in spirit.

It is clear that, independently of the moral judgement that each citizen may make on the question according to his or her personal code of ethics, the divergences in evaluating the phenomenon of corruption are many and the various observations that we have just outlined are far from being exhaustive. Disagreements are even more acute when we address the question of remedies or solutions to be provided. It is preferable at this stage to speculate about the explosion in corruption that has affected most countries over the last two decades.

New supply and demand where corruption is concerned

Interpretations of the causes of corruption are not just conflicting. Each of them is only partially satisfactory, and just when we think we have found a reasonable explanation, many different exceptions crop up that cast doubt on its overall validity. How can we get a clearer picture? Without claiming to provide a firm and final answer to the problem, we can start on the basis of the following observations:

Corruption is a widespread phenomenon, pervasive not only in space but also in time. But major variations, both spatial and temporal, may be observed in spite of the inadequacy and the lack of precision of the assessments. For instance, it is acknowledged that twentieth-century Great Britain is far less corrupt than it was a century ago, and that Scandinavia has fewer problems than Southern Europe. In the absence of quantitative studies that are almost impossible to carry out, given the subject, we know that public perception of corruption varies considerably, as several recent cases in Sweden, France, Italy and Spain have illustrated.)

The phenomenon of corruption is no longer, as in the past, primarily a national problem, intrinsic to a political system. Its international dimension is increasingly apparent.

The basic categories used in studying the phenomenon of corruption seem less and less valid, even if they continue to be of heuristic value: the contrast between democratic and autocratic systems, or the distinction between developed and developing countries, which for a long time was one of the main keys to interpretation, permits only a crude approach to the problem.

The forms and patterns of corruption have become much more sophisticated, to the point of rendering it almost invisible, or in any case not easily detectable.

These observations place us in a better position to examine the context in which corruption has spread and escalated in recent decades, in democratic and autocratic regimes alike and in both rich and poor countries.

Explosion of the phenomenon

Even if there is no yardstick by which to measure the extent of corruption with any accuracy, most observers concur in acknowledging the new growth of the phenomenon in the last two decades. Admittedly, the reasons often differ from one political system to another, but it is possible to identify constant factors, particularly context-related.

In western countries, where the state and democracy are in theory more firmly estab-

lished, corruption has nonetheless persisted in forms specific to each culture: almost systemic in Italy and marginal in Northern Europe.

In most countries, corruption seemed to stem more from individual misdemeanours than from general improbity in political and administrative circles. Things started to change because of the increasing needs of the political parties, their inability to meet their organizations' growing needs by regular means, and the staggeringly high cost of electoral campaigns. Until the 1960s, political parties were usually funded only by their activists' contributions (in time and in subscriptions) and by more or less generous donations from business people, professional organizations and trade unions. However, from the 1970s onwards, traditional resources diminished (a decline in militancy) while 'the Americanization' of electoral campaigns increased costs tenfold. Caught between these two conflicting developments, parties almost everywhere embarked on practices which were at best irregular, and at worst criminal. A first wave of reforms following tremendous scandals (the Flick scandal in Germany, the scandal of Nixon's electoral campaign, the resignation of the American Vice-President Spiro Agnew, the Lockheed scandal in Italy, Japan, the Netherlands, and so forth) created the impression that the miracle cure had been found, thanks to the public financing of parties and/or electoral campaigns, together with monitoring of the source and the use made of the funds. Unfortunately, it became apparent just about everywhere that this fresh influx of money only whetted appetites and intensified needs, giving rise to new forms of corruption or rule-bending (mushrooming of Political Action Committees in the United States and bogus parties in France).

In the former socialist regimes, in developing countries and indeed in many western societies, corruption emerged as the functional antidote to excessive regimentation and bureaucracy. Jean Cartier-Bresson (1993) aptly summarizes the position of neo-liberal economists on this issue. In regard to their viewpoint, he writes, 'The market always comes into its own again in the face of state intervention, and thus determines the development of black markets, on which a certain authoritarian legitimacy is conferred. In these circumstances, since governments are dominated by groups more interested in their own welfare than in collective welfare, an inevitable black market of state regulations governing the issuing of permits, licences, etc. is established, whose purpose is to appropriate windfall benefits through revenue hunters. Only a return to the inviolable principles of political rivalry and economic and social competition can curtail the phenomena of corruption.' Corruption, although in principle inadmissible, thus emerges as a safety valve, 'oil for the wheels', the functional tool to ease the workings of too rigid a society. This analysis lacks neither relevance, nor theoretical arguments, nor empirical substance, but it does have the drawback of underestimating the harmful impact of corruption on the entire social fabric. Corruption lingers and spreads even though the reasons which once 'justified' it have disappeared (cf. the former socialist countries, where corruption prospers despite the collapse of authoritarian and interventionist regimes).

The neo-liberal argument clashes with the opinion of those who see in the deregulation of the state (for good or bad reasons) the principal source of the development of corruption. They claim that the virulent attacks against state interventionism, the welfare state, and bureaucrats, have helped to blur the lines of distinction between collective and individual interest and between the public and private spheres. Conversely, the exaggerated importance attached to the market, profits and values such as productivity and competitiveness (to the deteriment of equality) have not only led to the undermining of the state as an abstract concept but, more commonly, cast doubt on the relevance and validity of its interventions and the status of its agents. Wherever public ethics was backed up by a series of conventions or internalized rules (*esprit de corps*, defence of the general interest, primacy of the public over the private), the downgrading of these values has resulted in a lowering, as it were, of the 'moral cost' of corruption.

This undermining of values in the public sphere and of the moral cost of corruption triggers the development of a vicious circle: as corruption spreads, so its very extension contributes to its social acceptance. In turn, corruption in high places renders corruption at lower levels more acceptable, and vice versa.

Corruption becomes a meta-system whose implications concern the whole of public life until its costs and its adverse effects spark off a reaction on the part of a fraction of the élite (the press or the judiciary) or the people (populism) against the élite in power.

The extent of corruption in the 1980s and 1990s becomes clearer if one considers the unprecedented opportunities that this period has afforded compared with other times in history, the reason being that the context is one of crisis; in other words, established situations are being challenged and becoming unstable, while at the same time new rules, values and principles of action are emerging.

This particular period is first and foremost one of major ideological change: the predominance of the idea of the market over that of the state. Originating in the United States, the neo-liberal wave then swept over Great Britain, South America and Asia, followed by continental Europe and even Africa, despite the specific problems of this last continent, more severely affected than others by underdevelopment.

The doctrine of the market has been endorsed by the economic achievements of Japan and the new Asian tigers, and reinforced, conversely, by the collapse of the socialist countries and the growing difficulties of the social democratic governments in coping with their costly Keynesian-based policies. Everywhere, under the impetus of neo-liberals or under the iron rod of the World Bank, or even of OECD, vigorous policies of deregulation and privatization have dismantled the state's legal, economic and financial control. Everywhere, new rules of the game have been imposed and new players have emerged. Old self-interested coalitions have been challenged under the impact of new ideas and increasingly pressing external constraints bound up with the formation of new regional blocs and the liberalization of world trade.

We are not much concerned here with debating whether these policies constitute in the long run the best remedy against corruption by introducing more competition and by reducing the revenue created by state intervention, or whether, on the contrary, they are only a Pandora's box opened by ill-advised market-worshippers, blinded by their anti-statism. We need only note that the challenging of old models

Nineteenth-century French print 'Gripardin, country attorney and councillor of Normandy'. Carnavalet Museum. Paris/ Lauros-Giraudon

and the introduction of drastic changes in ways of thinking and acting have created opportunities for considerable corruption in these 'in-between' times when conventions from the past are no longer in use or are no longer valid, while new rules of the game have not as yet been established or are unwelcome or reluctantly adopted. Neo-liberal policies are not a panacea for corruption, nor do they signify the end of it. Other conditions – which do not fall within the sphere of the market – must be met in order to halt or ward off corruption.

Recent corruption very much resembles past corruption. Its occurrence in a particularly propitious context (the transition from a command or socialist economy to a market economy), combined with inappropriate or unfamiliar new rules (the freedom of the economic actors often being equated with that of a fox in a henhouse), and the erosion of traditional values, have allowed it to attain an unusual degree of prominence both in its universal scope and in the importance of the interests at stake. However, there seems to be at least one new determining factor in the transformation of the problem: the internationalization of trade, in parallel with the internationalization of the machinery of corruption.

Internationalization

Corruption is a kind of parallel, covert exchange that is substituted for or added to market mechanisms or to public procedures for the granting of rights or resources. Corruption is therefore likely to thrive wherever normally transparent or codified operations are replaced by collusive transactions seeking to gain for their beneficiaries advantages that the workings of competition or the strict application of established standards would rule out. It is precisely what happens in a whole range of international transactions. Expedients that foster corruption are numerous: protectionist regulations that the exporter seeks to circumvent, such as the need to obtain a permit, authorization, licence, etc., on which political or administrative authorities are in a position to cash in; obligation when obtaining a contract to use the services of brokers, who are all too often concerned with creaming off a compulsory 'commission'; tied loans, obliging the recipient state to use these funds in the creditor country; intervention of the public authorities in the negotiation and conclusion of contracts, especially when supplier and client are themselves members of the public sector in their respective states. The long and turbulent history of relations between Africa and the former colonial powers bears witness to the antiquity and the persistence of these reprehensible practices. But the problem is not peculiar to Africa. Admittedly, its position of economic, military and often political dependence has facilitated the development of scandalously deviant practices. But in other parts of the world less dependent on the West, corruption has gone hand in hand with the expansion of trade. The Chinese Communist Party recently announced the exclusion of 500,000 of its members and leaders accused of corruption. And the indictment of the former Presidents of South Korea, Roh Tal Woo and Chun Doo-Hwan, brought to light considerable wheeling and dealing on the occasion of each major economic transaction: high-speed trains, armaments, major construction work, all of which were a pretext for the taking of substantial cuts by the leader or the élite in power.

Corrupt relations at the international level are particularly complex in that they combine private interests that are legitimate (those of the company) or less honourable (those of brokers) with the interests of political and administrative partners acting either on behalf of public interests considered to be legitimate (support for exports, defence of national positions) or as parties standing to gain directly from the illegal transaction.

In the name of the general interest, these deviant practices have often received the blessing of the highest state authorities; in France, for example, when exchange controls prevailed,

the Ministry of Finance authorized the export of currency to Switzerland (or to other similar tax havens) to cover the illegal commissions that the company had to pay. The law was therefore broken not only with complete impunity but also with the connivance of the tax authority. Moreover, this violation of ethical and market regulations has nothing specifically French about it. Only the United States, following the Lockheed scandal in 1977, penalized export practices involving bribery. The effectiveness of this policy is nevertheless doubtful, owing to the many different possibilities of evasion and the difficulty of providing proof of these illegal practices. The official remuneration of 'brokers' or the use of local subcontracted companies to carry out the 'dirty job' are among the simplest cunning ways of achieving the objectives sought without committing a statutory offence.

The expansion of international trade undeniably contributes to world prosperity and to strong growth in developing countries. But this favourable trend occurs in a political and commercial context that is doubly unsatisfactory. Firstly, this trade is increasingly giving rise to nothing short of economic war, in which sales arguments only partly comply with market regulations: contracts are signed in exchange for military or political protection, backhanders, and bribes to company directors, government officials or the political élite. Moreover, by a boomerang effect, the Western corrupters are in their turn corrupted when they accept donations or contributions for their electoral campaigns, not to mention allowing themselves to be kept on the payroll of those who have received bribes from them. Corruption is therefore not a one-way process, from the corrupt western company to the corrupt purchasing countries. All too often, corruption is practised within a complex network in which the corrupt transaction is multidirectional and systematic.

Secondly, unlike the situation that prevails in most states – at least where the law is concerned – corrupt exchanges at the international level take place in a world where the rule of law is a pious aspiration rather than a reality. Only national legislation can crack down on corruption. Apart from the fact that it is invariably difficult to prove the offence, it is illusory to expect repression to be very effective when very senior officials are sometimes among the ringleaders in the corruption. Despite the efforts of various international organizations (Council of Europe, OECD) which, when faced with this growing problem, became alarmed and made recommendations for its elimination, no real progress has been achieved. It is still to be hoped – but this again is a pious hope – that the new World Trade Organization (WTO) will be at pains to investigate one of the most striking cases of flouting of the rules of competition, not to mention the erosion of private and public ethics.

The internationalization of trade goes hand in hand with the internationalization of currency flow and the proliferation of banking centres where the secrecy of operations and anonymity of transactions and account-holders are the golden rule and undoubtedly the greatest comparative advantage. Switzerland, the traditional refuge for discrete operations, has had to make various minor concessions under pressure from the United States in its battle against drug trafficking and money laundering, but the slight changes that have taken place in Switzerland are offset or cancelled out by the proliferation of off-shore banks and the maze of criss-crossing transactions. The lack of transparency that prevails in this sphere has been only slightly remedied by a few investigations, specifically in France (after the affair of the financing of the Republican Party) and in Italy, where the *Mani Pulite* operation brought to light some of the highly sophisticated ways in which corruption money circulates. These investigations bore out what was suspected, namely that Switzerland and Hong Kong, Liechtenstein and the Cayman Islands, Jersey and Luxembourg are not merely innocent places designed to protect the security and privacy of legitimate economic transactions. But apart from this rather tame satisfaction, the progress achieved is limited, because once the general public's indignation against both bloodthirsty and corrupt dictatorial leaders dies down, a thick veil of silence enshrouds dubious national and international corruption operations. This phenomenon is all the more worrying in that various international drug, corruption, and organized crime mafias are able to rely on national protection at the highest level (thanks to the corruption of politicians and the police), while enjoying the new advantages derived from

both the internationalization of currency flow and the secrecy governing banking operations. In some Balkan and Latin American countries, collusion of the mafia with a fraction of the political and civil service élite has often been suspected and sometimes proved, giving a radically new dimension to the problem, since the urgent need is not so much to establish democracy – which has lost all meaning in this corrupt, mafia-ridden context – as to restore a minimum of state organization capable of re-establishing the preconditions for any kind of democratic construction, namely, security, legality and the separation of the public and private spheres.

Invisible corruption

These new aspects of the international corruption phenomenon bring out the increasing sophistication of the methods used. As has been emphasized several times already, corruption is a clandestine exchange. Basically, this assertion remains true – except in cases where corruption is such an everyday feature of life that there is no longer any need to take the precaution of concealing the exchange! However, it is becoming increasingly apparent that only the corruption pact remains clandestine; all other aspects of the exchange can easily take on the colours of legality and respectability. Examples of such corruption 'in the sunshine' are many and varied, and the cases exposed in France, Italy and Spain, to name only these three democracies in Southern Europe, have amply demonstrated that dens of corruption can be prosperous and highly respected. The corruption takes place via middlemen, brokers, and technical engineering and financing and banking agencies at the interface of the corrupter and the corruptee. The intervention of a go-between body is official, as is its remuneration. Only the service is fictitious or overvalued, the trading of favours masquerading as the anodine provision of services. The same applies to those politicians (centre stage) or their sidekicks (behind the scenes) who receive substantial remuneration, either as consultants, or as ostensible employees or managers of subsidiaries of large economic consortia. The most widespread corruption is also the least visible, since it takes the form of routine economic and social relations. One can no longer point to bribes or backhanders, *baksheesh*, *tangente* or *bustarella*, because every-thing has the appearance of normality and legal-ity except – as we have said – the unwritten, tacit, clandestine pact. The formal legality of the procedures whitewashes even the guilt of those primarily concerned, who sometimes feel unjustly persecuted and harassed in their private lives. That just goes to show how far the plethora of punitive measures and procedural safeguards are merely partial and inadequate counter-meas-ures. No penal sanction can solve the problem of corruption unless corruption is first of all perceived as a breach of the rules of public ethics. Observance of the rules of good conduct in the management of public affairs means more than refraining from committing crimes or offences. Under the rule of democratic law, prudential standards are called for, irrespective of any penal sanctions. They may be reduced to one simple rule: avoid a conflict of interests in whatever form, since corruption that is pun-ished is merely the most obvious and extreme expression of this basic rule in democratic sys-tems founded on the separation of powers and a system of checks and balances.

Conclusion

Almost everywhere in the world, corruption is no longer just a deplorable habit: it has become a political problem. It is tempting – especially for politicians – to see this new awareness as merely a kind of 'plot' by the media and the legal profession, and to denounce the unfair harassment of which parliamentary and govern-mental élites are victims. Of course, the press and the judges have been key players in the information process and in the new public awareness of the problems. Indeed, how could it be otherwise? The media have a crucial role in shaping public opinion, particularly on an issue that is by definition so secret and clan-destine. As for the pseudo 'persecutors' among the judiciary who are denounced by the persons incriminated, this is almost a joke: these prot-estations are above all symptomatic of the habits of impunity acquired by the ruling élite in many countries.

In our view, an explanation of the promin-ence given to the problem of corruption in recent years should be sought elsewhere.

The expansion of corrupt practices and their increasingly open (not to say at times quasi-official) character are what first give rise to this new awareness, since what was known at the outset only by very limited circles of the 'elect' (for instance, party leaders and some executives of large companies) eventually becomes an open secret when the corruption spreads, becomes pervasive, and affects more and more economic sectors. Where public morality is flexible and where the public generally has a fairly low opinion of politics, corruption is tolerated because it is considered to be an inevitable consequence of the exercise of power. This pessimistic outlook (Gaetano Mosca, 1977, wrote 'all feather their own nests by betraying the public interests that have been entrusted to them') is particularly deeply rooted in the countries of Southern Europe, where the Machiavellian view of politics is very much ingrained. In addition, this tolerance is strength-ened by the widespread practice of bribes, small commissions and clientelist policies; even if it is not everyone who gains from corruption, a collusive silence enshrouds departures from a system which is 'on balance favourable'. But this vicious circle is broken when a major scandal erupts and/or when this corrupt system falls into a trap of growing demands, inadequate resources and increasingly bitter internal con-flict. Italy is a striking illustration of this trend, in that, after decades of tacit complicity on the part of the élite and most of the general public, the corrupt system collapsed, a victim of its own imprudence and its arrogance on the one hand, and of its economic and financial cost on the other.

Exposure of corruption also takes place more vigorously during political and economic crises. The changeover of political power between parties or the possibility of upcoming, hotly contested elections are conditions parti-cularly conducive to the surfacing of scandals, when the opposition parties (or the new arrivals in power) are inclined to exploit the weaknesses of their opponents except, of course, if they are themselves deeply implicated in the system of corruption. Economic crises, by pricking the bubble of connivance and solidarity, produce the same effect: they discredit the economic and political élites in power and ultimately make it possible to put an end to the improper protection which they enjoyed (cf. the recent scandals in Mexico, Japan, Korea, Spain and Italy).

This destabilization of the ruling élite often benefits the opposition party or parties. But owing to the networks of connivance which extend far beyond the incumbents of official posts, it often happens that the leaders are reviled *en bloc* by the public. That 'politicians' are blamed emphasizes the fact that they constitute a privileged group and a class in their own right, a *nomenklatura*, greedy for its privileges, in contrast to popular and national virtues.

Anti-élitist views are increasingly fashionable nowadays in democratic systems. They are the consequence not only of corruption, but of the scandals that feed and sustain them. The prevailing populism, characterized by its confrontational attitude (anti-taxation, anti-immigration, anti-welfare, anti-élitism), is all the more influential in that the élites have lost the status that used to justify their power and, not infrequently, their privileges.

Translated from French

References

CARTIER-BRESSON, J., 1993. 'Corruption, pouvoir discrétionnaire et rentes'. *Le Débat*, no. 77, novembre-décembre.

CAZZOLA, F., 1988. *Della corruzione: fisiologia e patologia di un sistema politico*. Bologna: Il Mulino.

CLAEYS, P. H.; FROGNIER, A. P. (eds), 1995. *L'échange politique*. Bruxelles: Editions de l'Université de Bruxelles.

DELLA PORTA, D., 1992. *Lo scambio occulto. Casi di corruzione politica in Italia*. Bologna: Il Mulino.

DELLA PORTA, D.; MÉNY, Y., 1995. *Démocratie et corruption en Europe*. Paris: Editions la Découverte.

HEIDENHEIMER, A. J.; JOHNSTON, M.; LeVINE, V. T. (eds), 1989. *Political Corruption, A Handbook*. New Brunswick: Transaction Publishers.

MÉNY, Y., 1992. *La corruption de la République*. Paris: Fayard.

MOSCA, G., 1977. *Scritti politici* (a cura di G. Sola). Turin: UTET.

ROSE-ACKERMAN, S., 1978. *Corruption: A Study in Political Economy*. New York: Academic Press.

SÁNCHEZ, F. J., 1995. *Detras del escandalo político: opinión pública, dinero y poder en la España del Siglo XX*. Barcelona: Tusquets editores.

[19]

Democracy and 'grand' corruption

Susan Rose-Ackerman

Corruption scandals are a sign that a country recognizes the difference between the public and the private. A hallmark of modern democratic societies is a formal separation between the state and the rest of society. Politicians, bureaucrats, and judges are paid salaries and must make a sharp distinction between their personal finances and state revenues. Civil servants are hired to perform public duties and are barred from obtaining personal financial benefits from private individuals and firms. Corruption and self-dealing occur in such societies when officials use their positions of public trust for private gain. Thus in a newly emerging democracy corruption can be a sign of progress. Citizens' concern over bribes paid to public officials in return for favours indicates that citizens and government functionaries recognize that there are norms of fair dealing and competent administration, and that they can be violated.

High level or 'grand' corruption is impossible in a nation where state authority flows from the personality of the ruler. Such a ruler may lack legitimacy, but he cannot be corrupt. He and the state are intertwined. Low-level corruption can occur when functionaries enrich themselves at the expense of both the ruler and the citizens, but the ruler himself is immune. Observing kleptocratic behaviour at the top, lower-level officials seek a share, constrained only by the ruler's distress at losing a portion of the spoils. Payoffs to rulers are a symptom of a deeper problem of political legitimacy.

Democracy and the free market are not invariably a cure for corruption. A shift from authoritarian to democratic rule does not necessarily reduce payoffs. Rather it redefines the country's norms of public behaviour. A country that democratizes without also creating and enforcing laws governing conflict of interest, financial enrichment, and bribery, risks undermining its fragile new institutions through private wealth-seeking. A country that moves to liberalize its economy without a similar reform of the state, risks creating severe pressures on officials to share in the new private wealth.

Although malfeasance can occur at all levels of the political and economic system, the bribery of leading politicians and public officials is especially troubling. High level or 'grand' corruption involves large sums of money with multinational corporations frequently making the payoffs. If just 5 per cent of foreign direct investment in the developing world were paid as bribes, the total would average $2 billion annually. If 5 per cent of the value of merchandise imports were diverted into payoffs, the combined total would be $50 billion.[1] But corruption by multinational firms is not just a question of transferring monopoly profits from one pocket

Susan Rose-Ackerman holds a doctorate in economics from Yale and is the Henry R. Luce Professor of Law and Political Science at Yale University, Yale Law School, New Haven, CT 06515-2255, USA. She is the author of *Corruption: A Study in Political Economy* (1978), *Rethinking the Progressive Agenda: The Reform of the American Regulatory State* (1992), and *Controlling Environmental Policy: The Limits of Public Law in Germany and the United States* (1995). Her current research concerns corruption in societies making the transition to democracy and a market economy.

ISSJ 149/1996 © UNESCO 1996. Published by Blackwell Publishers, 108 Cowley Road, Oxford OX4 1JF, UK and 238 Main Street, Cambridge, MA 02142, USA.

to another. Nominally the bribe is paid by the multinational and accepted by officials in the foreign country. Ultimately, the cost of corruption may be borne both by the host country's citizens, creditors, and aid donors and by taxpayers in the multinational's home base. But corruption is not just a distributional issue. It has efficiency consequences as well. In a country seeking to establish democratic and market institutions in the face of powerful opponents, these distributive and efficiency effects can have political consequences if massive corruption undermines a government's legitimacy.

The problem is not just to locate the ultimate incidence of the bribe itself, but also to determine the consequences of bribery in terms of inflated contract terms, poorly conceived projects, distorted development priorities, and weakened government performance. The article begins by outlining the economic and income distribution impacts of corruption. The level of payoffs is not the most important measure of corruption's impact. The costs in lost investment funds and distorted priorities may be high even if the volume of payoffs is low. Next, it examines why multinational firms face incentives to pay bribes and how those incentives differ across industries and across countries, explaining why corruption's impact is not just a function of the services provided in return for bribes, but also depends on how the payoffs themselves are used. Bribes deposited in an offshore account or used to purchase real estate in New York City have a different impact from bribes that remain within the country.

The second part of the article links corrupt incentives with government structure and suggests reform strategies. It analyses the corrupt incentives that exist in both market-oriented democracies and autocracies and emphasizes how governmental stability interacts with independent outside checks to encourage or check corruption. The concluding section explores the conflicting pressures that exist in democratic governments. Both those in tough re-election fights and those who are at the end of their political life are especially vulnerable to corrupt inducements. However, the complex organizational structure of democratic legislatures and the formal separation of powers increase the costs of bribery and may deter all but the most valuable corrupt deals.

The impact of corruption

Corruption has first order and second order effects. First order effects are the inefficiency and unfairness introduced by the payment of bribes themselves. Inefficiencies include both the effects of bribes on the allocation of public benefits and costs, and the transactions costs of giving and receiving illegal payments. Second order effects concern the disposition of bribery revenues. The illegality of the payments may limit the way the funds are used and encourage their investment outside the country and in illegal business ventures.

The incidence of bribery and the inefficiency of corruption

Analysing corruption in otherwise legitimate business dealings is like studying the incidence of taxes. In both cases one wants to know not just how much was paid but the ultimate incidence of the payments and their impact on the allocation of resources. A tax on profits will not be entirely borne by a firm's owners. Some of it can be shifted to customers, creditors, and input suppliers. A bribe paid by a corporation may be shifted in the same way. The analysis of bribes, however, differs from standard tax incidence discussions in that the payments are always made in return for something. They are more analogous to user charges than to ordinary taxes. Because of the *quid pro quo* nature of bribes, the impact and level of corruption can be altered by the actions of greedy officials. They may redesign programmes or enforce the law in ways that maximize bribe payments. If the bribe payer is a multinational firm, these actions can shift the cost of corruption to the citizens and creditors of the host country or to the competitors of the bribing multinational. Such behaviour can compromise the efficiency of the country's economy and affect the allocation of resources between countries.

The value of a corrupt deal depends on the benefits received in return for payoffs. If net profits increase as a result of a payoff, kickback demands can stimulate investment and trade. Both the bribers and the bribee benefit, for example, from a payoff that exempts a firm from paying high tariffs on imported inputs. However, the benefits provided to investors may impose costs on the citizenry. In the above example, customs receipts fall. Even if bribery only leads to reductions in pointless red tape, corruption is costly since payoffs are a substitute for taxes that could be imposed on the investor in a world without counterproductive regulations. Bribery is always an inferior way of extracting economic rents from firms since the benefits largely go to a few individuals, not the mass of the population, and in many cases the search for payoffs destroys wealth. Furthermore, the corrupt state may need to rely on other less efficient and more regressive types of taxes if public officials have a lock on the rents of multinational firms and other large business enterprises.

At first glance it appears that bribery will be less distortionary if it is paid out of gross profits that are unaffected by the level of the payoff. Although this observation is correct, it misses an important aspect of the corrupt environment. The main difference between taxes and bribes is the lack of a fixed revenue constraint. Public officials can affect the level of rents available to them. High-level corrupt officials are like the Leviathan government posited by Geoffrey Brennan and James Buchanan (1980) that imposes taxes in order to expropriate as much private wealth as possible. Brennan and Buchanan recommend reducing the state's ability to extract rents. To them the best tax is one that is levied on goods and services that are elastically demanded or supplied. Few states fit this 'kleptocracy' model.[2] Most have laws outlawing bribery and other forms of self-dealing. Elections, public opinion, the media, accounting standards, and law enforcement check officials' unbridled search for private gain. Nevertheless, the basic lessons of Buchanan and Brennan's analysis apply to the struggle against corruption. Corruption can be reduced by a constitutional structure that limits the level of monopoly rents under the control of the state.

The endogeneity of corrupt gains in kleptocratic countries casts doubt on the claim that corruption favours growth in high red tape countries. Instead, the causation may run the other way. The possibility of obtaining bribes encourages officials to create red tape. This supposition is consistent with a study by Paolo Mauro (1995). Using a corruption index developed by a private investment advisory firm, he demonstrates that

high levels of corruption are associated with lower levels of investment. A one standard deviation improvement in the index was associated with a 2.6 percentage point increase in the investment rate over the period 1980 to 1985. Mauro's results are consistent with the claim that high levels of red tape are a function of the prevalence of bribe-seeking officials.

Mauro demonstrates that high levels of corruption are associated with low investment, but his data do not permit a detailed analysis of the mechanisms behind this link. To understand the impact of corruption on a country's citizens, consider two extremes. Suppose a project financed by a multinational firm involves the payments of bribes. At one extreme, suppose that bribes represent a transfer of rents from the excess profits of multinational corporations into the pockets of corrupt officials with no direct impact on the tax bills of the country's residents. At the other extreme, suppose that bribes increase the cost of the project, but do not reduce the profits of firms. The cost is borne by the taxpayers in the corrupt country and perhaps by international lending and aid organizations. Obviously, most real projects will fall into an intermediate category where the benefits are obtained by public officials and the costs are shared between multinationals and local taxpayers. It seems clear that for developing countries, the most harmful cases are those where the funds are ultimately raised from their own taxpayers. Conversely, since multinationals pay taxes on their profits in their home country and since most countries outside the United States permit the *de facto* deductibility of bribes, corruption that reduces profits is partly financed by the corporation's owners and partly by the taxpayers in the multinational's home country.

To interpret Mauro's results, however, one must look beyond the individual project. Corruption at the top can have a much broader impact. The search for bribes can affect the allocation of investment funds within a country and help determine the overall level of investment. If corruption increases costs and risks, it will discourage investment. If it reduces costs and risks, it will encourage investment. If the increase in investment occurs, not by eliminating pointless red tape, but by providing subsidies, developing 'white elephant' projects, or skimping on justifiable regulations, the populace will bear the costs. If such corruption is widespread and if bribes are not themselves used for productive investment, the overall impact on the economy may be negative even if each individual project's profits are improved by the bribes its sponsors pay.

Incentives for corruption in multinational business

All states, whether authoritarian or democratic, have benefits to dispense and costs to impose. They can create programmes that require widespread official discretion or ones that require few individualized determinations. They can control a large share of the GDP and regulate the remaining private sectors, or they can adopt a *laissez faire* attitude. The state has monopoly power, and state officials can use this power to seek private gain.

A multinational firm is vulnerable to corrupt demands from a country's officials if it is earning 'country-specific rents' that exceed its profits elsewhere. In other words, it would suffer a significant loss in profits from ceasing to do business in the corrupt country. Of course, these rents cannot be converted into corrupt payoffs unless the state has something of value to dispense. The most extreme case is where officials can simply expropriate all of the firm's country-specific rents in return for permission to operate. Most countries, however, are not so overwhelmingly corrupt. In less extreme cases, there are two broad situations in which governments provide valuable benefits.

The benefits of corruption differ depending on the relationship between government and foreign investors. In the first case, firms can act unless the state finds a violation of the law. Then bribes could induce officials to overlook legal violations or pursue the violations of one's competitors. Powerful officials can also extort bribes by threatening to find violations. Thus in this first category, there are three types of bribery incentives.

(1) If the firm violates the rules and if detection and punishment are likely without bribes, the firm may bribe in return for being ignored.
(2) The firm may pay to induce officials to pursue competitors' violations.

(3) Even if the firm has not violated the rules, officials may extort bribes in return for not harassing the firm with invented violations.

The key distinction is between the first two categories and the third. In the former pair the firm pays a bribe to induce the official to violate the rules. In the latter the official violates the rules and extorts a bribe in return for providing the firm with what it was entitled to in the first place.

The second general class of cases arises when the firm cannot take action unless the state has given its approval. The import or export of products may require licences and inspections. New construction may require zoning approval. A firm may be one of several bidders for a public construction or procurement project, or may be competing to purchase a state industry in the process of privatization. Bribes can then be used to induce officials to make a decision in the firm's favour. Bribes are not only a device for allocating a given benefit but may also influence the nature of the benefit. For example, officials may introduce excessive delay as a way of extorting larger bribes. They may privatize public firms with their monopoly power intact as a way of increasing the firms' value. They may propose massive, unnecessary capital projects as a way of accumulating bribes. An experienced observer of capital investment in the developing world claims that a large proportion of state-sponsored projects would not pass muster on cost-benefit grounds and have been carried out largely as bribe-generating mechanisms (Moody-Stewart, 1994). This may be an overstatement, but the phenomenon appears to be common.[3]

The potential supply of bribes is the inverse either of the demand for government benefits or of the demand to be free of government-imposed costs. The state may have a very complex regulatory system, but if no one wants to put themselves in the position of being regulated, bribery will not be high. An unscrupulous firm will have a willingness to pay equal to the benefit obtained from the payoff minus the expected costs of breaking the law. If one official has monopoly power over some aspect of government activity, the maximum willingness-to-bribe is the profits earned from obtaining the

Impeachment of Collor de Mello, Brazil 1992. A. Sassaki/Gamma

gross benefit minus the expected costs of bribery (i.e. the probability of detection times the expected penalty). The gross benefits are lower, the higher the likelihood that the benefit will be made available for free (or, for a law breaker, the higher the probability that no enforcement action will be taken even in the absence of a payoff). If more than one independent official has the authority to grant the benefit, the level of bribery will fall, since the marginal benefits provided by any one official falls. On the other side of the transaction, an official's willingness to accept bribes will also depend on the risk of detection and the expected level of punishment. Completely amoral officials may be honest simply because the net benefits of accepting bribes are negative (Rose-Ackerman, 1978).

If a country's autocratic top rulers accept payoffs, the risk of detection and punishment is zero in the ordinary sense of criminal enforcement. Even democratically elected leaders may be able to escape criminal liability, especially if the corruption is associated with close family members or business associates, not with the ruler him- or herself. However, that does not mean that the cost of accepting bribes is zero. If the bribery is revealed, it may undermine the regime's legitimacy and increase the threat of government overthrow. Large bribes may be more likely to be revealed than smaller ones and may have a more negative impact on the politician's future in office. Top officials, interested in retaining power, may refuse to accept bribes or may limit the level of payoff to limit the political fallout. A seemingly paradoxical situation may prevail in which corruption is uncommon in business dealings, but when it occurs, the bribes are very large. This result is simply an application of the familiar economic truism that demand falls when prices rise. If the supply of corrupt services is low at any given bribe, the equilibrium bribe-price may be high.

Country-specific rents

What is the source of country-specific rents? The firms with the lowest rents are those making new investments in manufacturing capacity that do not need to locate near sources of specialized raw materials, and firms in highly competitive markets seeking to sell goods produced elsewhere. When the extra earnings from doing business in any particular country are not large, firms in this category are in a strong bargaining position *vis-à-vis* a corrupt state. They may be able to resist corrupt demands because they do not benefit much from doing business in the corrupt country. Firms seeking to build manufacturing capacity can resist corrupt demands by threatening to locate elsewhere.

At the other extreme are firms with large country-specific rents. These include firms in the business of mineral extraction and oil production. A firm may shift from the first type to the second with the passage of time. Before picking a manufacturing location, a firm may be able to locate anywhere in the world. After fixed capital has been committed, the firm falls into the second situation. Because the second type is obviously much more vulnerable to corrupt demands, firms may try to leave as little as possible to future resolution when making large fixed investments. But it is almost impossible credibly to contract away future risks of corrupt demands. Countries known to be corrupt may, therefore, find it difficult to attract investment in immovable fixed capital. As an empirical matter, one should observe that, *ceteris paribus*, corruption is more prevalent in countries with a comparative advantage in capital-intensive or resource-intensive industries. Nevertheless, the capital intensity of economic activity is less in such countries than it would be in the absence of corruption. The alternative to corruption in these cases is legal taxation of a firm's profits, value added, or turnover. Thus corruption can result in higher taxes on a nation's citizens or lower levels of public services. From the point of view of a multinational, however, tax liabilities are a little like bribes in that a country may find it difficult credibly to promise not to raise taxes in the future.

Some firms with large country-specific rents may, nevertheless, be able to resist corrupt demands. These are firms that have monopoly power *vis-à-vis* the state. They supply something

that no other firm can provide as well. One example might be a specialized engineering firm that is the only one reliable enough to design a particular type of bridge.[4] Alternatively, a consumer product with brand recognition (McDonald's, Coca Cola) may be so popular with a nation's citizens or so much a symbol of successful development that corrupt officials cannot afford to risk antagonizing these firms.[5]

Vulnerability to corruption can also depend on the nature of the benefit wanted by the firm and the characteristics of the country. Country-specific rents depend not only on government policies but also on underlying characteristics such as a country's location relative to world markets and the characteristics of its labour force, transportation network, and raw materials. Countries that are closer to world markets are under stronger competitive pressures than those at a distance. Hence opportunities for corruption ought to be lower in the former than in the latter. A recent econometric study by Alberto Ades and Rafael Di Tella (1994) addresses these questions. Using a corruption index from the early 1980s supplemented by more recent information from the early 1990s, they ask how the competitiveness of the economy affects a country's corruption ranking.[6] They argue that more competitive countries should be less corrupt. Lacking a direct measure of competitiveness, they use various proxies and finds results consistent with their theory.[7] Their competitiveness measures include some under control of the state, such as antitrust enforcement, and some, such as distance from world markets, that are not.

Even when country-specific rents are low, bribes may still be paid, but they will raise the contract price, not reduce the firm's profits. The costs of bribery will be borne by the nation's citizens and creditors as officials create artificial benefits for investors. Payoffs may be made in exchange for special benefits that raise the multinational's gross profits and hence its ability to pay. Bribery will be particularly harmful in such cases, not only because the developing nation's citizens and the country's creditors will pay the cost, but also because corruption creates dead-weight losses and inefficiencies.

Firms with high country-specific rents are likely to pay bribes out of profits. New firms may seek the right to exploit a country's minerals or established firms with fixed capital in the country may seek a regulatory benefit or tax break. Such corruption will have resource allocation impacts if it discourages efficient investors from entering the country or if the transaction costs of extracting bribes are high enough to depress the efficiency of productive processes. For example, if the country's bureaucrats delay action until bribes are paid, this may lower the productivity of private workers. Nevertheless, paying bribes out of rents that might otherwise be shared between the firm and the country's citizens is a less serious problem than bribery that impoverishes a poor country even further.

Multinationals participating in the privatization of public corporations are in the same category as raw material producers. The state-owned railway, telephone company, or airline is much like a mineral deposit. One problem here is inefficient actions taken by government officials to increase the value of the public company, and hence the level of possible bribes. The most familiar examples of this are conditions on the newly private companies that restrict competition. For example, when Argentina privatized the state telephone company it divided the system in two, but gave each half a regional monopoly.[8] A national airline might be sold with the promise of exclusive access to certain lucrative routes. Furthermore, payoffs can undermine the tendering process itself leading to the sale of firms to inefficient or corrupt investors.

Such problems might also arise when mineral rights are allocated. For example, the state might favour an inefficient but corrupt bidder. It might build a road at taxpayers' expense that is useful only to whoever wins the extraction rights. If the resource is valuable enough, negative actions are possible. For example, bribes might be solicited that are essentially protection money paid to prevent arson, sabotage and kidnapping. The bribe is a transfer from multinational to official, given the level of rents associated with the project. Thus the unscrupulous official has an incentive to use public funds and take other harmful actions to structure the deal to increase rents.

There is, however, a limit to the rent-creating activities of officials. If they push too far, foreign investment will dry up, and local entrepreneurs will move into the shadow economy. One study of the Ukraine documented this phenomenon (Kaufman, 1994). The author developed an index of restraints on investors that included foreign

trade and foreign exchange controls as well as price controls. He estimated that the shadow, off-the-books economy grew in response to the restrictiveness of state controls. In such an economy corruption may be very high or very low. If the state retains some authority over the shadow economy, officials can demand bribes for overlooking violations of the rules. Conversely, when the state is very weak, officials may be unable credibly to threaten to enforce the law. Instead, payoffs to organized crime can substitute for bribery. Corruption is low because the state can neither make credible threats nor provide credible protection against private criminals. It has simply become irrelevant.

In short, a state with a low volume of bribery may nevertheless be one in which a vigorous anti-corruption campaign is justified. This seemingly paradoxical situation can occur when the state is so unstable and so lacking in outside constraints that the kleptocratic instincts of its officials succeed in choking off much investment and trade. Thus it is important to go beyond the volume of corruption to examine its impact on a country's citizens. The impact of corruption can be large even if the level of payoffs is low. If the probability of corruption is high and if corruption as a share of the value of each deal is large, investment may be discouraged and the overall volume of bribe payments may be low. The country faces a serious problem of corruption even though no massive scandals can be uncovered.

The disposition of bribes

The final issue, which raises both efficiency and equity questions, is the disposition of the bribes themselves. At first, one might think that the use of corrupt payments is irrelevant. The fact that money was received as a bribe should not affect one's desire to put it to the most productive use. This result does not necessarily follow if some uses of bribes attract the attention of the public and of law enforcement authorities more than others. The very process of converting payoffs into ordinary resources may be cumbersome and costly. Also since the money was obtained illicitly in the first place, it may be more easily available for investment in illegal business activities.

Bribery revenues may be invested abroad in a way that circumvents a country's own capital controls. Bribes from multinationals to top officials will be especially likely to contribute to capital flight. The funds can be paid directly into offshore accounts without ever falling foul of the country's own regulations. Of course, if bribes are simply a way of dividing the deal's profits between a country's leaders and multinational firms, ending corruption would not increase domestic investment; it would simply enrich outside investors. Nevertheless, in some cases the investment of bribes outside the country will reduce internal investment funds. Of course, one can criticize controls on the export of capital on economic grounds. They may, however, be a necessary second best response to other distortions in the country's macroeconomic policies. However, whatever their underlying merits, a system that permits a circumvention of such controls by top-level corrupt public officials while deterring others surely has little to recommend it.

Furthermore, corrupt officials may export capital even if profitable investments exist at home. If a lavish lifestyle is taken as evidence of corruption, officials may invest abroad even if good internal opportunities exist. Thus even if bribery represents a pure transfer from multinational firm profits to the ruler's pockets, its illegal character can distort investment priorities. Even money that remains in the country could end up being used for grandiose expressions of the ruler's personal power instead of being used for productive investment. In short, the overall impact of corruption includes not only the direct effects of using bribes to influence public sector performance, but also possible indirect effects on capital flows.

Democracy and the control of corruption

Short of improving the overall moral tone of society, there are two basic ways to limit corruption. The first is to reduce the monopoly power of officials within an existing political and bureaucratic structure. In a country with a functioning legal system, this strategy implies policies that push the bribe price low enough so that officials believe that the risk of detection and punishment outweighs the gains. Similarly, potential bribers must believe that the net gains from making payoffs are negative. Anti-corruption strategies should focus on policies such as reducing the

role of government in the economy, reforming government regulatory policies to incorporate market-based tests, and improving the law enforcement and administrative system to increase deterrence (Rose-Ackerman, 1978, 1994).

Programmatic and bureaucratic reforms are pointless, however, if corruption is endemic at the highest levels of the political system. Then the second option, reform in the basic structure of government, is the only effective cure. In fact, corrupt leaders may themselves seek to carry out the first strategy, i.e. limiting the discretion of subordinates in order to concentrate payoff opportunities at the top. 'Grand' corruption may occur even if lower levels are relatively honest, highly professional, and well paid. When systemic reform is at issue, one key question is the link between democracy and corruption. Do democratic institutions reduce or increase corrupt incentives? Before discussing this issue, however, I begin with two features of the political system that may be more fundamental: the stability of the system and the existence of independent outside checks.

Systemic reform: stability and independent checks

Systemic reforms constrain political and bureaucratic actors at all levels. The key variables are the stability of the governmental system and the existence of outside checks on official behaviour. Stability, however, is a mixed blessing that can deter or facilitate corruption depending on the circumstances. The interaction of these two factors will determine both the likelihood and magnitude of payoffs in any given deal along with total investment and the number of deals involving multinationals.

Let us begin with outside checks. Their role is to ensure that no one group or individual amasses too much power and that the exercise of power can be monitored and constrained. Checks are provided by the separation of powers within government and by the institutions of civil society. Independence is not sufficient, however. These sources of power must also be largely incorruptible themselves.

An independent, competent judiciary is a necessary check on executive and legislative power. The courts must be, however, not only independent but also enforcing laws that both effectively punish wrongdoers and avoid punishing the innocent. The effectiveness of the judiciary will be low if no one brings cases. Thus there must not only be tough statutes but also prosecutors willing to spend time on such cases. Otherwise courts may simply be called upon to uphold otherwise legal bargains based on hidden payoffs. Their very independence then plays into the hands of kleptocratic rulers seeking to guarantee the legitimacy of their deals.[9]

Similarly, a free press and an active civil society are of little use if the state does not respond to criticism and if prosecutors do not follow up the results of investigative journalism. Another option is the use of intermediate organizations such as independent auditing bodies, anti-corruption commissions, or ombudsmen. These bodies must, however, maintain a distance from state power. An anti-corruption commission reporting only to the country's leader risks becoming an instrument of repression rather than a force for clean government. A commission with veto power over who is permitted to bid on public projects can become just one more locus of payoffs.

The independence of private watchdog organizations must not be compromised by threats and intimidation from state officials. Laws that make it a crime to insult sitting politicians or that impose expansive definitions of libel can have a particularly chilling effect. Unfortunately, many democracies have such controls and the trend extends to some of the newly emerging democracies in Eastern Europe and Latin America.[10] Of course, outside organizations are not always paragons. The honesty of the judiciary, the press, and such non-governmental organizations as the church is not to be taken for granted. To the extent that they actually function as watchdogs, they are especially vulnerable. Journalists can be paid to write stories, civic groups can be captured by political agents, and independent institutions may become corrupt themselves. Thus they too must be subject to anti-corruption controls, and can themselves be the subject of muck-raking journalism. Nevertheless, regulations that threaten the independence of such organizations must be avoided in the name of preserving their independence, even if the result is sometimes painful for politicians.

In a democracy, opposition parties may also play the role of monitors and can threaten to make corruption a campaign issue. There is a risk, however, that the political system will focus on the moral and legal failings of the individual leaders rather than emphasizing inter-party differences on substantive policies and governmental reform. Thus it is not the electoral forms that are central, but the effectiveness of opposition politics. Corruption charges, well documented or not, have often brought down political leaders. However, the new regimes that take over frequently succumb to the same temptations. Furthermore, if the innocent have difficulty proving their honesty, accusations of corruption will not have much of a deterrent effect.

Another check on centralized power is a federal system. It enfranchises groups with an interest in monitoring the centre and gives them an independent power base from which to do it. Federalism may be rather a weak reed on which to rely, however, since corrupt incentives can exist at any level of government. In fact, some argue in favour of decentralization as a way of improving government performance (Ranis and Stewart, 1994), while others point to the heightened risk of favouritism at lower levels of government (Sánchez Morón, 1995). The problem is too complex to be analysed here, but the basic issues involve supply and demand. Federalism may limit corruption if it reduces the value of the benefits available to any government official (businesses will pay little to one low-level government if they can easily locate elsewhere) and it may reduce high-level corruption by giving low-level governments a stake in the honesty of the top. However, if decentralization is accompanied by the creation of a series of petty local monopolies, corruption may increase or be replaced by personal favouritism. The decentralization of the system will make corruption difficult to discover and prosecute. 'Grand' corruption may fall but the overall level of payoffs and their resource allocation consequences could increase.

The second dimension, systemic stability, by which is meant a high probability that the future legal and political system will be much like the present, at least along the dimensions of interest to business investors, plays a more complex role. Stability refers to one of two conditions. First, it may mean a high expected probability that current officeholders or their political progeny will remain in power. Thus

Page from a French comic strip *Sammy: Les gorilles et le roi dollar* telling a story of corruption. For non-francophone readers: the inspector receives a percentage of a deal from a local officer, and then on returning to the police station receives a telephone call from a senator arranging clear passage for an illegal delivery. The senator receives an advance from the criminals, with the remainder to follow after completion of the delivery. Berck, Cauvin and Editions Dupuis. R.R.

the Soviet Union until the Gorbachev era, Mexico since the 1920s, Japan under LDP rule, and Spain under Franco would have been viewed as stable. Second, it refers to countries with strong constitutional or legal traditions that imply that the contracts or regulatory benefits approved by one government have a high likelihood of being upheld by subsequent governments. These are 'governments of laws, not of men', where the identity and party affiliation of the rulers change over time but the underlying system remains relatively constant. Not all democracies are in this category. Some, such as the new democracies in Eastern Europe, are unstable since their laws are often non-existent or poorly defined and the constitutional situation is fluid.

Instability discourages investment whatever the level of independent checks.[11] Firms may seek to make payoffs to introduce some certainty into their business deals, but such bribery will not be an effective tool for investors if corrupt 'contracts' are not enforced. Thus stability can either deter or encourage corruption. A stable system with weak outside checks can be an engine for the generation of payoffs if top government officials can make credible threats and promises. Bribes may be worth paying since there is little risk. Like a monopoly firm, such a government can organize itself to maximize payoffs. The main problem faced by such governments is the difficulty of credibly committing to carry out their corrupt promises. Authoritarian governments can be arbitrary if they are not effectively constrained by legal rules. For example, a firm may make a payoff to obtain a monopoly franchise to sell automobiles only to discover that a second corrupt deal has been made with another automobile company. Even though a bribe has been paid, the first company may have a contract that appears valid. In a country with independent courts such a contract would be honoured so long as the bribery is kept secret. In regimes unconstrained by law, the rulers simply invalidate the contract, and there is no recourse. In such countries no deal may go through without corruption, but the level of bribes and the number of deals may be low if firms have alternatives. Thus bribes may be a high percentage of gross profits, but be low in dollar terms because the level of expected profits is low.

Conversely, corrupt governments with functioning independent courts, but no independent prosecutors specializing in white collar crimes, may be able to extract large shares of corporate profits in the form of bribes without discouraging risk-averse investors. A pure kleptocracy that sought to maximize bribe payments would limit investments, but only as a way of maximizing monopoly rents and hence the bribes paid out of them. Such a state could avoid potentially destructive competition between decentralized officials each seeking to maximize their own gain (Shleifer and Vishney, 1993). A kleptocracy with no serious opposition and a long-run perspective might be able to so institutionalize corruption that firms trust corrupt officials to keep their word. The trusting networks, which some see as a key source of competitive advantage (Barney and Hansen, 1994), can be converted instead to a system for maintaining corrupt relationships over time (Cartier-Bresson, 1995). In contrast, officials of a stable government with functioning outside checks, such as an independent court system, will have difficulty engaging in excessive kleptocratic behaviour so long as white collar crime is prosecuted with some degree of vigour.

This analysis suggests that the best situation both for investors in *legitimate* businesses and for the populace is a stable system with outside checks. Even in an autocracy stability may be better than instability. Instability lowers corruption because the state's commitments, corrupt or otherwise, are not credible. However, it also reduces investment since the risk is higher. When independent checks are combined with instability, corruption may be low but only because the benefits of bribery and the expected investment returns are low. State officials do not have control over much that is worth selling. Investors in *illegal* businesses, in contrast, prefer either an unconstrained captured autocrat or a weak state incapable of exercising effective power.

The two dimensions, stability and independent sources of authority, may be interrelated. Thus the stability of a rule-of-law state may be maintained by an independent judiciary and by a public willing to challenge the abuses of the regime in court and at the ballot box. If we add a dynamic element, another possible interconnection arises. A stable regime with a high level of corruption may find that bribery undermines the regime and produces instability with a consequent loss in investment funds and payoffs.

Democracy and corruption

How do democratic institutions map onto the categories of stability and independent checks? In democracies the desire for re-election will deter corruption so long as the electorate disapproves of the practice and has some way of sorting out valid from invalid accusations. But there are other factors that argue against uncritical optimism. We need to consider legislators' demand for bribes, the impact of legislative and government organization on corrupt incentives, and the supply of bribes.

There are two contrasting factors on the demand side which encourage both re-election-seeking politicians and 'lame ducks' to accept payoffs. First, elections themselves are costly, so candidates need to accumulate campaign funds or provide private benefits to constituents. These financial pressures can give politicians an incentive to accept payoffs. Politicians in most of the developed world are subject to these pressures, but countries with few constraints on campaign finance and constituents who expect lots of favours and help, face the most serious problems.[12] Second, politicians may sometimes find themselves in a situation where the likelihood of re-election is very low. This may occur because their popularity has declined since their election or because they are barred by law from seeking re-election. As the time of their retirement draws near, they have an incentive to extract as much wealth as possible from their remaining hold on power. Countries making a transition to democracy may be especially vulnerable if unelected sitting politicians doubt their ability to win the election, and if they have not been legally compensated by the new democratic politicians.

The second factor affecting the level of corruption is the method of political decision-making. If a favourable legislative decision is needed, then a majority must be persuaded to vote in favour of the briber's desired policy. Thus the level of bribery will depend on the willingness and ability of the legislature to

organize for extortionary purposes. Many decisions may be influenced by bribery, but the level of payoffs may be low if no stable corrupt coalition exists capable of extracting a high proportion of the private rents (Rose-Ackerman, 1978). If disclosure of corruption spells political death and if disclosure is more likely the higher the level of bribery, politicians may be unwilling to accept large bribes (Rasmusen and Ramseyer, 1995). This conclusion assumes, however, that the voters will focus on the level of the bribes accepted, not the distortionary costs to society of passing a law in return for payoffs. It also assumes that at some point the benefits of higher bribes are outweighed by higher costs. Under other conditions, there could be two possible outcomes: a no corruption regime in which re-election-seeking officials reject all offers, and a fully corrupt outcome in which bribes are high enough to compensate for the expected costs of accepting payoffs. In contrast, democracies with stable governing coalitions may not be much different, so far as bribery is concerned, from single autocrats. The regime can provide 'one-stop-shopping' and will handle the distribution of the payoffs to members.

Finally, consider the supply of bribes in a democracy. Are the benefits sought by those who make payoffs likely to differ between democratic and autocratic states? The answer depends both on formal constraints on state power and on the substance of rules and laws. Most democracies have some type of separation of powers. This reaches its most extreme form in the United States, but even parliamentary democracies, where executive and parliament are controlled by the same political grouping, usually have some degree of power diffusion. This may consist of an upper house based on different principles of representation, an independent judiciary, a constitution that can only be amended by supra majorities of the legislature or by other special procedures, a constitutionally protected bill of rights, including freedom of press and association, or a federal structure. Of course, authoritarian regimes may also be legally and structurally constrained, and not all democracies have all these features. Nevertheless, most democracies include at least some of them. These factors imply that democracy is not simply an instrument for imposing the will of the majority. Multiple sources of authority give the *status quo* some staying power and imply that no one individual or part of government has absolute power. A few countries with democratic forms have, however, experienced one-party rule for many years so, except for the periodic election requirements, the ruling party can operate like a constrained autocrat.

The constraints on legislative and executive power that exist in most democracies imply that obtaining benefits from government can be costly and complex. However, those wishing to preserve the *status quo* have an easy time since they only need to find one blocking group. In contrast, those wishing to effect a change need to influence numerous organizations. If the influence takes the form of corrupt payments, revelation of any one illegal payment is likely to doom the effort.

Critics of the impact of democracy on growth point to the redistributive pressures created by democracy which slow growth by retarding savings. They applaud efforts by economic interests to circumvent these pressures. Other observers, however, point to the value of democracy in ensuring that the benefits of growth are broadly diffused, thus setting the stage for long-term improvements. Corruption could undermine the extent to which growth benefits the populace, thus ultimately retarding development. Since these empirical issues have not been resolved and probably have no single, simple answer, the link between growth and democracy is unclear. Nevertheless, one can hypothesize that for a group which wants change or special treatment, the minimum price will be higher in a democracy than in an otherwise similar autocracy. Less corruption may occur than in an autocracy, but when it occurs, the cost will be high. Operating against this tendency will be politicians who refuse large bribes because of the political risks they present. For a group which wants to preserve the *status quo*, the price will be lower in a democracy than in an autocracy since the state has little monopoly power to exercise.

A similar contrast exists between the case where several sources of power must all agree before an action can be taken compared with one in which any entity can grant the request. For example, a law in the United States cannot be enacted unless House, Senate, and President

all agree or unless two-thirds of each house votes to overturn a presidential veto. The federal courts may also be asked to rule on the constitutionality of statutes. In contrast, a business need only find one state to agree to its locational plans and can threaten to go elsewhere if its first choice makes difficulties. Corrupt outcomes will be costly and difficult in the first instance. In the second, bribes may be unnecessary if the firm can credibly threaten to take its business elsewhere.

How, then, do democracies and autocracies compare insofar as corruption is concerned? An important distinction is between the minimum and maximum bribes officials are willing to accept, on the one hand, and the government official's bargaining power *vis-à-vis* the bribe payer, on the other. Thus officials in democracies may refuse to accept small bribes because of the fixed cost of corruption. If the fixed component dominates, eventually a range of bribe levels will be reached that is acceptable to the official. At some point costs once again dominate and the official refuses higher bribes. When very large payoffs are offered, however, some officials may simply decide to abandon their political careers and accept the payment in anticipation of leaving office. In an autocratic system without electoral constraints, the minimum bribe is lower and there is no threshold. Thus in a democracy the briber may be unable to pay off enough politicians even if he has a relatively high willingness to pay. For example, in a legislature operating through majority rule, less than 50 per cent of the re-election-seeking officials may be willing to be bought. If the law had no supporters in the absence of payoffs, only someone willing to pay bribes large enough to convert some officials into lame ducks will be successful. Thus in a democracy some corrupt deals will not be possible because not enough officials are corruptible at moderate payoff levels and marginal increases in bribe offers will decrease, not increase the number of corruptible officials.

The bargaining power of government officials determines not the incidence but the level of payoffs. It determines how the gains are divided between the bribers and the bribees. Compared to democracies, autocratic states are likely to be in a stronger bargaining position relative to bribers for the reasons outlined above. Thus if a bargaining range exists, the government officials can be expected to obtain more of it in an autocracy. It is, however, possible that the transaction costs of corruption are so much higher in a democracy that the ultimate benefits flowing to the briber are lower under democratic conditions. This in itself will discourage corruption by lowering the benefits. If the transactions costs have a large fixed component, corrupt projects with only moderate gains will be discouraged while highly profitable ones will still go ahead. Thus one might expect a concentration on two types of corrupt projects in a democracy, inexpensive ones and expensive ones, with few in the intermediate range.

Conclusions

Corruption in international business deals is especially troubling. It can produce short-term gains for some of the country's citizens by requiring the international firm to share its profits with the corrupt rulers. In a broader perspective, however, it substitutes for tax revenues and over time can discourage investments that further

economic growth. Multinational firms will still want to extract the minerals and pump the oil of corrupt countries, but investors with a choice will go elsewhere.

Reforms that move a country towards democracy can limit corrupt incentives, but the result is not inevitable. The costs of electoral campaigns may produce a new reason for politicians to extract economic rents from firms and wealthy individuals. Politicians who expect to lose may be corruptible due to their insecure tenure in office that is the hallmark of a well functioning democracy. In contrast, career politicians who seek re-election by people who disapprove of corruption will be deterred from taking payoffs. The independent sources of authority characteristic of most democratic systems, help limit payoffs both by multiplying the checks on government behaviour and by increasing the transaction costs for some types of corrupt deals. An electoral system is an insufficient deterrent to corruption, however. Also important are vigorous outside checks on power, a division of power within the state, and enforcement of the rule of law in commercial and political life.

Notes

1. The International Monetary Fund divides the world into industrial and developing countries. The former category includes members of the OECD plus Australia and New Zealand. This means that relatively underdeveloped countries such as Greece and Ireland are counted as developed and quite prosperous countries such as Singapore and Korea are in the developing category (International Monetary Fund, 1993, 1994). The IMF data on the countries of the former Soviet Union have been published in a separate document because they do not meet the requirements for incorporation into regular IMF publications. Not all FSU countries reported data for all

three years. I constructed estimates for these countries based on the growth rates of overall foreign direct investment and of imports. In general, data on direct investment is believed by IMF staff to be relatively inaccurate. Several countries reported no direct investment numbers to the IMF in recent years. They are included only to the extent that they are in the 'not elsewhere classified' category. The IMF total for direct investment in developing countries was $41 billion per year in current dollars. Adding in the estimates for the countries of the former Soviet Union raises the estimated total to $41.7 billion. Imports averaged $908 billion for the developing world. Adding in

the FSU raised the total to $955 billion.

2. The term apparently originated with Andreski (1968). For the example of Morocco, see Waterbury (1973).

3. For example, observers of Nigeria argue that a billion dollar aluminum smelter built with oil revenues fits into this category as well as a number of other large-scale projects in that country over the last several decades (Diamond, 1993; Werlin, 1994). Werlin also provides examples from a number of other countries.

4. For example, in Maryland kickbacks were frequently paid by

engineering firms in return for contracts with the state (*New York Times*, 11 October 1973). The article reports that 'a few companies developed in time a size, expertise, and stature that insulated them to some extent from this system [of corruption]. One or two developed an expertise, for example, in large bridge design, that other local companies could not match. One or two grew so large and had been awarded so many contracts that the state could not do without their services unless out-of-state consultants were employed. In these ways, a few companies in effect graduated in time from the system to a position of less vulnerability, and they could afford to resist, and perhaps in some instances, refuse to participate.'

5. A study of the experience of such companies' investments in Eastern Europe and Russia would be instructive. See 'Coke's Great Romanian Adventure', *New York Times*, 26 February 1995 (Business Section). The story describes Coke's successful domination of the soft drinks market in Romania. Its investment originated in a partnership with the former head of Romania's largest bottler of soft drinks who became general manager of Coke's operation in Bucharest and is described as 'riding around in a new Mercedes-Benz'.

6. Ades and Di Tella use a subjective index of corruption compiled by Business International (BI) from its correspondents throughout the world. The Economist Intelligence Unit, a proprietary firm which now owns BI, provided them with data from the early 1980s that it judged no longer of commercial value. The index, which covers 55 countries, ranks countries on a scale of 0 to 10 based on a judgement of how frequently corruption was required in business transactions. High numbers indicate low levels of corruption. The BI data also include numerous other measures of the climate for business. The

second index they used is from the *World Competitiveness Report* published by the EMF Foundation in Geneva. It covers only 32 countries. The indexes cover a limited group of countries. Those from the 1980s omit Eastern Europe and China. Neither index includes the Middle Eastern oil countries. The WCR data exclude Africa, Eastern Europe except Hungary, and Latin America except Mexico and Brazil.

7. Their proxies are the share of merchandise imports in GDP, the distance of the country from world markets, an index of labour power, and the strength of antitrust laws. They also include as controls measures of economic prosperity, educational levels, and political rights. As Ades and Di Tella themselves recognize, these measures all have weaknesses. The share of imports ought to take the size of the economy into account. The United States has a relatively small import share but is quite competitive because of the size of the internal market. Import share has a quite different meaning in China compared to Mali. In addition, the proxies ignore the competitiveness of export markets and the nature of the government contracting process.

8. 'Latin American Telecoms: Half-way There', *The Economist*, 4 February 1995, p. 63; Matthew Doman, 'Trying to Come in Line with Foreign Caller: Argentina Is Pressing Its Telecommunications Groups to Adjust Their Price Ratio', *Financial Times*, 20 September 1995. The shared monopoly arrangement expires in 1997, but is likely to be renewed until 2000.

9. Democracies can face the same problem. In the state of Georgia in 1795 all but one member of the legislature was bribed to authorize the sale of state land to private interests at a low price. When the deal came to light, all were defeated in the next election, but the contract itself was upheld by the US Supreme Court in *Fletcher*

v Peck (Coulter, 1933, pp. 187–92).

10. In Argentina, President Carlos Menem sent three bills to Congress that if passed would have restricted press freedom. So far these bills have not been enacted into law. One proposed law would make it a crime to offend the memory of the dead. Another increases the penalties for libel and slander, and the third would require news outlets to take out costly libel insurance. Opponents of the bills claimed that they were designed to intimidate the press and quash corruption investigations. The Justice Minister defended the proposed laws by saying that 'One of the most important precepts in our society is to protect the honor of an individual, because a person without honor is a person without liberty.' 'Press Protests "Gag" Bills in Argentina', *New York Times*, 19 February 1995. For examples of 'anti-insult' laws in Eastern Europe, see Tucker (1994).

11. Investment in start-up companies is risky in Eastern European countries such as the Ukraine because of the absence of a functioning commercial law system. Foreign partners may put up funds only to find themselves later squeezed out of joint ventures by dishonest local partners or excessive regulation. As a result in the Ukraine there are two types of investors: deep-pocket multinationals prepared to invest for the long haul and 'freewheeling individuals who have turned their taste for Ukraine's awfulness into a sort of competitive advantage over less patient rivals'. 'The Battle for Ukraine', *The Economist*, 11 February 1995, p. 56. Similar problems of foreign partners in joint ventures being squeezed out by local partners are reported to occur in China. The absence of a functioning legal system is also a contributing factor there. See Hao and Johnston (1995).

12. See, for example, the case of Korea described in Park (1995).

References

ADES, A.; DI TELLA, R., 1994. 'Competition and Corruption'. Draft, 13 June.

ANDRESKI, S., 1968. 'Kleptocracy or Corruption as a System of Government'. In *The African Predicament*, New York: Atherton.

BARNEY, J. B.; HANSEN, M. H., 1994. 'Trustworthiness as a Source of Competitive Advantage'. *Strategic Management Journal*, 15, pp. 175–90.

BRENNAN, G.; BUCHANAN, J. M., 1980. *The Power to Tax: Analytical Foundations of a Fiscal Constitution*. Cambridge: Cambridge University Press.

CARTIER-BRESSON, J., 1995. 'L'Economie de la Corruption'. In D. della Porta and Y. Mény (eds), *Démocratie et Corruption en Europe*, Paris: La Découverte, pp. 149–64.

COULTER, E. M., 1933. *A Short History of Georgia*. Chapel Hill: University of California Press.

DIAMOND, L., 1993. 'Nigeria's Perennial Struggle Against Corruption: Prospects for the Third Republic'. *Corruption and Reform*, 7, pp. 215–25.

HAO, Y.; JOHNSTON, M., 1995. 'Reform at the Crossroads: An Analysis of Chinese Corruption'. *Asian Perspectives*, 19, pp. 117–49.

INTERNATIONAL MONETARY FUND, 1994. *Balance of Payments Statistics Yearbook, part 2*. Washington, D.C.

INTERNATIONAL MONETARY FUND, 1993. *International Financial Statistics: Supplement on Countries of the Former Soviet Union*. Supplement Series No. 16, Washington, D.C.

KAUFMAN, D., 1994. 'Diminishing Returns to Administrative Controls and the Emergence of the Unofficial Economy: A Framework of Analysis and Applications to Ukraine', *Economic Policy* (December), pp. 51–69.

MAURO, P., 1995. 'Corruption and Growth'. *Quarterly Journal of Economics*, 109, pp. 681–712.

MOODY-STUART, G., 1994. 'Grand Corruption in Third World Development'. Working Paper, Transparency International, Berlin.

PARK, B.-S., 1995. 'Political Corruption in Non-Western Democracies: The Case of South-Korea Party Politics'. Draft, Kim Dae-Jung Peace Foundation, Seoul, Korea.

RANIS, G.; STEWART, F., 1994. 'Decentralization in Indonesia'. *Bulletin of Indonesian Economic Studies*, 30, pp. 41–72.

RASMUSEN, E.; RAMSEYER, J. M., 1994. 'Cheap Bribes and the Corruption Ban: A Coordination Game Among Rational Legislators'. *Public Choice*, 78, pp. 305–27.

ROSE-ACKERMAN, S., 1978. *Corruption: A Study in Political Economy*. New York: Academic Press.

ROSE-ACKERMAN, S., 1994. 'Reducing Bribery in the Public Sector'. In Trang (ed.), pp. 21–28.

SÁNCHEZ MORÓN, M., 1995. 'La Corrupcion y los Problemas del Control de las Administraciones Publicas'. Draft, Catedrático de Derecho Administrativo, Universidad de Alcalá de Henares, Spain.

SHLEIFER, A.; VISHNEY, R., 1993. 'Corruption'. *Quarterly Journal of Economics*, 108, pp. 599–617.

TRANG, D. V. (ED.), 1994. *Corruption and Democracy: Political Institutions, Processes and Corruption in Transition States in East-Central Europe and in the Former Soviet Union*. Budapest: Institute for Constitutional and Legislative Policy.

TUCKER, L., 1994. 'Censorship and Corruption: Government Self-Protection Through Control of the Media'. In Trang (ed.), pp. 185–89.

WATERBURY, J., 1973. 'Endemic and Planned Corruption in a Monarchical Regime'. *World Politics*, 25, pp. 534–55.

WERLIN, H., 1994. 'Understanding Corruption: Implications for World Bank Staff'. World Bank, OPR Consultant Report, unpublished manuscript.

[20]

Political Studies (1997), XLV, 417–435

Political Corruption:
Problems and Perspectives

PAUL HEYWOOD*

Introduction: On Why We Are All Now Concerned About Corruption

As the twentieth century comes to an end, one of the issues which has dominated its final decade – political corruption – shows little sign of diminishing in importance. The evidence is abundant. In the United States of America and the United Kingdom, two of the world's most well-established democracies, recent national elections have been punctuated by stories relating to corruption: in the former, President Bill Clinton has been dogged both by the so-called Whitewater scandal, and by questions over how his 1996 re-election campaign was funded; in the latter, John Major's Conservative government found itself caught up during the 1997 election campaign in allegations about 'sleaze', centring in particular on the 'cash-for-questions' issue.[1] In a rather less well-established democracy, Pakistan, the government of Benazir Bhutto was dismissed in early November 1996 by President Farooq Leghari, accused (amongst other things) of undermining judicial independence and engaging in massive corruption. The following day, India's former prime minister, Narasimha Rao, already accused of vote-buying and forgery, was charged with criminal conspiracy to cheat a businessman. In Russia, still struggling to establish democracy on a secure footing, President Boris Yeltsin admitted in March 1997 that '[o]ne of the main faults of the Russian authorities at all levels is corruption'.[2]

These examples (all of which have occurred since the original deadline for submission of manuscripts to this volume) are merely illustrative of a phenomenon which was seen until quite recently as being virtually the preserve of authoritarian or 'developing' nations – basically, that is, non-democracies (or, at best, proto-democracies). Where political corruption existed in democratic nations, certainly established *western* democracies, it was usually viewed as an aberrant deviation from the norm.[3] Such a view was undermined by the extraordinary revelations of systemic corruption which began to emerge in Italy

---

* I am grateful to Richard Aldrich, Anthony Butler, Ian Forbes, Lotta Hedman, Erik Jones, Chris Pierson, Sue Pryce, Lucy Sargisson and Mary Vincent for their valuable comments on this chapter.

[1] See R. J. Bartley (ed.), *Whitewater* (Dow Jones, 1994) and *Whitewater Vol. 2* (Dow Jones, 1997); David Leigh and Ed Vulliamy, *Sleaze: the Corruption of Parliament* (London, Fourth Estate, 1996).

[2] Quoted in *The Times*, 7 March 1997.

[3] See Arnold J. Heidenheimer (ed.), *Political Corruption. Readings in Comparative Analysis* (New Brunswick NJ, Transaction, 1970): although there are sections covering the United States and Western Europe, these cases are predominantly local level or else historical. In contrast, corruption in the developing nations – principally in South and South East Asia and Africa – is presented as being more systemic. Japan, where seemingly endemic political corruption has often been explained in culturalist terms, and Latin America receive virtually no attention in the Heidenheimer volume.

in the early 1990s: the entire Italian post-war body politic was revealed to have rested on a complex web of corrupt networks which encompassed politicians, bureaucrats and businessmen at the highest levels. But, even if the Italian example represented an extreme, endemic high-level political corruption could no longer be presented primarily as a problem of non-democracies. Instead, corruption scandals began to emerge with insistent regularity in several other European democracies – notably, Italy's southern neighbours Spain and Greece, but also France, Germany, Austria and Belgium. By the mid-1990s, it appeared that no nation was immune to the corrosive impact of political corruption. Academic interest in the phenomenon experienced a parallel upsurge, characterized by a proliferation of conferences devoted to the issue, with related publications.[4]

This volume obviously forms part of the trend. Its claim to distinctiveness lies in bringing together scholars working within a number of different areas of the social sciences, who have approached the issue of political corruption from a variety of analytical perspectives. The chapters which follow draw on insights from political science, philosophy, economics, sociology and law; the methodologies deployed include comparative approaches, game theory, focus group discussions, and case studies. Yet, whatever the distinctive merits or otherwise of this volume, the question arises of *why* political corruption has generated such interest in recent years. After all, as Alatas has commented, corruption is trans-systemic:

> it inheres in all social systems – feudalism, capitalism, communism and socialism. It affects all classes of society; all state organizations, monarchies and republics; all situations, in war and peace; all age groups; both sexes; and all times, ancient, medieval and modern.[5]

Part of the answer lies in the *perception* that the phenomenon has spread to new areas: no state any longer seems safe, not even the most mature democracy. The Italian revelations of the early 1990s acted as a form of catalyst to investigative journalists and, increasingly, magistrates in other democracies. Effectively, the Italian example produced a 'demonstration effect', sensitizing other western democracies to the issue of political corruption. It is hardly a coincidence that revelations of corruption scandals assumed a new momentum after the *'mani*

---

[4] It should be acknowledged that some seasoned observers of corruption had been driving this particular wagon long before others amongst us jumped aboard. See in particular, Arnold J. Heidenheimer, Michael Johnston and Victor T. LeVine, *Political Corruption. A Handbook* (New Brunswick NJ, Transaction, 1989), and the journal *Corruption and Reform*, which dates from 1986. Amongst recent publications, not all of which have resulted from conferences, see Donatella della Porta and Yves Mény (eds), *Démocratie et corruption en Europe* (Paris, Editions La Découverte, 1995; English version published by Pinter, 1997); F. F. Ridley and A. Doig (eds), *Sleaze: Politicians, Private Interests & Public Reaction* (Oxford, Oxford University Press, 1995); Walter Little and Eduardo Posada-Carbó (eds), *Political Corruption in Europe and Latin America* (London, Macmillan, in association with the Institute of Latin American Studies, University of London, 1996); M. Levi and D. Nelken (eds), *The Corruption of Politics and the Politics of Corruption* (Oxford, Blackwell, 1996); H. E. Bakker and N. G. Schulte Nordholt (eds), *Corruption and Legitimacy* (Amsterdam, SISWO, 1996); *International Social Science Journal, Corruption in Western Democracies* 149/3 (1996). In addition, a number of Internet sites which focus on corruption have been established; a useful site from which to begin exploring can be located at 'http://gwdu19.gwdg.de/~uwvw/'.

[5] Syed Hussein Alatas, *Corruption: its Nature, Causes and Consequences* (Aldershot, Avebury, 1990), pp. 3–4.

pulite' (clean hands) investigations were initiated in Milan. The rise in *exposure* of political corruption, rather than the fact of its existence, in turn became self-sustaining, prompting anti-corruption drives in several states.

However, the fact that corruption should have generated such public concern cannot be divorced from the wider political context within which it was uncovered. The early 1990s coincided with the collapse of the post-war order: until then, the Cold War had provided political actors with ideological and geo-strategic reference points. Its end destroyed the certainties which had charac-terized post-war Europe. Moreover, it contributed to the unravelling of a political settlement in Italy which had originally been based on an anti-communist coalition built around the Christian Democrats.[6] The revelation of widespread political corruption helped undermine one of the support structures – the claim to operate on the basis of public accountability – which had underpinned western democracies in the post-war world, and distinguished them from communist regimes. The lack of trust in public organizations associated with what has been termed the postmodern politics of fear and risk was exacerbated by the sheer scale of political corruption: without trust, democracy itself was threatened.[7] For some, therefore, political corruption is simply one more manifestation of the contemporary crisis of the nation state or, more particularly, western democratic states.

To others, such speculation may seem fanciful – or at best overblown. Rather more mundane reasons can be adduced for public concern about political corruption. For instance, it is possible that what changed in the early 1990s was the public's readiness to tolerate political corruption, the result in turn of a downturn in economic circumstances. Just as the proposals contained in the Maastricht Treaty began to meet with growing scepticism when they were used in several member states of the European Union to justify stringent controls on public expenditure, so political corruption may have assumed greater import-ance in the absence of a 'feel-good' factor. The readiness to accept shortcomings on the part of politicians may be inversely related to economic performance. It is difficult to track such responses, since political corruption did not figure as a central issue in opinion surveys until relatively recently.[8] Although this fact in itself may be taken as evidence that it did not elicit any great concern, on the other hand it may simply reflect a lack of awareness of its widespread existence. It does appear, though, that some of the major political corruption scandals of the 1980s – such as the P2 affair in Italy, the Carrefour du Développement and URBA cases in France, the Flick affair in Germany, or the Koskotas scandal in

---

[6] On the Italian case, see especially Donatella della Porta, *Lo scambio occulto. Casi di corruzione politica in Italia* (Bologna, Il Mulino, 1992); Donatella della Porta and Alberto Vannucci, *Corruzione politica e amministrazione pubblica. Risorse, meccanismi, attori* (Bologna, Il Mulino, 1994).

[7] See Nick Rengger, 'Beyond Liberal Politics? European Modernity and the Nation-State', in Martin Rhodes, Paul Heywood and Vincent Wright (eds), *Developments in West European Politics* (London, Macmillan, 1997). Joseph LaPalombara, 'Structural and institutional aspects of corruption', *Social Research* 61/4 (1994), p. 326 sees 'the widespread political turmoil associated with corruption ... [as] a manifestation of a much deeper and more pervasive loss of public confidence in the institutions and processes of democracy'.

[8] Cristina Bicchieri and John Duffy refer on p. 479 (fn. 10) to evidence from a small experiment on corruption and electoral support, conducted in 1977 by Rundquist, Strom and Peters, which lends support to the hypothesis that there is a tendency for voters to focus on corruption during periods of economic stagnation.

Greece – did not provoke the sense of alienation, distrust and disillusionment with the political class which had become commonplace throughout Europe by the mid-1990s.[9]

On the other hand, expectations of standards of behaviour amongst public servants may have changed as a result of greater – some may argue, more intrusive – media investigation. Since the early 1970s (and partly as a result of Watergate) politicians have been exposed to a much more intense media spotlight than were their predecessors. Again, this argument should not be overplayed: it may be more accurate – at least in regard to personal morality – in Anglo-Saxon nations than in continental European democracies, which appear to display a lower level of public prurience about their politicians' private lives. Nonetheless, one aspect of political corruption which has kept it in the public spotlight in recent years is that it makes for good news stories: there can be little doubt that 'scandal' appeals to the investigative instincts of journalists just as much as it does to viewers, listeners and readers of the mass media. Several political corruption scandals have involved such a degree of intrigue and, at times, sheer audacity, that following them can be akin to reading a good thriller.[10] For journalists, too, the prospect of uncovering a major scandal offers the promise of career advancement and financial reward.

Neither were investigating magistrates likely to be immune to the seductive appeal of the limelight which accompanied their every action.[11] In Spain, Baltazar Garzón, who led the investigations into the GAL affair, was dubbed 'Super Garzón' in the media – an image he seemed happy to cultivate as he rose to political influence. Similarly in Italy, several judges – notably Antonio Di Pietro – became household names and were able to launch their own political careers on the back of anti-corruption credentials.[12] Even in Britain, where the legal system differs markedly from the civil law tradition in most continental countries which allows judges also to act as prosecutors, names like Nolan and Downey came to public prominence as a result of their official enquiries into standards in public life and 'cash-for-questions' respectively.

The examples of corruption mentioned so far have all been drawn from a diverse range of democracies. This reflects in part the fact that there is growing concern about the apparent spread of political corruption to democratic states. However, it can also be argued, although not all the contributors to this volume would necessarily subscribe to such a view, that political corruption – particularly at high level – is more serious in democracies than in other forms of political system. This is not because political corruption matters 'more' in

[9] Ridley and Doig (eds), *Sleaze*, provides information on changing public responses to corruption in a variety of European countries. For details of the various scandals listed, see Longman, *Political Scandals and Causes Célèbres Since 1945: An International Reference Compendium* (Harlow, Longman, n.d., but December 1990?).

[10] This was particularly true of the Italian case, in which truth more than mirrored the fictional world of Rome-based police commissioner, Aurelio Zen, the hero of Michael Dibdin's crime thrillers.

[11] Véronique Pujas, a research student at the European University Institute, is currently working on how the notion of political scandal emerges as the product of social tensions. She argues that scandals result both from 'transversal' tensions between values and revealed behaviour, and also from 'sectoral' tensions between the political class, the judiciary and the mass media.

[12] See David Nelken, 'The Judges and Political Corruption in Italy', in Levi and Nelken, *The Corruption of Politics*, pp. 95–112. On Garzón, see Paul Heywood, 'Spain', in Ridley and Doig, *Sleaze*, pp. 178–89.

democracies than in non-democracies. Rather, it is because it does more damage to democracies: it is more undermining of their basic principles in a way which is not true for non-democracies.[13] The effects of corruption are especially disruptive in democracies: by attacking some of the basic principles on which democracy rests – notably, the equality of citizens before institutions (that is, the idea that individuals should be treated with fairness and respect by government officials) and the openness of decision making (that is, crucially, accountability) – corruption contributes to the delegitimation of the political and institutional systems in which it takes root. It is for this reason that political corruption is rightly a central focus of concern in contemporary democracies.

The Definitional Dilemma

The emphasis in this volume is on *political* corruption, as opposed to corruption more generally, and attention is therefore devoted primarily to the public sphere in which political actors operate. The critical emphasis here is on the 'public sphere': on corrupt activities which take place either wholly within the public sphere or at the interface between the public and private spheres – such as when politicians or functionaries use their privileged access to resources (in whatever form) illegitimately to benefit themselves or others. Boundaries are clearly critical: those activities which take place wholly outside the public sphere, such as private sector business and financial corruption (which are rife), lie outside the concerns of the analyses in this volume.[14] Naturally, there are substantial areas where public and private overlap: in some countries it is difficult to distinguish clearly, for instance, political corruption from organized crime. The case of Italy, in particular, as well as more recent developments in Russia, demonstrate that the interconnections between organized crime and politics can be extraordinarily close.[15] Equally, Donatella della Porta and Alessandro Pizzorno have talked of 'business politicians', a new breed of political entre-preneur who 'combines mediation in (licit or illicit) business transactions, first-hand participation in economic activity, and political mediation in the traditional sense'.[16] Further problems are posed by, for instance, police

[13] Michael Johnston, 'Comparing corruption: conflicts, standards and development' (paper presented to the XVI Congress of the International Political Science Association, Berlin, 1994), argues that any real notion of corruption depends on the existence of pluralism, without which the power of an autocrat or despot is not subject to any meaningful limitation: why bribe when you can bully?

[14] On the importance of boundaries – between state and society, public and private domains, politics and administration, personal and collective rights and interests, and within market, authoritarian and patrimonial mechanisms of allocation – see Michael Johnston, 'Corruption, markets and reform' (paper prepared for Conference on Anti-Corruption for Social Stability and Development, Beijing, 1995).

[15] In regard to Italy, there is a vast literature on the mafia. On its involvement in political corruption, see A. Vannucci, 'Politicians and Godfathers: Mafia and Political Corruption in Italy', in della Porta and Mény (eds), *Democracy and Corruption*, pp. 50–64; D. della Porta and A. Vannucci, 'Politics, the Mafia and the Market for Corrupt Exchange', in G. Mehrson and G. Pasquino (eds), *Italian Politics. Ending of the First Republic* (Boulder CO, Westview, 1995), pp. 165–84. On the Russian case, see F. Varese, 'The emergence of the Russian mafia' (unpublished D. Phil thesis, Unversity of Oxford, 1996).

[16] D. della Porta and A. Pizzorno, 'The Business Politicians: Reflections from a Study of Political Corruption', in Levi and Nelken, *The Corruption of Politics*, p. 75; D. della Porta, 'Actors in corruption: business politicians in Italy', in *ISSJ, Corruption in Western Democracies*, pp. 349–63.

corruption: insofar as the police operate within the public sector, they may be seen as possessing the potential to engage in political corruption when due legal processes are distorted – but the crucial issue here revolves around the extent to which such distortions are driven or motivated, or even directed, by *political* ends as opposed to personal, private or even corporate ones.

It would be impossible to develop one generalizable and uncontested definition of political corruption.[17] In fact, the entire enterprise is probably misplaced: as Mark Philp indicates in this volume (pp. 436–462), any definition of political corruption presupposes a notion of '*un*corrupt' politics. Such an observation implies normative judgements about the proper nature of politics, and its potential distortion. Philp's chapter highlights the difficulties involved in such an enterprise, but also underlines the need to be aware of how our definition of politics itself will affect our understanding of what political corruption entails. On that basis, it is possible to argue that the meaning of political corruption might vary with the nature of the political system in question. This is not to make an argument in favour of incommensurable relativism, in which it becomes impossible to make comparative judgements across any two political systems; rather, it is to suggest that political corruption in, say, a democratic polity may (or even must) take a very different form (or forms) to that in a non-democracy. The nature, scope and potential of political corruption will vary according to the type of polity in question, and its purposes. Thus, a wide-ranging generic definition can at best provide a starting point for identifying and analysing different *types* of political corruption.

Nonetheless, much of the literature on political corruption has followed Heidenheimer in distinguishing between public office-centred, public interest-centred, and market-centred definitions of political corruption.[18] In fact, only the first two of these really offer *definitions*, which in turn depend on normative – and, therefore, inevitably contestable – judgements as to the scope of public office, or the nature of public interest. In contrast, market-centred approaches, which are usually couched in terminology derived from economic analysis, tend to be more concerned with the mechanics of political corruption (which is viewed as a particular model of agency relationship), and the circumstances under which it becomes possible. To the extent that market-centred approaches offer an explicit definition, it tends to be minimalist or else based on a recourse to legal norms: political corruption occurs when an agent breaks the law in sacrificing the interest of a principal to his or her own benefit. Indeed, illegality is central to many definitions of political corruption, and the argument can be made that it is only by reference to legal norms that a basis for comparative analysis can be provided. Such an approach, however, confronts a two-fold problem: first, laws are not necessarily consistent in interpretation or

Alatas has observed that much political corruption is characterized by a dual and contradictory element: when engaging in bribes and backhanders, political officials and businesses may also be fulfilling their legitimate functions.

[17] See Michael Johnston, 'The search for definitions: the vitality of politics and the issue of corruption', *ISSJ, Corruption in Western Democracies*, pp. 321–35.

[18] Heidenheimer, *Political Corruption*, pp. 4–6. Johansen cites Lowenstein's caustic observation that the typical social science article or book on corruption begins with a definition of corruption and then proceeds to the empirical question without reference to the definition. Elaine R. Johansen, *Political Corruption: Scope and Resources. An Annotated Bibliography* (New York and London, Garland, 1990), p. 35.

application across different countries. What is illegal in one country may not be in another, leading to situations in which similar acts can be defined as corrupt or not according only to where they take place. The financing of political parties provides a good example: the rules on party financing in some countries are much stricter than in others, and there is little doubt that some well-established practices in Britain – such as voluntary private contributions, even from overseas, to party funds – would prompt investigation in several other democracies, as indeed would the existence of 'remunerated directorships' for sitting members of parliament.

Secondly, the recourse to legal norms in definitions of political corruption forgoes any possibility of capturing a more nebulous aspect of the phenomenon, one that depends on an inescapably normative notion of what defines democracy. As was argued above, all democracies must rest on some basic principles, one of which is the public accountability of decision making. The critical importance of this issue is difficult to exaggerate. Democracies depend upon their claim to accountability in a way which fundamentally sets them apart from all non-democracies (many other aspects of a government's activities, such as the elaboration, co-ordination and implementation of public policies, including the distribution of resources, are common to all polities). But accountability can be enforced only if government activity is transparent: citizens cannot hold their elected leaders to account for activities they are unaware of having taken place. This truism highlights one of the central conundrums in constructing a definition of political corruption. It could be argued that one of the most sinister forms of political corruption in a democracy is when the 'democratic transcript' is betrayed: that is, when members of the political class act in such a way as to prevent or circumvent the exercise of accountability, by actively seeking to ensure that the electorate is not properly informed about a given issue.[19] Thus, a case can be made for saying that certain legally-sanctioned uses of the resources of the state in a democracy could be defined as corrupt.

In commenting on the 1984 privatization of British Telecom, which involved an undervaluation of some £1.2 bn when measured by the rise in share prices at the end of the first trading day, John Vickers and George Yarrow observed:

> An important feature of the process is that the gainers know that they have gained, but the losers are less aware that they have lost. A windfall profit of £200 on BT shares is much more obvious than the effective loss of £20 to each of ten who failed to apply. John Kenneth Galbraith once remarked that few things enhance the overall feeling of wealth better than undiscovered theft. Without wishing to push the analogy too far, we would suggest that there is a common element in the two cases.[20]

As Alberto Ades and Rafael Di Tella have commented, one possible interpretation of this privatization (and, indeed, others) is that Mrs Thatcher's

[19] The parallel here with Lukes' notion of a third dimension of power – in which its exercise involves the manipulation of perceptions, cognitions and preferences – should be obvious; see Steven Lukes, *Power. A Radical View* (London, Macmillan, 1974). Against this, the argument could of course be made that all democratic governments are ultimately accountable in general elections.

[20] John Vickers and George Yarrow, *Privatization: an Economic Analysis* (Cambridge MA, MIT Press, 1988), p. 180. The example is borrowed from Alberto Ades and Rafael Di Tella, who used it in an unpublished appendix to their contribution in this volume.

government sought to use the state's resources in order to underwrite a massive redistribution of wealth and thereby help its own re-election chances. An alternative interpretation is that underpricing shares ensures wide ownership, which in turn acts as a 'bulwark against socialism' by reducing the likelihood that a future government will be able to re-nationalize the company: the primary objective on this analysis is to promote efficiency in the interests of the state. On this latter interpretation, the motives may be found objectionable – but they can hardly be seen as corrupt; the former interpretation, by contrast, raises much more serious questions about the legitimate ends of a policy designed to serve the best interests of a particular political party rather than the state.

Another approach to defining political corruption which also seeks to avoid recourse to legal definitions argues that it is socially defined: political corruption is what the public in any given state perceives it to be.[21] There are several difficulties with such an approach. First, it relies on public opinion being aware that actions which might be deemed corrupt are actually taking place; as has just been shown, one form of political corruption may involve precisely the attempt to keep the public from being properly informed about government activity. Secondly, it presupposes that public opinion can be freely expressed on any given issue – a questionable supposition even in democracies, but almost impossible (except perhaps at moments of regime crisis) in non-democracies. It might be argued that the inability freely to express opinions means that non-democracies are inherently corrupt, and therefore the distinction is meaningless. This, though, leads to a third difficulty: the reliance on a social definition of political corruption makes any comparative analysis pointless, since we cannot transpose conceptual definitions which are culture-specific. In Sartori's terms, such concepts do not travel.[22] A fourth problem concerns how we are to decide whose public opinion counts: for instance, does a simple majority suffice? Does the opinion of those closest to the event in question count more than that of those who are more distant? Again, recent experience in Britain provides a good example of the complex issues involved: opinion was clearly divided on whether the acceptance of cash for asking parliamentary questions was corrupt or not. As Dawn Oliver shows (pp. 539–558), the setting up of the Nolan Committee in November 1994 reflected a growing public concern, which had developed over some two decades, about standards of conduct in public life – but the distinction between 'ethical lassitude', sleaze and corruption was far from clear-cut.

Perception is clearly important. Heidenheimer drew a distinction between three types of corruption: one which is accepted and tolerated, its opposite, which is widely rejected and criticized, and intermediate forms which elicit different responses from different groups.[23] In practice, it is difficult to make

---

[21] Thus, 'a political act is corrupt when the weight of public opinion determines it so', Barry Rundquist and Susan Hansen, 'On controlling official corruption: election vs. laws' (unpublished manuscript, 1976), cited in Kate Gillespie and Gwenn Okruhlik, 'The political dimensions of corruption cleanups. A framework for analysis', *Comparative Politics*, 22/1 (1991), p. 93 (n. 3). See also Gurharpal Singh's chapter in this volume and Robert Williams, 'Watergate to Whitewater: Corruption in American politics', paper presented at 47th annual conference of the Political Studies Association of the UK, University of Ulster at Jordanstown (April 1997).

[22] Giovanni Sartori, 'Concept misformation in comparative politics', *American Political Science Review*, 54 (1970), 1033–53.

[23] Heidenheimer, *Political Corruption*, pp. 26–8. See also A. J. Heidenheimer, 'Perspectives on the Perception of Corruption', in Heidenheimer *et al.*, *Political Corruption*, pp. 149–64.

such clear-cut distinctions; on close inspection, corruption tends to fall within the intermediate category:

> The practice of giving gifts, regulated or forbidden in Europe in dealings between civil servants and private individuals, can be perfectly acceptable and integrated within African or Asian customs. Not offering a gift, or not ensuring that one's family, circle of friends or clan benefit from the advantages given by one's power and connections, can be just as shocking in some societies as accepting favours or bribes in others.[24]

Transparency International (TI), in association with Göttingen University, produces an annual Corruption Ranking, based on *perceptions* by people 'working for multinational firms and institutions' of the level to which corruption impacts on social and commercial life.[25] In spite of their somewhat disingenuous remark that '[t]heir perceptions may not always be a fair reflection on the state of affairs, but they are reality', the authors argue that the ranking tries to assess the degree to which public officials and politicians in particular countries are involved in corrupt practices. Corruption is defined by TI as being 'the misuse of public power for private benefits, e.g. the bribing of public officials, taking kickbacks in public procurement or embezzling public funds'. However, the index provides no evidence to indicate that those polled are operating with the same concept of corruption; nor, indeed, does it make a compelling case for privileging the views of those working for multinational firms and institutions. Nevertheless, the rankings produced by TI are widely cited and can be highly influential.[26]

It is clear that there exists a series of different forms and kinds of political corruption with a range of characteristics, which need to be mapped. The construction of a comprehensive taxonomy may run the risk of sacrificing analytical purchase for descriptive detail, but is probably an essential first step in providing a basis for meaningful comparison. Some such attempts have been made. Alatas, for instance, developed a broad-ranging typology on the basis of a minimalist definition: 'corruption is the abuse of trust in the interest of private gain'. He distinguishes between 'transactive' and 'extortive' corruption.[27] The former refers to a mutual arrangement between a donor and a recipient, actively pursued by, and to the mutual advantage of, both parties, whereas the latter entails some form of compulsion, usually to avoid some form of harm being

---

[24] Yves Mény and Martin Rhodes, 'Illicit Governance: Corruption, Scandal and Fraud', in Rhodes *et al.*, *Developments in West European Politics*, p. 98.

[25] The index is prepared on the basis of ten sources which include surveys prepared by the Institute of Management Development in Lausanne, Political and Economic Risk Consultancy in Hong Kong, Impulse, DRI/McGraw-Hill Global Risk Service, Political Risk Services in New York, and Göttingen University's own perception index which is based on *anonymous responses* to its internet service. In some cases, sample sizes are as small as 3 respondents per country (Impulse), 74 and 95 respondents across 10 and 12 Asian countries respectively (Political and Economic Risk Consultancy), and 190 respondents to Göttingen University's own perception index.

[26] As TI has commented, 'Our Corruption Index gained astonishing coverage worldwide'. A paper by Laurence Busse, Noboru Ishikawa, Morgan Mitra, David Primmer, Kenneth Doe and Tolga Yaveroglu of the Goizueta Business School at Emory University argues that there is a significant relationship between foreign direct investment and perceptions of corruption by potential investors: foreign investment is found to rise and fall according to whether exposure is followed by institutional reform. The paper is available via < http://userwww.service.emory.edu/ ~tyavero/ip/project2.html >.

[27] Alatas, *Corruption*, ch. 1.

inflicted on the donor or those close to him/her. Other types of corruption revolve around, or are the by-products of, transactive and extortive corruption. *Defensive* corruption is obviously related inversely to the extortive type, whilst *investive* corruption involves the offer of goods or services without any direct link to a particular favour, but with a view to future situations in which a favour may be required. *Nepotistic* corruption refers to the unjustified appointment of friends or relatives to public office, or according them favoured treatment. *Autogenic* corruption involves just one person, who profits, for example, from pre-knowledge of a given policy outcome. Finally, *supportive* corruption describes actions undertaken to protect and strengthen existing corruption, often through the use of intrigue (as in US machine politics) or else through violence. One advantage of Alatas' schema is that it offers a clear definition of corruption which is neither rule-bound, nor tied to society's prevailing moral conventions or norms. Extortive and transactive corruption can be identified in both complex and simple societies.

It is not difficult to conceive of other categories which could contribute to a typology of political corruption: distinctions could be drawn between high and low level ('grand' corruption versus 'petty'); the local and national level (the former being site of widespread corruption in regard, for instance, to municipal public works contracts); between personal and institutional corruption (that is, between corruption aimed at personal enrichment and that which seeks to benefit an institution such as a political party); between traditional and modern forms of corruption (for instance, nepotism and patronage versus money laundering through electronic means); and so forth.[28] Given the difficulties involved in stipulating a satisfactory definition of political corruption, as well as the inevitably normative nature of any such attempt, it is incumbent upon analysts not just to be aware, but also explicit, about the framework within which they are operating, and to be particularly sensitive to issues of cultural nuance. However, armed with an appropriate and suitably parsimonious generic conception of political corruption, it is possible to turn to the more empirical issues of how and why it occurs.

On the Causes of Corruption

The complexity of the phenomenon makes it impossible to provide a comprehensive account of the causes of political corruption. However, some central analytical issues can be outlined. A question which inevitably arises is why some countries appear more prone than others to political corruption: are there cultural causes of corruption, or does the emergence of political corruption depend upon more institutional factors? One possible response is to formulate the issue in terms of structure and agency. In such an approach, 'embedded local cultures' might be seen as a structural given: thus, rather than an appeal to some conception of national character, the nature of social practices in a country can be seen as a reflection of the long-term development and organization of its social and political system. In Europe, a divide is sometimes drawn between the

---

[28] Anthony Barker has sought to classify nearly 150 scandals in 20 democracies according to whether or not they relate to public duties; are lawful or unlawful; involve lapses in ethical or moral standards; involve politicians, public servants or private individuals; and how they are investigated. See 'The upturned stone: political scandals and their investigation processes in twenty democracies', *Crime, Law & Social Change*, 21 (1994), 337–73.

PAUL HEYWOOD   427

more corrupt southern states (Italy, Spain, Greece) and their less corrupt northern neighbours (particularly, Scandinavia, the Netherlands and Britain). As Mény and Rhodes have argued, institutional settings breed certain types of relationship and social practice – for example, the '*l'arrangiarsi*' of the Italians or '*l'arrangement à la française*'.[29] Similarly, Paul Hutchcroft (pp. 639–658) explores the development of formal structures of authority and shows how particular practices have become culturally embedded over the course of generations in South East Asia.

The 'structural' approach to political corruption places particular emphasis on the nature of state development. Administrative organization and efficiency are key variables, alongside the manner in which the political order becomes institutionalized. If the processes of social and political exchange are clearly separated from those of political and economic exchange, the penetration of politicians into bureaucratic structures becomes more difficult. In Britain, which has often been seen as free of endemic political corruption, one possible contributory factor may be the early institutionalization of its political parties and party system, separate from the administrative structure. In other European countries, notably those in the south, particularistic and personalized social structures remained in place as financially poor and administratively inefficient central states were forced to rely on 'regional brokers' at local level. In most of Mediterranean Europe, where the central state was weak, these regional brokers – *mafiosi* in Italy, *caciques* in Spain, *comatarhis* in Greece – mediated between centre and periphery on the basis of patronage networks which served as an important mechanism of social order. Strong patron-client networks ensured that the flow of favours and benefits was anchored in personal relations between individuals, a system which the deficiencies of the state administration ensured was largely self-perpetuating. Naturally, there are enormous variations in the nature of state development – even within Europe, let alone throughout other continents[30] – and it would be foolish to place too much weight on the inter-penetration of administrative and political structures as the principal explanatory factor in the incidence of political corruption. Nevertheless, the existence of strongly entrenched clientelistic networks may contribute to the development of a path dependency, in which it becomes almost impossible to escape from what Donatella della Porta has described as the 'vicious circles' of clientelism-corruption-clientelism and poor administration-corruption-poor administration.[31]

Della Porta has also distinguished in the Italian case between traditional forms of clientelism, involving localized relationships between patrons and clients, and clientelistic networks, which are linked to broad institutional contexts. This distinction highlights how forms of political corruption have changed and developed over time; it also links to an agency-based approach to explaining the causes of political corruption – one that rests on analysing the

[29] Mény and Rhodes, 'Illicit Governance', p. 103.

[30] See the thoughtful essay on 'bossism' and state formation in South East Asia by John T. Sidel, 'Siam and its twin? Democratization and bossism in contemporary Thailand and the Philippines', *IDS Bulletin*, 27/2 (1996), 56–63.

[31] For a detailed exposition, see Donatella della Porta, 'The vicious circles of corruption in Italy', in Della Porta and Mény, *Democracy and Corruption*, pp. 35–49. Della Porta's analysis draws out the relationship between the internal mechanisms of corruption and other 'pathologies' in Italy, such as clientelism, poor administration and organized crime.

motivations of those who become involved in political corruption. There are several variants of such an approach. One view is that the sense of public ethos which used to be highly developed amongst those who entered politics has been dissipated by the rise of a class of more self-interested (and therefore less ideologically motivated) 'career politicians'. Venality is hardly a recent phenomenon in politics, but the emergence of so-called 'business politicians', as described above, reflects a perceived tendency for a growing number to enter politics primarily for personal gain. A similar trend in North American politics was earlier identified by Rogow and Lasswell, who referred to 'gain politi- cians' – party bosses with little interest in national political issues.[32] An altern- ative perspective suggests that the low levels of financial reward for many in the public sector provides an impetus to engage in corruption: it follows that political corruption should be lower where financial rewards and incentives are highest. In fact, as Ades and Di Tella indicate (pp. 496–515), the evidence on this issue is far from clear-cut: in Singapore, for instance, which is often seen as relatively free of corruption, it is difficult to determine whether this is because of the very high salaries paid to public officials, or because of tough law enforcement measures.

An influential view, which derives mainly from within the discipline of economics, sees political corruption largely as the product of growing state intervention.[33] As the public sector has grown, particularly through an expansion of the welfare state, so ever more decisions – as well as control over ever greater financial resources – have been transferred into the hands of the political class. Instead of being subject to the discipline of market mechanisms, allocative decisions are bound by a series of rules and regulations which create incentives for both private individuals and public officials to circumvent them. The focus on personal motivation which is characteristic of such approaches tends to situate them within public choice theory, with an underlying emphasis on agency expressed through the methodologically individualistic belief in rational agents engaging in utility-maximizing behaviour. At one level, the proposition that market competition should reduce incentives to engage in political corruption appears persuasive; indeed, as Ades and Di Tella demon- strate, it finds empirical support in certain circumstances. If political corruption involves public officials acting either partly or wholly within the public sphere, then the more that decision-making capacity over resource allocation is removed from that sphere, the fewer should be the opportunities to engage in political corruption. It follows that privatization and deregulation should serve as powerful antidotes to political corruption.

In practice, the evidence is far from clear-cut. Mény and Rhodes have emphasized the importance of exploring 'political opportunity structures' in analysing variations in political corruption.[34] These refer to the institutional

---

[32] A. A. Rogow and H. D. Lasswell, 'Game Politicians and Gain Politicians', in J. A. Gardiner and D. J. Olson (eds), *Theft of the City* (Bloomington IN, Indiana University Press, 1974), pp. 289– 97.

[33] Susan Rose-Ackerman, *Corruption: a Study in Political Economy* (New York, Academic, 1978).

[34] The term is borrowed from Herbert Kitschelt, 'Political opportunity structures and political protest', *British Journal of Political Science*, 16: 1 (1986), 57–85, where it was used in a very different context; see Mény and Rhodes, 'Illicit Governance', p. 100. The argument developed here draws closely on Mény and Rhodes.

PAUL HEYWOOD 429

arrangements of political and administrative power: the extent to which they are transparent, open, subject to effective pressure, and so forth. Opportunity structures do not remain constant, but evolve over time in response to exogenous pressures. Amongst the most significant recent pressures – certainly in western democracies – are those which have derived from transnational developments, often associated with globalization or internationalization. In economic terms, restructuring has affected the nature of production and trade, the operation of financial markets, and the provision of services. The global economy places a premium on information, thereby privileging certain key posts at the interface of public and private sectors: the opportunities for insider trading and market manipulation have been transformed through processes of financial deregulation. It has become possible to organize transactions of extraordinary complexity, creating in turn new possibilities for a black market in corruption to flourish.[35]

In institutional terms, recent transformations have been equally profound. Alongside changes in regulatory mechanisms, which have become increasingly independent of national governments, the decline in influence of representative organizations such as political parties and trade unions, and the transfer of decision-making authority both upwards through transnational organizations (for instance, the European Union) and downwards through decentralization, the division between the public and private spheres has become increasingly blurred. One factor which has contributed to this development has been privatization. Rather than create a clear distinction between public and private sectors, privatization programmes have often been characterized by the emergence of a series of quasi-governmental regulatory agencies, quangos and 'third sector' organizations (voluntary, non-profit or charitable organizations which have become 'the private agents of public policy'). This process of 'agencification', linked to the doctrine of 'new public management', has created significant opportunity structures for influence-peddling, as well as removing many regulatory agencies from direct public accountability.[36] Similarly, public administrations in many western democracies have been faced with public choice onslaughts which have transformed organizational structures, shifting the emphasis away from due process (ensuring that all citizens benefit from respect for the rules) towards efficiency and output. Again, these changes have increased the scope for discretionary action, and – as Dawn Oliver underlines (pp. 539–558) – have further blurred the divide between public and private spheres.

Such developments cannot be divorced from the ideological context of the 1980s and early 1990s, in which the prevailing *Zeitgeist* devalued the state and public provision in favour of the market. This ideologically-driven approach perhaps reached its apogee in western responses to the former communist regimes of the Soviet bloc, in which aid was made conditional upon a transition to free-market mechanisms within an almost impossible time-scale. As Federico Varese demonstrates (pp. 579–596), the imposition of market mechanisms in

[35] See Yves Mény, ' "Fin de siècle" corruption: change, crisis and shifting values', in *ISSJ, Corruption in Western Democracies*, pp. 309–20.

[36] See Alan Doig and John Wilson, 'Contracts and UK local government: old problems, new permutations', paper presented at 47th annual conference of the Political Studies Association of the UK, University of Ulster at Jordanstown (April 1997). Doig and Wilson conclude that, 'In reality, the risks of corruption are greater under contracting out'.

the absence of adequate legal underpinnings created plentiful opportunities for rampant corruption in post-Soviet Russia.[37] Yet, even if Russia represents an extreme case, the exaltation of the market in established democracies has also engendered a certain disdain for regulatory mechanisms and established rules of conduct. In contrast, therefore, to those who see state regimentation and bureaucracy as the principal cause of corruption, it is equally plausible to make the case that deregulation has helped blur the lines between public and private spheres, whilst the emphasis on the market, competitiveness and profit has devalued a 'sense of state'. The belief in the pre-eminence of the market has spread across much of the globe: neo-liberal values, which first took firm hold in the USA under Reagan and the UK under Thatcher, have become dominant in most of Europe, most of Latin America, much of Asia (where the dramatic success of Japan and the 'tiger' economies has provided a further boost), and even parts of Africa. The introduction of new models of economic organization, which (as in the case of the former communist countries) has often been dramatic, has created new opportunity structures for engaging in political corruption. As Varese suggests, corrupt entrepreneurs have exploited the uncertainty associated with the transition to the market no less ruthlessly than corrupt officials exploited their control of the state apparatus under communist regimes.[38]

Much of the discussion so far has centred on the motivations and opportunity structures for individual actors to become involved in political corruption. Attention should also be devoted, however, to more institutional factors. In particular, the financing of political parties, and the funding of elections (especially in the USA and Japan), have become issues of central concern in relation to political corruption. Many of the major scandals in democracies in recent years have been linked in some way to campaign or party finance. The democratic political process costs money – in ever increasing amounts. Regulations over the funding of political parties and electoral campaigns vary widely, but in all democracies there has been an inexorable upward trend in election expenditure.[39] There are several reasons for the increasing cost of politics, the most obvious of which is the ever greater reliance on television advertising as a means of communicating with the electorate. In addition, fees to political consultants and expenditure on fund-raising initiatives have spiralled. Yet, the rise of the age of 'mediacracy' has occurred in parallel with a secular decline in membership of political parties: where once parties relied heavily on their activists for both subscriptions and voluntary work, they are now more dependent on expensive professional campaign teams, their approach

---

[37] See also Susan Rose-Ackerman, 'Democracy and "grand" corruption', in *ISSJ, Corruption in Western Democracies*, pp. 365–80.

[38] Johnston, 'Corruption, markets and reform' sees the connection between the rise of markets and the growth of corruption as particularly pressing in transitional periods: 'rapid change produces strange new connections between wealth and power, and people are confronted with new values and problems, opportunities and temptations', (p. 3).

[39] See C. Malamud and E. Posada-Carbó (eds), *Financing Party Politics in Europe and Latin America* (London, Macmillan, 1997). Susan Rose-Ackerman makes the point in this regard that 'Politicians who expect to lose may be corruptible due to their insecure tenure in office that is the hallmark of a well-functioning democracy', 'Democracy and "grand" corruption', p. 378.

largely driven by the 'Americanization' of the political process in most democracies.[40]

Even in periods between elections, political parties find themselves engaged in ever more costly battles to maintain a high public profile. In short, parties are over-extended and under-resourced. It is inevitable that they should seek to exploit all avenues in the search for funds. Which avenues are open will of course depend on prevailing regulations in any given country, but the search for additional revenue exerts an enormous pressure on political parties to find ways of circumventing, or at least bending, the rules. Public financing of parties or campaigns, once seen as a potential solution to the problem of escalating expenditure, appears to have little impact on the drive to seek out extra funds. In Europe, there have been several instances of 'parallel financing', such as the URBA case in France or the Filesa scandal in Spain, whereby bogus companies have been established to channel funds to parties by selling fictitious consultancy services; in the USA, concern has been expressed that political action committees (PACs) have changed from their original conception of being grass-roots groups, to working for special interests. The impact of the escalation in the costs of the democratic political process naturally varies according to the nature of the polity in question. In countries where candidates cannot rely on big party machines to cover most of their campaign costs, such as the USA and Japan, entry costs become much higher and the search for funds by candidates correspondingly more intense. Equally, in newly-established democracies political parties often have to subordinate the drive for membership to the search for votes, further increasing the need to secure funding from all means available. In practice, several of the corruption scandals which have emerged in Europe in recent years have involved political parties engaging in secret financing, rather than individuals seeking personal benefit.

Another potential cause of political corruption which merits attention is longevity in power, or at least the feeling that political power is not threatened by realistic challengers or alternatives. In non-democracies, the lack of formal independent mechanisms whereby power can be meaningfully challenged opens multiple possibilities for corruption by government officials and bureaucrats. In democracies, on the other hand, the institutional structures of the 'state of law' are designed to ensure public accountability. In practice, where governments come to feel that their hold on power is unassailable, the distinction between government and state can become blurred in the eyes of those in power, with the consequent risk of acting as if above the law. The Socialist Party in Spain under Felipe González, which ruled from 1982 until 1996, was often accused of arrogance in power and disdain for due processes, culminating in the so-called GAL scandal, whereby the government was alleged to have used reserve funds to set up death squads which executed members of the Basque separatist group, ETA. The Conservative government in the UK, in power from 1979 until 1997, was accused of presiding over a decline in ethical standards in public life, ultimately resulting in one former minister being challenged by an independent anti-corruption candidate, supported by both main opposition parties, at the 1997 general election. The Christian Democrats in Italy and the Japanese Liberal Democrats retained national hegemony for more than a generation

---

[40] Kay Lawson and Peter H. Merkl (eds), *When Parties Fail* (Princeton NJ, Princeton University Press, 1988); see also Sue Pryce, *Presidentialising the Premiership* (London, Macmillan, 1997).

before corruption scandals led to their downfall. In Mexico, the bizarrely titled Party of Institutional Revolution (PRI) has monopolized national power for over 60 years, its political dominance held together by 'the cement of corruption'.[41] This argument needs to be treated with some caution, however: not only can governments in power for short periods equally behave as if above the law (the GAL were set up in 1983, less than a year after the Spanish Socialists came to power), but also not all those which hold power for extended periods succumb to the danger of arrogance.

On Processes of Political Corruption

The discussion so far has centred on definitions and causes of political corruption. However, some of the most interesting recent research has been conducted on what might be termed the processes of political corruption. Several of the chapters in this volume analyse how political corruption operates, and how it is experienced – both from a theoretical point of view and on the basis of case-studies. Jean Cartier-Bresson (pp. 463–476) discusses the emergence of institutionalized socio-economic networks of corruption. These networks serve as a system of hybrid co-ordination for the exchange of widely diverse goods and services (which can be economic, political, social, symbolic and so forth). They also create standards – which are largely non-monetary or non-material – by which to measure these exchanges, and promote a value system which goes beyond the principles of purely market relationships. Cartier-Bresson investigates which organizational forms promote an expansion of corruption and encourage individuals to abandon legal frameworks in favour of corruption networks which, like all markets, are embedded in social structures. In practice, he contends, corruption networks vary in form not only according to how they are organized, but also according to their location (national, regional) and their activities.

Cristina Bicchieri and John Duffy adopt a game theoretic approach (pp. 477–495) to explain how corruption can become a cyclical phenomenon. They assume that there are two kinds of agent, politicians and contractors, who interact on a regular basis and can choose to be honest or corrupt. For politicians, they argue, generalized corruption represents a Pareto superior state – but with high anticipated initial costs. Contractors are assumed always to prefer the corrupt strategy, as the costs are borne by the politicians, even though generalized corruption is Pareto inferior for them. Over time, the politicians' penalty for corrupt behaviour declines and it is in their interest to become corrupt. In doing so, however, they must compensate contractors for placing them in a prisoner's dilemma, but their capacity to do so will depend on the resources they have built up during the period of 'honest' administration. When they run out of resources, they will be voted out of office. There thus develops a cyclical phenomenon of periods of honest rule followed by periods of generalized corruption, with the transition between the two occurring abruptly and rapidly. Bicchieri and Duffy's model is elegant, although – as with all such approaches – some will inevitably question the initial assumptions upon which it is based.

---

[41] Alan Knight, 'Corruption in Twentieth Century Mexico', in Little and Posada-Carbó, *Political Corruption in Europe and Latin America*, p. 231.

A very different methodology is adopted by Bill Miller, Tatyana Koshechkina and Åse Grodeland (pp. 597–625). They are concerned with low-level corruption, using focus group methods to analyse how citizens in two post-communist countries, Ukraine and the Czech Republic, view their interactions with officials. The data are subjected to both qualitative and quantitative analysis, and reveal that there is a discordance between general perceptions of increased bureaucracy and corruption in the Czech Republic and personal experience, which is much more positive; in Ukraine, by contrast, perceptions and personal experience of corruption have both increased, the result of officials no longer being afraid. These findings provide evidence that, at least from the point of view of citizens in post-communist regimes, the transition to a market economy has done little to reduce low-level corruption – even if the reality was not so bleak as suggested by the received wisdom. Gurharpal Singh (pp. 626–638) demonstrates how values and perceptions of corruption in India have been disrupted, and as a result made more transparent, by the political change and uncertainty which followed the decay of the 'Congress system'.

A case study of a rather different kind is John Peterson's analysis of fraud in the European Union (pp. 559–578), perhaps the first serious academic investigation of an issue which has attracted considerable media attention in recent years. Peterson's chapter demonstrates that political corruption, certainly if defined in terms of a deviation from formal public duties for personal gain, is relatively absent in the European Union. Fraud and waste, on the other hand, are rife.[42] In his explanation of this apparent paradox, Peterson lays stress on the importance of institutional structures: on the one hand, there are high barriers to entry to the EU's highly-trained and efficient bureaucracy, which is financially well rewarded; on the other hand, the institutional architecture of the EU ensures that there are inadequate policy tools with which to fight fraud. National practices remain sacrosanct within a *communautaire* political culture which, as Peterson argues, pools sovereignty but not accountability.

On the Consequences of Political Corruption

Given the difficulties in defining and, in consequence, measuring political corruption, it is unsurprising that there have been few empirical studies into its effects. Whilst most analysts are agreed that political corruption is morally reprehensible, there is far less agreement over its practical consequences – in either political or economic terms. In the 1960s, several analysts working within the framework of 'modernization theory' saw corruption as fulfilling a positive function in developing countries. In these countries, it was argued, corruption could provide a stimulus to investment, promote efficiency, and help cut through bureaucratic red tape and delays.[43] Corruption has often been depicted

---

[42] Fraud is defined by Peterson as 'improper or dishonest behaviour leading to the use of EU resources for unforeseen or unintended purposes', and is distinguished from corrupt activity aimed at personal benefit.

[43] For examples of this literature, best represented by authors such as David Bayley, Samuel Huntington, Nathaniel Leff, and J. S. Nye, see Heidenheimer, *Political Corruption*, part 4: 'Corruption and Modernization', pp. 477–578. Such views remain influential: see Jonathan Moran, 'From developing country to industrial democracy: the political economy of corruption in South Korea', paper presented to 47th Annual Conference of the Political Studies Association, University of Ulster at Jordanstown, April 1997.

as a lubricant, helping to foster social integration as well as economic development by providing a 'hidden incentive' which substitutes for the inadequacy of
official procedures. Paul Hutchcroft's discussion of the impact of rents,
corruption and clientelism on Third World development provides a nuanced
account of the complex issues involved (pp. 639–658): he demonstrates the
importance of assessing 'particular landscapes of special advantage'. In short,
there is no simple or straightforward correlation between corruption and
development in Third World countries.

In recent years, some economists have conducted empirical research into the
relationship between corruption and the components of government expenditure. Paolo Mauro, in particular, has sought to demonstrate systematically that
corruption slows economic growth in a number of ways: it lowers investment
since it acts as form of tax, leads to the misallocation of talent by distorting
incentives, diverts funds away from aid projects in developing countries, reduces
tax revenues to central government with consequent adverse budgetary
consequences, lowers the quality of infrastructure and public services, and
distorts the composition of government expenditure.[44] Alberto Ades and Rafael
di Tella (pp. 496–515) examine some of Mauro's propositions more closely,
notably the claim that there is a negative relationship between corruption and
investment regardless of levels of bureaucratic red tape. They find that, although
high levels of bureaucracy do have a negative impact on investment, the
evidence suggests that corruption acts mainly as sand in the machine rather than
as a lubricant: the level of bureaucracy makes little overall difference. One of
their most significant findings is that attempts to control corruption through
product market competition are most effective in countries where law
enforcement is lax.

A political analysis of the impact of political corruption is provided by
Donatella Della Porta and Alberto Vannucci (pp. 516–538). They argue against
functionalist accounts which stress the efficiency of corruption in short-
circuiting irrational administrative structures. The hypothesis that organizational efficiency is increased by paying a bribe to ensure that certain services are
provided which otherwise would not be (or else would be provided more slowly)
can be challenged on a number of grounds. First, if a service is provided more
quickly to one corrupt purchaser, then another equally deserving potential
recipient will be forced to wait: the advantage to one represents a disadvantage
to the other. Second, the decision-making process is distorted: some decisions
may be changed as a result of corruption, or else decision makers may devote
their energies towards appropriating revenue for personal profit, which is likely
to hamper organizational efficiency. Third, the resulting administrative inefficiency creates more opportunities to engage in corruption, so corrupt
administrators therefore have an interest in maintaining an inefficient system:
organizational structures come to reflect the interests of those who are corrupt.
Thus, even where corruption *appears* to favour efficiency (which must rest on a
definition of efficiency which is tied exclusively to economic ends), it necessarily

---

[44] Paolo Mauro, 'Corruption and growth', *Quarterly Journal of Economics*, 109 (1995), 681–712;
Paolo Mauro, 'The effects of corruption on growth, investment, and government expenditure', *IMF
Working Paper*, 96/98 (1996); Paolo Mauro, *Why Worry about Corruption?* (Washington DC,
International Monetary Fund, 1997). Mauro draws his data on corruption from Political Risk
Services, Inc., which publishes the *International Country Risk Guide*, and from Business
International, part of the Economist Intelligence Unit.

PAUL HEYWOOD   435

produces at the same time forms of inefficiency which negate its positive influence. Moreover, the assertion that corruption can be functional rests on the premise that existing procedures must be inefficient. For Della Porta and Vannucci, therefore, political corruption and maladministration feed upon each other. Political corruption generates social costs, as well as placing an increased burden on public accounts.

Much western political science in the 1960s and early 1970s was characterized by a certain confidence, bordering on condescension, in regard to high-level political corruption: essentially a problem of under-developed and non-democratic nations, its control and eradication depended upon institutional design, with liberal democracy providing the model towards which 'developing' nations would make (inevitable) progress. The contrast with the late 1990s is striking. The western triumphalism which followed the collapse of communism has been replaced by far more apocalyptic scenarios, increasingly pitched in terms of a 'clash of civilizations': confidence in 'westernization' being emblematic of 'modernization' has (at last) been eroded, but in its place has emerged a vision in which western civilization is facing a challenge from the morally integral alternatives of Islamic and Asian-capitalist states.[45] In such a scenario, growing corruption and decadence are symptomatic of western civilization in decline: what we are witnessing may be not so much political corruption *in* western liberal democracies as the political corruption *of* western liberal democracies. The danger of this second scenario should not be dismissed out of hand, but the chapters in this volume suggest a somewhat more sober view. Political corruption may be highly corrosive, especially in democracies, but it has always existed and its continued spread is not inevitable. By analysing how opportunity structures are created, as well as how processes of corruption operate in practice, steps can be taken to reshape institutional design in such ways as to render less favourable to corruption the structures of incentives available to actors. This is of course both an enormous and an eternal challenge, but the chapters which follow can hopefully serve as a contribution to establishing its current dimensions.

---

[45] See Samuel P. Huntington, *The Clash of Civilizations and the Remaking of World Order* (New York, Simon and Schuster, 1996).

[21]

Political Studies (1997), XLV, 639–658

The Politics of Privilege: Assessing the Impact of Rents, Corruption, and Clientelism on Third World Development

PAUL D. HUTCHCROFT*

'I am me,' explains Singaporean Senior Minister Lee Kuan Yew in response to criticism that he derived substantial personal advantage from a recent deal involving luxury condominiums. 'It's not a level playing field.'[1] To be sure, some element of particularistic privilege is found in all political systems – most clearly in those where corruption and rent havens predominate, but even in meritocracies such as that built up by Lee himself during his three decades as Prime Minister. While no 'playing field' is entirely level, however, it is equally obvious that landscapes of special advantage vary enormously in shape from one political economy to another: some varieties of unevenness may actually promote economic growth, while other types of rough terrain seem to pose enormous barriers to sustained development.

This paper takes initial steps toward building a framework able to explain why a range of related phenomena – variously described as rent-seeking, corruption, and clientelism – may be relatively more compatible or relatively more obstructive to the process of Third World development. In doing so, I will highlight how contrasting political settings spawn very different patterns of seeking – and dispensing – particularistic advantage. Moreover, I will seek to demonstrate that the process of creating such a broad framework benefits from an eclectic approach; specifically, it is valuable to draw insights from three literatures, with distinct lineages, that overlap but all too rarely interact: those relating to rents, corruption, and clientelism.

The first section of this paper discusses the utility of drawing on the three major paradigms, and the relative advantages and disadvantages of each in building a broad comparative framework. Second, I propose a preliminary framework for assessing the varying impact of major phenomena described by the literature on rents, corruption, and clientelism, focusing attention on seven

* Thanks to Don Emmerson, Jomo K. S., Mushtaq Khan, Andrew MacIntyre, Amado Mendoza, Jr, T. J. Pempel, Ansil Ramsay, Temario Rivera, and Joel Rocamora – as well as to participants in both a panel of the Association of Asian Studies annual meetings, 11–14 April 1996, Honolulu, Hawaii and the 'Rents and Development in Southeast Asia' workshop, 27–28 August 1996, Kuala Lumpur, Malaysia – for offering comments that contributed to this article. All errors, of course, are mine alone.

[1] *New York Times*, 5 June 1996. Lee was responding to a report that he and his son, Deputy Prime Minister Lee Hsien Loong, accepted discounts of more than $700,000 in a 'soft sale' of condominiums conducted before bids were opened to the public.

elements not fully captured in any one of the paradigms. Together, they examine the variability of the 'take' among comparable acts of corruption, the processes by which advantages are allocated, the way in which gains obtained are invested, the manner in which corruption affects the operation of markets, the impact of corruption on a state's capacity to execute a range of essential developmental tasks, the role that corruption may play in promoting or impeding the institutionalization of both state agencies and political parties, and the relative presence of factors able to mitigate or counterbalance the prevalence of corruption. The conclusion summarizes key lessons, and proposes paths that may be fruitful in further comparative research.

Surveying the Paradigms: Rents, Corruption, and Clientelism

The quest for and allocation of particularistic advantage has long been the subject of academic investigation, but the language and concepts employed in this process of inquiry have varied across time and across disciplines. Each of the major paradigms – rents, corruption, and clientelism – offers important insights to political economists, yet all would be enhanced by a more concerted effort at cross-fertilization. The following is a preliminary attempt to encourage useful hybrids.

The most recent addition to the theoretical repertoire is, of course, the literature on rents that has emerged from economics. The strength of this body of thought is its attention to market processes, and it is not surprising that rent theorists have achieved prominence in an era in which markets are widely praised and governments routinely reviled. Rents are, by definition, created when the state restricts the operations of the market. The processes of rationing foreign exchange, curbing free trade, and licensing some aspect of economic activity – to give just a few examples – serve to create 'rent havens' that can be captured by some combination of well-placed businesspersons and bureaucrats. The fight for privilege, known as rent-seeking, encourages 'directly unproductive profit-seeking' activities – sometimes legal (e.g. lobbying) and sometimes not (e.g., bribery). Overall, the focus is on 'the rent-seeking *society*'; analysis of the specific types of *state* structures in which this behaviour most thrives is commonly thwarted by distrust of states in general. Because rent-seeking is said to be 'directly related to the scope and range of governmental activity in the economy, and to the relative size of the public sector',[2] the solution is self-evident: 'the state's sphere should be reduced to the minimum, and bureaucratic control should be replaced by market mechanisms wherever possible'.[3]

Indeed, a major problem with the rent-seeking literature is its often strong ideological bias. The majority of theorists

> are obsessed with demonstrating the negative impact of government on the economy. They view competitive markets as the most socially efficient means to produce goods and services ... [and] do not treat the

[2] J. M. Buchanan, 'Rent Seeking and Profit Seeking', in J. M. Buchanan, R. D. Tollison and G. Tullock (eds), *Toward A Theory of the Rent-Seeking Society* (College Station, Texas A & M Press, 1980), p. 9.
[3] P. Evans *Embedded Autonomy: States and Industrial Transformation* (Princeton NJ, Princeton University Press, 1995), p. 24.

effects of government intervention as variable, sometimes reducing and sometimes stimulating social waste.[4]

This bias is best refuted by Peter Evans, who points out that many bureaucracies do indeed possess the capacity to restrain rent-seeking tendencies and promote collective effort among individual officeholders; 'strict adherence to a neo-utilitarian logic,' he asserts, 'makes the existence of a collective actor difficult to explain and the nightwatchman state [favoured by neo-utilitarians] a theoretical impossibility'. His analysis of the role of states in economic transformation, moreover, highlights major problems with the assumption that competitive markets 'are sufficient to the kind of structural transformation that lies at the heart of development'.[5]

Ideological bias aside, there are at least four other major deficiencies with much of the rent-seeking literature. First, even if a bureaucracy is pared down to a minimalist role, it is likely to retain ultimate responsibility for such basic tasks as building infrastructure and providing law and order. As long as bureaucrats continue to be tasked with supplying these goods, there remain 'rent havens'. In settings where (to quote Weber) individual bureaucrats can easily 'squirm out of the [bureaucratic] apparatus', the provision of public goods may bring significant opportunities for private profit.[6] Even in a minimalist state, for example, motor vehicle licensing authorities will potentially be able to extract an extra unofficial sum for a scarce resource, and police may be able to transform their public power into lucrative kidnap-for-ransom schemes. Privatization by no means resolves the dilemma: the process of bidding and negotiating with private companies seeking to build and maintain a road, for example, can provide enormous rent havens easily tapped by those with the most favourable political connections. Because rent theorists have little to say about such post-market-shrinking problems, the solution necessarily shifts away from market remedies and toward the realm of politics and public administration.

Second, the literature on rents generally neglects vitally important political elements of government-business relations. As Jomo and Gomez explain, there are major problems with the presumption that rents will be allocated solely according to market processes – and a 'certain irony' that

> the very people who assume that markets have been distorted with the creation of rents also seem to assume the existence of perfectly competitive markets for rent capture involving a fully competitive process. Rent-seeking may, in fact, not be very competitive – due to the clandestine, illegal, closed, exclusive or protected nature of rent capture processes – thus limiting rent-seeking activity and keeping down rent-seeking costs.[7]

The allocation is likely to be based not only on the market but also on a range of non-market considerations, including ethnic, regional, party, and old-school ties. Politics, not the market, provides the best clues to these processes.

[4] M. Levi, *Of Rule and Revenue* (Berkeley and Los Angeles, University of California Press, 1988), p. 24.
[5] Evans, *Embedded Autonomy*, p. 25. Fortunately, as Evans demonstrates, use of a rents framework does not require that one adopt the anti-statist perspective of a neo-utilitarian.
[6] M. Weber, *Economy and Society* (Berkeley and Los Angeles, University of California Press, 1978), p. 987.
[7] Jomo K. S. and E. T. Gomez, 'Rents, Rent Seeking and Rent Deployment in Malaysia'. Unpublished ms., Kuala Lumpur (1995), p. 3.

642 *The Politics of Privilege*

Third, and closely related, is the problem of determining the degree to which rents will be captured either by those in the state and those outside the state. This likely brings in even larger structural considerations, based on analysis of the historical development of state-society relations. Within Southeast Asia, I argue elsewhere, the ' "bureaucratic" capitalism' associated with the former bureaucratic polity of Thailand, for example, needs to be differentiated from the 'booty capitalism' spawned by the oligarchic patrimonial state found in the Philippines. In the first type of rent capitalism, the major beneficiaries of largesse are found in the state; in the latter, major beneficiaries have an independent economic base outside the state.[8]

Fourth, rent theorists rarely make a clear distinction between whether those who compete for advantage are seeking generalizable policy benefits (as when an exporters' association lobbies for reduced tariffs) or particularistic privileges (as when a family conglomerate bribes customs officials for lower duties on a specific importation, or lobbies congresspersons for the construction of a particular road). Taken together – whether lobbying or bribery, general or particularistic – all are seen as examples of unproductive rent-seeking activities.[9] For a purely market-based standpoint, it is no problem to aggregate such activities into one category; from the standpoint of political economy, however, there are certain disadvantages. Because such distinctions are largely reflective of the degree of institutionalization and differentiation of business interests, they are indeed important to those investigating larger questions of political power and future possibilities of political economic transformation. Moreover, because the relative incidence of bribery versus lobbying has an impact on the character of bureaucratic agencies, such distinctions are important to those analysing state capacity to promote developmental goals.

As useful as rent theory can be to understanding the allocation of particularistic advantage, its limitations suggest the need to search elsewhere for additional insights. Studies of corruption may have had their heyday in the era of modernization theory, but it is a mistake to suggest that corruption is merely a 'primitive' way of conceptualizing rent-seeking.[10] It is a distinct paradigm that, over the course of many years, has yielded many important lessons for contemporary analysis. Indeed, it is worthwhile inquiring into why the concept of corruption is often given only cursory scholarly attention – and sometimes eschewed in favour of other conceptual approaches. Because corruption is nearly omnipresent, some analysts seem inclined to treat it as an invariable element of the political economic woodwork; in other words, they are content to note that it exists almost everywhere without inquiring into how it varies in character and impact from one setting to another. Others, quite likely, have shunned the concept because it is more difficult to compile reliable empirical data on the often-shadowy world of corruption (based, quite inconveniently, on the 'what is') than it is to construct abstract models of how rent havens are created in the absence of perfect markets (based on the far

---

[8] P. D. Hutchcroft, *Booty Capitalism: the Politics of Banking in the Philippines* (Ithaca, Cornell University Press, forthcoming 1998).

[9] See for example, A. O. Krueger, 'The political economy of the rent-seeking society', *The American Economic Review*, 64 (1974), 291–303.

[10] Evans, *Embedded Autonomy*, p. 24.

less troublesome investigation of 'what is not').[11] 'Primitive' (i.e., early postwar) language, conceptual complexity, and dilemmas of data-gathering, however, are no excuses for throwing the baby out with the bathwater.

Corruption focuses attention on the public sector and on the distinction between official and private activity. Nye's oft-cited definition is a useful starting point: 'Corruption is behavior which deviates from the formal duties of a public role because of private-regarding (personal, close family, private clique) pecuniary or status gains; or violates rules against the exercise of certain types of private-regarding influence'.[12] With this as a starting point, one is able to go beyond the central concern of rent theorists (how states may distort markets) and move into other important terrain as well (e.g., how markets may distort states).

Theorists of corruption, as a group, cannot be accused of any strong ideological bias; on the contrary, one finds enormous variance in how to approach the issue. In the early days of modernization theory, corruption was commonly condemned on moralistic grounds but rarely accompanied by much careful analysis of its precise consequences (not to mention its causes, mechanics, or remedies). Later 'revisionist' approaches of the late 1960s found that corruption could, at least occasionally and sometimes systematically, have a beneficial impact on a range of important goals: 'nation-building,' economic development, administrative capacity, and democratization.[13] Subsequent literature continues the on-going evaluation of costs and benefits.[14]

Such attention to larger context is at once both a strength and a weakness of this body of literature. On the one hand, it is essential to view corruption as an element of broader political interactions, and understand that the prevalence of bribery may have both benefits as well as costs. On the other hand, in the course

---

[11] As one scholar noted thirty years ago, '[e]stimates of the extent of corruption practices in underdeveloped countries are, expectedly, very imprecise. Rumor abounds, facts are scarce', (D. H. Bayley, 'The Effects of Corruption in a Developing Nation', in A. J. Heidenheimer, M. Johnston and V. T. LeVine (eds), *Political Corruption: a Handbook* (New Brunswick NJ, Transaction, 1989 [1966]), p. 939.

[12] J. S. Nye, 'Corruption and Political Development: a Cost-Benefit Analysis', in Heidenheimer *et al.*, *Political Corruption*, p. 966. Alternative definitions are based on notions of the public interest and public opinion, but by far the most widely accepted definitions are based on legal norms. See the discussions of J. C. Scott, *Comparative Political Corruption* (Englewood Cliffs NJ, Prentice-Hall, 1972), pp. 3–5, and R. Theobald, *Corruption, Development and Underdevelopment* (Durham, Duke University Press, 1990), pp. 1–18.

[13] In 1965, Leys noted that 'the question of corruption in the contemporary world has so far been taken up almost solely by moralists ... Emotionally and intellectually, this seems to be in a direct line of descent from the viewpoint of those missionaries who were dedicated to the suppression of native dancing. The subject seems to deserve a more systematic and openminded approach.' C. Leys, 'What is the Problem about Corruption?', in Heidenheimer *et al.*, *Political Corruption*, pp. 52–3. The term 'revisionist' is derived from Cariño, who argues the need to combine analysis with moral judgements. 'Compare,' she writes, 'the outrage of American scholars against Nixon's indiscretions and their near-approval of more blatantly corrupt regimes in countries where they have worked.' L. V. Cariño, 'Tonic or Toxic: the Effect of Graft and Corruption', in L. Cariño (ed.), *Bureaucratic Corruption in Asia: Causes, Consequences and Controls* (Quezon City: College of Public Administration, University of Philippines, 1986). Among those who perceive at least occasional benefits to corruption are Nye and Scott (Nye, 'Corruption and Political Development'; Scott, *Comparative Political Corruption*); more systematic benefits are asserted in the work of Huntington and Leff: S. P. Huntington, *Political Order in Changing Societies* (New Haven, Yale University Press, 1968); N. H. Leff, 'Economic Development through Bureaucratic Corruption', in Heidenheimer *et al.*, *Political Corruption*.

[14] Cariño, 'Tonic or Toxic'; Theobold, *Corruption*.

of achieving breadth there is sometimes a lack of specificity as to which goals are being included in the cost-benefit analysis. Modernization theory's tendency to conflate distinct goals and presume that 'all good things go together' spills over into the Great Corruption Debate, as rival camps are at times over-eager to declare corrupt behaviour either an overall good or an overall bad. Many scholars who have contributed to this literature, however, are quite explicit as to how costs and benefits need to be evaluated in terms of specific goals.[15]

At the risk of simplifying what is indeed a very large body of work spanning a wide time period – from the earliest distinctions between private and public domains until present – there are at least four other advantages to building on previous studies of corruption. First, as noted above, the very definition of corruption focuses attention on the character of state agencies, specifically the degree to which any given system reflects a clear distinction between a public and a private sphere. The work of Max Weber not only highlights how polities vary enormously in the degree to which such a distinction is recognized, but also how corruption can have a different impact from one setting to another. Unfortunately, the potential for carrying forth Weber's nuanced comparative analysis of the interaction of politics, bureaucratic structures, and economies has been hampered in recent decades by disciplinary overspecialization: economists tend to treat all states as the same, political scientists rarely devote much attention to bureaucratic structures, and public administration specialists all too often ignore the larger political and structural contexts in which their subject agencies are situated.[16]

Second, the corruption literature almost universally recognizes that corruption can be expressed both according to non-market and market factors. Scott explains that

> [a]s ideal types, 'parochial' (nonmarket) corruption is a situation where only ties of kinship, affection, caste, and so forth determine access to the favors of power-holders, whereas 'market' corruption signifies an impersonal process in which influence is accorded those who can 'pay' the most, regardless of who they are. The real world, of course, rarely ever contains such pure cases. The proportion of market to parochial corruption, and hence the pattern of beneficiaries, varies widely among underdeveloped nations.

Modes of payment, he further explains, can be in cash or in kind; in electoral settings, they may of course include delivery of a bloc of votes.[17]

Third, the best of the literature on corruption insists that the concept can only be properly analysed 'within a broader analysis of a regime's political dynamics'.[18] Scott's own analysis leads him to suggest that its impact may at times be expected to have a counter-hegemonic influence by promoting the entry of new forces, but its more 'normal effect ... is to cement together a conservative coalition and hold back or cancel out the effects of growing

---

[15] Nye, 'Corruption and Political Development', J. Waterbury, 'Endemic and planned corruption in a monarchial regime', *World Politics*, 25 (1973) 533–55. Theobald, *Corruption*.

[16] See Fred Riggs' analysis of how 'the gulf between the study of politics and administration ... became institutionalized' both in developed and in developing countries. F. W. Riggs, 'The interdependence of politics and administration', *Philippine Journal of Public Administration*, 31 (1987), 418–38, p. 429.

[17] Scott, *Comparative Political Corruption*, pp. 88–9.

[18] Scott, *Comparative Political Corruption*, p. 6.

PAUL HUTCHCROFT   645

collective demands'.[19] Waterbury concludes that 'endemic and planned corruption' in Morocco 'serves only one "positive" function – that of the survival of the regime. Resources are absorbed in patronage and are drained away from rational productive investment'.[20] Whether or not other theorists agree with such conclusions, the very tendency to focus on how issues of politics and political power are played out among major social forces can be seen as welcome relief in an era in which the realm of macropolitics is often no longer the premier consideration of political economy.

A final advantage of employing the term 'corruption' is that it re-connects academics with real politics and real political discourse. There has probably never been a major political demonstration against rent-seeking, but popular disgust over corruption – the violation of norms based on a distinction between what is public and what is private – has in countless cases nurtured reform movements, provoked riots, and contributed to the downfall of regimes. As long as corruption scandals dominate the headlines of many national newspapers, it seems a worthy objective for academics to continue to investigate such phenomena.

Further political nuance comes from a third major paradigm, clientelism, which is above all a study of relationships of power. Persons of higher social status (patrons) are linked to those of lower social status (clients) in personal ties of reciprocity that can vary in content and purpose across time.[21] Patron-client ties may or may not be corrupt, but 'when a patron occupies a public position or extracts favours from those in public positions, patronage and corruption overlap'.[22] Conversely, purely market corruption has no element of clientelism: it is a one-time transaction lacking in affective ties. Although concrete empirical evidence may be elusive, it is probable that – contrary to the expectations of many economists – purely market corruption is far less common than other variants of corruption. Power and social relationships regularly interact with everyday market relations; in all likelihood, markets of a corrupt nature – involving the complex interplay of private and public spheres – are even more heavily infused with such ties. Integration of the clientelist paradigm into an analysis of the search for particularistic advantage encourages analysts to go beyond both the excessive attention to market transactions often found in economics and the legalistic-formalistic approaches commonly found in the field of public administration.

Along with the other two paradigms, however, clientelist literature generally gives insufficient attention to the role of coercion in the search for particularistic advantage.[23] Since coercion plays a major role in certain forms of corrupt behaviour (especially in extortion and in the delivery of a bloc of votes), it is important to supplement all three paradigms with careful consideration of the often prominent role of violence. Scott tends to treat corruption and violence as alternative expressions of political influence (the former 'a more peaceful route

[19] Scott, Comparative Political Corruption, pp. viii–ix.

[20] Waterbury, 'Endemic and planned corruption', p. 555.

[21] J. C. Scott, 'Patron-Client Politics and Political Change in Southeast Asia', in S. Schmidt et al. (eds), Friends, Followers, and Factions (Berkeley and Los Angeles, University of California Press, 1977 [1972]).

[22] Waterbury, 'Endemic and planned corruption', p. 537.

[23] See J. T. Sidel, 'Coercion, Capital, and the Post-Colonial State: Bossism in the Postwar Philippines', Ph.D thesis, Cornell University (1995), pp. 11–12.

to influence' than the latter),[24] but in practice the two often reinforce each other in quite effective ways. A New York mafioso, for example, may threaten an uncooperative city official with the proverbial 'swim with concrete overshoes' in the East River, or a Philippine influential may utilize state resources (the local police, or temporarily released and heavily armed prison convicts) to strike out at his or her political enemies.

Together, the three paradigms encourage careful analysis of the search for and dispensing of particularistic privilege. Rent literature focuses attention on what happens when state actions distort markets, corruption literature examines how public roles and private influences conflict within state agencies, and clientelism literature encourages clearer analysis of the relationships of power that permeate states, societies, and markets. The next task is to draw on these eclectic sources and begin to build a larger framework in which to analyse more effectively the very diverse impacts of the allocation of particularistic advantage.

Building an Eclectic Theoretical Framework

In varying settings, it was asserted at the outset, the range of related phenomena variously described as rent-seeking, corruption, and clientelism may be relatively more compatible or relatively more obstructive to the process of development. This paper does not aim to provide a generalizable framework able to explain when, where, why, and how the impact may be more or less positive, nor does it seek to provide a comprehensive new typology of the range of phenomena encompassed by these complementary paradigms. Rather, the purpose is to propose a series of initial questions that may build on previous insights – from eclectic sources – and contribute toward the longer term goal of building such a framework and such a typology. In other words, it is a preliminary treatment intended to promote discussion and further refinement of ideas.

There are seven sets of questions, I shall propose, that are useful in beginning to assess the differential impact of rents, corruption, and clientelism. It is important to emphasize that the focus here is *the impact of corruption on economic development*; separate assessments of the impact of corruption would be necessary if other goals (e.g., harmonious inter-ethnic relations, democracy, or political stability) are to be considered. Distinct analysis would also be required if one is investigating the causes or mechanics of corruption, or optimal strategies to curb the phenomenon.

Is Corruption Relatively More Variable or Calculable?

A key factor in understanding the diverging impact of corruption and bribery on capitalist growth, Weber suggests, is the variability of the phenomena: they have the 'least serious effect' when calculable, and become most onerous when fees are 'highly variable' and 'settled from case to case with every individual official.' Indeed, if bribery is a calculable element of a business firm's environment, its impact is no different than a tax; to the extent that a firm must devote major effort to negotiating each bribe, on the other hand, there is a high degree of unpredictability in the amount of time and resources to be expended. Overall,

[24] Scott, *Comparative Political Corruption*, pp. 34–5.

Weber expected that advanced forms of capitalism relied upon 'the rational, predictable functioning of the legal and administrative agencies'.[25] If correct, a major obstacle to the development of more sophisticated forms of capitalist accumulation is not corruption *per se*, but highly variable corruption.

What sort of polities are most likely to spawn highly variable types of corruption? Analysis of this questions begins with Rudolph and Rudolph's important distinction between authority (the formal roles conferred upon individuals in their official capacities) and power (when incumbents pursue 'values, interests, and goals of their own choosing that conflict with those of the administrative structure').[26] Few would disagree with Scott's observation, over two decades ago, that '[n]ominally modern institutions such as bureaucracies and political parties in Southeast Asia are often thoroughly penetrated by informal patron-client networks that undermine the formal structure of authority'.[27] For present purposes, it is worthwhile building on previous scholarship and examining further two key aspects of the interaction of power and authority within bureaucracies and parties.

First, what are the relative strengths of informal and formal power? Clearly, the formal structures of authority are stronger in some national settings than others; within any national administrative apparatus, as well, some agencies exhibit clearer lines of formal authority than others. By definition, the stronger the formal authority relative to informal networks the less prevalent will be the incidence of corruption.

Second, it is important to examine the process by which the power and authority interact: do patron-client networks tend to coincide with formal lines of authority, or do they constitute a competing source of orders and inducements? Higher degrees of coincidence, I propose, are likely to yield more predictable forms of corruption; conversely, the greater the degree of divergence between power and authority, the more variable is the form of corruption that is likely to emerge.[28]

In the former (pre-1980s) Thai bureaucratic polity, for example, formal bureaucratic authority was well developed and informal networks of power and formal status overlapped to a large degree;[29] in such a system, businesspersons were likely to have a good sense of whom to approach and what to expect from one transaction to another. In the Philippines, by contrast, lines of formal authority are weaker and the disjuncture between authority and power is often quite pronounced. In this loosely structured system, where patrons are as often found outside formal structures of authority as within them, there is likely less

[25] Weber, *Economy and Society*, pp. 240, 1095.

[26] L. I. Rudolph and S. H. Rudolph, 'Authority and power in bureaucratic and patrimonial administration: a revisionist interpretation of Weber on bureaucracy', *World Politics* 31 (1979) 195–227, p. 198.

[27] Scott, 'Patron-Client Politics'.

[28] Scott concurs that more predictable corruption is 'less likely to seriously retard economic growth'. Not only is the price more certain, but there is also greater 'probability of receiving the paid-for "decision" '. This type of corruption is more likely when: (a) 'The political and bureaucratic elites are strong *and* cohesive' and (b) 'Corruption has become "regularized" – even institutionalized after a fashion – by long practice' (Scott, *Comparative Political Corruption*, pp. 90–1). These insights, I will seek to demonstrate, are strengthened by analysis of the relationship between power and authority.

[29] J. L. S. Girling, *Thailand: Society and Politics* (Ithaca, Cornell University Press, 1981), pp. 37–8, 42.

regularization of corruption from one case to another. As Rose-Ackerman describes her category 'disorganized' bureaucracy,

> the official chain of command is unclear and constantly shifting and the decision-making criteria are similarly arbitrary and unknown ... While corrupt bureaucrats may be willing to accept bribes, applicants cannot be sure that officials have the power to perform their side of the bargain. Chaotic legal procedures increase the *demand* for more certain illegal ones, but if the disorganization of government is far advanced, no bureaucrats may be able to *supply* the requisite certainty even when offered a monetary incentive'.[30]

To what extent are rents 'dissipated' in the course of their allocation? In other words, to what extent (if at all) are resources wasted in processes that determine who obtains particularistic advantage?

Analysis of corruption and rents has focused considerable attention on the process by which particularistic privileges are allocated, but has unfortunately achieved little consensus as to the impact of these processes on development. Key elements of inquiry, as we shall see, involve the extent to which allocation is competitive and degree to which it generates efficiency.

Many economists – ever faithful to market processes – begin with the presumption that bureaucrats will allocate scarce resources such as licenses and other favours via 'competitive bidding among entrepreneurs'. Leff argues that within such a system 'favours will go to the most efficient producers, for they will be able to make the highest bids which are compatible with remaining in the industry'.[31] A decade later, Krueger developed a model which also tends to presume that that bidding will be competitive – but came to the opposite conclusion about efficiency. Competition for rents diverts resources toward such unproductive activities as lobbying and bribery, and in the end generates welfare costs for society as a whole.[32]

As discussed above, however, it is quite problematic to suppose that the allocation of privilege will be decided according to market processes. The recognition that rents can be allocated according to either market or non-market processes has led some neoclassical economists to propose – with further irony – that limits on competition might actually yield higher levels of efficiency. As paraphrased by Mendoza, these economists have argued that since less competition over the allocation of rents is considered less wasteful, 'the least wasteful situation is one where an absolute dictator who will brook no complaint will dispense rents as he sees fit'.[33] Campos argues that the costs of

[30] S. Rose-Ackerman, 'Which Bureaucracies are Less Corruptible?', in Heidenheimer *et al.*, *Political Corruption*, pp. 805, 816. Legal procedures, in fact, may be intentionally obscured in order to heighten the demand for illegal services. In such a system, moreover, those with specialized powers to interpret often opaque rules (i.e., lawyers) will likely play a prominent role.

[31] Leff, 'Economic Development', pp. 396–7, 393.

[32] Krueger, 'Political economy', pp. 292, 195.

[33] A. M. Mendoza, Jr, 'Notes for a Second Look at Rent-Seeking, Profit-Making, and Economic Change in the Philippines'. Unpublished ms, Quezon City (1995), p. 13.

directly unproductive profit-seeking (DUP) activities will 'likely be smaller in an environment in which only a limited elite can acquire rents'.[34]

Jomo and Gomez suggest, similarly, that 'the existence of rents, in itself, does not necessarily result in rent-seeking behaviour.' Because 'certain political groups, individuals, or institutions usually have much more influence on or even hegemony over the state,' some will likely do better than others in the process of securing advantage. Knowing that there is indeed 'uneven access to opportunities for rent capture,' many parties will not even bother to enter the market.[35] It is thus useful to make an analytical distinction between two broad forms of allocation: 'rent-seeking' and 'rent deployment.' Rents are sometimes obtained by persons or groups that actively seek out the advantage, and in other cases deployed from above to persons or groups who exert relatively little effort. To the extent that rents are deployed rather than sought after, there may in fact be far fewer wasted resources in the process of rent allocation than is commonly presumed.[36]

Just as Scott suggests that there are likely few cases of pure 'market' or pure 'non-market' corruption, so also are there likely few cases of pure 'competitive rent-seeking' or pure 'rent deployment'. A given claimant, for example, might have close affective ties to those who allocate privileges, and still have to expend considerable effort and resources to ensure that (a) the allocator does not forget to take care of what that claimant thinks is his/her due; and (b) this claimant's needs are taken care of before other claimants whose affective ties with the allocator are equally close. In short, both market versus non-market corruption as well as rent-seeking versus rent deployment are best conceived of as continua, across which one finds varying combinations of the two 'pure' types.

Overall, we can expect that the centralization of authority and/or power within a political economy will encourage a greater degree of rent deployment and a lesser degree of rent seeking. Rent deployment, in turn, seems likely to promote relatively less dissipation than rent-seeking and thus have the potential for more positive (or less detrimental) outcomes from the standpoint of development. Despite the considerable attention that these issues have received in the rents literature, however, it is quite likely that other elements of analysis may prove far more important in assessing developmental outcomes.

Once Gains from Corruption and Rents are Obtained, How are they Invested?

Whereas the previous question focuses attention of the processes by which rents are allocated, this question focuses attention on the purpose to which rents –

---

[34] J. E. L. Campos, 'The "Political Economy of the Rent-Seeking Society" Revisited: Cronyism, Political Instability, and Development', unpublished ms, Washington DC (1992), p. 15; see also Krueger, 'Political economy', p. 301 and E. S. De Dios, 'Parcellised capital and underdevelopment: a reinterpretation of the specific-factors model', *Philippine Review of Economics and Business*, 30 (1993), 141–55, p. 154. Other neo-classical economists, notes Mendoza in his review of the literature, acknowledge that rent-seeking is not always competitive yet nonetheless 'assert that a more competitive situation will reduce waste associated with rent-seeking' (Mendoza, 'Notes for a Second Look', p. 13).

[35] Jomo and Gomez, 'Rents, Rent Seeking and Rent Deployment', pp. 3–4.

[36] Jomo and Gomez do not provide a definition for their passing reference to the term 'rent deployment' (in their title as well as on pp. 21 and 22). I may be employing the term in a somewhat different sense than they originally intended, but I have taken the liberty to retain the term because it best suggests a systematic, purposive allocation of rents. The basic distinction between two types of rent allocation, however, derives from their discussion.

once obtained – are employed.[37] It has long been recognized not only that one of the 'benefits' of corruption may be to promote rapid capital accumulation, but also that one must inquire as to whether the capital itself is invested in productive ways.[38] At one end of the continuum, an entrepreneur invests his or her gains in a high-value-added industry that creates a great many positive externalities to the rest of the economy; at the other end of the continuum, advantages are hustled out of the country and into Swiss banks and Manhattan real estate.

There is no reason to expect that rents sought after in competitive environments will necessarily result in more productive investment than those that have been deployed. On the other hand, in the event that rents are deployed there is no reason to expect that either deployers – or those who obtain rents via deployment – are necessarily going to be interested in promoting productive investment. As asserted above, one must look at the larger context in which rents are allocated. I propose that there are at least three key variables to examine in assessing the productivity of privileges obtained: (1) what are the motivations of those who allocate and obtain privileges?; (2) presuming that rents are allocated in order to promote developmental goals, what is the capacity of the state to enforce or promote productivity criteria?; and (3) how secure is the environment in which a given entrepreneur is operating?

The motivations of those who obtain privileges through competitive rent-seeking are likely impossible to evaluate with any precision: some will be inclined to productive investment and some will not. In the case of deployment, however, one is by definition evaluating a systematic effort toward a clear objective. The nature of the objective, however, may have little to do with the promotion of explicit developmental outcomes – and may just as likely be oriented toward clearly political objectives. Such goals may in fact be relatively harmless – or actually promote – developmental objectives, as when privilege is extended to a particular region or ethnic group. In other cases, political goals may have a very harmful impact on the process of economic development, as when a highly unproductive businessperson is given a trading monopoly and extraordinary access to state credit in exchange for building political support for the regime in an important bailiwick. If the deployer is highly dependent on such local powerbrokers for political survival, it is particularly unlikely that developmental goals will figure prominently in the bargain.

Second, when rents are in fact allocated with clear developmental goals, what is the capacity of the state to enforce or promote such goals? In an optimal 'rent-seeking' scenario, those who obtain privilege through competitive bidding must invest them in productive enterprise. In an optimal 'deployment' scenario, those who give out the rents are not only very skilled in choosing the right entrepreneurs but also quite capable of enforcing strict performance guidelines from those they have provided a particular benefit. Entrepreneurs favoured by South Korea's Park Chung Hee, for example, were granted enormous privilege but at the same time forced to meet performance criteria (commonly in the form of export targets). In many cases, however, those who obtain advantages will be

---

[37] I am indebted to Jomo and Gomez for highlighting the important distinction between these two processes (Jomo and Gomez, 'Rents, Rent-Seeking and Rent Deployment', p. 5).

[38] Nye, 'Corruption and Political Development', p. 967.

able to pursue their own goals – which may or may not be oriented toward productive investment.

The clearest analysis, here again, requires careful examination of the broader configuration of authority and power within which rent allocation takes place. Privilege may be extended to collective interests (a particular region, ethnic group, political party, or military faction) or to far more particular interests (family members, fraternity brothers, golfing partners, etc.). It is necessary to examine the relationship of rent allocators to each of these types of interests. Moreover, one must note that while in some settings major beneficiaries will be found within the state (likely top bureaucrats and military officers), elsewhere major beneficiaries have an independent economic base outside the state. Overall, analysis of the ability of allocators to enforce and promote perform-ance criteria requires that one examine such basic issues as the distribution of political power, the character of bureaucratic agencies, and the institutional-ization and differentiation of business interests. Questions of enforcement cannot be understood without careful attention to the larger realms of power and authority.

Third, rent recipients operating in a very insecure environment may have little incentive to adopt a long-run strategy in the country where their advantage was obtained: capital flight, rather than productive investment of capital, will likely predominate.[39] To the extent that corruption and cronyism undercut the legitimacy of a regime, of course, they may at the same time undermine the overall stability in which rents are invested.

What is the Impact of Corruption and Clientelism on Levels of Competition and the Overall Functioning of the Market?

This question moves analysis from issues of investor productivity to those of market performance: does rent allocation, corruption, and clientelism tend to promote or discourage competition among firms? Doner and Ramsay contrast 'competitive clientelism' (in which competition among political élites keeps barriers to entry low and thus fosters business competition) with 'monopoly cronyism' or 'monopoly clientelism' (in which entrepreneurs can use their access to the state machinery to enforce higher entry barriers and reduce competi-tion).[40] Quite clearly the former can be expected to promote more favour-able conditions for capitalist development, particularly where the state lacks the regulatory capacity to ensure efficient performance from cartelized and monopolized sectors.

Second, and closely related, is the need to examine whether corrupt acts provide an end-run around policies that obstruct markets, or whether the acts themselves obstruct the efficient functioning of competitive markets. The first case is perhaps best illustrated by West African cocoa farmers evading laws that require them to sell their produce to state marketing boards, and smuggling

---

[39] Indeed, one could argue that an entrepreneur who benefits from a deployed rent (and is thus probably close to the regime in power) is likely more secure than an entrepreneur who has won out in a process of competitive rent-seeking. If the regime as a whole is in danger of collapsing, however, neither category of entrepreneur is likely to have much sense of security.

[40] R. F. Doner and A. Ramsay, 'An Institutional Explanation of Thai Economic Success', a paper prepared for the annual meetings of the Association for Asian Studies, Washington D.C., April 6–9 (1995), pp. 3–4. Scott *Comparative Political Corruption*, p. 91.

their produce to markets in neighbouring countries.[41] The second occurs when an anti-trust lawsuit is squelched through bribery of key officials.

What is the Impact of Corruption on the Capacity of State Agencies to Undertake Important Developmental Roles?

States have important tasks to achieve in promoting development. Even advocates of a relatively minimalist role for the state, such as the World Bank, assert that:

> governments need to do more in those areas where markets alone cannot be relied upon. Above all, this means investing in education, health, nutrition, family planning, and poverty alleviation; building social, physical, administrative, regulatory, and legal infrastructure of better quality; mobilizing resources to finance public expenditures; and providing a stable macroeconomic foundation, without which little can be achieved.[42]

To the extent that corruption inhibits the achievement of these vital foundations of laissez-faire capitalism, opportunities for sustained growth will be impaired. If one expects that promotion of late, late industrialization requires an even more extensive role for the state, quite clearly, it will be necessary to build up an even greater degree of capacity throughout the bureaucratic apparatus. For present purposes, however, it is possible to confine our attention to the impact of corruption on the basic political foundations of capitalist growth.

Some argue that corruption promotes development by promoting administrative responsiveness. 'Many economic activities would be paralysed,' wrote Myron Weiner of Indian politics in 1962, 'were it not for the flexibility which *bakshish* contributes to the complex, rigid, administrative system'. Huntington concurs: 'In terms of economic growth, the only thing worse than a society with a rigid, overcentralized, dishonest bureaucracy is one with a rigid, overcentralized, honest bureaucracy'.[43] Others introduce the distinction between 'speed payments' (involving 'bribes that *expedite* a decision without changing it') and 'distortive payments' (which 'change the decision and contravene formal government policy').[44]

From the standpoint of an individual businessperson or citizen, corruption does indeed grease the wheels of a bureaucracy; to be sure, 'honest bureaucracies' can be infuriatingly inflexible to those with a justifiable need to bend the rules, and 'dishonest bureaucracies' highly responsive to those who have the means and/or connections to do so. From a macro perspective, however, it is important to consider the impact of even seemingly innocuous 'speed' payments

---

[41] R. H. Bates, *Market and States in Tropical Africa: the Political Basis of Agricultural Policies* (Berkeley and Los Angeles, University of California Press, 1981).

[42] World Bank, *World Development Report 1991* (Oxford, Oxford University Press, 1991), p. 9.

[43] Huntington, *Political Order*, p. 69.

[44] Scott, 'Patron-Client Politics', p. 67. Fegan offers a broadly similar distinction between 'facilitative corruption' (in which the law is bent to the mutual benefit of both a bribing businessperson and a bribed bureaucrat, and neither has reason to complain to a third party) and 'obstructive corruption' (in which legitimate applications are blocked until a bribe is paid, and the businessperson is likely to complain to a third party). The former is 'probably a necessary lubricant to capitalist development', while the latter is an impediment (B. Fegan, 'Contributions from Sir Arthur Conan Doyle and Mick Inder to a Theory of Bureacratisation and Corruption in Southeast Asia'. Unpublished ms, Sydney (1994), pp. 4–5).

on the likelihood of a bureaucratic agency to deliver the services it was set up to deliver. Such payments can encourage systematic delays, precisely because slowing things down brings such handsome financial rewards to those in a strategic position within the bureaucracy. Corruption may in some cases be a valuable 'lubricant' to individual claimants, but one must not neglect the degree to which such incentives build more bureaucratic 'toll posts,' and in the end exacerbate delays in the system as a whole.[45]

Moreover, one must assess the longer term impact of corruption on administrative capacity to perform essential developmental tasks. Theobald asserts that:

> widespread venality, far from drawing together the different departments and areas of the public service, provokes fragmentation, dissension, inter- and intra-departmental rivalry ... the low levels of morale and paranoia which are typically associated with an acutely unstable work situation ... will have very marked consequences for job performance ... [A prevalence of] nepotism, political patronage and bribery ... [means] there is little incentive for functionaries to work efficiently or honestly.[46]

While not denying that corruption may have some 'positive consequences,' Theobald asserts that 'it is virtually impossible to confine corruption to those areas where its effects are deemed to be beneficial'.[47] Even Huntington, who sees many positive benefits to corruption, acknowledges that it 'naturally tends to weaken or to perpetuate the weakness of the government bureaucracy'.[48]

Aside from questions of flexibility and capacity one must consider the impact of corruption on government budgets. How much of an expenditure intended to promote certain developmental goals actually ends up being utilized for such purpose, and how much gets leaked to promote private gain? On the revenue side, as well, corruption may reduce the proportion of a given tax that actually ends up in public coffers; taxpayers can bribe the right officials to informally bargain down their tax burden or obtain a formal exemption. Either way, funds are diverted from public to private ends.

Leff argues that 'there is no reason to assume that the government has a high *marginal* propensity to spend for developmental purposes'; moreover, 'when the entrepreneurs' propensity to invest is higher than the government's, the money saved from the tax collector may be a gain rather than a loss for development'.[49] This begs the question, however, of whether the private hands that dip in the till will be investing their resources in the provision of public goods essential to the promotion of development. In many cases, even the most basic political foundations of economic development are severely disrupted by corruption: such tasks, for example, as law enforcement, fire protection, and the construction and maintenance of infrastructure. While entrepreneurs may invest some resources in provisioning themselves with these goods (private security guards, fire brigades, and roads), it will be rare for private investors to charitably provide

---

[45] S. H. Alatas, *The Sociology of Corruption: the Nature, Function, Causes, and Prevention of Corruption* (Singapore, Times Books, 1980), pp. 31–5.

[46] Theobald, *Corruption*, p. 46.

[47] Theobald, *Corruption*, p. 131.

[48] Huntington, *Political Order*, p. 69.

[49] Leff, 'Economic Development', p. 399.

public goods when governments fail to do so. As the World Bank explains, governments must do what markets alone fail to do.

A key question, then, is how much corruption actually reduces public expenditure on developmental goals (whether it be an irrigation project, a road, or a rural health clinic). Wade has provided an exceptionally detailed empirical portrait of how corruption in a South Indian system of canal irrigation impedes developmental goals. Irrigation engineers are able to raise 'vast amounts of illicit revenue' in the construction of irrigation works and in deciding how water is allocated; in the process, the 'economic well-being of local communities' is often poorly served.[50] Overall, one can expect that five per cent diversion of resources from public purpose to private hands is relatively harmless compared to ten per cent, and ten per cent far less damaging than 25 per cent and above.

Within any given country, some elements of the political machinery are likely to divert more resources than others: the actual incidence of corruption may vary, for example, depending on whether one is examining the upper level or the lower levels of a bureaucracy, Agency A or Agency B.[51] Huntington asserts that 'most political systems' exhibit a high incidence of corruption 'at the lower levels of bureaucratic and political authority,' and that as one moves to higher levels the frequency of corruption may – depending on the country – remain constant, increase, or decrease. In all cases, however, 'the *scale* of corruption (i.e. the average value of the private goods and services involved in a corrupt exchange) increases as one goes up the bureaucratic hierarchy or political ladder'.[52] Broad judgements as to whether upper- or lower-level corruption are likely to be more damaging to developmental prospects are difficult to make: bribes at the lower level involve less money per transaction, but may well prove more disruptive to the functioning of the overall legal and administrative order. One can presume, however, that corruption will have the most debilitating impact when it is pervasive throughout a system, not only obstructing the provision of basic services through petty corruption at the lower levels but also resulting in large-scale graft at the top.

From one agency to another, as well, there are commonly great variations in the prevalence of corruption and rent-seeking. 'Unable to transform the bureaucracy as a whole,' Evans explains of Brazil, 'political leaders try to create "pockets of efficiency"' in which universalistic norms governed recruitment and an 'ethic of public service' nurtured a 'clear esprit de corps'.[53] Doner and Ramsay similarly call Thailand a 'bifurcated state ... divided between politically well insulated macroeconomic agencies [including the Ministry of Finance and the Bank of Thailand] and highly politicized line agencies'.[54]

[50] R. Wade, 'The system of administrative and political corruption: canal irrigation in south India', *The Journal of Development Studies*, 18 (1982), 287–328, pp. 287–8.

[51] Insights can also be drawn from comparisons of the incidence (and impact) of corruption at the national level versus the regional level, or Region A versus Region B. The more decentralized a polity, the more important such analysis would be.

[52] Huntington, *Political Order*, p. 67, emphasis in original.

[53] Evans, *Embedded Autonomy*, p. 61.

[54] Doner and Ramsay, 'An Institutional Explanation', pp. 2–3. The relatively more efficient agencies may be more insulated from clientelistic pressures, but one should not presume that formal authority completely displaces informal networks of power. As Rudolph and Rudolph argue in their 'revisionist interpretation' of Weber's work on bureaucracy, effective administration depends not only on rational-legal authority but also on the persistence of patrimonial features able to '[mitigate] conflict and [promote] organizational loyalty, discipline, and efficiency' (Rudolph and

Moreover, the character – and hence impact – of corruption can vary according to whether or not democratic institutions are present. While some systems exhibit a clearer demarcation of administrative agencies and parliamentary bodies than others, in general one can say that the presence of representative institutions and electoral competition opens up the system to the influence of a wider array of actors: party leaders, politicians, and at least some element of a broader public. Moreover, electoral systems offer:

> noncorrupt channels for influence that simply do not exist in autocratic systems. For a businessman to give money to a civil servant is generally illegal, whereas the same amount given to a politician's campaign fund may 'buy' just as much influence over government decisions but is quite proper ... The over-all level of corruption (legally defined) is not necessarily lower in party systems, but the party system generally does legitimize certain patterns of influence that could only occur corruptly in a military/bureaucratic system.[55]

Finally, democratic institutions can in some cases provide new incentives for corruption. In his study of India, Wade concludes that 'it is likely that elective institutions have amplified the pressures towards corruption and made it more systematic ... because of the spiralling cost of fighting elections and nursing a constituency between elections'.[56] The relationship between democratic institutions and corruption, however, depends on a broad range of political dynamics: at the same time it enables more persons to seek a place at the trough, it can also provide greater influence to those trying to topple the trough.

Despite the analytical utility of locating where resources may be diverted from developmental goals, it is important to recognize how the various parts generally fit together as one single system of corruption. Wade criticizes those who 'treat "administrative" and "political," "high" and "low" level corruption as distinct and unconnected forms,' demonstrating that they are often 'systematically interconnected'.[57] Theobald, similarly, treats 'administrative and political corruption as dimensions of the same phenomenon, as different sides of the same coin'.[58]

Does Corruption Tend to Promote or Inhibit the Institutionalization of State Agencies? What is the Impact of Corruption on the Institutionalization of Political Parties?

In addition to examining the impact of corruption on the capacity of states to perform important developmental tasks, it is also valuable to consider whether certain types of corruption may promote the institutionalization of

Rudolph, 'Authority and power', p. 196). Evans argues that informal networks within developmentalist states 'reinforce the binding character of participation in the formal organizational structure rather than undercutting it in the way that informal networks based on kinship or parochial geographic loyalties would' (Evans, *Embedded Autonomy*, p. 59).

[55] Scott, *Comparative Political Corruption*, p. 94. I prefer the term 'electoral system' to 'party system', since (as discussed below) well-institutionalized parties may or may not play an important role within a system centred around competitive elections.

[56] Wade, 'The system of administrative corruption', pp. 318–9.

[57] Wade, 'The system of administrative corruption', p. 288.

[58] Theobald, *Corruption*, p. 18; see also Riggs, 'The interdependence of politics and administration'.

bureaucracies and militaries. Returning to the discussion above of the relationship between formal lines of authority and informal networks of power, I propose that a higher degree of convergence between power and authority may occasionally promote state institutionalization. In the late 1950s, for example, then-Colonel Suharto was transferred from his post as regional commander for Central Java because of involvement in a 'smuggling scheme ostensibly to raise funds for the "welfare" of his troops'. While personal gain was clearly a major factor, Indonesian generals engaging in such economic activities were also motivated to 'maintain the functioning of their units and the loyalty of their troops'.[59] State appropriations were insufficient to provision adequately the rank-and-file soldiers, and it was wise for patron-generals to share part of the gains from corrupt activities with a clientele located within the state apparatus.[60]

The second consideration is the impact of corruption on the institutionalization of political parties. This question draws on Huntington, who connects the achievement of more institutionalized parties with the demise of corruption itself:

> For an official to award a public office in return for payment to the official is clearly to place private interest over public interest. For an official to award a public office in return for a contribution of work or money to a party organization is to subordinate one public interest to another, more needy, public interest ... Corruption thrives on disorganization, the absence of stable relationships among groups and of recognized patterns of authority ... [It] varies inversely with political organization, and *to the extent that corruption builds parties, it undermines the conditions of its own existence* ... the incidence of corruption in those countries where governmental resources have been diverted or 'corrupted' for party-building is on the whole less than it is where parties have remained weak.

Historically, he continues, political parties of the West which were initially 'leeches on the bureaucracy in the end become the bark protecting it from more destructive locusts of clique and family'.[61]

As Huntington suggests, however, one should not presume that the mere contribution of money to a political party will necessarily strengthen the party itself. Just like bureaucracies, political parties combine formal lines of authority with informal networks of power. In some cases, grants of money obtained via corruption will promote the institutionalization of the party, but in other cases parties themselves are so riven along the lines of cliques, factions, and personalities that new resources are unlikely to have that result. Corruption can indeed contribute to the important goal of party-building, but weak parties may endure even when they are major beneficiaries of corruption. It is important to

---

[59] H. Crouch, *The Army and Politics in Indonesia* (Ithaca, Cornell University Press, 1988), pp. 40, 38.

[60] Overall, this period is of course known as one in which corruption in Indonesia lacked any real limits (Scott, *Comparative Political Corruption*, pp. 80–4). To the extent that institutionalization was taking place, it was seemingly almost entirely within a military that – after 1965 – came to 'backbone' the rest of the bureaucracy (D. K. Emmerson, 'The Bureaucracy in Political Context: Weakness in Strength', in Karl D. Jackson and Lucian W. Pye (eds), *Political Power and Communications in Indonesia* (Berkeley and Los Angeles, University of California Press, 1978); see also Crouch, *The Army and Politics* and B. Anderson, 'Old state, new society: Indonesia's new order in comparative historical perspective', *Journal of Asian Studies*, 42 (1983), 477–96.

[61] Huntington, *Political Order*, pp. 70–1, emphasis added.

take Huntington's observations a step further, and ask why 'corruption builds parties' in some settings but not others.

> *To What Extent is Corruption's Impact on Economic Development*
> *Counterbalanced by Other 'Growth-promoting Economic and*
> *Political Factors'? Does a Political System Generate an Internal*
> *'Sense of Limits' Able to Mitigate the Extent of Corruption?*

In assessing the impact of corruption on economic performance, it is commonly argued that other factors may insulate economies – at least temporarily – from its possibly detrimental effects. In some settings, as MacIntyre summarizes the argument, it seems that 'clientelism ... has been sufficiently counterbalanced by other growth-promoting economic and political factors that have enabled strong economic growth to continue in the face of rampant rent-seeking, or served to rectify the situation when the cumulative effect of rent-seeking activities threatened to endanger the economy.' Among these factors may be large endowments of natural resources, sizeable quantities of foreign aid, strong investor confidence, and the presence of nascent 'market-oriented reform coalitions'.[62] The basic notion of considering countervailing factors is valid, but as MacIntyre demonstrates this line of inquiry tends to raise as many questions as it answers. Indeed, a simple comparison of how Indonesia and Nigeria have utilized their oil resources and developed investor confidence returns analysis quite quickly to the question of how some political economies are better equipped than others in insulating themselves from the impact of 'rampant rent-seeking'.

A far more fundamental 'mitigating factor' is the extent to which a political system may be compelled to provide its own internal limits, however modest, to the prevalence of corruption. The presence of external threat is often a key factor in encouraging 'a sense of limits', explains Scott, and 'an elite which enjoys a measure of cohesion and security can develop a sense of its collective, long-run interest'. In many cases, however, 'limits are virtually absent'.[63] To the extent that corrupt practices become culturally embedded over the course of decades or even generations, it will likely be all the more difficult to promote a stronger sense that 'enough is enough'.

Conclusion

For many decades, scholars have inquired into the impact of corruption, clientelism, and rents on the process of economic growth in the developing world. This chapter has attempted to draw very broadly on some of the lessons developed in the course of past inquiry, and contribute toward a framework that can help us to understand better why a range of related phenomena may be relatively more compatible or obstructive to developmental goals. The content of the framework presented here is tentative, but in the process of construction I hope to have demonstrated the utility of an eclectic approach, able to extract

---

[62] A. MacIntyre, 'Clientelism and Economic Growth: The Politics of Economic Policymaking in Indonesia', a paper prepared for the annual meeting of the Association for Asian Studies Washington, D.C., 6–9 April (1995), pp. 10–6.
[63] Scott, *Comparative Political Corruption*, pp. 79–80.

valuable insights not only from recent contributions to the topic but also from those made in decades past.

Moreover, I hope to have highlighted how 'the politics of privilege' may vary in both character and impact from one Third World setting to another. Applying the framework above to a range of polities – each with its own particular landscape of special advantage – will likely yield very different conclusions about the impact of rents, corruption, and clientelism on developmental outcomes.[64] Admittedly, the model proposed above lacks parsimony; but so, for that matter, have many previous attempts at explaining these issues.[65] Perhaps a narrower or more abstract approach could produce greater simplicity – not to mention more scientific precision; but in all likelihood, some important aspects of (not surprisingly, complex and diverse) reality would be discarded in the process. For all the efforts that have gone into this line of inquiry in the past, it remains the case that corruption, 'a phenomenon which affects administration, politics, business, education, health and a host of other crucial areas of social life ... has been so little studied'.[66]

Future comparative research is necessary to prioritize the elements of analysis more clearly, and pursue major issues in greater detail. To the extent possible, it would be useful to develop measures of the variability of corruption, the dissipation of resources in the process of allocating particularistic advantage, and the diversion of budgetary resources from developmental purposes. It is also worthwhile to review the presence or absence of performance criteria across various sectors, and seek to understand more clearly the political processes by which barriers to competition are imposed and maintained. Finally, more research is needed to understand the interconnections of various forms of corruption as found throughout the entire political system, and the structural conditions that may promote (but by no means guarantee) a stronger 'sense of limits'. As inquiry continues, it is sure to be hobbled by many of the same obstacles that have long plagued the study of corruption. Research can only benefit, however, by drawing freely from the various literatures that have sought to answer, in the past, many of the same questions we are seeking to answer today.

[64] In P. D. Hutchcroft, 'Corruption's Obstructions: Assessing the Impact of Rents, Corruption, and Clientelism on Capitalist Development in the Philippines'. Paper prepared for presentation at the annual meeting of the Association for Asian Studies, 11–14 April 1996, Honolulu, Hawaii, I apply the various elements of this framework to the Philippines, a notoriously skewed, irregular political economic landscape long the playfield of both established oligarchs and favoured cronies. The country's particular configuration of political power, I conclude, has nurtured types of rent-seeking, corruption, and clientelistic ties that have proven generally obstructive to sustained economic development.

[65] See for example Nye, 'Corruption and Political Development'. Scott, *Comparative Political Corruption*, pp. 90–1. Theobald, *Corruption*, pp. 107–32.

[66] Wade, 'The system of administrative corruption', p. 288.

[22]

Political Studies (1997), XLV, 436–462

Defining Political Corruption

MARK PHILP[1]

I

In New South Wales in 1988, after more than 10 years of Labour Party rule, the Liberal–National Party coalition won a majority in the Legislative Assembly following a campaign which stressed the corrupt character of Labour's conduct of political office. In the first legislative session the new Premier, Nick Greiner, created the Independent Commission Against Corruption (ICAC), designed to prevent a range of corrupt practices, including the exercise of illicit political patronage. A further election in 1991, intended to increase the Government's majority, resulted in a swing to Labour and the election of four independent MPs. The Liberals remained in power, with 49 seats, facing a Labour opposition with 46 seats. One of the four Independents generally supported the Government, allowing Greiner to remain Premier. In October 1991 the other three independent members reached an understanding with the Government. At the same time, a Liberal MP, Tony Metherall (having resigned as a Minister in July following tax offences), resigned from the Party, remaining in Parliament as an independent. In January 1992, the Government's majority was further reduced after a by-election. The Greiner administration, in consequence, could rely on there being 47 votes for the government, and 47 against, with the balance lying with the five Independents of whom two (including Metherall) usually voted with the government.

In April 1992, after behind the scenes negotiation with the Greiner administration, Metherall resigned from Parliament. On the same day he was appointed to a well-paid position in the New South Wales public service. Following a public outcry, the ICAC investigated the matter and found that, pursuant to Section 8 of the ICAC act, Greiner and others had acted in a way which involved the partial exercise of official functions, and constituted a breach of trust, where this was sufficient to give (under section 9c of the Act) reasonable grounds for dismissing a public servant.[2]

[1] My thanks are owed for comments on earlier drafts of this paper to my editor and fellow contributors, and to Jerry Cohen, Liz Frazer, Barry Hindess, Doug McEachern, Philip Pettit and Vicki Spencer. The final version was written while I was a Visiting Research Fellow, in the Humanities Research Centre of the Australian National University.

[2] Section 8(1) identifies criteria of necessary conditions for conduct being corrupt (such as, adversely affecting the honest or impartial exercise of official functions, involving a breach of public trust, or the misuse of information of material acquired in the course of official functions). But these conditions do not constitute sufficient conditions for conduct being corrupt unless (under Section 9(1)) the conduct would constitute or involve, a criminal offence, a disciplinary offence, or reasonable grounds for dispensing with the services of a public official. The Commission, in effect, found that Greiner and the Minister for the Environment, Moore, had met the criterion of partiality under section 8 and that of reasonable grounds for dismissal in section 9.

Greiner and Moore commenced proceedings in the Supreme Court, but resigned before the hearings began because of Parliamentary censure. In August 1992 the Court of Appeal agreed that conduct fell within Section 8 of the Act, but, by a majority of 2 to 1, found that this conduct did not constitute reasonable grounds for dismissal under section 9. The initial report of the Commission was declared to be 'without or in excess of jurisdiction, and is a nullity'.[3]

In responding to the censure motion in the Legislative Assembly on 28 April 1992, Greiner argued:

> Ultimately, if what was done was against the law, then all honourable members need to understand that it is, for practical purposes, the death of politics in this State. (...) What the Opposition and media have opened up here is the very nature of politics itself – that is, the conflict between the demands of politics and the demands of public office. Under the English common law very serious obligations to act in the public interest are placed on those elected to public office, and yet our highest public officials are at the same time part of a political system which is about what is in many ways a largely private interest in terms of winning or holding a seat. (...) I am prepared to accept that community attitudes have changed, and that what is tolerated at one time is not acceptable at another. But every member needs to understand that the standards that are implied in this censure of me today are entirely new standards ... (and) I am not sure, when honourable members have considered them calmly in the bright light of day, that those standards are going to produce a workable system of democracy in our State ...[4]

The ICAC responded with a report which again raised the question of how corruption should be defined and whether the existing act had failed to draw a necessary distinction between corrupt and improper conduct – with the former requiring that conduct either be knowingly corrupt, or involve some direct personal benefit to the public official involved. In its third report, the Commission recommended the implementation of selection criteria for public sector recruitment based solely on merit.[5] Recommendations made in the wake of the Metherall case had still not been acted on by the end of 1996.

The Metherall case is only one among many throughout the world demonstrating the extent to which the investigation, prevention and prosecution of corruption is profoundly influenced not simply by how corruption is defined but, more deeply, by how we are to understand the character of politics. Similar questions have been raised, albeit with fewer results and declining interest, by the Nolan Commission in Britain; while, in America parallel concerns have been

---

[3] See, the three ICAC reports, written by Ian Temby, the Commisioner: *Report on Investigation into the Metherall Resignation and Appointment* (ICAC, Sydney, June 1992); *Second Report on Investigation into the Metherall Resignation and Appointment* (ICAC, Sydney, September 1992); *Integrity in Public Sector Recruitment* (ICAC, Sydney, March, 1993).

[4] ICAC, *Report on Investigation into ... Metherall*, pp. 92–3.

[5] See also the Discussion Paper, *Recruitment of Former Members of Parliament to the Public Service and Related Issues* (ICAC, Sydney, October 1992) and Ian Temby's 'Making government accountable: the New South Wales experience', unpublished paper to Edith Cowan University, W.A., 4.11.1994.

evident in the investigation of the Keating Five and a number of other cases.[6] Few other countries are without similar problems. Nonetheless, the Metherall case has raised publicly the issue of what understanding of the rules for the conduct of public office, with its related understanding of political corruption, is compatible with the realities of political life. Greiner's motives may be suspect, but there is no doubt that he was right in his claim that an intimate connection exists between how we understand corruption and how we understand politics. My aim in this paper is to show both how deep this connection is, and how our acknowledgement of it must result in substantial revision to the way we define and understand political corruption.

II

The Metherall case is complex. The ICAC judgement that a case of political corruption existed was contentious, as the Court of Appeal decision demonstrated. In the course of the first and second reports several criteria were appealed to as relevant to the judgement. The statutory provisions of the Independent Commission Against Corruption Act 1988, and sections 8 and 9 in particular, were critical to a finding of corrupt behaviour. Nonetheless, the interpretation of such clauses in section 8 as 'the honest and impartial exercise of official functions' (S.8.1.a.), 'dishonest or partial exercise' (S.8.1.b), and 'conduct ... that constitutes or involves a breach of public trust' (S.8.1.c), is extremely difficult. So is the interpretation of Section 9.1.c, where the conduct is judged to constitute 'reasonable grounds for dismissing, dispensing with the services of or otherwise terminating the services of a public official'.[7] Moreover, the Commission found Greiner to have contravened the Act despite the fact that he did not knowingly engage in wrongful conduct, that he made no clear private and personal gain from the transaction, and that he could make a case for his behaviour being a normal part of the political process within the traditions of New South Wales' political culture. Each of these three elements raises serious issues in the definition of political corruption.

In responding to criticisms about the definition of corruption extending beyond knowingly wrong conduct the second ICAC report claimed that:

> The whole point of the legislation was to combat a corrupt culture, a culture that regards nothing wrong with things like jobs for the boys, or giving a Government contract to a mate, and accepts corruption as part of the way things are done. To let through the net those who are sufficiently amoral

---

[6] Cf., *Standards in Public Life: First report of the Committee on Standards in Public Life*, Chairman Lord Nolan (HMSO, Cm 2850 I and II, May 1995), especially I, p. 14; and Dennis F. Thompson, 'Mediated corruption: the case of the Keating Five', *American Political Science Review*, 87(2), 1993, 369–81, and his *Ethics in Congress: from Individual to Institutional Corruption* (Washington DC, Brookings, 1995). In the Keating Five case, five members of Congress were accused of improperly assisting a major campaign contributor. However, they were not levying an income from Keating, and their lobbying in his favour was in many respects indistinguishable from the kind of lobbying which takes place throughout the American political process. Nonetheless, they were acting corruptly – a judgement based on a finely nuanced conception of what kinds of services a politician can perform for someone without undermining or side-stepping the democratic process as understood in contemporary America. In this, as in the Metherall case, it is not a requirement that the person acting in ways deemed corrupt was aware in advance that he or she was so doing.

[7] Cf., ICAC, *Second Report ... Metherall ...*, p. 3.

© Political Studies Association, 1997

that they do not recognize wholly unacceptable behaviour would be to abrogate the central charter the Commission tries to fulfil.[8]

The suggestion that the appropriate standard to take is the law, rather than knowledge and intention, or existing cultural norms, was also rejected by ICAC on the grounds that they had already had to investigate cases in which public officials had been able to abuse their position for personal gain in ways on which the law was currently silent but which constituted a clear breach of trust.

The fact that Greiner sought no private gain from the transaction was discussed in the second ICAC report in terms of whether a distinction could be sustained between improper and corrupt conduct. Although the Commission did not seek to resolve the issue it commented that 'partial, dishonest or wrongful exercise of public office can be equally dangerous and harmful to the community, irrespective of whether the public official concerned gets a kick-back'. In Dennis F. Thompson's terminology, Greiner's conduct looks like institutional corruption:

> Legislative corruption is *institutional* insofar as the *gain* a member receives is political rather than personal, the *service* the member provides is procedurally improper, and the *connection* between the gain and the service has a tendency to damage the legislature or the democratic process ... Recognizing institutional corruption is not always easy because it is so closely related to conduct that is a perfectly acceptable part of political life.[9]

But institutional corruption is a deeply contestable concept which implies a clear set of criteria for identifying the borderline between politically proper and improper conduct. On what resources and criteria are such judgements to draw – prevailing mores, legal rules, institutional norms, or publicly endorsed standards? In the midst of this uncertainty one thing which did seem clear to the Commission was that to insist that corruption must involve direct and personal gain would be unacceptably restrictive. Yet, their reluctance to do so was precisely what prompted Greiner's complaint about the death of politics.

Greiner's speech raises a further problem in defining corruption when he points both to the changes that can take place in community attitudes, and to the way that the historical traditions of a political culture shape its current institutional mores and practices. On *his* understanding of the character of politics in the political culture of New South Wales, what he did was no more than what needed to be done – given the implicit rules of the game. The public outcry it provoked is dismissed as arising from the machinations of the Opposition and media. But, even though Greiner might be said to have been proved wrong about the character of that culture, he could have been right. And if he had been right, then we seem committed to saying that there was nothing wrong with his conduct. Indeed, the ICAC itself seems committed to that proposition:

> It must be said that what is 'corrupt', i.e. the wrongful exercise of public duty in any community, will depend on what the correct duty is determined to be. That will be influenced by cultural issues and accepted behavioural standards within the community. There may be behaviour that is 'right' in

[8] ICAC, *Second Report ... Metherall ...*, p. 13.
[9] Thompson, *Ethics in Congress*, p. 7.

one country, and 'wrong' in another. The very first step must always be to determine and clearly signpost the standards of behaviour that are required to be observed by public officials.[10]

Can progress be made on the definition of corruption, given these difficulties? The three most commonly cited definitions are public office-centred, public interest-centred, and market definitions. (Public opinion and legal norms have also been cited, but they can be subsumed under the other cases). In the two works which have dominated the study of corruption over the last twenty-five years, Heidenheimer's *Political Corruption* (1970), and its successor volume edited by Heidenheimer, Johnston and LeVine (1989), these three definitions are proposed as different ways of identifying the scope of the concept of political corruption. The public office conception of corruption is exemplified by Nye:

> Corruption is behavior which deviates from the formal duties of a public role because of private regarding (personal, close family, private clique) pecuniary or status gains; or violates rules against the exercise of certain types of private regarding influence. This includes such behaviour as bribery (use of reward to pervert the judgement of a person in a position of trust); nepotism (bestowal of patronage by reason of ascriptive relationship rather than merit); and misappropriation (illegal appropriation of public resources for private-regarding uses).[11]

Nye explicitly excludes considerations of the public interest so as to avoid confusing the phenomenon with its effects. Others, however, have sought to define political corruption precisely in terms of a conception of the public interest. Carl Friedrich, for example argues that:

> ... corruption can be said to exist whenever a power-holder who is charged with doing certain things, i.e., who is a responsible functionary or office holder, is by monetary or other rewards not legally provided for, induced to take actions which favour whoever provides the rewards *and thereby does damage to the public and its interests.*[12]

Although there is an issue about confusing the phenomenon with its consequences, the view that corruption involves the subversion of the public interest or common good by private interests is one with an impeccable historical pedigree: Machiavelli is hardly alone in understanding corruption as the decay of the capacity of the citizens and officials of a state to subordinate the pursuit of private interests to the demands of the common good or public interest. Indeed, even Nye's public office account, in which corruption deviates from the formal duties of the public role, implicitly recognizes the public interest dimension by insisting that the deviation must be for private regarding gains – thereby covertly introducing a public interest component.

---

[10] ICAC, *Defending the Fudamental Political Values of the Commonwealth Against Corruption* (report for the Consideration of Commonwealth Law Ministers, Mauritius, November 1993), p. 3. Interestingly, no attempt is made to explain, or resolve, the inverted commas around 'right' and 'wrong'.

[11] J. S. Nye, 'Political Corruption: a Cost-Benefit Analysis', in A. J. Heidenheimer, M. Johnston and V. LeVine (eds), *Political Corruption: a Handbook* (New Brunswick NJ, Transaction, 1989), p. 966.

[12] Heidenheimer *et al.*, *Political Corruption*, p. 10, emphasis added.

Both public office and public interest definitions of corruption must show which view of the character and scope of public office or public interest should be accepted. It is not immediately obvious which norms should flesh out these subsidiary concepts. The potential sources are manifold but they share the difficulties which can be identified with the three main candidates: public opinion, legal norms, and standards derived from modern western democratic systems.

Public opinion is an important element in the identification and understanding of political corruption but, as the Metherall case shows, it raises a number of difficulties. To whose opinion do we give most weight? The norms of a local community may differ from those insisted on by a central authority or a political élite and they may differ between sections of the local population (either vertically [e.g., between different classes] or horizontally [different ethnic groups or segmented communities] or both). More damagingly, we need to recognize that opinion may be disjointed from behaviour – that is, people may say one thing and do another. Moreover, relying on public opinion means that we risk omitting cases where the casualty of corruption is the capacity of the citizenry to recognize a distinct set of public norms or a conception of the public interest. Something like this worry is conveyed by the ICAC's sense of its mission as being 'to combat a corrupt culture'.

Appeal to the law is equally fraught with problems. In few states does the law define a category of acts as 'political corruption' – focusing instead on the definition of various sub-sets – such as bribery, fraud, or electoral malpractice. But even here, the law is an inadequate guide – not only because it may not cover cases which are widely perceived as corrupt (such as receiving cash payments or favours for asking Parliamentary questions), but also because the law can itself originate in corrupt practices: that an act is legal does not always mean that it is not corrupt. Moreover, laws regulating political conduct rest on prior assumptions about the character of political office. At best, laws express such principles, and it is this normative or principled structure which must be regarded as the baseline from which we should work to flesh out definitions of public office or public interest, although these principles are open to very similar objections to those raised against norms. The final objection to using law as the determining standard for conduct is that the actions of those engaged in politics cannot be exhaustively settled by systems of rules. There is inevitable indeterminacy in politics, both for bureaucrats in the conduct of their administrative offices, and for politicians in the conduct of their political ones – and many public scandals are prompted by cases where, although the law does not prohibit an action, the action violates the public's sense of appropriate conduct for public officials.

Because the identification of the norms and principles which give a determinate content to the concept of the public interest, or which govern the exercise of public office, is fraught with difficulty, many political scientists in the 1960s and 1970s came to the view that there was no alternative but to plump for a definition which was clear and could be applied with a degree of objectivity – even if it meant they had to fall back on assumptions about politics and its corruption which rested heavily on western views of the central values of democratic societies. More recently, many political analysts have sought to avoid imposing the cultural prejudices of western democratic systems by arguing that what counts as a wrongful exercise of public duty must have some reference to accepted standards of behaviour within a community. The net result is that the analysis of political corruption is left caught between the equally repugnant options of stipulative definition following western norms, or a relativist appeal to local norms or standards.

The relativism which we risk is not simply moral relativism; that might seem like a price worth paying to avoid western stipulation. But the danger of this move is that the damage to one's analysis spreads beyond moral relativism to a conceptual relativism.

Consider the case of bribery. In most western cultures bribery is defined in terms similar to Nye's – 'the use of reward to pervert the judgement of a person in a position of trust'. In different western cultures, different understandings will exist as to when something meets these criteria: what counts as rewards, what sorts of influence are held to pervert judgement, what defines positions of trust, and how far other components of an individual's life are held to be constrained by the responsibilities associated with that trust. But, while such differences are tolerable, it would be another matter entirely if a culture claimed to have the concept of bribery without believing that there was anything wrong with it. On the modern view, if it is bribery, then there is something wrong with it. To believe otherwise verges on incoherence. It has been claimed that 'The (ancient) Greeks did not have a word for bribes because all gifts are bribes. All gifts are given by way of reciprocation for favours past or to come'.[13] The Greeks did have terms (*dōron, lemma, chresmasi peithein*) for bribes although they were terms which also meant gift-giving or receiving, or persuasion. That there are a number of neutral terms for giving, receiving and persuading in ancient Greek literature implies a tolerance for much that we would now regard as bribery. But do these terms recognizably denote bribery? They do not imply that someone's judgement has been perverted, even where they recognize that it has been influenced; and since it is not perverted, but influenced, it is difficult to see them as indicating that a trust has been betrayed. If these were the only terms for bribery in the Ancient Greek world we would have to take the view that there is a basic untranslatability of the terms between us and them – that they not only failed to distinguish gifts and bribes, but that they also had no real concept of public office or trust.

In fact, although there were a number of terms for bribery which were essentially neutral, there were also powerfully negative terms, such as *diaphtheirein,* which implied the destruction of a person's independent judgement and action.[14] There is also ample evidence that the Greeks could recognize both the concept of a public trust, and the use of gifts to subvert the ends of that trust. There was a general law in Athens concerning bribery which laid down penalties for giving or taking bribes to the detriment of the interests of the people, and 'cata-political bribery' was accorded the most powerful condemnatory adjective in Greek, namely *aischorn,* or shameful.[15] Although this means that there are common elements between modern and ancient understandings of bribery, we should recognize the implication of the thought

[13] A claim cited and refuted by J. T. Noonan, *Bribes* (Berkeley CA, University of California Press, 1984), and commented on by Jon Elster, *The Cement of Society* (Cambridge, Cambridge University Press, 1989), p. 267.

[14] David Harvey, 'Dona Ferentes: some aspects of bribery in Greek politics', *History of Political Thought,* VI (1/2), 1985, 76–117, p. 86.

[15] Harvey, 'Dona Ferentes', pp. 111 and 109.

that there might not have been. If we rely wholly on local norms we end up risking a fundamental incommensurability between ourselves and the local normative and conceptual vocabulary.

The use of local norms and judgements must, then, be handled with care – they have a role in identifying what types of activity are understood as corrupt, but they cannot be accepted as the only criteria, since this would be to embrace a conceptual relativism which renders any cross-cultural analysis of corruption incoherent. Consider, for example, the entry for 20 August 1664, in Samuel Pepys's Diary in which he reports that he went to his office 'where I took in with me Bagwell's wife; and there I caressed her, and find her every day more and more coming, with good words and promise of getting her husband a place, which I will do'. Mrs Bagwell makes frequent appearances in the Diary in pursuit of a career for her husband, which lies in Pepys's disposal – an objective she failed to achieve despite Pepys raping her in her own home. Pepys does occasionally show qualms about his treatment of Mrs Bagwell, but it is unclear how far this arises from a sense that he is exploiting her, and how far from residual guilt about his adultery.

It is certainly not difficult to find Pepys's behaviour abhorrent (although scholars have been astonishingly tolerant towards him), and although some part of this reaction arises from Pepys's transgression of norms of sexual conduct which it may be anachronistic to apply to the late seventeenth century, there remains a sense that he was exploiting a position of power and influence for personal gain. The same must be said of the way Pepys gleaned a fortune from back-handers and gifts from provisioners of the navy. His use of his office was not especially remiss compared to that made by others, and there was clearly some partly shared understanding that certain types of public office were a form of property which could be used to generate financial or other forms of personal gain. As such, Pepys was simply exacting an 'income' from his office. But in both cases Pepys was fully aware that his conduct could not withstand public scrutiny. Even if we believe that Pepys did not think there was anything corrupt about his conduct, and even if many of his contemporaries would have agreed, this does not mean we have to endorse that judgement in full. While local norms provide evidence about what people accept and reject, they should not be permitted to impinge upon the deeper sense of corruption, which Pepys and his contemporaries certainly recognized, involving the violation of the norms of public office for private and personal gain. Indeed, Pepys himself believed that corruption was an evil and was full of praise for the 1618 commission on the provisioning of the Navy which sought to reduce corruption in the earlier Stuart reign.[16] Where they differ from us is not on what it is about corruption which makes it corrupt, but on what particular activities are identified as corrupting.[17]

Market-centred definitions have sometimes offered themselves as a morally neutral way of avoiding the kind of complexities involved in this delicate balancing of objective or universalist components with local and relative standards. The term 'market-centred' is not entirely felicitous. What such definitions broadly share is the application of social or public choice methods to the analysis of corruption – or, more crudely, the use of economic methods and

---

[16] Cf., Linda Levy Peck, *Court Patronage and Corruption in Early Stuart England* (Routledge, London, 1993), p. 111.

[17] Pepys is a very complex case – see Noonan, *Bribes*, pp. 366–91.

models for the analysis of politics. Not all theorists who use rational choice methods claim a distinctive rational choice definition of political corruption,[18] but many do. Consider, for example, the definition offered by Leff:

> Corruption is an extralegal institution used by individuals or groups to gain influence over the actions of the bureaucracy. As such the existence of corruption *per se* indicates only that these groups participate in the decision making process to a greater extent than would otherwise be the case.[19]

Van Klaveren is also cited as advancing a market-centred conception:

> ... corruption means that a civil servant abuses his authority in order to obtain an extra income from the public ... Thus we will conceive of corruption in terms of a civil servant who regards his office as a business, the income of which he will ... seek to maximize. The office then becomes a 'maximizing unit'.[20]

Although such accounts seem dedicated to the task of conceptual clarification, the view that they can offer an alternative definition of political corruption is itself conceptually muddled. Market-centred definitions are certainly one way of *understanding* corruption; they may also provide a fruitful model for the explanation of the incidence of corruption, but they are not a way of defining it. Indeed, Van Klaveren's analysis starts from the view that the occurrence of corruption is contingent on the development of a system in which the people are subject to the control of officials, where there exists a 'regulating principle which gives to the officials and other intermediary groups a public existence with a purpose of their own'.[21] Thus, what defines an act as corrupt is not that it is income maximizing, but that it is income maximizing in a context where prior conceptions of public office and the principles for its conduct define it as such. Which means that Van Klaveren, at least, cannot be identified with a market-centred definition.

Leff is similarly vulnerable. Despite his impressive commitment to nominalism in the identification of corruption, Leff's account is also predicated on a prior conception of public office and the norms for its exercise. The very identification of the extra-legal character of corruption introduces into the definition a conception of public office and its principles of conduct which acts as the standard from which corruption deviates. Both Leff and Van Klaveren are implicitly appealing to public-office conceptions of corruption in defining corruption, even if their subsequent accounts of the conditions for its emergence and persistence might differ substantially from other public-office centred accounts.

---

[18] See, e.g., Susan Rose-Ackerman, *Corruption* (New York, Academic, 1978), p. 7, Jens Chr. Andvig, 'The economics of corruption', *Studi economici*, 43, 1 (1991), 57–94 and, with Karl Ove Moene, ' How corruption may corrupt', *Journal of Economic Behaviour and Organisation*, 13 (1990), 63–76. See also Francis T. Lui, 'A dynamic model of corruption deterrence', *Journal of Public Economics*, 31 (1986) 215–36, and Oliver Cadot, 'Corruption as a gamble', *Journal of Public Economics*, 33 (1987) 223–44.

[19] Nathaniel Leff, 'Economic Development through Corruption', in Heidenheimer *et al.*, *Political Corruption*, p. 389.

[20] Jacob van Klaveren, 'The Concept of Corruption', in Heidenheimer *et al.*, *Political Corruption*, pp. 25–6.

[21] Jacob van Klaveren, 'Corruption as a historical phenomenon', in Heidenheimer *et al.*, *Political Corruption*, p. 75.

This conclusion is of more general applicability to economic definitions of corruption, and can be generalized also to accounts which rely upon modelling public office in principal-agent terms or in terms of rent seeking.[22] To ask if a civil servant or politician is acting corruptly when s/he acts in an income or interest-maximizing way, or when s/he sacrifices her principal's interest to her own,[23] we have to show what makes this use of office a member of a distinct set of cases identifiable as corrupt, as opposed to non-corrupt. Not all cases of income or interest maximizing need be corrupt (witness cases where office is understood as a certain type of property). To be able to point to those cases of interest/income maximizing which are also politically corrupt, one has to appeal to constructions of public office and the public-interest which draw on norms and values which are external to the market model – that is, to the set of normative constraints on income or interest maximizing which picks out the full set of politically corrupt acts. Market-based accounts might well show under what conditions it becomes more or less likely that people will break those constraints, but it has to take those constraints as a given – and it is these which distinguish corrupt from non-corrupt behaviour.

On this account, we are reduced to the alternatives of public-office and public-interest definitions of political corruption. There is, however, some pressure towards further reduction. There are two major sources of this pressure. The first comes from the recognition of the open-ended character of much public office. Some civil servants have tightly defined and constrained activities, but many do not. Similarly, politicians do not act simply as functionaries to fulfil promises made to an electorate fully cognisant of its interests. Rather, politics is partly about the contestation and projection of conceptions of the public interest. Part of the conception of the role of leaders is to lead, not to act as wholly impartial mechanisms for the adjudication of interests and the production of the social optimum. Public office and public interest are, then, intimately connected. The open character of much public office is structured by principles and expectations that demand office holders be guided by considerations of the public interest. To ask whether a politician acts corruptly we must be aware that the characterization of public office will inevitably point beyond the compliance with rules to the principles underlying those rules – principles which come into play to cover cases on which formal rules are silent.

The second pressure comes from the recognition that definitional disputes have obscured the basic point that the term 'corruption' is not in itself problematic: it is rooted in the sense of a thing being changed from its naturally sound condition, into something unsound, impure, debased, infected, tainted, adulterated, depraved, perverted, etcetera. The problem arises in the application of this to politics. Definitional problems are legion because there is hardly a general consensus on the 'naturally sound condition of politics'. The contest between public office and public interest definitions is not over what corruption is, so much as over how to derive the standard for identifying the naturally sound condition from which corrupt politicians deviate.

---

[22] Edward Banfield, 'Corruption as a feature of governmental organisation', *Journal of Law and Economics*, 18 (1975), 587–605, and Andrei Shleifer and Robert W. Vishny 'Corruption', *Quarterly Journal of Economics*, August (1993), 599–617 use principal-agent terminology to explore corruption. On 'rent-seeking', see Gordon Tullock, *Rent-Seeking* (Aldershot, The Locke Institute, Edward Elgar, 1993).

[23] Banfield, 'Corruption as a feature of governmental organisation', p. 587–8.

We should not mistake the nature of this pressure towards reduction. It does not allow us further to refine and delimit the definition of political corruption so as to pick out a core conception. On the contrary, we are forced to accept that to identify political corruption we must make commitments to conceptions of the nature of the political and the form of the public interest. One line definitions of political corruption are inherently misleading because they obscure the extent to which the concept is rooted in ways of thinking about politics – that is, of there being some 'naturally sound condition' (variously described) from which corrupt acts deviate.

There should be little surprising in this. Few if any concepts in social and political science or theory can claim a wholly factual content, and given the core meaning of the term 'corruption' it should not be surprising to find that identifying its political form will implicate us in a range of commitments about the nature and ends of the political domain. Moreover, this recognition must also be tied to an acknowledgement that the perspective on politics from which we generate our conception of corruption will play a major role in shaping the explanations we offer. The philosophical and practical upshot of all this is that while the original trinity of definitions collapses under a little pressure to a single core set of concerns, these concerns in turn generate a wide range of views as to the nature and causes of political corruption.

III

I have argued that definitional disputes about political corruption are linked directly to arguments about the nature of the healthy or normal condition of politics. Greiner's comments about what the Commission's judgement implied for the continuation of politics epitomize this conclusion: their clash is appropriately understood as one between contrasting conceptions of the nature of parliamentary and party politics. Nor is it a clash between a view in which anything goes and one which is more restrictive. After all, Greiner founded the Commission with an apparently genuine wish to clear up some of the more egregious practices of the previous administration. Nor, more generally, is the debate over different definitions of political corruption best understood as running along a continuum from the less to the more restrictive. On the contrary, debates on the 'naturally sound condition of politics' often draw on such dramatically divergent social, economic, anthropological and philosophical theories that their differences cannot be ranged along a single axis.

Faced with these definitional difficulties it is not surprising to find political scientists willing to forego the niceties of philosophical and methodological disputes by stipulatively defining a class of events for study as politically corrupt. This is a prudent move, with considerable utility for studies of phenomena within a single culture or political system. But even studies with such moderate ambitions will find it difficult to avoid moving from identification of cases of rule infraction to more general questions about what such infractions mean within that political culture – and, thereafter to questions about the character of politics. Small questions have a way of leading to big ones and the broader questions almost inevitably raise deeper normative and ethical issues.

I say 'almost inevitably' because there are frameworks for the analysis of politics which can avoid such commitments. They do so by denying any degree of autonomy to politics as a sphere of activity. If politics can be reductively analysed in terms of some more basic intentional or causal feature of the context, then it is possible to reject the view that there is some naturally sound condition of politics.

In at least two versions of public choice accounts of democratic politics the analysis is unable to give any account of what a naturally sound condition of politics might look like. This is because the models assume that 'the preferences of citizens are exogenous and fixed, and equilibrium is reached instantaneously. Hence there is neither need nor place for any kind of a process: preferences will not be altered and the outcome is known directly from preferences and constraints'.[24] As Przeworski shows, in both the Chicago and Virginia public choice schools politics is, at best, 'noise' – serving to distort the processes of equilibrium formation. Politics must always be inferior to the market because of its imperfections. On this view, then, politics is already corrupt – but it is so because the naturally sound condition is seen as a non-political state of spontaneous market equilibrium. The only acceptable form of politics is one which prevents the corruption of that more natural state of equilibrium.[25] A basic difficulty with such accounts is that once we allow that politics is in part a process which shapes and guides preference formation, then the concept of a unique social optimum disappears, and arguments about the rankings of alternative stable optima must rely, not on the quantitative account of aggregate preference satisfaction, but on an alternative account of preferableness – one which appeals to some conception of real interests or the good.[26] Of course, public choice accounts can adopt a public office or legal definition of corruption, but doing so without acknowledging the deeper definitional questions leads to tension between the definition and the methods. Asking how individuals in public office can best maximize their interests tends to favour an analysis based on incentive structures. The tendency is to discount norms and values, relegating them either to the side of costs, or to the side of preferences. Yet, this model of agency simply rides rough-shod over the way that public office and its associated culture can shape and direct people's conception of the ends of their activity. Indeed, it assumes a tactical attitude to law-keeping/breaking which, on republican theories of politics (and others), would itself be seen as an indication of corruption. Given such assumptions, it is not surprising that these accounts find little reason for optimism about the stability of political and legal orders and favour a shift from politics to the market so as to make fewer demands on self-restraint. A new generation of political theorists, attracted to the rigour of rational choice methods, have begun to produce more subtle accounts of the micro-processes of corruption in recent years, but there remains a basic problem in characterizing how politics is to be distinguished from other spheres of action. If it is not distinguished, the political disappears; but if it is distinguished only by reference to formal structures and rules, which agents must negotiate, corrupt intent is seen as ubiquitous and differences in levels of corruption are largely a function of differences in opportunities.

[24] Adam Przeworski, *The State and Economy under Capitalism: Fundamentals of Pure and Applied Economics* (New York, Harwood Academic, 1990), p. 23.
[25] E.g., William C. Mitchell and Randy T. Simmons, *Beyond Politics: Markets, Welfare, and the Failure of Bureaucracy* (Boulder CO, Westview, 1994), p. 66.
[26] Although see James S. Coleman, *Foundations of Social Theory* (Cambridge MA, Harvard, 1990), who suggests that maximum aggregate satisfaction can only be identified with a constitutional distribution of control over actions among agents.

A similar problem occurs with historicist or materialist accounts which see politics as epiphenomenal to economic or social forces. Without some distinction between politics and economics – indeed, without some recognition of politics as an autonomous sphere – it is impossible to make any sense of the idea of a naturally sound condition of politics. The more reductionist the account of politics (for example, in Marxism's account of the determining character of economic interests), or the more scientific in aspiration the theory is, the more marginal to the theory does the concept of political corruption become. One index of its marginality in modern political science is the extent to which political corruption is most frequently analysed in terms of individual motivation and pathology, and has lost the sense of its systemic character which marked the republican model of politics in the seventeenth and eighteenth centuries.[27]

IV

Once we have seen that problems in defining political corruption revolve around competing conceptions of the nature of politics we have to recognize that our earlier concern about falling prey to either Occidental arrogance or cultural relativism militates against agreement on the nature of politics in exactly the same way that it undercuts the ground for agreement on public office or public interest theories. We are left with the problem of knowing what norms or standards of politics we should accept.

In this and the final section of this paper, I sketch a number of features of political rule which seem to be more or less constant, and a range of theories in which these features are seen as resolving certain types of conflict or problem. Each theory works with a broadly similar understanding of the character of political rule, but has a different view as to what is required to maintain such rule (and as to why this maintenance is desirable) together with a sense of the forces which threaten it. Each understands the natural condition of politics differently, and each consequently sees political corruption in a distinct light. I make no attempt to argue for one or other of these theories – nor do I present these theories as competing foundational philosophical anthropologies. Rather, I suggest that they are better understood as partly empirical theories whose explanatory and normative force depends to some extent on the culture under examination. My aim in sketching their features in broad terms is to provide a richer theoretical context for the understanding of what political corruption involves and why, and to what extent, it should be condemned.

A necessary first step is to distinguish politics from other spheres and types of allocation, exchange and decision making. One way of doing so is to see politics as involving a distinct type of relation, distinguishable from, for example, communal, market, patron-client or kinship relations. Although boundaries between these different relations are not easily drawn, we can contrast them in the following, ideal-typical, terms.

Communal relations give rise to spontaneous solidarity rooted in familial and group relationships. These relationships are ascriptive in character – belonging

---

[27] See J. G. A. Pocock, *The Machiavellian Moment* (Princeton NJ, Princeton University Press, 1975) and my 'Liberalism and republicanism: on leadership and political order', *Democratization* 3 (4) (1996).

MARK PHILP 449

is not a question of will but of 'nature'. Exchange within such relationships is often heavily symbolic in character and freighted with issues of esteem, trust and status. To violate the norms of exchange, or those governing relations between members of the group is to act shamefully, and so invoke penalties or demands for ritual cleansing. Members of such groups seek respect, which is won by conformity and leadership appeals to tradition and status.

Market relations involve dispersed competition, between firms or individuals, who are formally equal, and who enter relations to maximize profit. Relationships within the market are wholly instrumental; individuals' motives are straightforwardly interest-maximizing. Economic exchanges, ideally, produce benefits which are calculable and one-off, involving no commitment for future transactions and giving rise to no permanent relationship. In a situation of pure market exchange, familial or other communal relations would be valued only so far as doing so maximized the individual's advantage. Leadership has no place within such a system, since no collective action is sought, and prices achieve all desired coordination.

Gellner outlines the features of patron-client relations as follows:

> Patronage is unsymmetrical, involving inequality of power; it tends to form an extended system; to be long term, or at least not restricted to a single isolated transaction; to possess a distinctive ethos; and whilst not always illegal or immoral, to stand outside the officially proclaimed formal morality of the society in question ... What makes a patronage society is not the sheer presence of this syndrome, but its prominent or dominant position, to the detriment of other principles of social organization.[28]

Patron-client systems are favoured where we find an incompletely centralized state, a defective bureaucracy or a defective market. The patron acts as a means of access to goods and services which the client requires but which cannot be provided by either the state or the market; the client pays for the services his patron delivers usually by a willingness to perform some service for the patron when requested. The exchange is not symmetrical, since the patron has considerable power and influence and the client has little or none; but the patron gains in status and often more tangibly as well by having his clients in a position of dependence and indebtedness.

Politics concerns the craft of rule. Political relations are neither communal nor market in character – although they have similarities to both. Like communal relations, they involve a form of hierarchical ordering and the creation of patterns of authority; unlike them, their legitimacy does not rely solely on tradition and solidaristic norms. The justification for political authority involves a broader claim for legitimacy. Politics is unlike the market in that, although it may invoke consent as a part of the claim for legitimacy, the consent is not individuated to particular acts of the state but is taken as generating a *prima facie* right to rule which may legitimately exercise coercion. So those who rule expect those whom they rule to comply, not because so doing is interest-maximizing but because they claim a right to rule, and some recognition of this right on the part of citizens. True political authority rests not on the threat of punishment, nor on persuasion through argument, but on the citizen conceding

---

[28] Ernest Gellner and John Waterbury (eds), *Patrons and Clients in Mediterranean Societies* (London, Duckworth, 1975), p. 4.

to the commander a right to rule.[29] Moreover, strictly political authority is
neither solely instinctive nor habitual but grounds its claim to rule on some
principled basis – most commonly, by appeals to consent, public utility or
welfare, or the common good. Although claims may also draw on the history of
the society or on tradition or founding acts, in each case a distinction is
acknowledged between the office and the individual occupant of the office. The
relation of commander to complier is one mediated by a claim to the authority
which derives from his/her office, and, implicitly, by an appeal to the general
and public ends the office serves.

The view that political relations are authority relations which involve a claim
of the right to rule, where this claim is grounded in a general, public-regarding
justification, is essentially a development of an older distinction, at least as old
as Aristotle, between personal and political forms of rule. The rule of a despot
or tyrant is personal. He treats his state as his personal property for disposal as
he sees fit. How far tyrants in fact behaved in so unconstrained a way is another
question, but the theoretical construction of this type of rule as a limit case was
important in developing a contrasting set of norms and claims distinctive of
political forms of rule. Inroads into this personal form of rule were made
historically at times when the ruler found himself subject to countervailing
forces within his state which had to be conciliated to preserve his position; but
these constraints took a more permanent and public form when a distinction
developed in the public language of rule between the king qua person and the
king qua sovereign. In this process of development from rule as a private activity
to rule as a public function, we can recognize an expansion of the criteria of
legitimacy from the will of the individual ruler through to a collective and public
sense of the appropriateness of the action and its end. The force of the requirement that rule be referenced to the public is that it imposes a different character
of discourse on its participants than does civil society or the household.
Justification within the public realm appeals not to the force and strength of
personal preferences but to more generalizable principles of right and the
common good. A crucial distinction between political authority and other
forms of relation or exchange is that it necessarily appeals to public standards of
justification and appropriateness. In asking both who rules and in whose
interests, or in distinguishing the king from the crown, political argument
emerges as a field of legitimation and justification where claims must be couched
with reference to the distinctive rights and responsibilities of the political body
and of those subject to it or citizens of it.

However, political relations do not necessarily determine the basic structure
of a society or its institutional form, nor do they necessarily trump other
principles of exchange. We can notionally identify a threshold of politics, above
which political norms are sufficiently powerful either to order, or at least to
resist being ordered by, the social, ethnic, patrimonial and other exchange
relations of a community, but below which political norms operate in relatively
circumscribed areas of jurisdiction, in which they may be trumped by other
norms. This raises the question of at what point, under what conditions, and to

---

[29] 'The authoritarian relation rests neither on common reason nor on the power of the one who
commands; what they have in common is the hierarchy itself, whose rightness and legitimacy both
recognize and where both have their predetermined place. Hannah Arendt, *Between Past and
Future: Six Exercises in Political Thought* (Harmondsworth, Penguin, 1992), p. 93.

© Political Studies Association, 1997

what extent, political relations and norms become autonomous (as a sphere from other spheres) or dominant (as a sphere over other spheres of activity) as a mode of order and exchange within a community.

What distinguishes politics from other forms of relation and systems of exchange is the type of general, public-orientated justification used to legitimate its claims – something which also gives it, however tentatively, a conception of the state as an entity, and its people as a unity. For us to be able to say that political rule exists, it must be practically sustainable in the face of competition from these other forms. This does not mean that it will be differentiated from these other forms consistently across all cultures. In some systems it may not be seen as incompatible with the ends of politics for public offices to be filled by patronage, favouritism or nepotism, or for those holding office to make large personal fortunes; in others, anything less than a perfect meritocracy and an absolute scrupulousness about financial matters may be deemed corrupt. But what is required is that the ends which a political system recognizes, and which are acknowledged in its creation of public office, are able to curtail the scope of other principles of exchange when these encroach on the political domain.

How far this is possible raises two types of counter-factual question. The first asks how far, with, for example, a different system of appointment to office or with a different type of office or set of ends, the political system would act more effectively; the second asks, how far things could in fact be other than they are. The first relies on a richer conception of the ends of politics to be discussed in the next section. The second is an empirical question about how far there is, within the social and political culture of a society, the resources to support that richer conception. Indeed, this second question may also take the form, where there is a consistent disjunction between the official norms and rules of a political culture and its practices, of asking, counterfactually, how far the norms and rules of the political sphere are viable given the social, economic, and cultural conditions in which they must operate. It does not take a great deal of imagination (nor a particularly extensive knowledge of life in post-Soviet Russia), to recognize that political norms for the conduct of office can become inoperable under certain socio-economic conditions. The kind of benefits generated by a political system – security, the rule of law, citizenship, and so on – are not easily quantified or weighed against other types of good, and they are invariably long-term in character. As a result, their achievement requires a relatively integrated and stable political culture. When these benefits are threatened by political chaos, or social or economic disruption, there comes a point at which it is irrational not to seek other gains or more partial, less general forms of political goods – for example, by seeking profit that can be turned into hard currency, by building a following (or seeking a patron) so as to provide some of the benefits of a stable political system, albeit in a less general form, or by falling back on kinship or other types of communal relations for the delivery of goods and services. To think of these activities as corrupt requires that there be some other way people could act – and where it requires a degree of saintliness or heroism to take the moral high road, we must discount that as a relevant counter-factual. The still more difficult judgement to make in this case is whether we are dealing with a non-political system, or whether we should recognize the state as itself corrupt. That judgement requires a still more complex assessment of the forces which have brought the state to this point.

On this view, the study of political corruption cannot be wholly straight-forward – as we have seen, we cannot rely uncritically on official norms or laws. We have to recognize that 'ought implies can', and that in some circumstances properly political rule becomes impossible, while in others what can be achieved may fall far short of the objectives formally proclaimed by the political system. We need to ask of states, not whether they have political rule, but to what extent they have it and under what conditions. To answer these questions we need to recognize the causal conditions under which certain types of political authority become capable of consolidation, and thereby able to constrain the operation of other principles of allocation and exchange, as well as the conditions under which politics ceases to be possible because it can deliver too little in terms of its control of other spheres;[30] or where, by demanding too much of politics, it becomes incapable of supplying the minimum (as the breakdown of the communist regimes of eastern Europe and the Soviet Union might indicate).

Political rule is not a once-and-for-all achievement. A stable political culture can be efficiently self-reproducing and yet can be destabilized and destroyed by forces beyond its control – such as economic crisis or war. Moreover, states in which political relations are systematically subverted by other forms of exchange are not necessarily corrupt. Indeed, we might state categorically that they are not corrupt unless, counterfactually, they could be otherwise than they are – were it not for the way that political norms and rules are being ignored or bent by a faction, group or individual to maintain their dominance and secure their interests over and against the political and broader cultural norms of the community. It is difficult to establish these counterfactuals, but not impossible.

In his defence of his wheeling and dealing with Metherall, Greiner implies that the Commission's view of public office is one which is apolitical – where the political system is understood as being about 'what is (in Greiner's view) in many ways a largely private interest in terms of winning or holding a seat ...'. Nothing I have said thus far challenges Greiner's view of politics (although I have placed more emphasis than he does on the consequent obligations of those who achieve public office). There is a difference between the rules which structure public offices and those which govern how they are to be filled. Thus, political appointments to the House of Lords, or to certain positions in the US Federal Service, are seen as compatible with sustaining a recognition of the responsibilities of public office. Nonetheless, such appointments, or Greiner's view that achieving political office is a private interest, clearly could undermine the impartiality with which public office is exercised, and where it does so, the understanding of politics advanced here would require that the concern to sustain the character of public office must delimit the range of acceptable practices determining appointment to such office.

V

What is so good about political rule? Political theorists range from those who seem willing to deny that politics ever has sufficient ethical pull to trump the individual's other commitments, to those who emphasize the morally superior

[30] Judith Chubb, *Patronage, Power and Poverty in Southern Italy* (Cambridge, Cambridge University Press, 1982), for example, suggests the Christian Democrats in the north effectively surrendered control of the party in the south to opportunists with Mafia connections.

character of agency under political rule. Moreover, history is discomfitingly generous with cases in which political rule has imposed horrific costs upon domestic and foreign populations, whereas clean, beneficial and humanitarian political orders have been rather less in evidence. Clearly, we cannot on every occasion assume the ethical superiority of political rule. Rather, we should recognize that political rule is attractive as a solution in certain circumstances.

We can distinguish four views of the necessity for political rule:[31] one which sees it as offering a constitutional solution to the civil war that arises from the socially heterogeneous character of the polity; one for which it offers a quasi-juridical device which substitutes the sovereignty of the state (with its creation and protection of individual rights and liberties) for a war of all against all; one in which it provides a way of organizing the public powers so as to avoid conflict between those entrusted with public power and those subject to it; and one in which its defining moment involves the successful assertion of sovereignty against other sovereign units or groups claiming sovereignty.

From each perspective, the short answer to the question of what it is that gives moral precedence to political rule over other forms of exchange is 'war'. Politics takes normative precedence because it orders otherwise irresolvable forms of social and interpersonal conflict, and the form of political rule and the character of its concerns about corruption, is a function of how it understands these conflicts. This claim about the ethical necessity of political rule, however, presumes that authority is exercised appropriately. It is impossible not to recognize that political authority can be exercised cruelly, violently, or vindictively, or that those who rule may do so incompetently. In each case, these activities will damage the capacity of that authority to secure a stable order of rule capable of resolving conflict. But political corruption is distinctive as a form of dereliction: if political authority is desirable because it orders fundamental conflicts between interests, the suborning of that authority to serve one particular set of interests covertly reinstitutes the domination which that authority is designed to avoid. Other activity does so incidentally, through incompetence, or bad luck; but corruption strikes at the root.

Each of these views sees politics as a response to potential disorder, but understands the sources of this disorder in a different way. Moreover, since corruption involves the perversion, decay or destruction of the natural condition of politics, and these accounts offer different understandings of that condition, each also differs in its identification of those activities which most fundamentally threaten politics and its understanding of the forces which lie behind those activities. The emphasis on the socially heterogenous composition of the body politic, common to republican accounts, sees the predominant risk as one of factional strife, or *stasis*, and sees the political order as enabling the collective pursuit of the common good. That pursuit is framed by a constitutional structure, in the form of mixed government, which contains the threat of domination of one class and its interests, and is coupled with a variety of mechanisms to promote civic virtue and the pursuit of the common good. On this model the sources of corruption are manifold – luxury, commercial

---

[31] Drawing on Pasquale Pasquino. 'Political theory of war and peace: Foucault and the history of modern political theory', *Economy and Society*, 22 (1) (1993), pp. 77–88; and Carl Schmitt (G. Schwab, trans.), *The Concept of the Political* (New Brunswick NJ, Rutgers University Press, 1976). Although these accounts draw on concerns found in European and Anglo-American political thought, they are certainly not exclusive to these traditions.

activity, foreign subversion, extremes of inequality, failures to recognize the services of leading politicians, and the constant tendency for civic *moeurs* to be undermined by ambition, pride and the more destructive human passions. In each case it is manifested in the erosion of the collective capacity to pursue the common good. For republicans, political corruption has less to do with individual rule infraction, and more to do with the systematic decay of the political culture. Moreover, there is no conception within republican thought of a social order without politics. As a result, corruption unleashes an internal war which, if not stemmed, results in the complete breakdown of order. Hence the tendency to associate corruption with the decline of the state.[32]

The Hobbesian repugnance for the war of all against all results in an insistence on the resignation of individual sovereignty to a common power which enforces a common law and set of procedures. Hobbes has little room for political activity, which he sees as for the most part destabilizing; rather, he embodies political rule in the exercise of the sovereign power – and by implication sees corruption as whatever tends to the weakening of that power. Indeed, Hobbesians so fear the triumph of individualism over the formal order of the state that they embrace a version of nominalism: corruption is simply what people accuse each other of when they see them acting against their interests in some way – it has no moral content. What distances Hobbes from outright political realists is his belief that the ultimate end of this sovereignty is the public good. If Hobbes's commitment to absolute sovereignty distances him from our third, liberal, model, his commitment to the contractarian principle that the ultimate justification for sovereignty is its ability to allow us peaceably to pursue our interests distances him from the more decisionist realism of our final perspective drawn from Schmitt.

The liberal model of politics shifts the emphasis from a concern with the destructive tensions inherent in the social order to a concern with how the powers of the state can be exercised in ways inimical to the liberty and security of its subjects. The emphasis on constitutional order and the separation of powers is not concerned with tensions in the entire social body, but instead focuses on ways of ordering the structures of rule so that those entrusted with political power will act in the interests of those whom the state was founded to protect and will not usurp that power for their own ends – although liberals are, after 1789, also much concerned with popular encroachments on the orderly exercise of political power. The liberal model sees corruption in terms of the weakening of ethical constraints on individual conduct in public office and consequent abuse of political power for individual gain. Liberals have more or less demanding views as to the conditions which are necessary to ensure that the occupants of political office are devoted solely to the public interest. It is possible to insist that all appointments be made on the basis of merit; equally, less rigorous criteria may be tolerated on the grounds that effective government relies on a degree of coordination which can only be brought about by allowing some partisan interest within political institutions. Moreover, where some liberals have been wholly concerned with mechanisms for ensuring that public

---

[32] See Patrick Dobel, 'The corruption of a state', *American Political Science Review*, 72 (1978), 958–73, J. Peter Euben, 'Corruption', in Terence Ball, James Farrar and Russell Hanson (eds), *Political Innovation and Conceptual Change* (Cambridge, Cambridge University Press, 1989); and Hannah Arendt, *The Human Condition* (Chicago, University of Chicago Press, 1958).

servants do not act beyond their powers (those, for example, who follow the separation of powers principle) there are others (not least Montesquieu) for whom political rule must be understood in relation to the society and culture of which it is a part and who remain sceptical about simple formulae for ensuring uncorrupt and stable political rule.[33]

The decisionist conception of the state, as expounded by Schmitt, sees the exercise of state sovereignty in determining the line between friend and foe as essential to avoid the subordination of the state to other states or to other groups willing to make and enforce that distinction. Schmitt owes a good deal to Hobbes, but he differs in the existential character of his thought. The emphasis he gives to the friend/foe distinction is a function of the utterly arbitrary character of such divisions: 'The high points of politics are simultaneously the moments in which the enemy is, in concrete clarity, recognized as the enemy'.[34] Schmitt's approach takes it as axiomatic that it is the political decision as to whether or not another entity poses a threat to one's own way of life which dominates all other relations in the state. In Slagstad's apt phrase, 'the *Machstaat* overrides the *Rechsstaat*'.[35] Without this moment of absolute and norm-creating sovereignty the state would fall prey to an internalization of the political: 'If one wants to speak of politics in the context of the primacy of internal politics, then this conflict no longer refers to war between organized nations but to civil war'.[36]

Schmitt's account is deeply pessimistic. It is decisionist because all that matters is that the decisive distinctions can be drawn and sustained by sovereign entities – there is no right or wrong in any particular state's decision. But the underlying normative project in Schmitt's account is the existential view that it is only through the identification of friend and foe that life becomes endowed with meaning and purpose.[37] *The Concept of the Political* is in large part an attack on de-politicization, particularly in the form of pacifism and liberalism, both of which threaten to eradicate the political, to evade 'political responsibility and visibility' and thereby to eliminate the most serious and central concerns of human life.[38] This account rests on two presumptions. The first is that the political is threatened when its realm of action becomes displaced or obscured by systems of exchange or by pretensions to shared ethical principles which deny its decisive content. The resulting state of peace and security rests on a refusal to recognize that there are fundamental disagreements

---

[33] See, for example, the intense debates within French liberal circles in the early nineteenth century, G. A. Kelly, *The Humane Comedy: Constant, Tocqueville and French Liberalism* (Cambridge, Cambridge University Press, 1992).

[34] Schmitt, *The Concept of the Political*, p. 67.

[35] Cited by Rune Slagstad, 'Liberal Constitutionalism and its Critics', in Jon Elster and Rune Slagstad (eds), *Constitutionalism and Democracy* (Cambridge, Cambridge University Press, 1988), p. 116.

[36] Schmitt, *The Concept of the Political*, p. 32.

[37] See Leo Strauss 'Comments on Carl Schmitt's *Der Begriff Des Politischen*' given as an appendix to Schwab's translation of *The Concept of the Political*, pp. 98–9.

[38] Schmitt's conception of the centrality and inevitability of the political is captured in his discussion of theories which suggest the eventual displacement of politics by economic exchange. 'A domination of men based on pure economics must appear a terrible deception if, by remaining nonpolitical, it thereby evades political responsibility and visibility. Exchange by no means precludes the possibility that one of the contractors experiences a disadvantage and that a system of mutual contracts finally deteriorates into a system of the worst exploitation and repression.' *The Concept of the Political*, p. 77.

over the proper ends of life and no such refusal can be stable, since its inevitably partial disposing of differential costs and benefits must eventually generate attempts at resistance. The second is his view that: 'all genuine political theories presuppose man to be evil, i.e., by no means an unproblematic but a dangerous and dynamic being'.[39] Or, put less objectionably: 'Political thinkers such as Machiavelli, Hobbes, and often Fichte presuppose with their pessimism only the reality or possibility of the distinction of friend and enemy'. And included in this presupposition is the view that what it is to make this distinction is to recognize 'the ever present possibility of conflict'.[40]

Where Hobbes saw the major threat to sovereignty as arising from the tendency for the nobility and the political élite to usurp sovereignty,[41] Schmitt, responding to a more democratic era, sees state unity as supremely expressed in the rejection of forces inimical to its sovereignty both within and outside the state. Consequently, corruption involves the weakening of the state's ability to draw this line, either through the introduction of conflict into the institutions of the state, or through its subversion by or subordination to foreign powers, or in the failure to achieve a shared political will behind this distinction: 'everywhere in political history, in foreign as well as in domestic politics, the incapacity or the unwillingness to make this distinction (friend/foe) is a symptom of the political end'.[42] Indeed, it is not difficult to find in Schmitt the view that liberalism is the ultimate form of corruption – 'liberal concepts typically move between ethics ... and economics ... From this polarity they attempt to annihilate the political as a domain of conquering power and repression'.[43]

These four positions are certainly not exhaustive of possible accounts of the ethical value of political rule. Nonetheless, they help us to recognize a threshold for politics: a theory which sees no lines of conflict between social groups, no threat from individual self-government, no distinct conception of the state the powers of which can be subject to abuse, and no sense of the potential subversion of sovereignty, will see no need for political rule and will have no standard by which to assess its corruption. Where we recognize one or more of these fundamental forms of social conflict, political rule has normative weight because it offers a way to resolve conflict in a way which is not simply a case of one side winning. Even if we want to build more ambitious accounts of the possibilities of politics, this basic solution can be valued independently because by ordering conflict it offers a degree of security and freedom from fear and domination, thereby ensuring (within inevitable limits) the avoidance of radical harm or evil. On this account, then, politics exerts ethical pull only under certain conditions, or certain characterizations of the 'human condition'. Politics, then, turns conflict into order – albeit perspectives differ on what balance of *Recht* and *Macht* are required to achieve this. But even where, as with Schmitt, *Macht* is predominant, its purpose is to define an arena which is subsequently relatively free of the need for it. Moreover, for all these positions, what makes political corruption an evil is that it undercuts the ability of politics to provide such a solution. Of course, there are many more appealing accounts of this 'pull', but

---

[39] Schmitt, *The Concept of the Political*, p. 61.

[40] Schmitt, *The Concept of the Political*, pp. 65 and 32.

[41] Deborah Baumgold, *Hobbes's Political Philosophy* (Cambridge, Cambridge University Press, 1988).

[42] Schmitt, *The Concept of the Political*, p. 68.

[43] Schmitt, *The Concept of the Political*, p. 71.

their scope of application is usually far more restricted and, prosaic though my suggestion is, it is likely to serve most of our purposes.[44]

VI

I have sketched in very broad terms four possible ways of understanding the ethical appeal of politics. It should be clear that each position (and others) offers only a background set of assumptions against which more detailed debate about the practices of a state must take place. Views as to which institutional structures and political practices, what social and economic preconditions, and what balance between political and other forms of exchange, must be in place for politics effectively to order the identified area of conflict, will vary greatly. On Hobbesian and republican grounds it is possible to believe that an absolute sovereign or a dictator is necessary – but it is also possible for an essentially similar understanding of politics to generate much more moderate models of the state. Moreover, the scope of the political is not fixed by these four positions, since political theorists will disagree about how far political rule can resolve certain types of conflict. Pepys's nasty proclivities with respect to Mrs Bagwell can be seen as being of marginal significance in a view of politics which is concerned with welding together different interests and classes within a polity divided between court and country, and which sees the civil service largely as an adjunct to a patronage machine. But, in a view in which the fundamental political problem is securing freedom from domination,[45] Pepys's activities could be condemned as a deeply corrupt extension of political power into the private sphere – corrupt because self-serving and violating the injunction against arbitrary power.

More modern concerns that the personal be recognized as political, in many cases, involve the recognition that apparently consensual arrangements are often sustained by the insidious, illicit and exploitative exercise of power by one group over others. In these accounts, activities which might otherwise be thought of as irrelevant to the political process can fundamentally challenge its legitimacy.[46] Furthermore, because each account perceives the need for political rule differently, what one account will see as resolving conflict, another will see as corrupt. Thus, where a state takes draconian action against an internal faction in the name of sustaining its sovereignty, it is open to challenge from an interpretation driven by a distrust of those exercising power. While Machiavelli

---

[44] This has to be understood as a first move in the argument. There are accounts of the political, such as the Aristotelian, which ground its ethical value in the particular way of life it offers its participants. But it should be recognized that Aristotle's account assumed that slaves and mechanics were incapable of political life. We thus risk a trade-off between the force of the ethical pull which a theory delivers and its inclusiveness. Taking the view I have adopted here seems closer to one central feature of the western liberal tradition (which Judith Shklar described as 'The liberalism of fear', in Nancy Rosenblum, *Liberalism and Morality* (Cambridge MA, Harvard University Press, 1989), pp. 21–38) than does the Aristotelian account, but it does leave open the question of how stable a political culture can be in which 'satisficing' on the avoidance of radical harm is the predominant motivation of citizens.

[45] Philip Pettit, *Republicanism: a Theory of Freedom and Government* (Oxford, Oxford University Press, 1997).

[46] See, for example, Toni Morrison (ed.), *Race-ing Justice, En-gendering Power: Essays on Anita Hill, Clarence Thomas, and the Construction of Social Reality* (London, Chatto and Windus, 1993).

can celebrate Borgia's skill in dealing with Romerro de Orca,[47] or Schmitt *might* have recognized that it was necessary for Hitler to 'execute' Ernst Rohm, liberals, concerned with the way that political power quickly becomes arbitrary and self-serving, would see both as threatening to corrupt the character of true political authority. This does not mean that we are dealing with a core set of concepts – politics, authority, corruption – which are theory dependent and thereby essentially contestable.[48] On the contrary, through the use of counterfactual speculation, detailed historical research, and careful theoretical construction, the student of politics can construct a case by identifying the type of imperatives these states really faced, the extent to which the political authority they sought to exercise was (or could have been) directed to resolving these imperatives, and the degree to which the actions of those in power came to be subverted by a range of aspirations and motives which imposed avoidable costs on those subject to them. It is extremely difficult to construct such arguments – not least in an academic culture increasingly dedicated more to publishing than to thinking – but it is in principle possible so to do. To resign oneself to the essential contestibility of politics and its corruption is to deny one's intellectual responsibility to establish the best possible case.

In conclusion I want briefly to address three problems in the study of political corruption to see how far our understanding of them can be advanced by the arguments developed here. The first concerns how we draw a distinction between corruption and incompetence; the second asks how far we can admit the view that political corruption may be functional; and the third re-opens the debate on how we should analyse the Metherall case.

Most commonly, political corruption involves substituting rule in the interests of an individual or group for those publicly endorsed practices which effect an ordered resolution to conflicting individual or group interests. Understood in this way it is easy to see the normative appeal of the political, and equally easy to see that a distinction can and should be drawn between corruption and, say, incompetence. Incompetence can be directly harmful, it can contribute to delegitimation, and it can undermine the efficacy of political solutions to conflict. But it differs from corruption, not because corruption involves intentional wrong-doing (since, as in the Greiner case, that intentionality may be doubtful), but because corrupt action directly subverts the distinction between the interests of the individual or group and the responsibilities of the office, and thereby erodes the very distinction upon which the domain of politics relies for its capacity to resolve conflict. Greiner may not have intended to act corruptly but, in believing that he had the right to appoint public officials so as to shore up his party's control of parliament he was denying that a distinction should be drawn between political appointees and employees in the public service. The Commission clearly believed that that distinction was central to sustaining the legitimacy of parliamentary and administrative activity.[49]

---

[47] Machiavelli, *The Prince*, ch. VII.

[48] Cf. William Connolly, *The Terms of Political Discourse* (Lexington MA, Heath, 1974), ch. 1.

[49] The Court of Appeal majority judgement was that the Commissioner went beyond his jurisdiction in finding Greiner's behaviour 'reasonable grounds for dismissal' because the grounds for such a judgement must be legal and objective. The dissenting opinion was that the conduct could constitute reasonable grounds for dismissal. So the disagreement was not over whether the distinction should be drawn, nor over whether Greiner's conduct violated that distinction, but over whether the appropriate standards for judging reasonable grounds must be objective legal standards or can be more subjective and intuitive in character.

Superficially, because it can have similar results, incompetence may seem like a type of corruption, but it does not put into question this distinction – it may lead to open conflict, but it does not declare it in the heart of the political system. As we have seen, what is taken to be central to sustaining that distinction will vary, and may be vigorously contested, in political systems. Moreover, a great many activities enjoined by law, or not prohibited by it, may lead to the erosion of that distinction and the outbreak of conflict, so we need to distinguish a core set of cases of corruption, in which intentionality, illegality, and the substitution of private for public interests are all present, and a set of penumbra cases where more complex judgements have to be made about whether and to what extent these different criteria are met. But this broader analysis has to be informed by the recognition that what distinguishes corruption from other forms of destructive political behaviour is that it works by eroding the distinction between private and public concerns and interests. Extreme incompetence may lead to the collapse of political authority, but it does so because of its consequences, not because the actions of public officials actively suborn that authority so as to pursue interests in a manner which that order is expressly designed to resist. This is why terrorist movements, although they introduce war, are not corrupt – because, while they deny the validity of the existing political system, they implicitly project a conception of a political solution in which the distinction between the public and their private concerns is sustained. Similarly, authoritarian regimes, such as Hitler's Fascist state, may come to pursue goals which are so grandiose, and so appalling in their consequences, that we may be tempted to describe them as corrupt. But, while many individuals within such states are deeply corrupt, not all are, and for many there remains a clear sense that in accepting office they were accepting certain public responsibilities. It is, however, another issue as to whether these men and women, by refusing to ask questions about what was happening elsewhere in the state, by putting their self-protection above a broader sense of public responsibility, or, by allowing themselves unreflectingly to indulge their prejudices and passions, increasingly sacrificed the integrity which public office requires, resulting in the eventual corruption of the entire political order. We need to distinguish carefully between the question as to whether or not a type of political authority (with an associated conception of public office) is being preserved, and the question of whether there is any ethical standing left attached to that authority. Many things may erode the ethical force of political authority, without that authority being corrupt.

The view that corruption can be functional is one which has caused a good deal of contention. In his brief but elegant discussion of the thesis, Jon Elster identifies two premises upon which the objection to the arguments for the functionality of corruption can be founded: that corruption is only useful when there is not too much of it, and that corruption feeds upon itself.[50] If both hold, as seems plausible, then what initially looks like the best solution, moderate levels of corruption, begins to seem unfeasible. The two stable equilibria are limited corruption and heavy corruption – moderate corruption is not an equilibrium position. Or, as Elster puts it: 'Beyond a certain threshold, the whole fabric of society may unravel'.

---

[50] Jon Elster, *The Cement of Society*, pp. 268–72.

Elster's argument is, within limits, persuasive. Moderate corruption can only
be functional if it does not encourage heavy corruption; but where it is tolerated
it inevitably produces widespread corruption, and where it is systematically
penalized it tends to limited corruption. Nonetheless, the suggestion that
corruption can be functional is not necessarily incompatible with the argument
advanced here. The most common claims for functionality are made with
respect to economic development. The account I have given has assumed that
the political order of a state is roughly appropriate for the conditions of that
state. Obviously, this is not always the case. State-socialist societies in eastern
Europe were, for the most part, very inefficient and deeply riven with corruption – necessarily so because people were often unable to meet targets and
deliver services without systematically breaking the rules.[51] Under these
circumstances, corruption was clearly functional both to the economy and to
continuing political stability – albeit in the short to medium term. But, in such
cases, there is such a divergence between the official and the unofficial culture
that it is clear that the political system of authoritative allocation is for the most
part a sham and could only be implemented by the state declaring war on its
society. Short of this, something like a take-over occurs of various areas of
political allocation by covert marketization or, more commonly, by some form
of patrimonial or patron-client type exchange, and this subversion can result in
economic progress, and may also force political changes.[52] However, this
process is not costless: although open conflict may not result, covert patterns of
domination by some groups or individuals over others do tend to emerge, and
there is a danger that the corrupt but functional activity becomes so widespread
that it makes it extremely difficult to re-establish the political order on a new
footing.

Moreover, claims for functional corruption remain troubling wherever the
official culture continues to command lip-service and where, consequently,
discovery of covert activity can result in costs. Under these conditions, even
where there seems no alternative but to engage in bribery, black-marketeering
etc., the result is rarely pure marketization of exchange. On the contrary,
exchanges come with hooks on them – one's willingness to engage in certain
activities means that others have information which you would prefer them not
to use, which means it has a price. In that respect it differs markedly from
legitimate forms of market exchange. The residue of the transaction is a price
which is paid by the transaction remaining open ended – with the participants
remaining exposed to others and to potential future costs. This is less of a
problem the more equal the two participants are in their attitude to the political
order. Two equally unwilling rule violators pay equivalent prices in their
exchange. But where one violator has behind him a syndicate for organized
crime, while the other seeks a one-off exchange outside a system of rules to
which he remains committed in principle, the real prices paid may be radically
different. Under the pressures of circumstance, people may engage in activities
in which they effectively attach little cost to potential future consequences but,

---

[51] As clearly did happen in certain areas in Russia once the communist system began to fall
apart – see Leslie Holmes, *The End of Communist Power: Anti-corruption Campaigns and Legitimation Crisis* (Carleton, Melbourne, Melbourne University Press, 1993).

[52] This does not mean that the scope of politics is fixed. What was appropriate in the civil war in
the USSR after the revolution was not necessarily appropriate later – the boundaries between, e.g.,
politics and economics are not set in stone.

while such transactions may be functional to economic development or unfreezing a politically strangled economy, they can set in place relations in which some groups are able systematically to shape the behaviour of others in the future. Shedding one's tainted past is not easily done. In effect, moderate to widespread corruption requires that people make a gamble on future immunity – but that gamble does not always pay off, and they then become prey to those who hold information they want to keep secret. Moreover, it creates incentives for those who have discounted future punishment to block the establishment of any system in which they may be held responsible for their past activities – and this is true not only for those committed to non-political solutions, but also for those who are not so committed but who have an interest in avoiding any political solution in which they may have to bear costs for past activities. Alliances between Mafia gangs and politicians with an interest in avoiding certain types of control mechanism and public accountability can produce very weak forms of political control within a state.

Greiner's characterization of politics (as I understand it) is that it is a process of struggle for the exercise of sovereignty, by groups who have to use the distribution of office and patronage as a way of consolidating their grasp on the powers of the state. To take away those powers of patronage would be to destroy the government's capacity to hold together otherwise atomistic and factional tendencies within its political institutions. One way of characterizing the disagreement between Greiner and the Commission is that the latter was working with a more classically liberal set of concerns about politics serving the public interest and not being exercised in an arbitrary manner. But there is a much deeper issue at play here concerning the balance between the legitimacy of outcomes being guaranteed by procedures and the legitimacy being guaranteed by effects. The more discursive conceptions of politics, in which public deliberation and collective understandings play a substantive role in ensuring the legitimacy of the outcomes of the political procedures are in stark contrast to a more Schmittian realism with respect to the political process as a struggle for the assertion of sovereignty over a territory. The disagreement between Greiner and the Commission, if couched in such contrasting terms, reveals deeply conflicting conceptions of politics. Nothing I have said here denies such conflict. It may be that if we understand the political process in a certain light we will see it as essential that what many liberals would see as 'rules of the game' should be regarded as themselves open to strategic manipulation by the players. But that argument would not involve denying the distinctive character of political authority. Even the insistence that politics must get dirty depends on a particular understanding of the imperatives which face attempts to establish political authority. Political realism bows to what it recognizes as political necessity. And while there are philosophical anthropologies and a range of foundational commitments behind both realism and its alternatives, there are also more empirical issues in play – issues which might, for example, lead us to endorse Schmitt's account as capturing the central feature of politics in the Weimar Republic, or in many European states after 1914, without thinking that the account works across all conditions. As such the case for or against realism is one which we have to recognize as to some extent empirical.

In the case of Greiner, we have to ask whether the political, economic, and cultural conditions of New South Wales were such as to necessitate the politicization of public appointments to the degree Greiner claimed, or whether

462   *Defining Political Corruption*

he was falling back on political reflexes appropriate to an era in which the grip of the political order over its citizens and the political leadership over its supporters was substantially more fragile. The Commission's judgement clearly challenged the long-standing, partly self-serving, but increasingly contested norms of an élite political culture, and it sought to put an end to the use of public resources by politicians in their struggles for power – struggles which can so blind the participants that they come to confuse their activity with the pursuit of the common good – but it did so not to abolish politics, but to preserve it in a more democratic and accountable form. And in a choice between Greiner's version of politics and the Commission's, the latter seems both to meet the requirement of practical feasibility and to have greatest ethical weight.

[23]

Review of African Political Economy No.76:221-240
© ROAPE Publications Ltd., 1998
ISSN 0305-6244; RIX #7605

Misunderstanding African Politics: Corruption & the Governance Agenda

Morris Szeftel

Corruption has become an African epidemic. It is impossible to overstate the poisoning of human relations and the paralysing of initiative that the corruption on the African scale brings.

> - Matthew Parris, *The Times*, 8 August 1997

And they beat each other's heads all bloody
Scuffling over booty,
Call the other fellows greedy wretches,
They themselves but do their duty.

> - Bertolt Brecht, *The Song of the Waterwheel*

The plundered
Point to you with their fingers, but
The plunderer praises the system ...

> - Bertolt Brecht, *Germany*

Political corruption – the misuse of public office or public responsibility for private (personal or sectional) gain – has been an important theme of the neo-liberal policies of adjustment, conditionality and democratization in Africa. Having identified the state as 'the problem', and liberalization and democratization as 'the solution' to that problem, it was inevitable that efforts to eradicate and control the widespread corruption characterising post-colonial politics would be given a high priority by 'the donors'. From the outset, proponents of structural reform linked political corruption to authoritarianism as an explanation of developmental failure, thereby identifying the arguments for democratization and 'good governance' with those for liberalization. This paper explores the way in which corruption has been understood in this 'governance' agenda and the efforts that have been made to control it by improving institutional performance and policing – greater transparency and accountability, more effective oversight and punishment – and by building a political culture intolerant of corruption. In general, however, legal and administrative reform has produced disappointing results and corruption has flourished and even increased. Failure has compounded cynicism and weakened faith in democratic change. Such failures suggest: firstly, that the anti-corruption strategies pursued by international donors and imposed on African debtors are inadequate because of weaknesses in their conception of the state; secondly, that the

222   Review of African Political Economy

reforms introduced through liberalization (a weakening of the state, deregulation and privatization) create new conditions in which corruption can flourish; and, thirdly, that fundamental features of African politics will need to change before such anti-corruption measures can hope to succeed.

Corruption has become an increasingly important issue for most countries in the aftermath of the cold war. Once complacently viewed in the West as 'being virtually the preserve of authoritarian or "developing" nations', the perception has grown, in the last decade, 'that the phenomenon has spread to new areas: no state any longer seems safe, not even the most mature democracy' (Heywood, 1997:1,2). The evidence for this changing perspective has been accumulating fast. Even in Italy, where corruption has been a normal feature of all levels of the state, there was still shock at revelations that a Masonic order (P2) – including many leading political, administrative, military, judicial, business and media leaders – ran a 'secret' or 'parallel' state involved in widespread corruption, criminal activities and violence (Chubb and Vannicelli, 1988). The scandals also touched the Vatican and linked the political class directly to organised crime. One former prime minister was convicted *in absentia* of serious corruption offences, another was accused of being a longtime servant of the Mafia. Scandals pointing to high-level corruption in Greece, Spain, France (where the most senior judge is presently under investigation), Germany, Austria and Belgium dominated the headlines in the nineties. In the United States, the Clinton administration has been besieged by a range of accusations of sexual and financial impropriety. In Britain, a succession of scandals – involving gerrymandering, MPs taking money in return for asking parliamentary questions, abuses of office, bribery, and the usual crop of sex frolics – required the appointment of a commission to redefine standards of public morality (Doig, 1996a & 1996b; Oliver, 1997; Ridley & Doig, 1997). Altogether more sinister events, involving arms sales to Iraq and the unlawful diversion of budgeted aid to provide sweeteners for arms sales to Malaysia (the so-called Pergau Dam affair) and Indonesia were reviewed by the Scott inquiry which (despite an 1800 page report calculated to obscure rather than reveal) nevertheless found clear evidence of government misconduct (Norton-Taylor et al., 1996). The issue of secret financial contributions to political parties remains to be tackled.

In Asia, corruption has hardly been out of the headlines either. In India, the Jain *hawala* scandal in 1995 and 1996 implicated a number of politicians of involvement in systematic receipt and extortion of funds from local and foreign business, of accepting bribes in return for tailoring policies to the needs of contributors and of other major abuses of electoral and criminal laws. The scandal touched politicians in opposition as well as in government and ultimately claimed the then Prime Minister, Narasimha Rao. In the wake of the *hawala* scandal, evidence emerged of other cases of serious looting of public resources – most notably in Bihar, where the state administration purchased expensive stock-feeds for extremely hungry animals which apparently required up to forty years of normal feed each month – despite the fact that many of them did not actually exist. In South Korea, recent democratic reforms have resulted in the prosecution of former senior government officials, including two former presidents, on charges of having received bribes totalling hundreds of millions of dollars while in office. And in China, White (1996: 41) observes that by late 1993

> *one of the main officials in charge of countering corruption ... admitted that corruption 'is now worse than at any other period since New China was founded in 1949. It has spread into the Party, government administration and every part of society, including politics, economy, ideology and culture'. US and European business people interviewed in Hong*

Kong in 1995 ranked China's 'business corruption performance' as Number 1 in Asia along with India and Indonesia (with Japan and Singapore ranking the lowest).

The seal of relative honesty bestowed on Japan will no doubt be a welcome surprise to a citizenry buffeted by a chain of high-level corruption scandals – Lockheed and Recruit among them – stretching back to the seventies. Similar instances could be cited for Latin America (Little, 1996; Little & Posada-Carbo, 1996). In Russia, the wholesale plunder of the carcass of the old Soviet economy and state has become a thing of wonder. The result, everywhere, has been an increase in public distrust of the state, politics and politicians.

Set against corruption on this scale, Africa's experience of the problem seems relatively modest. The scale of the examples mentioned above far exceeds what is possible given Africa's meagre resources. Indeed, those looting the African state can only envy the size of the 'pot' available to those in other countries. So it is perhaps the more ironic that it is in Africa that corruption is widely regarded as posing the most serious threat to both development and stability. It is in Africa that corruption (along with ethnic conflict) is seen as 'the political disease' by indigenous and foreign observers alike.

There is a pervasive cynicism in many international circles about the corruption of African states, a view that it is in the nature of things African, that there may even be 'a culture of political corruption' (LeVine, 1993:274) in which corruption is the normal stuff of politics. It is reflected in the comment, quoted at the start of this article, from the former British Tory MP, Matthew Parris, which appeared under the subheading: 'Corruption is so widespread that African leaders no longer disappoint us; we no longer expect anything'. And mirrored, too, in the comment attributed to an American diplomat that 'you can no longer buy an African state, you can only rent one by the day' (Charlton & May, 1989:13). And in popular belief among ordinary people throughout Africa, too. And in the way in which many public officials seem almost to believe that this is how they should behave, this is the way it is done, while they are in office: it is difficult to think of a military coup or a political movement which did not accuse their opponents in government of corruption (or later themselves not face – and merit – similar charges). This, perhaps, is why Bayart's book (1993) – with its tendency to reduce African politics to personal accumulation and patronage, devoid of ideals, struggles for justice, notions of equality, and so on – has been so influential. It is also why the donors have been so quick to include anti-corruption measures among the conditionalities required for aid and balance of payments support. External intervention against corruption was not invented in Africa; the 'war on drugs' and efforts to stem international money laundering (see, for instance, Gilmore 1995) have a longer history. But it is in Africa (not Korea or Venezuela or India) that attempts have been made to use aid topress and even force governments to take steps against general public office corruption within their own administrative structures.

Corruption and the 'Governance' Agenda

From the start, therefore, political corruption has been at the forefront of the issues raised by the economic restructuring of the last 25 years and the (more marginal) tide of democratization of the last decade. It has been an issue on which all Africa's creditors (or 'donors' as they prefer) could agree. Those primarily concerned with debt repayment and economic reform (especially the IMF and World Bank) regarded corruption as a threat to good governance because of its potential to 'redirect' aid, subvert policy reforms and undermine market institutions. And those more interested in using conditionality to foster democracy and human rights (such as the Nordic countries, the Netherlands and, since 1997, Britain) focused on the role of corruption in the abuse of power, the unfairness of resource distribution and the negation of citizenship rights. For both, a bloated, unaccountable and authoritarian state promoted endemic corruption.

This view also helped to link the donor agenda to the demands of African democratic reformers in the eighties and nineties. The idea that corruption flourished in one-party or military regimes where accountability was lacking and, in turn, produced inequality, dishonesty, stagnation and debt was a constant theme of critics of the old oligarchies. Economic liberalization and multi-party democracy were presented (by donors to African elites and by elites to voters) as the most effective means of combating corruption. It was the means to remove and punish those who lined their pockets and abused their power and also to prevent their successors from getting their own snouts too deeply into the trough. The proposition that democracy can limit the worst excesses of corruption by making it easier to scrutinise and regulate the operation of the state – because public institutions are more responsible, transparent and accountable and because political and legal costs are more easily imposed on corrupt officials – is the core language of conditionality, liberalization, good governance and democratization, of donor and local democrat alike.

These themes were clearly set out, for example, at a 1992 conference in Washington on *Limiting Administrative Corruption in the Democratizing States of Africa* – some of the papers being published in a special 1993 issue of *Corruption and Reform*, edited by Robert Charlick, a senior adviser to the Africa Bureau of USAID. In a keynote paper (1993:177), Charlick observed that:

> With the end of the Cold War in Africa international donor agencies have begun to say openly what they could previously only mutter – that corruption, rent-seeking, or other such euphemisms, is a major impediment to the economic development of many African countries. Perhaps, just as important, it is a threat to donor programs as well. Not only are taxpayers and their representatives displaying an increasing impatience with the waste of public resources which systematic administrative corruption entails, private sector actors are decreasingly willing to tolerate the high cost of doing business in societies where the 'informal' transaction costs are so steep.

Corruption and Rent-seeking

'Rent-seeking' has indeed become a euphemism for 'corruption' among many political scientists. But for multilateral donors and their economists, 'rent-seeking' is more than a euphemism; it is at the core of their critique of the role of the state. Paolo Mauro, an IMF economist, explains economic rent as 'the extra amount paid ... to somebody or for something useful whose supply is limited either by nature or through human ingenuity' (1997:2), that is, the incremental price that has to be paid for scarcity or monopoly of supply. Some rents are 'natural' in that they derive from the unique talents of their producers (for Mauro, interestingly, it is Mike Tyson's purse that comes to mind). Other rents are 'artificial', the result of manipulated shortages created, for instance, by import restrictions. At the heart of these artificial rents is the capacity of government to interfere with the market: 'every day private firms spend vast amounts of money attempting to convince legislators to grant monopolies or otherwise restrict competition so that some industry or individual can realize a rent'. Moreover, it is in the nature of the state that public officials will use this capacity to extract rents for themselves:

> *Throughout the world bureaucrats and people in authority are indefatigably manoeuvring to position themselves in a tiny monopoly where they can be bribed for issuing a license, approving an expenditure or allowing a shipment across a border.*

For the World Bank (1998: 4) corruption is a function of the capacity to seek rents:

> *The dynamics of corruption in the public sector can be depicted in a simple model. The opportunity for corruption is a function of the size of the rents under a public official's control, the discretion that official has in allocating those rents, and the accountability that official faces for his or her decisions.*

The concept therefore neatly links state regulation to corruption. The rent-seeking behaviour of the state is deemed objectionable because it imposes economic and social costs – whether the rents are extracted legally or corruptly. For the Bank, corruption flourishes where 'institutions are weak and government policies generate economic rents'. For Mauro its causes are found in trade restrictions, subsidies, price controls, multiple exchange rates and foreign exchange allocation schemes, which permit rents to be extracted, and in low civil service wages which encourage rent-seeking activities. Two other sources of rents and corruption which he identifies are especially interesting for Africa: resource rich economies where high rents can be extracted by the regulation of exports; and societies where ethnic and linguistic divisions which encourage public officials to favour their own group. As for the consequences of these activities, the Bank argues that corruption will reduce macroeconomic performance, undermine fdi, harm small business and the poor and endanger the environment. Mauro suggests that rent-seeking and corruption are likely to lower investment and retard growth, to direct skills towards rent-seeking activities, to reduce the effectiveness of aid flows, to reduce tax revenue and hence state capacity, to lower the quality of infrastructure and public services and to distort the composition of government spending by encouraging officials to favour activities where the pickings are high. The implications are clear – the alternatives to corruption and rent-seeking are the same, namely, deregulation, less state and more market.

It is not surprising, then, that the international financial institutions concerned with adjustment and restructuring should be concerned about corruption. In 1996 the managing director of the IMF called on governments to 'demonstrate their intolerance for corruption in all its forms' (Mauro, 1997:1) while the president of the World Bank, James D Wolfensohn, spoke of the need to 'deal with the cancer of corruption'. He went on to issue this call to arms:

> *In country after country, people are demanding action on this issue. They know that corruption diverts resources from the poor to the rich, increases the cost of running businesses, distorts public expenditures, and deters foreign investors. They also know that corruption erodes the constituency for aid programs and humanitarian relief. And we all know that corruption is a major barrier to sound and equitable development. Solutions can only be home-grown. National leaders need to take a stand. Civil society plays a key role as well.(World Bank, 1997: http://www.worldbank.org/html/prddr/trans/so96/art3.htm)*

The theme is further developed in the Bank's 1997 *World Development Report*:

> *The state's monopoly on coercion, which gives it the power to intervene effectively in economic activity, also gives it the power to intervene arbitrarily. This power, coupled with*

access to information not available to the general public, creates opportunities for public officials to promote their own interests, or those of friends or allies, at the expense of the general interest. The possibilities for rent seeking and corruption are considerable. Countries must therefore work to establish and nurture mechanisms that give state agencies the ... incentive to work for the common good, while at the same time restraining arbitrary and corrupt behaviour ... (World Bank, 1997:98).

Corruption and Democratization

So the 'cancer of corruption' is identified as threatening economic restructuring and as stemming from 'unrestrained' state power. For the donors, therefore, liberalization requires also a democratization strategy to restrain state power: the liberal economy needs a liberal state (1). The main concern of the 1992 Washington conference mentioned earlier was to identify ways in which corruption might be limited by democratic change. Corruption, over-regulation and economic crisis were seen as characteristics of authoritarian regimes and their ultimate unpopularity had paved the way for political reform. As Riley (1993: 258) noted:

A major impetus for change has been the economic, social and moral costs of the administrative corruption involved in the single-party regimes presided over by aging nationalist figures. High levels of administrative corruption have been associated with authoritarian politics in many, but not all, of such regimes.

Others were more categorical. Thus, Alison Rosenberg of USAID (1993:173) observed that:

Thirty years of highly centralized, one-party authoritarian regimes wielding major discretion over the personal and economic lives of their citizens ... have created deep frustration among many Africans. Centralized controls over the economy, a lack of transparency and accountability, and flawed judiciaries have made Africa a breeding ground for corruption ...

Conversely, democracy – understood as political pluralism and multi-party electoral competition – was simultaneously the antithesis of single-party or military oligarchy and of dishonest and incompetent authority. Thus, LeVine (1993:271) suggested that

... while administrative corruption cannot be eliminated, it can be limited in [democratic] states. The operative consensus [of the conference], with which I agree, is that attempts at limitation are more likely to succeed the further the country is along the democratization path. The more democracy, the more likely that mechanisms will have been put in place to monitor the performance of administrators and bureaucrats ...

And, despite entering several important caveats about factors which might weaken the capacity of reform to reduce corruption, LeVine held firmly to the central proposition that more democracy meant less corruption. Indeed, the persistence of corruption was an indication not of democratic failure but rather of *incomplete* democratization, arising from the need to 'wipe the old states clean' and eradicate old vested interests:

It may well be that a nation can have many of the appurtenances of democracy ... yet have to put up with a sclerotic administrative system, pervasive corrupt practices, and massive resistance to reform, as the case of the Soviet Union since 1985 amply reveals. It may also be that a government with a massive electoral mandate, such as Lee Kwan Yew's ... in

Singapore in 1965 ... could use that mandate to institute a complete overhaul of the administrative system and sack half the country's bureaucrats. But that is a risky strategy, simply because African bureaucrats, when threatened, have already demonstrated impressive capability to defend themselves ... (Ibid. 272).

The survival of these 'residues' of the old order thus make corruption a threat to the process of democratization. Hence, alongside the proposition that democracy and the market can combat corruption effectively, is placed another hypothesis, its seeming opposite: unless corruption can be tackled effectively, it will inevitably threaten the consolidation, even survival, of reform and democracy. Given the claims made for pluralism and the liberal state at the start of this decade, this is a significant irony. Yet it is no more than a recognition of the reality on the ground and of the accumulating evidence that 'good governance' made little headway against systematic private appropriation of state resources. In turn, this has intensified concern about corruption and the need for effective counter strategies.

Attacking the Problem: The Governance of Corruption

It is all a far cry from the rather cavalier attitudes of western governments and academics towards corruption in the sixties. Then, apologists for corruption were occasionally rather derisive about those 'moralists' who condemned corruption as invariably against the public interest and as harmful of political stability, efficient development and administrative capacity. For Huntington (1968) corruption was sometimes a symptom of 'modernization', of efforts made by enterprising strata to circumvent the stultifying dead weight of oppressive states, to 'cut red tape'. In certain circumstances, especially where elites reinvested the proceeds of corruption (in contrast with lower level corruption which was invariably consumed) official dishonesty might even generate private investment (Leff, 1964). And even where it did not do so, corruption might play a role in redistribution (for instance, redressing low tax revenues raised by the state) or in making the state accessible to otherwise excluded groups (Huntington, 1968; Bayley, 1966). While, for the most part, the literature on Africa and Latin America viewed the consequences of corruption negatively, research in Asia – in those countries of the Pacific rim where rapid growth was matched by high levels of corruption – tended to hold open the possibility that corruption might have positive consequences for development. It was a matter of keeping an open mind and adopting a cost-benefit analysis of the process (Nye, 1967).

That was then. The world has changed. In part this is because renewed concern with corruption in the west, to which we referred at the start of this essay, has made observers more sensitive to its consequences. In particular, the decline of political trust experienced in Britain, Italy, Spain and France (where the far-right gained political ground because many voters agreed with LePen's slogan that 'they're all at it') caused widespread concern. For Della Porta and Meny (1997:5-6), corruption undermines institutions and 'by striking at the very roots of democracy, compromises the values of the system'. It 'substitutes private interests for the public interest, undermines the rule of law, and denies the principles of equality and transparency'. In Italy, Della Porta sees corruption as central to a series of 'vicious circles' which sustain clientelism, electoral fraud, administrative inefficiency and criminal activities (1997:36-44).

In part, it is also because corruption is no longer viewed as something predominantly aimed against a collectivist, authoritarian state. During the cold war there was a temptation for some to see corruption in the Soviet Union or in an African one-party state as an act of defiance, an assertion of individualistic entrepreneurship rather than an instance of furtive dishonesty. If the 'entrepreneur' used corruption to jump to the front of the queue that had been set up by the bureaucrats, that was a reward for enterprise and tough luck on those pushed to the back of the line. Now the boot is on the other foot and corruption has lost much of its buccaneering charm. If it is an act of political defiance, it is one exercised against the conditionalities of the donors. The price it imposes is levied not only on the hapless African citizen but also on western businesses, donor aid and free market aspirations. Not surprisingly, then, it is now condemned as a threat to development and democratization. If a few voices still hold open the possibility of positive consequences (Hutchcroft, 1997) most do not.

The World Bank is clear that 'while costs may vary and systemic corruption may coexist with strong economic performance, experience suggests that corruption is bad for development' (1998:1). And while recognising that private sector fraud can undermine confidence in privatization and financial markets, it asserts that 'public sector corruption is arguably a more serious problem in developing countries, and controlling it may be a prerequisite for controlling private sector corruption' (Ibid. 3). Concerned to shape a 'market friendly' environment for business, it has no doubts that corruption seriously undermines its project:

> *A survey of 3,600 firms in 69 countries carried out for the* 1997 World Development Report *provides further evidence of the widespread existence and negative effects of corruption. As noted in the report: the survey confirmed that corruption was an important – and widespread – problem for investors. Overall, more than 40 percent of entrepreneurs reported having to pay bribes to get things done as a matter of course. ... The consequences of corruption often do not end with paying off officials and getting on with business. Government arbitrariness entangles firms in a web of time-consuming and economically unproductive relations ...* (Ibid. 8).

One area towards which aid (particularly from bilateral donors) has been targeted is institutional development capable of improving monitoring and policing of corruption. Some of these initiatives go back to the early days of debt rescheduling and conditionality. In the eighties, for instance, Britain gave financial and expert assistance to the creation of an Anti-Corruption Commission (ACC) in Zambia. After 1991, when the MMD came to power, there was some suspicion of the ACC among elements of the new government as a result of its institutional position within the Office of the President from where it had been used to harass political opponents. In 1993, there was talk of downgrading it by merging it into the Police. Its survival owed much to strong support by Britain's ODA and political conditionality. Instead of its marginalization, the MMD government has given it independent statutory powers alongside a Drug Enforcement Commission and a Human Rights Commission. While these reforms were accompanied by a degree of donor pressure, there was also appreciation within government that the pressure had been exercised in a way that was helpful (Interviews, 19 and 21 January 1998). Similarly, elsewhere donor sponsorship of police training and aid for increased facilities for the judiciary and legal system are not generally controversial.

In addition to institutional reform of this kind, there has been a strong emphasis on creating an international climate of intolerance of corruption through anti-corruption conferences and through international exposure. The compilation and dissemination of material about corruption is taking place on an unprecedented scale. In addition to the efforts of USAID and the IFIs in sponsoring meetings and in putting out material (notably on the internet), the Center for Institutional Reform and the Informal Sector at the University of Maryland (IRIS) has been prominent in sponsoring a conference and, more permanently, producing a practical handbook on combating corruption (IRIS, 1996). Most significant of all, however, has been the emergence of Transparency International (TI), an NGO based in Berlin and dedicated to 'curb corruption through international and national coalitions encouraging governments to establish and implement effective laws, policies and anti-corruption programmes', building public support for anti-corruption programmes and encouraging 'all parties to international business transactions to operate at the highest levels of integrity' (Mission statement, 21 July 1997). Working closely with aid agencies and the World Bank (which commends its 'integrity workshops' and the building of an 'integrity infrastructure' to combat corruption as set out in the TI Source Book – World Bank, 1998:9). TI has produced a Source Book (1997) which seeks to serve as a manual of institutional measures that can be mobilised to reduce corruption. It has also created an international network of TI chapters throughout the world (there were 18 in Africa and 72 worldwide in mid-1997) bringing together concerned political, professional and business people (some of them connected with wider human rights issues). Its most prominent British figure, the retired businessman George Moody-Stuart has produced a most readable popular manual (1997) of the way in which 'grand corruption' (that is, high-level corruption) works and the way in which business and government leaders feed off each other in a mutual dance of bribery and extortion. Ultimately, like most contributions from TI, it seeks the use of moral pressure and institutional oversight to check the cycle of abuse. The use of public pressure has been a major feature of TI's work – in May 1997 it called for Mobutu's assets in Europe to be seized and also gave prominence to the call by prominent European corporate executives for tougher international curbs on bribery.

Most interesting has been the creation of an annual international Corruption Perception Index ranking countries according to their levels of corruption, produced by TI in collaboration Gottingen University in Germany (http://www.transparency.de.press/1997.3.1.7.cpi.html). The index is compiled from a number of other indices produced from surveys undertaken by a number of polling organisations and business risk consultancies. It is not exhaustive – it does not cover all countries – and not all countries are given scores each year. In 1996 and 1997, Nigeria rated worst of the 54 countries ranked and Kenya was third in 1996 but not recorded the next year. Cameroon was 6th in 1996 but also missing in 1997. South Africa was 32nd in 1996 but had worsened relatively to rank 20th in 1997. Essentially the index codes the responses of businessmen, diplomats and journalists who travel and work in various parts of the world. It therefore presents the perceptions of an element of the western capitalist and state elite and it is likely that it suffers from the biases and cultural distortions which its sources make inevitable. But as an example of the process of putting pressure on the South to conform to the new 'global' standards being imposed through governance and restructuring, it is an impressive case of 'naming and shaming'.

An important part of this effort by agencies and NGOs has been the sponsorship of anti-corruption conferences. In 1997, for instance, TI organised conferences in Pakistan, India and Peru and had a role in a number of others. As for Africa, in Cotonou in September 1993 and in Entebbe in December 1994 conferences were held on 'Corruption, Democracy and Human Rights' (in West Africa and in East and Central Africa respectively). They were organised by the Africa Leadership Forum (ALF) in collaboration with TI (the ALF chair is General Obasanjo who is also an advisory member of Transparency International) and sponsored by the European Commission. In March 1996, a seminar on 'Good Governance and the Economy in Francophone Africa' was held in Dakar sponsored by USAID/Senegal and by IRIS. In 1997, a conference on public sector ethics and governance was staged in Windhoek by the Namibian government in collaboration with Transparency International.

The emphasis at these meetings has been on reinforcing the anti-corruption agenda and focusing policy makers on the measures which can be taken to control corruption. They have provided opportunities for discussion between experts drawn from academe, the World Bank, USAID, IRIS and TI (such as Robert Klitgaard, Susan Rose-Ackerman and Patrick Meagher) and African leaders concerned about corruption. For donor representatives, they have been an opportunity to restate the main governance concerns. In the foreword to the proceedings of the Dakar conference, for instance, Anne Williams, the USAID Mission Director in Senegal, observes that

> *Africans today are beginning to talk openly about ... 'the climate of corruption'. ... From the highest levels where substantial bribes and Swiss bank accounts are a way of life, to the lowest levels where obtaining simple documents requires a cadeau, Africans see public officials using their offices for private gain. ... For Africa to move into the global economy of the 21st Century, it must develop a different climate, one of good governance, where transparency and effective management become the rule of the day* (http://www.inform.umd.edu/iris/tlktfore.html)

And to the extent that Africans have been able to speak at these conferences, they have tended to be no less critical of corruption in Africa than the donors. Aderinwale's report of the Entebbe conference notes that the effects of corruption on development, democracy and human rights 'have been particularly pernicious' (1994:6) and that 'corruption across the board is systemic in many African countries, arising from the corruption of leadership' (Ibid. 9). And among the conference's recommendations was a call for the state in Africa to be 'restructured' (Ibid. 13). Yet sometimes these interventions have been sharply critical of western behaviour and intentions. The Entebbe conference was critical of the effects of adjustment policies on governance and condemned the role of the North in fostering corruption in the South. Obasanjo, for example, took up the question of foreign companies using bribery to do business in the South and was critical of the way they were able to claim tax exemptions at home on bribes as business expenses (Aderinwale, 1994:59-60). Interestingly, this issue was taken up in March 1995, at an OECD Symposium on Corruption and Good Governance held in Paris, where Robert Klitgaard urged OECD members to make corruption abroad illegal in their home countries (something only the United States has done with the Foreign Corrupt Practices Act) as a means of reducing both the cost of corruption to international business and, more pressingly, the systematic corruption of legal systems, economic management and public service delivery which this created.

Yet not all interventions have been as co-operative and amicable as these – along with carrots there have been sticks. Concerned about the immediate problem of corruption in subverting democratic reforms and siphoning off aid into private pockets, the donors have sought to attach anti-corruption measures to the conditionality package – specifically by making some aid provision, balance of payments support (and hence debt rescheduling) conditional on the implementation of such policies by African governments. As noted, bilateral donors have directly tied aid to democracy, governance (D/G) and human rights policies which include anti-corruption programmes, whilst the World Bank and IMF have encouraged or demanded action against corruption to ensure that financial support goes where it is supposed to go and that debts are repaid abroad rather than recycled locally. Over time, attitudes have hardened in cases of perceived non-compliance by debtor countries and aid support has been withheld in some cases. The annual Consultative Group meetings in Paris, at which the donors review progress and determine the level of aid to be disbursed, have made governance issues a key – and controversial – item of the agenda.

Perhaps the most startling and dramatic instance of corruption being used as a condition for aid came at the CG meeting of December 1993 when the donors 'expressed concern' about 'drug-trafficking in high government circles' in Zambia. The Zambian government delegation to Paris made the content of these discussions public, as a result of which three members of the government resigned pending an investigation (*The Post*, Lusaka, 12 May 1995). In 1994, in an interview with the BBC, the government promised a commission of inquiry into the allegations but none has been appointed. The episode embittered relations between the government and the donors, with the former feeling that debt relief had been used to make an unwarranted intervention in internal political matters lying outside the remit of CG meetings. In 1996, after elections, the President expressed bitterness that donor pressure had not permitted the reappointment of the three individuals. The matter also poisoned political relations within the ruling MMD with the ousted leaders feeling that they had been the victims of a tribal 'mafia' (namely, the ministers who had attended the Paris meeting) and also that the CG meeting had been highly selective in its moral indignation, ignoring the corruption of others (presumably including those they felt had accused them). The complaints were combined when one of them reportedly addressed a meeting of the National Executive Committee of the MMD on 22 April 1995, thus:

> For better or for worse, there is a public perception that we as leaders have been accepting bribes and that we have become very rich through land issues, tenders, contracts and other transactions. The donor community have been talking about corruption and when the issue of corruption and drug-trafficking was raised in Paris the main focus by those who made the accusations from our government was on drugs, almost to the total exclusion of corruption which was conveniently sidelined. ... I am not saying that the allegations of corruption in the government are necessarily true, but it is important to understand that in politics, public perceptions matter more than reality. This perception will simply not go away in the absence of an explanation as to how certain leaders who entered the government poor all of a sudden become affluent on their meagre salaries and allowances (The Post, 12 May 1995).

The drug scandal undermined what had previously been a collaborative relationship between the Zambian government and the donors. It marked the start of a steady deterioration in relations culminating in the suspension of balance of payments support in 1996 as a result of concern about the integrity of voter registration and allegations of electoral fraud (at the time of writing, major debt service obligations loomed but there had been no resumption of support after 18 months and CG meetings had been twice postponed). Both donors and government leaders agreed that it was issues of 'governance' rather than 'economic reform' which blocked disbursement of support (Interviews, 15, 16, 19 and 21 January 1998). Similarly, in Kenya, allegations of corruption and abuse of power led to a suspension of balance of payments support in 1996 and widespread concern about electoral fraud during the 1997 election campaign threatened to influence future dealings over debt servicing and aid.

The linkage of anti-corruption measures – albeit as one of several democracy and governance issues – to aid is particularly interesting in the Zambian case because it can be regarded as something of a 'showpiece' in the recent wave of democratization in the continent (2). Whereas political conditionality has been imposed on many governments against their will and despite their open resistance, Zambia represents one of a small number of countries where democratic reform has been initiated from within rather than imposed from without (Namibia, South Africa and Uganda also come to mind). Moreover, in the Zambian case, the constitutional agenda adopted by the MMD was almost a textbook model of liberal democratic reform. Thus the standards by which the donors judge D/G performance (including controlling corruption) are ostensibly those laid down in the MMD manifesto of 1991 and the concerns of the donors about corruption and other abuses of power have increasingly made them the keepers of the MMD's conscience. In addition, the institutional reforms since 1991 have been significant – not least in the creation of independent anti-corruption, drug enforcement, human rights and electoral commissions. The government thus felt aggrieved by the sanctions imposed over governance because, it believed, its record compared favourably with other African countries (Interviews, 19 and 21 January 1998).

This brings us to the heart of the dilemma facing the agencies and governments seeking to promote the liberal democratic agenda in Africa. There can be no doubt that anti-corruption pressures have had a significant effect. They have produced or facilitated a degree of institutional change, not least in the proliferation of anti-corruption and drug enforcement agencies around the continent. They have publicised the problem of corruption and disseminated the values of open and accountable government throughout Africa. This in turn has encouraged scrutiny by emboldened journalists, human rights organizations and the political opposition. The linkage that has been established between corruption and aid constrains what the political class does (or, at least, appears to do), something politicians must include in their calculations in dealing with the outside world. Yet these efforts are more noteworthy for their limits than their successes. Where governments have had been determined to ignore conditionality, as in Nigeria, conferences and moral sermons have had little effect and private capital has negated official sanctions. Even where dependency has given the donors a great deal of leverage, as in Kenya and Zambia, government resistance to imposition has produced an impasse which brings the efficacy of the whole governance strategy into question. Most importantly, despite all the conferences, commissions and conditionalities, corruption has continued to flourish and even to grow. In the nature of the subject, evidence is necessarily anecdotal and impressionistic but no one claims that corruption is less of a problem in 1998 than it was in 1990, and most would consider that it has increased in frequency and scale.

Misunderstanding the State: the Corruption of Governance

Partly, this dilemma was, and is, inevitable. It was never going to be possible to make a major impact on the problem in the space of a few years. Anti-corruption measures need to contend with entrenched interests and existing lack of capacity. Investigating corruption is one thing, bringing miscreants to book quite another. A bloated bureaucracy is likely to resist attempts to reduce its share of the social surplus. Nor is it surprising, given low salaries and rapid inflation, that petty corruption is widespread among rank-and-file civil servants, a problem worsened by continuing economic crisis. For example, in August 1997, the estimated cost of the monthly 'food basket' (excluding rent, clothes, transport, etc.) for a family of six in Lusaka was

K172,800, while the highest General Professional Scale salary in the civil service was K152,107 and the highest General Administrative Scale was K149,488 (*The SAP Monitor*, July/August 1997, Catholic Commission for Peace and Justice, Lusaka, p.6). In such circumstances, low level corruption should surprise no one and whether there is a multi-party or single-party state, a market or command economy, is not likely to make the slightest difference.

In part, however, the resilience and increasing scale of corruption, particularly high-level corruption, owes something to the disruptive nature of the reforms being imposed on African countries and the weakness of the remedies against corruption which these reforms embody. Seminars, handbooks and education are important and uplifting, and economic sanctions worrying for *governments*, but they are unlikely to influence *individuals* being offered thousands of dollars by multinationals or by drug dealers. More importantly, structural adjustment, liberalization and even democratic reforms have played a significant part in weakening the regulatory capacity of the state by removing oversight capabilities. By reducing state funding and excluding it from various areas of activity, adjustment programmes have undermined the possibility of improving auditing, investigation and enforcement. Governments trying to meet CG conditionalities have to meet demands for improved standards of public conduct with fewer resources.

In particular, deregulation has weakened the capacity of the state to control corruption while privatization has created a host of opportunities for personal accumulation. Deregulation – almost by definition – reduces the capacity of government to tighten rules governing government-corporate relations. In Africa, where the rules have traditionally been poorly observed and enforced, deregulation reduces government capacity still further and makes it particularly difficult to control interactions between private interests and public officials. It also creates opportunities for public figures to use their positions to obtain privileged access within the marketplace. Privatization of agricultural marketing, for example, ends the opportunity of officials to loot state marketing boards but it creates new opportunities for private contractors, either selling inputs or buying output, to defraud peasant producers and allows politically well-connected transporters and distributors to make profits from the import of food (sometimes even of drought or famine relief). In the last decade or so, there has also been the emergence of what might be called 'political banks'. Deregulation of the financial sector opens up new opportunities to set up private banks which, in some cases, can use political connections to obtain public sector accounts, such as payrolls previously lodged in state banks, which can then be used for personal investment. Privatization, one of the central tenets of adjustment programmes, has also produced opportunities for acquiring public resources. Instead of a programme of commercialization of run-down state corporations before privatization, adjustment conditionalities and donor deadlines frequently forced a rapid divestment of physical assets at knockdown prices. This permitted politicians and officials to use their 'insider' positions to buy them up. It has generated a great deal of resentment about high-level corruption; it has managed both to encourage corruption and reduce the legitimacy of democratization.

The problem here is that the donors proceed from the ideological assumption that political corruption is simply the product of growing state intervention (Heywood, 1997:12, quoting Rose-Ackerman). There is much to this, of course. It would be ridiculous to pretend that one-party states and parastatal companies did not provide officials with a whole host of opportunities to treat public resources as their personal property. But it is also clear that liberalization creates a set of new problems while not always eradicating the old sources of dishonesty. The use of patronage and bureaucratic 'rent-seeking' have not been ended by market reforms; rather they have been joined by new kinds of graft. Heywood notes that changes in regulatory mechanisms often move oversight functions out of government and hand them over to independent organizations from which representative democratic interests (such as trade unions) are often excluded. Such changes often blur the distinction between public and private interests (for instance by appointing business executives or political allies to such regulatory agencies) and so create 'significant opportunity structures for influence-peddling' (Ibid. 13). The process has been identified as a source of corruption even in Western Europe where state capacities to control corruption are much stronger than in Africa. Della Porta & Meny (1997:176) note that 'the actual point of privatization and deregulation seems to be characterized by an increase in the opportunities for corruption'. And Heywood (1997:14) observes that

> ... *the imposition of market mechanisms in the absence of adequate legal underpinnings created plentiful opportunities for rampant corruption in post-Soviet Russia. Yet even if Russia represents an extreme case, the exaltation of the market in established democracies has also engendered a certain disdain for regulatory mechanisms and established rules of conduct. In contrast, therefore, to those who see state regimentation and bureaucracy as the principle cause of corruption, it is equally plausible to make the case that deregulation has helped blur the lines between public and private spheres, whilst the emphasis on the market, competitiveness and profit has devalued a 'sense of state'.*

The separation of the 'public and private spheres' is at the heart of conceptions of the modern liberal democratic state and of contemporary notions of corruption (Theobald, 1990:chapter 2). Corruption – especially when combined with clientelism – acts to eradicate this distinction by conducting public office for private gain. Governance conditionalities attempt to restore or create anew the separation by reducing the size and activities of a state that is 'too big' and fostering the growth of a 'civil society' of NGOs and associations which at present is 'too small' and 'too weak'. Democracy and markets need 'less state' and 'more civil society'; the creation of an 'intermediate' layer of associational structures occupying the space between the state, on the one side, and ethnic and kinship networks, on the other (LeVine, 1993:276) is seen as a means of counter-balancing the interventionist state and so reducing rent-seeking behaviour.

As a way of ensuring accountability and reducing corruption, the strategy seems seriously flawed. Firstly, the crude antithesis of state and civil society has no basis in reality; democracy rests on a dynamic and effective state as much as on 'civil society' (Glaser, 1997). Secondly, it is difficult to believe that this watchdog role can be performed by a donor-sponsored 'civil society' of civic and human rights associations dependent on foreign funding (Allen, 1997). Thirdly, and most important, efforts to reduce the size of a state that is 'too big' also undermine a state that is 'too weak' (that is, lacking in capacity to implement policy or provide strategic direction for development). Conditionalities require a reduction in the *size* of the state (through 'Public Sector Reform' programmes) but do little to improve its *strength* (audit structures, organization, salaries, educational and management skills, and so on). It is telling that public sector reform is classified as an *economic* conditionality, not as a *governance* problem; the policy is to reduce its activities to make space for capital and has little concern with its possible role in a sovereign, democratic country.

The shrinking of the state sector, without any complementary strengthening of state institutions and skills, turns a bloated weak state into a small weak state, further reducing its capacity to check corruption. Worse, the *combination* of a weak 'civil society' and weak state allows small, predatory political machines the more easily to dominate an unorganised electorate (through clientelist and ethnic factionalism) and take control of the institutions of the state. In such circumstances, government becomes a means of access to public resources which, unprotected either by internal structures or by organized social interests capable of checking official misconduct, is available to be plundered. The governance agenda thus risks promoting what it seeks to eradicate – more corruption and greater instability. As Reno observes in his study of corruption in Sierra Leone (1995:12) structural adjustment tends to strengthen the very features of African governance which they are intended to address. There is some indication that the donors are beginning to recognise and respond to such problems – as signalled by the World Bank devoting its 1997 development report to the state (including the problem of corruption). Yet the approach is still on liberalization strategy; honesty and democracy are considered only as a means to that end. And where liberalization results in the state being too weak to control corruption, well, says the Bank, the donors will just have to take over the job on its behalf (1997:99):

> *Sustainable development generally calls for formal mechanisms of restraint that hold the state and its officials accountable for their actions. To be enduring and credible, these mechanisms must be anchored in core state institutions; if these are too weak, external mechanisms, such as international adjudication may substitute temporarily.*

Misunderstanding African Politics: Clientelism, Corruption, Class Formation

If 'governance' rests on a crude simplification of the role of the state, there are problems also with its assumptions about the nature of African politics. The lack of separation between the public and private spheres, which encourages corruption, is often ascribed to 'neo-patrimonialism' – the personalized character of African politics, in which formal constitutions and organizations are subordinate to individual rulers (the president or 'big man') and personal relationships are 'the foundation and superstructure of political institutions in Africa'. Such systems are typically presidentialist and clientelist and use state resources to gain political support. Although 'neo-patrimonial practices can be found in all polities, it is the core feature of politics in Africa' (Bratton & van de Walle, 1997:62). This representation is echoed to some extent in Bayart's notion of 'the politics of the belly' (1993). In essence, this kind of notion understands African politics as a reflection of the way in which traditional institutions and cultural values respond to and appropriate the institutional arrangements of a modern state. Corruption then becomes one of the ways in which 'big men' employ traditional forms of patronage and clientelism to access state resources which they use to reward supporters or appropriate as personal tribute.

There is an implication, doubtless unintended, in this kind of characterisation with which I am uncomfortable; namely, that the modern state is somehow alien, that corruption is somehow a 'foreign' concept invented to fit western political practice, of little relevance to the values which direct everyday African politics, that notions of the separation of public duty and private interest lie somewhere outside the cognition of African politicians and administrators. It is a premise that chimes with anti-corruption measures adopted by the governance agenda, an assumption that values of honesty and transparency must be 'taught' through the pressures imposed by globalization and by persuasion, conferences, educational materials and, if necessary, sanctions and public condemnation. This kind of view is found in much western writing about corruption in non-western societies. The literature on corruption in

Asia, for instance, devotes much space to traditions of gift-giving, family solidarity and deference against which 'foreign' notions of honesty must contend (see the examples in Heidenheimer et al., 1993). Clearly such customs are important in creating pressures for special treatment or access (as are masonic societies, 'old school ties' and family loyalty in western countries). Yet, for all that, there is widespread disapproval of corruption in all countries, even (perhaps especially) in those where corruption is rife, and, no matter how systemic high-level (or 'grand') corruption may be, it is still practised furtively. It is not difficult for researchers to interview politicians who are involved in corruption but it is far more difficult to find one who does not understand the difference between what is corrupt and what is not. We noted at the outset that when regimes take power in Africa they denounce the corruption of their predecessors and promise to clean things up; it is part of the justification for their claim on office. They then invariably behave in the same way as those they succeeded. This suggests, firstly, that there is public concern about corruption and leaders sense that they must be seen to be against it and, secondly, that once in office, they are driven by the same imperatives as their predecessors. Unless we assume that everyone in politics is simply a liar, we must ask why, regardless of motives and intention, corruption is so resilient.

While the elements which comprise 'neo-patrimonialism' (presidentialism, clientelism, the appropriation of state resources) are easily identifiable on the ground in Africa, the concept offers us a descriptive label rather than an explanation of process and structure. What produces such systems? Similar patterns of political power are found in a variety of social environments and countries which have no cultural similarity (the Mediterranean basin, India, the Philippines, Haiti, and parts of the former USSR as well as much of Africa, for example) and in urban as well as agrarian settings (many urban 'political machines', from early-century Boston to contemporary Bombay, Lagos and Karachi, manifest similar characteristics of personalist leadership and clientelist factionalism). And, given the great range of cultural forms across the continent, it is difficult to accept that there is some 'African neo-patrimonialism' which somehow reflects a uniform African political culture. If it is indeed 'the core feature' of African 'historicity' (an assumption which is debatable, but not here) then the reason why it is so, why corruption is so deeply rooted in political practice, must be found outside it.

A much more fruitful approach to understanding the combination of clientelism, centralised rule and corruption so frequently found in African politics (but *not* inevitably or exclusively) would need to include a more holistic and coherent view of the various forces that shaped them. It might start from Allen (1995) who identifies the roots of clientelism and presidentialism in two elements of the decolonization process which were designed to ensure government passed into the hands of conservative interests: firstly, independence constitutions concentrated power in the executive to ensure order; and secondly, hastily organized elections encouraged the development of support through ethnic and regional networks. These networks were readily available, structured perhaps by the 'bifurcated' colonial state with its 'decentralized despotism' of 'native authorities' controlling rural society (Mamdani, 1996, especially 3-34, 287-294). This political order was built on the foundations of an historical experience of capital accumulation which produced underdevelopment, deprivation and racial exclusion and which consequently made power, 'the political kingdom', and access to the state's resources the primary focus of material expectations and aspirations (Szeftel, 1982, 1987). The 'shadow state' which Reno finds in Sierra Leone (persuasively from Siaka Stevens onwards, less so before that) rested heavily on the existence of a colonial export economy, the patronage structures of electoral mobilization in a 'bifurcated' administration and the existence of a powerful central authority which could be used to maximise the returns afforded by political access. In such circumstances, access is everything and its absence means exclusion from the resources provided by office. Politics becomes a winner-takes-all game in which power allows private appropriation of state resources (to satisfy personal ambitions and factional loyalties). The process becomes self-defeating, increasing social divisions and corruption and finally culminating in 'a crisis of clientelism' (Allen, 1995:305). The result is increasing authoritarianism as leaders cling to power, a shift into what Allen calls centralised-bureaucratic politics and/or spoils politics. Viewed in this light, clientelism provides a mechanism for mobilizing support *and* controlling the electorate in a political economy in which socially and economically excluded rural producers and urban migrants predominate. Africa is not unique in this respect; clientelist politics have served in this way all over the world during the last century. Corruption – 'the politics of the belly', 'neo-patrimonialism', whatever – are not just 'the African problem'.

In any case, African politics are not reducible to clientelist factions jockeying for access to state resources. This kind of politics underpins a more fundamental process of local capital accumulation and class formation. Given the context of underdevelopment and the power of foreign capital, political office in Africa becomes a means of entry into business (particularly commerce, finance and services). Given the depth of the economic crisis, the ability to use office to access and manipulate state resources and foreign aid opens up possibilities of entry into the bourgeoisie. Thus, Iyayi (1986) has suggested that corruption might represent a form of primitive accumulation in which the plunder of state resources was a means of transferring surplus from peasants and workers to bureaucrats and businessmen. The process also works the other way around; the state is a resource through which capital can seek market privileges, public contracts, monopolies or other rents. The 'shadow state' of Sierra Leone, which Reno describes, involves the use of the state to control illicit economic activities not only to ensure a continuing hold on power but also for purposes of personal accumulation.

Corruption, all too often, arises where capital and state intersect. Moody-Stuart (1997:13) describes how the size of contracts may determine the nature of the bribery needed by business to influence officials: 5% of $100 million may net a head of state, 5% of $10 million may interest a minister and key staff, 5% of $1 million and one is down to permanent secretaries, and so on. The 'Goldenberg scandal' in Kenya, involving some $300 million being syphoned from the public exchequer to assist mineral exports which never occurred, has implicated Cabinet ministers as well as private businessmen with close political links to government. In a 1996 report on corruption in Tanzania, Justice Joseph Warioba identifies business connections (not clientelism or an over-weening state) as the primary source of corruption:

> The growth in corruption in the 1990s was accentuated by the close relationship between Government and Political leaders on the one hand and businessmen who engage in corruption on the other. ... Leaders who are supposed to take important national decisions are bribed by businessmen in order for them to take decisions which are in the interest of those businessmen ... (Warioba, 1997:198,201).

Not surprisingly, such problems play little part in the concerns about corruption discussed in governance papers, except insofar as they arise from the problem of state 'gatekeepers' charging rents. Structural adjustment is primarily concerned with the stabilization of what might be called 'a bourgeois order' (markets, private enterprise, the liberal state, urban and middle class 'civil society'). The process of accumulating private property is not a problem in its discourse. More seriously, it leads to those tackling corruption largely ignoring the role of political economy, electoral competition and inherited institutions in corruption. The concern is with the role of state intervention, not with crises of underdevelopment and debt peonage in the context of international accumulation, still less with the opportunities for corruption which markets, privatization and deregulation create. Corruption has survived and prospered despite efforts at institutional political reform, precisely because such change has not affected the structural forces which give rise to it and, frequently, has not even addressed it.

Conclusion

We can confine our conclusion to just two observations. Firstly, the governance agenda tackles corruption as if it were the cause of democratic and development problems rather than a symptom or consequence of them. Thus it fails to address the deeper political and class forces which drive the politics of clientelism and corruption. And secondly, in their demonization of the state and determination to substitute themselves for the state to force adjustment through, the donors and international agencies undermine the institutional development needed to sustain a more democratic, transparent and accountable political system. The result is that the important institutional structures and principles they seek to mobilize against corruption are unlikely to take root.

Morris Szeftel is in the Department of Politics, University of Leeds, UK.

Endnotes

1. The broader issue lies outside the scope of this paper. The argument is brilliantly set out in Ellen Meiksins Wood, *Democracy Against Capitalism*, Cambridge UP, 1995 (especially chapter 7), and Karl Polanyi, *The Great Transformation*, Boston: Beacon, 1944 (especially chapters 12-14). Working from different perspectives, both evaluate the limited nature of the liberal democratic state and, in particular, the way in which citizenship is emptied of economic content in order to protect private property from democratic interference.

2. Material on corruption has been gathered in the course of wider research on aid and democratization in a collaborative study of 'Aid, Political Conditionality and Democratization in Africa', undertaken by members of the Centre for Democratization Studies in the University of Leeds, funded by the ESRC (R000234986).

Bibliography

Aderinwale, Ayodele (ed.) (1994), *Corruption, Democracy and Human Rights in East and Central Africa*, Entebbe: Africa Leadership Forum (with Transparency International), Summary Report of a Seminar Organised by Africa Leadership Forum and sponsored by the European Commission in Entebbe, Republic of Uganda, 12-14 December, 1994, 167pp.

Allen, Chris (1995), 'Understanding African Politics', *Review of African Political Economy* 22, 65, pp. 301-320; (1997), 'Who Needs Civil Society?' *Review of African Political Economy* 24.73, pp. 329-337.

Bayart, J-F (1993), *The State in Africa: The Politics of the Belly*, London: Longman, 370 pp.

Bayley, D H (1966), 'The effects of corruption in a developing nation' in A J Heidenheimer et al. (eds.), *Political Corruption: A Handbook*, New Brunswick, NJ: Transaction Publishers, 1993, pp. 935-952 (first published in *Western Political Quarterly*, 19.4, 719-32).

Bratton, M & N van de Walle (1997), *Democratic Experiments in Africa*, Cambridge: Cambridge UP, 307 pp.

Brecht, Bertolt (1947), *Selected Poems*, New York: Harcourt Brace Jovanovich, translation & introduction by H R Hays, pp. 88, 113.

Charlick, R B (1993), 'Corruption in political transition: a governance perspective', *Corruption and Reform* 7.3, 177-187.

Charlton, Roger & Roy May (1989), 'Warlords and militarism in Chad', *Review of African Political Economy* 45/46, pp. 12-25.

Chubb, J & M Vannicelli (1988), 'Italy: a web of scandals in a flawed democracy' in I A Markovits and M Silverstein (eds.), *The Politics of Scandal: Power and Process in Liberal Democracies*, New York: Holmes and Meier, pp. 122-150

Della Porta, Donatella & Yves Meny (1997), *Democracy and Corruption in Europe*, London: Pinter, 208 pp. [ISBN 1-8567-367-3].

Della Porta, Donatella (1997) 'The vicious circles of corruption in Italy' in Della Porta, Donatella & Yves Meny, *Democracy and Corruption in Europe*, London: Pinter, pp. 35-49.

Doig, Alan (1996a), 'Politics and public sector ethics: the impact of change in the United Kingdom' in Little, Walter & Eduardo Posada-Carbo (eds.), *Political Corruption in Europe and Latin America*, London: Macmillan, pp. 173-192; (1996b), 'From Lynskey to Nolan: the corruption of British politics and public service?' in M Levi & D Nelken (eds.), *The Corruption of Politics and the Politics of Corruption*, Oxford: Blackwell

Gilmore, William C (1995), *Dirty Money: The evolution of money laundering counter-measures*, Strasbourg: Council of Europe, 317pp.

Glaser, Daryl (1997), 'South Africa and the limits of civil society', *Journal of Southern African Studies*, 23.1, pp. 5-25.

Harriss-White, Barbara & Gordon White (eds.) (1996), Liberalization and the New Corruption, *IDS Bulletin* 27.2, April, Institute of Development Studies, University of Sussex.

Heidenheimer, AJ et al. (eds.) (1993), *Political Corruption: A Handbook*, New Brunswick, NJ: Transaction Publishers, 1017 pp. [ISBN 0-88738-163-4].

Heywood, Paul (1997), 'Political corruption: problems and perspectives' in P Heywood (ed.), *Political Corruption*, Oxford: Blackwell/The Political Studies Association, pp. 1-19.

Heywood, Paul (ed.) (1997), *Political Corruption*, Oxford: Blackwell for the Political Studies Association, 250 pp. [ISBN 0-631-20610-8].

Huntington, S P (1968), 'Modernization and corruption' in AJ Heidenheimer et al (eds.), *Political Corruption: A Handbook*, New Brunswick, NJ: Transaction Publishers, 1993, pp. 935-952 (and in *Political Order in Changing Societies*, New Haven, Conn.: Yale University Press, pp. 59-71)

Hutchcroft, P D (1997), 'The politics of privilege: assessing the impacts of rent, corruption, and clientelism on Third World development' in P Heywood, ed, *Political Corruption*, Oxford: Blackwell & The Political Studies Association, pp. 223-242

IRIS (1996), *Governance and the Economy in Africa: Tools for Analysis and Reform of Corruption*, Center for Institutional Reform and the Informal Sector (IRIS), University of Maryland. Based on the proceedings of 'Good Governance and the Economy in Francophone Africa', sponsored by USAID/Senegal in conjunction with IRIS, Dakar, 5-7 March 1996. Website: http://www.inform.umd.edu/iris/toolkit.html.

Iyayi, F (1986), 'The primitive accumulation of capital in a neo-colony: the Nigerian case', *Review of African Political Economy*, 35, pp. 27-39.

240   Review of African Political Economy

Klitgaard, Robert (1995), 'National and international strategies for reducing corruption', paper presented to OECD Symposium on Corruption and Good Governance, Paris, 13-14 March 1995 (mimeo).

Leff, N H (1964), 'Economic development through bureaucratic corruption' in A J Heidenheimer et al. (eds.), *Political Corruption: A Handbook*, New Brunswick, N J: Transaction Publishers, 1993, pp. 389-403.

Levi, Michael & David Nelken (eds.) (1996), *The Corruption of Politics and the Politics of Corruption*, Oxford: Blackwell, 169 pp. [ISBN 0-631-20014-2] published simultaneously as *Journal of Law and Society* 23.1, 1996.

LeVine, V T (1993), 'Administrative corruption and democratization in Africa: aspects of the theoretic agenda', *Corruption and Reform* 7.3, 271-278.

Little, W (1996), 'Corruption and democracy in Latin America' *IDS Bulletin* 27.2, pp. 64-70.

Little, Walter & Eduardo Posada-Carbo (eds.) (1996), *Political Corruption in Europe and Latin America*, London: Macmillan, 314 pp. [ISBN 0-333-66310-1].

Mauro, Paolo (1997), *Why Worry About Corruption?*, Economic Issues Series, No. 6, Washington: International Monetary Fund, 13 pp. [ISBN 1-55775-635-x].

Moody-Stuart, George (1997), *Grand Corruption: How Business Bribes Damage Developing Countries*, Oxford: World View Publishing, 116 pp. [ISBN 1-872142-31-1].

Norton-Taylor, R, M Lloyd & S Cook (1996), *Knee Deep in Dishonour: The Scott Report and Its Aftermath*, London: Victor Gollancz, 207 pp. [ISBN 0-575-06385-8].

Nye, J S (1967), 'Corruption and political development: a cost-benefit analysis' in A J Heidenheimer et al. (eds.), *Political Corruption: A Handbook*, New Brunswick, NJ: Transaction Publishers, 1993, pp. 963-983 [first published in *American Political Science Review* LXI,2 (1967)].

Oliver, D (1997), 'Regulating the conduct of MPs. The British experience of combating corruption' in P Heywood (ed.), *Political Corruption*, Oxford: Blackwell & The Political Studies Association, pp. 123-142.

Reno, William (1995), *Corruption and State Politics in Sierra Leone*, Cambridge University Press, 229 pp. [ISBN 0-521-47179-6].

Riley, Stephen P (1993), 'Post-independence anti-corruption strategies and the contemporary effects of democratization', *Corruption and Reform* 7.3, pp. 249-261.

Rosenberg, A P (1993), 'Corruption as a policy issue', *Corruption and Reform* 7.3, 173-175.

Szeftel, M (1982), 'Political graft and the spoils system in Zambia', *Review of African Political Economy* 24, pp. 4-21; (1987), 'The crisis in the third world' in R Bush et al., *The World Order: Socialist Perspectives*, Oxford: Polity, pp. 87-140.

Theobald, Robin (1990), *Corruption, Development and Underdevelopment*, London: Macmillan, pp. 191.

Transparency International (1997), *National Integrity Systems: The TI Source Book*, Berlin: Transparency International or website: http://www.transparency.de/

Warioba, James (1997), 'Corruption and the State – The Warioba Report', *Soundings* 7, pp. 198-208, extract of English language summary of the Warioba Report 1996, Tanzania.

White, Gordon (1996), 'Corruption and market reform in China', *IDS Bulletin* 27.2, pp. 40-47.

The World Bank (1997), *World Development Report 1997: The State in a Changing World*, New York: Oxford University Press, pp. 265 [ISBN 0-19-521114-6]; 'Helping countries combat corruption: the role of the World Bank', World Bank website, April 1998, http://www.worldbank.org/html/extdr/corruptn/cor02.htm

[24]

Crime, Law & Social Change **29**: 113–159, 1998.
© 1998 *Kluwer Academic Publishers. Printed in the Netherlands.*

A framework for the analysis of corruption

A.W. GOUDIE[1] & DAVID STASAVAGE[2,*]
[1] *Department for International Development, London, UK;* [2] *Centre for the Study of African Economies, Oxford University, Oxford, UK*
(* *corresponding author*)

Abstract. The article sets out a framework within which the problem of corruption may be analysed in any specific country. It does not seek to establish the importance of such activity in a general sense, or seek to propose particular economic policy or institutional programmes that should be pursued in order to reduce the impact on the development process. Rather, the objective is to provide a structure for two distinct areas of analysis. Firstly, it considers the investigation of the determinants of corruption, emphasising the environment in which corruption evolves – whether shaped by international, national or specific institutional factors – and the manner in which the different parties to corruption interact and organise themselves in conducting these activities. Secondly, the article focusses on the importance of corruption for economic development by considering the different forms of corruption and the characteristics of these forms that are most critical for economic activity. Here, the distortions that are introduced into on-going economic activity are identified, together with the manner in which these distortions redirect activity in sub-optimal directions. In addition, the nature of the uncertainty attaching to these differing forms of corruption is considered, and especially the degree to which a form may be considered anarchic or structured in character: the former reflecting a system of intense uncertainty, and the latter one of less uncertainty – perhaps, only minimal uncertainty – as a predictable and stable set of relationships between parties is established. Finally, the article reviews the empirical work that has been undertaken in this field. This article, therefore, seeks to identify how detailed case study analysis, focussed on individual countries – and, indeed, on specific institutions or sectors within those countries – could valuably complement these existing studies, and provide a framework for those seeking to design policy that is appropriate to any individual circumstance.

Introduction

The establishment of good governance is now widely accepted as a critical element in securing stable economic development. In this context, the control of rent-seeking and corruption are of central importance, as has been noted by the World Bank (1995): "good governance – that is, the practice by political leadership of accountability, transparency, openness, predictability, and the rule of law – .... has been shown to be a virtual pre-requisite of the enabling environment for market-led economic growth".

Within the OECD, the problems surrounding rent-seeking and corrupt practices have been accorded more importance over recent years, especially in the context of the relationships between OECD economies and the developing countries. The OECD Recommendations of the Council on Bribery in International Business Transactions (adopted May 1994) set out several key elements for OECD Member states to address in the immediate future. The concern of the Recommendations is focused on the legal sanctions that might be imposed in order to deter corruption and on the transparency of organisational systems through enhanced accounting and recording procedures and through improved taxation structures. It is less immediately concerned with the fundamental incentives and motivations that stimulate corrupt activities and with the broader questions of what types of economic policies and state institutions are likely to foster corruption. Similarly, the OECD Recommendation with respect to Anti-Corruption Proposals for Bilateral Aid Procurement (endorsed by OECD's Development Assistance Committee (DAC) in May 1996) focuses on the provision of anti-corruption clauses in procurement contracts. On the other hand, the DAC publication *Orientation on Participatory Development and Good Governance* (1994) goes much further in identifying many of the primary causal factors that underlie and contribute to the basic problem. Indeed, it stresses the importance of addressing these underlying determinants in addition to the efforts to regulate the conduct of business transactions.[1]

The rationale and objectives of analysis

In order to complement ongoing efforts within the OECD and elsewhere, the article focuses on four basic research questions on corruption. Firstly, what are the main causes of corruption and what explains the observed international diversity in forms of corruption, and how might economic policy and the design of state institutions be altered so as to reduce the opportunities and incentives to engage in corruption? Secondly, how does corruption affect economic development and what types of corruption are likely to be the most damaging to economic growth? In view of the wide range and severity of the obstacles to growth identified in the poorest countries, it is appropriate to consider the relative importance of corrupt activities in influencing their economic development. Despite the widespread assumption that corruption can hinder economic growth, there have been relatively few attempts by economists to undertake empirical studies of this phenomenon in developing countries. A third question is how might donor assistance be better deployed so as to reduce the risk of corruption? A fourth and final question is how might corruption tend to lead to political turmoil and instability?

A FRAMEWORK FOR THE ANALYSIS OF CORRUPTION   115

Definitional considerations

There have been a number of different attempts at defining corruption. Some seek to provide a formal comprehensive definition, while others are not strictly designed to define corrupt activity *per se* but are deployed to isolate those activities that are the subject of the author's concern. A further complication is that corruption is most commonly referred to as a public-sector phenomenon, but it is also an important fact of life in the private sectors of both developed and developing countries.

One possible definition of public-sector corruption is that proposed by Bardhan (1996): "the use of public office for private gains". The problem here is how to differentiate corruption from mere patronage politics or favouritism for electoral reasons, since the basic assumption underlying political economy work, in general, is that officials use their office not to maximise social welfare, but to serve their individual interests. Most observers would, for example, agree that when a customs official demands a bribe for letting a product enter the country duty free, it is corruption, but what about when a politician decides whether or not to devalue based on whether it will suit his political supporters?

One approach to addressing this problem is to suggest that there are two different types of corruption: firstly, administrative or bureaucratic corruption which involves the use of public office for pecuniary gain and, secondly, political corruption involving the use of public office by politicians both for pecuniary gain and for purposes of remaining in office (Tanzi 1994, Rose-Ackerman 1978). This distinction, however, does not separate out standard interest group or patronage politics from corruption. An alternative definition which does help separate these two phenomena is that proposed by Shleifer and Vishny (1993) – "the sale by government officials of government property for personal gain" – where personal gain is restricted to the direct financial benefit accruing to government officials or politicians. This definition might be extended to include the purchase of government goods from the private sector. Cases where government goods are distributed so as to maximise political support, or where policy choices are made so as to maximise political support, would not be seen as corruption according to this definition. Shleifer and Vishny distinguish further between "corruption without theft" and "corruption with theft". The former occurs when an official demands a bribe but passes on the regular payment to the government. This could happen if an official charged a bribe in addition to an import license fee, but then passed the license fee on to the state treasury. Corruption with theft involves instances where the regular payment is not made to the government. An example here would be when customs officials let goods enter the country without paying a duty in exchange for a bribe.

For the purposes of the article, corruption is broadly defined as the use of public office for private gains, but with the following limitations. First, the definition is confined to public-sector corruption: that is, where the receiver of the corrupt payment is a government official although it is apparent that, with economic policy reform leading many economies to move, albeit somewhat slowly in Africa, towards a rebalancing of economic activity away from the state, the importance of private-sector corruption is arguably becoming of increasing relevance. Secondly, activities that may be perceived as corrupt in the sense that they lead to a personal benefit, but which are conducted by a single party without involving a process of negotiation with any other external parties, are excluded. Thus, crime – and particularly theft – that is conducted unilaterally is excluded. In addition, policy decisions taken by an official on his/her initiative alone are not considered, even though they may be corrupt in the sense of being motivated for personal gain rather than strictly being the implementation of government policy. The third limitation is with respect to the nature of the gain accruing to the government official. This might be considered to be, first, pecuniary or in kind; secondly, to be for personal benefit or for the benefit of personal friends, family, social or political grouping; or, thirdly, direct (as where the benefit takes on a negotiated and precise valuation) or indirect (as where the benefit may not be agreed precisely at the time of the negotiation, but accrues at a later time). In principle, each of these instances are important, although, for empirical study, analysis would be expected to focus on the more direct forms of personal gain.

Within this context the article discusses a framework for the analysis of the determinants of corruption based on principal-agent theory. It then considers alternative conceptions of the determinants of corruption before assessing the organisation of corruption and then analysing the implications of different structures of corruption for the economic environment and economic growth. Finally it takes a more detailed look at the empirical work that has been undertaken to date.

The determinants of corruption from a principal-agent perspective

Ultimately, corrupt practices must be analysed from the perspective of the two parties that negotiate such agreements within a specific institutional framework as a condition for the fulfillment of a particular transaction. However, each corrupt act is necessarily set within a national and an international context in which broader characteristics play a critical determining and constraining role. Such characteristics are common to all transactions within the national economy and are determined externally to the institutions within which specific acts of corruption take place. For this reason, the approach followed in this section is first to present several basic elements of a theory about the causes of corruption, followed by a look at how these elements present themselves at the international level, the national level and at the level of individual state institutions. Moreover, it is instructive to draw a distinction between those elements which may be seen to provide opportunities for corrupt acts to be perpetrated and those which create an incentive for such opportunities actually to be exploited.

The basic theory

Economic analysis of the determinants of corruption has typically drawn upon principal-agent theory. The principal is defined to be the top level of government and the agent is a government official designated to carry out a specific task. In the case of high-level corruption – perpetrated at the centre by the elite of the political or administrative structures – one might consider the citizens who elect a politician as the principals and the politician as the agent. The work of Rose-Ackerman (1978, 1994) and of Klitgaard (1988, 1989, 1995a, 1995b), drawing heavily on this framework, is especially pertinent here. Klitgaard particularly stresses three dimensions of institutional structure that he considers most critical in bearing on the opportunities for corruption:

- the monopoly power of officials;
- the degree of discretion that officials are permitted to exercise;
- the degree to which there are systems of accountability and transparency in an institution.

Monopoly power

The question of whether officials have monopoly power over provision of a government good is crucial for explaining the incidence of corruption without theft. Monopoly power could exist for the legal reason that a certain official is the only person charged with performing a certain task. In some cases it could exist because of shortages which are themselves the result of government regulations of prices or quantity of good produced. In others, the official himself may create the shortage in order to create opportunities for bribery. Conversely, for some types of corruption the presence of competition reduces opportunities for corruption on the part of public officials. When more than one government agent can issue the same license, competition among different officials will drive the bribe price down to zero (if one allows for the fact that even a few officials in a large population will not engage in bribery for moral reasons, this will be a further factor reducing the level of corruption (Rose-Ackerman 1978). These issues are considered in relation to social norms are below). One remedy to the problem of monopoly power that is suggested by Rose-Ackerman is the creation of overlapping jurisdictions for official duties.

The above argument about the benefit derived from introducing competition between government officials in the provision of a good applies for corruption without theft, as in the case where an official demands a bribe for provision of a government license but then passes on the regular fee to the government. It does not apply in the case of corruption with theft, as when an official accepts a bribe in exchange for non-payment of an import duty. In this case, corruption reduces overall costs for businesses in addition to lining the pockets of government officials, so businesses have an incentive to seek out corrupt state agents. It is also important to note that competition *among businesses* in this case will lead to the spread of corruption, since businesses which do not reduce costs through bribery will be at a disadvantage. Competition among government officials to be posted to a certain position may also increase the prevalence of corruption in this case, since an honest official will not be able to obtain a transfer, if doing so requires a cash payment. (Shleifer and Vishny 1993).

Discretionary power
Whether an official will be in a favourable position to extract bribes from clients depends not only on whether they have a monopoly over their particular activity, but also upon the rules and regulations regarding the distribution (or purchase) of government goods. The greater the amount of discretion which is given to an agent, the more opportunities there will be for agents to give "favourable" interpretations of government rules and regulations to businesses in exchange for illegal payments. Strict rules and regulations that spell out all the details of a particular question would seem an appropriate antidote to the problem of excess discretion, but this assumes that formal rules will actually be followed. Moreover, in many cases, rules can often be made too rigid or too unrealistic, inciting non-compliance, and a large amount of *de facto* discretion for officials (Tanzi 1994). A more useful solution is to simplify rules and regulations whenever possible.

Monitoring and accountability
Asymmetries of information present principals with a challenge in that they often find it difficult to monitor the actions of agents effectively and hold them accountable for their actions when they fall to carry out an assigned task (Rose-Ackerman 1978, Laffont 1995). The extent of imperfections in monitoring and accountability will depend upon the effectiveness of the institutional structures that are designed to deal with the problem, but it is not exactly clear which institutional structures are best suited for this goal. Reinforcing hierarchical control through state institutions is one way in which

governments can address this problem, but those who are paid to monitor the actions of lower-level officials can themselves be bribed not to blow the whistle, leading to a redistributionary chain within the bureaucracy that simply transfers corruption to the next level of responsibility. Increasing hierarchical control can also exacerbate the problem of informational asymmetries if officials far removed from the actual activities taking place are called upon to make judgements which depend upon having accurate information (Gould & Amaro Reyes 1983, Rose-Ackerman 1978). An alternative to increasing hierarchical control is to privatise certain government functions, but this presumes that adequate institutions exist for corporate governance in the private sector, without which privatisation will simply mean trading the problem of public-sector corruption for inefficiencies elsewhere.

Perhaps because there is no general rule about broad questions, such as whether increasing hierarchical control will reduce corruption, much of the literature on monitoring and accountability focuses on more specific technical measures that have proven themselves effective, within individual institutions (Klitgaard 1988). Failure to rotate agents between posts, failure to use outside auditors, and lack of consultation of clients of a particular bureaucratic agency are three among the numerous more technical aspects mentioned as increasing opportunities for corruption. Another issue concerns the appropriate level of penalty to apply to officials who are caught.

Summary

In summary, these aspects provide a succinct way of evaluating the extent to which there are opportunities for officials to engage in corruption. One might add to this the question of what incentives are offered for staying "clean". Chief among these is does public-sector employment pay well relative to pay available for similar duties in the private-sector? It is also important to consider whether there are provisions for internal promotion based on merit so that officials have some indication that obeying the rules today will lead to greater rewards in the future (Evans & Rauch 1995).

The international context for corruption

One critical dimension of corruption in African economies is the role of transactions with multinational enterprises. Observers like Transparency International have argued that it is the competitiveness of international markets, in general, and in the provision of capital projects, in particular, that is one of the key elements in the promotion of corruption in developing countries. This follows what Shleifer and Vishny (1993) suggest for competition among businesses as a source of corruption. For the competing enterprise from a de-

120   A.W. GOUDIE & DAVID STASAVAGE

veloped country, the cost of bribing government officials or ministers must be seen in the context of exploiting market opportunities. In the face of competitors themselves engaging in bribery, competitive bribery may be considered unavoidable, and, possibly, even a more cost-effective strategy than competing through lower costs or profit margins. The securing of a contract may often not be a function of the competitiveness of the product, but a function of the competitiveness of the bribe. Certainly, there may be bounds to the product competitiveness that must be observed, if for no other reason that typically third parties will be involved, but, within limits, this may not be the decisive factor.

Enterprises from developed economies that engage public officials in corrupt activities have many incentives to resist reform in this area. To the extent that established relationships with key public officials may have been cultivated over many years and their preferential treatment vis-à-vis their competitors may be firmly established, there would necessarily be considerable resistance to any measure that might jeopardise this investment of time and energy. Any programme to eliminate corrupt payments and restore genuine international competitive processes to procurement would imply the establishment of uncertain market forces and the potential loss of the market. It might be anticipated that an enterprise which bribes to secure a contract, while already having a product competitiveness advantage, would welcome a move to eliminate corruption, since it would be expected to retain the contract in a freely competitive environment. This, however, overlooks the risk that this strategy entails, particularly within a dynamic product market. In reality, securing a long-term hold on a country's market through bribery may be significantly more cost-effective.

Underlying all the discussion of the international corruptor's attitude to the outlawing of corrupt practices is the fundamental and predominant fear that other competitors will not adhere to such a regime even if formally agreed to at the inter-Governmental level. The gains to any free-rider may be considerable if such a break from an accord facilitates the establishment of a long-term relationship with a ministry or official.

One further issue that has an important international dimension – but which need not solely be seen in this context – concerns the wealth of the country and, particularly, its access to a rich resource such as oil or diamonds, and its role in fostering corruption. The examples of Nigeria and Angola support the view that such wealth has the potential to stimulate high-level corruption on a massive scale, facilitated, if not encouraged, by the participation of multinational companies in the exploitation of the resource in collaboration with the government. On other hand, the case of Botswana, with its massive diamond exploitation since the end of the 1960s, suggests that, with more democratic political structures and a more participative civil society, corruption need not overwhelm such economies.

The national context for corruption

The national context is necessarily instrumental in the evolution of corruption. First, the national context may constrain the evolution of opportunities for corruption at the institutional level and the ability of individuals to exploit such opportunities. Secondly, given that one of the major objectives of this work is to understand the inter-national diversity of corruption, national factors would be anticipated to play a major role in explaining observed differences in patterns of corruption between different countries.

In all societies political structure is a critical element in the evolution of corruption. Indeed, it is not merely the degree of political centralisation and the extent of democratic accountability that characterise the governing regime which are important, but also the manner in which the regime interacts with, and exercises political control or influence through, the institutional structures. Political structures where representative processes to enforce Governmental accountability are weak or absent would be expected to provide the greatest opportunities for corruption in view of the absence of the political mechanisms through which governments that tolerate, condone or participate in rent-seeking and corrupt practices might be dismissed. The lack of this ultimate power would imply that the popular rejection of corruption would typically lack an appropriate means of expression and, therefore, fail to compel the implementation of necessary legislative and organisational steps by government. Four key elements may be identified and these are considered in detail below: three concern the structure of the society – namely, the relationship of the government with the civil-service, the judicial structures, and with civil society – while the fourth concerns the basic economic development strategy of the government.

The government – civil-service relationship

The relationship that is established between the political leaders and the civil-service administration is important in considering why corruption might emerge both on the part of civil servants abusing their posts for private and on the part of politicians abusing their office for private, pecuniary gain. For civil servants, the reward structure within the state administration has traditionally been seen as one of the key determinants in the evolution of corruption. In most developing countries, the form of these rewards is resolved centrally and not left to the discretion of decentralised units.

Thus, from the perspective of this analysis, their structure may be seen as being determined externally to the local institutions within the civil-service structure. If officials are paid wages comparable to those available for similar duties in the private sector, and are compensated according to performance, the potential gains from engaging in corruption may not be large enough in relative terms to make it worth the risk. If, instead, officials in the public sector are paid wages well below those for similar duties in the private sector, then the opportunities for corruption may become the principal reason for choosing a public sector post (while acknowledging the link between levels of remuneration and incentives to engage in corruption, Besley and Maclaren (1993) offer a somewhat different argument. They suggest that for a government which is unable to monitor its civil servants, it may be cost-effective to pay civil servants a very low wage, with the tacit expectation that they will supplement their income by engaging in corrupt activities). Klitgaard (1995b) notes that government accountants in the Gambia are paid only one-third to one-sixth of what private sector accountants are paid. For lower-level officials if, in absolute terms, a public sector wage is too low for an official to support himself and his dependants above the poverty level, then the incentives for corruption will be considerably greater. Many authors have suggested that the erosion of real wages in the public sector in African countries since the early 1980s has been responsible for increased corruption. It is the fact that governments undertaking stabilisation programs have preferred to reduce total wage expenditures in real terms, rather than reducing the number of personnel, which has created the incentive problem.

From the solely economic perspective, individuals would be expected to assess the net potential gains from engaging in corrupt practices by comparing the anticipated gross benefits of such behaviour (as given by the expected monetary value of the bribe received from the initial act, and the anticipated future flow of payments from the establishment of a long-term arrangement with the payer) with the potential costs of so doing (as given by the expected costs of exposure). This economic calculation would be expected to assume a very different complexion, depending on the nature of the corrupt activity under consideration. For example, in the case of major international corruption, involving high-level, low-incidence corrupt acts, it is likely that the magnitude of the potential economic benefit from the acceptance of a bribe may dwarf the apparent economic costs. In many African contexts, where this situation certainly prevails, the structure of the civil service administration, together with the package of salaries and conditions, may appear of little relevance. This argument does not, of course, imply that other non-monetary determinants will not dominate and outweigh these (potentially massive) monetary net gains. Nor, indeed, does it imply that more appropriate compensation structures are not important in tipping the balance of monetary plus non-monetary benefits towards foregoing corruption opportunities.

In contrast to these situations of high-value corruption possibilities, the balance of the economic arguments may be considerably more delicate at the lower levels of bureaucracies, with the potential net economic benefits being far from clear cut. Here, the internal salary structures and benefit systems may be highly significant, as equally may be the opportunities from additional part-time employment in the unofficial sectors.

Viewing this relationship from the perspective of the politician, an ability to manipulate the actions of the civil service can provide a major opportunity to intervene in individual decisions in exchange for illegal payments. As a consequence, instead of leaving politicians a large amount of discretion in their decision when to intervene in civil service affairs, it is important to establish clear rules that will make bureaucratic agencies independent from excess political interference. Independence of the civil service is important in three specific regards: first, in the appointment and dismissal of officials at all levels; secondly, in the internal structuring and organisation of the service; and, thirdly, in the implementation of specific legislation. Inevitably, the on-going relationship between politicians and official creates opportunities for political influence to be exerted in all three of these areas in any state, and – especially in the third of these areas – political influence would often be seen as legitimate in many respects. To the extent that political influence evolves into political management of the service, however, the independence of the civil-service is rapidly eroded, and the risk of corruption is increased.

The opportunities for collusion between politician and administrator are typically smaller within meritocratic structures where the officials are appointed through internal procedures and where the number of political appointments is very small. On the other hand, where appointments at the highest level do reflect the political outlook of the ruling party, issues of civil service independence re-emerge, albeit in a less severe form than under less representative systems. Generally, the risk of exposure will increase as the degree of separation of powers increases and where the motivation of senior civil servants does not encompass political considerations. In less meritocratic environments, the potential for political interference in the civil service is considerably greater. Political appointments to the civil service and the designation of key officials by political leaders are characteristic of highly politicised civil services in which collusion between political and administrative decision makers may become explicit, and even open, rendering the mechanics of implementing acts of corruption considerably easier.

While these issues of civil service independence would be expected to bear on the nature of high-level corruption in both the civil service and in the higher political echelons, it is less clear that the separation of powers influences lower-level opportunities for corruption to the same degree. The impact that derives from the observed integrity of top civil servants and politicians may be a key factor, but, otherwise, the political influence in low-level corruption is likely to be restricted and important only insofar as political power plays a significant role in establishing the structure and internal organisation of the civil service.

The government – judiciary relationship

The judicial system can play an important role in limiting corruption both at the highest and lowest levels of government by monitoring both civil servants and politicians and by holding them accountable in the event of wrongdoing. Three characteristics of the established judicial structures may be isolated as playing a key role in this context: first, the degree of separation of power between judiciary and government; secondly, the effectiveness of the security and law enforcement officials in the implementation of the law; and, thirdly, the integrity and management of the security and law enforcement officers themselves. Moreover, it is the *de facto* nature of these elements that will ultimately be most crucial in this context, rather than the strict constitutional or legal situation.

While these three elements necessarily vary between economies, several generalisations would appear *a priori* to be reasonable. For instance, political leaders who maintain very tight controls over the judiciary and law-enforcement sector will typically have the capacity to undertake corrupt acts with impunity. Even if the risk of detection at the highest levels is significant, and, at the extreme, corrupt acts are openly acknowledged, the costs of that exposure will typically be small, both in terms of any legal sanction and in terms of the repercussions for political responsibility. Similarly, if this control is accompanied by the maintaining of highly effective enforcement operations, then the capacity to deter decentralised corruption will be considerable: here, the fear of exposure is likely to dominate the potential gains from corruption, particularly if the costs of exposure are high. On the other hand, societies characterised by the same lack of separation of powers between the ruling regime and the judiciary, but with a relatively lax security and law enforcement system may additionally see the evolution of decentralised corruption.

In addition, the integrity of the security and law enforcement officers will also be a major factor insofar as the officials engaged in these operations may themselves be major players in the perpetration of corrupt acts. To the extent that these officers do engage in such practices, their tolerance of corruption in general throughout the economy might be expected to be high, thereby facilitating wider-scale corruption. On the other hand, a combination of corrupt security and law-enforcement officers, implementing controls on civil society with excessive force and violence, is by no means unknown.

In contrast to these expectations of autocratic societies, it could be anticipated that more representative Governments would be substantively constrained in each of these regards. Opportunities for collusion between government and judiciary would typically be greatly reduced, while, with the ruling government being deemed responsible for both the conduct and effectiveness of the security and law-enforcement sector, the scope for major abuses of power and the failure to implement policy is smaller, though certainly nonnegligible. As is considered later, the opportunities may remain substantial but the cost of exposure will undoubtedly have escalated.

The government – civil society relationship

The importance of the government-civil society relationship for influencing corruption is perhaps best illustrated through considering the role and power of the non-governmental organisations, and particularly the crucial impact that the media may have. While the media has the opportunity to expose corruption in democratic societies – although, for different reasons, it may not always choose to exercise this opportunity – the conduct of the media in autocratic political structures will be heavily dependent on the precise form of these structures. In this context, there would be an expectation of a close relationship between the role of the media and the nature of the judicial and security services that the government maintains: a tight and hard-line security stance generally being associated with a tight control of all forms of media, and vice versa.

At lower levels of government, where corrupt acts tend to be low-value and high-incidence, media interest and concern would be anticipated to be weak, thereby exercising little deterrent effect. This discussion presupposes, of course, that, irrespective of the nature of the ruling government, civil society would be able to play an effective monitoring role. In practice, many African countries lack such a coherent civil society with the capacity to fulfil the functions envisaged in this section. It may be, however, that in the face of the vested interests of the political and judicial establishment, the various bodies within civil society are the only practical channels through which corruption might be reduced.

The basic development strategy of the government

The economic environment contributes to the evolution of corruption to the extent that established economic strategies and policy instruments, together with institutions for the implementation of economic policy, provide different opportunities for the pursuit of corrupt practices. Moreover, beyond this somewhat static framework – and of immediate relevance to many African states – the process of economic reform provides significant new opportunities for corruption.

The common judgement is that more liberal economic systems, founded upon market-orientated behaviour and a smaller role for the state, generate fewer opportunities than do economies where the administrative allocation of resources and the central direction of economic activity dominate. Greater bureaucratic control over the economy will, all other things being equal, increase problems with monitoring and accountability, because a greater share of economic planning decisions will be dependent on bureaucrats who do not receive information from functioning markets (Olson 1995). This assumes that effective institutions exist for corporate governance in the private sector. However, reducing the scope of government intervention in the economy is clearly not a sufficient condition for the control of corruption, because there are many activities which are left to government administration in even the most market-based economic systems. Revenue-raising objectives, as in the customs service and in the domestic tax collecting agencies, necessarily continue to be integral to government policy, and they remain major areas prone to corruption. Similarly, the provision of public goods or the favouring of policies to meet other indisputable instances of market failure are commonly pursued for economic efficiency purposes and/or to meet social objectives. There is, it would seem, an unavoidable trade-off in some policy decisions between satisfying efficiency and equity objectives, on the one hand, and reducing the risk of public sector corruption on the other.

The transitional period in which economic reform is being implemented is one of considerable interest in the analysis of corruption. From one perspective, there may be an incentive to preserve pre-reform structures if they facilitate the undertaking of corrupt activities that are of direct or indirect value to the ruling party. Conversely, there is an important question of what in practice stimulates the ruling government to initiate reforms in an area of policy in which the benefits to the leadership *per se* will be substantively reduced, even if the benefits to the economic development of the country as a whole are more readily identifiable. Equally, if the reforms are clearly counter to the vested interests of those outside government, but on whose support the government depends, the mechanisms by which reform are initiated are again of considerable interest. In general, an understanding of the factors that provoke a change in policy is crucial. However, as many examples throughout the world have demonstrated, despite these seemingly insurmountable obstacles to reform, economic reform – although perhaps not explicitly anti-corruption reform – has often proceeded against the apparent interest of the ruling leadership itself.

A FRAMEWORK FOR THE ANALYSIS OF CORRUPTION 127

The nature of the opportunities for corruption to develop is necessarily heavily contingent on the specific areas of economic activity at issue. It is, therefore, instructive to define the primary categories of activity in the public sector from the perspective of the broadly similar opportunities that they provide for corrupt practices to be undertaken (see Appendix). All the activities share a common characteristic in that they entail a significant degree of administrative responsibility and decision-making power on the part of a public sector official or politician in the authorisation of economic transactions.

One of the clearest examples of the evolution of corruption in response to economic reform is in the domain of enterprise ownership and control. While reform in this area has become a major element of most adjustment programmes, principally for reasons of fiscal adjustment and economic efficiency, it has important implications for the conduct of corrupt activities, themselves, and for the fundamental attitude of the government towards corruption. The process and mechanism by which privatisation has been undertaken in many economies has been severely criticised for the opportunities it afforded for inequitable resource allocations to be made and for the manipulation of the asset valuations and asset payments. Moreover, with many of the state monopolies being transformed into private monopolies, the scope for rent-seeking has, in many instances, remained unchecked, and, with the new owners and managers being initially determined by the government, the scope for abuse has persisted. Few developing-country governments have the capacity to establish the essential regulatory bodies to monitor and control the activities of newly created private monopolies, leaving few remaining controls to prevent the exploitation of these powers, albeit without need to resort to corrupt practices *per se*.

In conclusion, it could be argued that reform programmes to move away from state-led development will generally reduce opportunities for corruption, but, to see to what extent this is true, it would be necessary to take a close look at the reform process and at privatisation, in particular.

Determinants of corruption in individual institutions

Irrespective of the role played by national-level considerations in shaping the broad structure and management of the civil service administration, it is also necessary to consider the manner in which individual institutions and agencies are organised, because there is ample reason to believe that corruption is more of a problem in certain agencies within the same country than others. As at the national level, the causes of corruption here can be considered in terms of the degree of monopoly and discretionary power awarded to officials and

128   A.W. GOUDIE & DAVID STASAVAGE

the opportunities for monitoring officials and holding them accountable for their actions. Three specific areas of government activity are considered.

Key determinants of corruption in customs administrations

The question of the extent of monopoly power does not have a major bearing on the level of corruption in customs, to the extent that corruption in customs is of the form of corruption with theft, that reduces costs for private-sector operators who pay bribes (although it might be the case in some ports that corruption results in blackmail that, in fact, raises the costs involved). As a result, they have no incentive to seek out honest officials. What is likely to make more of a difference for corruption in customs is whether there are effective systems of monitoring and accountability and whether substantial discretion is afforded to customs officials.

In terms of monitoring, many developing countries today face a dilemma between attempting to make their own customs services more effective through internal reforms, or by instead contracting the services of a Pre-Shipment Inspection (PSI) company. Thailand has been an example of successful customs reform that remained an internal government initiative, while other countries like Indonesia, Senegal, and Mozambique have attempted to reform customs via contracting of a PSI firm. PSI companies can offer several different levels of service, the most basic of which involves inspecting shipments in the exporting country to verify their value, quality, quantity, and tariff classification. This can help customs officials in the importing country crack down on importers who make false declarations but who do not seek to bribe a customs official to do so. It does less to reduce the incidence of importers paying bribes to customs agents in exchange for lower duties, because customs officials can often simply ignore the information supplied by the PSI firm. The next level of involvement for a PSI firm involves an ex-post reconciliation to examine, shipment by shipment, whether the PSI firm's recommendations were followed by customs officials or not. This further improves monitoring, but problems remain of both a technical and political nature. For one, in some systems customs officials can enter the number from the pre-shipment inspection certificate incorrectly into the customs computer system, making it more difficult to know on which shipments fraud occurred. In addition, political authorities in the importer country may fail to act on the information provided to them through the reconciliation process. The third level of involvement for a pre-shipment inspection service is actually to require that the PSI company official is shown that the duty has been paid, an option first chosen by Indonesia in the 1980s and more recently chosen by African countries like Cameroon. This makes it yet more difficult to engage in corruption in customs, but still far from impossible. Finally, the bottom line with PSI is that it costs a significant amount of money, and it needs to be carefully considered at what point countries might do better to use scarce resources to improve their own internal systems of monitoring and accountability.

In terms of the level of discretion, when a customs agent is allowed to apply one of several tariff rates to a product, or when a tax inspector is given substantial leeway to decide whether companies are given deductions or not, there will be an incentive to demand a bribe in exchange for offering favourable treatment. The best strategy for minimising these problems seems to be to move towards a simplified tax and tariff structure which will leave less room for discretion on the part of customs officials. Efforts also need to be made to minimise possibilities for *ad hoc* exemptions to be granted for certain categories of goods, and the case of exemptions which are maintained because they serve an important purpose, efforts should be made to see that they are not easy to abuse. For example, in Mozambique personal belongings repatriated by Mozambican miners working in South Africa have enjoyed an exemption from paying duties but customs officials were for a long time given wide latitude in determining exactly what constituted miners' belongings. In other cases, even when formal rules and regulations are altered so as to restrict potential abuse of exemptions, top politicians have been known to intervene and declare that certain import shipments should be exempted from duties, and they have presumably done this in exchange for illegal payments. It would seem that this sort of abuse would be resistant to virtually any formal institutional change.

Key determinants of corruption in business regulation

Both foreign and domestic businesses in many developing countries have to deal with a large number of regulations that concern both the initial investment in a business and subsequent operations. In many African countries, such regulatory frameworks are a legacy both of the colonial state and of efforts towards central planning of economies during the 1960s and 1970s. Opportunities for corruption in the area of government regulation occur when a single individual (or single agency) has monopoly power over provision over a certain good (like an operating license) and when there is substantial discretion in how the good is provided.

Both of the above types of reform are likely to prove particularly difficult in African economies because they require an increase in the capacity of the state administration in order to be effective. On the other hand, there are some reforms which could reduce corruption in the area of business regulation and actually free up state capacity. This would involve simplifying useful regulations and doing away with unnecessary regulations in order to reduce

130   A.W. GOUDIE & DAVID STASAVAGE

opportunities for corruption. For African countries, like Mozambique, which
have a huge number of regulations on business activity and yet which lack
trained personnel to administer these regulations effectively, simplification
seems to be the most logical near-term route for reform.

Key determinants of corruption in foreign aid projects
The determinants of corruption in the administration of public aid can be examined from the same framework as with other areas of government activity.
As is true with customs, arrangements for improved monitoring of foreign
aid projects can follow two basic routes. On one hand, efforts can be made
to strengthen those agencies within the developing-country government (like
an auditing department) so as to improve monitoring and accountability internally. On the other hand, given the virtual absence of auditing and control
procedures for public expenditure in many African countries, donors have often opted for improving monitoring and accountability externally, by relying
exclusively on their own auditing and control procedures. The problem with
this, as is true with customs reform that involves contracting a pre-shipment
inspection company, is that it threatens to mitigate against the possibility that
the auditing and control departments in the developing country administration
might become allies of the donors in the effort to improve aid effectiveness.

Further conceptions of the determinants of corruption

Multiple equilibria, or "contagion", models of corruption
In the framework for the emergence of corruption outlined above, for a given
set of opportunities for engaging in corruption and incentives not to engage
in corruption, there should be only one equilibrium level of corruption. A
number of recent papers provide an alternative vision of the persistence of
corruption and its transformation from one degree of intensity to another.
Common to all of these models is the idea that, once a high-level corruption equilibrium is reached as a result of a temporary change in the nature
of opportunities and incentives, widespread corruption may be very hard to
eradicate even if the situation with regard to opportunities and incentives
subsequently returns to normal.

Some of these models (discussed by Bardhan, 1996) have frequency dependent equilibria where, as the percentage of officials engaging in corruption
increases, the potential costs for any new officials to begin engaging in corruption (loss of reputation, chances of being caught) decrease. The result is
that a temporary shock may permanently raise the level of corruption (Andvig
1991, Andvig & Moene 1991). Collier (1995) presents a similar model, based
on the idea that corrupt practices spread through a social learning process

that is likely to follow a contagion S-curve. Murphy, Shleifer, and Vishny (1991) present a model where individuals divide their time between rent-seeking, cash crop production (which brings a high return but is more subject to rent-seeking), and subsistence agricultural production (which brings a low return but is more immune to rent-seeking). The model has two stable equilibria, the outcome of which depends upon the quality of property rights protection: one where all individuals are engaged in cash-crop production and there is no rent-seeking and another where activities are split between rent-seeking, cash-crop production, and subsistence agriculture. As in the frequency-dependent models, once a low-level equilibrium is reached it takes a major effort to get out of it.

Overall, these ideas present the most rigorous treatment yet of the popular adage that 'corruption feeds on itself', but they may remain most useful as a heuristic, because it is unclear exactly how one would conduct a thorough empirical test of their validity. One way of evaluating these explanations in a preliminary sense might be to see if there are cases of countries or bureaucracies where the level of corruption has changed dramatically but without a permanent change in terms of monopoly, discretion, levels of pay, or risk of detection and punishment.

Social norms as explanations for corruption
While the factors highlighted in relation to the determinants of corruption from a principal-agent perspective, from both the national and institutional perspectives contribute to an explanation of the role played by formal rules and institutions, they do not address the possibility that informal institutions or social norms may have a major influence on government behaviour. To a large extent, the answer to this question lies beyond purely economic considerations and in determinants that others have analysed concerning cultural and social norms and acceptable and unacceptable standards of behaviour.

There is, therefore, ample reason to believe that informal societal institutions or social norms can also promote or deter corruption.[2] Social norms might emphasise an individual's allegiance to ethnic, religious, or other collectivities over his responsibility to act as a rational bureaucrat in the Weberian mould (Gould & Amaro-Reyes 1983, Ekpo 1979, Tanzi 1994). Gould and Amaro-Reyes talk about 'norms of the collectivity rather than the individual'. Tanzi (1994) suggests that, in many developing countries where family ties retain a greater importance than they do in Europe or North America, officials in public office will be less able to escape demands that they extend special favours to family and friends. Other authors have looked at the manner in which traditional practices of gift-exchange can fuel corruption, as government officials become drawn into such networks. From a similar per-

132   A.W. GOUDIE & DAVID STASAVAGE

spective, Ekpo (1979) considers how the language involved in such varieties of gift exchange has facilitated the development of corruption in the modern state apparatus. Common to all these arguments is that social norms do not serve an economic function and they represent holdovers from a traditional past.

There are several significant problems with this sort of argument as an explanation for the emergence of corruption in a given country. First, social norms encouraging corruption are sometimes seen as being universal in African countries, but vocal opposition to corruption and anti-corruption campaigns have existed even in many traditional societies, like 19th century Nigeria, as noted by Smith (1979) and by Obasanjo (1994). Secondly, norm-based arguments tend to invite tautology. Without clear specifications of exactly what norms are or without any means of demonstrating (rather than just positing) their existence, one risks arguing that because a country had high corruption, its social norms must have been such that they favoured corruption. A final problem with the argument about social norms is that it does not consider how ethnic, religious, or other ties among individuals can serve important economic functions, and that they even might help reduce corruption. Putnam (1993) suggests that the same 'norms and networks' of civic association which others have seen as promoting corruption are actually highly correlated with lower levels of corruption in local government in Italy. Speculating about how Putnam's argument might be applied to the developing countries (although not specifically for explaining corruption outcomes), Bardhan (1994) suggests that norms and networks of civic association in East Asian states may have been stronger than in countries like India.

What seems clear from this is that the debate on the importance of social norms remains open, and the old argument that social norms necessarily favour the development of corruption is too simplistic. No one disputes the importance played by informal norms and institutions in influencing individual behaviour but until methods are developed actually to measure the existence of norms independent of the consequences which they are portrayed as having, it will be difficult to assess how important they have been in either promoting or deterring corruption. In the future, it may be useful in asking how norms may promote or reduce corruption, to establish clear distinctions between the 'norms of civic association' to which Putnam refers and 'norms of kinship' which may be more likely to promote corruption.

Income distribution and trends in standards of living
Several additional factors of a broader economic-policy relevance may be identified as potentially providing incentives for the pursuit of corrupt practices (this issue has not been extensively analysed with respect to corruption,

but the link between income distribution and growth has been studied, as for example in Alesina and Rodrik [1994]). These factors would include, first, the prevailing nature and extent of poverty in the economy and the national distribution of income and wealth, in general, as well as the recent trends in these distributions. Second, the recent aggregate performance of the economy and the trends in real incomes – perhaps, consequent upon the implementation of economic stabilisation or structural adjustment programmes, or upon a significant exogenous shock to the system – would be *prima facie* important if they reveal substantive disparities amongst different social groupings. Indeed, the presence of major absolute deprivation alone may be significant.

To the extent that expectations in either an absolute or relative regard are frustrated, specific social groupings, and individuals within these groupings, could be motivated by the prospect of improving their status to undertake corrupt practices. This argument is, however, only relevant to those individuals or groupings which have the opportunity to exploit possible openings for corruption. Clearly, the poorest groupings, for whom the incentive may be greatest in this context, will typically have almost no opportunities. Rather, questions of absolute or, more likely, relative deprivation in a society will be of relevance to those in, for example, lowly government positions, where the remuneration is exceptionally poor, but where the work provides possibilities for corrupt activities.

The nature of the political leadership

The role of the political leadership – and especially of the most senior leaders – is arguably one of the most critical elements in determining the evolution of corruption in any single country. Their tacit sanctioning of higher-level corruption will greatly facilitate the contagion at lower levels. One chain of contagion might be from the incidence of high-value corrupt acts, perpetrated at the highest levels of the political regime and the civil service, typically deriving from contact with multinational enterprises in the negotiation of major capital investment projects, to lower level officials. The latter will typically be aware of these specific acts and this may provide a sufficient incentive for bribes to be demanded by these officials in their own areas of power and responsibility. As long as corruption is limited to high-level acts involving international parties, the impetus for corruption to spread domestically *may* be more limited: the lower-level officials may be envious – and this may indeed be a sufficient condition to motivate contagion effects – but will not bear a direct cost. However, as soon as corruption spreads to acts involving purely domestic transactions, the impetus for contagion effects will rise sharply: domestic individuals come increasingly to bear the costs of corruption in a very direct sense and this provides the incentive to pass on the 'tax'.

134 A.W. GOUDIE & DAVID STASAVAGE

While this line of reasoning would suggest that corruption would tend in all economies to evolve towards a generalised systemic form, the existence of many economies in which a reasonably stable form of corruption, that is relatively predictable and certain in its impact, suggests that other determining factors must indeed play a highly significant role and counteract this form of contagion effect. For example, such demonstration effects may be contained or eliminated by other deterrents, as where the internal security forces are particularly effective in exposing and punishing acts of corruption or where highly developed networks prevail to manage corruption.

The organisation of corruption

In addition to the range of potential determinants of corruption identified above, it is important to consider the mechanisms by which these factors combine to establish particular structures of corruption, each with a specific impact on the economy. In this respect, there are two dimensions of organisation that are important insofar as that they shape both the form and impact of corruption:

- The degree to which, in the absence of Troperty rights to guarantee the enforcement of bribery contracts, there is an alternative means of enforcement between government officials/politicians and the other parties to the corruption.
- The degree to which individuals in the civil administration act independently in demanding bribes, or as part of centralised arrangements, or according to certain 'rules of the game'.

In general, when corruption is well-ordered, centralised, and predictable, it will likely have a less damaging effect on the economy than when corruption is anarchic. However, even centralised and predictable forms of corruption will still have a number of negative effects on the economy.

The absence of property rights for corruption contracts
Unlike regular commercial contracts, corruption contracts are not subject to formal property rights (Shleifer 1994). In the absence of corrupt practices, entrepreneurs would ideally know which state agency has the authority to sanction specific functions, what charges would be levied by the agency, and, once payment is made, there would be certainty that the good would be delivered. In the presence of corruption, once an entrepreneur has paid a bribe for a certain service the official who has accepted the bribe may be unable to guarantee delivery of the good if other officials can then intervene and demand a bribe for provision of the same good. There is also no guarantee

that the official will not accept the bribe and renege on the contract. In both cases, there is no formal enforcement mechanism for the entrepreneur.

Depending upon how corruption networks are organised, there may be informal mechanisms through which contracts can be enforced. Borner, Brunetti, and Weder (1995) suggest that it is inevitably more effective to have an impartial third-party (the state) enforce contracts rather than having the two contracting parties attempt to find an enforcement arrangement by themselves. The principal argument they make is that the effectiveness of the state in playing this role will depend not so much on the precision of its legal arrangements but on having a history of institutional stability and on several mechanisms through which governments can reduce problems of time-inconsistency in policy making. In the case of corruption, this third-party enforcement is not possible because of the need for secrecy, but even when third-party enforcement does not exist to regulate commercial exchanges, there are numerous forms of two-party enforcement that can substitute, albeit less effectively. One of the most successful of these arrangements is engaging in commerce with familial relations. Another option is to create clubs where members meet frequently and exchange with each other. In both of these cases the high number of face to face interactions between individuals will increasing the costs of breaching a contract, because with better exchange of information other members are more likely to find out and those who breach the contract will be more certain of losing their reputation.

It is possible that corruption networks could operate in a similar manner. If there were mechanisms through which business leaders and government officials demanding bribes associated frequently, this might improve flows of information about bribery practices and lead to the establishment of reputations for officials who demanded reasonable bribes and did not renege on contracts. The positive effect would be to reduce the uncertainties inherent in corrupt transactions. A potential negative effect might be to create a clique of 'insider' firms that co-operate closely with government officials while the 'outsiders' are at a disadvantage. Small and medium-size enterprises would likely be excluded from such organisational forms and, hence, from the same benefits. Thus, even in the presence of a well-organised and predictable form of corruption, an important section of the economy would be subjected to high degrees of uncertainty on account of corrupt practices. Of particular significance is the effect that such uncertainty might have on innovation, to the extent that innovation would originate in smaller firms or new entrants to markets (Alam 1990).

One example of this phenomenon from Indonesia is what the World Banks' *East Asian Miracle* study (1993) calls 'informal networks linking senior officials with major enterprises'. The report continues, "little is known about

136   A.W. GOUDIE & DAVID STASAVAGE

these networks, but they appear to have produced a high degree of cooperation in the economy. In contrast to the deliberation councils, where rules are more transparent, these networks are more susceptible to capture by participants and corruption" (p.185). Presumably, increased possibilities for corruption derive from the secretive nature of these networks, and as argued above, the formation of secretive corruption cartels may exclude new firms that provide important innovations.

To help account for differences in growth between African and East Asian countries, this explanation would depend on showing not only that such associations existed between domestic businessmen and government officials, but that there also exist mechanisms through which foreign businesses associate with government officials. One likely possibility is that foreign businesses will associate themselves with domestic entrepreneurs that have an established relationship with the government. This then raises the question of how contracts between foreign businesses and these local intermediaries are enforced. Overall, one would expect these mechanisms to be more successful in reducing uncertainty when associative groups were small in number, because smaller size would lead to improved flows of information. Without corruption one would expect small size to be less important, because information could be distributed openly. Fewer ethnic, linguistic, or other social barriers between government officials and businesses should also improve chances for success.

A collective dilemma facing officials engaged in corruption
While the previous section focused on how corruption is organised between government officials and the entrepreneurs who pay bribes, there is also a second and related issue that involves a collective dilemma for government officials collecting bribes. Shleifer and Vishny (1993) work from the presumption discussed in the principal-agent models above that corruption involves individual government officials having monopoly and discretionary power over distribution of a good or service. They then propose a model for how the organisation of corruption will influence economic growth outcomes when entrepreneurs need several complementary government goods or services to conduct business. The basic conclusion is that when officials are able to collude and set bribes at a certain price they will maximise total bribe revenue and at a lower bribe price than if they acted as independent monopolists. When acting as an independent monopolist each official will ignore the externality that as he raises the bribe price for the good he provides, the demand for other complementary government goods will decline and total bribe revenue will decline. The way out of this problem is by collusion, in which case officials co-operate to set all bribes at the price which will max-

imise total bribe revenue. This will also benefit businesses via a lower bribe price. From this model one derives the implication that corruption organised in this manner will have a less harmful effect on economic growth than in countries where bureaucratic agencies or politicians conduct their corruption separately. The basic logic of this argument is similar to Mancur Olson's discussion of 'narrow' vs. 'encompassing' interests (Olson 1982, 1995). Collusion between officials demanding bribes will also likely mitigate the effects of corruption on growth in another way, by minimising the problem of 'free entry' into the market for bribes that is described above.

Collusion between bureaucratic agencies or politicians will be easier to enforce when deviations from the agreed bribe level are easily detectable. This would be the case when the corruption network has an effective 'policing machine' to detect offenders and to punish those who deviate from the agreed price, when the ruling elite of a country is small, and when society is homogeneous. Finally, collusion will have a greater effect to the extent that it is centralised. In fact, these conditions are quite close to those which should favour the functioning of networks between businesses and government officials.

For their empirical example of collusion in bribe-taking, Shleifer and Vishny (1993) refer to corruption in Soviet Russia, where different bureaucracies co-operated in setting bribe levels and in sharing the proceeds, while the KGB was used to monitor attempts to deviate. Another potential example of collusion in bribe-taking has been revealed by the recent scandal in Korea, where major companies reportedly made contributions to a central slush fund that was then distributed between different politicians. This kind of system would address both the uncertainty effect of corruption referred to above and the dilemma encountered by independent monopolists engaged in corruption.

A related consideration in this context is the definition of the motivation of the official receiving the corrupt payment. Much theoretical analysis assumes explicitly the presence of profit-maximizing officials, and analyses both individual decision-making and decision-making in the presence of collusion within this framework. It is, however, far from evident that this is a generally valid assumption in view of one of the fundamental distinctions between the market for corrupt acts and the standard form of market in economic analysis: namely, the critical importance of secrecy and the fear of exposure. These characteristics suggest that, once established, an understanding between an official and an external party to corruption may be stabilised through minimal further negotiation. Moreover, without information on similar forms of corrupt practice, convergence on a maximizing solution may be absent. In these circumstances, the government official's behaviour may be more appropriately equated with that of the satisficing enterprise in theories of the firm in which objectives – other than that of purely profit – are maximised.

The effects of corruption

The effects of corruption on the economy can be thought of in terms of the distortionary effects on the allocation of resources – that is, the extent to which on-going economic activity is redirected and rendered less efficient – and the disincentive effects – that is, the degree to which risk and uncertainty are introduced into the economic environment and thereby deter prospective economic activities and, especially, investment.

The distortionary effect of corruption

The undertaking of a corrupt act may entail the redirection of economic activity from one transaction to another, or it may permit the conclusion of the transaction that would have occurred in the absence of any such act but on different terms. The implication of these two outcomes for economic efficiency and economic development in a broader sense will vary significantly. Indeed, these repercussions may be looked at from three different perspectives: the economic transaction; the broader economic impact; and the corrupt payment per se. Before considering these three aspects, however, it is interesting to begin with an old debate over whether, under certain circumstances, corruption might actually improve allocative efficiency.

Corruption as a facilitator of growth ?

Nathaniel Leff's 1964 article "Economic Development Through Corruption" is the most frequently cited source for the argument that corruption in the form of bribery can be an important arm in the hands of entrepreneurs seeking to do business with a hostile or indifferent government and may, indeed, stimulate the development process (see also Nye [1967] and Huntington [1968]). Leff's general perception was that many developing-country governments have imposed excessive bureaucratic control and regulation on their economies, and that many of these regulations create serious uncertainty for entrepreneurs. Corruption in the form of bribery allows bureaucrats to get around excessive regulations and to minimise uncertainty over enforcement. For Leff and other authors, the other main potential advantage of corruption comes in cases like that where several entrepreneurs are vying for a single government license or permit. Rather than award the license based on *ad hoc* criteria, corruption can set up an auction mechanism whereby the most efficient firm will be able to pay the highest bribe and will be awarded the license or permit. The fact that the bribe payment goes directly to a bureaucrat instead of to the government will have negative economic implications, but allocative efficiency will actually be improved, since the lowest-cost firm wins out when it might not have otherwise. Finally, some authors have argued that corruption can help speed up the pace of bureaucratic activities when some sort of waiting period or queue occurs.

The idea that corruption can set up an efficient auction mechanism has not gone unchallenged. Potential problems cited with this idea are that entrepreneurs considering giving bribes may not have full information about other potential bribers, and furthermore, bribes may represent a sunk cost that cannot be reclaimed if surpassed by other offers. However, as Bardhan (1996) notes, others have provided game-theoretic models showing that, even under these conditions, the most efficient firm will win out. Bardhan (1996) and Andvig (1991) also review several of the considerations of corruption's effect on speeding up queues, and they both conclude that current models have so far failed to capture effectively the dynamics of bribery.

In part, this debate continues due to the apparent success of many economies despite, or perhaps because of, the presence of extensive corruption. Commentators have looked to the impressive performance of the East Asia economies between 1965 and 1997, often achieved in an environment characterised by widespread corruption, and raised the question of whether corrupt activities were, in fact, a positive contributory factor in this success. Several issues are raised by this argument. Firstly, a simple comparison of the growth performance of African and East Asian economies is necessarily unsatisfactory: higher growth in East Asia arguably results from an array of factors and the prevalence of corruption does not imply anything about its value to growth.

The crucial issue in any determination of whether corruption has the potential to accelerate development through one or other mechanisms is how efficient the economic system is at the outset. It can be argued that, if the initial condition is one of extreme inefficiency, then corrupt practices may stimulate more efficient behaviour that is beneficial to growth. On the other hand, if the starting point is relatively efficient, then corruption may indeed be detrimental and distortionary. Even if the former environment prevails, two questions arise: first, it is questionable whether the introduction of another distortion – that is, corruption – has the capacity to counter the first distortion or whether it merely exacerbates it through the introduction of another distortion or the substitution of one distortion for another; and, secondly, even when corruption can potentially counter the initial distortion, whether it is the appropriate instrument to ameliorate the existing environment if alternative instruments are available. Here, it could be argued that, even if the latter were true, it is the fact that the government fails to undertake these alternatives that renders corruption as a private initiative to be the appropriate response. That is, it is a second-best solution given that the first best (government policy improvements) is unavailable.

Moreover, the analysis of any single act of corruption is too partial to be meaningful in this context, and it is necessary to take account of the wider impact, and specifically the contagion implications of corruption. While it might be apparent that one specific corrupt activity is itself beneficial, it remains doubtful that this act may be isolated and that contagion effects can be averted. More probably, the act will contribute to the entrenchment of a more systemic and comprehensive form of corruption. For example, as noted above, the use of corrupt payments to accelerate the paper work of officials may prove highly effective for one transaction, but, if – as is arguably inevitable – the practice spreads to encompass all transactions, the net impact on efficiency is probably zero: the productivity of the official remains unchanged and efficiency may not be enhanced through any re-ordering of the queue.

The immediate economic impact

The corrupt acts at issue here are those that relate to specific economic transactions, such as the purchase or sale of an asset or service, the licensing of an economic activity or the allocation of a scarce economic resource. While attempts to model the bribery process to gauge its effects on efficiency have led to inconclusive results, there are several major reasons why it is unlikely that corruption will have a positive effect on allocative efficiency:

- The risk of exposure prevents bribery from being conducted as a truly market auction. If corruption contracts necessarily must remain secret, then officials demanding bribes will deliberately restrict the sort of information which would be necessary to set up an efficient auction, and they may well choose those giving bribes based on confidence that the arrangement will be kept secret as much as by ability to pay. As noted above, the need for secrecy with corrupt activities may mean that governments collude with a coterie of established firms and are unwilling to bring innovators into the circle.

- The risk of exposure will encourage corrupt officials to bias their activities towards those which minimise the risk of detection but which might actually increase overall costs for the economy. Shleifer and Vishny (1993) cite the example of countries tendencies to import high-cost machinery when a more generic machine might do. The more expensive machine is less likely to have a commonly known price, improving possibilities for overinvoicing and kickbacks that leave the government with inappropriate technology.

- Irrespective of the risk of exposure, if economic transactions are conditioned on the reaching of agreement on corrupt payments, then this additional cost may lead to the preference of alternative transactions rather than that which would have occurred in the absence of corruption (such issues are discussed in, for example, Krueger [1974]). On the assumption that the original use was preferable on efficiency grounds – and this is, of course, a relatively strong assumption – the distortion introduced would reduce efficiency overall.

- There is, moreover, a further potential efficiency loss in that the same transaction may occur but with a different party. For example, an operating license may be issued for the same activity, but, on account of the corrupt act, it may be issued to a different individual or enterprise than otherwise. Here, there is the potential for the economic activity to which the corrupt act gives authority to be conducted less efficiently by the corrupt licensee. The quality loss in contract licensing for building projects, attributable to corruption, was dramatically illustrated recently in Korea.

- Innovation may be deterred, because new firms which provide most innovation are more in need of government-supplied goods (licenses, permits, etc.) than are established firms.

In sum, the view that corruption can actually improve allocative efficiency seems flawed.

The broader economic impact

The broader distortionary implications that arise from corruption may be summarised as follows:

- Multiplier effects: any redirection of economic activity carries multiplier implications for the economy as a whole, and these will be directly related to the factors identified in the preceding section. Their identification will be particularly problematic, but, in the case of major capital investment projects, for example, they may be substantive. The loss of a road linkage to one region of a country – attributable to an act of corruption – in favour of an irrigation project in a different region would entail measurable and substantial multiplier opportunity costs.

- Competitiveness effects: if the nature of the corruption constitutes a bias against one group of enterprises, then there will be competitive bias that distorts the structure of economic development. For instance, in the situation where international trade tax is evaded through corruption, domestic producers may well face a more costly overall tax regime vis-à-vis importers.

- Fiscal effects: some forms of corruption will impact on fiscal objectives, in part through direct mechanisms whereby the government loses income directly from a corrupt act, but also indirectly through the tendency of corruption to drive economic activity into the black economy and outwith the administration of the tax authorities. Adverse effects may be substantial, both in terms of a loss of aggregate fiscal discipline, and in a reduction of the effectiveness with which different public expenditures are prioritised.

- Debt effects: some corrupt acts will add to national indebtedness as costs are unnecessarily incurred in international transactions. The servicing of this excess debt burden presents a long-term burden.

- Growth and investment: while the impact of the efficiency issues, raised above, may only be qualitatively rather than quantitatively definable, the ramifications for the volume and quality of investment and for growth may, nonetheless, be cumulatively highly significant.

Corrupt payments

Corrupt payments may be considered as implicit transfer payments between individuals or enterprises, with an opportunity cost that results from the modified income distribution and, in consequence, the modified pattern of consumption, saving and investment that it generates. Any single transaction is likely, in a macroeconomic sense, to be marginal in its impact, but, cumulatively, transactions may generate significant distributional effects.

Several alternative patterns of transfer may be envisaged. A transfer from one multinational enterprise to a government official may be seen from one perspective as an external capital inflow and as equivalent to a private-sector transfer payment. Thus, it might be seen as adding to the real disposable income of government officials and thereby boosting domestic consumption and domestic savings potential. However, this apparent stimulus to growth would most probably be negated on two counts: firstly, to the extent that the external bribing of a government official is effectively financed from donor external assistance, as is often the *de facto* case (the payment to the official from the multinational would appear as an inflated costing in seeking donor assistance), the opportunity cost will be the foregoing of another externally-financed project (assuming – as is typically the case for most bilateral and multilateral donors – that there is a fixed annual ceiling on the allocations to any single economy). Secondly, it is highly probable – at least in the instance of corruption at the highest levels – that the payment in foreign currency may never enter the domestic economy, thereby being of no benefit to the local economy and, insofar as it diverts scarce resources, clearly leaving the economy worse off.

In the case of corrupt practices involving only internal parties, the effects of the purely domestic transfers would depend on how the pre-corruption income distribution is modified. As in the growth model literature (as, for example, in the early work of Kaldor (1960), different personal sector social groupings with differentiated savings ratios may be identified. In this framework, transfers to higher saving ratio groupings would, for example, enhance domestic savings and investment and reduce the real incomes and consumption of lower saving ratio groupings. On the other hand, if transfers effectively flow from domestic enterprises to officials, then the reduction in corporate profits might be expected to curtail investment in the absence of access – or highly restricted access – to other sources of corporate finance.

In each of these forms of transfers – which would be expected to incorporate most of such flows – the task of identifying the primary flows is necessarily highly problematic, not to mention the assessment of their magnitude relative to other non-corrupt flows. However, in principle, it is the evaluation of these corrupt flows that determines the allocative implications, and thus the growth implications, of corrupt payments.

The disincentive effect of corruption

In addition to the distortionary impact that reduces the efficiency of present economic activity, the prevalence of corruption arguably acts on the economic environment in a far more insidious manner through the creation of significantly higher levels of risk and uncertainty in economic transactions, particularly when corruption is not organised in any of ways described in section four. This, in turn, acts to deter economic activity, in general, and capital investment in productive assets, in particular. Uncertainty is present both in the context of individual economic transactions and in terms of heightened fears about future developments in the broader economic environment in question.

The idea about the link between uncertainty and investment comes from recent literature which emphasises that the irreversibility of many types of investments drastically increases the importance of uncertainty as a potential deterrent. When this is the case, the net present value idea that one should invest when the value of a unit of capital is at least as large as the purchase and installation cost of the unit is no longer applicable. The new formulation suggests that the value must exceed the purchase and installation cost by an amount equal to the value of keeping the firm's option open to invest these resources elsewhere, which might be substantial if new information was expected (in an uncertain environment) (Pindyck 1991). As a result, both foreign and domestic investors will have a greater propensity to keep their money invested in developed-country financial markets unless they have credible assurances about the return that they will receive on investing in developing countries. The net effect will be lower accumulation of capital and there will also be an important effect on efficiency of allocation as investment is biased towards short-term, high-return activities, like trading.

144   A.W. GOUDIE & DAVID STASAVAGE

A single transaction

The risk and uncertainty that attaches to a single transaction may be characterised by several parameters, including:

- The lack of information *ex ante* regarding the number of corrupt acts that
  must be negotiated with different parties to complete the transaction as
  a whole. This may be illustrated by a customs department where the
  number of officials having the opportunity to engage in corrupt acts
  – and choosing to exercise that power – may be unknown and highly
  volatile. Alternatively, it may be illustrated by the unknown number of
  road blocks that obstruct the free passage of trade. The more anarchic
  the structure, the greater the uncertainty.

- The effective rate of corruption, having consolidated all the costs resulting from the corrupt act(s) that are involved in the single economic
  transaction. From this cost perspective, the overall effective rate is more
  important than how many times a corrupt act occurs, although an administrative 'overhead' cost no doubt accrues with each negotiation (equally,
  there may be economies of scale from corrupt acts: for example if the
  payment has a flat-rate element rather than being purely *pro rata*). The
  rate may vary from, at one extreme, a system of *ad hoc* rates dependent
  on the whim of the official, to, at the other extreme, an highly structured
  pattern of rates that has been established over time and which is rigorously and consistently observed by all parties. In this latter instance,
  there may, indeed, be effective sanctions within the structure for those
  attempting to deviate from the established system.

- The probability of attaining the desired outcome by completing the transaction as a whole.

- The risk of exposure of the corrupt acts.

- The likelihood of legal sanctions being imposed and the costs of that
  sanction. In addition, the other costs of exposure – for example, those
  resulting from the loss of employment or political office – will be relevant.

- The delay that is incurred in negotiating with corrupt parties in completing the transaction as a whole.

It is the combined impact of the above factors that generates an economic
environment in which uncertainty can deter entrepreneurship and thereby restrain development. At one extreme, corruption poses a relatively mild degree
of uncertainty if all the key parameters are known *ex ante*. In contrast, if these
parameters are *ex ante* unknown, any transactions are entered into on the basis
of extreme risk, not only in terms of cost, but also in terms of the probability
of attaining the desired outcome.

Decision making and investment

The uncertainty, as analysed above, that surrounds any *single* transaction that an enterprise would undertake in the course of its business activities, is only one aspect of economic uncertainty. More critical for the development process of any economy will be the impact of the prevailing structure of corruption on the uncertainty that characterises the economic environment in a more fundamental and more generalised sense. Such uncertainty will be a key determinant in long-term corporate planning, and especially in investment decisions. Here, four crucial factors may be isolated that will have profound importance in establishing uncertainty:

- The cumulative impact of the distortionary and disincentive effects generated by many individual transactions, as noted above.

- The risk of the evolution of more severe forms of corruption. To the extent that the prevailing structure of corruption is perceived as unstable or as fragile in the face of anticipated future shocks to the system, there will be a considerable risk of corruption's escalating and perhaps evolving into more uncertain and costly forms.

- Discriminatory behaviour in the treatment of competitors. This aspect relates to the structure of corruption that a particular enterprise perceives to be relevant to its competitors, for it is far from certain that all competitors in the same product market will face the same structure. Relatively random changes in the degree of uncertainty faced by an enterprise as between different transactions may, of course, occur: for instance, the effective rates may vary arbitrarily or some corrupt payments may be erratically demanded. More problematic for an enterprise, however, is the situation where it perceives discrimination by officials systematically to bias competitiveness against itself. With all structures of corruption having the capacity to differentiate between competitors, an added uncertainty derives from the possibility that any established pattern of corruption – if such there is – will move to the detriment of the enterprise concerned. This may apply to both domestic and international transactions: indeed, one important example is that in which corruption within the customs service evolves to facilitate the avoidance of import taxes in return for corrupt payments to officials, and thereby undermines the competitiveness of domestic producers. In economies in which import taxes are a very substantial proportion of total costs, this is a major consideration.

- Political and economic risk. Where corruption is perceived as having the potential to undermine the political stability of the state, through the provocation of social unrest or, more seriously, through the instigation of coup d'états and civil war (see below for an elaboration of this point), this enhanced degree of political risk may significantly deter business activity. Equally, where corrupt activities are perceived to be instrumental in disrupting macroeconomic policy to a substantive extent, the danger of macro destabilisation – or, in the context of an on-going stabilisation programme, the threat that macroeconomic stabilisation may not be attainable – may once again create increased uncertainty in the business environment.

It is important to set these sources of uncertainty in the context of more traditional sources of uncertainty, as are commonly associated with the economic and political risk that enterprises have always faced in their operations in LDCs. There has always been a significant probability of political destabilization, with the potential threat of asset destruction or asset expropriation on terms highly disadvantageous to the previous owners. In traditionally politically unstable economies, corruption may not greatly augment the existing risks, but in those economies that have been more politically sound, the impact on the prospects for development is likely to be more significant.

The impact of corruption on the political climate

Earlier discussion focused on the manner in which political structures contribute to the evolution of a particular form of corruption, but the reverse causality is equally important in many developing countries. Low-value, high-incidence corruption alone is less likely to feed through into political instability in a substantive manner, but the prevalence of major opportunities for access to high-value, low-incidence rent-seeking acts may provide a powerful incentive for the securing of political power and influence. This form of instability might be anticipated in autocratic structures. It may also, however, be expected in weak democratic structures, in which the overthrow of an existing regime through undemocratic means may be feasible. In view of the fragility of democracy in many African states that have sought to introduce more representative government, this threat may be a reality.

Many examples from around the world illustrate that the potential gains from corrupt practices at this highest level are sufficiently vast to motivate both existing ruling parties and opposition groupings in many countries. Not only does this prospect motivate opposition coup d'états or other more protracted and more violent attempts at overthrowing both democratically-elected and autocratic regimes, but it impacts on the existing policy of ruling governments. This latter situation can be observed in a variety of policy decisions. On the political side, it motivates efforts to resist moves to greater representative government or to delay that process – as is apparent now in Nigeria – or to manipulate the democratic processes in order to sustain the ruling government. This is seen in government-inspired efforts, such as the rigging of elections or the blocking of the participation of opposition leaders in elections. Equally, it is observed in the manipulation of economic policy in order to favour specific factions or social groupings, or, indeed, through the corruption and bribery of key figures in society. In the former case, such manipulation does not refer to the standard attempts by all governments to synchronise the economic cycle with the political cycle, or the efforts to attract political support through specific, relatively marginal policy measures, such as targeted tax cuts and the like. Rather it refers to major redirections of policy with a blatant political objective and, typically, of a type that would not find support within a representative constitutional body (the border between marginal electioneering and political manipulation of budgetary policy may, at times, seem indistinct and is certainly highly subjective, but, in practice, extreme abuses of economic policy – and especially public expenditure policy – to this end are easily recognisable). More obviously, it motivates repressive policy that seeks to eliminate any threat to the ruling party. Here, the entire political and social policy of the government focuses on control by the security forces and the total subjugation of the judiciary and other organs of civil society. This, as we have seen itself impacts on the form of corruption that evolves.

The establishment of a ruling government that is motivated by the wish to retain the privileges that facilitate corruption also leads to the favouring of specific economic policies that facilitate that corruption. Thus, policies that favour opportunities for corruption are accorded a greater priority, irrespective of whether those choices accord with the national interest and the articulated economic development strategy – if such exists – of the government. One instance of this would be the favouring of external capital assistance. Certainly, such a policy stance may be consistent with the optimal policy stance in the absence of corruption, but such flows are typically regarded as major contributors to the facilitation of corrupt practices. The exploitation of domestic mineral resources by multinational enterprises through direct foreign investment, or the negotiation of contracts for other major capital investment programmes are the classic examples that are usually provided. In the former instance, it is clear that, not only does the external assistance provide the technology and skills to exploit the national resources, but also provides the mechanisms through which foreign exchange can be generated for personal benefit. However, for economies with no obvious natural resource to attract such foreign investment, a policy of maximising external donor aid plays a similar role. Thus, just as earlier it was concluded that donor flows form a major determinant of the structure of corruption, so it is clear that corruption – and the wish to create further opportunities for its pursuit – can drive a policy of aid dependence.

148 A.W. GOUDIE & DAVID STASAVAGE

Existing empirical studies

The first thing to note about the empirical literature on corruption is that it is not nearly as extensive as the theoretical literature on corruption. Many writings are mostly theoretical with a small section on empirical examples, while little effort has been made to conduct systematic tests of the various hypotheses. That empirical material which does exist could be divided into three categories:
- case studies which are used to propose a theory about corruption;
- case studies that are essentially descriptive in nature; and
- papers which attempt to construct systematic tests for hypotheses about corruption and growth.

With few exceptions, the papers in this third group use cross-country regressions based on indices of corruption formulated by country risk services.

Case studies that propose a theory
Some of the most interesting empirical work on corruption appears in papers whose primary purpose is to use a single case as an illustration to propose a theory about corruption. As a result, these papers do not provide ideas about how corruption hypotheses might be tested in a systematic manner, but they do provide material which can be used to ask whether the theories proposed above seem relevant.

Perhaps the most interesting of these examples is Robert Wade's 1985 article on the market for public offices in the irrigation agency of an unnamed Indian state. After presenting a description of an agency plagued by problems of corruption where officials demand bribes from villages in exchange for irrigation services, Wade focuses on how corruption is organised hierarchically. Officials demand bribes from villages, but in order to be posted to a position where they can demand bribes they themselves need to make payoffs to a superior, and so on, in a chain of corruption that reaches to the level of local politicians who can influence bureaucratic postings and who need bribe money for campaign finance.

According to Wade, the basic causes of corruption in this system are similar to those outlined above. Wade also adds a third causal factor, in that even honest officials may need to become corrupt to get sufficient money for transfer to a higher post. In terms of effects on growth, there are substantial negative effects on the Indian economy and environment, Wade argues, primarily because officials under pressure to raise money create new opportunities for bribe collection by managing the irrigation network so as to maximise opportunities for bribes. This includes using capital intensive techniques that improve opportunities for graft, which supports the theoretical argument made above about corruption biasing the activity of bureaucrats.

Wade also cites numerous examples of how the quality of service provided by the irrigation department, was eroded by prevalent corruption.

The one important aspect of corruption where Wade does not come to a firm conclusion is with the issue of organisation. At the outset of the paper he refers to corruption in this case as 'a smoothly functioning market kept in place by a strongly centralised hierarchy of authority'. Later on he acknowledges that there is actually a substantial amount of uncertainty in the system. What seems clear from his description is that this system is organised in the sense that bureaucrats have to pay to be transferred to a post where they can extract bribes from the populace, but once in their positions, officials operate as independent monopolists, which should have a negative effect on the economy. There is also no apparent form of association between officials and village representatives which might reduce uncertainty.

Apart from Wade's contribution, there are several other articles which have used a single case to illustrate an interesting theory. Olson (1995) refers to the former Soviet Union to present an argument about the emergence of corruption and its effects on economic growth. Corruption in the USSR emerged from excess bureaucratic control and an absence of private property. To function efficiently, the Soviet planned economy required an immense amount of information to be transmitted from the level of the shop floor to party bureaucrats. There were inevitably problems of monitoring in this system, as top officials could not know whether production targets set by lower-level bureaucrats were realistic or whether they were kept artificially low by bureaucrats who would then skim off a percentage of the good produced to sell on the black market. The fact that top officials might receive information from several different lower-level bureaucrats who produced the same good provided opportunities for checking up, but Olson argues that over time lower-level bureaucrats were able to collude to defraud the centre.

For Shleifer and Vishny (1993) the Soviet Union (and, since 1990, the countries of the former Soviet Union) is also a paradigmatic case upon which to draw in formulating theories about corruption. They are in accord with Olson in stressing the importance of excess bureaucratic control as a cause of corruption during the Soviet period, but they differ fundamentally in suggesting that corruption will have a more or less significant effect on economic growth depending upon how it is organised. Olson paints a picture of a decentralised form of corruption in Soviet Russia that undermined the party hierarchy, while Shleifer and Vishny emphasise the critical role played by the Communist Party and the KGB in running a centralised system of corruption. Olson does not suggest that the organisation of corruption in post-Soviet Russia has changed dramatically from Soviet days, while the central argument of Shleifer and Vishny is that corruption today is much less organised than in the Soviet period and as a consequence more detrimental to economic growth. The argument made by Shleifer and Vishny seems more convincing in the sense that they have a ready explanation to account for the apparent transformation in corruption following the breakdown of Communist rule, but Olson's argument poses problems for their account of the Soviet period. If the origins of corruption in Soviet Russia lay in the failures in monitoring inherent to a planned economy under bureaucratic control, then why didn't the system of well organised corruption that Shleifer and Vishny describe succumb to the same problems?

Descriptive case studies
Many of the case studies on corruption which use a more descriptive and qualitative type of analysis seem to have been written in the 1970s and early 1980s. While contributing partial insights, these studies do not present much of an idea about how a study on corruption that seeks to test hypotheses systematically might be organised. Two of the more interesting contributions from this group include Szeftel (1982) on Zambia and Gould (1980) on Zaire. Szeftel presents a number of examples to demonstrate that corruption in Zambia is perhaps not as endemic as in other African countries. It has been fostered by an expansion of the central state administration and parastatal sector. The main consequence of corruption has been the creation of an "indigenous owing class" which has accumulated wealth through that state rather than through private enterprise. Gould (1980) presents evidence from Zaire of massive corruption in a bureaucracy that no longer functions even remotely as it is supposed to.

Systematic tests of corruption hypotheses
Three recent studies investigate the *causes* of corruption in a systematic manner across regions or across countries. There are also several studies which investigate the *effects* of corruption on investment and economic growth as part of a broader effort to investigate the relationship between institutions and growth.

Studies which investigate the causes of corruption
Of the three available studies which look at the causes of corruption in a systematic manner, Putnam (1993) treats the issue of corruption indirectly. Evans and Rauch (1995) investigate the effect of bureaucratic rules and procedures on the emergence of corruption. Their basic argument is that when bureaucracies have 'Weberian' criteria of meritocratic recruitment and internal promotion, they will suffer from less corruption. Using survey questionnaire responses from 26 developing countries, Evans and Rauch find that more 'Weberian' bureaucracies are significantly correlated with lower levels

of corruption (as indicated in indices produced by risk assessment agencies). Their measures of bureaucratic rules and procedures are, however, not significantly correlated with common measures of economic performance like private investment or per capita GDP growth. Ades and Di Tella (1995) look at the relationship between certain structural variables in the economy and the extent of corruption. They find that the size of monopoly rents in an economy, attributable either to policy factors or distance from trading partners, is significantly correlated with the level of corruption as measured in indices provided by risk assessment agencies.

Studies which investigate the effects of corruption on growth
The four studies which perform cross-country regressions to examine the effect of institutional efficiency and corruption on growth use two types of data:
- indices of corruption from private firms that analyse country risk for investors; and
- indices based on survey questionnaires which the authors prepared.

While this conclusion is not unanimous, the overall evidence from these papers provides some support for the the proposition made above that similar levels of corruption may have different effects on economic growth, depending upon how corruption is organised.

Keefer and Knack (1993) ask whether inadequate legal, political, and regulatory institutions can be an obstacle to economic convergence in poorer countries. The primary effect of inadequate institutions that they emphasise is via the problem of insecure property rights which will discourage investment and growth. For data on institutional effectiveness, Keefer and Knack use indices compiled by two country risk services (the ICRG covering 97 countries and BERI covering 47 countries). Indices for risk of expropriation, repudiation of contracts by governments, contract enforceability, and risk of nationalisation cover the issue of property rights directly. When placed in regressions with other variables commonly used in endogenous growth regressions, these institutional variables remain statistically significant as explanations of economic growth over the period 1960–89. Keefer and Knack use a separate regression to assess the importance of indices for bureaucratic quality, bureaucratic delays, and corruption and government. The indicator for corruption proved significant, but an interaction term designed to measure the interaction between corruption and the initial income gap was not statistically significant.

Keefer and Knack (1994) uses the same data from ICRG and BERI but makes the advance of directly investigating the effect of institutions on investment as well as on economic growth. The results are statistically significant and the values of the coefficients indicate an effect of the same magnitude as that of education on growth for some of the variables. This effect is also present even when investment is controlled for, which the authors interpret as suggesting that the quality of institutions affects growth both through the channel of accumulation of capital as well as through allocative efficiency.

A third contribution, Mauro (1995) focuses more directly on the effect of corruption on growth. He uses data from Business International for 68 countries for the period 1980–83 including nine separate indices measuring institutional efficiency and political stability.[3] While the methodology with which the BERI and ICRG indices are compiled remains somewhat opaque, the system for constructing the Business International indices is clearer, depending on subjective reports from individual country experts that are asked the same specific set of questions. From the nine basic indicators Mauro constructs one index for bureaucratic efficiency (legal system, red tape, corruption) and a second index for political stability (using the remaining six indicators).

Placing countries in order according to these two indices and then looking at their economic growth performance 1960-85 shows some interesting exceptions to what one might expect. Thailand was reported as the most corrupt country in the BI data set between 1980 and 1983, yet it enjoyed enviable growth performance. Another feature Mauro highlights is that the indices for political stability and bureaucratic efficiency are highly correlated, although again there are some interesting exceptions. Indonesia was rated as a very stable country but as having a 'corrupt, cumbersome bureaucracy'.

In the regressions relevant to corruption, Mauro finds that both the individual corruption variable and the bureaucratic efficiency index are statistically significant determinants of the average level of investment over the period 1960–85, even when controlling for other determinants of investment. A one standard deviation improvement in the bureaucratic efficiency index is association with a 4.1 percent of GDP increase investment, or 3.3 percent GDP for the same change in the corruption index. While the bureaucratic efficiency and corruption indices are both significantly correlated with economic growth, when further tests are conducted, the relationship with the bureaucratic efficiency index is shown to be robust while that with the corruption variable is not. As a final step, Mauro tests the influence of his variables on allocative efficiency by including the level of investment on the right-hand side of the growth repression. The result is that the bureaucratic efficiency index remains statistically significant but the value of its coefficient is reduced by a third. The corruption variable loses its statistical significance. It should also be noted that Brunetti (1995) uses Business International data to test the importance of the same political variables as Mauro (1993) using the same indices but different specifications for the regression and per capita growth 1980–1990 (instead of 1960–85). In this specification, none of the variables are statistically significant.[4]

Brunetti (1995) follows an approach different from Keefer and Knack and Mauro by using data from a questionnaire distributed to entrepreneurs in different developing countries that was created for Borner, Brunetti and Weder (1995). The 12 questions in the questionnaire were designed to measure the degree of uncertainty which entrepreneurs perceived as a result of institutional instability and of corruption. Separate indicators for each of the twelve questions were constructed based on six possible step-wise answers. Data were retained from 28 different countries where there were at least three respondents to the questionnaire. Two problems with this method are:
- the fact that ideally one would have responses from entrepreneurs from the beginning of whatever period of growth was considered; and
- the fact that the questionnaires were answered anonymously by mail rather than being administered.

All four indicators designed to measure aspects of corruption failed to prove statistically significant as determinants of either growth, investment or allocative efficiency over the period 1960–85 (as did a composite indicator that was the average of the four). In contrast, indicators designed to measure the degree of uncertainty in institutions and policies were statistically significant, and retained this significance in the growth regression under the extreme bounds analysis test (extreme bounds analysis was apparently not performed for the regressions where investment and allocative efficiency was the dependent variable). Duplicating the result obtained by Mauro, this analysis also finds that Thailand and Indonesia were very corrupt, but without an apparent negative effect on economic growth. In Thailand in particular it was noted that bribery was endemic, but payment of a bribe to a government official virtually guarantees the right to get what one paid for. Brunetti interprets this as meaning that both countries had very low levels of uncertainty in their institutional framework, and that this supports the prediction that corruption will not have as negative an economic growth when it occurs in an organised and regular manner.

Conclusions

This article has attempted to propose a general framework for analysing the causes of corruption, derived from principal-agent theory. The framework puts a strong emphasis on concrete aspects of developing-country economies that might be observed by future empirical analysts in order to test corruption hypotheses. We conclude that it will be useful to consider separately the causes of corruption at the international level, at the national level, and within individual institutions. At the international level, the extent to which the competitiveness of international markets gives multinational companies an incentive to offer bribes to gain an advantage on their competitors needs to be considered. This factor may be most important in resource-rich economies like Nigeria or Angola. At the national level, analysts should consider how the basic development strategy of the government affects opportunities and incentives for corruption and how three principal-agent relationships do the same: the relationship between government and civil service, between government and judiciary, and between government and civil society. Finally, three specific areas of government activity are proposed as possibilities for considering the sources of corruption at the level of individual institutions: the customs administration, business regulation, and management of foreign aid.

In addition to proposing a framework for analyzing corruption, the article's second objective has been to consider several further explanations of corruption, based on models with multiple equilibria, socials norms, income distribution, and the importance of political leadership. For the moment, these explanations are less promising for those intent on conducting empirical research. There is every reason to believe that each of these further explanations provides substantial insight into understanding why corruption exists in some environments and not in others, but given that the empirical study of corruption is at such an early stage, it may be most useful in the near term for empirical studies to focus on the basic hypotheses which can be derived from principal-agent theory.

The article's third objective has been to propose a framework for considering the effects of corruption on the economy. There is little support for the argument that corruption can actually facilitate economic growth, and there are in fact a number of reasons to believe that it can have a strong distortionary and disincentive effect on economic activity. These two effects will be most pronounced in cases where corruption is anarchic in form, as seems to be the case in many African countries.

Finally, the review of the existing empirical literature on corruption reveals that there have been a number of descriptive studies on corruption and a number of more recent studies which analyse corruption with the aid of cross country regression and indices for corruption published by organisations that evaluate risk. The next logical step for empirical research on corruption is to conduct case studies which will offer more detail of how corruption actually functions than does the cross-country work but which are designed to test specific corruption hypotheses. This could be done either by considering corruption in a country as a whole, or, more plausibly, by investigating corruption within an individual institution in a given country, like the customs administration. As far as the choice of countries is concerned, existing work suggests that it would be particularly interesting to compare one or more African cases with one or more East Asian ones, since corruption seems to have been equally prevalent in both these groups but the impact of corruption on the economy has varied considerably. This is a common proposition in both the policy and academic community. It would be useful to subject it to a rigorous test.

Typology of public-sector corrupt practices.

	Primary activities of public-sector	Elements of activity open to corrupt practices	Elements of economic development most affected
A	The implementation of established public expenditure strategies: including the manner in which expenditure allocations are determined across sectors and regions, and the manner in which humanitarian aid is managed.	Regional and sectoral allocation of real, financial and administrative resources, Prioritisation of expenditures and of programme implementation. Determination of expenditure quality. Diversion of goods for personal use.	Adherence to, and compatibility with, the macroeconomic and sectoral objectives of the Government economic development strategy. Cohesion and consistency of sectoral strategy. Compatibility with economic incentive strategy.
B	The purchase of assets or services: this includes the procurement both of current goods and services and of capital assets within the fiscal expenditure programme. The purchases may be made in the context of self-financed projects or externally financed under donor assistance programmes.	Negotiation with domestic and multinational operators. Selection of suppliers, contractors and operators. Pricing of procurement.	Adherence to government economic strategy (see A. above). Cost effectiveness of expenditures. Opportunity cost of external capital assistance.
C	The licensing of entities to undertake specific economic activities: this may incorporate licenses authorising the right to trade in certain products or in certain regions of the country, or to import and export particular products, to produce specified products, or to exploit particular natural resources.	Selection of entities (especially if rationing). Determination of supply level. Pricing of licenses.	Efficiency of allocation process. Quality of capital asset accumulation. Supply impacts on competitiveness of markets (according to market size). Disincentive to new starts and expansion.

156   A.W. GOUDIE & DAVID STASAVAGE

Typology of public-sector corrupt practices.

	Primary activities of public-sector	Elements of activity open to corrupt practices	Elements of economic development most affected
D	The allocation of resources through centrally administered structures: this form of activity ranges from the allocation of foreign exchange to financial credit under systems of non-market administered control.	Selection of recipient. Determination of values of allocation. Pricing of allocation. Management of default situations.	Efficiency of allocation process.
E	The sale of public assets to private-sector interests under programmes of privatisation.	Determination of asset valuation. Determination of terms and conditions of sale. Selection criteria of buyer.	Efficiency of allocation process. Return on sale for alternative use.
F	The regulation and management of private sector economic activities.	Determination of pricing. Controls on scale and location of operation. Environmental controls.	Consumer purchasing power Efficiency of pricing policy and sub-optimal production levels Environmental degradation.
G	The administration of the tax revenue system (for both internal and international transactions).	Determination of liabilities and their collection.	Fiscal policy objectives: * macroeconomic compatibility; * expenditure policy objectives; * incentive structure compatibility; * equity/distributional objectives; Competitive impact of tax avoidance.
H	The operations of the public enterprise sector: including the purchase and sale of goods and services, and their pricing.	Invoicing of imports and exports.	Access to domestic savings if capital flight.

Notes

1. Another indication of the growing concern to address the problem of corruption was provided in the establishment of the internationally-supported NGO Transparency International in 1993. See, for example, Eigen (1995) and Transparency International (1995).
2. We consider cases here where norms are exogenous. Collier (1994) presents a model where social norms are important short-run determinants of the level of corruption but which are themselves in the long-run endogenous to other variables.
3. They include: political change, political stability, probability of opposition group take-over, stability of labour, relationship with neighbour countries, terrorism, legal system ("efficiency and integrity of the legal environment as it affects business, particularly that of

A FRAMEWORK FOR THE ANALYSIS OF CORRUPTION   157

foreign firms"), bureaucracy and red tape, ("the regulatory environment foreign firms must face when seeking approvals or permits. The degree to which it represents and obstacle to business"), corruption "the degree to which business transactions involve corruption or questionable payments".

4. As an additional point, Mauro also makes an attempt to deal with the possibility of joint endogeneity. He does so by using data from an index on ethnolinguistic fractionalization, which it turns out is highly correlated with institutional inefficiency, and he suggests that one can assume ethnolinguistic fractionalization to be exogenous both to economic variables and to institutional inefficiency.

References

Alberto Ades and Rafael Di Tella (1995a) "Competition and Corruption", unpublished, Oxford University.

Alberto Ades and Rafael Di Tella (1995b), "The New Economics of Corruption: a Survey and Some New Results", unpublished, Oxford University.

M.S. Alam (1990) "Some Economic Costs of Corruption in LDCs", *Journal of Development Studies*, Vol. 27, No. 1, October.

Alberto Alesina and Dani Rodrik (1994) "Distributive Politics and Economic Growth", *Quarterly Journal of Economics*, Vol. 109.

J.-C. Andvig (1991) "The Economics of Corruption: a Survey", *Studi Economici*, Vol. 46, No. 43, pp. 57–94.

J.-C. Andvig and Karl Ove Moene (1990) "How Corruption may Corrupt", *Journal of Economic Behavior and Organisation*, Vol. 13, pp. 63–76.

Pranab Bardhan (1996) "The Economics of Corruption in Less Developed Countries: a Review of the Issues", OECD Development Centre, Paris.

Silvio Borner, Aymo Brunetti and Beatrice Weder (1995) *Political Credibility and Economic Development*, Macmillan, London.

Aymo Brunett (1995) "Political Variables in Cross-Country Growth Analysis", unpublished, Department of Economics, Harvard University.

Timothy Besley and John Mclaren (1993) "Taxes and Bribery: the Role of Wage Incentives", *The Economic Journal*, Vol. 103, pp. 119–141, January.

Paul Collier (1995) "The Domain of African Government", paper prepared for the *SAREC International Colloquium on New Directions in Development Economics – Growth, Equity, and Sustainable Development*.

Peter Eigen (1995) "Coalition Building for Islands of Integrity", paper presented to the *OECD Symposium on Corruption and Good Governance*, Paris.

Peter B. Evans and James Rauch (1995) "Bureaucratic Structures and Economic Performance in Less Developed Countries", *IRIS Working Paper* No. 175, August.

Monday Ekpo (1979) "Gift-Giving and Bureaucratic Corruption in Nigeria", in Monday Ekpo (ed), *Bureaucratic Corruption in Sub-Saharan Africa, Causes Consequences, and Controls*, University Press of America, Washington DC.

David Gould and Jose Amaro-Reyes (1983) "The Effects of Corruption on Administrative Performance: Illustration from Developing Countries", *World Bank Staff Working Papers*, No. 580.

Arnold J. Heidenheimer (1970) *Political Corruption: Readings in Comparative Analysis*, Holt, Rinehart and Winston, New York.

Philip Keefer and Stephen Knack (1997) "Why Don't Poor Countries Catch Up?: a Cross-National Test of an Institutional Explanation", *Economic Inquiry*, Vol. 35, No. 3, July.

Philip Keefer and Stephen Knack (1994) "Institutions and Economic Performance: Cross-Country Tests Using Alternative Institutional Measures", *Economics and Politics*, Vol. 7, No. 3, November.

Robert Klitgaard (1995a) "National and International Strategies for Reducing Corruption", paper presented to the *OECD Symposium on Corruption and Good Governance*, Paris.

Robert Klitgaard (1995b) "Institutional Adjustment and Adjusting to Institutions", *World Bank Discussion Paper*, No. 303.

Robert Klitgaard (1988) *Controlling Corruption*, University of California Press, Berkeley.

Anne Krueger (1974) "The Political Economy of the Rent-Seeking Society", *American Economic Review*, June.

Jean-Jacques Laffont (1995) "Controles de Prix et Economie des Institutions en Chine", unpublished.

Nathaniel Leff (1979) "Economic Development through Bureaucratic Corruption", in Ekpo ed. (1979)

Paolo Mauro (1995) "Corruption and Growth", *Quarterly Journal of Economics*, Vol. 109, August, pp. 681–712.

Kevin Murphy, Andrei Shleifer and Robert Vishny (1991) "Why is Rent-Seeking so Costly to Growth?", *American Economic Review*, May.

Kevin Murphy, Andrei Shleifer and Robert Vishny (1991), "The Allocation of Talent: Implications for Growth", *Quarterly Journal of Economics*, Vol. 107.

J.S. Nye, (1979), "Corruption and Political Development: a Cost Benefit Analysis", in Ekpo (ed.).

Obasanjo, O. (1994), Letter to the *Financial Times*, 14 October.

OECD (1994) Recommendations of the Council on Bribery in International Business Transactions, May.

OECD (1994) DAC Orientation on Participatory Development and Good Governance.

Mancur Olson (1982) *The Rise and Decline of Nations*, Yale University Press, New Haven.

Mancur Olson (1995) "Why Poor Economic Policies Must Promote Corruption: Lessons from the East forAll Countries", paper presented at the *Conference on Institutions and Economic Organisation in the Advanced Economies: the Governance Perspective*", Rome.

Robert Pindyck (1991) "Irreversibility, Uncertainty, and Investment", *Journal of Economic Literature*, Vol. 29, pp. 1110–1148.

Robert Putnam (1993) *Making Democracy Work*, Princeton University Press, Princeton NJ.

Susan Rose-Ackerman (1994) "Reducing Bribery in the Public-sector", in Duc V Trange ed. *Corruption and Democracy: Political Institutions, Processes and Corruption in Transition States in East-Central Europe and in the former Soviet Union*, Institute for Constitutional and Legislative Policy, Budapest.

Susan Rose-Ackerman (1995) "Proposal for Research on the Level and Impact of Corruption in International Business", unpublished.

Susan Rose-Ackerman (1978) *Corruption: a Study in Political Economy*, Academic Press, New York.

Andrei Shleifer and Robert Vishny (1993) "Corruption", *Quarterly Journal of Economics*, Vol. 108, No. 3.

Andrei Shleifer (1994) "Establishing Property Rights", in *Proceedings of the World Bank Annual Conference on Development Economics 1994*.

Michael Smith (1979) "Historical and Cultural Conditions of Political Corruption among the Hausa of Nigeria", in Ekpo ed.

Morris Szeftel (1982) "Political Graft and the Spoils System in Zambia: the State as a Resource in Itself", *Review of African Political Economy,* Vol. 24, May–August.

Vito Tanzi (1994) "Corruption, Governmental Activities, and Markets", *IMF Working Paper* No. 94/99.

Transparency International (1995) *Building a Global Coalition Against Corruption.*

Robert Wade (1985) "The Market for Public Office: Why the Indian State is not Better at Development", World Development, Vol. 13 No. 4.

World Bank (1995) *A Continent in Transition: Sub-Saharan Africa in the Mid-1990s,* Oxford University Press.

World Bank (1993) *The East Asian Miracle,* Oxford University Press.

[25]

Third World Quarterly, Vol 20, No 3, pp 491–502, 1999

So what really is the problem about corruption?

ROBIN THEOBALD

ABSTRACT *The past five years have seen a torrent of writings, pronouncements, warnings, statements of intent, programmes of action and suchlike by a range of agencies both national and international on the theme of corruption and what to do about it. Paralleling the outpouring of public utterances, social scientists have also addressed themselves to analysing the phenomenon and reflecting upon its apparent causes. Not infrequently these analyses have been centred around the notion of the neo-patrimonial state and by implication its converse, some loosely conceived 'modern' state. By means of an exploration of the nature and extent of neo-patrimonialism in both less developed (LDCS) and developed (DCS) countries, this article suggests that not only is the underpinning dichotomy merely descriptive and therefore analytically unproductive, but the consequent policy implications may be both misplaced and inappropriate.*

The title of this article refers consciously to a significant early attempt to grapple critically with the phenomenon of corruption by Colin Leys, which appeared more than 30 years ago.[1] Leys begins his article by identifying a gap in the social science literature which had hitherto failed to produce a systematic analysis of the phenomenon of corruption. In fact, in so far as corruption had been addressed, this had either been in the form of historical studies, documentation from inquisitorial investigations or sociological studies which dealt with corruption only incidentally. For these reasons the discussion of corruption in relation to contemporary societies had tended to become the preserve of moralists. Firmly in this genre was a book by Wraith and Simpkins entitled *Corruption in Developing Countries*.[2] Mainly concerned with West Africa, the authors' stance with regard to the phenomenon is abundantly evident when they refer to it as the 'scarlet thread of bribery and corruption' which 'flourishes as luxuriantly as the bush and weeds which it so much resembles, taking the goodness from the soil and suffocating the growth of plants which have been carefully, and expensively, bred and tended'. Corruption embodies a 'jungle of nepotism and temptation' which has dangerous and tragic consequences, replacing the enthusiasm of the young African civil servant with disenchantment and cynicism. Wraith and Simpkins spend a large part of their book examining British history and seeking an explanation of the transformation from the situation of pervasive graft of the 18th century to the eventual institutionalisation of administrative probity 100

Robin Theobald is at the Westminster Business School, University of Westminster, 309 Regent Street, London W1R 8AL, UK.

0143-6597/99/030491-12 © 1999 *Third World Quarterly*   491

ROBIN THEOBALD

years later. Their aim: to discover an answer to the question, 'Why does the public morality of African states not conform to that of the British?' Their answer seems to boil down to one simple cause: avarice! Leys, however, feels that the explanation is bound up with the different economic social and political characteristics of these states, together with their specific historical experience. Leys maintains that the results of corrupt transactions are not necessarily bad, while their elimination will not necessarily yield positive outcomes. The funds rescued from the grasp of the corrupt public servant or politician will not necessarily be spent on good causes, eg education, health facilities for the poor. He is, none the less, well aware of the potential of widespread corruption for undermining the development effort—creating economically stagnant societies in the grip of self-seeking and corrupt elites. The escape from this impasse for Leys seems to depend upon the emergence of a nucleus of 'puritans' drawn from the professional and middle classes who will exert pressure to apply 'disregarded public codes of ethics'. However, Leys goes on to acknowledge that a major problem for new states is the relative absence of such independent middle and professional classes because of economic backwardness.

This paper will argue that despite the torrent of writings on the theme of corruption which have appeared over the past 30 years, mainly during the last five, our treatment of the phenomenon has not moved very far beyond the insights offered by Leys. That is to say, in spite of the implicit recognition in much writing on corruption that the West's historical experience is distinctive, unique and unrepeatable, this experience continues to provide the model of the 'modern' state to which premodern or less developed forms must aspire. This line of thinking is most apparent in the heavy dependence of the development literature on the notion of the patrimonial or neo-patrimonial state. The allegedly fundamental contrast between the neo-patrimonial state, and its converse the developed and implicitly rational–legal state, continues to pervade much of the writing on Third World politics generally and corruption specifically. But does simply labelling such states neo-patrimonial tell us much about them and about why abuse of public authority is apparently at such a high level? Is the contrast with developed states really all that helpful, especially given their distinctive route to modernity, plus the fact that they too are widely held to display not insignificant patrimonial features? In addressing these questions the aim here is to relocate the problem of corruption in less developed states and, by implication, comment critically upon contemporary policies aimed at its containment.

Patrimonialism

Since a great deal has already been written around the theme of patrimonialism, an extended elaboration in this context is not required.[3] Suffice it to say that a patrimonial administration is one in which the public/private boundary, central to the concept of modern administration, is to say the least unstable, and in many cases barely exists at all. The private appropriation of the spoils of office in the form of taxes, customs, gifts, land and the like is normal and not regarded as illegitimate. As Weber pointed out, despite wide variations across time and region all pre-industrial states were basically patrimonial in character. The processes of industrialisation and modernisation are held eventually to have led to the emergence of modern administration with its strict separation of the public from the private, as captured in Weber's ideal-type of rational–legal bureaucracy. However, the development of modern administration is generally accepted to have been contingent upon the existence of certain socioeconomic conditions. Not the least of these was a monetised economy, together with a rising bourgeois class spearheading a reforming civil society.[4] Although such socioeconomic conditions were and, in many respects, still are confined to a minority of developed states, the *discourse* of public administration has been disseminated throughout the world. This means that states which are constrained by a radically different conjuncture must subscribe at least formally to the tenets of neutrality and universalism. To describe the situation in which the public/private distinction is recognised but allegedly seldom observed, the term 'neo-patrimonialism' has been widely employed.[5]

Despite its potentially deleterious consequences for administrative capacity, neo-patrimonialism is none the less seen by some to make a major contribution to political stability. The distribution of the spoils of office plays a significant role in the integration of the centre. That is to say, strategically placed elites and sub-elites are incorporated into the regime by the ruling individual or faction, through the judicious distribution of jobs, contracts, loans, development grants, useful information and other opportunities for self-advancement. This mode of integration is thought to be especially suited to societies that are deeply fissured along communal lines. Ethnic, religious, regional and other 'primordial' big men along with their followings are suborned by a national 'political machine' along rather similar lines to the urban machines which allegedly pulled the US cities together during the early years of the twentieth century.[6]

By the 1980s, however, a number of commentators had come round to taking a more jaundiced view of patrimonial or neo-patrimonial regimes. Just as more perceptive analyses of city machines and other clientelist systems have highlighted their essentially manipulative and repressive character,[7] so also with neo-patrimonialism. Several writers have emphasised the pronounced tendency for the spoils to circulate only within hegemonic groups, with the mass of the population marginalised from this process. This marginalisation may arise from geographical and cultural isolation, as is the case with backward peasantries. More often it is the outcome of deliberate policies of intimidation and repression—Brazil 1964–84, Indonesia 1965–98 for example—often combined, in more developed economies, with a degree of low level co-option (eg of trade union leaders), as well as populist manipulation. In the case of more backward economies, neo-patrimonial regimes often descend into pervasive and unabashed theft of public resources, large-scale institutional paralysis and, in some situations, state collapse.[8]

Overall, there seems to be general agreement that neo-patrimonialism, in the sense of the appropriation of public resources for private ends, is a major problem for Third World states. Whether these ends are directed to rewarding supporters, buying off opponents, or straightforward personal accumulation or rentseeking, the general consequences for policy making, investment, public authority, the poor, democracy and overall development are decidedly negative.

493

ROBIN THEOBALD

Accordingly, the much needed establishment of good governance requires *inter alia* the elimination of patronage and cronyism and the enthronement of merit-based principles in recruitment and promotion in the public service.[9]

Notwithstanding apparently widespread agreement that the neo-patrimonial character of the Third World state is the core of the problem, there is a danger that we are simply describing the symptoms rather than identifying underlying causes. There is after all a certain lack of specificity in the concept in the sense that it has been employed in such a range of empirical contexts—from Brazil to Zaire, from Paraguay to the Philippines—which raises serious questions about its analytical utility.

An obvious example of this uncertainty relates to the long-established nation-states of Latin America, which political scientists have tended to regard as falling under the rubric of corporatism: that is to say, they tend to have regimes under which social and economic groups are compulsorily and separately organised into monopolistic state-run and funded national organisations.[10] Brazil under Vargas and Mexico under Cardenas were precursors, to be followed in the 1960s by Peru (1968–75) and Bolivia (1964–82) and, for some, Chile after Pinochet's coup in 1973.[11]

The relationship between corporatism on the one hand, and neo-patrimonial-ism on the other, has not always been clearly delineated. Brazil, for example, seen by some as unequivocally corporatist,[12] is viewed by others through the lens of patrimonialism.[13] The main difference seems to be that in the more developed states of Latin America neo-patrimonial principles articulate with bureaucratic structures which are to a degree institutionalised along rational–legal lines. Thus in Mexico the end of every *sexenio* sees a complete change of personnel at the upper echelons of the state, while lower levels of the administration operate on more or less meritocratic lines.[14] How this differs from the situation in many developed states, particularly the USA, is not entirely clear.[15] Leaving this question aside for the moment, we note that some writers have seen sub-Saharan Africa as predominantly neo-patrimonial, while Latin America has moved through the stage of what we might term 'raw' patrimonialism—evident during the era of *caudillismo*—to corporatist mode.[16] The corporatist model was eventually refined into Guillermo O'Donnell's conception of bureaucratic autho-rianism. This had the advantage of linking the authoritarian state to unfolding stages in the process of economic development. The bureaucratic–authoritarian stage succeeds its populist predecessor and embodies the need, in the interests of capital accumulation, for the state to contain the social forces unleashed under populism.[17]

Notwithstanding the sophistication of O'Donnell's approach, there lay within this and much of the strong state literature on Latin America a contradiction. Implicit in the concept of bureaucratic authoritarianism is precisely the notion of bureaucratic structures which are capable of implementing the kinds of economic and social policy that are appropriate to a given stage of development. We are in other words talking about stable, efficient and institutionalised formal organ-isations. And yet the literature on the state in Latin America is replete with references to the pervasiveness of patron–clientelism and other forms of person-alism, the essence of which is institutional instability and weak administrative capacity.[18] In the light of this, Hammergren has questioned the applicability of the notion of the corporatist state to Latin America. Though not denying that corporatist policies were introduced into a number of Latin American countries in the 1970s, she maintains that these are best understood in terms of Huntington's notion of the 'praetorian' character of the political contest in these societies. In the absence of strong central institutions and widespread agreement on the rules of the political game, social forces within them are in a state of permanent confrontation and politics takes the form of a zero-sum game. 'Corporatist' structures, thus, represent an attempt precisely to contain these social forces, not least those which express the needs and frustrations of the masses. Latin American political reality, for Hammergren, is composed of persisting low levels of national integration and the existence of large areas and populations outside the control of the national political system. In fact, such is the gap between real and formal control in Latin America as to have inspired speculation over whether there is a peculiarly Latin American attitude towards the law. One of the most obvious examples of this gap is to be found in the extremely limited success achieved by Latin American governments in their attempts to garner revenues. Despite elaborate and sophisticated tax laws and appropriately complex organisations to implement them, the level of popular compliance remains remarkably low.[19]

In the face of such difficulties over the significance and extent of neo-patrimonial relationships, it might be helpful to focus upon the other side of the equation by turning to the case of developed states and considering the decline or rather alleged decline of patronage in that orbit.

Modernisation and the 'decline' of patronage

With regard to the literature on patronage and its so-called decline, it has become conventional to distinguish between two forms: community or peripheral patronage on the one hand and patronage at the centre on the other.[20] Community patronage (Patronage I) refers to the traditional patron–client relationship, usually between a high-status landlord and a low-status peasant, in which scarce resources such as land, loans, intercession with outside agencies are exchanged for labour, deference, information, votes, perhaps armed support. Sometimes referred to as 'lopsided friendship', the traditional patron–client relationship endures over time, often across the generations.[21]

Patronage at the centre (Patronage II) is usually understood to refer to the more familiar exchange of favours for political support. Whether at national or local levels, jobs contracts, contacts, useful information, protection form the law are exchanged by politicians for material and other forms of support—contributions to campaign funds, use of property or vehicles, banks of votes, favourable articles in newspapers and so forth. The two forms of patronage mirror each other, except that Patronage II links tend to be less clearly inegalitarian and less enduring than their counterparts at the periphery. The linkages between the two levels intensify as we move into the modern era of elections and party politics, with the need to mobilise votes, funds, staffing and the like.

Ultimately patronage is held to decline as societies industrialise and modern-

ROBIN THEOBALD

ise. The explanations for this decline, however, vary. So far as Patronage I is concerned a standard explanation is that, in the context of the modern state particularly under welfare capitalism, this form of relationship is no longer needed. In developed societies, that is to say, the affluence and security afforded by advanced capitalism, together with the accompanying recognition of rights of citizenship, render obsolete the need for relationships of personal dependence, ie for lopsided friendship. Thus Lemarchand and Legg observe towards the end of their extensive conceptual discussion of patron–client ties: 'most individuals in an industrial polity do not require personalized political relationships: affluence and opportunity have diminished insecurity'.[22]

In the case of Patronage II, it is usually argued that, since the logic of industrial capitalism and the market demands efficiency and optimality, then principles of rationality and universality must necessarily extend to all areas of social or rather public life. This means that patronage is necessarily superseded by meritocracy in recruitment to, as well as movement within, modern organisations.[23]

But neither explanation is entirely adequate. As for Patronage I being no longer needed, one could observe that, so far as the not insubstantial numbers of unemployed, poor and homeless in developed states are concerned, it manifestly is needed. The key point is rather that such patronage is no longer *on offer*. This is because a necessary consequence of industrialisation and economic expansion is the restructuring of social relationships along mass lines. This means that social exchanges outside immediate family and friends are generally and unavoidably transacted through the structures of formal organisations, eg firms, trade unions, professional associations, interest groups and the like.

Turning once more to Patronage II, on closer examination the much-vaunted meritocratic principle seems to operate in a somewhat attenuated form. This is evident from a wealth of studies flowing from a wide range of developed societies which reveal the continued significance of patronage-type ties, particularly in relation to exchanges within and between elites. Whether we are talking about 'old boy networks' in the UK, alumni of Ivy League universities in the USA, *gadzarts* drawn from the *grandes ecoles* in France, *jinyaku* ('veins in the rock') groups from Tokyo University, or Masonic, Rotary, Buffalo, 'quango' or other such personal links and connections—the flow of resources along exclusive networks continues to play a central role in developed states.[24] How do we explain this? The principal reasons appear to be as follows.

First, the higher we ascend organisational hierarchies, the more unspecific become the required qualifications for entry and performance. Although there will doubtless be essential technical qualifications, these will not suffice to separate the potential 'leader', 'highflier', 'troubleshooter', 'entrepreneur' or 'innovator', from his/her peers. Inevitably subjective measures intrude.

Second, the fact that incumbency of such positions yields highly valued rewards in terms of often exceptional opportunities for self-aggrandisement in the form of six-figure salaries, directorships, knighthoods, flights in private jets and the like, means that demand for them vastly exceeds supply. This further amplifies the need for subjective, non-specific, if not vague, criteria of appointment and, by implication, *exclusion*.

496

Third, members of such elites must routinely take far-reaching decisions which may often affect the lives of thousands if not millions. Such strategic significance renders them potential targets of public scrutiny and criticism, thereby generating a tendency to surround themselves with circles of trusted supporters and protectors.[25]

Last, the fact of the departure from conventional merit principles in associated appointments, together with the scale of the rewards that usually accrue, increases the premium on trustworthiness of those who are 'chosen'. They must be the 'right type', 'one of us', discreet, 'chaps' (invariably *chaps*) who will 'not rock the boat'.

What is particularly interesting about the persistence of this type of patronage in developed states is that it is not generally seen as a problem unless too many of its beneficiaries do indeed 'rock the boat' in the sense of flagrantly undermining the dominant values of universalism and merit. This is primarily because these values are firmly institutionalised within the wide range of formal organisations in which most exchanges are transacted in developed states.

However, this is not to argue that these formal organisations operate entirely or even mainly on the basis of rational–legal principles. In fact the substantial literature on modern organisations, both public and private, indicates unequivocally that they do not; that informal personal exchanges embodied in networks, cliques and factions articulate with and in many cases predominate over formal rules and procedures. In this respect the neo-patrimonial/rational–legal dichotomy significantly underplays the role of informal personal relationships in modern organisations and societies.[26]

But if personalism—one may even talk of patronage or neo-patrimonialism— is normal at all levels of formal structures in developed states, how then do these differ from less developed counterparts? In real life they obviously do differ in that both public and private bureaucracies in DCs are generally better able to deliver goods and services than their counterparts in LDCs. But simply to fall back upon the ideal-type analysis by proposing that this is because the former are located towards the rational–legal end of the continuum, while LDCs are overwhelmingly neo-patrimonial, is merely descriptive and ultimately tautological. Three major differences need to be highlighted.

First, and most significant, the very socioeconomic complexity of DCs as expressed in a plurality of social and economic organisations means that profit or rent seeking are not targeted upon a single sphere, ie the state apparatus, but are diffused across a range of institutional areas. Most significant among the latter is of course a developed business sector which constitutes an obvious focus for (legal or illegal) self-advancement. Hence in DCs the plunder of the state's resources is relatively unusual, while theft in the private sector is not (think, for example, of Robert Maxwell's fleecing of various pension funds, the not entirely reliable Bank of Credit and Commerce International, the Barings debacle, the Savings and Loans scandal and the 1996 $3 billion copper scam—to mention only the better known and more sensational.)[27]

Second, it has to be admitted that merit principles probably intrude into neo-patrimonial links to a greater degree in developed states than in their counterparts in the Third World. In other words such relationships are less likely to be based upon ascriptive principles (ie kinships, clanship, ethnicity) alone. Despite this we need to be wary of overstating the importance of merit mainly for two reasons: it is by now well established in the literature on organisations that there are serious limits to rationality in decision making;[28] and second, no doubt relating to this, a good deal of evidence on top management, in both public and private sectors, emphasises the importance of presentational and political skills.[29]

Third, and despite the conditions outlined under the last point, it is obviously the case that routine public administration in DCs generally operates at an acceptable level of efficiency and is not subject to the levels of abuse that appear to be normal in many LDCs. The standard explanation of why this is the case centres upon the existence of a deeply rooted ethic or culture of public service in Western public administration. This culture is held to be the product of a prolonged period of continuity and stability during which, through specialised training and general socialisation, a professional ethic of service has been disseminated to, and inculcated in, successive waves of public servants.

But culture, whether at the societal or organisational level, does not float freely in the ether but both reflects and reacts upon a given pattern of structural arrangements. The culture of public administration in DCs is not therefore something that has simply been implanted but has evolved reciprocally with administrative structures and, particularly important, the resources that underpin them. Not least among these are material resources, particularly in the form of a stable salary structure with associated pension and other rights. Without wanting to reduce the ethic of public service to the size of a wage packet, one wonders how long it could be sustained were Western public servants to remain unpaid for months on end as is often the case in LDCs.[30] A more immediate question (but one which cannot be explored here), relates to the continued health and viability of this ethic given the imposition upon the administrative systems of most DCs of a business-focused New Public Management.[31]

Conclusion

In addition to the outpourings of academics, the past five years have seen a positive deluge of interest and concern about corruption. Many international organisations, including the World Bank, the International Monetary Fund, the United Nations, the Organisation for Economic Cooperation and Development, the European Union, the G7 group of industrial nations and others, have declaimed upon the urgency of dealing with the problem. What is remarkable about the current clamour is its contrast with the eerie silence which prevailed during most of the previous 30 years. Explanations are not difficult to formulate. Clearly, the ending of the Cold War exposed to criticism the regimes of former allies whose peccadillos had previously been ignored for strategic reasons. The evaporation, furthermore, of the triumphalism that followed the collapse of the Soviet Bloc, the realisation that history had not after all ended, called for a discourse which would explain the increasingly apparent shortcomings of the international capitalist system. Not least among these is the manifest inability to deal with the escalating polarisation between rich and poor. In its cruder forms

SO WHAT REALLY IS THE PROBLEM ABOUT CORRUPTION?

contemporary discourse identifies corruption as the principal cause of poverty, with greedy Third World politicians targeted as the main culprits. At a more sophisticated level, the theory of the neo-patrimonial state is in danger of following the same logic. The point being made here is that the preoccupation with the neo-patrimonial character of the Third World states is achieving little more than describing a salient feature of social organisation in a context of underdevelopment. The specific manifestation of personalistic ties in LDCs is primarily a *symptom* of a conjuncture in which escalating demands for goods and services are targeted, by default, mainly upon a single area: the state. In developed economies by contrast, such demands are diffused via established formal organisations across a range of institutional areas. A brief example will illustrate this point: in 1997 the US-based banana grower, Chiquita, was extremely fortunate in persuading US trade representative, Mickey Kantor, to raise its case against European Union tariffs with the World Trade Organization (WTO). Whereas Chiquita had hitherto been only a modest contributor to Democrat Party funds, the day after Mr Kantor asked the WTO to examine the corporation's complaint, Chiquita transferred more than $500 000 to Party coffers. A key aspect of the transaction was that the route was suitably discreet: not to central party funds, where it would have been recorded openly, but to state-level organisation. The main point is that, although transacted through the structures of formal organisations, this series of exchanges was probably no less personal or covert than the those embodied in what might be regarded as traditional patron–client relationships.[32]

But this is not to argue that, since corruption seems to be a symptom of underdevelopment, the only course open to us is to wait for these societies to develop. Such Olympian detachment would be vacuous as well morally reprehensible. The fundamental point of this article is that our dependence upon a particular conception of a state whose origins lie in the unique historical experience of the West may be clouding the issue of the real problem of underdevelopment and how it might be addressed. Instead of asking whether the Third World state can be de-patrimonialised, we should perhaps be asking whether we should be focusing upon the state in the first place. Without wanting to strike an overly pessimistic note, given the resources that are likely to be available to them in the immediate future, is it feasible that the sprawling panoply of ministries, agencies and bureaux which form the state apparatuses of LDCs can be seriously reformed and reconstructed? More to the point, under the current distribution of power both within states and between them and trans-national coalitions, what are the chances of the massive influx of resources that would be needed for reconstruction ever percolating down to the masses?[33]

Under such circumstances, might it not therefore be more productive to shift the reforming focus and the resources that are likely to follow to another level altogether? Here the *city* would seem to be an obvious candidate. As we enter the next century, cities—and not only cities in the less developed world—are increasingly likely to be the focal points of international movements of capital and the primary beacons of the ebb and flow of economic activity.[34] Cities are also certain to be the eye of the storm of poverty, social conflict and upheaval. According to Wally N'Dow, who was secretary-general of the United Nations

499

ROBIN THEOBALD

Habitat II Conference held in Istanbul in 1996, 'a low grade civil war is being fought every day in the world's urban centres … The problems are staggering. There are now more than 600 million people officially homeless or who are living in life-threatening urban conditions. More than a billion lack sanitation and a further 250 million have no easy access to safe water.'[35] Along the same lines two years later, the United Nations Food and Agriculture Organisation published a report which painted an extremely bleak picture of the prospects for urban dwellers in LDCs. Infrastructure in these burgeoning mega-cities is unable to keep pace with the demand for food. Their citizens are being forced to spend up to 80% of their income on vital food items, while paid employment is increasingly scarce or non-existent. Overall the urban poor now outnumber the rural poor in many countries, a trend that is likely to continue as global urbanisation proceeds apace.[36] Confronted with what appears to be a looming catastrophe, the apparent obsession of international agencies with reforming the *state* along what are assumed to be 'Western' lines may be somewhat misplaced. Perhaps, therefore, we need to be wary, given our preoccupation with the neo-patrimonial character of less developed states, of not acquiescing too far in the policy preferences of these agencies.

Notes

[1] C Leys, 'What is the problem about corruption?', *The Journal of Modern African Studies*, 3(2), 1965, pp 215–224.
[2] R Wraith & E Simpkins, *Corruption in Developing Countries*, London: Allen and Unwin, 1963.
[3] A list of writers in whose analyses the term has occupied a central role would, to say the least, be lengthy. For useful general surveys see M Bratton & N van de Walle, *Democratic Experiments in Africa. Regime Transitions in Comparative Perspective*, Cambridge: Cambridge University Press, 1997; and P D Hutchcroft, 'Oligarchs and cronies in the Philippine state: the politics of patrimonial plunder', *World Politics*, XXXXIII, 1993, pp 414–450.
[4] M Weber, *Economy and Society*, Vol 2, New York: Bedminster Press, 1968, pp 968–1015.
[5] J-F Medard, 'The historical trajectories of the Ivorian and Kenyan states', in J Manor (ed), *Rethinking Third World Politics*, London: Longman, 1991, pp 185–212.
[6] For a typical statement of the alleged functionality of the old city machines, see J C Scott, 'Corruption, machine politics and political change', *American Political Science Review*, 63(4), 1969, pp 1142–1159.
[7] See, for example, J Chubb, 'The social bases of an urban political machine: the Christian Democrat Party in Palermo', in S N Eisenstadt & R Lemarch (eds), *Political Clientelism, Patronage and Development*, London: Sage, 1981, pp 91–124; and R Theobald, 'On the survival of patronage in developed societies', *Archives Européennes de Sociologie*, XXXIII, 1992, pp 183–191.
[8] See, for example, H Crouch, 'Patrimonialism and military rule in Indonesia', *World Politics*, 41(4), 1979, pp 571–587; R Roett, *Brazil: Politics in a Patrimonial Society*, New York: Praeger, 1992; M C Newbury, 'Dead and buried or just underground? The privatisation of the state in Zaire', *Canadian Journal of African Studies*, 18(1), 1984, pp 112–114; and W Zartman (ed), *Collapsed States: the disintegration and restoration of legitimate authority*, London: Lynne Rienner, 1995.
[9] The problem of nepotism in the public sectors of less developed states and the necessity of reducing it figures prominently in current policies of reform. See especially World Bank, *World Development Report 1997. The State in a Changing World*, Oxford: Oxford University Press, 1997; and R Klitgaard, 'Cleaning up and invigorating the civil service', *Public Administration and Development*, 17, 1997, pp 487–509.
[10] P Schmitter, 'Still the century of corporatism', *Review of Politics*, 36, 1974, pp 85–121.
[11] For critical views of the applicability of 'corporatism' to Latin America, see L A Hammergren, 'Corporatism in Latin American politics: a re-examination of the "unique" tradition', *Comparative Politics*, 9, 1977, pp 443–461; and H Schamis, 'Reconceptualising Latin American authoritarianism in the 1970s: from bureaucratic authoritarianism to neoconservatism', *Comparative Politics*, 23(2), 1991, pp 201–220.
[12] See, for example, K P Erickson, 'Corporatism and labour in development', in H J Rosenbaum & W G Tyler

SO WHAT REALLY IS THE PROBLEM ABOUT CORRUPTION?

(eds), *Contemporary Brazil: issues in economic and political development*, New York: Praeger, 1972; and P Schmitter, 'The 'Portugalisation' of Brazil?' in A Steppan (ed), *Authoritarian Brazil*, New Haven, CT: Yale University Press, 1973.

[13] Roett, *Brazil.*

[14] See M Grindle, *Bureaucrats, Politicians and Peasants in Mexico*, Berkeley, CA: University of California Press, 1977.

[15] See, for example, M-F Toinet & I Glenn, 'Clientelism and corruption in the 'open' society: the case of the United States', in C Clapham (ed), *Private Patronage and Public Power*, London: Frances Pinter, 1982, pp 193–213. See also P C Light, 'Federal ethics controls: the role of inspectors general', in H G Frederickson (ed), *Ethics and Public Administration*, London: M E Sharpe, 1993, pp 100–120. Light notes that 'with political appointees now moving … five steps down into the bureaucratic hierarchy – and with no prospect that Congress or the president will act to stem the tide, the IG [Inspectors General] concept may be the last best hope for a durable counterweight to the short-term thinking that often prevails among political appointees' (p 118).

[16] See especially T M Callaghy, 'Politics and vision in Africa: the interplay of domination, equality and liberty', in P Chabal (ed), *Political Domination in Africa: Reflections on the Limits of Power*, London: Cambridge University Press, 1986, pp 30–51.

[17] G O'Donnell, *Modernization and Bureaucratic–Authoritarianism: Studies in South American Politics*, Berkeley, CA: University of California Press, 1973.

[18] See, for example, A Hennessy, 'Fascism and populism in Latin America', in W Laqueur (ed), *Fascism: a Reader's Guide*, London: Penguin, 1976, pp 248–299.

[19] In addition to Hammergren, 'Corporatism in Latin American Politics', see especially W Little, 'Political corruption in Latin America', *Corruption and Reform*, 7, 1992, pp 41–66: 'The problem of underfunding of key state agencies is acute throughout Latin America and is clearly evident in the fiscal sphere. The capacity to raise tax lies at the core of the state's power … and is clearly rudimentary in much of Latin America. Argentina is a case in point. There the revenue departments are understaffed, badly-paid and demoralized. They have no coherent data bases, no modern technology, conduct few audits, detect little evasion, and fail to successfully prosecute the few they do detect.' (p 58) See also Callaghy's comments on Latin America, 'Politics and vision in Africa', p 40, 'Nowhere are constitutions more elaborate and less observed'.

[20] See especially J D Powell, 'Peasant society and clientelist politics', *American Political Science Review*, LXIV, 1970, pp 411–425; and A Weingrod, 'Patrons, patronage and political parties', *Comparative Studies in Society and History*, VII, 1968, pp 377–400.

[21] J Pitt-Rivers, *People of the Sierra*, London: Weidenfeld and Nicolson, 1954.

[22] R Lemarchand & K Legg, 'Political clientelism and development: a preliminary analysis', *Comparative Politics*, IV, 1972, pp 149–179. See also J Boissevain, 'When the saints go marching out. Reflections on the decline of patronage in Malta', in E Gellner & J Waterbury (eds), *Patrons and Clients in Mediterranean Societies*, London: Duckworth, 1977, pp 329–342.

[23] Probably the best-known statement of this line of argument is in C Kerr *et al*, *Industrialism and Industrial Man*, London: Penguin, 1962.

[24] For an excellent recent survey which highlights the salience of patronage and cronyism in developed states, see H Perkin, *The Third Revolution: Professional Elites in the Modern World*, London: Routledge, 1996. For copious examples of cronyism in US politics, see H Smith, *The Power Game. How Washington Works*, New York: Random House, 1988: 'It [ie one-to-one lobbying] is Bob Strauss's note to Treasury Secretary Jim Baker to help a friend seek appointment to the World Bank. It is Howard Baker's contact with an old Senate colleague to see that some client gets a break on the "transition rules" of a tax bill. It is Bob Gray's phone call to the White House to ask the president to address some convention or wangle an invitation to a state dinner for an industrial bigshot. It is breakfast with a committee staff director who is drafting intricate legislation. It is little favours such as tickets to a Washington Redskins football game or helping Ed Meese's wife get a job. It is knowing which buttons to push.' (p 232)

[25] See, for example, L I Rudolph & S H Rudolph, 'Authority and power in bureaucratic and patrimonial administration: a revisionist interpretation of Weber on bureaucracy', *World Politics*, XXI(2), 1979, pp 195–227. For the world of top managers, see also R Jackall, *Moral Mazes. The World of Corporate Managers*, Oxford: Oxford University Press, 1988.

[26] See especially M Eve, 'Comparing Italy: the case of corruption' in D Forgacs & R Lumley (eds), *Italian Cultural Studies: an Introduction*, Oxford: Oxford University Press, 1996, pp 34–51. Eve convincingly demonstrates that the widely accepted dichotomy between allegedly particularistic and patronage-ridden Italian society on the one hand, and so-called universalistic England on the other, is significantly overdrawn. See also the substantial body of literature in the general area of the sociology of organisations both public and private, eg M Dalton, *Men Who Manage*, New York: John Wiley, 1959; A Downs, *Inside Bureaucracy*, Boston, MA: Little, Brown, 1967; and M I Reed, *The Sociology of Organizations*, London: Harvester Wheatsheaf, 1992. Whereas Bratton & van de Walle, *Democratic Experiments in Africa*, p 62, locate

ROBIN THEOBALD

personal relations on the 'margins' of bureaucratic systems, these latter writers (as well as numerous others) see them as the core of modern formal organisations.

[27] See especially M Punch, *Dirty Business*, London: Sage, 1996.

[28] On the limitations on decision making in organisations, see especially J March & H Simon, *Organizations*, Oxford: Blackwell, 1993; and C E Lindblom, 'The science of "muddling through" ', *Public Administration Review*, 39, 1979, pp 517–526. On the alleged rationality of 'modern' organisations, one might have anticipated this to be most pronounced in the case of international banks, with their highly developed accounting systems. Yet, when we reflect upon the lending policies of several world leaders in the field during recent years, it is hard to disagree with J K Galbraith's conclusion that such institutions seem to have been driven primarily by a combination of 'greed and sophisticated stupidity'. On the significance of 'cronyism' in high-level financial transactions in the West, see J Plender, 'Western Crony Capitalism', *Financial Times*, 3 October 1998; and B Cumings, 'The Korean crisis and the end of late development', *New Left Review*, 231, 1998, pp 43–72, esp p 58.

[29] In addition to Jackall, *Moral Mazes*, see A M Pettigrew, *The Awakening Giant: Change and Continuity at ICI*, Oxford: Blackwell, 1985; and M I Reed, *The Sociology of Management*, London: Harvester–Wheatsheaf, 1989.

[30] Accordingly, in contemporary literature on administrative reform there is a heavy emphasis upon an adequate and stable salary structure. See, for example, World Bank, *World Development Report 1997*; and Klitgaard, 'Cleaning up and invigrating the civil service'. See also F Stapenhurst & P Langseth, 'The role of the public administration in fighting corruption', *International Journal of Public Sector Management*, 10 (5), 1997, pp 311–330.

[31] See especially B G Peters, *The Politics of Bureaucracy*, London: Longman, 1995; and J B Christoph, 'The remaking of British administrative culture', *Administration and Society*, 24(2), 1992, pp 163–181.

[32] 'Rotten Bananas', *Guardian Weekly*, 5 October 1997.

[33] R W Cox has observed that, 'as the proportion of state revenue going into debt service rises, governments have become more effectively accountable to external bond markets than to their own publics'. Cox, 'Global restructuring: making sense of the changing international political economy', in R Stubbs & G R D Underhill (eds), *Political Economy and the Changing Global Order*, London: Macmillan, 1994, pp 45–59. See also J Nef, who maintains that for much of Latin America, 'the state has become the receiver and debt collector of a bankrupt economy on behalf of translational creditors'. Nef, ' "Normalization": popular struggles and the receiver state', in J Knippers Black (ed), *Latin America, its Problems and its Promise: a Multidisciplinary Introduction*, Boulder, CO: Westview Press, 1991. Nef is quoted by M T Berger, 'The end of the "Third World"?', *Third World Quarterly*, 15(2), 1994, p 268.

[34] 'World cities are the keyboard of the global economy.' Cox, 'Global restructuring', p 47.

[35] 'Global warning: cities harm people', *Guardian Weekly*, 16 June 1996.

[36] 'Rural poor are overtaken by urban underclass', *Guardian Weekly*, 20 December 1998.

502

[26]

The Journal of Modern African Studies, 37, 1 (1999), pp. 25–52
Printed in the United Kingdom © 1999 Cambridge University Press

A moral economy of corruption in Africa?

J. P. Olivier de Sardan*

ABSTRACT

As far as corruption in Africa is both conspicuous and generalised, it has to be studied from the viewpoint of the participants. This article starts with six general theses on corruption in Africa, which place it within a broader 'corruption complex', and emphasise its routine nature, the stigmatisation of corruption despite the absence of effective sanctions, its apparent irreversibility, the absence of correlation with regime types and its legitimacy to its perpetrators. Corruption is then shown to be socially embedded in 'logics' of negotiation, gift-giving, solidarity, predatory authority and redistributive accumulation. Any anti-corruption policy must face up to these realities.

INTRODUCTION

The rampant corruption affecting the totality of African countries has scarcely become a bona fide object in the sociological or anthropological study of Africa, in which corruption is barely mentioned except in the course of studies dealing with other themes, usually African political systems.[1] The types of corruption in West Africa, characterised by their conspicuousness and their generality, and which obviously bear some resemblance to the Asiatic and Latino-American types, deserve particular attention because of the specific nature of contemporary African states, and the depth of the crisis which affects them.[2] Besides, international organisations, investors and public opinion are often reminded of the scope of this problem, which is currently considered to be fundamental to 'good governance'. Unfortunately, beyond declarations of principle, pathetic or exasperated acknowledgements and moralistic condemnations, the social mechanisms of corruption are scarcely explored, nor are its processes of legitimation *seen from the actors' point of view*. This is why this article uses the term: *moral economy*, which may appear surprising when attached to a term as unanimously stigmatised as amoral or immoral. The intention here is to insist on as subtle as possible a restitution of the value systems and cultural codes,

* Professor at the Ecole des Hautes Etudes en Sciences Sociales (EHESS–CNRS), Marseille. A first and curtailed version of this paper has been published in French in *Politique Africaine* 63: 97–116, 1996. My thanks are due to Antoinette Tidjani Alou for the English translation.

26   J. P. OLIVIER DE SARDAN

which permit a justification of corruption by those who practice it (and who do not necessarily consider it to be such – quite the contrary), and to anchor corruption in ordinary everyday practice.

However, the use of the expression 'moral economy', which makes an obvious reference to a certain intellectual tradition (Thompson 1971; Scott 1976), does not imply any intention to adopt a 'culturalist' point of view. Although reference is made to the *cultural embeddedness* of corruption, this is not done in the name of any monolithic or determinist theory of culture. Our intention is rather to pinpoint certain *social norms* widely represented in modern Africa, which 'communicate' with or influence the practices of corruption. It is, in a manner of speaking, a question of 'slants' which leave a certain room for manoeuvre to the actors who operate within or around certain 'logics', often combining them, sometimes dissociating or refuting them. These logics seem to have a 'family resemblance', a certain relation of affinity with 'corruption'-type practices, but are not in themselves corruption. Their role is simply to provide a better understanding of the reasons why corruption finds, in contemporary Africa, such a favourable ground for its extension and generalisation, in short for its banalisation.[3]

Needless to say, this moral economy is 'post-colonial' (see Mbembe 1992) and fundamentally syncretic. It in no way reflects on 'traditional' or pre-colonial culture, even though ancient cultural elements, transformed and recombined, are undeniably amalgamated with numerous elements inherited from the colonial period, as well as others produced during the independence era. The process of state-apparatus building during the twentieth century, a process that is far from being achieved (see Olivier de Sardan and Bierschenk 1998), is obviously fundamental not only for the production of corruption itself, but also for the production of a cultural embeddedness of corruption.

Before entering into these diverse logics in which corruption appears to be embedded, some extended preliminary remarks will be made in the guise of six general theses on corruption in Africa.

SIX THESES ON CORRUPTION IN AFRICA

Thesis 1: The moral economy of corruption in Africa does not merely concern corruption in the strict sense of the word, but rather the 'corruption complex' in a wider sense, which covers a number of illicit practices, technically distinct from corruption, all of which none the less have in common with corruption their association with state, parastatal or bureaucratic functions, and also contradict the official ethics of 'public property' or 'public service', and likewise offer the possibility of illegal enrichment, and the use and abuse to this end of positions of authority.

It is necessary, of course, to make an analytical distinction between the various components of this vast complex of corruption, so as to avoid confusion between the bribe given to a civil servant in return for some favour, the abusive use of public funds to a personal end, or simple dipping into the public purse. This is why jurists make careful distinctions between these various forms, rightly so since they correspond to what one may call different 'techniques'. From the legal point of view, corruption (in the strict sense of the word) is for example neither embezzlement nor abuse of public property. Sociologists and political scientists, on the other hand, have attempted to reveal what these various 'techniques', generally resorted to by the same individuals in pursuit of identical objectives, have in common, thus enlarging the notion of 'corruption'. This is the case of Nye's now classical definition (1967: 419): 'behaviour which deviates from the formal duties of a public role because of private-regarding (personal, close family, private clique) pecuniary or status gains; or violates rules against the exercise of certain types of private-regarding influence'.[4] This definition has in turn been criticised as being too narrow and excessively concerned with the illegality of such practices, defined from a modern, Western point of view (these practices can be perfectly legal in other historical and social contexts, such as modern Saudi Arabia). Nevertheless, the illicit character of these diverse practices, from a juridical point of view, must apparently remain an unavoidable element of this definition, seeing that the law of African countries is in this respect directly copied from current French and English law. In reality the core of the sociological problem of corruption is to be situated in the distance between juridical condemnation of certain practices and their frequency, their banalisation or indeed their cultural legitimacy.

From this perspective, the notion of corruption may be broadened into what may be termed a 'corruption complex', in other words beyond corruption in the strict sense of the word, to include nepotism, abuse of power, embezzlement and various forms of misappropriation, influence-peddling, prevarication, insider trading and abuse of the public purse, in order to consider what these various practices have in common, what affinities link them together, and to what extent they enter into the same fabric of customary social norms and attitudes. Besides, they are often considered by the populations as belonging to the same behavioural category: the term 'bouffer' is thus of current use in French-speaking Africa in reference to all illegal modes of enrichment through positions of authority (cf. the equivalent 'to chop' in pidgin English). Numerous other variations exist on the basis of this common metaphor. In songhay-zarma, a venal civil servant is said to have 'his mouth wide open' (*a miiyo ga hay*), while the expression 'to grease the paw' becomes 'to grease the mouth', as after a good meal (*miiyo fiisendi*).[5] Stuffing ('bouffer') corresponds emically to the whole range of practices falling within the corruption complex. A customs officer 'stuffs' and so does a minister. The way in which each manages to 'sort himself out' is of little importance in this context: bribes or direct misappropriation in one case, private use of special funds or influence-peddling in another.[6]

Thus all references to 'corruption' in this study, except where otherwise specified, cover the whole 'corruption complex', including similar practices technically different from those already mentioned above.

Thesis 2: Corruption (that is to say the 'corruption complex') has become, in almost all African countries, a common and routine element of the functioning of the administrative and para-administrative apparatus, from top to bottom. This being the case, corruption is neither marginal nor sectoralised or repressed, but is generalised and banalised.

For clear analysis it appears necessary to make a distinction between the various spaces in which corruption comes into play, the different types of social actor and the financial sums involved. Big-time corruption, the type practised at the summit of the state (presidents, ministers, directors of important offices, directors of public or parastatal enterprises), involving millions or even billions of CFA francs, has nothing in common, in terms of scale, social space and type of protagonist, with the 'petty corruption' of policemen, clerks, nurses or customs officers. The latter is extremely familiar to ordinary mortals, who come into contact with it, exploit it or become its victims, on an everyday basis. Everyone in Africa has routine experience in dealing with corruption (and the like), this being a part of the social landscape. It has even become a part of popular know-how, at the base of good usage of administrative services, and is indispensable for survival in the post-colonial milieu. However, this bottom rung corruption is doubtless of secondary economic importance compared to corruption at the top. The latter constitutes the ground for the type of analysis which associates corruption with neo-patrimonialism – the draining off of public resources by a 'state elite' or a 'political aristocracy' (see Harsch 1993). Although its results are quite visible (the vertiginous increase in

A MORAL ECONOMY OF CORRUPTION   29

the wealth of high civil servants and officers of state), by contrast with 'petty corruption' it possesses hidden mechanisms, being practised between high officials according to procedures that are impervious to the non-initiated. For all that, it is none the less notorious, as indicated by recurrent rumours on this topic in the newspapers as well as in private conversations, in town and country. The difference in nature and scale between petty corruption and major corruption should not however prevent us from considering them at the same time as being two poles of a continuum, nor from trying to discover the possible existence of common factors that favour or legitimise both.

Thesis 3: The stigmatisation of corruption, as well as recriminations against it, are a central element of all discourses, public or private, at all levels of society, and have punctuated all the political phases since independence. Corruption is therefore as frequently denounced in words as it is practised in fact. But the verbal stigmatisation of corruption rarely leads to legal proceedings or sanctions. If there is officially a 'public domain', there is almost no 'practical ethic of the public service'.

The transition from the one-party state to military regimes at the end of the sixties and seventies was made in the name of the fight against corruption, widely mobilised as a means of legitimising military coups.[7] The passage from military to democratic regimes at the end of the eighties was also made in the name of the fight against corruption, which was a central theme of the national conferences. Finally, at the present time, disappointment with democratic regimes, which has sometimes opened the way to the men and means of the past, thrives on generalised accusations of corruption brought against democratically elected politicians.

At the everyday level, there is scarcely a conversation without hostile or disgusted references to corruption, either the petty type of which one claims to have been a victim, or the upper crust type about which one has rumours to spread. This widespread stigmatisation of corruption, public as well as private, must be taken seriously, and not just brushed off as mere superficial rhetoric. The complex of corruption is almost unanimously experienced as an evil, or even as a calamity. Many current problems of African societies are attributed to it, by just about everyone, in a way that is not evidently insincere (see Bayart 1992: 70).

This stigmatisation is not limited to the educated or to intellectuals, whom one may suppose to have appropriated Western norms of public interest, but also exists in the popular, non-educated milieu, among those who are fed up with being swindled by politicians and bureaucrats, or disgusted at rumours of illegal enrichment by the elite.

It is true that such stigmatisation is often fatalistic, and just as true that it has nothing to say about effective personal practice: it is none the less real and widespread.

The contrast between this generalised discourse on the illegality of corruption, and the almost overwhelming impunity enjoyed by those given over to these practices, is particularly striking. There is rarely any evidence of trials of the guilty, or of consistent and effective legal or political campaigns against the corruption complex.[8] The flagrant lack of prosecution is evident at all levels, and applies as much to 'big-time corruption' as to 'petty corruption'. First of all, let us look at the latter level, by taking into account a 'public space', which is not in itself a part of the state, but which integrates the category which has above been termed 'parastatal', in the broad sense of the word. Take, for instance, community funds at the village level. Generally instituted under direct or indirect pressure from development institutions, or in the hope of obtaining help from them, and concerning different areas (cooperatives, community cereal stores, peasant groups, village pharmacies, small land-holdings, etc.) these community funds give rise at one moment or another to accusations of misappropriation: for example, such and such an overseer, treasurer or president has 'gobbled up' the money from the cashbox. Obviously, without police investigation (which never occurs, as there is never any complaint), there is no proof that these accusations are justified. We are in a realm of rumours and suspicion (see Blundo 1996). However, field research often proves the embezzlement to be real. But the culprit is rarely prosecuted. In general, he is simply relieved of his functions. There is impunity. This is not because of lack of interest or absence of moral condemnation, quite the contrary. Although the affair is concealed from strangers (especially if they happen to be potential donors), it is a source of anger, rancour and distrust at the local level. However, in a 'face to face' society, the price of open conflicts is too high. It is unthinkable to denounce to the police a relative, a neighbour, the relative of a friend, that is, someone with whom one has a personal tie, even a weak one: social disapproval would be too heavy.

The impunity enjoyed by important individuals is clearly on another scale, and belongs to another order. Most, if not all, have compromised themselves and are best advised not to denounce their own personal practices when encountered elsewhere. In the eventuality of an embezzlement hunt in high places, the majority of African politicians would stand to face trial.[9] But is the network of solidarity within this small techno-political and political world so far removed from village solidarity? Both social universes are torn apart by antagonisms, jealousy and quarrels. Both, however, protect themselves from external interference and hinder justice. Neither has internalised any shared conception of public domain in its daily practices.

The scarcity of an 'ethic of the public service' within African civil services (not in words, but in practice) has often been pointed out. The youthfulness of these states and of their apparatus, as well as the traumatising experience of colonialism, are to some degree responsible. The lack of enthusiasm manifested by the political elites of all types, which have succeeded each other since independence, for the promotion of such an ethic, illustrated by their own example, bears a part – a great part – of the responsibility. Another factor, neither of greater nor lesser importance, which comes under this moral economy shared by African societies, is the general lack of a tradition of the 'public domain'.

Once again let us take a look at village space. In numerous regions of Africa, despite appearances, there is no village property, or any equivalent of the former 'communal holdings' of rural European societies. If such holdings do have 'proprietors' or 'masters', who act in the interests of a 'group', these 'groups' are usually private ones, so to speak, claiming their rights against other groups of the same village, by asserting their own supremacy: the lineage of the descendants of the first settlers, or the founders of the well, or the first conquerors, or the last conquerors, or the first chiefs of the colonial administration, or the last chiefs of the independence administration, and so forth. Village infrastructures are not usually 'communal' or public, even if their usage happens to be public (and though there are strong moral constraints governing their accessibility). They either depend on the representative of an eminent local group, a more or less customary authority, or belong to the state, that is to the outside world, and therefore to nobody. The difficulty that NGOs and Northern aid agencies have in the execution of their community programmes bears witness to this frequent absence of public property on the village level Most African villages are conglomerates of specific sub-communities (families, peer groups, ritual societies, etc.), often existing in a climate of rivalry and antagonism, with no culture of 'general interest', partly because the village chiefs supposed to promote or represent this general interest were put in place by colonialism or were colonial agents.

The extrapolation of this state of 'non-communalism' from the village scale to that of the state is doubtless excessive, but there is something in it. The barriers which in Europe, since the nineteenth century, have generally quelled (without, of course, completely

32 J. P. OLIVIER DE SARDAN

abolishing) the private appropriation of the state, the excessive personal or factional use of authority, the transformation of a public function into a private affair, play but a minor role in Africa. These states, created from scratch by a foreign occupier, excluded 'indigenous' peoples from their management, and even more so from the co-ownership of the country. Independence witnessed the hasty construction of a new bureaucracy in the place of the colonisers, concerned above all with the exercise of their privileges and the consolidation of their status in as short a time as possible.

Thesis 4: Corruption is a cumulative and expansionist process, which is hardly reversible and mostly spreads from the top down. The factors favouring its diffusion cannot be reversed so as to produce its regression.

The more corruption develops, the more it becomes engrained in social habits (the more deeply it becomes inscribed in the 'moral economy') and the less possible it becomes to retreat. Though Africa provides numerous examples of countries showing a rapid development and spread of corruption, it provides none of the reverse. In a certain sense, the expansion of corruption produces a kind of 'corruption culture' with a tendency to permanence. Many known structural and contextual factors favour the spread of corruption. Three sets of factors, though by no means the only ones, are among the foremost and most prevalent.[10]

First, the crisis of the African state (the massive employment of unproductive civil servants, followed by the bankruptcy of the employer-state, the irresponsibility and cupidity of the ruling elite) have all contributed to the exposure in broad daylight of corruption in high places, and the incapacity of the state to control 'petty corruption'.

Second, the 'under-payment' of civil servants, whether in comparison to their northern counterparts (with whom, owing to 'globalisation', they increasingly share the same training and aspirations to a similar style of life), or in the light of the economic crisis (indebtedness, devaluation and structural adjustment), has obliged them to look elsewhere for the resources which are no longer provided by their salaries.

Third, development aid has played a somewhat similar role to that of the incomes of the drug and diamond economy, by inducing an inflow of assistantship and clientelism favourable to corruption. The 'project system' and the multiplication of NGOs, which have attempted to correct this bias by a greater control of the use of these resources and by partly short-circuiting the state, have amounted to the creation of parastatal enclaves, which secrete in turn their own particular form of corruption. The enormous gap between the salaries paid by development projects and those paid by the state also incites government civil servants to seek complementary resources by illegal means.

But even in the (improbable) event of the suppression of these three sets of factors, it is not clear how a regression of corruption could thereby be produced; 'not enough state' produces no less corruption than 'too much state'; nor do the improvement of economic conditions or a reduction in development aid seem likely to produce a reduction in corruption.

As for anti-corruption measures, these contribute to the generalisation of corruption, in accordance with what one may call the 'driving licence formula'. In almost all African countries, a driving licence can be bought from the inspector, during the test. Attempts have been made, from time to time, to take firm measures in order to put an end to these practices: in Niger a policeman is in attendance during the test. The obvious result is that one has to bribe the policeman as well as the examiner.

But in this process of expansion which looks like a one-way trip, responsibility is not equally shared on all sides. 'Big-time' corruption, long since established at the summit of the state, and the consequent incapacity of politicians to carry out any kind of credible campaign in favour of the public welfare or the public service, has certainly been a decisive factor in the extension and generalisation of corruption. After all, the example is given in high places. However, beyond a certain limit, it would seem that the effect of acquired habits and the normalisation of commonplace practices renders the situation more or less irreversible.

Thesis 5: There is no obvious correlation between the extent of corruption, on the one hand, and the types of political regime, their degree of despotism and their economic effectiveness on the other.

It would certainly be nice to think that with the transition from a dictatorial to a democratic regime, a country would experience a recession in corruption; or that states which respect human rights would be less corrupt than those which do not; or that a country whose economic machinery is more or less functional would experience a lower rate of corruption than one in the midst of crisis. Unfortunately, none of these propositions have any demonstrable empirical foundation, seeing that examples to the contrary exist in each case. No conclusive data (in a domain in which one disposes of little more than impressions) can be cited. Whether states have pro-Western one-party regimes, socialist or Marxist–Leninist one-party regimes, military regimes, more or less face value democratic regimes, or democratic regimes which play the game, one can distinguish none that has been more or less preserved, due to its 'nature', from either big-time or small-scale corruption.

Some African personal dictatorships have been less corrupt than democracies, and vice versa. As for economic efficiency, the hypothesis has been sustained that corruption is not an impediment to business, but, on the contrary, allows for economic transactions despite the odds, and functions like the grease necessary for turning the wheels of a notoriously inefficient bureaucracy (see Nye 1967; Bayart 1992). One might as well say that corruption is a result of the incompetence of the state apparatus (or even a palliative for this), as well as its cause and agent of reproduction. It is true that each type of regime develops its own particular form of corruption: electoral corruption is linked to democracy, in the same way that the black market is linked to bureaucratic forms of exchange control. But beyond these specific forms, the extension, banalisation and generalisation of corruption seem to accommodate themselves to just about any kind of regime.[11] One might consider that the modes of governance, or the policies involved, *within a given regime*, have some effect on the forms assumed by corrupt practices, but that is another matter.

Thesis 6: The practices that come under the complex of corruption, while being legally culpable and widely reproved, are none the less considered by their perpetrators as being legitimate, and often as not being corruption at all. In other words, the real borderline between what is corruption and what is not fluctuates, and depends on the context and on the position of the actors involved.

In one sense, 'corruption is someone else'. Only the practices to which one falls victim or from which one is excluded are denounced as being corrupt. Those in which one plays a role oneself never give rise to condemnation. Let us take the example of the 'corrupter/corruptee' pairing. It is obvious that it takes a corruptor to produce a corruptee. The former is as guilty in the eyes of the law as the latter. We are all actors in corruption, for anyone who lives in Africa spends some time perpetrating corruption, to various degrees, according to the position one occupies: one bribes a policeman to avoid a fine, a customs officer to avoid overtaxing, a telephone service agent to finally come by a line, a *directeur de cabinet* to obtain an authorisation, a minister to get hold of a market, etc. Whoever practices corruption auto-legitimates his own behaviour, by presenting himself, for example, as the victim of a system in which he is bound to this kind of practice to avoid wasting time and/or an insupportable amount of money, being penalised or condemned to inactivity. And at any rate, doesn't everyone do it? Nor is this completely false.

It is clear that the borderline between a legal and an illegal commission (a 'bribe') tends to be appreciated in a different light, according to whether one is oneself a beneficiary or not. There is a continuum rather than a gulf between bribing someone and thanking someone for services rendered. Between obtaining a favour from a friend in the civil service, which favour will be 'returned' later on, and slipping a bank note in return for the same favour to a civil servant whom one does not know, there is only a difference of form, be it monetary or not, in the exchange. A minister who uses public agents and public material to build his villa presents a scandal only to those who are poorly lodged or who not stand to benefit from these 'facilities', but is merely gaining a fringe benefit similar to the use of an office car, in the eyes of the beneficiary, who considers that the services rendered to his country are far from being recompensed at their proper worth. In other words, the briber, embezzler or corrupter often has 'good reasons' for his actions and carries them out with a clear conscience.[12] Their attitude is not illegitimate as far as they are concerned, but is only perceived as such by those on the outside, or by participants who might stand to lose in the transaction, or by those who are placed at a disadvantage. At this point, one could easily fall into a mere relativism, thus legitimising any act of delinquency.

This relativism can be looked at from two sociological perspectives:

First, a description of the universe of legitimation peculiar to a given sub-culture in a given space-time: this will include, for example, an identification of the way in which a 'delinquent' sub-culture – corrupted civil servants, or elsewhere gangs of young burglars, drug dealers, mafiosi, computer pirates – produce specific forms of self-justification (see Whyte 1955, or Becker 1963, on gangs in the USA).

Second, an analysis over time of the fluctuations in official as well as in practical norms.[13] That is, how formerly legal practices now fall under the rigours of the law (such as the sale of public offices in eighteenth-century Europe); how formerly tolerated actions are currently 'repressed' (such as the prosecution of enterprise managers in modern France for abuse of public property); or how the clandestine

36   J. P. OLIVIER DE SARDAN

practices of yesterday are now carried out in the light of day (such as
bribing a traffic policeman in Niger).

But I would like to propose yet another perspective, which will
depart for a while from the ambiguous 'stigmatisation/self-justifi-
cation' dichotomy. It consists in pinpointing a number of current social
practices which, in themselves, have nothing to do with corruption, but
none the less provide a favourable ground for its generalisation and
banalisation. It will then be possible to reintegrate the practices of
corruption, defined *a priori* in a negative light, in terms of illegality, into
the larger fabric of everyday practices, expressing positive logics from
the perspective of habitual local social norms.

THE CULTURAL EMBEDDEDNESS OF THE CORRUPTION COMPLEX

Six logics, profoundly engrained in current social life, and underlying
a number of common behavioural traits, seem to influence the complex
of corruption. Others surely exist. We will subsequently consider the
existence of two 'facilitators', which cut across these logics and
accelerate their effects.

The logics of negotiation

Corruption has, of course, long since been analysed as a transaction,
and, as such, the cost of the transaction is obviously a subject of
'bargaining', that is a commodified form of negotiation regulating
almost all forms of current exchange in Africa. But we would like to go
beyond this particular aspect of the matter. Bargaining is not only
pertinent to the pricing of commercial transactions. It enters into the
larger configuration of everyday negotiations, commodified or not,
which does not only concern a simple matter of negotiation within the
limits of a set of stable rules, accepted on all sides, but is extended to a
negotiation of the rules themselves.[14]

Marriage provides a significant example, especially in the urban,
lower-middle-class or aristocratic milieus: not only is there constant
negotiation on the expenditure that the prospective husband has to face
(as well as the sum that must be given in return), but there is also
permanent negotiation between both families and within each, on the
very nature of the dues to be taken into account. There is no consensus
on many of the rules of this 'game', which are selected, arranged,
modified and reinvented along the way.[15]

A MORAL ECONOMY OF CORRUPTION 37

The history of African countries obviously provides for an under-standing of the current instability of these norms. This is evident in the juridical domain, where there is a superimposition of various types of law, inherited over several eras: pre-colonial (common law, Muslim law, for example), colonial ('customary law', 'indigenous law', French law), and post-independence (national law, constantly modified). None of these legal forms, however, is completely 'abolished' in practice, and all can be called into service according to need. The same holds true in the political domain, successive forms of political power having been piled one upon the other, and reorganised in relation to one another, without there being any question of substitution (coexistence of politico-religious authorities of pre-colonial origin with administrative chiefdoms, regional administrators of colonial origin, mayors and representatives of political parties and other mass structures of post-colonial origin, and so forth).

The practice of corruption benefits from this logic of negotiation and bargaining. Not only is corruption in the strict sense of the word an object of bargaining, thus affecting the form of normal, customary commercial transactions; it also takes the shape of a simultaneous negotiation on rules, their pertinence and modes of interpretation. Petty corruption, which we all recognise for having practised it, always has a necessary rhetorical dimension and often occurs in the form of verbal sparring (one cannot just give a 1,000 CFA note without saying a word: there has to be some kind of verbal exchange concerning the traffic law that has more or less been violated). In a sense, this negotiation is indispensable, if the 'illegal' transaction is to become banal, exempt from reprobation, if it is to become a part of everyday negotiations. In more general terms, vagueness concerning the laws governing the coexistence of various normative systems obviously favours the diffusion of corrupt practices, by widening the margin of negotiation.[16]

The term 'brokerage' (Bailey 1969; Boissevain 1974), in a sociological sense, designates social actors situated at the interface of two sociocultural universes, and endowed with the capacity to establish links among themselves, be they symbolic or economical, material or political. Contemporary Africa is a privileged site for this function, particularly so in the sphere of development. It suffices to mention local development brokers, who drain off development projects towards their village, their region or neighbourhood, and act as intermediaries between donors and northern NGOs, on one hand, and the populations that they coordinate or organise, in order to meet the expectations of the former, on the other, thus allowing for the redistribution of the 'development income', without passing through the crisis-stricken state structures (Blundo 1995; Olivier de Sardan & Bierschenk 1993). The cultural logics of brokerage thus operate by means of an historical syncretism between pre-colonial practices (cf. the traditional role of mediators in family or political negotiations), the colonial heritage (cf. the necessary breaching of the gap between the colonised and the colonisers), and post-colonial transformations (cf. development aid).

The practices of corruption, however, make use of brokers in the strict sense of the word.[17] One readily says in songhay-zarma *ir ma faaba ceeci* ('let's look for help'), which means let's find 'a useful relation' for any given kind of mediation, which clearly implies a bribe, a commission or a 'gift'. Brokers often organise transactions themselves, relieving the corrupter or the corruptee of the annoying aspects of these proceedings, while placing them in the circuit of everyday practices. When in need of anything, one gets in touch with a middle man, and leaves it up to him to 'sort out the matter' (*muraado feeri*), without having to bother oneself with whether the affair is legal or not. The generalised recourse to intermediaries makes it difficult to distinguish and interpret the practices of corruption by drowning them in common practices.

The logics of gift-giving

In Sahelian countries one would say 'kola' (*goro*). The giving of 'little gifts' is one of the thousands of actions of everyday life, mostly as thanks for service rendered. This 'kola nut' is not a fixed or negotiated price of remuneration, nor is it a brokerage commission; it is above all a moral duty. The beneficiary of whatever kind of aid has the duty to make some gesture of thanks. This duty to give a 'kola' goes even beyond the mere rendering of service. Aren't the inevitable gifts given to *griots* who flatter one a contributing factor to the extension of the field of application of these logics of gift-giving? There exists an entire crop of names designating one type or another of these common, more or less solicited gifts. Is it not right to offer a gift to the bearer of good news (cf. *tukunci* in hausa and songhay-zarma: symbolic gifts to a bearer of glad tidings), or to the witness of an important transaction, the purchase of a car or a house, for example (*alaada nooru*, 'customary money')? Shouldn't someone who goes to the market bring back 'something' to his relatives (*habiize*: 'a market product'), who have the right to claim this in case of non-execution? Doesn't this also apply to the traveller who returns home? Shouldn't the passer-by or visitor give something to women encountered in the act of hair braiding (*turguru nooru*: 'braiding money') or engaged in collective work (*yuubi*)?

Gift-giving is practised equally in the direction of 'superiors', equals or 'inferiors'. The holders of traditional power, for example, are receivers as well as donors. In Niger (where chiefs retain official entitlement to local power and are paid by the Ministry of Home Affairs), a gift is brought to the customary chief when one goes to greet him, even in the absence of any precise request; this is the 'done thing', and has the additional value of entering into his good graces or assuring his goodwill in the future. For an enthroning (as for a marriage or baptism) everyone brings his 'contribution' (*kambu-zaa*, which means, more or less, 'to give a hand').

Nowadays gift-giving is usually a question of money. The general monetarisation of everyday life has transformed the giving of kola into the giving of money. One must constantly have one's hand on one's purse. Many practices of petty corruption enter into this 'gift' category: one owes a 'little something' by way of thanks to a compliant or helpful civil servant. If, out of kindness, he has refrained from applying in one's disfavour the rigours of the law, doesn't he typically become one of those to whom one is obliged to give something, out of good manners? He himself will not forget to claim his 'kola' or rightful 'part', as occurs when the potential donor seems distracted or recalcitrant.

Of course the 'gift' is sometimes given in advance, as a preventive measure in view of conciliating the good graces of the civil servant in question, in order to give 'weight to the file' confided to him, and as a means of preventing the documents from 'disappearing into thin air'. But this practice is not without its counterparts outside of corruption. Whoever goes to see a marabout in order to set him to 'work' (therapeutic or magical) will first give what can be called 'money for the ink' (this ink is used by the marabout for the tracing of verses of the Koran which will serve in the making of the amulet). If the amulet turns out to be effective, one will then give more ample 'thanks' to the marabout. The transition from this practice to corruption is in fact made in popular speech. Thus, in songhay-zarma, *kalam dene* (the quill of the pen) which describes this preliminary gift to the marabout, is now applied to the 'advances' given to a bureaucrat in charge of one's case.[18]

One must also realise that to refrain from giving the 'kola' when deserved is not only a sign of avarice or of bad manners, but also carries the risk of attracting misfortune. Quite apart from the fear that can be inspired by a griot of marabout who has been mistreated or cheated of his recompense, anyone who has been thus frustrated can bring you back luck, even despite himself. One might consider, for example, the current practice which consists in giving 'something' to the cashier when withdrawing a large sum at the post office or at the social security office: this gift is called *moo daabu* in songhay-zarma (which means, approximately, 'to prevent the evil eye', which, in the absence of a gift, the envy of the cashier might send you, or *moo baa* ('the eye's share'). Obviously it is also a matter of paving the way for future collaboration. Here, once again, the borderline between corruption and everyday practices is quite thin. The multiplication of 'gifts' in everyday practice leaves room for the drowning of illicit gifts within the mass.[19]

The logics of the solidarity network

There are a multitude of solidarity networks in Africa. These are of course far from being negligible in Europe, where, however, their extension is clearly inferior: factors such as the withdrawal of the nuclear family, confinement of friends and close acquaintances to limited circles, the absence of relations between neighbours, among others, result in a weaker sociability in the North than in the South. The importance of these networks of sociability in Africa, in particular in urban areas, goes far beyond the family framework, which is however, as we all know, widely extended and replete with pressures and solicitations which can hardly be ignored. Links created within peer groups (primary school, secondary school and college friends) last until retirement. Comradeship, good neighbourliness and work relationships also multiply this 'strength of weak ties' (Granovetter 1975). Solidarities that arise from adherence to a common association, church or confraternity, to the same party, to the same faction within a party, also play their role, as does the fact of originating from the same region or district.

However, not only are these various forms of interrelations particularly extended, providing each person with a capital of social relations far exceeding that of other continents, they also include an almost general obligation of mutual assistance. One cannot refuse a service, a favour, a bit of string-pulling or compliance to a relative, neighbour, party comrade or friend. Nor ought one to refuse the same to someone who is 'sent' by any of the above. The circle of individuals to whom one feels obliged to render services is thus astonishingly wide. One must add the converse, that there is also a great number of persons to call upon. The system thus becomes one of a 'generalised exchange' of services, big or small, often in the shape of an officially illicit favour.

Let us employ the conventional term 'network' to qualify these multiple forms of belonging.[20] Each individual is integrated into various networks, each of which entails solidarities and therefore corresponding pressures. The problem is that the solidarity exacted by the network is so rigorous that anyone who fails to respect his obligations to a member of one of the networks to which he belongs suffers reproach, and becomes the object of considerable and sustained pressure from all members of the network. Should he persist, he becomes the cause of scandal, and his reputation soon becomes detestable.

Moreover, in the context of a dysfunctioning administrative and bureaucratic apparatus, and a dramatic scarcity of resources, the multiplication of interventions in favour of one person or the other progressively becomes the normal mode of management of such affairs and cases. Woe betide the man who knows no one, either directly or indirectly.[21] He is left with no solution but bribery, if his means permit. Instead of acting like everyone else, through an exchange of favours, combined or not with 'little gifts', he will be obliged to make a monetary 'purchase' of the required service, directly or through the mediation of a broker. Engrained, commodified corruption is, in this perspective, a mere symptom of the lack of an activatable network, a temporary deficit in 'social capital'. The resource to bribery is merely a sub-set of the recourse to 'favours'.[22] But the omnipresence of 'personal favours' (though often liable to legal action, if the law were to be applied, and while remaining an undebatable constituent of the corruption complex) is simultaneously a functional necessity (conditioning the effectiveness of all administrative undertakings), and a normative necessity (the foundation of all forms of sociability).

The logics of predatory authority

While the preceding logics share obvious elements of complementarity, and concern just about everyone, the two that follow are somewhat different, and are linked to functions of authority. The first concerns the right that many persons holding positions of power accord themselves to proceed to various types of extortion, to the detriment of their 'subjects', that is to those who must toady to them. These royal prerogatives, which their victims describe as rackets, appear in the eyes of the beneficiaries, not simply as a matter of personal choice, but

Explaining Corruption 499

42 J. P. OLIVIER DE SARDAN

rather as a rightful aspect of their office. The latter therefore 'naturally' entails a predatory dimension. A policeman has the right to deduct his dues from transporters, in the same way that a *directeur de cabinet* has the right to dip into special funds, or the customary judge the right to exact fees from offenders.

Bankruptcy of the state and non-payment of salaries explain in part why public servants holding the slightest bit of authority fatten themselves on the other man's back. But one can go further in history in search of more general causes. Might one not consider the banalisation of despotic extortion as a prolongation of certain pre-colonial habits (raids, tributes of war which were at time a part of the social landscape)? But the current context is so different (the modern African state has little or no resemblance, whatever may be said to the contrary, to the chiefdoms, kingdoms and emirates of yesterday) that one needs to turn instead towards colonial customs, from the military conquest and the all-powerful 'commandant', to administrative chiefs appointed by colonialism and to indigenous auxiliaries, who have always enjoyed a wide margin for arbitrary actions.[23] As for post-colonial regimes, these have propelled into existence and into sudden omnipotence a local elite wearing the boots of the European dominators, flattered by both camps of the Cold War, without any counterbalance to their despotic or predatory temptations (see Darbon 1990). From the top to the bottom of the state apparatus, the assimilation of positions of power with the right to levy tribute has undergone rapid extension (despite the existence of a few remarkable exceptions, whose exceptional character is thus noted by one and all). The change to democracy seems, in this regard, merely to have introduced the possibility of openly attacking practices (by means of a denunciation of 'prebend' and 'racket'), without modifying them; those who criticise them today, when in opposition or without power, will adopt them tomorrow when in power or possessing influence.

The current semantic difference in songhay-zarma between *kom-yan* (to despoil) and *zey-yan* (to rob) might be elucidating. A chief, prince or 'big man', a man of power, or of force, is *kom-yan*, he despoils, takes, serves himself, openly, impudently (isn't authoritative levying to be linked with power?). A poor man, without resources or power, for his part, can only have recourse to *zey-yan*, that is to theft, cheating and shameful sneaking around.

A MORAL ECONOMY OF CORRUPTION   43

The logics of redistributive accumulation

A civil servant who accedes to a prestigious position, a post of responsibility, and of course to an appointment considered to be 'juicy', must, in the sight of his relatives, profit from this and spread the benefit around. It is obviously a question of making a fortune, that is of displaying the outward signs of wealth (villas, luxurious cars, private schools for the children, jewels for the wives, etc.), and at the same time making this of benefit to his extended family, his acquaintances, his village, his dependants by means of numerous and visible signs of largesse. To refuse to grab such an opportunity to make a fortune is to make oneself an object of reproach in some cases or of mockery in others. Illegal enrichment and nepotism are definitely supported by positive social values, namely the necessity to seize all opportunities allowing for a manifestation of cardinal virtues, such as generosity, largesse and gratitude to all those who in the past, when you were unimportant, weak, in need, provided help, encouragement and support. Now, for a civil servant, positions of power provide the only means of coming into any kind of wealth. To refuse them is to make a simultaneous show of ingratitude, egoism, pride, naiveté and even stupidity. Social pressure is very strong in the direction of the accumulation of wealth in view of redistribution.[24]

This cultural logic, like others mentioned, does not come down directly from the past. It is clear, particularly so in the present case, that the factors originating in pre-colonial culture of ostentation are of some importance (see Nicholas 1986); the pre-colonial chief was obliged to show largesse to all, and thus to allow for public praise of his generosity. Here the capacity to redistribute was of course founded on patrimonialism, which regulated traditional power in the context of a confusion between the wealth of the state and that of the sovereign. But these customs had to be recycled under colonial and post-colonial periods, in order to come down to us in the present day, while retaining their power in a world which has undergone such enormous transformation.

One other factor is 'rivalry'. Contrary to various communal illusions, contemporary African societies are remarkably 'agonistic', from a real or symbolic point of view (cf. sorcery). Redistributive accumulation finds a particularly powerful additional propellant in the 'jealousy' of a neighbour, colleague or relative, and in the imperious necessity to best him as far as possible. It suffices to remark on the importance of ostentatious distribution (cf. the role of griots in the Sahel), whose

44   J. P. OLIVIER DE SARDAN

competitive aspects are evident. The anxiety to build one's 'reputation' easily takes the form of an effort to out-do others.

CULTURE AND CORRUPTION

The role played by all these logics in the banalisation of corrupt practices seems undeniable. They are usually combined, thus dissolving juridically reprehensible practices into the fabric of similar and socially commonplace practices, which happen to be accepted and even esteemed.[25] Of course corruption is not produced as such by these logics – except perhaps, to some extent, by the last two. Neither permanent negotiation nor the prevalence of brokerage, nor the practice of frequent gift-giving, nor solidarity with the social networks to which one belongs, *automatically* give rise to illicit practices, and there are examples of particularly vigilant, and relatively atypical public servants, who, at least for the most part, refuse to indulge. However, these logics, while exerting continuous pressure on social actors, help to accord a cultural acceptability to corruption. Should one therefore impute corruption in Africa to some kind of 'African culture'? Nothing would be more absurd. The notion of culture is extremely polysemic, and many of its interpretations are, to my mind, unacceptable. Nowhere is there any Value System, soaring above the populations and inducing their deportment, be it on an 'ethnic', national or 'African' level. 'Culturalism', to the extent that it occasions an excessive homogenisation of the way in which practices are perceived, to the extent that it transforms the abstract construction of the researcher into a Subject, to the extent that it deduces from social actions a kind of cultural 'tablet of the law', is indefensible. On the other hand, the converse, denial of the existence of common normative pressures exerted on actors, or a refusal to take into account shared social codes which act as a foundation for modes of social recognition or modes of intelligibility of interrelations, would imply falling into the opposite excess. The logics here enumerated thus attempt an avoidance of both of these opposed and symmetrical stumbling blocks: an explanation by 'culture', or the denial of any 'cultural factor' whatsoever. 'Cultural factor' is as vague an expression as one may encounter. The notion of logics therefore seems to be more analytically operational, in that it refers to normative configurations which influence actors' strategies. All these logics are syncretic, none is 'traditional', none comes directly from any so-called pre-colonial culture.

This brings us to the following proposition: *in the modern process of its generalisation, induced to a great extent by the bankruptcy of the political elite, corruption benefits from a favourable terrain for its routinisation and banalisation, owing to an encounter with widespread behavioural logics within post-colonial societies.*

A few other favourable factors need to be mentioned. I will call them 'facilitators' for want of a better word, to the extent that they integrate each of the above mentioned logics, by 'facilitating' the erosion and dissolution of the separation line between legal and illegal everyday practices, through an accentuation of social pressures inciting a disregard of this barrier. One may distinguish at least two such facilitators, each having a very distinct nature.

First facilitator: over-monetarisation

The permanent search for cash in contemporary African societies has already been underlined above.[26] If the economic crisis is quite clearly among the primary causes, due to the scarcity of resources available, it is not the only one. The inflation of outputs in relation to family ceremonies (marriages, baptisms in Muslim cultures, funerals in others), and to other social festivities (Christmas, Tabaski, etc.) is definitely a 'social problem', generating an infernal mechanism which everyone deplores but which no one can stop. An example among several others is that of the haussa *buki*: a custom and term which has also passed into songhay-zarma, a recent system according to which the presents received by a woman for a baptism (or at times for a wedding), and which she has carefully recorded, must be returned *doubled* to the respective donors, on similar later occasions.

All these outputs have since taken a monetary form, transformed either directly into cash or into consumer goods bought for the occasion. Personal relationships also take on a permanent monetary form. Whereas in Europe everyday forms of consumption require a constant dipping into one's pocket, everyday forms of sociability shy away from monetary support. In Africa, on the contrary, they require quite a lot of cash: giving of 'taxi fare' to a visitor, giving coins to the children of friends, giving money for the purchase of a length of African print to a cousin going to a school party, giving a bank note to your step-mother when running into her in the street, giving 500 CFA to a colleague at work to buy cigarettes, helping out a neighbour or a vague acquaintance in need; this monetarisation of everyday forms of sociability is the object of much exertion of pressure. Thus, well beyond

46   J. P. OLIVIER DE SARDAN

the mere logics of gift-giving analysed above, the over-monetarisation
of everyday life obliges all and sundry to engage in a permanent quest
for 'means', and blurs the distinction between legally admissible and
legally condemnable ones. The illicit purchase of an administrative
favour or the embezzlement of public money are all the more visible in
Europe – and all the more condemnable – according to the degree to
which they assume a monetary form (the 'bribe' or 'suitcase full of
bank notes') in domains from which money is normally excluded.
Entire sectors of social life function through a minimisation or
condemnation of the circulation of money. In Africa, on the contrary,
there is no domain (matrimonial relations included) in which money
does not play a permanent role.[27]

Second facilitator: shame

One might expect the feeling of 'shame' to be an impediment to
corrupt practices. The opposite is nearer the truth. Let us reconsider
the problem in a more general light. 'Shame' is, in the majority of
African cultures, a powerful means of social control. Any behaviour'
which breaches good breeding, which provokes a scandal, which
engenders humiliation, which displays bad manners, which ridicules
local moral values, is a generator of shame and must, as far as possible,
indeed at all costs, be avoided (see Olivier de Sardan 1982). Shame is
a social morality, a morality based on other people's opinions, rather
than one based on an individual examination of conscience.

Shame relates first of all to the disapprobation of others, and above
all of one's family circle. As already mentioned, denouncing a relative
or an acquaintance guilty of embezzlement generates shame. To refuse
a favour to a 'recommended' person generates same. To refuse a gift in
return for help generates shame. To stand out or to distinguish oneself
in public (by rejecting the 'privileges' of one's status, for example)
generates shame.

On the contrary, slipping a banknote to a civil servant, taking one's
cut to the detriment of 'clients', 'borrowing' from the cashbox,[28]
abusing 'office' material, obtaining illegal favours, none of this
generates shame, even though the abuse of power or extortion will
sometimes be considered as 'shameful' and as incompatible with the
norms of aristocratic conduct.

The engrainment of corruption into social habits has the remarkable
characteristic of displacing the barriers of shame. An intransigent
attitude in the face of all forms of corruption would marginalise its

A MORAL ECONOMY OF CORRUPTION 47

author by reason of the shame that would inevitably befall his relatives, and which could be interpreted as his pride, his scorn for others, his lack of compassion, his rejection of family or friends, his hostility towards social norms.

In other words, the stigmatisation of corruption mentioned above (Thesis 3) is unconnected to the feeling of shame, which one might have expected to impede individual recourse to practices which are deplored on another level. Stigmatisation is general, concerns public morality, is usually abstract, and when nourished by reference to personal experiences, this is often in a context where the complainant see himself as a 'victim' and/or considers that the rules of proper behaviour have not been respected; shame, which is fundamentally situational, plays upon another register, that of the pressure of the family circle and its networks, that of 'what will people say', and this register favours rather than impedes the practices of the corruption complex.

These 'facilitators' help to dissolve the borderline between sociocultural logics and corrupt daily practices. Of course, the norms of the public service or the legal definitions of corruption in Africa are the same as in Europe, being directly derived from the European model. But in Europe this model is in part the product of rather different sociocultural logics, inaugurated in the nineteenth century, on the basis of a distinction between public and private affairs, on puritanism, on egalitarian and individualistic demands. In Europe, in other words, the norms of the public service and the legal definitions of corruption correspond or harmonise, even if only approximately, with the predominant sociocultural logics.[29] In Africa, on the contrary, there is a glaring discrepancy.[30] As a result, the functioning of the administrative apparatus, entirely copied from the European pattern, is of a schizophrenic type. In law, official functioning and budget it is totally Western. In practice, it is otherwise, traversed by logics in drastic contradiction with the original model. Thus what is considered to be corruption from the perspective of official norms is not, or very little, viewed in the same light from the perspectives of practical norms and of practices. The type of generalisation of corruption peculiar to Africa makes 'petty corruption' particularly conspicuous. This is certainly not the most significant nor the gravest aspect of the matter, from an economic point of view. But its embeddedness in wider sociocultural logics produces in Africa, as opposed to Europe, a

48   J. P. OLIVIER DE SARDAN

continuum or a resemblance between petty corruption and major corruption.

Civil servants also find themselves in a schizophrenic situation. Their administrative and professional legitimacy is derived from their training in modern European administration (which is now a world-wide standard) and therefore in its values concerning the 'public service'. But their social legitimacy implies, on the contrary, that they act in conformity with more or less contradictory 'sociocultural' logics. The very widespread adherence to abstract official norms of European origin, advocating the impartiality of the state and the necessity of an ethic of the general interest, thus coexists peacefully with an equally prevalent pattern of behaviour in conformity with social norms in favour of the preeminence of private and partisan interests. Everyone is sincerely in favour of respecting the public domain, and wants the bureaucracy to be at the service of the citizens, but everyone participates by means of everyday actions in the reproduction of the system he denounces.

Hence the general feeling of helplessness in the face of an infernal mechanism. And hence this hypothesis, which is also a risk: the development of movements of a 'puritanical' tendency, intended to bring about a reform of public morals (which can assume, in Islam as in Christianity, a fundamentalist hue) may be among the ultimate means, in the absence of an improbable self-reformation of the political elites, to attempt to change the present course of affairs. Any 'anti-corruption' policy must face up to these realities.

NOTES

1. J. F. Bayart (1989, 1993) with his analysis of 'the politics of the belly', characteristic of the modern African state, and J. F. Médard (1991, 1992) in his studies concerning neo-patrimonialism, are, obviously, those that come closest. To the best of our knowledge, G. Blundo (1998), alone in francophone africanist literature, has attempted systematic research, from an empirical point of view, on the theme of local corruption in Africa (based on Senegalese working material). An article here and there touches directly on the subject, but usually on a quite general level: Bayart (1988, 1992, 1996), Bayart *et al.* (1997), Morice (1991, 1995), Amselle (1993), Elwert (1994), Sindzingre (1994) or Médard (1995). On the anglophone scene, the studies are more substantial by far. See among others Smith (1964), Greenstone (1966), Le Vine (1975), Gould (1980), Szeftel (1982), Joseph (1983, 1987), Klitgaard (1988), Charlton (1990), Pepinsky (1992), Tignor (1993), Harsch (1993) and Reno (1995). As for corruption in other contexts or in general, there is a very abundant literature, particularly in the areas of political science and economics.

2. Of course no society possessing a state and bureaucracy, ancient or modern, is exempt from corruption. But from one society to another, or from one type of society to another, corruption varies in scope and extension, assumes different forms, more or less perceptible or tolerated, sectoralised or generalised. This opens the way for a discussion of the characteristic forms of corruption in developing countries, as distinct from European and North American forms. Cf. the early works of Leys (1965) and Scott (1969).

3. Although reference is made to general tendencies, which seem quite widespread on the African continent, this does not imply an ignorance of specific national and sectarian distinctions. Each country (and in some instances each administration) obviously has its own 'style' in corruption, in the same way that it has its own political culture (the examples here refer to West African countries in general and to Niger in particular). The forms assumed by its generalisation and banalisation are also variable and can present more or less obvious exceptions (cf. e.g. Good's remarks on Botswana, 1994).

4. Méry (1992: 10–11) proposes a similar definition: 'a form of secret social exchange through which those in power (political or administrative) take personal advantage, of one type or another, of the influence they exercise in virtue of their mandate or their function'.

5. Our examples in popular semiology about corruption are taken from songhay-zarma, spoken in Niger, Mali and Benin, which has been familiar to the author since 1965. But the logics we describe are present in very different West African countries.

6. Bayart (1989) is of course the first to have insisted on this aspect. However, we are not in entire agreement with his systematic (almost explanatory) association between 'belly' metaphors linked to corruption and those linked to witchcraft or sorcery (Bayart 1992). Power and corruption are of course related, as are power and witchcraft. But these two relations are by no means to be confused or superposed, under the excuse of metaphorical closeness. One has to be suspicious of 'over-interpretation' (Olivier de Sardan 1997).

7. One might go back to the period before independence. Tignor (1993) shows that, immediately after the Second World War, the theme of corruption was a central element of political debate in Nigeria, as much on the British side (against nationalist leaders) as well as on the Nigerian side (one against each other).

8. Sarassoro (1990) refers to anti-corruption campaigns in Africa as a mere flash in the pan destined to failure.

9. However, one must bear in mind that the threat of prosecution is often brandished, and constitutes in certain cases a means of pressure and of systematic blackmail at the disposal of a dictator or man of power, who thus controls his allies and enemies (the rare cases of prosecution in the higher spheres thus correspond to the legal 'execution' of an undesirable individual). This mechanism (pinpointed by Bayart 1989, 1992) also has a wider application and can be encountered on other levels: the threat of denunciation, or in some cases, the act itself, is always to be interpreted in the context of political or factional combat (cf. Blundo 1998), local or central (and in the relation between the local elite and the centre). In this perspective, a 'corrupted' individual is, above all, a loser.

10. Other more local or sectoralised cases include the presence here or there of easy money, due to the petroleum income controlled by high officials; connections with the drug economy or smuggling (Bayart 1996); compliance or connivance with multinational enterprises; and underhand manipulation by former colonial powers, mostly French.

11. Unfortunately, there is no justification for Sarassoro's optimism, when he repeats the declaration of the chairman of the OAU in 1990: '*l'instauration de la démocratie est le seul moyen de sortir l'Afrique de la corruption*' (1990: 206).

12. This has been emphasised by Le Vine whose corrupted interviewees do not express the slightest amount of guilt. Le Vine (1989: 368).

13. The official norms in question are those defining corruption in terms of illegality; the practical norms are those that regulate practices that are illegal but which are culturally legitimate or tolerated. Generalised cultural legitimacy corresponds to what Heidenheimer (1989: 161) calls 'white corruption'.

14. Cf. S. Berry (1994) who has pointed out this particularity of contemporary Africa. Lund (1998), for his part, develops an example on the subject of property conflicts. It has already been noted (e.g. Padioleau 1975: 45) that the coexistence of several systems of norms is a factor favourable to corruption.

15. There is of course a general agreement on certain usages which remain or have become unavoidable, for example the bride price and 'suitcase' in Niger (the latter being a tradition of recent invention); but beyond these scant guidelines, the notable variations in local custom and the numerous changes that have intervened over the years, have opened up the list of possible references, thus leaving elbow room that 'uncles' and 'aunts' do not ignore, each in their own interest.

16. Scott (1969) has produced an analysis which goes partly in the same direction. In his opinion, certain practices of corruption in the South are the functional *ex-post* equivalent of *ex-ante*

50   J. P. OLIVIER DE SARDAN

parliamentary lobbies in the North. The latter carry out collective negotiations on the terms of a law to be passed, in the interest of a group whose mandate they execute, which law will be relatively well applied, while the practices of corruption in the South, where the political class is more estranged from the civil society, and where group and professional interests are rarely organised collectively, where laws are not very familiar or well adapted, allow for individual negotiation on the level of the process of application of laws and regulations.

17. Morice (1995) has pointed out the link between the system of corruption and the emergence of a mediator class, in Guinea and Brazil.

18. Brownberger (1983: 221–3) uses the term 'polite corruption' in reference to traditional gift-giving, to which he accords only a minor role in the practices of corruption. But this is because he perceives only the traditional aspects of gift-giving (if gift-giving is obviously of traditional origin, it now assumes completely new and modern forms), and because he makes it out to be a particular form of corruption, divorced from other such practices. Here, on the contrary, we consider gift-giving as constituting a wider cultural logic.

19. Leys (1965: 225) had already noted the degree of inconspicuousness in the passage from the traditional gift in kind to the monetary bribe ('the precise nature of the rule of infringement is partially concealed by the continuity with the older custom'). He makes reference to a case in which a chicken given in the open becomes a bank note given in half-secrecy.

20. Though the term is vague, it seems preferable to excessively rigid anthropological designations such as 'corporate groups' or 'primary solidarities'.

21. Le Vine (1975) has underlined, in the case of Ghana, the hyper-personalisation of political and administrative relations. No affair is ever handled before an anonymous institution, but before 'relations' of which one disposes in these institutions. Here again it is a question of a well-known phenomenon in the North (the French system of '*énarques*', for example, reposes for the most part on this personalisation), but this is, in general, restrained to networks of peer groups of equivalent training and competence, and does not therefore entail the same generality, tranversality or extension as in Africa. The essential point is to demonstrate that there is a continuum rather than a rupture between an 'exchange of services' and 'bribes'. Padioleau (1975), referring to the United States elite, is therefore right to insist on the importance of 'corruption through exchange of favours'.

22. Thus the limit of the opposition between 'parochial corruption' and 'market corruption' (Scott 1969: 330).

23. Wangrin obviously comes to mind, a scarcely fictive hero of the well-known book by Amadou Hampaté Bâ. For a sociopolitical analysis of colonial despotism in western Niger, based on the accounts of peasant victims, see Olivier de Sardan (1984).

24. Chinua Achebe's novels *A Man of the People* and *No Longer at Ease* are remarkable illustrations of this.

25. Several authors have already pointed out this characteristic; note, for example, Heidenheimer (1989: 159): 'all the activities considered "routine corruption" by official Western standards are standard practices deeply rooted in more general social relationships and obligations'.

26. Raynaud (1977) has long since demonstrated the importance of cash circulation in one African society (a Hausa village society) even when resources are scarce and cash is rare.

27. G. Elwert (1984) has analysed in a stimulating text what he refers to as the generalisation of 'venality'. But, to my mind, he confused two processes, the 'monetarisation' of social life and its 'commodification'. Over-monetarisation does not imply that relationships in which there is a circulation of money obligatorily become commodified relationships. The money given to a prostitute comes under venal love, but this is not true of the money given to one's wife.

28. The importance of 'borrowing' and especially of the unreturned and unclaimed loan (it is sometimes more 'shameful' to ask a debtor to reimburse than for the latter to refrain from doing so) merits development, and one might consider this as yet another 'logic', favouring the banalisation of practices of corruption.

29. Of course, there are places and sectors, in Europe, where corruption is ordinary. But these practices are confined to a number of particular domains (public works, and construction, for example, or the financing of political parties, not to mention the recycling of dirty money and the drug economy). Corruption is 'sectoralised', whereas it is 'generalised' in Africa.

30. Médard (1995) rightly points out that it is not only a matter of contradiction between norms and practices, but one of a contradiction between the norms themselves.

A MORAL ECONOMY OF CORRUPTION   51

REFERENCES

Amselle, J. L. 1993. 'La corruption et le clientélisme au Mali et en Europe de l'Est: quelques points de comparaison', *Cahiers d'Etudes Africaines* 128.

Bailey, F. 1969. *Strategems and Spoils: a Social Anthropology of Politics*. London: Basil Blackwell.

Bayart, J. F. 1988. 'La corruption en Afrique: l'"invisible" et le partage du gateau', *Africa International*. 209: 64.

Bayart, J. F. 1989. *L'Etat en Afrique: la Politique du Ventre*. Paris: Fayard.

Bayart, J. F. 1992. 'Argent et pouvoir en Afrique Noire', *Projet* 232: 6–70.

Bayart, J. F. 1996. 'L'Afrique en voie de malversation', *Croissance des Jeunes Nations* 389: 50.

Bayart, J. F., S. Ellis & B. Hibou. 1997. *La Criminalisation de l'Etat en Afrique*. Paris: Editions Complexe.

Becker, H. 1963. *Outsiders: Studies in the Sociology of Deviance*. New York: Free Press.

Berry, S. 1994. *No Condition is Permanent: the Social Dynamics of Agrarian Change in Sub-Saharian Africa*. Madison: University of Wisconsin Press.

Blundo, G. 1995. 'Les courtiers du développement en milieu rural sénégalais', *Cahiers d'Etudes Africaines* 137: 73–99.

Blundo, G. 1996. 'Bavardages, rumeurs et accusations: d'une ethnographie de la corruption?' ms.

Blundo, G. 1998. Elus locaux, associations paysannes et courtiers du développement au Sénégal: une anthropologie politique de la décentralisation dans le Sud-Est du bassin arachidier (1974–1995). Lausanne, thèse de doctorat.

Boissevain, J. 1974. *Friends of Friends: Networks, Manipulators and Coalitions*. Oxford: Basil Blackwell.

Brownsberger, W. 1983. 'Development and governmental corruption: materialism and political fragmentation in Nigeria', *Journal of Modern African Studies* 21, 2: 215–33.

Cartier-Bresson, J. 1992. 'Eléments d'analyse pour une économie de la corruption', *Revue Tiers Monde* 131: 581–609.

Charlton, R. 1990. 'Exploring the byways of African political corruption: Botswana and deviant case analysis', *Corruption and Reform* 5: 1–27.

Darbon, D. 1990. 'L'Etat prédateur', *Politique Africaine* 39: 37–45.

Ekeh, P. 1975. 'Colonialism and the two publics in Africa: a theoretical statement', *Comparative Studies in Society and History* 17.

Elwert, G. 1984. 'Markets, venality and moral economy', ms.

Elwert, G. 1994. 'Lorsque l'argent remonte vers le pouvoir: la corruption en Afrique', *Développement et Coopération* (Frankfurt) 2: 23–6.

Gould, D. 1980. *Bureaucratic Corruption and Underdevelopment in the Third World: the Case of Zaïre*. New York: Pergamon Press.

Granovetter, M. 1973. 'The strength of weak ties', *American Journal of Sociology* 78, 6: 1360–80.

Greenstone, J. D. 166. 'Corruption and self interest in Kampala and Nairobi', *Comparative Studies in Society and History* 8: 199–210.

Harsch, E. 1993. 'Accumulators and democrats: challenging state corruption in Africa', *Journal of Modern African Studies* 31, 1: 31–48.

Heidenheimer, A. 1989. 'Perspectives on the perception of corruption', in A. Heidenheimer, M. Johnston & V. Le Vine, eds. *Political Corruption: a Handbook*. New Brunswick: Transaction Publishers.

Joseph, R. 1983. 'Class, state and prebendal politics in Nigeria', *Journal of Commonwealth and Comparative Politics* 21, 7: 21–38.

Joseph, R. 1987. *Democracy and Prebendal Politics in Nigeria: the Rise and Fall of the Second Republic*. Cambridge: Cambridge University Press.

Klitgaard, R. 1988. *Controlling Corruption*. Berkeley: University of California Press.

Lautier, B., C. de Miras & A. Morice. 1991. *L'Etat et l'informel*. Paris: L'Harmattan.

LeVine, V. 1975. *Political Corruption: the Ghana Case*. Stanford: Hoover Institution Press.

Leys, C. 1965. 'What is the problem about corruption?', *Journal of Modern African Studies* 3, 2: 215–30.

Lund, C. 1998. *Law, Power and Politics in Niger*. Hamburg: Lit. Verlag.

Mbembé, A. 1992. 'Provisional notes on the post-colony', *Africa* 62, 1: 3–37.

Médard, J. F. ed. 1991. *Etats d'Afrique Noire: Formation, Mécanismes et Crise*. Paris: Karthala.

Médard, J. F. 1992. 'Le "big man" en Afrique: esquisse d'une analyse du politicien entrepreneur', *L'Année Sociologique* 42: 167–92.

52   J. P. OLIVIER DE SARDAN

Médard, J. F. 1995. 'La corruption politique et administrative et les différenciations du public et du privé: une perspective comparative', in Borghi and Meyer-Bisch, eds, *La corruption: l'envers des droits de l'homme*. Fribourg: Editions Universitaires.

Mény, Y. 1992. *La Corruption de la République*. Paris: Fayard.

Morice, A. 1991. 'Les maîtres de l'informel: corruption et modèles mafieux d'organisation sociale', in Lautier *et al. L'Etat et l'informel*.

Morice, A. 1995. 'Corruption, loi et société: quelques propositions', *Tiers Monde* 141: 41–65.

Nicolas, G. 1986. *Don Rituel et Échange Marchand dans une Société Sahélienne*. Paris: Institut d'ethnologie.

Nye, J. 1967 'Corruption and political development: a cost-benefit analysis', *American Political Science Review* 56.

Olivier de Sardan, J. P. 1982. *Concepts et Conceptions songhay-zarma (Histoire, Culture, Société)*. Paris: Nubia.

Olivier de Sardan, J. P. 1984. *Les Sociétés songhay-zarma: Chefs, Esclaves, Guerriers, Paysans*. Paris: Karthala.

Olivier de Sardan, J. P. 1995. *Anthropologie et Développement: Essai en Socio-anthropologie du Changement Social*. Paris: Karthala.

Olivier de Sardan, J. P. 1996. 'La violence faite aux données: autour de quelques figures de la surinterprétation en anthropologie', *Enquête* 3: 31–59.

Olivier de Sardan, J. P. & T. Bierschenk. 1993. 'Les courtiers locaux du développement'. *Bulletin APAD* 5: 71–6.

Olivier de Sardan, J. P. & T. Bierschenk. 1998. *Les pouvoirs au village. Le Bénin rural entre democratisation et décentralisation*. Paris: Karthala.

Padioleau, J. 1975. 'De la corruption dans les oligarchies pluralistes', *Revue Française de Sociologie* 17: 33–58.

Pepinsky, H. 1992. 'Corruption, bribery and patriarchy in Tanzania', *Crime, Law and Social Change* 17, 1: 25–52.

Raynaut, C. 1977. 'Circulation monétaire et évolution des structures socio-économiques chez les Haoussas du Niger', *Africa* 47, 2: 160–71.

Reno, W. 1995. *Corruption and State Politics in Sierra Leone*. Cambridge: Cambridge University Press.

Sarassoro, H. 1990. 'La corruption et l'enrichissement sans cause en Afrique aujourd'hui', *Afrique Contemporaine* 156: 195–206.

Scott, J. 1969. 'The analysis of corruption in developing nations', *Comparative Studies in Society and History* 11: 315–41.

Scott, J. 1976. *The Moral Economy of the Peasant: Rebellion and Subsistence in Southeast Asia*. New Haven and London: Yale University Press.

Sindzingre, A. 1994. 'Etat, développement et rationalité en Afrique: contribution à une analyse de la corruption'. Bordeaux: CEAN, Travaux et Documents, 43.

Smith, M. G. 1964. 'Historical and cultural conditions of corruption among the Hausa', *Comparative Studies in Society and History* 6: 164–94.

Szeftel, M. 1982. 'Political graft and spoil system in Zambia: the state as a resource in itself'. *Review of African Political Economy* 24: 5–21.

Thompson, E. P. 1971. 'The moral economy of the English crowd during the eighteenth century', *Past & Present* 50: 76–117.

Tignor, R. 1993. 'Political corruption in Nigeria before independence', *Journal of Modern African Studies* 31, 2: 175–202.

Whyte, W. 1955. *Street Corner Society*. 1st edn. Chicago: Chicago University Press.

[27]

Third World Quarterly, Vol 20, No 3, pp 503–513, 1999

New concepts for old?

ROBERT WILLIAMS

ABSTRACT *There has been an explosion of interest in corruption in the past 10 years and the literature on the causes, consequences and control of corruption is now substantial. But there has not been a corresponding concern with the concept of corruption and how it can be defined and refined. Dissatisfaction with the approaches used in earlier decades has, in the 1990s, encouraged many analysts to turn to other, primarily economic, concepts. This article explores how the concept of corruption has evolved in contemporary social science and examines whether the new concepts constitute an important advance on the approaches used in earlier studies. It concludes that the new concepts are attempts to explain the circumstances most likely to give rise to corruption rather than original ways of defining it.*

Interest in corruption has grown rapidly in the 1990s. Academic journals, newspapers and magazines are full of articles on corruption. Government departments, international financial institutions and supranational political bodies have all published policy statements emphasising the significance of corruption. The 1990s have been the decade of corruption as an academic and policy topic and there is no indication that popular, academic, professional or political interest is beginning to flag. The literature is voluminous and varied but most accounts share a common characteristic: a reluctance to say what they mean by corruption. This issue is either avoided completely or dismissed in a cursory fashion.

There is, it seems, a desire, even impatience, to get on with the tasks of detecting its causes, assessing its consequences and evaluating means to bring it under control. It is unusual for authors to take time to examine the concept but, when they do, they find it vague, elusive and unsatisfactory. Yet it is a curious state of affairs when an academic mini-industry and the policy agendas of development professionals are dominated by a concept which most participants in the debate are reluctant or unable to define.[1]

Dissatisfaction with the term has driven a number of analysts to seek other concepts to employ as alternative or auxiliary means of achieving greater clarity and precision in their accounts. Corruption has no fixed disciplinary allegiance and analysts have ransacked the cupboards of anthropology, economics, law, organisation theory, philosophy, political science and sociology in their efforts to find ways of making the concept more robust and useful. Others have abandoned the quest and merely pay lip service to the need to define corruption

Robert Williams is Head of the Department of Politics, University of Durham, Durham DH1 3LZ, UK.

0143-6597/99/030503-11 © 1999 *Third World Quarterly*

before embarking on empirical studies which make no connection with the definition offered at the beginning of the analysis.

This article has two main aims: to examine how the concept of corruption has evolved in contemporary social science and to consider whether the term has outlived whatever usefulness it ever had. In addressing these issues, it will be necessary to say something about the conceptual rivals to corruption before reaching a judgment as to whether the new concepts constitute an advance on more established ones.

It is a normal preliminary in social inquiry to identify the key terms employed in the analysis. If they are to serve a useful role in the subsequent analysis, definitions of social phenomena need to be capacious yet discriminating. If they are too narrowly drawn, they will not be comprehensive. If they are broad, they may be seen as vague and imprecise. The task of finding a suitable definition of corruption which can be used for purposes of comparative analysis has proved fraught with difficulty. It is possible to stipulate a definition derived from one context and apply it to another, but the question arises as to whether the assumptions on which it is based have any resonance in the other context. In the context of developing countries, the stipulative definitions of Western social scientists can easily be interpreted as another form of cultural imperialism. The alternative seems to be to reject the comparative quest in favour of some form of moral, cultural and conceptual relativism, where different contexts demand different definitions of corruption.

Before it became subject to the rigours of modern social science, corruption was used primarily as a term of moral condemnation. In moral terms, to corrupt means to pervert, degrade, ruin and debase. In the moral realm, an act identified as corrupt is something to be condemned. To say that corruption is wrong is rather like saying that murder is wrong. Both statements express what is, in effect, a conceptual truth or grammatical necessity.[2] Moral standards are applied to, rather than emerge from, particular situations. They are external, not intrinsic, to disputes about the nature of corruption. Implicit in the moral meaning of corruption is the judgement that corruption essentially privatizes moral life. As a consequence, social relations are dominated by self-interest and fellow citizens are seen as instruments, obstacles and competitors. In the morally corrupt society, civic virtue and social responsibility are displaced and discarded in favour of an intense competition for spoils. Such a characterisation is as applicable to parts of modern Africa as it was to 15th century Florence.

With isolated exceptions,[3] modern social science has largely eschewed the moral perspective on corruption. The first and most enduring approach favoured an essentially legalistic understanding of the term. The legal meaning of corruption appeals to rules and laws. It relates corruption to the violation of a rule, while legal adjudication relates acts to rules in ways intended to reveal the contravention of specific rules by particular acts. But legal judgements only apply in the context of the administration of justice to individuals who are already, *prima facie*, thought to have contravened rules or laws prohibiting corrupt behaviour. For those seeking a more general application of the term, the early appreciation that legal codes varied from country to country discouraged analysts from adopting a purely legal approach.

504

The legal approach raises other problems: the law may be silent on conduct which is widely perceived by political actors, the media and the public to be corrupt. More seriously, it depends on the notion that legal frameworks are somehow neutral, objective and non-political. But laws regulating political and bureaucratic conduct derive from assumptions and beliefs about the nature of politics and the character of public office. Laws are generally made by the politically powerful who can determine what conduct is declared improper. Equality before the law remains at best an aspiration in many jurisdictions. If legality is a matter for the politically powerful, using only legal criteria to define corruption is to endorse the authority of the strong rather than the just.

The dominant definition of corruption from the 1960s to the 1980s was a legally derived approach—the public office definition. This built on a crucial distinction between the public and private realms, which gradually evolved as arbitrary, autocratic and absolutist government in Europe gave way to more limited, representative and accountable forms. This was a complex process but suffice it to say here that, in the political order, the vital change was to create barriers to the expropriation of public resources by the officials responsible for administering them. On Weberian lines, public officials were compensated by regular salaries rather than by permitting them to make private use of public monies. As the notion of public office crystallised, so too did the understanding of corruption as theft from the state by state officials.

Even approaches which explicitly reject the public office definition have to confront it and, when they do, it is almost obligatory to cite the formulation offered by Nye over 30 years ago.

> corruption is behaviour which deviates from the formal duties of a public role because of private regarding (personal, close family, private clique) pecuniary or status gains; or violates rules against the exercise of certain types of private regarding influence.[4]

Although this definition has been heavily deconstructed to expose its ambiguities, limitations, assumptions and prejudices, it should be recognised that its author was well aware of the problems it raised in terms of inclusiveness of behaviour and relativity of standards. Nye argues both that it had the merit of identifying specific behaviour generally called corrupt by Western standards and that such standards had at least a partial relevance to most developing countries. The public office definition has many appealing characteristics: it speaks directly to official conduct and the centrality of duty; it seems to embrace bribery, nepotism and embezzlement; it avoids confusing the phenomenon with its effects; and, unlike a narrowly legal approach, it appears to offer the possibility of meaningful comparative analysis.

Although Nye's formulation sounds neutral, it nevertheless stems from a desire to condemn as corrupt conduct which furthers private interests. Other analysts have been more explicit and simply asserted that corruption involves the subversion of the public interest or common good by private interests. The association here is between a notion of a public, a citizenry, which has distinct interests and the corresponding idea that these interests will be damaged when and if public servants engage in what Nye terms 'private regarding' conduct.

505

Thus the public office and public interest definitions of corruption share the understanding that the common good is best served when officials adhere to 'the formal duties of public roles' and do not lapse into conduct designed to secure 'private regarding gains'. But the problems remain of how to determine public and private roles and which view of the public interest to adopt. While the politically powerful can manipulate the definitions of public office and can seek to impose their view of what is in the public interest, one potentially countervailing force in shaping these conceptions is public opinion.

In one obvious sense, corruption is socially defined: it is what the public in a country think it is. But public opinion is not monolithic. It is often divided, unstable, ambiguous and ignorant. Public awareness is often low, access to mass media is limited and state censorship is common. The values of rural communities may be incommensurate with those of urban elites or there may be clashes between the opinions of different religious or ethnic groups. Where there is no clear public perception of a set of principles governing the conduct of public office or there is an inability to identify and specify the public interest, the contribution of public opinion to clarifying the public office and public interest definitions is correspondingly reduced.

Attempts to break away from public office conceptions were rare before the 'corruption eruption' of the 1990s but one early and influential attempt is that of Leff. In his determination to avoid the language of approval or disapproval, or what Philp terms 'his impressive commitment to nominalism in the identification of corruption',[5] Leff absorbs corruption into an appreciation of actual decision-making processes. In Leff's view:

> Corruption is an extra-legal institution used by individuals or groups to gain influence over the actions of the bureaucracy. As such, the existence of corruption *per se* indicates only that these groups participate in the decision making process to a greater extent than would otherwise be the case.[6]

In effect, Leff argues that corruption is part of the difference between formal political and bureaucratic procedures and the way they actually work. But despite his desire to avoid condemnation, it can be seen that Leff's suggestion that corruption is an 'extra-legal institution' actually depends on a prior notion of public office and of principles of official conduct. It seems that all definitional roads lead back to the notion of public office, with its attendant problems of vagueness, cultural relativity and elasticity.

When the upsurge of interest in corruption began, the old definitions seemed unsatisfactory. As many of the new analyses were produced by economists, a corruption vocabulary rooted in law and government was alien and corruption was recast in theoretical frameworks which were more familiar and congenial to economists.

The prime exponents of the new approach to corruption are Rose-Ackerman[7] and Klitgaard,[8] who tend to see government through an economic prism and interpret its workings as akin to private business monopolies. Economists argue that monopolies exploit their positions to make excessive profits or, in economic jargon, economic rents and the monopoly position of government as owner and regulator similarly provide numerous opportunities for rent seeking. Rents are defined in economics as returns in excess of a resource owner's opportunity cost. They arise in market systems by adjustments of price through demand and supply changes and constitute short-term profit maximisation. They last only until the market readjusts through the entry of new suppliers. But government actions can generate long-term rents by creating artificial shortages, setting a state price below market prices and organising monopolistic trading opportunities.

Rent seeking is a key concept in the economic approach to corruption and it is important to note that it is predicated on assumptions about the motivation of individuals.[9] We are, it is suggested, driven by self-interest and concerned to maximise our self-interest, which can be narrowly construed as financial benefit or, more broadly, as a maximisation of an individual's general position. One problem with the notion of rent seeking is that, even accepting this characterisation of human motivation, it does not help us discriminate between corrupt and non-corrupt means of interest or income maximisation. To identify which forms of self-interest maximisation are corrupt, we need some sense of public office and associated norms. Market-driven approaches do not offer an alternative definition of corruption because they implicitly accept the notion of public office and the constraints on official conduct. Although they superficially appear to offer a distinctive conceptual perspective, their real focus is not on defining corruption but on explaining the economic imperatives and political circumstances which encourage breaches of the rules and norms of public office.

This gives rise to another conceptualisation: the modelling of public office in terms of principal–agent theory.[10] Agency theory uses the same assumptions about human behaviour as rent seeking. It suggests that we are concerned to 'maximise' our self-interest and that, if government officials are presented with opportunities to engage in corrupt activity, they will do so unless they are closely supervised and controlled. Principal–agent analysis shifts the focus away from abstract considerations of how to judge whether or not particular conduct is corrupt and instead situates the analysis in the interaction and interrelations which exist within and without public bodies. The approach identifies organisational roles and characterises them as either principals or agents: the party labelled the principal is the authority figure and those who contract to carry out specified tasks for the principal are the agents. In return for fulfilling their part of the contract, agents are paid salaries.

Public organisations do not exist in a vacuum. They interact with society and economy and, in addition to the principals and agents, there are also customers or clients outside the organisation who are in need of help and cooperation from agents. The problem arises because the principal, the agent and the client are all striving to maximise their self-interest and these interests will rarely coincide. The pursuit of self-interest will override the contract between the principal and agent and such breaches of contract take place because closely monitoring the agent is too costly to the principal. Thus, from the principal–agent perspective 'corruption occurs when an agent betrays the principal's interest in pursuit of their own'.[11]

Principal–agent analysis has influenced the way government agencies and international financial institutions have understood corruption in recent years. Even scholars who do not make use of the principal–agent framework in their own work have suggested that it offers a new way of looking at corruption. One leading authority argues that it shifts the focus to the significance of officials' and clients' conduct within an institutional setting. He further suggests that it usefully includes the issue of accountability in the conduct of public office, as well as making room for the notion of the public interest by associating it with the principal's interest.[12]

But principal–agent analysis is not an answer to the definitional problem because such analyses, like that of rent seeking, are concerned to identify what conditions are most and least conducive to people acting corruptly. They take as given the constraints on the use of public office which are central to traditional definitions. On its own terms, principal–agent analysis only recognises interest or income maximising behaviour and is unable to discriminate between the corrupt and the non-corrupt. It raises more elementary problems: who is the principal and who is the agent? Can principals be agents and vice versa? Identities are, in this form of analysis, slippery, shifting and uncertain.

In applying the principal–agent perspective, analysts assume the problem lies with the agent; the political or managerial problem is thought to be to find ways in which agents can be controlled. But, given the model's own assumptions, it is evident that principals are equally prone to corruption. Its assumption that corruption is the consequence of uncontrolled agents betraying their principals' trust is profoundly conservative and does not reflect the actual distribution of resources and power.[13] Like rent seeking, it uses highly contestable assumptions about human motivation. Yet we know that, outside economic models, markets are imperfect, rationality is bounded and maximising is impossible when information is incomplete. Organisation theory suggests that much administrative behaviour is better characterised as 'satisficing' rather than maximising. The rational egoist beloved of economic theory seems more and more a creature of fiction as we understand more about the extent to which corruption is socially conditioned and sustained by complex and enduring social networks. In short, economic analyses import assumptions about motivation in market situations to the political and administrative arena. This article is not concerned to deny the role of economics in helping to understand the incentive structure underlying many corrupt transactions, but its contribution to the clarification of the concept of corruption remains problematic.

If economic approaches actually depend on public office-type definitions of corruption, it is important to examine Nye's contention that such definitions identify specific behaviour and facilitate comparative analysis. The approaches to defining corruption discussed above all focus on bureaucratic rather than political corruption. By implication they relate to situations where rule following is anticipated and where there are guidelines on what constitutes improper or 'private regarding' conduct. Bureaucratic organisations characteristically operate on the basis of clear lines of authority and accountability and, in principle, it is possible to distinguish formal duties from private regarding conduct. But even here problems arise. For example, there are often no effective prohibitions or limits on bureaucrats receiving additional sources of income. When bureaucrats have extensive private business interests, the potential for conflicts of interest necessarily increases.

NEW CONCEPTS FOR OLD?

But the major problem with the public office definition is how to deal with politics. Bureaucrats are monitored and controlled by other bureaucrats. The most senior officials are answerable to politicians who set the acceptable boundaries of private regarding conduct and have the authority to regulate or remove officials they judge to be corrupt. But, however elaborate and strict the definitions of public duties are for officials, the world of politics is likely to be more uncertain. Principal–agent analysis identifies corruption as occurring when agents betray principals but it leaves open the question of how to determine what constitutes corruption by principals. The omission is a reminder of how concepts of corruption fit awkwardly with political practice.

If corruption involves private regarding conduct or, to use Hutchcroft's formulation, 'particularistic privilege',[14] then how do we understand machine politics, alliance building and other forms of developing a political following? Patronage, cronyism and clientelism pose similar problems. While bureaucracy is formally committed to public service, politics is inherently partisan, with winners and losers, supporters and enemies. How can any form of partisanship be reconciled with public duty?

In the US Congress there is a strict prohibition on legislators employing their relatives but, in the UK House of Commons, many MPs routinely employ their spouses to assist them in their official functions. This highlights the problems inherent in any notion of private regarding conduct. Does it refer only to individuals and their families or should it be extended to class, clan, race and gender? In focusing on individuals and families rather than on social, ethnic, institutional and ideological loyalties, there seems to be an attempt to insist on atomisation and autonomy. Presumably, such an assertion is thought preferable to the alternative position of saying that all political activity is, by definition, corrupt.

Classifying conduct as corrupt requires a context and some reference points. It forces us to say something about the character of politics and the legitimacy of government. The nature of the political order and its stability, the limits and sources of political power, the forms and types of political organization, and the opportunities and processes of political reform are all relevant to a consideration of the meaning of corruption. Our understanding of corruption is formed by the political process, as is our general sense of what is politically legitimate. If taking corruption out of politics is generally thought desirable, taking politics out of our understanding of corruption would be a mistake. Much of the debate about defining corruption is really about competing conceptions of the nature of politics.

In a variety of contexts there can be a conflict between partisan advantage and the public interest. Some will argue that these are not incompatible or that seeking partisan advantage is necessary for building and sustaining governing coalitions. The need to reward allies and supporters is at the root of the call 'to the victors the spoils'. The spoils are usually public resources, positions or opportunities which are allocated on a basis of 'particularistic privilege'. In extreme cases the notions of public office and duty are so remote from the realities of political life and so alien to the experience of both officials and citizens that is it questionable whether it is sensible to use a term like corruption.

In situations where shortages are acute, where violence is rife and where instability is the norm, politics and government break-down and so too does our ability to identify the corrupt. In countries beset by civil war, insurrection and terrorism, there may be a number of competing claims for political legitimacy and this lack of agreement or consensus will similarly extend to what constitutes corruption.

The public office and public interest notions of corruption appear to rest on the existence of settled, agreed political orders. It is clear that many developing countries are deeply divided and the struggle for political supremacy is so intense that it precludes agreement on political principles and processes. Such circumstances dictate that corruption will become a term which is more useful in political invective than in political analysis.

Where agreed, settled political orders do exist, it is possible to think of corruption not only in terms of the individual misconduct of public servants but also in terms of its consequences for political institutions.[15] In this context, most commentators tend to neglect the second part of Nye's public office definition: behaviour which 'violates rules against the exercise of certain types of private regarding influence'. The emphasis here is not on the gains, usually financial, made by allegedly corrupt bureaucrats or politicians but on the notion of improper influence. The important point is that influence is improper when the opportunity to influence is not open to all, when it is secret and when it undermines the purposes of the organisation.

It is therefore both possible and desirable to link the search for a definition of corruption to questions about the character and vitality of the political process. It can then be argued that corruption is a term that can be used to describe political institutions as well as individuals. The concern is less with the motives of individuals or the extent of personal enrichment than with the damage done to the standing of government and the quality of the representative system. Transactions between citizens and politicians can be judged corrupt when they subvert or circumvent a democratic process and its associated values of openness, equality, equity and accountability.

The above line of argument takes the definitional debate full circle. It has been recognised that stipulative definitions drawn from an idealised version of Western experience are unhelpful when applied to the realities of many developing countries. It has consequently been suggested that defining corruption requires an appropriate political context but it is also apparent that in some contexts it is difficult to see how any notion of corruption could be meaningful. The implication is that to have any notion of corruption, certain basic conditions are required. Such conditions are not susceptible to precise measurement or quantification but, at a minimum, they involve having a known government, a continuing administrative apparatus, containable levels of violence and disorder and a regular source of public revenue. When government disintegrates or otherwise succumbs to challenges to its authority, attempts to define corruption have as much relevance as rearranging the deckchairs on the Titanic.

One conclusion might be that public office notions of corruption are derived from Western-style liberal democracies and are wholly inappropriate in non-democratic settings. But it should be noted that the conditions listed above are not synonymous with the tenets of liberal democracy. The conditions stipulated are not those of any particular form of political regime but rather seek to identify the minimal conditions necessary for the survival of any form of political rule. Many developing countries experience periods of instability, domestic disturbance, bureaucratic chaos and revenue shortfalls but these problems do not amount to an irretrievable breakdown of the political order. Without underestimating the enormous difficulties experienced by developing countries, there are many examples where stability has been restored, where unrest has been defused or dissipated, where bureaucratic efficiency has been improved and where the flow of revenues is sufficient to fund the day-to-day workings of government. In such circumstances, public office definitions need not be as inappropriate as arguments in favour of cultural and conceptual relativism would suggest.

Perhaps corruption has become a catch-all concept which embraces all manner of political and administrative difficulties. In essence, the explanatory burden is too much to bear and the concept buckles under the weight of analytical expectations. When a concept seems inadequate to the task, one temptation is to discard it in favour of another—for example, rent seeking in place of corruption. Yet, as noted above, the new concepts raise other, equally intractable difficulties. Their focus may not even be relevant to the inquiry. For example, economic approaches to corruption deal with the ways in which governments influence or distort the operation of markets, whereas the analytical concern may be with the ways markets influence or distort government.

A recent contribution to the conceptual debate suggests that, instead of putting all our eggs in one conceptual basket, there is a need to examine a range of related concepts. Hutchcroft identifies the major paradigms as corruption, rents and clientelism and he argues that, although each offers important insights, 'all would be enhanced by a more concerted effort at cross-fertilization'.[16] On this account, particularistic advantage takes a variety of forms in different circumstances and to capture the nuances we need to develop hybrid concepts. Such concepts, it is hoped, will enable us to compensate for the analytical weaknesses of corruption, rents and clientelism. But such work is at a preliminary stage and it is too soon to say whether the hybrids will prove fertile or sterile.

Conclusion

It has been suggested that defining terms is an important preliminary stage in any social inquiry and that the study of corruption has been handicapped by the inadequacies of existing definitions. New conceptual approaches have begun to dominate the thinking of academics and policy makers but, as we have seen, these new approaches are actually based on the old definitions and concepts they were intended to replace. The way forward, as Hutchcroft suggests, may be to combine concepts to compensate for their individual inadequacy. But, whatever direction future studies take, we should remember that definitions are not true or false. They are not statements of fact but more like conventions which apply only because of agreement or consensus that they are relevant to the phenomenon under consideration.

ROBERT WILLIAMS

No doubt some analysts still hope that, somewhere in the conceptual ether, there exists a definition of corruption which is sufficiently capacious and nuanced to compensate for the limitations of existing definitions, yet which is brief enough to slip into the introductory paragraph of official reports on corruption. To date, no all-purpose definition is available and there are grounds for believing that the search is futile. Corruption is complex and multifaceted and resists simple labelling. How corruption is defined depends on the context in which it is located, the perspectives of the definers and their purpose in defining it. Different questions demand different responses and the choice of question depends on what it is we are trying to identify and understand.

Choosing a definition of corruption is not an irrevocable exclusive commitment. Selecting a definition is not like entering a strict monastic order in which we have to abandon all other possibilities. Public office definitions may be appropriate for those interested in the gap between Weberian expectations of the ideal-type bureaucracy and real life bureaucratic conduct, but the public opinion approach will be more relevant to ascertaining whether the clientele served by the bureaucracy shares the public office conception. In other words, in seeking to identify and understand corruption, it may be necessary to define it in different ways. Corruption resists simple definition because it is not a discrete, hermetically sealed phenomenon and, although it is important to be clear about what we mean, it is not compulsory, and may not be desirable, to adhere rigidly to only one meaning. What is more important in any analysis of corruption is that we are clear about which meaning is being used at any particular point in the analysis. The choice of definition is intimately related to the focus of analysis but, by exaggerating the problems of definition, it is possible to mistake definitional molehills for explanatory mountains. The defining of terms is a preliminary to, not a substitute for, explanation and, however defined, definitions should be aids not obstacles to understanding corruption. As an important feature of political and economic life, corruption demands awareness of, and sensitivity to, a variety of perspectives. Such awareness requires us to evaluate new concepts and approaches to the subject not in the expectation that they will resolve long-standing issues but in the hope that they will help provide a richer and fuller understanding of corruption.

Notes

[1] An important recent exception to this rule is M Philp, 'Defining political corruption', *Political Studies*, 45(3), 1997, pp 436–462.

[2] For an elaboration of these definitional issues, see R Williams, *Political Corruption in Africa*, Aldershot; Gower Publishing, 1987, pp 12–15.

[3] 'Corruption is above all a moral problem, immeasurable and imponderable'. R Wraith & E Simpkins, *Corruption in Developing Countires*, London: Allen and Unwin, 1963, p 17.

[4] J S Nye, 'Corruption: a cost–benefit analysis', *American Political Science Review*, LXI(2), 1967, p 419.

[5] Philp, *Defining Political Corruption*, p 444.

[6] N Leff, 'Economic development through corruption', in A J Heidenheimer (ed), *Political Corruption*, New York: Holt, Rinehart and Winston, 1970, p 510.

[7] S Rose-Ackerman, *Corruption*, New Haven, CT: Academic Press, 1978.

[8] R Klitgaard, *Controlling Corruption*, Berkeley, CA: University of California Press, 1988.

[9] G Tullock, *Rent Seeking*, Aldershot: Edward Elgar, 1993.

NEW CONCEPTS FOR OLD?

[10] The earliest example is E Banfield, 'Corruption as a feature of government organization', *Journal of Law and Economics*, 18, 1975, pp 587–605.

[11] Klitgaard, *Controlling Corruption*, p 24.

[12] M Johnston, 'The search for definitions: the vitality of politics and the issue of corruption', *International Social Science Journal*, 48(3), 1996, pp 321–335.

[13] For a useful critique of agency theory, see C Perrow, 'Economic theories of organization', in S Zukin & P Di Maggio (eds), *Structures of Capital: the Social Organization of the Economy*, Cambridge: Cambridge University Press, 1990, pp 121–152.

[14] P Hutchcroft, 'The politics of privilege: assesing the impact of rent, corruption and clientelism on Third World development', *Political Studies*, 45(3), 1997, p 639.

[15] For the consequences for a developed nation, see D Thompson, *Ethics in Congress: From Individual to Institutional Corruption*, Washington, DC, Brookings, 1995.

[16] Hutchcroft, 'The politics of privilege', p 640.

[28]

What Can Be Done about Entrenched Corruption?

Michael Johnston

Corruption is not a problem that "happens to" otherwise healthy societies, nor does it necessarily lead to social, political, or economic collapse. Rather, it is one of a constellation of development problems, endogenous to societies and often a symptom of deeper difficulties. In the most serious cases—entrenched political and bureaucratic corruption—it represents equilibrium, a tightly organized and internally stable system that creates and is sustained by insufficient political competition, slow and uneven economic growth, and a weak civil society. Countries can move from a high- to a low-corruption equilibrium, however, by guaranteeing civil liberties and basic economic rights, enhancing economic and political competition, nourishing a strong civil society, and adopting legal and institutional anticorruption measures. While difficult, such transitions do not require fully democratic systems or advanced economic markets. Aid partners can help fight corruption by judiciously applying conditions to aid and by using program design, delivery, and evaluation to encourage and reward necessary changes.

Corruption is often spoken of as a serious illness—a cancer or, as one official recently put it, "the AIDS of democracy"—spreading relentlessly from official to official and agency to agency, undermining institutions until the political system they represent collapses. In this view corruption must be eradicated so that the system can return to health or—better yet—corruption must be stopped before it starts.

The attraction of such metaphoric language is understandable. Corruption can be a frightening problem: governance and social conditions deteriorate, and venality seems to be everywhere. Moreover, the illness metaphor grabs headlines—no small consideration for a problem that once drew little serious attention. Still, it is misguided to think about corruption in this way. In some countries, such as Singapore and the United Kingdom, eras of entrenched corruption eventually gave way to honest politics

Michael Johnston is professor of political science at Colgate University.
Annual World Bank Conference on Development Economics 1997
©1998 The International Bank for Reconstruction and Development / THE WORLD BANK

and administration. Others, such as Germany and the United States, have been able to prosper through long periods of moderate corruption. Major scandals in Italy have led to positive changes in electoral and judicial institutions. In China an outbreak of corruption has accompanied rapid economic growth, while the political regime, though under considerable stress, has changed relatively little. Even more remarkable are countries like Bangladesh and Nigeria, which have experienced prolonged episodes of extreme corruption without ever reaching the point of total collapse. Corruption does not always undermine regimes and institutions: sometimes it does its harm by propping them up past the time when basic changes are needed, as in the former Soviet Union and its member states. Ironically, those countries now face new forms of corruption growing out of political and economic reform.

Illness metaphors likewise do not facilitate reform. Corruption is not something that "happens to" otherwise healthy societies: no country has ever been free of it, and those that reduce it still have other problems. Rather, corruption is one of a constellation of interrelated development problems endogenous to societies and the changes they experience. It is not only worrisome in its own right but also a symptom of deeper difficulties (Rose-Ackerman 1997). This view is supported by empirical analysis: corruption is associated with slow economic growth (Mauro 1997), reduced investment, feeble property and contract rights, ineffective institutions (Knack and Keefer 1995), limited social interaction and weak rule of law (Cooter 1997), poor economic competitiveness (Ades and di Tella 1994), deep ethnic divisions and conflicts (Easterly and Levine 1996), low popular participation in politics and weak protection of civil liberties (Isham, Kaufmann, and Pritchett 1995, 1996), low educational attainment (Mauro 1997), and closed economic and political systems (Elliott 1997). Thus while it will always be important to combat corruption, it is also crucial to understand the broader context in which it occurs and with which it interacts. For aid agencies this means not only combating abuses within programs but also using programs to fight corruption as a development problem.

The Most Difficult Cases

All countries have corruption, but in more developed systems reformers have several advantages. Corruption is usually the exception, not the rule. Anticorruption laws, agencies, and nongovernmental organizations and independent courts, auditors, and news media are generally in place. Anticorruption efforts receive political and popular support, and the basic vocabulary of reform—what is public or private, and which actions are considered abusive—is generally agreed. The government can draw on a fund of political capital—legitimacy, credibility of basic policies and the rule of law, established lines of accountability, and laws consistent with social norms—in its pursuit of reform. If these efforts fail, the government can be changed without destroying the political order (Przeworski and Limongi 1993).

In many of the countries that borrow from the World Bank, however, corruption is entrenched, embedded in a social setting that both shows its consequences and helps sustain it. Entrenched corruption can be political, bureaucratic, or both, though these variants differ and the relationships between them are important. Entrenched corruption is not necessarily more visible—watchdogs may be too weak to make an issue of it—or frequent. Indeed, it is often marked by a shift to fewer but significantly larger cases of self-dealing (Rose-Ackerman 1996). Nor is it necessarily disruptive: entrenched corruption is tenacious because it generates a kind of equilibrium.

Entrenched corruption is of particular concern to the World Bank because it grows out of and helps perpetuate the development problems—feeble and sporadic political competition, slow (or negative) and uneven economic development, and a risky investment climate—found in many of the poorest nations. In such a setting many citizens and investors see corruption as inevitable and reform as futile. There are few alternatives to dealing with corrupt officials on their terms. Those officials preserve that situation as long as they can, and few citizens or businesses are willing or able to confront them directly. Entrenched corruption diverts development resources and saps the political and social vitality societies need to use aid effectively. Moreover, entrenched corruption resists many of the institutional and civil service reforms commonly deployed in more advanced nations. For all these reasons it is a particularly challenging worst-case scenario: if we are serious about corruption as an aid and development issue, we must confront it in countries where the odds of reform seem least favorable. It is in such cases that corruption does the most to keep poor nations poor.

While entrenched corruption is one kind of equilibrium, it is possible to move to other, lower-corruption equilibria. Analyzing corruption in terms of multiple equilibria is not new (Rose-Ackerman 1996, 1997). But my approach differs in scope— I suggest that we can produce, and institutionalize, such a transition "from without," by changing the environment in which corruption is embedded—and emphasizes political as well as economic and legal reforms. While the reform scenario outlined here has never been pursued in its entirety in any one country, it is based on the kinds of changes that helped shift some of today's low-corruption societies out of "corruption traps."

Entrenched Corruption and Its Social Settings

Entrenched corruption, far from being the endgame of a long slide into chaos, is well organized and embedded in a political and economic context that both reveals its effects and helps sustain it. At times these extended aspects of the problem—such as extended clientelism and the dependency it can foster—are as harmful to development as the corrupt actions themselves. Thus entrenched corruption is best thought of as an equilibrium—or, to borrow a less strict term from complexity theory, as a "settling point"—an understanding of which can help explain its origins and tenacity. But it is not the only possible equilibrium: by altering the political and economic environment it is possible to shift toward low-corruption, higher-growth equilibria that benefit from and help sustain accountable politics and administration. Aid agencies are well placed to help with this process, using their resources, staff, and knowledge of the countries in question.

Although political and bureaucratic corruption differ, I consider both entrenched if they are pervasive, organized, and monopolistic. *Pervasive* means that corruption is so common—throughout an entire country or subunit—that there are few practical alternatives to dealing with corrupt officials. This does not necessarily mean that every citizen encounters corruption every day; indeed, as corruption becomes entrenched the most significant abuses often shift upward to elite levels. Moreover, the perception that corruption is pervasive may be as much a matter of expectations as a matter of fact—expectations possibly cultivated by political and bureaucratic middlemen with a stake in maintaining public dependence on their services (Oldenburg 1987; Sacks 1976). Still, corruption that is pervasive is no longer an exception to the political or administrative norm.

Organized corruption involves internal coordination, shared knowledge, and a vertical exchange of benefits. It facilitates (and, in its structure, reflects) an internal economy linking principals and agents. Principals provide protection, make major decisions, control agents' discretion and powers, and confer or withhold shares of the take. Political or bureaucratic agents pay for their spoils through loyal support— by rigging the count at the neighborhood polling station, for example, or by providing services to clients in exchange for payments to be shared with the principals. Organized corruption closes off clients' alternatives, giving the organization more leverage. It creates a network of operatives sharing not only rewards but also risks; thus operatives have a stake in keeping corruption hidden, increasing its proceeds, and freezing out critics and noncorrupt agents and clients. Well-organized corruption is often a sign that political opposition, bureaucratic checks and balances, and private economic alternatives have been weak for some time.

Monopolistic means that corruption faces no meaningful political opposition or economic competition, making it harder to eradicate and allowing corrupt operatives to generate maximum benefits over a long period. Officials enjoying a monopoly on corruption can deliver important benefits in exchange for large payments from major economic interests, who have few alternatives to engaging in corruption on the officials' terms. The monopoly dimension of entrenched corruption is complex, differing between the political and bureaucratic realms and potentially creating instabilities.

These three features of entrenched corruption—pervasiveness, organization, and monopolistic control—are not necessarily related: some corruption is pervasive without being organized, monopolistic without being pervasive, and so on. But when the three characteristics combine—when corrupt officials extend their activities throughout a jurisdiction, organize their practices, and drive out their political or bureaucratic competitors—corruption is especially damaging. Moreover, it creates an equilibrium that is difficult to eradicate, particularly if only administrative and personnel remedies are used.

Entrenched Political Corruption

No example illustrates all these ideas with perfect clarity. Still, when mass politics and policymaking are affected by corruption—including bribery, extortion, election fraud, abusive patronage, and official intimidation of opposition groups—the effects can be classified according to corruption's degree of entrenchment (table 1).

When political corruption is entrenched, political activity is dominated by a monopolistic organization or faction that maintains its power in part through corruption and reaps large rewards from it. Haiti's Tonton Macoute, with its mix of violence and intimidation, is one example. Political machines—found at various times in U.S. cities and elsewhere—are another (Scott 1972; Chubb 1981; Theobald 1992). When the leaders of such organizations have effectively eliminated their competitors, they can extract monopoly rents from their official roles and functions without fear of political reprisal.

Where many factions compete for power, it is difficult to build and maintain a disciplined following: supporters have many political alternatives, and competitors may buy them off. Leaders must bribe their supporters and tolerate disloyalty and suboptimal political support. Meanwhile, their chances of winning lasting power, and therefore their leverage for extracting rents, are small. Discipline can be tighter in a political oligopoly because disgruntled followers have fewer political alternatives. But organizational maintenance will still draw off significant resources, and leaders, facing fewer but better-organized competitors, may still find power difficult to win and to hold.

A political monopoly, however, means that dealing with the organization's leadership, on its terms, is the only political game in town. Leaders can extract monopoly rents, while supporters must work long and hard before seeing any but the most trivial rewards. The focus of corruption shifts from broadly based petty patronage toward fewer but much larger deals at the top: machine leaders demand large payments in exchange for utility franchises and construction contracts, for example, while those seeking such benefits have no reason to believe that the next election will put anyone else in office. Such organizations are not entirely stable, however: leaders face internal conflicts for which patronage or harsh political discipline are awkward remedies, and they may distribute rewards in counterproductive ways or draw off too many resources for personal enrichment (Johnston 1979). Monopoly rents can theoretically rise to infinity, choking off economic activity (Shleifer and Vishny 1993) and turning those who must pay into potential enemies.

Still, the ability of such organizations to close off political alternatives means that their corrupt influence can extend deep into government and society. The leadership not only can politicize the bureaucracy; through arbitrary policies and regulations it can also keep economic growth tightly controlled and uneven. Rent-producing sec-

Table 1. Degrees of Entrenchment of Political Corruption

Is political corruption	1	2	3	4
Pervasive?	No	Yes	Yes	Yes
Vertically organized?	No	No	Yes	Yes
Monopolistic?	No	No	No	Yes

Source: Based on Sherman 1974.

tors may be allowed to grow in order to channel more wealth to corrupt elites, while overall growth is held down to maintain mass dependence on political favors—keeping the costs of political discipline low—and to protect politically favored enterprises from competition. Monopoly political organizations will also fight potential competitors for the loyalties of the public even when the competitors are not seeking official power. Many U.S. political machines, for example, were hostile to the settlement-house movement, which offered the poor aid without a political price tag, and to the early stirrings of labor unions (Rosenbaum 1973). Surveys of African-American community leaders in the late 1960s found that they were much less independent and critical in their political views in Philadelphia, a machine city, than in Detroit, a city without a machine tradition (Webman 1973).

Meanwhile, those harmed by entrenched corruption are more likely to adapt to it than combat it. Alam (1995) identifies three kinds of "countervailing actions" that losers from corruption might take: evasive actions, to reduce dependence on corrupt officials (relocating, finding alternative goods, or forgoing goods altogether); direct actions, to raise the cost or risk of corruption to officials (protest, political action, complaints to oversight bodies, or violence); and illicit actions, to fight corruption with corruption. Where corrupt organizations have eliminated political competition and reduced economic alternatives—and particularly where they protect their monopoly using intimidation or violence—direct action is risky. Evasive and illicit responses are more attractive but will do little to reduce corruption or create effective opposition to it.

Entrenched Bureaucratic Corruption

The situation for corrupt bureaucrats is somewhat different. Most do not face full-blown competition from other governments or agencies performing identical functions (partial exceptions include some over-the-counter services such as passport issuance and a state enterprise that competes with privatized enterprises). Several agencies might deal with one sector of the economy, but in specialized ways: one might regulate working conditions, another inspect products, and yet another collect taxes. These agencies usually cannot abolish one another or drive each other out of the corruption business. But they can collude, creating lasting and lucrative corruption networks that feed on and help sustain economic and political dependence (table 2).

Where bureaucratic corruption is not pervasive, some officials may take bribes as opportunity allows. Most do not, however, nor do they systematically seek them out. Indeed, many deals are initiated by private individuals, such as motorists seeking to avoid fines. Payments, and the discretion they buy, are likely to be modest. By contrast, corruption is pervasive when it occurs (or is perceived as occurring) more often than not. More members of the public may offer payments, and individual functionaries or small groups may seek out bribes and practice extortion on a regular basis. They may share the take and perform specialized roles ("bagman," "enforcer," accountant), but what is taken at the street level or at the front counter stays there. Agents do not share with principals, and rents are likely to be moderate.

Table 2. Degrees of Entrenchment of Bureaucratic Corruption

Is bureaucratic corruption	*1*	*2*	*3*	*4*
Pervasive within an agency?	No	Yes	Yes	Yes
Vertically organized?	No	No	Yes	Yes
Horizontally coordinated with other agencies?	No	No	No	Yes

Source: Based on Sherman 1974.

Vertically organized bureaucratic corruption, however, is a significant step toward entrenchment. Here a portion of the agents' take is shared with principals. This may begin as protection payments to superiors, but it can evolve into a condition of employment (Rose-Ackerman 1996). Emphasis also shifts from "corruption without theft" to "corruption with theft" (Shleifer and Vishny 1993). In the first case agents keep a side payment but pass the full nominal price of a good (say, a license fee) on to the public treasury. In the second case agents keep some or all of the fee and the treasury receives little or nothing. Low-level agents who do not enjoy protection will find corruption without theft easier to conceal or will at least keep theft within limits to avoid notice. But with vertical organization, corruption with theft grows rapidly, both because of the increasing number of claimants to the take and because of the official protection that corruption enjoys. Indeed, where bureaucrats' salaries are unrelated to the cost of living, organized corruption with theft may be a matter of survival. But barring close integration of bureaucratic and political corruption (see below), theft is still unlikely to be total: for political reasons, tax collectors must generate some revenue and police must make some arrests.

Specialization can be a source of instability in pervasive, vertically organized bureaucratic corruption. If many agencies with specialized functions can extract monopoly rents—theoretically, without upper limits—from the same industry, they can kill off the source of bribes. A business might relocate or close, or shippers might move to another route or port—examples of Alam's (1995) evasive actions. As a result rents would collapse. But if agencies coordinate corruption among bureaucratic functions or levels of government, creating a joint monopoly instead of independent monopolies, the result could be smaller individual payments, but a much larger take over time:

> A helpful analogy is to tollbooths on a road. The joint monopoly situation corresponds to the case of one toll that gives the payer the right to use the entire road. The independent monopolists solution means that different towns through which the road passes independently erect their own tollbooths and charge their own tolls. The volume of traffic and aggregate toll collections fall. In fact, they fall to zero when any party can erect its own tollbooth on this road. The competitive case corresponds to multiple booths competing with each other for the right to collect the toll, or alternatively to the case of multiple roads. In this case, the volume of traffic is obviously the highest, and toll collections the lowest. (Shleifer and Vishny 1993, p. 608)

Independent monopolies can persist if one agency, such as the police, deals with many economic activities, or if a business cannot easily move or is itself a monopoly. But pervasive, organized, and coordinated corruption is stable and difficult to uproot. As with monopoly political corruption, opportunities for large, high-level deals grow, and coordinated bureaucratic harassment and selective law enforcement can be used to pressure those who are reluctant to pay. Unless political leaders send credible signals that critics of corruption will be protected and supported, direct countervailing action will be rare. In this way corrupt bureaucrats extend their influence outward into society, creating an unfavorable economic and investment climate whose shortage of alternative opportunities can further solidify their power.

A Low-Corruption Equilibrium

Entrenched corruption is persistent and difficult to combat not only because of its inner workings but also because it is embedded in a wider political and economic environment that helps sustain it as an equilibrium. Can this environment be altered to create incentives for officials to reduce corruption and for groups in society to combat it and begin to move toward a low-corruption equilibrium? Yes—and international aid, trade, and political organizations can help. Reform need not rely on virtue alone, but can offer real rewards and incentives of its own (which, as George Washington Plunkitt would observe, is essential): in a changed political and economic setting many of the interests now engaged in entrenched corruption can be enlisted to help fight it.

Reformers have more options in countries where corruption is less entrenched. In these countries resistance to corruption is based not just on fear of punishment but also on legitimate norms and traditions that have evolved over time and are shared by contending political and economic interests—interests that help hold the state and private actors in check. Political and economic opportunities are sufficiently plentiful that there is less need to use wealth to buy political power or to use power to extract wealth (Huntington 1968; Johnston 1997). The political officials who oversee bureaucrats know that they can lose power because of corruption or ineffective policies. Supervision from above, scrutiny from without, and structural checks and balances mean that individual officials or small groups do not possess monopoly discretion and find it difficult to organize and coordinate corruption on a large scale. The result is a different sort of equilibrium: corruption may occur, but it is kept within limits and does not become entrenched. This is not the only possible low-corruption scenario: tight political control, as in Singapore and Pinochet's Chile, is the basis of others. But the situation sketched out above is more desirable on political and social grounds and is more feasible in countries larger than city-states.

Moving between Equilibria

Variations on the low-corruption equilibrium can be found in many politically and economically advanced parts of the world—Canada, New Zealand, Scandinavia—

and often reflect long processes of political and economic contention that brought past periods of extensive corruption to a close. There is no quick recipe for this transition, and it will always require supporting legal and institutional reforms. But it is a manageable transition: starting it does not require wholly democratic politics or an advanced market economy, and aid partners can help by adopting policies that change the political and economic setting of entrenched corruption. The goal is to encourage developments that undermine the monopolies and organization of entrenched corruption while strengthening the forces that help sustain low-corruption equilibria. Stronger political and economic competition can increase accountability, open up alternatives to dealing with corrupt networks, and create incentives for political leaders to fight corruption. Reduced corruption can encourage economic growth, further broadening economic alternatives and strengthening interests in civil society while weakening the political and bureaucratic leverage underlying entrenched corruption. Over time this virtuous circle of development fosters a low-corruption equilibrium and entrenches reform, not corruption, in the broader political and economic system (figure 1).

As noted, this process does not require the establishment of a fully institutionalized democracy. Meaningful civil liberties are a good starting point (Isham, Kaufmann, and Pritchett 1995, 1996). An independent press, opposition groups, and an active civil society are more likely to develop if they can express themselves publicly and are free from intimidation. Civil liberties are also essential if the losers from corruption are to confront it in direct, rather than evasive or illicit, ways (Alam 1995).

On the economic side credible property and contract rights, which in the short to medium term help increase investment and weaken incentives to extract short-term profits (Keefer 1996), are a first step analogous to meaningful civil liberties. The economic alternatives that this move would generate would make it easier for firms, investors, and individuals to avoid corrupt officials and harder for officials to keep such groups dependent on their favors. The move to such rights would also, over time, strengthen civil society and social interaction. Here again a full transition

Figure 1. Transition to a Low-Corruption Equilibrium: Elements and Linkages

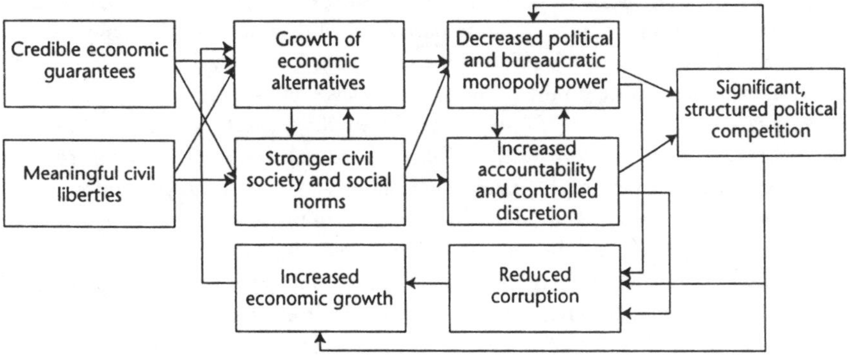

to prosperity is not essential: aid for emerging sectors of the economy and for growth in a country's most deprived regions (admittedly complicated tasks) can create new economic opportunities outside of established corrupt networks and empower new political constituencies.

Broadened political alternatives also can weaken corrupt monopolies. A first step is to establish independent arenas in which appeals against corruption and other abuses can be filed—mainly the courts but also investigative agencies, inspectors general, and ombudsmen open to public complaints and scrutiny. The goal is to encourage, protect, and follow through on direct countervailing actions, thus strengthening checks and balances. The second, longer-term task is to foster significant and institutionalized political competition, creating opportunities for political forces to win or lose power through open, public processes. Competition is beneficial even if the main political groups do not represent all citizens. England's seventeenth-century parliaments, for example, were strikingly unrepresentative by modern standards, yet they played major roles in resisting the abuses of royal patronage both before and after the civil wars (Peck 1990). Competition must be meaningful but structured: one party offers no choice, but twenty or thirty parties are unlikely to have agendas much broader than the personal interests of their leaders or to win enough power to govern effectively. Indeed, small and numerous parties are more likely to indulge in corruption, both for self-enrichment and to build a political following.

An important distinction between political competition and insecurity applies here. Many scholars have noted that political insecurity leads to voracious corruption, since officials do not know how much longer their power will last (Knack and Keefer 1995; Scott 1972). Why should the threat of losing power through political competition be any different? The answer lies in the way in which power is lost and won, and in what happens next. Insecurity—the threat of a coup, for example—means that the identity and strength of one's opponents, and their timing and tactics, may be difficult to know or predict. Uncertain timing is of particular importance because it creates an incentive to enrich oneself as quickly as possible. The issues and grievances involved are likely to be personal or factional and thus are resistant to negotiation or compromise because they are aimed at overall dominance. When power is lost, it is lost altogether and permanently: rather than remaining as an opposition group or coalition partner, the losers may be killed, imprisoned, or exiled. Thus the contest is not just for spoils, but for survival.

Political competition, on the other hand, involves known opponents, tactics, and timing. The broad outlines of competitors' strengths, appeals, and support are discernible, and competition, if well institutionalized, takes place within agreed rules and social norms. Many of the main issues can be addressed through routine policy, are open to compromise, and can be made matters of public commitment—facts that encourage accountability and careful political oversight of policy formation and implementation. While the winners obtain agreed powers for a limited period, the losers remain to fight another day—an incentive in itself to refrain from last-minute looting of the public purse. Unlike political insecurity, political competition creates incentives to avoid rather than to indulge in corruption. But such competition is a matter of contending forces, not just institutional architecture: where opposition is weak, elected elites engage in entrenched corruption. The point is that orderly competition can undermine political monopolies and create incentives to control corruption.

Interconnections between Bureaucratic Corruption and Political Corruption

Political corruption and bureaucratic corruption can flourish in each other's absence. France, for example, experiences political corruption but retains a highly professional bureaucracy. In Poland, by contrast, former Communist Party figures have created personal bureaucratic fiefdoms, while political activity is open and competitive. But in most cases the two types of corruption coexist and may be interlinked. Political corruption can intrude into the bureaucracy, as when a police department or an inspectorate is staffed with patronage appointees. And bureaucratic corruption can become a factor in politics, as when agencies grant favors to the politically connected to maintain cover for their own corruption. Different connections between political and bureaucratic corruption produce different patterns of extended clientelism in society, as Khan (1997) argues in his comparison of countries in South and Southeast Asia.

The more serious either type of corruption becomes, the less likely it is to exist independently. An interlocked system of entrenched bureaucratic and political corruption is a powerful force: rents can be coordinated and shared across both realms, while monopoly power allows politicians to preempt opposition. Economic policies can maximize corruption while curtailing competition. There will be few opportunities for direct countervailing actions, and illicit responses will require the indulgence of corrupt officials (Alam 1995). Indeed, the functional distinction between political and bureaucratic corruption might all but disappear.

China comes close to this situation: official and market activities, roles, and resources are tightly interlocked—and corruption flourishes—in a large gray area neither wholly public nor wholly private. The same agency or official may deal in consumer goods, access to bureaucratically controlled commodities, and Party preferments, often in collusion with private entrepreneurs (Hao and Johnston 1995; Solinger 1992). Public resentment runs deep, and officially orchestrated anticorruption campaigns are common. But attempts to confront the issue directly are confined to small groups of dissidents willing to criticize the political order (Johnston and Hao 1995).

In other cases political leaders may have the formal duty and power to confront bureaucratic corruption but do so only in response to compelling problems or crises. McCubbins and Schwartz (1984) term this "fire alarm" oversight and compare it with a continuing "police patrol" approach. Despite their argument that the fire alarm model is not altogether ineffective, unsystematic oversight after the fact is an inadequate safeguard. If networks are sufficiently organized and coordinated, corrupt bureaucrats can respond by covering up their dealings more effectively.

Whatever the model of oversight, political initiatives against bureaucratic corruption will depend on the balance of power between the two realms, and in this competition bureaucrats have significant advantages. In the absence of compelling domestic or international pressure, political leaders may tolerate bureaucratic corruption if it:

- Allows them to share in its spoils or if their position is weak or compromised.
- Benefits favored interests or helps buy off potential opponents.
- Provides enough income to bureaucrats to make tax increases (or the systematic collection of the taxes that are on the books) less necessary.
- Helps build support for political leaders' desired policies or cushions their impact.
- Moderates conflicts among bureaucratic factions, particularly if corruption cleanups seem likely to mobilize elite opposition.

Similarly, if reform seems likely to produce major economic disruption, as was arguably the case in the final decades of the Soviet Union, politicians may conclude that its immediate costs outweigh its prospective, long-term benefits.

Indeed, the first result of reforms that break up the organization or coordination of corrupt networks may be corruption that is more visible and disruptive than the entrenched practices had been. Or reforms could yield an independent monopolies situation (Shleifer and Vishny 1993) likely to be damaging to the economy. Would-be corruption fighters must be confident that reform efforts, economic growth, and their careers could survive such a crisis. On the other hand, political leaders who draw broadly legitimate mandates from institutionalized political competition will have reasons to fight bureaucratic corruption, and can do so from a stronger position. Other motives may reinforce this determination: politicians may act if bureaucratic corruption protects a hostile faction or makes the bureaucracy unresponsive and unaccountable. Also, as Rose-Ackerman (1996) points out, secure political leaders may find it advantageous to fight corruption as a way to increase economic growth.

Countering Bureaucratic Corruption

Once political leaders take on bureaucratic corruption, they must do several things. One problem is material: reforms will fail if bureaucrats are paid so little that they must steal in order to survive. But the salary problem is not easily addressed. Besley and McLaren (1993) show that the "reservation wage" for tax inspectors—the wage they would earn working in the private sector—is substantially higher than the "capitulation wage" that drives them to corruption. An "efficiency wage" comparable to what they earn from bribes would be even higher. An interim step might be to create a legal schedule of fees for services, payable by citizens directly to bureaucrats. These would raise pay, reward efficiency, and create accountability to the client. Such payments might be difficult to supervise and regulate, but enabling a number of officials to compete to provide a service, shifting their postings frequently, and monitoring for signs of collusion could help. Direct payments also would be more difficult for higher-level officials to tap into, both for logistical reasons and because agents who do not need high-level protection to collect payments will fight to protect their living wage.

Many of today's low-corruption countries passed through a phase when payment of direct fees to constables, inspectors, and tax and customs officials was not only common but was viewed as a reform (Johnston 1993)—an important step on the road to comprehensive, professional bureaucratic roles. Still, fee-for-service arrangements should be allowed only on a selective basis and only for routine bureaucratic functions. Rose-Ackerman (1996, p. 14) argues that the best candidates are "cases where corruption's only efficiency cost stems from its illegality." Fees for services can also be introduced through careful and honest privatization or by franchising various functions to officials or private bidders. This franchise approach could be modeled on seventeenth-century English "customs farmers," who paid large fees for the right to collect customs duties.

Political leaders will also need to attack the vertical organization and horizontal coordination of corruption. Increasing agencies' independence from one another and encouraging competition among them where possible will be important, though waste, duplication, and contradictory policies may result. Placing new agency managers and powerful inspectors general into each major agency and making them accountable to top political leaders might also be worthwhile, though this can encounter strong bureaucratic resistance. These new principals can reform relationships among agents and clients (Klitgaard 1988; Rose-Ackerman 1978), changing the monopoly-plus-discretion nexus and increasing accountability.

Attacking bureaucratic corruption is a task fraught with costs and dangers (Anechiarico and Jacobs 1996). But there are also many opportunities to use incentives analogous to those created by competition in the political arena. Bureaucrats' motivations are complex and critical to the question of political accountability (Gruber 1987). Most bureaucrats care about the functions they are supposed to perform; once assured of a living wage they will respond positively to changes that increase their effectiveness and provide clear evidence to them, and to the public, that administration is honest and accomplishes worthwhile social goals. Professional status, a sense of personal security, and meaningful autonomy with respect to illegitimate pressures from above and below are important as well. Klitgaard (1988) demonstrates the effectiveness of raising morale and status and (in some cultures) of shaming those engaged in corruption.

Performance-linked incentive schemes also must be carefully considered. Mookherjee (in this volume) argues that these schemes are often ineffective or even counterproductive. Klitgaard (1997), while acknowledging that circumstances in many developing countries are not favorable to performance-linked incentives, suggests that finding new ways to measure performance and making creative institutional adjustments can make such schemes more likely to succeed. This debate can hardly be resolved here, but careful analysis of and judicious experimentation with incentive schemes can teach political leaders and top officials about the origins of corruption and the prospects for reform, convey to bureaucrats (and their private clients) that their superiors are serious about corruption, and alleviate (at least) the worst "incentive traps" that leave many individuals with little alternative to corruption.

Finally, government officials and powers should be subject to checks and balances—separate routine powers or, in parliamentary systems where full separation is not feasible, independent courts, oversight bodies, and client advocates. If these agencies and the government in general are accessible by opposition politicians, journalists, and members of the public, then checks and balances will not only help fight corruption, they will also draw on powerful forces in society. Hong Kong's Independent Commission Against Corruption, for example, used its extensive legal and investigative powers and adopted innovative social strategies to significantly reduce corruption and alter public attitudes toward it (Clark 1985; Manion 1996).

The Role of Civil Society

The political and economic problems that corruption engenders seriously weaken civil society. Civil society has become a buzzword in recent years, and many claims on its behalf will require further research. But the concept dates back to de Tocqueville's ([1835] 1945 ed.) discussion of "intermediate institutions" in the United States in the 1830s and highlights important aspects of political life in low-corruption countries. Here I use it to refer to organizations and public activities between the level of individuals or families and the state. Organized, active groups in civil society can be a check on the state and on one another, as well as a basis for direct countervailing action. They are critical to accountability because "transparent" procedures mean little if there is no external monitoring: corrupt states abound in inspectors, commissions of inquiry, and record-keeping requirements that create and conceal corruption rather than reveal it, because no one outside the state can demand a meaningful accounting. Without a strong civil society to energize them, even a full set of formally democratic institutions will not produce accountable, responsive government.

A strong civil society also encourages and protects free social interaction. Cooter (1997) uses game theory to show that where people freely interact on a repeated basis, they are likely to form strong mutual expectations of conduct and legitimate social norms (see also Keefer 1996 and Milgrom and Roberts 1982). Surveys of popular conceptions of corruption suggest that most citizens judge public officials, as well as one another, by social norms learned in those everyday interactions (see data and bibliography in Johnston 1991). Moreover, where civil society is strong, a range of social groups—trade and professional associations, community groups—function as "law merchants" (Cooter 1997). They promulgate codes of good practice and can impose modest, but socially significant, anticorruption sanctions relatively quickly using a lower burden of proof than that required for criminal penalties. Particularly when it exists within a legitimate state, an active civil society can thus help form a network integrating legal and social norms—a comprehensive value system more likely to be obeyed than laws alone would be.

The transition to a low-corruption equilibrium takes time and requires sustained support. As noted, during its initial stages reform will likely produce an apparent surge in corruption, as formerly concealed practices come to light, elite consensus breaks down, whistleblowers and media investigators begin to speak, and organized corruption gives way to more fragmented and disruptive practices. But these are indicators of a breakdown of the old entrenched system. Sustained political leadership and international support are crucial during this phase. Over time, however, increased political and economic competition and alternatives, a stronger civil society, and improved government and economic performance should develop considerable synergy. There is no guarantee that the system will never revert to its old ways, but once a low-corruption equilibrium is attained, important political and economic interests will have a stake in sustaining the new situation.

Helping Countries Get There: The Role of Aid Partners

The above reform scenario is obviously an idealized account. If there were an easy or obvious way to control corruption, many nations would have done it already—though it is worth remembering that many of today's low-corruption countries overcame serious corruption through similar processes of political and economic development (Johnston 1993). Still, the question remains: What can international aid organizations do to make such transitions more likely and to get them over with in a matter of years, not generations?

Conditionality requirements have an obvious appeal, but they must be carefully conceived. Linking aid directly to reductions in corruption may produce short-term or cosmetic results, perhaps through repression or the manipulation of scandal. But this would be a step away from the enhanced economic and political competition and revival of civil society central to a low-corruption equilibrium. (Similarly, anti-corruption coups, even when sincerely aimed at the problem—as they almost never are—rarely reduce corruption on a lasting basis because they preempt political contention and weaken civil society.) Moreover, conditionality of this sort could lead to a situation in which few programs are funded or renewed, or in which conditions must routinely be waived, making them an empty gesture. Where conditionality links aid to processes, however—expansion of civil liberties, reform of institutions, and enhancement of political and economic competition—it may be considerably more beneficial, particularly when supported by technical assistance for implementing and monitoring those processes.

It is also possible to pursue reform through more positive incentives that encourage leaders to reduce corruption, weaken clients' acceptance of it, and strengthen the social forces supporting such changes. While the goal is a broad transition, the measures themselves must be applied selectively because of variations among countries and their corruption problems.

One factor that will differ is the balance between competition and institutionalization in a nation's economic and political system. The transition away from entrenched corruption will weaken political and bureaucratic links, in part because it is intended to do so. Moreover, the transition requires increased political contention and economic competition and entails a strengthening of interests and organizations in civil society. Where corruption has been entrenched, however, institutions and their links to society will likely be weak, as real power will have been held by corrupt networks behind the organizational facade. Even honest leaders may resist anticorruption strategies that risk greater political insecurity or that increase contention without also increasing the state's capacity to deal with it. For this reason my proposals are divided into the very rough categories of competition-enhancing and institution-enhancing measures. Some address both problems. Together they can attack the monopolies and weaken the organization underlying entrenched corruption while strengthening the institutions and social forces that would benefit from and help sustain a low-corruption equilibrium.

Competition-Enhancing Measures

As noted, meaningful civil liberties are the first political step toward the enhanced political and economic contention needed to break through entrenched corruption, and credible property and contract rights are the first economic step. Aid partners can make these changes criteria for program approval and renewal. Later, overall economic and political competition, with an emphasis on a vital civil society, could become additional criteria for aid and be included in project design, evaluation, and delivery.

Progress toward these goals can be measured by the treatment of the press and of dissidents, the openness and honesty of elections, the status of women and minorities, and the viability of trade and professional associations and other private bodies. On the economic side, aid agencies should reward secure property and contract rights, protection for small businesses, honest privatization (where appropriate), and policies encouraging the free movement of capital and resources and fostering transparency in banking, customs, and taxation. Moreover, allowing various segments of society to assess this process will contribute to a stronger civil society and counteract political and bureaucratic monopolies.

To ensure that aid agencies have continuing anticorruption leverage, they should impose such standards gradually, perhaps emphasizing them at the evaluation and renewal stages of programs rather than as criteria for original support. And at least for all but the slowest-reforming countries, trends should be considered more important than absolute levels of attainment, creating incentives to sustain positive change rather than requiring high thresholds that must be reached before aid can be given or renewed. The threshold approach would punish many of the countries suffering the worst ravages of corruption while playing into the hands of corrupt officials currently feeding off the status quo.

Increased political and economic competition and openness should also be major considerations in program design. Aid for emerging sectors of the economy and economic development in regions and for groups previously left behind are not only desirable but can also strengthen emerging political interests, economic alternatives, and social interaction. So too can microcredit initiatives at the community level. Literacy programs, particularly for women and girls and for peripheral regions and groups, can increase the demand for political participation and help individuals recognize, resist, and take action against corruption. Protection and encouragement for labor unions, trade and business associations, and other groups in civil society are also positive steps.

Requiring public consultation and participation in service delivery and securing guaranteed access for journalists and social organizations would also enhance accountability and transparency. In this regard the World Bank's recently revised procurement processes, including a greater emphasis on broad institutional assistance for all public procurement in borrower countries, are a welcome change; an additional, probably controversial, step would be to publish widely the results of project and procurement evaluations, thus making it easier for opposition groups to turn corruption problems into political issues or for governments to benefit politically from anticorruption successes.

Within the bureaucracy a competition-enhancing measure that could help break down organized, coordinated corruption is Transparency International's idea of "islands of integrity." Briefly, bidders on government contracts mutually undertake not to pay bribes—commitments that bidders back up by posting sizable bonds subject to forfeiture should violations occur. If bureaucrats engage in corruption (or keep silent) because they fear reprisals or because they see no point in honesty when everyone else is on the take, and if some firms pay up because they see no alternative, these "islands" might be useful, creating processes beyond the control of corrupt official networks. The potential difficulty, obviously, is one of follow-through. Without it, islands of integrity might become another way to cover up corruption, or at least to divert attention from it. Still, the approach has been implemented in Argentina and Panama. Close scrutiny of such cases will tell us much about creating alternatives to entrenched bureaucratic corruption.

Changes in the overall structure of administration and service delivery also can weaken monopolies. Federalism can have major benefits—opponents to political machines in U.S. cities often found support at the state level—though such a major constitutional change may not be feasible or desirable. Moreover, fragmented federalism can provide nooks and crannies for hiding or coordinating corruption. Decentralizing public agencies might be a better way to inhibit horizontal coordination. Similarly, jurisdictions at the same level could share or merge various bureaucratic functions, but in differing geographical patterns, inhibiting both coordination and vertical organization of corruption.

Institution-Enhancing Measures

Stronger institutions are required if greater openness and competition are to produce maximum benefits and minimal disruption, particularly during the early stages of anticorruption reforms. One essential step is improved and more systematic tax collection—a measure that helps create a predictable investment and economic climate and yields more revenue with which to upgrade official salaries. Much like fee-for-service arrangements, a better tax system can increase social demands for accountability and transparency. In some high-corruption countries real tax burdens are negligible for many. As a result the state is seen as an independent source of benefits to be plundered rather than as an institution using social resources to pursue common goals.

Greater emphasis on the rule of law is also important, because it replaces arbitrary personal power with predictable institutionalized authority and defines the ways state and society can (and cannot) interact. Enforcing the rule of law requires a strong, independent judiciary, investigative and auditing bodies, and legitimate paths of access between state and society. Where the rule of law is weak, even states with great power, such as China, can have serious problems of state capacity and governance.

Fee-for-service arrangements can increase accountability while bringing bureaucrats nearer to a real living wage, perhaps enabling them to resist corruption. Privatization that shifts commercial activities, such as a national airline, into the private sector can reduce the exposure of the public bureaucracy to market pressures. Greater institutionalization of bureaucracies and a stronger rule of law help build more secure, predictable, and autonomous economic markets. Such an environment enables and encourages individuals and firms to plan for the long term and renders corruption an expensive, unreliable, and ultimately unnecessary form of influence. Thus the same private economic motives that encourage corruption in one setting discourage it in another.

Institutionalized political competition is also important. Parliaments and electoral systems merit particular scrutiny. Do they encourage and reward competition, make public the sources and uses of funds, and offer an effective way of expressing political demands and support? Do elections offer real choices, building a broad base of interests into the legislative process while producing decisive results? Do campaign finance laws protect the political process from international manipulation while allowing new interests and groups to enter politics without unduly splintering government and parliamentary bodies? Do parliamentary processes exacerbate ethnic divisions or encourage groups to work together? What works well in one country may be counterproductive in another; still, consider cases such as Italy, where in the wake of the Mani Puliti and Tangentopoli scandals a fragmented proportional representation system was replaced by one awarding half the parliamentary seats on a first-past-the-post basis. The goal was to replace the old elite stalemate (which had tolerated and concealed corruption for years) with increased political competition by offering fewer but more broadly supported parties the chance to gain or lose real power. Campaign financing and representation systems should be made explicit parts of governance criteria but must be backed up by extensive technical assistance and research.

Perhaps, too, it is time to rethink governance itself. The World Bank (1992, p. 3) has defined governance as "the manner in which power is exercised in the management of a country's economic and social resources for development." There is little to quarrel with here, but the concept could also include the strength of civil society, the vitality of political and economic competition, the security of civil liberties and basic economic guarantees, and the capacity of the system to foster and cope with the changes implied by the notion of sustainable development. Bräutigam (1992), for example, identifies three dimensions of governance: accountability, openness and transparency, and predictability and the rule of law. The Organisation for Economic Co-operation and Development (OECD 1995, p. 14) likewise proposes three features of governance: "the form of political regime; the processes by which authority is exercised in the management of a country's economic and social resources; and the capacity of government to formulate and implement policies and discharge government functions."

A broader definition of governance emphasizing the expansion of freely available political and economic alternatives, a balance between the accessibility of government institutions and the autonomy that enables them to govern (Johnston 1997), and well-institutionalized paths of access and demarcations between government and market forces could shift the emphasis in both aid and governance away from projects and toward a broader-gauged assessment of a country's capacity for development. One such definition of governance might be the degree of institutionalization and openness of the political and economic processes through which social development decisions are made; doubtless better ones can be devised. The point is to think of governance in ways that help us increase the precision and internal coordination of aid programs, and to encourage and reward the kinds of changes that historically helped reduce corruption in many countries.

Conclusion

It is worth emphasizing again that corruption is just one of many interrelated problems—one that does not account for all that is wrong or overwhelm all that may be right in a developing country. And again, the transitions envisioned here are medium to long term in nature and will involve many reversals, just as was the case in many of today's low-corruption countries. Short-term increases in corruption, and in more visible and disruptive varieties of it, may be unavoidable. A balance between institutionalization and competition at all points in the process is unlikely. The energies and dedication of anticorruption watchdogs will always be valuable, and the amount of corruption in any society will never be zero—nor would that be an optimal outcome (Klitgaard 1988). Still, an understanding of corruption as a problem endogenous to development, of what sustains it where it is entrenched, and of the forces that inhibit it where it is low may show us how the political and economic interests that sustain corruption can be used to fight it. To that end extensive research on different types of corruption and on their origins and effects in different sorts of societies might be an excellent investment for any agency concerned with development.

These findings offer major challenges and opportunities for the World Bank and other aid agencies—challenges that are political, economic, and administrative in nature. Sustainable reductions in corruption require solidifying political interests and competition, as well as steadfast leadership to see a country through the rocky transition from a high- to a low-corruption equilibrium. Policies encouraging these developments and their practical consequences for the countries concerned will never be politically neutral: some interests, leaders, and followers will gain considerably, while others will lose.

Is the World Bank, by virtue of the restrictions on political involvement laid out in its Articles of Agreement, closed out of this arena? Not if we think in terms of the capacity-oriented definition of governance proposed above. Indeed, the Articles, as well as the broader idea of faithful stewardship of development resources, require the Bank to consider and, where possible, to enhance the political aspects of countries' capacity to use those resources. The case becomes clearer if we think of politics not as the day-to-day contention among elites and their followers but as a fundamental set of competitive processes just as essential to building development capacity as the growth of market economics. Prohibitions against direct partisan involvement and against political favoritism in Bank programs remain eminently sensible and in no way contradict the reform strategy I have proposed. That strategy involves using aid to enable political groups and processes, to provide mutual paths of access between state and society as well as an outlet for social reactions to the stresses of change, and to encourage the institutionalization of political and economic competition in ways that are likely to make Bank programs more effective.

In such efforts the Bank possesses important resources. These include not just its capital and its unique role as a global development agency, but also its continuing presence in developing countries, its regulations, and its personnel. Most of the reforms discussed here—in political and economic processes, civil society, and the quality of leadership, institutions, and administration—have long been Bank concerns. Similarly, a number of administrative strategies, such as procurement controls and the threat of canceling projects, have always been at hand. The Bank's recent emphasis on corruption is welcome, and the debate it is certain to encourage offers an important opportunity to reexamine familiar elements of policy in terms of their impact on corruption, to use anticorruption sanctions more aggressively, and to combine old and new ideas into a comprehensive policy on corruption. The Bank can pursue such a policy on an international and regional basis—avoiding singling out specific nations for disgrace while encouraging intraregional cooperation—and can facilitate greater integration between countries pursuing genuine reform and their international trade partners.

Looked at this way, corruption is not just a development problem but a central issue in development policy; not a discrete problem with self-contained solutions but an endogenous process that must be attacked using comprehensive strategies. Many countries have overcome serious corruption in the past; those experiencing entrenched corruption today can do much to alleviate it. The task begins by understanding not only corruption but also how it shapes and can be sustained by the broader social and economic environment.

References

Ades, Alberto, and Rafael di Tella. 1994. "Competition and Corruption." Working paper. Oxford University, Institute of Economics and Statistics.

Alam, M.S. 1995. "A Theory of Limits on Corruption and Some Applications." *Kyklos* 48 (3): 419–35.

Anechiarico, Frank, and James B. Jacobs. 1996. *The Pursuit of Absolute Integrity.* Chicago: University of Chicago Press.

Besley, Timothy, and John McLaren. 1993. "Taxes and Bribery: The Role of Wage Incentives." *The Economic Journal* 103 (January): 119–41.

Bräutigam, Deborah. 1992. "Governance, Economy, and Foreign Aid." *Studies in Comparative International Development* 27 (3): 3–25.

Chubb, Judith. 1981. "The Social Bases of an Urban Political Machine: The Christian Democrat Party in Palermo." In Shmuel N. Eisenstadt and Rene Lemarchand, eds., *Political Clientelism, Patronage and Development.* London: Sage.

Clark, David. 1985. "Dirigisme in an Asian City-State: Hong Kong's ICAC." Paper presented at the Thirteenth World Congress of the International Political Science Association, 12 July, Paris.

Cooter, Robert D. 1997. "The Rule of State Law and the Rule-of-Law State: Economic Analysis of the Legal Foundations of Development." In Michael Bruno and Boris Pleskovic, eds., *Annual World Bank Conference on Development Economics 1996.* Washington, D.C.: World Bank.

de Tocqueville, Alexis. 1945. *Democracy in America.* New York: Alfred A. Knopf.

Easterly, William, and Ross Levine. 1996. "Africa's Growth Tragedy: Policies and Ethnic Divisions." World Bank, Policy Research Department, Macroeconomics and Growth Division, Washington, D.C.

Elliott, Kimberly A. 1997. "Corruption as a Global Policy Problem: Overview and Recommendations." In Kimberly A. Elliott, ed., *Corruption and the Global Economy.* Washington, D.C.: Institute for International Economics.

Gruber, Judith E. 1987. *Controlling Bureaucracies: Dilemmas in Democratic Governance.* Berkeley: University of California Press.

Hao, Yufan, and Michael Johnston. 1995. "Reform at the Crossroads: An Analysis of Chinese Corruption." *Asian Perspective* 19 (1): 117–49.

Huntington, Samuel P. 1968. *Political Order in Changing Societies.* New Haven, Conn.: Yale University Press.

Isham, Jonathan, Daniel Kaufmann, and Lant Pritchett. 1995. "Governance and Returns on Investment: An Empirical Investigation." Policy Research Working Paper 1550. World Bank, Policy Research Department, Poverty and Human Resources Division, Washington, D.C.

———. 1996. "Civil Liberties, Democracy, and the Performance of Government Projects." World Bank, Policy Research Department, Poverty and Human Resources Division, Washington, D.C.

Johnston, Michael. 1979. "Patrons and Clients, Jobs and Machines: A Case Study of the Uses of Patronage." *American Political Science Review* 73 (2): 385–98.

———. 1991. "Right and Wrong in British Politics: 'Fits of Morality' in Comparative Perspective." *Polity* 24 (1): 1–25.

———. 1993. "Political Corruption: Historical Conflict and the Rise of Standards." In Larry Diamond and Marc F. Plattner, eds., *The Global Resurgence of Democracy.* Baltimore, Md.: The Johns Hopkins University Press.

———. 1997. "Public Officials, Private Interests, and Sustainable Democracy: Connections between Politics and Corruption." In Kimberly A. Elliott, ed., *Corruption and the Global Economy.* Washington, D.C.: Institute for International Economics.

Johnston, Michael, and Yufan Hao. 1995. "China's Surge of Corruption." *Journal of Democracy* 6 (4): 80–94.

Keefer, Philip. 1996. "Protection against a Capricious State: French Investment and Spanish Railroads, 1845–1875." *Journal of Economic History* 56 (1): 170–92.

Khan, Mushtaq. 1997. "Corruption in South Asia: Patterns of Development and Change." Paper presented at a workshop on corruption and development sponsored by the University of Sussex's Institute of Development Studies, 6 May, Brighton.

Klitgaard, Robert. 1988. *Controlling Corruption.* Berkeley: University of California Press.

———. 1997. "Information and Incentives in Institutional Reform." In Christopher Clague, ed., *Institutions and Economic Development*. Baltimore, Md.: The Johns Hopkins University Press.

Knack, Stephen, and Philip Keefer. 1995. "Institutions and Economic Performance: Cross-Country Tests Using Alternative Institutional Measures." *Economics and Politics* 7 (3): 207–27.

Manion, Melanie. 1996. "Policy Instruments and Political Context: Transforming a Culture of Corruption in Hong Kong." Paper presented at the annual meeting of the Association for Asian Studies, 11–14 April, Honolulu.

Mauro, Paolo. 1997. "The Effects of Corruption on Growth, Investment, and Government Expenditure: A Cross-Country Analysis." In Kimberly A. Elliott, ed., *Corruption and the Global Economy*. Washington, D.C.: Institute for International Economics.

McCubbins, Matthew D., and T. Schwartz. 1984. "Congressional Oversight Overlooked: Police Patrols vs. Fire Alarms." *American Journal of Political Science* 28 (1): 165–79.

Milgrom, Paul, and John Roberts. 1982. "Predations, Reputation, and Entry Deterrence." *Journal of Economic Theory* 27 (2): 280–312.

OECD (Organisation for Economic Co-operation and Development). 1995. *Participatory Development and Good Governance*. Paris.

Oldenburg, Philip. 1987. "Middlemen in Third-World Corruption: Implications of an Indian Case." *World Politics* 39 (4): 508–35.

Peck, Linda Levy. 1990. *Court Patronage and Corruption in Early Stuart England*. Boston: Unwin Hyman.

Przeworski, Adam, and Fernando Limongi. 1993. "Political Regimes and Economic Growth." *Journal of Economic Literature* 7 (3): 51–69.

Rose-Ackerman, Susan. 1978. *Corruption: A Study in Political Economy*. New York: Academic Press.

———. 1996. "When Is Corruption Harmful?" Background paper to *World Development Report 1996: From Plan to Market*. World Bank, Washington, D.C.

———. 1997. "The Political Economy of Corruption." In Kimberly A. Elliott, ed., *Corruption and the Global Economy*. Washington, D.C.: Institute for International Economics.

Rosenbaum, Alan. 1973. "Machine Politics, Class Interest, and the Urban Poor." Paper delivered at the annual meeting of the American Political Science Association, 4–8 September, New Orleans.

Sacks, Paul Martin. 1976. *The Donegal Mafia: An Irish Political Machine*. New Haven, Conn.: Yale University Press.

Scott, James C. 1972. *Comparative Political Corruption*. Englewood Cliffs, N.J.: Prentice-Hall.

Shefter, Martin. 1976. "The Emergence of the Political Machine: An Alternative View." In Willis D. Hawley, ed., *Theoretical Perspectives on Urban Politics*. Englewood Cliffs, N.J.: Prentice-Hall.

Sherman, Lawrence W. 1974. *Police Corruption: A Sociological Perspective*. New York: Doubleday.

Shleifer, Andrei, and Robert W. Vishny. 1993. "Corruption." *Quarterly Journal of Economics* 108 (3): 599–617.

Solinger, Dorothy J. 1992. "Urban Entrepreneurs and the State: The Merger of State and Society." In Arthur Rosenbaum, ed., *State and Society in China: The Consequences of Reform*. Boulder, Colo.: Westview.

Theobald, Robin. 1992. "On the Survival of Patronage in Developed Societies." *Archives Européenne de Sociologie* 33 (1): 183–91.

Webman, Jerry A. 1973. "Political Institutions and Political Leadership: Black Politics in Philadelphia and Detroit." Yale University, Department of Political Science, New Haven, Conn.

World Bank. 1992. *Governance and Development*. Washington, D.C.

Name Index

À Becket, T. 177, 283
Achebe, C. 35–6, 41, 44, 507
Aderinwale, A. 412
Ades, A. 296, 326, 335, 343, 348, 354, 461, 522
Agnew, S. 314
Alam, M.S. 196, 445, 526–7, 529, 531
Alatas, S.H. 338, 342, 345–6, 370
Alcibiades 148, 155, 161
Aldrich, R. 337
Alesina, A. 231–2, 443
Allen, C. 416, 418–19
Alou, A.T. 482
Amaro-Reyes, J. 213, 224, 429, 441
Amsden, A. 304
Anderson, B. 373
Anderson, D. 138
Andreski, S. 87–8, 334
Andrews, F. 107
Andvig, J.C. 255, 384, 440, 449
Anechiarico, F. 533
Anzelmi, F.J. 191
Arendt, H. 390, 394
Aristotle 138, 140, 145–9, 151, 154, 158–65, 179, 281, 390, 397
Arrow, K.J. 114
Duke of Athens 144, 162
Aubrey, H.C. 25
Auerbach, H. 190
Avelino, J. 79
Azikiwe, N. 35

Bâ, A.H. 507
Bagwell 383, 397
Bailey, F. 90, 183, 494
Bailyn, B. 139
Baker, H. 480
Baker, J. 480
Bakker, H.E. 338
Balfour 31
Ball, T. 394
Banfield, E. 35, 47, 58, 65, 79, 114, 116–17, 124, 212, 385
Bardhan, P. 425, 440, 442, 449
Barker, A. 346
Barnard, C.I. 120
Barney, J.B. 331
Barro, R.J. 224, 231, 242, 244–5, 247–9, 251,
253, 256–7
Bartley, R.J. 337
Baterina, V.F. 68, 79
Bates, R.H. 369
Batista 49, 199
Baumgold, D. 396
Bayart, J.-F. 405, 417, 486, 491, 506
Bayley, D. 45, 47, 53, 175, 189, 207, 353, 360, 409
Becker, G.S. 108, 110, 119, 212–13, 216
Becker, H. 492
Ben Barka, M. 104
Ben Messaoud, O. 93
Ben-Dor, G. 190
Benham, F. 49
Bentham 287
Berg, E. 48
Berg, L.L. 290
Berliner, J.S. 113
Berlusconi 264, 277
Bertram, C. 263
Besley, T. 432, 532
Bhagwati, J. 300
Bhaskar, V. 306
Bhutto 277
Bhutto, B. 337
Bicchieri, C. 339, 352
Bierschenk, T. 483, 495
Bill, J. 85
Blundo, G. 487, 495, 506
Boissevain, J. 87–8, 92, 494
Borgia 398
Borner, S. 445, 463
Bousquet, G.-A. 83
Braibanti, R. 27, 46
Brasz, H.A. 62
Bratton, M. 417
Bräutigam, D. 539
Brecht, B. 403
Brennan, G. 323
Bretton, H. 51
Brewster, D.B. 108
Brezhnev 221
Brooks, R.C. 114, 121, 183
Brownberger, W. 507
Browning, E. 301
Brunetti, A. 445, 462–3

Plato 138, 140, 145–50, 160–62, 164–6, 172, 179, 281
Plunkitt, G.W. 528
Plunkitt, S. 174, 186
Pocock, J.G.A. 139, 157, 388
Polanyi, K. 420
Posada-Carbó, E. 338, 350, 352, 405
Posner, R.A. 299
Primmer, D. 345
Pritchett, L. 522, 529
Pryce, S. 337, 351
Przeworski, A. 387, 522
Pujas,V. 340
Putnam, R. 232, 236, 255, 442, 460
Pye, L. 28, 46, 50, 86, 373

Rajaratnam, S. 189
Rambo, A.T. 48
Ranmsay, A. 356, 368, 371
Ramseyer, J.M. 332
Ranis, G. 329
Rao, P.V.N. 264, 337, 404
Rasmusen, E. 332
Rauch, J. 429, 460
Raynaud, C. 507
Reagan, R. 350
Rebelo, S. 248, 256
Reisman, M. 288
Renelt, D. 232, 244, 248, 250–51
Rengger, N. 339
Reno, W. 417–19
Rhodes, M. 339, 345, 347–8
Ridley 404
Ridley, F.F. 338, 340
Riggs, F. 63, 68, 90, 94, 133, 135, 361, 372
Riley, S. 173, 408
Riordan, W. 33, 55, 174
Rivera, T. 356
Roberts, C. 287
Roberts, J. 534
Roberts, M. 176
Robinson, M.R. 182
Rocamora, J. 356
Rodrik, D. 443
Rogerson, W.P. 299
Rogow, A. 286, 288, 348
Roh, T.W. 295, 297, 317
Rohm, E. 398
Roosevelt, F.D. 175
Rose, R. 64, 73–4
Rose-Ackerman, S. 106, 174, 184, 186, 212, 216, 232, 282, 284–5, 291, 300–301, 306, 309, 321, 325, 328, 332, 348, 350, 365, 384, 412, 415, 425, 427–9, 513, 522–3, 527, 532–3

Rosenbaum, A. 526
Rosenberg, A. 408
Rosenblum, N. 397
Rottenberg, S. 109
Roubini, N. 232
Rousseau, J.-J. 138, 140, 144–5, 147–50, 152–4, 156, 158, 160, 164–8, 179
Royce, J. 143, 155
Rubinstein, J. 118
Rudolph, L.I. 364, 371
Rudolph, S.H. 364, 371–2
Rundquist 339
Rundquist, B. 344

Sacks, P.M. 524
Sah, R.K. 255
Sánchez, F.J. 310
Sánchez Morón, M. 329
Sandbrook, R. 87
Santhanam, K. 60
Sarassoro, H. 506
Sargisson, L. 337
Sartori, G. 344
Savonarola 167
Saxonhouse, A. 138
Sayre, W.S. 116
Schaffer, B.B. 133
Schmidhauser, J.R. 290
Schmidt, S. 362
Schmitt, C. 393–6, 398, 401
Schulte Nordholt, N.G. 338
Schumpeter, J. 48
Schwab, G. 393, 395
Schwartz, A.C. 188, 191
Schwartz, T. 531
Scott, J. 84, 86–8, 92, 201, 208, 282, 287, 360–64, 366, 368–9, 372–5, 483, 505-7, 525, 530
Seko, M.S. 236
Selden, R.T. 108–9
Senturia, J.A. 282
Sforza, F. 168
Sherman, L.W. 525, 527
Shils, E. 23, 48, 53
Shklar, J. 397
Shleifer, A. 215, 231–2, 237, 243, 255–6, 301–2, 306, 331, 385, 425, 428–9, 441, 444, 446–7, 450, 459–60, 525, 527, 532
Shumer, S.M. 281
Sidel, J.T. 347, 362
Siffin, W.J. 89
Silva Michelena, J.A. 90
Simmons, R.T. 387
Simpkins, E. 29–32, 34, 36, 40, 45, 49, 57, 59, 63, 71, 127, 287, 470, 519